LATINOS AND THE POLITICAL SYSTEM

Latinos and the Political System

F. Chris Garcia, editor

UNIVERSITY OF NOTRE DAME PRESS
NOTRE DAME, INDIANA 46556

Manufactured in the United States of America

Library of Congress Cataloging-in-Publication Data

Latinos and the political system.

1. Hispanic Americans—Politics and government.
2. United States—Politics and government—1981—
I. Garcia, F. Chris.
E184.S75L368   1988   323.1'168'073   87-40616
ISBN 0-268-01285-7

Contents

Preface

AMERICANS OF HISPANIC DESCENT, or Latinos, have been perceived as important participants in U.S. politics for about a quarter of a century. Since the activist period of the Chicano movement, beginning in the early 1960s, Latinos have been actively and visibly involved in the United States political system. Prior to that time, Latino politics were somewhat localized, often defensive, and not in the system's mainstream. With a few notable exceptions, particularly in New Mexico and the lower Rio Grande valley, Latinos' successes in electoral politics had been minimal. The momentum of the activist politics of the 1960s has been sustained, with more or less intensity and in varying forms, into the "decade of the Hispanics," the 1980s. Significant achievements have been attained, although Latinos are still far from being full participants in and beneficiaries of the United States political system.

Scholarly recognition of ethnic politics in general and Latino politics in particular, has lagged behind their recognition by the popular media, practicing politicians, and those involved in marketing. In my preface to *La Causa Politica,* the Chicano politics reader published by Notre Dame Press in 1974, it was noted that there were very few scholarly materials available which would enable students, or the interested lay person, to view comprehensively Chicano politics in the United States. This situation has improved somewhat over the past several years, yet there are still relatively few such materials. This anthology is intended to provide a systematic overview and perspective on the involvement of the three major Latino groups — Mexican-Americans, Cuban-Americans, and Puerto Ricans — in the politics of the United States. There are two major differences from our earlier volume of readings. In addition to focusing now on the three major Latino groups, these articles are illustrations primarily of conventional or accommodational politics. This reflects the tenor of the times, as the predominant style of ethnic politics has changed from the nonconventional, more radical politics of the movement. Every attempt has been made to select articles which are interesting, "classic," in that they stand the test of time,

ix

and either comprehensive in nature or narrower but exemplary of research on an important topic. The articles have been placed in a systematic framework as a heuristic exercise, that is, to help readers conceptualize the overall, dynamic relationship of various elements of system politics one to another. The use of the Eastonian model does not imply a bias toward accommodation rather than radical politics—indeed, radical politics can be analyzed using the system paradigm—but rather is utilized as an organizing conceptual framework, the elements of which can accommodate any political style.

As with any work of this nature, several debts of gratitude must be extended toward several contributors. First and foremost, my sincerest appreciation goes to the fine scholars and colleagues whose research and writings are contained in this volume. Another major debt of thanks goes to the staff of Notre Dame University Press, in particular, its administrative director, John Ehmann, whose patience, support, and consideration over an extended period of time made this volume possible; and Carole Roos, whose meticulous editing was a major contribution. The superb secretarial work of Virginia Ortiz was essential for all this to come together. The constructive criticisms of the anonymous reviewer added considerably to the quality of the manuscript. Finally, to Flaviano P., Crucita I., Sandra D., Elaine L., and Tanya C.—the Garcias, to whom this book is dedicated—goes my deepest gratitude.

F. Chris Garcia
The University of New Mexico

Introduction

ONE OF THE MANY characterizations attributed to the 1980s in the United States is "the Decade of the Hispanics." This appellation first appeared in the late 1970s in conjunction with the upcoming 1980 census in advertising campaigns and in major media, such as national news magazines, prominent newspapers, and network television. The timing of this was somewhat ironic. One would have expected national media publicity to be focused on Hispanics several years earlier. The decade from 1965 to 1975 was a period in which Hispanics were actively and intensely engaged in attempts to affect public policy. This period of the "civil rights movement" found Hispanics engaged in unconventional political tactics which included sit-ins, walk-outs, boycotts, marches, strikes, and other confrontational or, at least, highly dramatic political activities. Leaders and spokespersons for the movement included Jose Angel Gutierrez in Texas, Corky Gonzales in Colorado, Reies Lopez Tijerina in New Mexico, Cesar Chavez in California, and many less known but equally effective spokespersons for "la causa." Americans became familiar with the names of such hitherto unknown towns as Delano, California; Crystal City, Texas; and Tierra Amarilla, New Mexico. Groups, such as the Brown and Black Berets, organized along paramilitary lines and espousing militant self-defense tactics, were established throughout the Southwest. Similar political activity occurred in other parts of the country, such as the Midwest, particularly in the Chicago area, where Latinos formed organizations to seek redress of their grievances, and also in the Northeast, particularly the New York area, where Puerto Ricans also challenged the system of ethnic and racial inequality. Chicano and Latino Studies programs and activist student organizations sprung up on our college and university campuses.

This era was one of general social activism, and Latinos found allies among liberal Anglo individuals and groups, with other ethnic and racial groups, such as the blacks, Indians, and Asians, and with some powerful mainstream organizations such as unions and churches. Governments responded sometimes with token appointments and policies, at other times

1

with more meaningful substantive policies, and sometimes with repressive reactions. The general American public, if not always supportive, was at least attentive and often sympathetic. This period also was marked by political activism against our involvement in Vietnam, for the protection of our environment, and on behalf of other "progressive" policies.

As the United States moved into the 1970s, much of the steam ran out of the various social and political movements, the war came to an inglorious and uncertain end, and the mood of the American public grew less open to "progressive" movements. Social observers talked about this period as being one of retreat into a "me" philosophy as the public, particularly the young, seemed more concerned with their own personal material advancement than with sociopolitical affairs. The public seemed to have grown tired of the exciting and frenetic civil rights and anti-war agitation.

Indicators of socioeconomic well-being for the underprivileged such as Latinos had improved during the late 1960s and early 1970s. However, these tapered off in the mid- and late 1970s. Many Latino leaders, still concerned about the relatively disadvantaged position of their people, lamented the lack of progress and the seeming lack of concern among the public and even among Hispanics themselves. It was during this hiatus of the late 1970s when the media began to designate the upcoming decade as one of special significance for Hispanics. Perhaps it was a belated recognition of the changes that had occurred several years earlier; perhaps it was the increased attention, necessarily national in scope, given to troublesome developments in Latin America and especially in Mexico, focusing on the latter country's petroleum reserves and the flow of undocumented workers into the United States. In any case, it is somewhat paradoxical that just as the momentum seemed to have gone out of the Hispanic political movement for a few years the national media focused in on this group and its present and future position in the United States.

The 1980 census fed into this characterization. Population figures indicated that the Hispanic population had grown tremendously over the past ten years and that the rate was such that Latinos probably would become the largest distinctive ethnic group by the first quarter of the twenty-first century. The implications of this for United States society were very significant. The political potential of these numbers was a factor in the 1984 presidential election.

Given the attention then being focused on Hispanics, many persons were curious as to the political status and potential of Latinos. Because of the past lapse of attention, there seemed to be little information available about the current condition of Hispanics. Had the political objectives of the late 1960s and early 1970s been attained? Had the movement been

so successful that all grievances had been redressed and all inequality eliminated? Were Hispanics truly a potentially powerful and pivotal political
force in this country? Were Latino political activities still continuing? If
so, in what forms would they be manifested? And, importantly, what kind
of government responses were being solicited, and what policies were forthcoming from governments in the United States? This volume examines these
questions and provides some answers to them.

The purpose of the book is to examine Latinos' places in the United
States political system. To help comprehend Latino politics in the United
States during the decade of the Hispanics, a well-known and much used
conceptual framework is employed to help structure our information. Our
organizing theme is modeled on the political system paradigm, most notably conceptualized by David Easton in his various works on political systems.[1] The political system can be schematized as follows:

THE POLITICAL SYSTEM

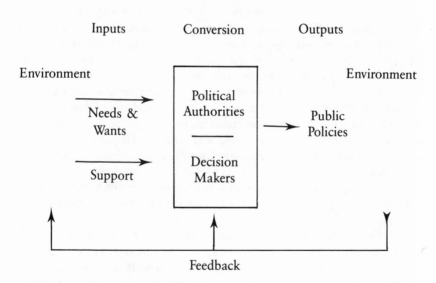

	Inputs	Conversion	Outputs

Environment Environment

Needs & Wants → Political Authorities

Support → Decision Makers

→ Public Policies

Feedback

Four basic elements of the system include (1) the setting or environment
in which the political system operates, i.e., the contextual factors, (2) in-

puts into the system, (3) conversion, and (4) system outputs or outcomes. The political system is one of many systems, such as the economic and social systems, operating interdependently and simultaneously in any society. The political system is distinctive in that it operates to allocate values and goods authoritatively, that is, to make binding decisions by choosing from among many possible policies and legitimizing some of those alternatives in the form of public laws or other kinds of public policies.

The context in which any system operates has a great impact on that system, and this is certainly true of the political system. A complete understanding of the operation of the political system is not possible if one is ignorant of its history, the condition of other coexisting systems, such as the economic system, the prevailing psychological mood of the system's populace, and other major contextual factors. Therefore, with regard to understanding Latino politics, one must have some familiarity with the setting in which Latinos are interacting with the political system. Therefore, section one includes five articles which briefly illuminate the environmental setting, especially the history and demography, in which Latino politics in the United States currently are operating.

Most of the manifestations of Latino politics occur on the *input* side of the system. Hispanics attempt to engage the system by presenting to it their needs and wants. Latino desires are aggregated into some kind of a collective form, and they must be communicated to the authorities, that is, articulated to the political system decision makers. In the Movement era, much of this was done through militant or radical forms of action and organization, such as boycotts, demonstrations, separate political parties, paramilitary groups, separatist movements, and other forms of political protest. In the 1980s, the predominant mode of political input has been conventional, that is, primarily electoral in nature. Hispanics continue to organize "interest groups" at all levels. Latinos also continue to work through the grand coalitions called political parties which represent their interests best, and a great deal of attention is being given to voter registration and participation. Other means of presenting Latino interests include taking Latino interests into the courts, that is, litigation.

Once Latino interests have been communicated to the public officials and placed on the public agenda, then the *conversion* process begins. The system can respond to myriad pressures upon it and selects some of those, which then at least will be placed on the public agenda for consideration. It is at this point that the authoritative decision makers or public authorities must decide which interests shall be legitimized by government, that is, which shall become binding public policy. Historically, and continuing to the current time, Latinos have had disproportionately few government officials of their own to represent their interests. The question of Latino representation at all levels of government, including positions in the bureaucracy, is one of continuing interest, the theory being that Latino "passive" representation is likely to be conducive to the promotion of Latino interests, i.e., "active" representation. Several selections in this volume dealing with the conversion process examine the subject of Latino representation in the legislative and executive branches of the various levels of government.

The paramount payoff for Latino politics comes in the formulation and promulgation of public policy, that is, in the outputs of the system — laws, regulations, and the policy outcomes which ensue from those. From the viewpoint of a socioeconomically depressed ethnic group, most of the desired outcomes revolve around the topics of exclusion, inequality, socioeconomic deprivation, and a related cluster of issues, such as bilingual education, employment, lack of public services, crime, immigration, and to a lesser extent United States foreign policy toward Latin America. Policy outputs and outcomes are examined in the final section of selections.

This volume should provide an opportunity to the reader to assess the current state of Latino politics in the "Decade of the Hispanics" and perhaps formulate a prognosis, at least for the immediate future, of Latinos in the United States political system. Unfortunately, there has been a diminution of research into Hispanic politics over the past several years compared to the activist era. Particularly in short supply are studies dealing with the politics of Latinos outside the southwestern United States, such as in the Midwest, as well as research which focuses on Latino nationality groups other than Mexican-Americans, such as Puerto Ricans and Cuban-Americans. Also lacking are comprehensive but in-depth investigations into the attitudinal bases of the Latino political community. We are pleased to include a few excellent examples of such writings in this volume.

It is hoped that not only will this volume lead to increased awareness and understanding of Latino politics but that it might also encourage more attention to and research on the continuing disadvantaged position of Latinos in the United States.

NOTE

1. David Easton, *A Framework for Political Analysis,* (Englewood Cliffs, N.J.: Prentice-Hall, Inc. 1965); *A Systems Analysis of Political Life,* (New York: John C. Wiley and Sons, 1965). The schematic diagram used here is a slightly modified and greatly simplified version of the Eastonian political systems model.

PART I
The Setting:
History and Demography

LATINO POLITICS DO NOT EXIST in a vacuum. The political activities of persons of Latino/Hispanic ancestry in the United States are conditioned by the societal environment in which they take place. That environment is the product of a history the understanding of which is crucial to comprehending the current political status and activities of Latinos in the U. S. Not many people in the United States know much about the history of one, much less most, Latino groups. Throughout most of the history of public education in the United States, for example, Mexican-Americans have not been taught the centuries-long history of their own ancestors and the impact of that history on their current lives, but instead have been presented exclusively with the historical developments on the eastern seaboard. One manifestation of this has been that not only have Latinos felt cut off from their own "roots," but non-Latinos have had a difficult time understanding why the political orientations, objectives, and activities of Latinos sometimes take the unconventional forms which they do.

The articles included in this section describe the setting in which Latinos engage in politics. Their thrusts are largely historical and demographic, presenting the political development of various major Latino groups in the United States and describing past, present, and possible future demographic trends. Some of the most salient common threads are (1) the racism and prejudice which these groups have encountered and to some extent still are experiencing, (2) historical experiences which in some ways are diverse but in many ways are leading toward some significant commonalities among these groups, and (3) the rapidly expanding Latino population in the United States.

Concerning the latter point, some demographers have projected a doubling of the Hispanic population in the United States over the next twenty years and its tripling in the next forty years. In less than one hundred years, the Latino population is projected to constitute twenty percent

7

of the nation's total population. These considerations hold many significant implications for Latinos' involvement in politics in this country.

Some of the significant political implications of the growth of the Hispanic community are presented in the article written in 1979, just before the beginning of the "Decade of the Hispanics," in which authors Pierce and Hagstrom observe that Latinos were on the verge of becoming a major consideration in the domestic and foreign policies of the United States. A brief history of the three major Latino groups—Mexican-American, Cuban-American, and Puerto Rican—is recounted. The relative isolation or invisibility of these groups is noted, yet because of the demographics of the Latino populace, particularly its rapid increase in size, it is inevitable that Latinos will become a major consideration for the nation's policymakers. The political potential of these groups is perceived as being tremendous. Because of this, political parties should be making concerted efforts to bring these new forces into their ranks. Traditionally, the Democratic Party has been a more comfortable organization for Mexican-Americans and Puerto Ricans than has the Republican Party. On the other hand, because of more compatible orientations in the area of foreign policy, most Cubans have been closer to the Republican than to the Democratic Party.

With regard to policy issues, that of immigration, both a domestic and foreign policy matter, is seen as the most salient. Foreign policy concerns focus on relations with Central and Latin America and, most particularly, with the three mother countries of the three major Latino groups. Domestic agenda priorities include concerns with Latinos' treatment in the criminal justice system; the quality of education, particularly bilingual education; unemployment and underemployment; and poverty.

There is some speculation that some cultural and socioeconomic traits work against increasing the political potency of Latino groups. Certainly an increase in voter registration and electoral participation is essential for this empowerment. A pan-Latino political force naturally would be of great significance in both regional and national politics.

The article "Chicanos in the United States: A History of Exploitation and Resistance" explores the history of the social, economic, and political relations which have profoundly shaped the status of Mexican-Americans in the United States today. The entrance of Mexican-Americans into the United States society through means of conquest, with the resulting social and economic displacement of Mexicans, is surveyed for each of the states of the Southwest. Reactions by Mexicans to the imposition of the new order took several forms, including active resistance and force. The period from 1900 to World War II is particularly important because of the large immigration from Mexico, the extensive use of the new immigrants as laborers in road construction, mining, and agriculture, and the reflection of these factors in the public policies of national and state governments, including immigration laws and repatriation activities. The World War II period featured some well-publicized confrontations between Mexicans and Anglos as well as attempts to stabilize the agricultural labor relations between the two countries; it also led to some important organizational self-defense activities by Mexican-Americans.

The more outwardly militant and visible political activities of the Chicano movement period, 1965–1975, are reviewed and assessed, particularly in terms of the transformation of the organizational base of the Chicano community. Finally, demographic characteristics, including the rapid rise in Hispanic population and its dispersal throughout the country, as well as the socioeconomic achievements of Chicanos, are reviewed.

Although Puerto Ricans are the second largest Latino group and are all citizens of the United States, by and large their influence has not been commensurate with their numbers and citizenship status. James Jennings' study elaborates on the reasons why this has been the case, particularly in New York City where, until recently, most Puerto Ricans resided. Paradoxically, Puerto Ricans participate in elections to a very high degree on the island of Puerto Rico, yet on the mainland participation is extremely low. Puerto Ricans have seen themselves as "temporary" immigrants coming to the United States for reasons which are primarily economic with the intention of returning to the island as soon as their economic lot is improved. The United States political setting has not offered Puerto Ricans the political opportunities provided to other immigrants early in our history. Institutions such as the Democratic Party, and even the fabled urban political "machine," did not help in integrating or even co-opting Puerto Ricans as they had earlier immigrant groups. Very little political community identity was developed among the Puerto Ricans, who are mainly from the lower socioeconomic class and consider themselves as temporary work visitors. Little or no ethnic political identity developed in the Puerto Rican communities until the civil rights era of the 1960s.

In discussions of Latinos in the United States, it is often pointed out that Cubans are quite different in many respects from such other Latinos as Mexican-Americans and Puerto Ricans. The brief history of Cubans in the United States by Maria de los Angeles Torres explicates the reasons for this phenomenon. Cubans in the United States have a very distinctive history, rooted as it is in the foreign policy of the United States and, more specifically, its relationships with right-wing governments in Latin America. The Cuban Revolution of 1959, with the consequent takeover by Marxist Fidel Castro, produced a large conservative exile community in the United States, particularly in Miami, Florida. The concerns of most of this group, relatively well-off socioeconomically, were almost exclusively with counter-revolutionary activities. Yet, as the Castro government became better ensconced in Cuba, hopes for a counterrevolution or attack on the island faded. Along with this came increased concern of Cuban-Americans with their status as a distinctive ethnic minority in the United States. The Carter administration's more liberal foreign policy and the rise of a younger generation of Cubans who felt less attached to Cuba have begun to affect the attitudes and ideologies of the Cuban-American population.

As time passes, Cuban-Americans have become increasingly concerned with their status as minority group Latinos in the United States, and although they are still quite distinctive politically in their relationship with the Republican Party, many of the domestic local issues facing the Cuban-American community are similar to those faced by other Latino communities in the United States.

The selection by Richard Santillan on Latino politics in the Midwest is particularly interesting for several reasons. First, many people are under the impression that Latinos are concentrated in the West and Southwest, Florida, and New York. However, there is a large and significant population of Latinos in the midwestern United States. The political life of Latinos in the Midwest has been significant at the individual, organizational, and community levels. Moreover, it is in the Midwest that certain characteristics of the Latino situation appear that may hold great significance for Latinos' involvement in *national* politics. It is in the Midwest that several different Latino nationality groups exist side by side, none of them being a majority, and, in most cases, with the combined Latino groups forming less than a majority of the population. Thus, Latinos there must function in a setting which places them as true numerical as well as ethnic minorities, minorities which also are relatively powerless. The settings for these particular minority politics are rural and small town as well as metropolitan in nature. Thus, different strategies must be employed, including the all important option of coalition politics.

In sum, one finds in the Midwest virtually all the features which would apply to Latinos on a national basis. It may well be that lessons learned from the Latino political microcosm of the Midwest will be most important in developing Latino political strategies and tactics in the national political arena.

These selections should provide the reader with a broad overview of the past and present political status and goals of Latinos in the United States. How these background factors affect political inputs into the system, what form these take, and how they are communicated forms the rationale for the next section of readings.

1. The Hispanic Community—A Growing Force to Be Reckoned With

Neal R. Pierce and Jerry Hagstrom

THE SCENE WAS THE HUGE ballroom of the Washington Hilton Hotel. Nearly nine hundred Mexican-Americans, Puerto Ricans, Cubans, and other Hispanics from around the country were gathered for the first of a planned series of annual fund-raising dinners for the Congressional Hispanic Caucus.

For the leaders of America's Hispanic community, estimated to number between twelve million and sixteen million people, the dinner last September 20 was a significant event. For the national news media, it was not.

The gathering, in fact, was largely ignored by the national press. The next day's news pages contained no accounts of the "state of Hispanic America" nor any mention of the $80,000 raised to benefit the caucus's research and education programs. The Style section of *The Washington Post* did note the presence of Rosalynn Carter at a party to celebrate "the start of a new Hispanic unity."

Future platforms for Hispanic leaders in Washington are likely to command more attention. From Miami to the Rio Grande, from the migrant labor camps to the big cities where 85 percent of America's Hispanics now live, the burgeoning Hispanic community is becoming increasingly powerful and is preparing to take American domestic and foreign policy in new and uncharted directions.

The Hispanic presence in North America is not new. Before Jamestown or Plymouth Rock, while most of what is today the United States slumbered through its last age of innocence, Spanish conquistadores pushed through Mexico and deep into what is now the southwestern United States.

From *National Journal*, April 7, 1979, pp. 548–555. Reprinted with permission of *National Journal*.

They mingled their blood with the native Indians to form what is roman-
tically called La Raza, the Cosmic Race. Yet "Anglo" America, once formed,
traditionally regarded Hispanics as a people to be conquered or ignored.
After the United States waged war with Mexico and acquired California
and the southwestern states in 1848, the Mexican people living there were
expected to adopt the Anglo culture.

Likewise, Puerto Ricans on the island and the mainland and Cubans
who fled to this country after Fidel Castro took power in 1959 were expected to blend into American society. In fact, despite their mixture of European, Indian, and African blood, Hispanics for generations were officially considered white.

But the acculturation has not taken place — both because the larger
American society discriminated against Hispanics and because Hispanics
themselves clung to their language and culture.

Instead, a pattern of exploitation and discrimination was established.
"The Mexican-American has been the black man of the Southwest," said
Ronnie Lopez, executive assistant to Arizona Governor Bruce E. Babbitt.
"There have been rapings and lynchings. We couldn't use swimming pools.
People's land was taken from them."

Washington policymakers are now beginning to pay attention to Hispanic issues for three important reasons:

- Because of high birth rates and legal and illegal immigration, Hispanics have become the fastest growing minority group in the country and may well outnumber blacks sometime between 1980 and
  1990 — although the Census Bureau lacks the data to be sure.
- Though their current voter participation rates are extremely low,
  Hispanics represent an enormous source of political power, especially in Florida, California, Texas, and New York.
- Domestic policies affecting Hispanics may play a vital role in U.S.
  access to Mexico's huge oil and gas reserves.

The long-term effect of an increased Hispanic influence on American politics and federal policy can only be guessed at. A poll by Louis Harris and Associates Inc. has shown that non-Hispanic Americans are still
somewhat puzzled by the Hispanic phenomenon. The study found that
almost two-thirds of non-Hispanic whites "deny the extent to which Hispanics have faced discrimination," and 62 percent of non-Hispanics have
no real contact with the Hispanic community.

"Only in the West and in the big cities can majorities be found among
whites who know any Hispanics," Harris said. "The irony is that when
whites come into contact with this minority group, they find the experience highly positive."

As the Hispanic population increases, however, some sections of the country are beginning to find it difficult to cope with a non-English speaking, sometimes dependent population for which they have not planned. State and local officials and members of Congress from heavily Hispanic districts are turning to the federal government for help with health, education, and employment problems.

The growing Hispanic influence on all sides of American life is also being recognized in official quarters, although Hispanics continue to hold little political power in Washington. Only six Hispanics, including the non-voting resident commissioner of Puerto Rico, sit in the House, and no Hispanic has served in the Senate since Senator Joseph Montoya, a Democrat from New Mexico, was defeated in 1976. Nor are there any Hispanic governors, though Hispanics recently were chief executives of Arizona and New Mexico.

The Hispanic banner is carried in the executive branch, however, by President Carter's 107 Hispanic appointees in administrative posts and 68 Hispanics on boards and commissions. They are working with Hispanic leaders around the country and with lobbying groups in Washington to increase the community's political clout in the capital.

The Hispanic influence has already been felt on such issues as the Panama Canal treaties, immigration legislation, and plans for the 1980 census. Relationships with Mexico alone have become so critical that the Carter Administration has set up extraordinary mechanisms to coordinate foreign and domestic agency ties with the country's southern neighbor. In addition, a few agencies have begun to make special attempts to serve a constituency that they might have ignored in the past. A task force on Hispanic-American arts, for example, has been established to help the National Endowment for the Arts funnel more money to the Hispanic community.

Nevertheless, a lengthy agenda of unresolved issues and mounting problems remains to be dealt with by government officials and the various branches of the Hispanic community.

POLITICAL POTENTIAL

Future relations between the federal government and the Hispanic community are certain to be colored by one overriding demographic fact: in the next decade, Hispanics are expected to replace blacks as the nation's largest minority.

But this demographic reality may not automatically be translated into political power.

"If we're going to be the largest minority, we'll be like a river that runs and changes course," said Arizona's Lopez. "But unless we're able to grab that river with a dam so we can use the water, it serves no purpose."

As Lopez suggests, Hispanics have a long way to go to achieve the voting power and unity that could make them a powerful bloc in national politics.

In 1976, according to a study by the Southwest Voter Registration Education Project, there were 6.3 million Hispanics of voting age; 23 percent of them, however, were noncitizens, leaving only 4.9 million eligible to vote. Only 55 percent of the eligibles registered to vote, and of that number, 69 percent turned out at the polls in the presidential contest.

Many reasons have been given for the perennially low turnout of Hispanic voters—the phenomenon of the "sleeping giant." Besides the citizenship factor, the list usually includes the lack of a two-party tradition in Mexico, the fear of revealing "undocumented" (illegal) household members, and the fact that so many Mexican-Americans with long histories as migrant workers have never had a chance to establish voting residences. William G. Velasquez, director of the Southwest project, argues that poverty and poor education are more responsible for the low voting patterns than any ethnic characteristic.

Hispanic leaders become angry when it is suggested that they must become politically organized before they can change their marginal status. "To tell a colonized people you're not getting what you want because you haven't voted is the height of social pathology," said Raquel Marquez Frankel, executive director of the Congressional Hispanic Caucus. "People don't see that for ages, every single law was designed to prevent voting by the 'undesirables.' Registration was ten miles away in the county seat and in English."

Hispanic voter participation is being encouraged now, however, by the federal Voting Rights Act, which was amended in 1975 to include Spanish-speaking areas.

Since that year, the Southwest project has conducted voter registration drives in six states—Texas, New Mexico, Arizona, Colorado, California, and Utah—adding over 260,000 persons to the voting rolls.

Mexican-American voting is bound to increase in the future, Velasquez said, because the community has an unusually youthful population that is still too young to vote or not yet inclined to do so.

Not all Hispanic leaders are as optimistic about achieving political gains. "Political power isn't going to flow automatically because Mexicans historically have been one of the slowest groups to naturalize," said Leonel J. Castillo, chief of the Immigration and Naturalization Service. "Many don't ever become citizens because of the proximity to Mexico and the pride that says they want to die in Mexico. They will assume economic and social influence, but political power will come more slowly."

Hispanics have made significant gains in state and local elections—either with particularly attractive candidates or in areas where their numbers were so large that it was not necessary to seek support from the mainstream of society. The Southwest project has concentrated its registration efforts on local races in the belief that most crucial issues facing Mexican-Americans—education and street and sanitation improvements in long-neglected neighborhoods—are decided locally. The Congressional Hispanic Caucus estimates there are 5,000 Hispanic local and state officials.

After generations of Anglo dominance, Chicanos have begun to achieve substantial power in such southwestern cities as San Antonio and Phoenix. But many Mexican-American leaders are concerned about the failure to make breakthroughs in other areas where their numbers are large. The most egregious cases of disproportionately low political gains appear to be in California and Texas.

Mexican-American political development at the local level has also been aided by a string of community development corporations and protest groups inspired by the late radical activist Saul Alinsky in East Los Angeles and San Antonio.

Community development corporations financed by the Ford Foundation and the federal government have proven particularly important in the development of Hispanic leaders who can cope with complex business and political situations. Arizona Senate President Alfred Gutierrez got his start in Chicanos Por La Causa, a Phoenix community development corporation. A number of Carter Administration political appointees, including White House political aide Rick Hernandez; Arabella Martinez, assistant secretary of Health, Education and Welfare (HEW) for human development; and Alex Mercure, assistant secretary of Agriculture for rural development, came out of the community development corporation movement.

Mexican-Americans are trying to gain political influence by backing Anglo candidates, said Arizona's Lopez. Governor Babbitt won their support, Lopez said, by speaking Spanish, guaranteeing access to the governor's office on all issues, and promising to hire Mexican-Americans for state jobs and appoint them to boards and commissions. California Governor Edmund G. (Jerry) Brown Jr., a Democrat, has been similarly successful with strong appeals to Mexican-Americans and significant numbers of high-ranking appointments for Hispanics.

To date, voting participation among Cubans and Puerto Ricans has also been low, though improving. A Cuban turnout has been hampered for years by the conviction of many Cubans that they will be returning home eventually and should therefore not take out U.S. citizenship.

Many Puerto Ricans, who vote at rates of 80 to 85 percent in the island's heated elections, see themselves as only temporary stateside residents and accordingly fail to become involved in mainland politics, explained Representative Robert Garcia, a Democrat from New York.

Hispanic professionals are beginning to achieve political power by organizing around the fact of being Hispanic, according to Raul Yzaguirre, president of the National Council of La Raza. Hispanic professionals used to disappear into the mainstream, but a younger professional generation, influenced by the student movement of the 1960s, is more inclined toward racial solidarity and willing to give money and to volunteer time to further Hispanic causes, he added.

Even if Mexican-Americans, Puerto Ricans, and Cubans do achieve substantial electoral power, they still face the job of unifying to take advantage of their combined numbers as a national political force and lobbying bloc in Washington. Separated by geography and history, the three largest groups have founded a string of separate national organizations. Central and South Americans are even more disjointed and have organized by country groups only at the local level.

One effort at unity, Hispanic-American Democrats, is being launched by White House political aide Hernandez, in preparation for the 1980 presidential campaign. To counter the usual divisions, the group is being organized by state. The Puerto Ricans and Cubans have already acknowledged the predominance of the Mexican-Americans, who make up 60 percent of U.S. Hispanics. The group of prominent Hispanic Democratic officeholders and political activists has elected as its temporary chairman David Lizarraga, president of the East Los Angeles Community Union, a community development corporation.

Hernandez is also using his White House position to arrange informal meetings of Hispanics so that they may rid themselves of stereotypes such as that Puerto Ricans are interested only in statehood and that all Cubans are rich businessmen.

Among themselves, Mexican-Americans are trying to overcome a tendency toward factionalization and in-fighting that has often held them back politically. Mexican-American politicians themselves tell the story of the crab vendor whose crabs were all moving slowly toward the side of a tub and forming a pyramid by stacking themselves one upon the other. A tourist worried that the crabs might escape, but the vendor dismissed his concern. "Oh, don't worry," the vendor said. "Those are Chicano crabs. When one finally gets ready to make it over the top, the others will pull out from under it."

Graciela Olivarez, head of the Community Services Administration (CSA), the federal anti-poverty agency, shares the feeling:

We find all sorts of lame excuses for not supporting candidates. If [a candidate] emerges, he may have looked at you sideways or you didn't like him when he was at such and such a place. If he happens to live in a better neighborhood, he doesn't represent our interests. If he happens to have gone off to school someplace else and comes back, he doesn't have any sensitivity. And if we manage to get a group to support the candidate, then we have the problem of getting people out to vote. It's very frustrating. We're going to have to get rid of some cultural hang-ups about politics and politicians.

The tendency toward in-fighting is decreasing, however, as Hispanic professionals in their twenties and thirties assume leadership positions in the community, noted William Medina, a Puerto Rican who is assistant secretary of Housing and Urban Development.

The Cubans and Puerto Ricans are also split. The Cubans are divided into pro- and anti-Castro camps. There is almost no connection between Puerto Rican island politics and the "Nuyoricans" in New York, except that they move back and forth frequently, noted Cesar Perales, head of the HEW regional office in New York.

IMMIGRATION

On any list of issues of concern to the Hispanic community, immigration must rank at the top. Not only does it affect the largest number of interest groups, but it is also by far the hardest problem to solve.

People who migrate from one country to another without permission defy accurate counting, but a series of studies have placed the number of undocumented aliens in the United States at somewhere between four million and seven million, about 80 percent from Latin America and the Caribbean. Mexicans in this group are estimated at three million to six million.

The State Department believes that one million to two million aliens cross the U.S. border every year without documents, including 500,000 to 1.25 million Mexicans. (Analysts also note, however, that between half and two-thirds of the Mexicans return home each year.)

The U.S.–Mexican border may well be the world's most porous. The legal two-way flow of people across what some call the "Tortilla Curtain" is almost 160 million a year—nearly twice that through the U.S.–Canadian border.

Through Mexico and by other means, hundreds of thousands of illegal Central and South American immigrants also enter the United States annually. Studies indicate the largest numbers are from the Dominican Republic, El Salvador, Guatemala, Colombia, and Ecuador.

Undocumented workers are perceived in two quite different ways. On the one hand, the argument is made that they contribute to U.S. society by providing hard-to-get labor for menial agricultural and service work; that they reduce inflation and encourage small business by accenting low wages; and that they pay income, sales, and social security taxes while rarely using government services.

The other viewpoint, pressed chiefly by organized labor and some environmental and population control groups, is that hard-won U.S. standards in minimum wage, job security, and labor, health, and safety laws and regulations are endangered by a large influx of workers willing to accept lower standards; that their availability reduces incentives for U.S. employers to make menial jobs more attractive; and that they add to the crime rate and the level of communicable diseases even if they do not make use of government services.

A variety of American interests—state and local officials, employers, environmentalists, civil rights advocates, population control groups, labor unions, and Hispanic lobbies—are trying to resolve the immigration problem. All agree that the continuous violation of U.S. border law sets a bad precedent, but beyond that, the groups disagree among themselves about the severity of the problem and its potential solutions. And the reaction against proposed solutions has so far outweighed public outcry over the problem.

The Carter Administration in 1977 proposed sanctions against employers who hire undocumented workers while offering amnesty to illegal aliens living in the country since 1970. But the proposal was roundly attacked by a panoply of groups, including business leaders and the Mexican-American Legal Defense and Education Fund.[1]

Since then, the various interests appear to have settled back to study the issue further. "We are in the process of building a new consensus on this issue," said Matthew Nimetz, counselor of the State Department. "The migration issue will increase in difficulty as we face the next decade, and it's important we start dealing with it now."

State and local officials in the Southwest have difficulty facing the issue with equanimity and seem to have little inkling of what a national consensus on the issue developing in Washington might be—or mean for them.

Returning from a trip to Mexico, San Jose Mayor Janet Gray Hayes—whose city is 20 to 22 percent Hispanic—noted with alarm that half the population of Mexico is under fourteen years of age and that Mexicans are willing to accept living conditions far below accepted U.S. levels. "Down there, I saw people living 10, 12, and 14 in two rooms. And if we have 8 and 10 in four rooms, which is unacceptable by our standards, it's heaven by their standards." Anticipating a major continued influx of Mexican emigrés into her city, Hayes said she had no idea how community centers or health facilities, as well as the city housing stock, could accommodate the new burden.

There is no way, Hayes believes, that the United States can prevent an impending immigration wave that would change the whole complexion of California and the Southwest. "If we put up a wall, you're really encouraging a revolution in Mexico. They see that border as a safety valve."

Even with the strongest economic development programs to make Mexican life more attractive, officials fear that Mexico cannot absorb the estimated 600,000 to 800,000 new workers entering the country's job market yearly. At present, the Mexican economy is providing only 400,000 new jobs each year, leaving a shortfall of 200,000 to 400,000.

Some environmentalists paint a doomsday picture if illegal immigration is allowed to continue. Projections by the Environmental Fund indicate that a lax policy on illegal immigration would add 40 million people to the U.S. population by the year 2000 and require the importation of an additional 2.3 billion barrels of oil per year. It would also lead, the Fund alleges, to annual increased consumption of 32 metric tons of grain valued at $4.42 billion, reversing the country's present grain export balance and undermining one of the factors alleviating the country's serious international payments imbalance.

Hispanic leaders, along with some other population groups, challenge the assumptions behind these projections. They also note that increased Hispanic population would add new productive wealth to the U.S. economy.

Some circles welcome illegal immigration. Many Anglo businessmen and ranchers, for instance, find undocumented workers hard working, profitable, and necessary. Even though they generally favor restrictive immigration policies, labor unions have also begun to organize undocumented workers in California and Arizona. Hispanic Americans fear that the presence of illegal aliens encourages discrimination, but are unwilling to turn their back on unfortunate relatives. (An Immigration and Naturalization Service study of Texans' attitudes toward illegal immigration has shown, however, that Hispanics near the border have much less sympathy for the illegals than do Hispanic residents of inland cities.)

On the side of restrictive immigration, Phyllis Eisen of Zero Population Growth advocates long-term U.S. policies of aid for economic development and birth control in other countries, sanctions against U.S. employers who hire undocumented workers, documentation cards for U.S. residents, and stricter enforcement of immigration laws, the Fair Labor Standards Act, and the Occupational Safety and Health Act.

The speed with which the immigration issue will be handled may depend to some degree on an oil and gas deal with Mexico. During Carter's February visit to Mexico, he promised Mexican President Jose Lopez Portillo that he would consult him on any new immigration proposals.

Debate on the subject may soon shift to the new Select Commission on Immigration and Refugee Policy, a two-year study group created by Congress with orders to report by September 1980. The commission, including representatives from Congress, the executive branch, and the private sector, is headed by former Florida Governor Reubin O'D. Askew.

Interviews with responsible U.S. officials reveal that the government has no hard estimates of the degree with which immigration from Mexico and other Latin American countries could be expected to increase in the coming years, and no studies whatever gauging the effect of such immigration on the U.S. economy or on conditions in the southwestern states.

Members of Congress from the southwestern states are expected to introduce legislation to allow Mexicans to travel to the U.S. as documented workers, but not to become citizens.

FOREIGN POLICY

The increasing number of Hispanics in the United States is also turning U.S. policy toward Latin America into a complex foreign and domestic policy drama.

Relations with Mexico are the most complicated. "No U.S.–Mexican issue is exclusively foreign policy," said a National Security Council staff member. "The border issues and the trade issues do not fall into typical categories and affect all Americans."[2]

To improve U.S.–Mexican relations, the White House has taken the unusual step of creating the position of ambassador at large to coordinate the work of a number of federal task forces that have been working with Mexican officials on problems affecting the affairs of both nations. The Carter Administration considered but rejected the idea of transferring Ambassador to Mexico Patrick J. Lucey to the post.

Beyond the issues of immigration and oil, U.S.–Mexican relations are complicated by a host of issues arising in the increasingly populous border areas of the two countries. Local officials on both sides are worried about law enforcement, air and water pollution, drug trafficking, exchange of prisoners, the need to share electrical energy, and the constant flow of people back and forth.

Under the aegis of the Southwest Border Regional Commission, a federally financed agency established in 1977, the governors of the region have become involved in U.S.–Mexican relations. They will meet with their counterparts from the northern Mexican states in Tucson, Arizona, in June. The meeting could turn into a forum of criticism of the Carter Administration by California's Brown and Texas Governor William P. Clements Jr., a Republican. Both men have made their own official visits to Mexico and have criticized Carter for not moving quickly enough to establish a new relationship with Mexico based on the importance of oil and immigration questions.

Brown has gone so far as to propose a Common Market among the United States, Canada, and Mexico. "North America is the most powerful economic unit in the world," Brown told his fellow governors at a February meeting of the Southwest Commission in Washington. "As the economies of Europe and Asia regionalize, we have to build our strength at home as a very high level of priority."

The political-economic ties that Brown envisages exist already in Miami, which Mayor Maurice Ferre says has become "a new Cuban capital" through its immense influx of Cuban refugees in the past decades. But the Cuban population surge is now a multinational Latin affair. Made to feel comfortable by the Cuban beachhead, Central and South Americans have flocked to the city to shop and do business, some to live. Hundreds of firms operate in the Miami area (including 76 branches of multinational firms in suburban Coral Gables) for no other reason than to do business with Latin America.

Of Dade County's 1.6 million people, 660,000 to 700,000 are estimated to be Latins—primarily Cubans, but also Puerto Ricans, Colombians, Venezuelans, Dominicans, even Brazilians. Of the 5.7 million foreign air passengers who arrive and depart from Miami International Airport each year, about 90 percent are going to or coming from Latin America. South African, Dutch, German, and British business interests have also opened offices in the Miami area to establish permanent access to Latin America. Miami and South Florida, said Frank Soler, editor of El Miami Herald, the Miami Herald's successful three-year-old Spanish-language edition, have gone beyond being simply a gateway to the Americas to becoming a kind of Latin American capital in North America.

As the memory of the Bay of Pigs era recedes, fervent anti-Castroism has diminished in Miami's Cuban community, though strongly hostile sentiments remain among a vocal minority. No one will venture a clear prediction of the future foreign policy implications of the thriving Hispanic community in southern Florida, but some have suggestions. House Banking, Finance, and Urban Affairs Committee chairman Henry S. Reuss, a Democrat from Wisconsin, for instance, has visited Cuba, Colombia, Costa Rica, and other Latin American countries and reached the conclusion that "there is a great foreign policy future for a close relationship of the nations that border on the Caribbean." South Americans of African and Spanish ancestry, Reuss said, have close cultural ties with American blacks and Hispanics. But an Afro-Latin "good neighbor policy would mean coming to terms with Castro."[3]

In less specific terms, there are signs that the Hispanic community in the United States, despite its diversity and the poverty of many of its people, is taking an increased interest in the government's Latin American policy. "The [Roman Catholic] Church holds us together. More and more, the theology of liberation seems to be permeating into a Pan-Hispanic consciousness," suggested Yzaguirre of the National Council of La Raza.

Hispanics are also being encouraged to take a greater interest in foreign policy by two high-level Carter Administration political appointees— Ralph Guzman, deputy assistant secretary of State for inter-American affairs, and Abelardo Valdez, the Agency for International Development's assistant administrator for Latin America and the Caribbean.

Hispanic interest in foreign policy has also been sparked by the appointment of Gabriel Guerra-Mondragon as the first Hispanic career foreign service officer to work in the office of the Secretary of State.

Valdez has worked hard to increase AID's budget for Latin America from $180 million per year when Carter took office to a proposed $230 million for fiscal 1980.

Valdez has also been trying to broaden the constituency for aid to Latin America by making speeches before such groups as the Houston Committee on Foreign Relations and the Texas House of Representatives. "For too long, the foreign relations of the United States have been the concern— and the preserve—of a more narrow constituency in the East," Valdez said. "In today's world, it's the South and the Southwest that have the most at stake in our relations with Latin America."

The Hispanic community got its feet wet in foreign policy when the Carter Administration recruited its support in the campaign for Senate ratification of the Panama Canal treaties. The Hispanic groups proved to be an effective, if small, lobbying force, Administration sources said.

Falling into the cracks between domestic and foreign policy is the status of Puerto Rico. Stateside Hispanics say they will wait for the islanders to decide upon statehood or commonwealth or independent status, but will then use their newfound political strength to mount a campaign to gain congressional approval.

DOMESTIC AGENDA

Of more immediate concern to most Hispanics is a lengthy domestic agenda that reflects the usual poverty concerns—better housing, education, jobs, public health—but with unique twists and turns that stem from Hispanics' desire to preserve their language and culture.

The principal concern of Mexican-Americans, said White House aide Rick Hernandez, is police brutality. Attorney General Griffin B. Bell has reversed a Justice Department policy under which the federal government usually did not prosecute civil rights crimes that violated both state and federal laws as long as there was state prosecution. Hispanic groups contend, however, that the government is still moving too slowly.

Hispanics are very concerned about improving both bilingual and general education programs.

The debate over whether bilingual education helps Hispanic children or keeps them out of the mainstream continues, but the major issue at the present time, Hernandez said, is getting bilingual education money from Washington to local schools.

"There are a lot of school districts in Texas that don't apply for bilingual funds," he said. "We can't make those school districts take it, and they don't really want the conditions under which we give it to them."

The high dropout rate for Hispanic high school students makes some Hispanic professionals despair. "We are losing great numbers of our kids through drugs, alcoholism, and problems with poverty," said Fernando Torres-Gil, a University of Southern California professor now serving as a White House fellow and special assistant to HEW Secretary Joseph A. Califano Jr.

The dropout problem is intensified, Torres-Gil said, by a decline in the availability of federal and state grants for minority students and by the fears of colleges and universities of *Bakke*-style reverse discrimination lawsuits.

Bilingual and bicultural health care also holds a high priority among Hispanics. Anglo members of Congress and health professionals, the Hispanics charge, do not understand the roles of folk medicine, religion, and the extended family in Latin culture. The conflicts between Anglo and Hispanic culture make mental health problems a particular anguish, Torres-Gil said.

With the Hispanic unemployment rate at 8.2 percent, compared with

5.7 percent in the population as a whole, jobs and economic development remain another high priority. The federal government now spends $1 billion annually on jobs programs aimed at Hispanics, according to Hernandez's calculations, but the generally low level of official interest is reflected in the fact that the Bureau of Labor Statistics only recently began keeping monthly statistics on Hispanic unemployment.

Olivarez, the anti-poverty head, says more emphasis must be placed on rural development since Hispanics are continuing to leave rural areas for the cities, even when few job opportunities await them there.

Hispanics are particularly annoyed by the federal government's slow gains in employing Hispanics. Hispanics make up about 5.6 percent of the total population, but hold only 3.7 percent of federal jobs—and even smaller shares of professional slots. The Hispanic goal is "population parity" in federal jobs.

POLITICAL LEANINGS

What would increased Hispanic political power mean to national politics and federal policy? Hispanic political development is too fresh to make broad speculations, but a few trends are apparent.

In the short term, Hispanic groups are falling in line with liberals and other minorities in criticizing the Carter Administration. Hispanic relations with the Carter camp started off well, said Al Perez of the Washington office of the Mexican-American Legal Defense and Education Fund, but declined when Carter proposed an unacceptable immigration plan and failed to make broad changes in the areas of federal employment and police brutality. Hispanic leaders are also upset that Carter has met with them directly only once, before his visit to Mexico.

In 1976, Hispanics gave 81 percent of their votes to Carter and provided "crucial" margins in Texas, New York, and Ohio, according to the Southwest Voter Registration Education Project. The question for 1980—if Carter seeks reelection—is whether he can hope to count on anything like this level of support.

Rick Hernandez broadly defends the Administration's record on Hispanic issues, citing increases in jobs programs and bilingual education funds. But he acknowledges that the Administration has had a hard time conveying its pro-Hispanic stance to the community.

Thus Carter's decision to appoint Hispanics to substantive positions of assistant secretary and below in the Cabinet departments, rather than create symbolic positions for Hispanics, "is going to entrench [Hispanics]. But that doesn't do any good for him politically," Hernandez said.

Hispanics have a long-standing affection for Senator Edward M. Kennedy, a Democrat from Massachusetts, because of his Catholicism, his extended family, and his charisma, and their leaders often point to him as a presidential alternative to Carter. Hispanics have also formed close ties with Governor Brown, who has supported the United Farm Workers' initiatives and appointed a number of Hispanics to high-level posts in the California government. Hispanics have become nervous, however, about Brown's balanced budget amendment campaign because they fear that social programs benefiting them would be hurt.

Over the long term, increased Hispanic voter participation is almost certain to help the Democratic Party and could create a new constituency for an expansion of the party's traditional liberal agenda.

The vast majority of Hispanics are so concerned with economic development that they appear unlikely to align themselves with conservatives who may try to appeal to them on the issues of abortion and birth control. In fact, the Hispanic conservative attitude toward birth control also appears to be waning.

"Population control is no longer an issue that we can be apathetic about," said Yzaguirre. "There isn't a left or right position. It's no longer an ideological question."

Most Hispanics remain opposed to abortion, he added. Yet even conservative Republican presidential candidate Ben Fernandez said in an interview that "abortion has no place in a presidential campaign."

Despite the odds, Republicans tried hard to woo Mexican-American voters in Texas in 1978 and are planning a major effort in 1980.

The most troublesome possibility for sociologists and for Anglos in heavily Hispanic areas is that Hispanics may push bilingualism and bicultural life to the point that America experiences the separatist problems of Canada and Belgium. Most Hispanic leaders active on the Washington scene play down the possibilities of a separatist movement.

Whether or not the increased Hispanic presence in the United States leads to a separatist movement, it is clear that expanding Hispanic political power, along with continued ties to Latin America, will create situations that defy traditional political analysis.

As Arizona's Governor Babbitt said of the growing Mexican-American community in his state: "They're tied to their motherland and their mother country by an umbilical cord across a common border, and there's going to be more coming through that umbilical cord than there is melting at the other end. We'll have ethnic pluralism; the melting pot isn't going to happen out here."

The Growing Hispanic Population

Officially, there are about 12 million people of Spanish origin in the United States. That's what the Census Bureau reports.

Unofficial estimates, however, which take into account illegal aliens and probably undercounting by the Census Bureau, range up to and beyond 16 million.

The differences are highly significant. Using the higher count, Hispanics are likely to exceed blacks as the largest minority group in the country within about a decade. The Census Bureau still uses the lower figure, however, and projects that blacks will continue to outnumber Hispanics through the year 2000. The calculations on Hispanics are hampered by inadequate birth and death records and the impossibility of estimating illegal immigration.

Of the 12 million official Hispanic residents as of March 1978, 7.2 million were of Mexican origin, 1.8 million of Puerto Rican origin, 700,000 of Cuban origin, 900,000 of Central or South American origin, and about 1.5 million of other Spanish origin.

Hispanics are concentrated in five states—New Mexico, California, Texas, New York, and Florida—with significant populations in Arizona and Colorado. But a Congressional Hispanic Caucus study has shown that Hispanics make up at least 5 percent of the population in 98 congressional districts in those states plus Illinois, Indiana, New Jersey, and Utah. Although the image of the Hispanic is often that of the migrant agricultural worker, about 85 percent of all Spanish-origin families live in metropolitan areas, compared with 65 percent of other families.

The Hispanic population grew from 9.3 million in 1970 to 12 million in 1978, a rate of 29 percent, while the rest of the population rose by 6 percent. The Hispanic population is also younger than the rest of the population—about 42 percent were 18 or younger in 1978, compared with only 29 percent of the rest of the population—and in the next generation will make up a larger proportion of the adult U.S. population. Over all, Hispanics have already increased from 4.5 percent of the population in 1970 to 5.6 percent in 1978.

A profile of Hispanic Americans by *American Demographics* magazine has shown that Hispanics are less educated, lower paid, more urban, and more likely to be unemployed than the total population.

Younger Hispanics are more likely to have stayed in school, however, than their elders. Some 57 percent of the Spanish-origin population aged 25 to 29 had completed a high school education in 1978, compared with only 30 percent of those 45 to 64 years old.

About 21 percent of Spanish-origin families had incomes below the poverty level in 1977, while only about 9 percent of families not of Spanish origin were officially poor.

The Census Bureau uses a system of self-determination to find out the number of persons of Spanish origin in the country. On census questionnaires and in interviews, people are asked if they fit one or more of three criteria: Spanish ancestry, Spanish spoken in the home during childhood, or Spanish surname. Portuguese and Brazilians are not considered Hispanics.

For its official records, the Census Bureau still uses the term "Spanish origin" and will also begin to use the now-popular "Hispanic" for the first time in 1980. (The terminology varies widely around the country. Although "Hispanic" is gaining nationwide acceptance as the name that includes all the groups, some people in the Southwest refer to themselves as "Mexican-Americans" while others prefer "Chicano," a term that came into use in the militant 1960s. In cities with large concentrations of Central and South Americans, the terms "Latin" and "Latino" are often heard.)

Hispanic advocacy groups and politicians have complained bitterly that state governments, the bureau, and other federal agencies do not gather the statistics the community needs to demonstrate its size, income status, and problems. Only 19 states currently identify Hispanic births and only 20 record deaths; this covers about 59 percent of Hispanic births and 62 percent of deaths nationwide. These figures are basic to population projections and health studies, and the National Center for Health Statistics is urging the states to improve their data collection.

"Statistical visibility is policy visibility," said Representative Edward R. Roybal, a Democrat from California, chairman of the Congressional Hispanic Caucus and father of the 1976 Roybal Act, which requires federal agencies to collect and publish statistics on the social, health, and economic conditions of Hispanics.

In preparation for the 1980 census, the Census Bureau has established an advisory committee on Spanish population and is making plans to hire indigenous census takers in heavily Hispanic areas and to conduct an extensive public relations campaign to encourage Hispanics to stand up and be counted.

NOTES

1. See *National Journal,* September 3, 1977, p. 1379.
2. For background, see *National Journal,* February 19, 1979, p. 208.
3. For background on U.S. Cuban policy, see *National Journal,* May 13, 1978, p. 762.

2. Chicanos in the United States: A History of Exploitation and Resistance

Leobardo F. Estrada, F. Chris Garcia,
Reynaldo Flores Macias, and Lionel Maldonado

THIS ESSAY SEEKS TO PROVIDE material that will contribute to an understanding of Chicanos[1] in the United States today. The task calls for a historical perspective on the Mexican people within the context of the U.S. political economy

It is essential to examine first the early and continued influence of Mexicans in the development of what is today the southwestern United States. Unlike those who believe that social, political, and economic influences in the region were largely the result of Anglo penetration, we argue that practices and institutions indigenous to Mexicans were largely taken over by colonizing Anglos.[2] The military conquest of the Southwest by the United States was a watershed that brought about the large-scale dispossession of the real holdings of Mexicans and their displacement and relegation to the lower reaches of the class structure. Anglo control of social institutions and of major economic sectors made possible the subsequent exploitation of Mexican labor to satisfy the needs of various developing economic interests.

Mexicans were not passive actors, simply accepting Anglo domination. Mexican resistance to exploitation has taken a great variety of forms since the conquest, contributing to the maintenance and perpetuation of cultural patterns among Mexicans living in the United States. These cultural patterns include: a national identity built around an "Indian" past; an Indianized Catholicism (*La Virgen de Guadalupe*); racial miscegenation (*mestizaje* — Indian and Spaniard — although almost as many Africans as Spaniards were brought to Middle America during the colonial period);

Reprinted by permission of *Daedalus,* Journal of the American Academy of Arts and Sciences, vol. 110, no. 2 (Spring 1981), Boston, Massachusetts.

and a regional, single language, Spanish. These patterns and practices, which distinguish the Mexican population from other groups, have persisted even among those who left the Southwest for other regions of the United States.

THE MILITARY CONQUEST

Mexicans were incorporated into the United States largely through military conquest. The period that brought the northern reaches of Mexico under the U.S. flag begins approximately in 1836 with the Battle of San Jacinto and ends in 1853 with the Gadsden Purchase. The military conquest was preceded by a period of Anglo immigration.

In 1810 Mexico began its struggle to gain independence from Spain, an objective finally achieved in 1821. Mexicans, recognizing the advantage of increasing the size of the population loyal to its cause, granted permission to foreigners in 1819 to settle in its northern area, what is now Texas. Two years later Stephen Austin founded San Felipe de Austin. By 1830, one year after Mexico had abolished slavery, it is estimated that Texas had about twenty thousand Anglo settlers, primarily Southerners, with approximately two thousand "freed" slaves who had been forced to sign lifelong contracts with former owners.[3] This trickle of immigrants soon became an invading horde.

Immigrants into the territories of Mexico were required to meet certain conditions: pledge their allegiance to the Mexican government and adopt Catholicism. The settlers' initial acceptance of these conditions, however, soon turned to circumvention. The distance of the settlements from Mexico's capital city, together with the internal strife common in the period, made enforcement of these settlement agreements difficult, almost impossible. The foreigners' attitudes toward their hosts only aggravated the situation. Eugene C. Barker, a historian, wrote that by 1835 "the Texans saw themselves in danger of becoming the alien subjects of a people to whom they deliberately believed themselves morally, intellectually, and politically superior. Such racial feelings underlay Texan-American relations from the establishment of the very first Anglo-American colony in 1821."[4]

A constellation of factors—attitudes of racial superiority, anger over Mexico's abolition of slavery, defiance of initially agreed-upon conditions for settlement, and an increasing number of immigrants who pressed for independence from Mexico—strained an already difficult political situation. Direct and indirect diplomatic efforts at negotiation failed. The result was the Texas Revolt of 1835–1836, which created for Anglo-Texans and dissident Mexicans the so-called independent Texas Republic, which was to exist until 1845. This republic, while never recognized by the Mexican government, provided the pretext for further U.S. territorial expansion and set the stage for the war between Mexico and the United States (1846–1848).

Despite significant and conflicting regional interests in the war, imperialist interests allied with proponents for the expansion of slavery carried the day. When the United States granted statehood to Texas in 1845, almost a decade after recognizing it as a republic, war was inevitable; it was officially declared on May 13, 1846. It has been argued that U.S. politicians and business interests actively sought this war, believing Mexico to be weak, a nation torn by divisive internal disputes that had not been resolved since independence.[5]

When hostilities ended in 1848, Mexico lost over half its national territory. The United States, by adding over a million square miles, increased its territory by a third. Arizona, California, Colorado, New Mexico, Texas, Nevada, and Utah, as well as portions of Kansas, Oklahoma, and Wyoming, were carved out of the territory acquired.

The Treaty of Guadalupe Hidalgo, signed on February 2, 1848, officially concluded hostilities and settled the question of sovereignty over the territories ceded. A new border was established, and the status of Mexicans in the newly acquired U.S. territory was fixed. Mexicans were given one year to decide whether to relocate south of the new border, maintaining their Mexican citizenship, or remain on their native lands, accepting U.S. sovereignty. The treaty explicitly guaranteed that Mexicans who elected to stay in the United States would enjoy "all the rights of citizens of the [United States] according to the principles of the Constitution; and in the meantime shall be maintained and protected in the free enjoyment of their religion without restriction."

Mexican property rights were further defined once the treaty had been approved by both governments. A Statement of Protocol, drafted by U.S. emissaries when the Mexican government reacted strongly to changes unilaterally made by the U.S. Senate, said:

> The American government by suppressing the Xth article of the Treaty of Guadalupe Hidalgo did not in any way intend to annul grants of lands made by Mexico in the ceded territories. These grants preserve the legal value which they may possess, and the grantees may cause their legitimate [titles] to be acknowledged before the American tribunals.
>
> Conformable to the law of the United States, legitimate titles to every description of property, personal and real, existing in the ceded territories, are those which were legitimate titles under the Mexican law

of California and New Mexico up to the 13th of May, 1846, and in Texas up to the 2nd of March, 1836.

Subsequent events soon indicated that these "guarantees" were specious.

A final portion of Mexican land was acquired by the United States through purchase. James Gadsden was sent to Mexico City in 1853 to negotiate a territorial dispute arising from the use of faulty maps in assigning borders under the Treaty of Guadalupe Hidalgo. Mexico's dire need for funds to rebuild its war-ravaged economy influenced its agreement to sell more land. Gadsden purchased over 45,000 square miles in what is now Arizona and New Mexico, land the United States wanted for a rail line to California. The Gadsden Purchase territories were in time seen to contain some of the world's richest copper mines.

The importance for the United States of this imperialist war and the later Gadsden Purchase cannot be overstated. Vast tracts of land, rich in natural resources, together with their Mexican and Indian inhabitants, provided conditions very favorable to U.S. development and expansion. The United States had done very well in its "little war" with Mexico.

DISPOSSESSION AND DISPLACEMENT

To make matters worse, the social and economic displacement of Mexicans and their reduction to the status of a colonized group proceeded rapidly, in clear violation of the civil and property rights guaranteed both by treaty and protocol. In Texas, a wholesale transfer of land from Mexican to Anglo ownership took place. That process had started at the time of the Texas Revolt and gained momentum after the U.S.–Mexico War. Mexican landowners, often robbed by force, intimidation, or fraud, could defend their holdings through litigation, but this generally led to heavy indebtedness, with many forced to sell their holdings to meet necessary legal expenses. With depressing regularity, Anglos generally ended up with Mexican holdings, acquired at prices far below their real value.[6]

The military conquest, the presence of U.S. troops, racial violence, governmental and judicial chicanery—all served to establish Anglos in positions of power in economic structures originally developed by Mexicans. Anglos adopted wholesale techniques developed by Mexicans in mining, ranching, and agriculture.[7] Because this major transfer of economic power from Mexicans to Anglos varied by region, it is important to say something about each.

Texas, responding to a significant expansion in the earlier Mexican-based cattle and sheep industries, was quick to cater to increased world demands. Acreage given over to cotton also expanded, helped greatly by improvements in transport facilities. These industries helped create and develop the mercantile towns that soon became conspicuous features on the Texas landscape.[8] Mexicans, instead of reaping the economic rewards of ownership, found themselves only contributing their labor. Mexicans were increasingly relegated to the lower ranks of society. By the end of the century, ethnicity, merged with social class, made Mexicans a mobile, colonized labor force.

The social structure of *New Mexico* in the beginning was quite different from that of Texas. The state, sparsely populated, was more densely settled in the north, in and about Sante Fé, than in the south; communal villages with lands granted to each community were common in the north. Communal water and grazing rights were assigned by community councils; only homestead and farming land were privately owned. Southern New Mexico, by contrast, boasted *haciendas* that had been established by grantees. This system consisted of *patrónes*, with settlers recruited to perform the necessary chores. It was a social structure organized on a debt-peonage system.

Anglo penetration into New Mexico after the war was more limited and did not occur on a large scale until the mid-1870s. Indian and Mexican defense of the territory served to keep out many settlers. Only an established U.S. military presence in the area made it at all accessible to Anglo cattlemen and farmers. Encountering a diversified class structure among the resident Mexicans, the Anglos generally chose to associate with the U.S. armed forces, creating a quasi-military society in the process. By the early 1880s, however, the railroads had helped to stimulate a new economic expansion. There was a further swelling of the Anglo population, and as pressure for land increased, the process of Mexican dispossession also dramatically accelerated.

The dispossession process in New Mexico was achieved in part through taxation. The Spanish-Mexican traditional practice had been to tax the products of the land. Under the new Anglo regime, land itself was taxed. With agricultural income fluctuating greatly with climatic conditions, fixed land taxes placed severe burdens on both farmers and ranchers. Small-scale subsistence farmers were unprepared and generally unable to raise the capital to meet the newly imposed tax liabilities. The practice of transferring the title on land on which delinquent taxes were owed to the person making such payment caused many Mexicans to lose their land. Fraud, deceit, and manipulation were common. An associate justice of the Court of Private Land Claims wrote:

> A number of grants have had their boundaries stretched and areas marvelously expanded. But this has been done mostly by Yankee and English purchasers and not by the original Mexican owners. Where

boundaries were made by natural landmarks, such as a "white rock," and "red hill," or a "lone tree," another rock, hill or tree of like description could always be found a league or two farther off, and claimed to be the original landmark described in the grant documents.[9]

Toward the end of the century, federal policies also operated to dispossess Mexicans of their land. The National Forest Service, for example, began taking over millions of acres from northern villages, which were rarely compensated for their losses. Inhabitants were now compelled to pay grazing fees on land that had originally belonged to the villages. The granting of large tracts of land to the railroads served further to confine Mexicans to increasingly smaller land bases.

The Court of Private Land Claims, established in 1891 to resolve conflicts over land claims in New Mexico, Colorado, and Arizona, existed for thirteen years; its Anglo judges had a very limited knowledge and understanding of Mexican and Spanish landowning laws, traditions, and customs. Their judgments, based on Anglo legal practices, greatly contributed to the dispossessions. In time, Anglos came to own four-fifths of the New Mexican grant areas,[10] and this loss of land relegated the vast majority of Mexicans to a bleak economic and social existence.

Twenty or so prominent Mexican families in New Mexico joined with the Anglo interests in banking, ranching, and the railroads, expecting to maintain their own political, economic, and social advantages.[11] The alliance, however, was controlled by the Anglo faction, and was therefore always unequal.[12] In any case, efforts by this small proportion of the original Mexican families to hold on to their advantaged status had no positive effect for the vast majority of Mexicans. As in Texas, ethnicity and class merged, and Mexicans, dispossessed of their holdings, saw them taken by the Anglo elites that dominated the political and economic activities of the society.

Arizona offers the example of the development of a colonial labor force in yet another mode. Arizona, not a separate entity at the time of conquest, was originally part of New Mexico, administered from Santa Fé. The small Mexican population was concentrated in the south, largely in Tucson and Tubac. One of the reasons for the sparseness of the settlements was the failure of the Spanish missionaries to impose Christianity on the nomadic Indian inhabitants; another was the aridity of the soil, which made agricultural pursuits difficult. The presence of the U.S. Army in the 1880s began to have its effects on the region. The Army fought the Indians, allowing the mining of copper and silver to resume; it was soon to become a large-scale economic enterprise. As with other industries, Anglo ownership was the norm; Mexicans contributed their labor, employing the

familiar techniques they had developed long before.[13] Railroads accelerated the migration of Anglos and the establishment of new towns. The
growth of all these major industries called for a cheap wage labor pool.
Mexicans who migrated north, mostly to work in these industries, discovered that the wages they received for tasks identical to their Anglo
counterparts were considerably lower. Restricted to menial and dangerous work and forced to live in segregated areas in the mining and railroad
communities that had created their jobs, they felt the indignity of their
situation.[14]

California differed from the other regions: New England clipper ships
had established very early ties with California; Franciscans, founding missions in the area in the 1830s, forced Christianized Indians into agriculture and manufacturing, to work alongside mulatto and *mestizo* Mexicans. This labor force helped to make California—economically, politically,
and socially distant—independent of Mexico City. Excellent climate and
abundant natural resources contributed to make this the most prosperous
province in Mexico. Strong ties bound the missions to the *ranchos*. Missions, given large parcels of land to carry out their Christianizing enterprise, were neighbors of private individuals who owned vast tracts of land.
Eventually, however, the privately owned *ranchos* established their suprem-
acy throughout the province.

Urban settlements also developed: Monterey was the center of northern California; *el Pueblo de Nuestra Señora, la Reina de los Angeles de
Porciúncula,* the economic and social center of southern California. Other
towns sprung up around the major forts and missions. The rigid feudal
system of *patrón* and *peón,* typical of southern New Mexico, did not
develop in California. The class system that emerged was three-tiered:
wealthy landowners enjoyed political, economic, and social power, and constituted about 10 percent of the population; artisans, small-scale landowners, vaqueros, herders, and soldiers constituted the bulk of Californian society; Indians and lower class *mestizos* stood at the bottom of the
class hierarchy.

A few Anglos had come to Alta California before the U.S.–Mexico
War; some were recipients of land grants, and many of them apparently
assimilated into Mexican society. After the Texas revolt, however, Anglo
foreigners coming to California were more reluctant to mingle or assimilate and openly showed their antagonism towards Mexicans. The U.S. government was at the same time stepping up its efforts to secure California.
In 1842, in fact, the U.S. flag was prematurely raised in Monterey when
Commodore Thomas Jones imagined that the war with Mexico had already begun.

The transfer of land titles from Mexicans to Anglos in California differed significantly from the transfer of title in other areas conquered by the U.S. forces. To begin with, the vast majority of Mexicans did not own land in California. The original *Californios* began to lose title to their lands to better-financed Anglo newcomers very early; there was no possibility of competing with wealth established through banking, shipping, railroads, and other such enterprises. The holdings of these new elites ran into the hundreds of thousands of acres early in the nineteenth century.[15]

Congress established the Land Commission in 1851 to judge the validity of grant claims made by *Californios* whose titles came down through the Spanish and Mexican periods. The commission served mainly to hasten the process of dispossession. Litigation costs often involved a contingent lawyer's fee of one quarter of the land in question. Some Mexican landowners borrowed money at high interest rates to carry on their legal fights, and frequently found themselves in the end selling their lands to meet their debts. Anglo squatters only added to the burden; they formed associations to apply political pressure favorable to their own interests, and were generally successful in retaining land forcefully taken from Mexicans.[16] Violence and murder in California, as in other parts of the conquered territories, were the order of the day.

Gold discoveries in 1849 in northern California brought a massive influx of Anglo gold-seekers. Although Mexicans had been working claims in the area for some time, those who now arrived entered as laborers. The Anglo-American foreigners, inexperienced and ignorant of mining techniques, depended on the Mexican/Spanish/Indian mining experience in Arizona, northern Mexico, and California for the technical knowledge required to develop mining in California. Large-scale borrowing of mining techniques, tools, and language, not to speak of geological knowledge, took place between 1840 and 1860. The highly prejudiced Anglo miners treated Mexican miners as they did Chinese laborers; illegal taxation, lynchings, robbings, beatings, and expulsion became daily occurrences. Gold-mining lasted only a short time. When it was over, Anglos in great numbers turned to agricultural pursuits. The Mexican and Chinese populations migrated to California's towns to become landless laborers.

Southern California showed a very different face. *Rancheros* managed to hold onto their land for at least a generation after the Gold Rush. But climate, in the end, defeated many of them. Floods, followed by severe droughts, undercut the economy of the region in the 1860s and again in the 1880s. These were not "good times" for California agriculture.

By the turn of the century, Mexicans had been largely dispossessed of their property. Relegated to a lower-class status, they were overwhelmingly dispossessed, landless laborers, politically and economically impotent. Lynchings and murder of both Mexicans and Indians were so common that they often went unreported. Long-term residents of the region were reduced to being aliens in their native lands. The common theme that united all Mexicans was their conflict with Anglo society. The dominant society, profoundly racist, found it entirely reasonable to relegate Mexicans to a colonial status within the United States.

POLITICAL, MILITARY, AND CULTURAL RESISTANCE

Mexican resistance to Anglo hegemony took many forms. A great deal has been made of what individuals like Tiburcio Vásquez and Joaquín Murrieta were able to do; they, and others like them, became legendary for their resistance to Anglo domination. While many others resorted to the courts, a militarily conquered people, dispossessed and relegated to a subservient economic and political status largely justified by notions of racial inferiority, have seldom been successful in pressing their grievances to any equitable solution through a legal system controlled by the conquerors.

The political resistance that occurred varied from region to region, but almost always involved an accommodating elite who wanted to force the conqueror to stick to the "rules"—to abide by the Constitution, the Treaty of Guadalupe Hidalgo, and the like. In some areas, Mexicans went as delegates to constitutional conventions, winning at least *some* of the battles that the treaty negotiators had not been able to guarantee. In California, for example, it was significant that the franchise was *not* limited to white males. Legal recognition of the Spanish language was achieved for various periods in certain areas. Such political victories were won through struggle and resistance, yet they were rarely long-lived. Once there was Anglo control over a region—through military or police action, by economic advantage, or population size—there was no possibility of such "victories" being sustained.

The military resistance of Mexicans was never "official." Such actions were most often responses to individual or collective Anglo acts of violence against a Mexican, whether through lynching, rape, murder, or arson. The first person hanged in occupied California was a Mexican woman, three months pregnant, who had been raped by a drunken Anglo assailant. Her Mexican lover/husband who killed the Anglo was exiled; she was lynched.

The atrocities of the U.S.–Mexico War, especially along the Texas-Mexican border, continued; the Texas Rangers in time assumed the role once taken by the U.S. Army in Texas. Jacinto Treviño, Joaquín Murrieta, Chino Cortina, and Las Gorras Blancas are all examples of the "people's revolt" continuing well into the early twentieth century. Although Anglos called such men bandits, outlaws ("Mexican outlaws"), and desperados (from *desesperados* — those without hope, those who are desperate), Mexicans considered them heroes, often aiding and abetting their activities, if for no other reason than because they saw them as the only friendly force between themselves and the Anglo gun.

Many Anglos saw the Mexicans as a natural resource of the region that was to be domesticated and exploited. The Mexicans refused such a characterization; their resistance was a struggle to maintain their identity — control over their language, family, art, and religion — that involved them in a continuing relation with Mexico.

MEXICO AND ITS RELATIVE STANDING

Mexico, a nation with a long history of striving for social, political, and economic stability, seemed farther than ever from its goal after its war with the United States. The French invasion of Mexico in 1860 and the ensuing political instability only served to exacerbate many of Mexico's problems. When Porfirio Díaz became president of Mexico in 1876, he inaugurated policies that were intended to lead to rapid economic development. Federal government policies encouraged European and U.S. investments in railroads, mining, oil, and agriculture, especially cotton, sugar, coffee, and rubber. The attraction of foreign capital and investment was, however, too successful. By the time of the 1910 Revolution, foreigners owned three quarters of Mexico's mines, more than half of its oil fields, and massive tracts of land. Huge cattle ranches, particularly in northern Mexico, were owned by foreigners. Five major rail lines in northern Mexico, built and owned by U.S. interests, were characteristic foreign investments. Foreigners, in sum, owned more capital in Mexico than its citizens.

It was one thing to be successful in attracting foreign capital; it was another to reap significant benefits from such a policy. The effects of large-scale foreign investment were neither anticipated nor always beneficial to Mexico. The five rail lines, for example, did little to integrate Mexico's national economy. All five ran unerringly north, connecting Mexico's markets and labor supply with ranching and commercial centers in the U.S. Southwest. Mexico's products made their way into the world market economy; they were not intended for internal markets and thus brought no great advantage to Mexicans, whose industrial economy remained massively underdeveloped.

Meanwhile, mechanization in agriculture displaced many Mexican workers; few could be absorbed into the modest industrial sector. Prices for food and related commodities doubled, and in some cases tripled, in the decades just before the 1910 Revolution. Real wages declined; inflation was consistently high. At the same time, Mexico's population was growing rapidly; it increased by 50 percent between 1875 and 1910. Not surprisingly, such pressures led to great discontent and ultimately to the Revolution of 1910. That event, in turn, created a large-scale movement of Mexicans unable to fit into the restricted Mexican economy. Galarza, in his moving autobiography, *Barrio Boy*,[17] tells how Mexicans in the interior were forced from the land, sought work wherever they might find it— generally on the railroads—and gradually made their way northward, along with products extracted from Mexico, with scant compensation.

The U.S. Southwest and Beyond, 1900–1930

Foreign capital investments in Mexico retarded its economic independence. Far more was extracted than was left for internal development. The situation was made even more serious by events within the United States, particularly in the Southwest, where the local economy was developing and expanding. Initial U.S. demands for labor were large, particularly for agriculture, but also for sheep and cattle ranching. Between 1870 and 1900 the land given over to farming increased from 60,000 to nearly a million and a half acres.[18] Protective tariffs for agricultural products helped to expand the acreage under cultivation. The more powerful influence, however, was the effort by the federal government to bring water to arid regions. The Reclamation Act of 1902 significantly bolstered the struggling agricultural economy of the Southwest; the building of dams and reservoirs in the desertlike area created new prospects for a highly labor-intensive agricultural enterprise. Large areas in California, Texas, Arizona, and New Mexico were turned over to the cultivation of cotton, a commodity of increasing demand for the new industrial sectors of the world. When war came in 1914, Allied needs gave additional incentives for such agricultural expansion. Southwestern agriculture diversified; sugar-beet cultivation was another labor-intensive enterprise bolstered by a protective tariff and improved irrigation; California, Colorado, and Utah all profited. Fruits and vegetables—citrus, lettuce, spinach, beans, carrots, dates, cantaloupes, and nuts—became important commodities, particularly in California.

Agriculture played its own procreative role. It helped create industries for the processing, canning, packing, and crating of agricultural products. These tied in nicely with an expanding rail system that first linked east with west, and later, and more pragmatically, crisscrossed the Southwest to transport its products to new markets. Sheep and cattle ranching continued, creating yet new industries in meat processing and shipping.

Mining gained new momentum and new dimensions during this period. The manufacturing of machinery for one extraction and processing became vitally important, first, with copper in Arizona and New Mexico, then, with quartz in Nevada, Colorado, and Arizona, and later, with petroleum in Texas and California. The petroleum industry had a multiplier effect; it rapidly became a major component in the nation's burgeoning chemical industry.

The lumber industry also grew. Texas, California, Arizona, and New Mexico identified timber-cutting very early as a profitable economic activity that called for new modes of processing and distribution. These in turn developed still other industries.

The common denominator for all this rapid growth in the Southwest was the availability of cheap labor. The majority of European immigrants flowing into the United States through New York were absorbed in the industrial economies of the Northeast and Midwest. The Southwest had its own source of readily available and exploitable labor in the colonized Mexicans who filled the lower ranks of the economic order. They were still developing communities throughout the Southwest and would in time become increasingly visible also in the Midwest.

The conditions that greeted new immigrants from Mexico were essentially like those that Mexicans already in the United States know only too well. There was powerful racial hostility; Mexicans were thought to be inferior beings and inherently unassimilable and foreign. Their economic niche was insecure; their work was often seasonal in nature. In agricultural and related pursuits they were forced into a dual-wage system where they received low wages, frequently below those received by Anglos for the same type and amount of work. Many found themselves barred from supervisory positions. The situation in mining and related industries was not much different.

The railroad companies offered only slightly better conditions. By 1908 the Southern Pacific and the Atchison, Topeka, and Santa Fe were each recruiting more than a thousand Mexicans every month. The vast majority worked as section crews, laying track and ensuring its maintenance. The major difference between this industry and others in which Mexicans found work was that it seemed somewhat more stable and less seasonal; wages, however, were uniformly low.[19]

The Southwest was growing; its urban centers — in most instances, expanded versions of earlier Mexican towns — were often inhabited by Mexicans overwhelmingly concentrated in the lower range of the urban occupational structure. The wage differentials common to the rural sector were not as obvious in the urban areas. Access to particular occupations and industries, however, was limited and channeled. There was no mobility out of the unskilled and semiskilled positions in which Mexicans found themselves. They formed a reserve labor pool that could be called up as the situation dictated. When the economy expanded and jobs were created, these might be filled by Mexicans in specific sectors. Contractions of the economy relegated Mexicans quickly to the ranks of the unemployed; it was then they were reminded that they could be technically subject to another "sovereign," Mexico.

Mexicans served the industrial economy in other ways also. As a reserve labor pool, employers used them as a sort of "strike insurance," much as female and child labor were used to undercut unionizing efforts in other parts of the country. Such policies tended to generate ethnic antagonism between working-class Mexicans and working-class Anglos. Trade union practices, which excluded Mexicans and contributed to their exploitation, also helped to maintain them as a reserve labor pool, forcing them in the end to organize their own unions and associations.

While the beginnings of a middle class among Mexicans is discernible at this time, it is important to emphasize that most of those who made up this incipient class were self-employed in small-scale service businesses (newspapers, retail stores, and the like) while a few were "professionals," mostly elementary and secondary school teachers (in segregated schools). This class was never absorbed into the general economy. Rather, these business ventures tended to be restricted overwhelmingly to the Mexican community. On a social level, members of this emerging middle class encountered substantial barriers to their acceptance in the larger society, further perpetuating the prevailing patterns of residential and social segregation.

The Mexican government regularly lodged formal complaints with the State Department, protesting the abusive treatment its citizens received from industrial, mining, and agricultural enterprises. Those protests went largely unheeded; the U.S. government generally chose not even to verify the assertions, let alone make efforts to correct abuses.

By the early 1920s Mexicans began to settle outside of the Southwest. Many were recruited by northern manufacturing interests: meatpacking plants and steel mills in the Chicago area; automobile assembly lines in Detroit; the steel industry in Ohio and Pennsylvania; and Kansas City's meat-packing plants. By 1930 about 15 percent of the nation's Mexicans were living outside the Southwest. In addition to the recruitment of Mexicans from northern Mexico and the American Southwest by the industrial sector, many others chose to settle out of the principal migrant agricultural stream. Regular routes had become established that connected South Texas with the Great Lakes and Plains states. Many Mexicans continued their odyssey, following the crops west through the northern tier of states, finally arriving in the Northwest, and then turning south again. Others journeyed from Texas to the South, then north along the Eastern seaboard. Still others went west for agricultural work. Mexicans in California worked the crops north through that state, into the Northwest, and then east through the Mountain states. Many settled out of the migrant stream in areas where they found work.[20]

MIGRATION 1900–1930

No precise figures are available on the number of Mexicans who migrated north (or south) across the paper-made border between Mexico and the United States before 1900. The fact is that the border was open to unrestricted immigration until the creation and organization of the Immigration and Naturalization Service (and the Border Patrol) in 1924. Even then, however, large parts of the 2,000-mile border were unguarded, making the accuracy of all immigration figures somewhat questionable. One estimate is that from 1901 to 1910 approximately 9,300 Mexicans, principally from central and eastern Mexico, came to the United States each year.[21] In the second decade of the century, Mexicans came principally from northeastern and west-central Mexico. It is thought that 1,900 or so came annually between 1911 and 1914, and about 2,750 migrated annually from 1915 to 1919. Economic factors and the Revolution of 1910 spurred migration during this period. The third decade witnessed a very heavy Mexican migration to the United States. Between 1920 and 1924, more than 135,000 Mexicans (about 27,000 on an annual basis) left for the United States. Migration then tapered off to just under 109,000 between 1925 and 1930, about 18,000 per year. In all, about a quarter of a million Mexicans arrived in the United States during the first three decades of the twentieth century. No comparable figures are available on return migration.[22]

Included in the large wave of Mexican immigrants were a number of merchants, landowners, and intellectuals, many of whom had been displaced by the Revolution of 1910. Many settled in Texas; others established themselves in the Midwest, in cities like Kansas City; some went as far north as Milwaukee. Many, continuing with activities they had pursued in Mexico, became entrepreneurs in the United States. A greater number of Spanish-language newspapers, pamphlets, books, and articles appeared; analysis of the political effects of the Mexican Revolution became a staple item of such publications. Many Mexicans who crossed the border at this time, including this group of entrepreneurs, saw themselves as temporary expatriates who would one day return to Mexico when conditions there were more settled.

The population flow from Mexico during these decades represents one of the largest movements of people in the history of the world. The reasons are easily discoverable: there was an active labor recruitment by mining, railroad, and agricultural interests in the American Southwest, who justified their policies by arguing that Mexicans were uniquely suited for work that Anglo workers refused to do. The labor shortage resulting from U.S. involvement in World War I was another reason for the large upturn in demand. Mexico's Revolution of 1910 also induced many to leave. The net result, however, was that economic interests in the Southwest found an abundant source of cheap and exploitable labor.

The United States has been quite deliberate in permitting access to all immigrants except Asians. This policy of unrestricted immigration had significantly furthered national development. Immigrants took jobs in the industrial Northeast and Midwest that natives would not take, frequently at wages that tended to undermine unionizing activities. Immigrants served other purposes as well; for example, they traditionally constituted a disproportionate number of the enlisted men in the U.S. military forces.

Between 1917 and 1924, however, a combination of events caused the open-door policy to be changed, and free access to the United States was thereby ended. The sixty-year struggle of nativists and xenophobes to control the foreign population stimulated restrictionist legislation and promoted Americanization programs. The uneasy peace after World War I nurtured fear and distrust of all that was foreign, ranging from the League of Nations to immigrants. Old Yankee families in New England viewed with some misgivings the rising percentage of foreign-born around them. Organized skilled labor felt that its interests could be protected only by sharply curtailing cheap foreign labor. There were blocs of Southerners, Populists, and Progressives, each with its own reasons, wanting immigration to end.[23]

These groups were successful. Legislation passed in 1924 set national quotas on European immigrants to the United States. The year used as a base for calculating national quotas was 1890, a date chosen with care and deliberation, for in that year many more of the "older" immigrants from Northern and Western Europe had arrived in the United States. The law thus discriminated openly against the "new" immigrants from Eastern and Southern Europe. Justification for restrictive immigration was provided by the detailed study of the Immigration Commission. Appointed in 1907 by President Theodore Roosevelt and chaired by Senator Dillingham, the commission issued its conclusions in 1911 in an impressive forty-two volume report, which was soon widely quoted. Its principal message was that the new immigration was essentially different from the old and that new immigrants were less capable of being Americanized. Oscar Handlin, critically reviewing the commission and its work, cites the overt bias of the commission's report, beginning with the acceptance of the very assumptions it was ostensibly charged with investigating:

> The old and the new immigration differ in many essentials. The former was . . . largely a movement of settlers . . . from the most progressive sections of Europe. . . . They entered practically every line of activity. . . . Many of them . . . became landowners. . . . They mingled freely with the native Americans and were quickly assimilated. On the other hand, the new immigration has been largely a movement of unskilled laboring men who have come from the less progressive countries of Europe. . . . They have . . . congregated together in sections apart from native Americans and the older immigrants to such an extent that assimilation has been slow.

> Consequently the Commission paid but little attention to the foreign-born element of the old immigrant class and directed its efforts almost entirely to . . . the newer immigrants.[24]

The commission's report reflected the racial bias and attitudes of the time. Handlin cites from *The Passing of the Great Race,* the immensely popular book by the distinguished anthropologist Madison Grant on these newer immigrants:

> The new immigration contained a large and increasing number of the weak, the broken, and the mentally crippled of all races drawn from the lowest stratum of the Mediterranean basin and the Balkans, together with hordes of the wretched, submerged populations of the Polish ghettoes. Our jails, insane asylums, and almshouses are filled with human flotsam and the whole tone of American life, social, moral, and political, has been lowered and vulgarized by them.[25]

These beliefs, although vigorously debated in scientific circles, were given validation by their wholesale incorporation in the Dillingham Commission's report. They gave intellectual support for restrictive immigration legislation.[26] If the Rogers Act, passed in 1924, was silent on the matter of Mexican immigrants who continued to arrive in great numbers, there was no comparable reticence by the Dillingham Commission, which had said of Mexicans:

> Because of their strong attachment to their native land, low intelligence, illiteracy, migratory life, and the possibility of their residence here being discontinued, few become citizens of the United States. . . . In so far as Mexican laborers come into contact with native or with European immigrants they are looked upon as inferiors. . . .

Thus, it is evident that in the case of the Mexican he is less desirable as a citizen than as a laborer.[27]

The Dillingham Commission, in common with later immigration legislation, officially sanctioned the social and economic niche of Mexicans: they were not good enough for citizenship but certainly acceptable as manual laborers. Why such "tolerance"? To begin with, there was a great social distance between the Mexican of the Southwest and the nativists of the Midwest and Northwest. Also, the continued expansion of the region's economy, particularly in railroads and agriculture, made the availability of a large labor force imperative. Social distance and the emerging economic needs of the Southwest resulted in a lax policy toward Mexican immigration when the country was otherwise obsessed by its restrictionist mood.[28]

The passage of the 1924 Immigration Act made Mexicans conspicuous by their continued free access to the United States. Debate on the issue continued to agitate Congress. A report prepared for the 1928 congressional hearings on Western Hemisphere immigration, which argued against Mexican immigration, suggests how some, at least, saw the Mexican:

> Their minds run to nothing higher than animal functions — eat, sleep, and sexual debauchery. In every huddle of Mexican shacks one meets the same idleness, hordes of hungry dogs, and filthy children with faces plastered with flies, disease, lice, human filth, stench, promiscuous fornication, bastardy, lounging, apathetic peons and lazy squaws, beans and dried chili, liquor, general squalor, and envy and hatred of the gringo. These people sleep by day and prowl by night like coyotes, stealing anything they can get their hands on, no matter how useless to them it may be. Nothing left outside is safe unless padlocked or chained down. Yet there are Americans clamoring for more of these human swine to be brought over from Mexico.[29]

The Indian racial mixture was clearly a part of the cultural perception, little distinction being made between the two. The nativist drive for racial purity, emphasizing the superiority of the "white" race, denigrated the racial mixture characteristic of Latin America generally and of Indian nations like Mexico in particular. Yet no action was taken to curb the flow of Mexican immigrants. The powerful economic arguments for the continued importation of Mexican laborers had been articulated two years earlier before a congressional committee by John Nance Garner, who was to become Franklin Roosevelt's vice president: "In order to allow land owners now to make a profit of their farms, they want to get the cheapest labor they can find, and if they can get the Mexican labor it enables them to make a profit."[30]

At the same time, control of the "immigrant" population came to include measures that could be applied to the domestic Mexican population. The Americanization activities of the early twentieth century spread throughout the country and were used to bleach all ethnic vestiges in the national flock. These activities included intensive English instruction—with retribution for those who chose to speak other tongues—and success defined as a capacity to speak as did the English-speaking middle class; and intensive "civics" classes to socialize the "foreign" population. The norm for success became the Anglo middle class, and standardized IQ and achievement tests measured this success. The widespread institution of high schools that tracked the population into occupational or college preparatory curricula, with immigrants and racial minorities tracked into the former—when they entered high schools at all—became common. English oral proficiency became a requirement for immigration, as did English literacy for voting. The latter was also aimed at blacks in the South and spread throughout the United States as a mechanism of social control. Legislation mandating English instruction in the schools and English proficiency as a prerequisite to employment was targeted for various groups in different parts of the country. Segregated Mexican schools were maintained. In the early 1930s, through federal court litigation, segregation based on race was challenged, and segregation based on grouping for language instruction was initiated and legitimated.[31] Statehood for Arizona and New Mexico (which together had been one territory) was denied several times at the beginning of the century, in part because there were too many Mexicans in the territory. References were made to their "mongrel racial character," their inability to speak English, and therefore, presumably, their dubious allegiance to the United States. Despite racial conflict, physical abuse, cultural genocide, and economic exploitation, the Mexican population grew; however, where restrictionists had failed to limit Mexican immigration, the Great Depression succeeded.

THE GREAT DEPRESSION AND REPATRIATION

The decade of the Great Depression was another watershed for Mexicans. Social forces during this period significantly shaped the lives of Mexicans and are in many ways still responsible for their status half a century later. The decade began with a massive economic collapse that started late in the 1920s and continued until World War II. There was a major decline in economic activities, with wage rates in both industry and agriculture suffering, and rampant unemployment. With this came a major acceleration of government intervention in social welfare, with bureaucracies developing and expanding to meet the urgent needs of a dislocated populace. There was also a large-scale westward migration out of the Dust Bowl. In the Southwest, this was a time of accelerated rates of concentration into larger and larger units in both agriculture and mining, where increased mechanization led to a further displacement of labor. The industrial sector in the Southwest lagged behind the rest of the nation and could contribute little to absorb either the locally displaced labor or the dust-bowl migrants. These major economic dislocations fell on Mexicans with even greater force than on other groups. Already relegated to a marginal status, Mexicans were particularly vulnerable. The situation worked to eliminate for all practical purposes further northward migration from Mexico.

The Great Depression had another sobering effect: it engendered a collective social atmosphere of insecurity and fear that set the tone in allocating blame for the major social and economic traumas. Mexicans were singled out as scapegoats and made to bear the guilt for some of the ills of the period. It was not long before great numbers of unemployed Mexicans, like other citizens in the country, found themselves on the rolls of the welfare agencies.

One response to the strain placed on limited economic resources throughout the country was the demand for large-scale repatriations. To reduce the public relief rolls and agitation to organize labor, the Mexican became both the scapegoat and the safety valve in the Southwest. It is estimated that in the early years of the Depression (1929–1934) more than 400,000 Mexicans were forced to leave the country under "voluntary repatriation." Those who applied for relief were referred to "Mexican Bureaus," whose sole purpose was to reduce the welfare rolls by deporting the applicants.[32] Indigence, not citizenship, was the criterion used in identifying Mexicans for repatriation.

A 1933 eyewitness account of a Los Angeles repatriation scene suggests the mental frame of those responsible for the program:

> It was discovered that, in wholesale lots, they could be shipped to Mexico City for $14.70 per capita. The sum represented less than the cost of a week's board and lodging. And so, about February 1931, the first trainload was dispatched, and shipments at the rate of about one a month have continued ever since. A shipment consisting of three special trains left Los Angeles on December 8. The loading commenced at about six o'clock in the morning and continued for hours. More than twenty-five such special trains had left the Southern Pacific Station before last April.

> The repatriation programme is regarded locally as a piece of consummate statecraft. The average per family cost of executing it is $71.14, including food and transportation. It cost one Los Angeles County $77,249.29 to repatriate one shipment of 6,024. It would

have cost $424,933.70 to provide this number with such charitable assistance as they would have been entitled to had they remained — a savings of $347,468.40.[33]

Repatriations took place both in the Southwest and Midwest, where Mexicans, recruited to the area by employers with promises of work, had lived since the early twenties. Approximately half of the "returnees" actually were born in the United States.[34] Shipment to Mexico was a clear violation of both their civil and human rights. The Immigration and Naturalization Service, in concert with the Anglo press, identified the Mexican labor migrant as the source of (Anglo) citizen unemployment, for the increase of public welfare costs (and taxes), and as having entered the country "illegally" and in large numbers. The scapegoating tactics of an earlier nativist generation, with its xenophobic memories and myths, were used against the Mexicans. There was a good deal of sentiment also against Mexico's expropriation and nationalization of its oil industry, which U.S. oil companies had once controlled. Repatriation caused widespread dissolution of family and community, and contributed to an even more acute distrust among Mexicans of all government—local, state, or federal.

Some small efforts at organized resistance were made. Strikes and organizational campaigns were started in the agricultural and industrial sector. *La Unión de Trabajadores del Valle Imperial* and *La Confederación de Uniones Obreras Mexicanas* began late in the 1920s to try to ease the blow of the unfolding Depression through labor organizing and self-defense. There were similar, but less successful, efforts made in the mining industry. *La Confederación Regional Obrera Mexicana,* a Mexican industrial union affiliated with the American Federation of Labor, sought to encourage the formation of unions in California.

Mexican consuls, meanwhile, continued to lodge complaints with the federal government, protesting the treatment of Mexican citizens recruited to work in the United States. Official protests by Mexico generally were ignored, and the abuses went unchecked.

Despite all such efforts, the social and economic standing of Mexicans was seriously eroded by the Great Depression. Families were forcibly broken up by the repatriation efforts, as were communities. The overall economic impact of trade union activities was limited, and failed to modify the underlying problem of relegating Mexicans to the lowest levels of the economic system.

WORLD WAR II TO 1960

World War II brought many changes. In the economic upturn that followed, there was a new demand for both industrial and agricultural labor. The movement to the cities accelerated. Regional economic needs and interests reasserted themselves; they were again instrumental in shaping national legislation in the agricultural arena. The bracero program, reestablished in 1942 and patterned after a similar program in effect from 1917 to 1920, was based on a bilateral agreement between Mexico and the United States and was intended to supply labor for agriculture. The United States underwrote Mexicans' travel costs, insured a minimum wage, and guaranteed their just and equitable treatment. Agricultural interests were required to post a bond for every bracero and to abide by the agreements negotiated by the two governments. The program, in effect, was a federal subsidy of agriculture's labor needs.

Although intended only as a limited-term war measure to meet specific labor shortages in the agricultural sector, the advantages of the bracero program to both countries suggested its continuance. For Mexico, it was a temporary solution for high levels of unemployment and made for a significant flow of capital to Mexico in wages earned and sent home. For U.S. agriculture, it gave promise of a steady supply of labor that was readily controlled and minimally paid, and for whom no long-term responsibilities were assumed.

The program, extended annually after the war, was formalized in 1951 as Public Law 78. The reasons given for the extension were labor shortages stemming from U.S. involvement in the Korean War; it is better understood as a continuation of the traditional U.S. manipulation and control of the flow of Mexican labor. The program was terminated in 1964, when annual immigration quotas of 120,000 were established for all the nations of the Western Hemisphere.

Large-scale abuses were common in the program.[35] Mexico protested these abuses and each time the agreement was renegotiated sought to protect its citizens from inequitable wages and overt discrimination in working conditions, housing, and general treatment. The U.S. government relinquished the determination of wage rates to the agricultural employers, but continued to take responsibility for contracting and transporting Mexican laborers across the border. Nearly 5 million Mexicans came to the United States as a result of the program. The peak years were from 1954 to 1962, when 70 percent of all Mexicans involved in the program were working in the United States. We have no figures to tell us how many of these laborers returned to Mexico.

A steady flow of undocumented workers paralleled this importation of braceros. The undocumented proved to be a mixed blessing for agricultural interests. On the one hand, they were generally hired for wages substantially below the modest levels that agribusiness established for braceros, and bonds were not required to be posted for them. They were widely used as strikebreakers to thwart unionizing activities in agriculture. But there were obvious drawbacks. A labor pool made up of largely undocumented workers was very unstable. Since such workers were under no binding agreement to any employer, they were free to seek the highest wage, within the restrictions imposed by specific jobs and particular industries and under the continuous threat that the employer would terminate the job by calling the Immigration and Naturalization Service just before he was to meet the payroll. To the extent that agribusiness failed to establish a uniform wage, there was a constant temptation for undocumented workers to move on in search of better employment. Moreover, since the undocumented worker was not covered by an agreement restricting him to agricultural tasks, he would always be attracted by industrial jobs in cities, where wages and working conditions were generally better. During World War II, the informal agreements between industry and agribusiness that prohibited the hiring of Mexican labor for factory work were in abeyance.

We understand today how an initial bilateral agreement between Mexico and the United States to supply braceros became in time a unilateral program dictated by U.S. agricultural interests, supported by the federal government.[36] Once agricultural employers took control of the bracero program, they sought to expand their control also over the undocumented worker. Agricultural entrepreneurs ended up by transporting undocumented workers to the border, where they were immediately rehired as braceros, thereby transforming what was once an unregulated labor supply into a legal and semicontrolled work force bound to the agricultural sector.

After a regulated labor pool was firmly reestablished for agribusiness, in 1954 the Immigration and Naturalization Service vigorously launched "Operation Wetback." Undocumented workers, unstable and intractable as a labor source, were now to be removed. An astonishing 3.8 million Mexican aliens (and citizens) were apprehended and expelled in the next five years. Of the total number deported during that time, fewer than 2 percent left as a result of formal proceedings. The vast majority were removed simply by the *threat* of deportation. "Looking Mexican" was often sufficient reason for official scrutiny. The search focused initially on California and then Texas; it soon extended as far as Spokane, Chicago, St. Louis, and Kansas City.[37]

For urban Chicanos and Mexicans, World War II had effects similar to those for their rural cousins. On the positive side, war industries provided the semblance of occupational opportunity for many, though often in unskilled, semiskilled, and low-level service capacities. Still, the rigid tie between class and ethnicity seemed somewhat weakened.

World War II posed a major dilemma for the United States. In its official pronouncements and acts, the country strongly condemned the racism explicit in Nazism. Yet at the same time, the United States had a segregated military force. This was also a time when President Roosevelt issued Executive Order No. 9066, which authorized the internment of Japanese who were U.S. citizens and whose sole "crime" was living and working on the West Coast.

This contradiction also manifested itself in ugly confrontations between Mexicans and Anglos. The press, for its part, helped to raise feelings against Mexicans. The violent confrontations between servicemen and local police against Mexican residents began late in 1942 and continued until mid-1943. The overt racial bias of the press with regard to Mexicans has been thoroughly documented. It suggests the power of the press in shaping public opinion and in justifying major abuses by law enforcement and military personnel. The so-called zoot suit riots illustrate the power of the press in mobilizing prejudice:

> The zoot-suiters of Los Angeles . . . were predominantly Mexican youth with some Negro disciples, between the ages of sixteen and twenty. They wore absurdly long coats with padded shoulders, porkpie hats completed by a feather in the back, watch chains so long they almost touched the ground, and peg-top trousers tapering to narrow cuffs . . . at best, as one pundit observed, they were "not characterized primarily by intellect." They formed themselves into bands with flamboyant names: the "Mateo Bombers," "Main Street Zooters," "The Califa," "Sleepy Lagooners," "The Black Legion," and many more. Their targets for physical harm were members of the armed forces, with a special predilection for sailors. The latter fought back with devastating effect. The situation quickly deteriorated to the point that the Navy declared Los Angeles out of bounds. The city council outlawed wearing of zoot suits for the duration and the city simmered down.[38]

Some investigators, more objective than the press, have reversed the roles, with the navy on the offensive and the Mexican young obliged to defend themselves. The firsthand accounts show that the police actually encouraged and supported the servicemen's aggression. And not only did the police refuse to halt the violence, they often contributed to it.[39]

Another celebrated incident was the so-called Sleepy Lagoon case in 1942. A Mexican youth was killed as the result of gang conflict. A sensationalist press soon gave the incident a wholly false character; it was thought to be the beginnings of an incipient crime wave led by insurgent Mexicans. Public pressure led the police to massive roundups. Twenty-four Mexican youths were arrested; seventeen were indicted and tried for murder. The defendants, beaten by the police and forced to appear in court in their unkempt and disheveled states, received scant sympathy. Despite the lack of tangible evidence, nine were convicted of murder, eight, of lesser crimes. These decisions, reversed two years later by the California District Court of Appeals as a direct result of efforts by outraged civil rights lawyers and activists, tell much of the temper of the times. They also suggest why Chicanos and Mexicans are so suspicious of the U.S. law enforcement and legal systems. Mexicans believe that they consistently receive harsher sentences than Anglos for the same crime. They also believe that this explains their disproportionate representation in U.S. penal institutions.[40]

The Mexican community, in responding to the situation of World War II, acted as it had done in previous times of hostility and exploitation —with organizational efforts and litigation, and occasionally with armed resistance. Unity Leagues, created in the early 1940s, had as their principal purpose the election of Mexicans to city councils in Southern California communities; they also conducted voter registration drives, attempted fund-raising, and worked to get voters to the polls. The basic theme uniting these leagues was the fight against racial discrimination, particularly in the schools. The League of United Latin American Citizens (LULAC), founded in South Texas in 1928, expanded into a national organization in the post-World War II period, and was soon heavily involved in anti-discrimination activity, again particularly in the educational arena.

A landmark court decision in 1945 (*Méndez v. Westminster School District*) barred *de jure* segregation of Chicano students. A similar legal action in Texas in 1948 was also successfully pressed. The results of both court actions, as well as others during the 1950s, helped set the stage for the Supreme Court's *Brown v. Board of Education* decision in 1954, and clearly established the illegality of the deliberate segregation of Chicano and Mexican schoolchildren on the basis of race, and of bilingual education as a partial remedy for segregation. The success of these efforts served to encourage civil rights suits in other areas, notably against job discrimination in New Mexico.[41]

The refusal of local officials in Corpus Christi, Texas, in 1948, to allow the burial of a Chicano war hero in the local "for whites only" cemetery was the specific catalyst for the creation of the G.I. Forum. The Mexican community proudly emphasized two facts: Chicanos received the largest number of Congressional Medals of Honor during World War II, and despite forbidding interrogations by the North Koreans and Chinese during the Korean War, no Chicano soldier ever "broke down." The collective memory of such Chicano military contributions fed the Mexican distaste of continued political gerrymandering, economic exploitation, physical abuse, and cultural repression at home.

The Mexican-American Political Association, formed in 1959, had as its goal "the social, economic, cultural and civic betterment of Mexican Americans and all other Spanish-speaking Americans through political action." The association established chapters in voting districts with large concentrations of Mexican residents and endorsed candidates for public office who could be counted on to work actively for social improvement.

Large numbers of Mexicans migrated to urban centers in the decades after World War II. There was a general optimism that life in the cities would be better than in the rural setting. The cities seemed to hold out the promise of better jobs, more adequate housing, and new educational possibilities. These early migrants to the cities came with visions of expanded opportunities and believed that if they themselves did not achieve their aspirations, their children surely would. This optimism made tolerable the thwarted aspirations so many of these urban migrants soon came to feel. Since they outnumbered Mexicans already living in the cities, their optimism spread to the larger group.

Many of the postwar organizations were primarily self-protective, mutual-aid associations. They were formed principally to protect their numbers by offering services consistent with Mexican cultural traditions, in effect compensating for services withheld by the larger society. Organizations such as the G.I. Forum and LULAC entered the activist period of the 1950s and 1960s with an organizational base redirected toward activism. Their resources were considerable—a growing constituency, established legitimacy, and a solid leadership core. Their past history of noninvolvement in political affairs, their emphasis on assimilation, or working within the system, and their passive, nonactivist stance, drew criticism in the 1970s. Such groups, however, provided the foundation for attempts to improve the condition of the Mexican people.

THE CHICANO MOVEMENT 1965–1975

In the 1960s and early 1970s, activist, sometimes radical, organizations appeared. These organizations came to be known collectively as the Chicano movement. Often very critical of certain of the basic assumptions of U.S. society, they sought fundamental transformations in the distribution of power in the United States. Many promoted radical alternatives, preferring socialism, for example, to the prevailing economic and political system. Others hoped to create various kinds of alternative or separatist institutions, with alternative schools, community control of law enforcement, health, educational, and political institutions, and the like. They were looking, in short, for a radical and equitable transformation of a racist society. Almost all such groups emphasized the distinctiveness of Mexican culture. They actively promoted Chicano cultural norms and values. Chicano culture represented the common ground that bound together all the members of the group. Political terms such as "Chicano" and *La Raza Nueva* were used to symbolize unity, and were intended to increase the cohesiveness of otherwise diverse elements.

Charismatic leaders appeared. Reies López Tijerina hoped to restore lost Spanish and Mexican land grants in New Mexico through the widely publicized and often dramatic activities of the *Alianza Federal de Pueblos Libres*. Rodolfo "Corky" Gonzales, former prizefighter and disaffected Democratic party official, organized the Crusade for Justice and established several alternative community institutions in the Denver area. The miserable working conditions of Mexican agricultural laborers became the special concern of the United Farm Workers Organizing Committee, led by César Chávez.

Throughout the Southwest and Midwest, political and educational issues sparked new organizing activity. In Texas, José Angel Gutiérrez and others overthrew the minority Anglo-dominated governments of several South Texas cities and counties, primarily through a third party, *El Partido de La Raza Unida*. To secure educational change, students in secondary schools and colleges formed Chicano organizations to stage massive school walkouts. These organizations served as foci for various kinds of diffused activities; they brought a variety of grievances under a single banner, and made a collective approach to these grievances possible.

Anglo decision-makers, reacting to the politics of direct action and confrontation, were sometimes repressive, sometimes progressive; many of the gains made could be attributed to the "threatening" activities of such militant organizations. The protest groups, however, were often short-lived. They called for a great expenditure of time and effort and involved considerable risk.

The student groups were ideologically very diverse: some were moderate-liberal; others were radical. The Mexican-American Youth Organization, a precursor in Texas to the *Raza Unida* party, gave José Angel Gutiérrez, Mario Compeán, and others apprenticeship training in community-based and campus-based politics. *El Movimiento Estudiantíl Chicano de Aztlán*, a campus-based organization, was fairly radical and had many chapters throughout the Southwest; it was very active in support of the farm workers' movement and many other nonschool issues. The United Mexican American Students and the Chicano Youth Organization were other prominent student organizations during the period. Although such organizations often worked off-campus, they pushed also for increased recruitment of Chicano students and faculty, for opening new educational opportunities to Chicanos, and for curricula more relevant to

Chicano concerns. Many of these demands were embodied in the new Chicano Studies programs developed in many colleges and universities.

The importance of these campus-based organizations cannot be overemphasized. They provided invaluable resources for both on-campus and off-campus activities. Many interacted with both staff and faculty. Student groups were effective agents of political mobilization; they had the idealism, ideological commitment, and the relatively supportive environment necessary for sustained organizational activities. Many of these campus organizations, however, were unable to contend with the rapid turnover of student populations, with increasing administrative intransigence, and internal division created by law enforcement *provocateurs* and ultraleftist organizations.

Prior to the 1970s there were few Chicano professional associations, which is not surprising, given the small number of Chicano professionals. As the system yielded to pressure, however, and greater numbers of Chicanos became teachers, lawyers, physicians, and business managers, organization became viable. Many started with less than a dozen members; in many of the academic disciplines, the formation of Chicano/Latino caucuses in major Anglo professional organizations was a necessary first step. Public and private foundations, responding to demands for increased numbers of Chicano professionals, provided support to foster organizational activity. Among these were the *Southwest Council de la Raza,* the Mexican-American Legal Defense and Educational Fund (MALDEF), and the *National Task Force de la Raza.*

Until 1970 Mexicans were traditionally concentrated in the nonunion ranks of the U.S. economy. Starting in the early 1920s they attempted to form their own unions or to affiliate with unions in Mexico and the United States. The leadership of established industrial unions in this country was never Chicano, although some change is now taking place. Latino workers — Mexicans, Puerto Ricans, and others — are beginning to coalesce in organizations such as the Labor Council for Latin American Advancement.

With the establishment of "national" offices based in Washington, several Chicano organizations began to grow in the mid-1970s. Interorganizational cooperation between Chicanos and Latinos in general has become more common. There have been several attempts to weld "Hispanic" organizations together in some sort of federation, notably the newly created Forum of National Hispanic Organizations and the Hispanic Higher Education Coalition. In the late 1970s such Washington-based groups as the *National Council de la Raza,* MALDEF, and the Mexican-American Women's National Association could coordinate to express the common concerns of Chicano organizations.

Chicanos have gravitated toward public employment, having found opportunities there, particularly in lower-status positions, somewhat more open than in the private sector. Organizations within the public sector, such as IMAGE, a nationwide group of employees that seeks to enhance the working conditions and positions of Chicanos and other Latinos within the government, have emerged. Although there are few high-level government officials of Mexican origin, organizations of Latino officials have come into being. The National Association of Latino Elected and Appointed Officials tries to increase communication between Chicano and Latino decision-makers, particularly on the local level. The Congressional Hispanic Caucus, consisting of the six Latino members of Congress, is the group with the highest governmental status at the federal level.

Two broad coalitions of interests make up the major political parties in the United States, and in general, Chicanos have been exploited by both. Many of the successes of the Democratic party can be attributed to the 70 to 90 percent electoral support regularly given by Chicano voters. Minimal rewards, in the form of minor patronage and policy concessions, have been returned to the Chicano community by the Democratic party, which for the most part has taken the Chicano vote for granted. In very close elections, Democrats have made extravagant promises to Chicanos, but once the election is over, the Anglo Democratic leadership has generally failed to follow through. The Republican party has only limited appeal for Chicanos; Republican leaders have not made a very serious effort to broaden their base by attracting Chicano participation.

Minor parties, including socialist and Marxist-oriented parties, have not been very successful in recruiting Chicanos to their cause. The most successful third party movement for Chicanos, El Partido de la Raza Unida (LRUP), at the height of its influence in the early 1970s played a pivotal role in determining the outcome of several local elections, primarily in South Central Texas. In small localities with large Chicano populations, it succeeded in school, town, and county government elections, often stressing the unresponsiveness of the major parties, and arguing for cultural nationalism. The Partido provided an alternative that threatened the customary hegemonic position of the major parties. Both the Democratic and the Republican parties reacted by supporting minor institutional reform: they set up "Hispanic" offices within their party organizations, and the Democratic party went so far as to guarantee Chicano representation in its party structure. Conflicts within its own ranks over strategic issues led La Raza Unida to fragment into smaller locally based units. Punitive measures sponsored by the State of Texas and specifically aimed at breaking up the Partido contributed to its decline. Modifications in electoral laws proved problematic to third parties that attempted to place their candidates on the ballot. By raising the number of required petition-signers or votes received to qualify for inclusion on the ballot, third parties could be excluded.

By the late 1970s the organizational base of the Chicano community had been largely transformed. Many of the more radical and ideological organizations had either disappeared or were mere shadows of their former selves. Leaders who cut their political teeth in such organizations have become part of older, more broadly based organizations or have joined the new professional organizations that continue to advocate, with renewed spirit, specific political reforms. The organizational structure changes as collective and individual political sophistication continues to grow.

GROWTH AND NATIONAL VISIBILITY

The structural characteristics of the Chicano population suggest why Chicanos have gained national visibility. All demographic description starts by emphasizing the youthfulness of the Chicano population, the median age for Chicanos being seven years younger than the national population. A youthful population is one that will be active for a longer period, with the bulk of its members in an early phase of labor force participation, or only just beginning to prepare for that phase. A youthful population has its future before it; schooling, family formation, and child-rearing are crucial issues. And given their rapid numerical growth, Chicanos must play an increasingly important role in the United States in the next decades.

With journalistic phrases like "people on the move," "awakening giant," "emerging minority," and "sleeping giant," writers have drawn attention to the "sudden" visibility of Chicanos. Some are surprised by this visibility. Even the most casual traveler through the southwestern United States has observed the centuries-old Spanish and Mexican influence on architecture, cuisine, language, art, music, and the very layout of towns and cities. Chicano presence in the Southwest has never been hidden. It is the sudden awareness that Chicanos also reside outside these traditional southwestern enclaves and that Chicano issues are not simply regional in nature that has drawn the continuing attention of the mass media. Indeed, the rapid *growth* and continuing *dispersion* of the Chicano population is producing the new national awareness.

The Chicano population has grown substantially over the last decade. Although this growth is attributed in part to improved methods of survey and enumeration by gathering agencies such as the Census Bureau, the greater part of the increase comes from the real growth of the Chicano population. This growth rate has been conservatively estimated at 2.2 percent per year; a more liberal estimate is 3.5 percent per year. The first figure indicates a doubling of the Chicano population every twenty-five to twenty-seven years; the second, a doubling in less than twenty years.

This phenomenal rate of growth is in stark contrast with decreasing growth rates for the U.S. population as a whole. While U.S. birth rates are stabilizing at just above replacement level, the Chicano population is maintaining the highest rate of growth of all major racial and ethnic groups in the country. Early marriage and the emphasis placed on family accounts for these high fertility rates. Chicano families are generally about 25 percent larger than the average American family, and one in every five Chicano families consists of six or more persons.

There is, however, a trend toward lower birth rates. Younger Chicanas are having fewer children and spacing them out longer over the childbearing years. Still, even among younger and better-educated women, the emphasis on childbearing appears to remain strong; voluntary childlessness among married Chicanas, or those who were married, is virtually unknown.

The high fertility rates of Chicanos suggest major structural differences between them and the Anglo population. Although the Anglo birth rate has decreased owing to later marriages, birth spacing, and the use of contraceptives to synchronize childbearing with the demands of increased female employment, this has not always been the case. From the late 1930s to the early 1940s the United States had high rates of immigration and fertility; the two together produced a period of high population growth. The Chicano population explosion today is in many ways reminiscent of that earlier era, with high rates of immigration (both legal and undocumented) and birth rates. All signs point to a significant growth of the Chicano population in the 1980s.

There is now considerable discussion regarding total Hispanic population growth in the United States and whether this collective group will overtake blacks as the largest national minority group. Precise projections are impossible since they depend on how long current high rates of growth in the Hispanic population are sustained. Still, it is now expected that the Hispanic population will become the largest majority in the United States in the foreseeable future. Further, since Chicanos make up the majority— 60 percent—of this population group, they will be among the more visible elements in what is increasingly referred to as the "Hispanization" of the United States.

If high birth rates are important, so also is immigration. The century-old relationship between the United States and Mexico continues to affect both nations. Immigrants, natural resources, and profits continue to flow north. Legal immigration from Mexico to the United States at present allows between forty and fifty thousand visas each year for permanent residence. Those looking for "commuter status," which allows them to work in the United States while living in Mexico, have to endure, barring political connections, a three-year waiting period.

Mexican workers caught in Mexico's economic sluggishness are aware that wages in the United States for identical work are sometimes seven times higher than at home, and many are thus led to risk illegal entry. Such illegal entry is only increased by the active recruitment by "coyotes," who transport Mexicans across the border for a fee. Undocumented workers are a significant part of the U.S. labor force, particularly for work that most American citizens regard as demeaning, low paying, dirty, and unstable. Undocumented workers have always come to the United States in circumstances of multiple jeopardy, as minorities unprotected from employer exploitation and abuse. Such conditions continue unabated today.

A majority of the undocumented workers in the United States come as sojourners in search of economic opportunity; few have any desire to remain here as permanent residents. Despite the widespread impression that Mexican undocumented workers come across the border in search of the promised land, *corridos,* or ballads, by and about them celebrate the less hostile, more familiar ambience they plan to return to.

The flow of immigration, both legal and undocumented, is extensive: more than a million persons annually are apprehended by the Border Patrol for seeking entry without inspection. Annual deportations, both voluntary and involuntary, continue to increase steadily. These statistics suggest improved enforcement capabilities; they also measure, however crudely, the growth in the number of Mexicans wanting to cross the permeable U.S.–Mexico border. That flow increases in part because of labor force needs. Jobs are available to Mexican migrants largely in the secondary labor market, where the lack of fringe benefits makes these low-paying, seasonal jobs unattractive to domestic workers. The Mexican worker historically has been desirable. Mexicans—particularly without legal rights and privileges—are especially desirable for agribusiness, marginal industries, seasonal work, or in businesses quickly affected by economic downturns.

Although only a small fraction of the undocumented workers come to the United States with any intention of staying, there is no reason to believe that Mexican immigration will cease, at least in the foreseeable future. The flow of nearly a century and a half, responding to the need for labor by U.S. employers, seems to argue against the possibility of immigration being terminated. The growth of the Chicano population, because of higher fertility and continued immigration, is increasingly visible. The continued dispersion of the Chicano population out of the Southwest into the industrial Midwest, particularly into cities like Chicago, Gary, Ham-

mond, Kansas City, Detroit, Flint, and Saginaw, will go on. It is not difficult to understand the attraction of the Midwest: a Chicano worker with
a high-school education will earn approximately $4,000 more per year there
than his cousin can expect to earn in the Southwest.

Such differentials in income are significant. The Midwest, highly
unionized and with a long-established industrial base, is very different from
the Southwest, which is only now beginning to unionize, and where light
manufacturing is still the rule. In the Southwest, also, labor-intensive industries in agriculture and mining are giving way to high-level service industries in aerospace, electronics, and petrochemicals that require a labor
force that is technically trained. This new labor force tends to be made
up largely of transplanted Easterners.

Chicanos in the Midwest, Pacific Northwest, Florida, and other parts
of the United States need to be seen as a vanguard. Although farther removed from their origins, they still maintain and perpetuate their Mexican heritage. Their entry into an area is almost always followed by the
rapid opening of small Chicano businesses that specifically cater to their
needs. Spanish-language mass at the Catholic Church typically follows,
along with Spanish-language radio programs and bilingual programs in
the schools. The taking root of Chicano businesses, services, and traditions produces a Midwestern version of the Southwestern or Mexican environment. The ability of Chicanos to transfer their ethnic preferences from
one location to another tells something of the strength and durability of
their cultural ties.

Midwestern Chicanos, finding themselves among non-Chicano Latinos, necessarily interact, but not always easily or without hostility and
suspicion. New patterns, however, are becoming evident as efforts at
cooperative ventures are made. Chicanos in Milwaukee, Chicago, and Detroit, for example, discovering that they face problems very similar to those
of other Latinos, seek to create coalitions that form the basis for a national Latino thrust. These contacts have understandably progressed further among Cuban, Puerto Rican, and Chicano leaders at the national level
than at the local level, particularly as the strategy of nationally organized
coalition-building has spread.

The dispersal of Chicanos has had positive and negative effects, making it obvious that Chicano issues cannot be dealt with simply as a regional (Southwestern) matter. Chicanos now reside in every state in the
Union; the 1980s will undoubtedly see almost half the Chicano population
residing outside the five southwestern states. Had the dispersal of Chicanos
not occurred, most of the southwestern states would be overwhelmingly
Chicano. Although the size of population does not automatically translate
into political power, political negotiation and coalition-building would

have taken very different forms if the Southwest had become a single and greater Chicano enclave.

CURRENT STATUS

Chicanos lag behind the rest of the U.S. population by every measure of socioeconomic well-being—level of education, occupational attainment, employment status, family income, and the like. Some say that Chicanos are no different from other immigrants who arrived in the United States impoverished, and who managed by hard work to gain advantages for their children, taking the first important step toward assimilation. The substantial achievements of the American-born first generation over that of the immigrant generation are thought to be conclusive. Such an optimistic view overlooks major changes in the society and the historical relationship of over a century and a half of racial discrimination and economic exploitation. Although economic expansion and dramatic social change characterized the postwar years, economic contraction and dislocation, possibly exaggerated by the new conservative retrenchment, are the hallmarks of more recent times. When the economy was productive and growing, Chicanos participated in that growth, at least through their labor. A close examination, however, suggests that the modest gains made in average income and occupational status during the 1950s and 1960s were lost in the 1970s. As one scholar explains:

> When the 1975 occupational employment distributions for Anglos and Chicanos are compared to the Labor Department's revised estimates for 1985 employment opportunities, it is clear that the [1975] recession hurt the future income potential of Chicanos as well as their current incomes. In general, the recession has forced Chicanos into occupational groups for which future employment is expected to decline relative to the employment, and in which relative wages can be expected to fall as well. Similarly, while Anglos were moving into those occupations that are expected to have the greatest future income potential, Chicanos were moving out, thus losing the ability to share in the expected relative wage increases that growth usually brings. By 1975, only 33 percent of Chicanos were located in expanding occupations. . . . The evidence supports the conclusion that our latest recession had a definite racial bias and that Mexican Americans received more than their share of economic hardship.[42]

Although second-generation and later Chicanos made large gains relative to those of the first generation, such gains did not allow for their thorough absorption into the economic and social structure of U.S. society. The data of the late 1970s suggest how different generations of Chicanos have fared.[43] The median education for second-generation Chicanos was 11.1 years, only two years more than for U.S. born first-generation, but decidedly more than for the immigrant generation (5.8 years).

All generations of Chicano males are underrepresented in white-collar jobs; Mexican-born males are least likely to be found in such positions. Farm labor is the one area where there is a significant difference between the U.S.-born and immigrant Chicano populations.[44] Over 15 percent of Mexican-born men are employed as farm laborers, twice the number for sons of Mexican immigrants, five times the number of second-generation Chicanos. Labor force participation figures, however, also show that second-generation Chicanos had the highest unemployment rate, while the immigrant generation had the lowest. The data on incomes indicate first-generation Chicano families as having the highest median income, with the second-generation following, and the Mexican-born as having the lowest incomes. The range, however, was not great—about $1,500.

That Mexicans who have resided for the longest time in the United States—second generation—have the highest unemployment rates and only very modest representation in white-collar, professional, and managerial categories suggests the limited structure of opportunity for Chicanos. They are entering the industrial sector at a time when its socioeconomic structure is increasingly tertiary, demanding highly trained personnel in high-technology industries such as aerospace, communications, and the like. Although Chicanos may be making "progress" relative to their immigrant parents, they are actually falling farther behind when looked at in the context of the opportunity structure in an increasingly postindustrial social order and compared to the dominant population. Also, there is evidence that Chicano technical and occupational skills will increasingly limit them to the secondary labor market, with its unfavorable wage rates, limited fringe benefits, and general instability. These conditions do not promise either full equity or full participation for Chicanos in the decades immediately ahead. Still, that the Anglo population growth is at or near a steady state, with its income-generating population increasingly aging, suggests that the younger and expanding Chicano work force will be shouldering a growing and disproportionate burden in the future. Social Security, Medicare, Medicaid, and the myriad of other social programs funded from taxes on the work force will be more and more borne by youthful employed Chicanos.

Historically, Chicanos' economic rewards have been disproportionate to their contribution to U.S. industrial development. Now that the society is increasingly postindustrial, Chicanos find themselves still carrying the burden. The federal government, which played a prominent role throughout the history of Mexicans in the United States, has often been repressive, supporting industries and employers, and generally frustrating Chicanos' efforts to advance. Many of the organizations developed by Chicanos were direct responses to these negative influences. The prediction seems to be unremitting governmental policies that will continue to deplete the resources of the Chicano community or leave it as disadvantaged as ever. But Mexico's new wealth, particularly its energy resources, may somewhat alter that prognosis, especially if Mexico retains control over those resources. A nation tends to treat descendants of foreign stock, even a militarily conquered population, with greater responsibility when it is obliged to negotiate with that foreign nation on an equal footing.

Still, the outlook for Chicanos is not very encouraging. Efforts by Chicano organizations to obtain justice and equality and to share in society's bounties have not been overwhelmingly successful. Whether these efforts stand a better chance of succeeding when external forces are more active in helping such efforts, only the future can tell.

NOTES

This essay is a joint effort by the authors. The listing of names on the title page in no way indicates the extent of contribution. Rather, all four authors contributed equally.

1. The terms "Chicano" and "Mexican" are used interchangeably in this essay, because the U.S. Southwest and northern Mexico were initially a cultural and geographic unit, the border being only an invisible line between the two nations.

2. The term "Anglo" will be used to refer to U.S. residents of European origin. It is used, for convenience, as a generic term for all European immigrants of the United States.

3. Rodolfo Acuña, *Occupied America* (San Francisco: Canfield Press, 1972), p. 11.

4. Eugene C. Barker, *Mexico and Texas, 1821–1835* (New York: Russell and Russell, 1965), p. 52.

5. Acuña, *Occupied America.*

6. Ibid., p. 44ff; Mario Barrera, *Race and Class in the Southwest* (South Bend, Ind.: University of Notre Dame Press, 1979), pp. 7–33; Matt S. Meier and Feliciano Rivera, *The Chicanos: A History of Mexican Americans* (New York: Hill and Wang, 1972), pp. 88–94.

7. Carey McWilliams, *North from Mexico* (Philadelphia: Lippincott, 1949).

8. Joan W. Moore, with Harry Pachon, *Mexican Americans,* 2d edition (Englewood Cliffs, N.J.: Prentice-Hall, 1976), pp. 13–14.

9. Barrera, *Race and Class in the Southwest,* p. 25.

10. Meier and Rivera, *The Chicanos,* p. 107.

11. Moore, with Pachon, *Mexican Americans,* p. 15.

12. Barrera, *Race and Class in the Southwest,* pp. 23–30.

13. McWilliams, *North from Mexico.*

14. Peter Baird and Ed McCoughan, *Beyond the Border: Mexico and the U.S. Today* (New York: North American Congress on Latin America, 1979); Barrera, *Race and Class in the Southwest;* Meier and Rivera, *The Chicanos.*

15. Ibid.

16. Barrera, *Race and Class in the Southwest,* p. 20.

17. Ernesto Galarza, *Barrio Boy* (South Bend, Ind.: University of Notre Dame Press, 1971).

18. Meier and Rivera, *The Chicanos,* p. 124.

19. Barrera, *Race and Class in the Southwest,* pp. 84–86.

20. Vernon M. Briggs, Jr., Walter Fogel, and Fred H. Schmidt, *The Chicano Worker* (Austin: University of Texas Press, 1977); Meier and Rivera, *The Chicanos.*

21. Manuel P. Servin, "The Pre–World War II Mexican-American: An Interpretation," *California Historical Society Quarterly* 45 (1966): 325–38.

22. The migration figures at this time are characterized by imprecision. Leo Grebler, for example, in *The School Gap: Signs of Progress* (Advance Report 7, Mexican American Study Project [Los Angeles: University of California Press, 1967]), has figures that are 20 percent higher than Servin's (ibid.), and Barrera, in *Race and Class in the Southwest,* indicates that a comparison of Mexico's emigration statistics with U.S. immigration figures shows still higher numbers.

23. Oscar Handlin, *Race and Nationality in American Life* (New York: Anchor Books, 1957), pp. 93–94.

24. Ibid., pp. 101–2.

25. Ibid., p. 97.

26. Ibid., pp. 93–138.

27. William Paul Dillingham, *Report of the Immigration Commission,* vol. 1 (Washington, D.C.; Government Printing Office, 1911), pp. 690–91.

28. Acuña, *Occupied America,* pp. 123–50; Baird and McCoughan, *Beyond the Border,* pp. 21–35; Barrera, *Race and Class in the Southwest,* pp. 72–75.

29. "Mexican Immigration: A Report by Roy L. Garis for the Information of Congress," *Western Hemisphere Immigration,* Committee on Immigration and Naturalization, 71st Congress 2d session, 1930, p. 436.

30. Committee on Immigration and Naturalization, *Seasonal Agricultural Laborers from Mexico,* 69th Congress, 1st session, 1926, p. 24.

31. Moore, with Pachon, *Mexican Americans,* p. 40.

32. Meier and Rivera, *The Chicanos,* p. 163.

33. Moore, with Pachon, *Mexican Americans,* pp. 41–42.

34. Ernesto Galarza, *Merchants of Labor: The Mexican Bracero Story* (Santa Barbara, Calif.: McNally-Loftin, 1964).

35. Ibid.

36. Ibid.

37. Ibid.

38. McWilliams, *North from Mexico,* pp. 227–58.

39. Roger Daniels and Harry H. L. Kitano, *American Racism: Explorations of the Nature of Prejudice* (Englewood Cliffs, N.J.: Prentice-Hall, 1970), p. 76.

40. Armando Morales, *Ando Sangrado: I Am Bleeding* (LaPuente, Calif.: Perspectiva Publications, 1972).

41. Meier and Rivera, *The Chicanos,* pp. 242–43.

42. Tim D. Kane, "Structural Change and Chicano Employment in the Southwest: Some Preliminary Changes," *Aztlan* 45 (1973): 383–98.

43. Ibid., p. 29.

44. Philip Garcia and Lionel Maldonado, "America's Mexicans: A Plea for Specificity," (mimeo); Philip Garcia, "Nativity, Bilingualism and Occupational Attainment among Mexican-American Men," (in press). The data summarized here are from a more detailed analysis of the 1970 Decennial Census and the March 1978 Current Population Survey. This section borrows from that more detailed analysis. Chicanos' attainments on selected racial characteristics are presented in terms of Mexican immigrants, first-generation and subsequent-generation Chicanos.

3. The Puerto Rican Community: Its Political Background

James Jennings

BY 1970 OFFICIAL ESTIMATES of the number of Puerto Ricans living in New York City varied between 850,000 and 1,200,000.[1] Although Puerto Ricans first began to migrate in significant numbers to New York City in 1917 after the passage of the Jones Act,[2] they were not living in large residential clusters until the 1930s. During that decade between 53,000 and 70,000 Puerto Ricans came to the city, settling first in the Brooklyn Navy Yard vicinity, then in East Harlem. By 1950 this latter area had become the one with the largest concentration of Puerto Ricans in New York City. From 1950 until 1963 the number of Puerto Ricans migrating to the United States reached an average of 50,000 per year. Unofficial reports estimate that there are at least one and a half million Puerto Ricans living in the City today.

The emigration of Puerto Ricans has been basically a fluctuating lower-class movement. The optimum level of Puerto Rican migration to New York City is achieved when there is an "economic pull" in the city, and when the economic conditions in Puerto Rico do not favor lower-income sectors. C. W. Mills, in his still relevant work *The Puerto Rican Journey,* explained that the "economic pull" force was a stronger variable in explaining Puerto Rican migration trends than the "economic push" factors in Puerto Rico.[3] He tried to show this by first showing a relationship between migration and the economic motivation of the migrant, and second, by showing a level change in migration movements that is closely correlated with the Business Activity Index of New York City.[4]

Another source, however, states:

From *Puerto Rican Politics in New York City* (Washington, D.C.: University Press of America, 1977), chap. 2. Reprinted with permission of the author.

The immigration of such a huge proportion of the country's population, an exodus of people which comprises one of the largest movements of people in modern history, may simply be viewed as constituting an escape valve to reduce the social pressures created in the
colonial super-exploitative economic transformations in Puerto Rico.
But it is more. It is, further, a systematic process of exporting cheap
labor to the United States and controlling the total working class.[5]

Thus various political factors must also be considered in a discussion on
migration. Although 80 to 90 percent of Puerto Rican "deciders" migrate
to the United States for economic reasons, the decision to leave Puerto Rico
should not be analyzed as an "individual" one, but as resulting from broad
social and political factors. The decision to come to the United States is
a decision that in a real sense is "encouraged" upon the Puerto Rican lower
class by the governments of Puerto Rico and the United States.

C. W. Mills attempted to show that the early Puerto Rican migrant
was similar to other ethnic immigrants in the respect that they all came
to New York City primarily for a better economic life. Though economic
motivations were important in explaining the immigration to the United
States of earlier ethnic groups, individual political motivations also played
a substantial part. Oscar Handlin writes on this account:

> The Jews who migrated were set in motion by a combination of re-
> ligious and economic factors. In Russia, persecution made their posi-
> tion untenable. Discrimination prevented them from leading normal
> lives, and occasional outbreaks of violence emphasized the precarious
> nature of their existence. Moreover, their economic situation dete-
> riorated both there and in the Austrian Empire, where persecution
> was less important. The development of large-scale agriculture and
> industry destroyed their role as intermediaries between the peasants
> and the landlords and the urban markets. Thousands became super-
> fluous and fled to America where about half of them settled in New
> York.[6]

Puerto Ricans leaving their country for the United States were encouraged by the particular economic relationship between the mainland
and the colony, a situation unlike what earlier ethnics experienced.[7] Part
of the government's strategy in Puerto Rico was to establish a "safety valve"
for the economic costs of industrializing Puerto Rico.[8] The Puerto Rican
migration can be perceived as "involuntary" in that it was organized between the governments of the United States and Puerto Rico. For no other
migrant group, except perhaps for the Mexicans under the Bracero Program, has the United States government systematically and over a period

of decades arranged entry into this nation.[9] Manuel Maldonado-Denis claims that to see the Puerto Rican migration as purely voluntary is inaccurate. He writes:

> It would be a futile intellectual exercise to see Puerto Rican migration to the United States as abstracted from the social and historical conditions within the island itself that have fostered such a migration. It should be evident even to those that submit to a policy of "benign neglect" with respect to non-white peoples that something must have happened in a country in which almost one-third of its population has now settled in the United States, a social phenomenon that has occurred at a hectic pace during the last two decades. As a matter of fact, the problem of Puerto Rican migration should be seen as part of a problem "that transcends the relationship between Puerto Rico and the United States."[10]

Puerto Rican migration was partially created by the displacement of "jibaros" from their small farms by the monopolizing operations of the huge American sugar and coffee corporation. Maldonado-Denis continues:

> The social result of this process of progressive deterioration of Puerto Rican agriculture has been the mass exodus of the peasant population to the cities and to North American ghettos. . . . Many of the displaced campesinos that flocked to the urban areas did so as an intermediate step towards migration to the mainland. . . . The labor shortage in the post-war United States served as a magnet for Puerto Ricans, who in increasing numbers migrated to the mainland.[11]

The mass exodus of Puerto Ricans from Puerto Rico was legally encouraged. Laws such as the Foraker Act (1900), the second Organic Act (1917), and the Federal Statute of Relations with Puerto Rico Act (1944), all prohibited the enforcement of the Sherman Anti-Trust Act in Puerto Rico. This was a booster shot for sugar monopolies to run rampant. But in order to establish sugar plantations, thousands of small farmers had to leave their farms. Conveniently, one might add, this displacement occurred at times when New York City needed cheap labor to run the factories and the service industries in the city. The War Manpower Commission recruited workers from Puerto Rico during World War II, just as the later Commonwealth Office would do in the 1950s. In this sense, Puerto Rican migrants did perform a "cheap-labor" function for expanding urban economics as had earlier immigrant groups.

Many cities in earlier periods recruited cheap migrant workers to help subsidize economic expansion. According to Constance Green,

Cheap immigrant labor, whether European, French Canadian, Mexican, or Oriental, provided the means of expanding some towns into cities and enlarging established manufacturing centers. While Northern and Midwestern communities drew upon European peasants and "habitants" from Province Quebec, on the West Coast, . . . coolie labor supplied a downward, if indirect, effect upon industrial pay rates.[12]

Some immigrants presumably came to New York City hoping that one day they would be citizens, while other immigrants had intentions of returning to their homeland. However, the European immigrants could not return as quickly as the Puerto Ricans. Another related difference is the process of gaining citizenship. If European immigrants decided to stay in America they had to manage a political process to gain citizenship, whereas the Puerto Rican was already a citizen—legally, at least. These apparent differences between the migration of Puerto Ricans and that of other ethnic groups has had major consequences in the ensuing development of Puerto Rican politics in New York City. It has not only retarded the pace of electoral activism in the Puerto Rican community relative to other ethnic groups, but it has contributed to a unique pattern of ethnic politics.

Italians, as an example of the earlier ethnic groups, not only migrated to America for the economic opportunities supposedly available in the United States, but also in search of a permanent home. Though "as many as a third of the immigrants returned to their homelands" some came here with intentions of staying.[13] The attitude of Italian immigrants upon arriving in New York City was that this city would be a new Italy, a new community to which they would have to become accustomed psychologically, socially, economically, and therefore, politically. Humbert S. Nelli, writing on the Italian immigrant experience, says:

> Identification with the colony and use of its facilities and institutions signified not only a movement away from homeland outlooks, but also, for many newcomers, a necessary step in Americanization. . . . Some chose to make use of a few or all existing community institutions and gradually identified themselves with the Italian group, a concept that did not exist for them before their immigration; others saw immigrant churches, journals and societies as intermediaries through which to learn American customs and ideals. Often members of this assimilation-oriented group arrived as children or young adults and absorbed (or consciously adopted) American habits and speech from the outside community—from schools, settlement houses, criminal gangs, and political organizations.[14]

Politics for the Italian community became a stepping stone into American society but it was also a way to consolidate the Italian community. "Italians, who in Italy never considered the possibility of cooperation with compatriots from other towns and provinces, found that in the absence of the old family ties and services, they could solve many problems only as members of organized groups."[15] Italian politicians or power brokers sprang up almost immediately in Italian communities. The Italian political leader had the responsibility to speak for the social, economic, and cultural needs of the community and to assist the emerging businesses in the neighborhood. This is unlike the Puerto Rican case; the Puerto Rican community, until recently, did not perceive the necessity for electoral organization in order to respond to community needs.

The type of leaders that first arose in Puerto Rican communities tended to be ministers of small churches and small businessmen. From this group were chosen the early civic leaders of the Puerto Rican community. But even these early civic leaders were for the most part apolitical in the electoral arena. Early civic leaders in the 1950s did not have to become political—the needs of the community were expressed by the Commonwealth Office in New York City. Only in the late 1960s does one see developing in significant numbers the "grassroots," indigenous leader with interests in electoral politics.

Unlike earlier ethnic groups who upon arriving in New York City attempted to form cohesive voting communities and build political machines, the Puerto Ricans did not organize themselves electorally to satisfy some of their needs as an ethnic community. Patricia Sexton writes that,

> Although the social improvement clubs of the slums have given new force and responsibility to the poor of Detroit and other parts, these organizations have not penetrated East Harlem. . . . In other communities of New York City, the political clubs have established incomes [but] relatively only a few poor people of East Harlem participate in these organizations. . . . In East Harlem the older political clubs of immigrants, despite their defeats, helped to organize the immigrant. Now the old Italian machine has been weakened in East Harlem . . . and there is yet a good substitute.for the new Puerto Rican and Black inhabitants.[16]

The history of other immigrant groups also reflects differences in their community's early political development compared to that of the Puerto Rican community. In his classic work, *Who Governs?*, Robert Dahl states that generally "an ethnic group passes through three stages on the way to political assimilation." In the first stage, the ethnic group is proletarian and homogeneous, "they are low in status, income and influence. For leadership they depend on influential politicians who have come from previously assimilated ethnic groups. Members of the new group serve sometimes as intermediaries between the group and the older leaders, acquiring in the process moderate influence and experience as subleaders."[17] The Puerto Rican community in New York City can be characterized by this stage only in the sense that presently, it is "low in status, income, and influence." In many ways this first stage that Dahl describes is not applicable to the Puerto Ricans.

Early settled Puerto Ricans did not turn to politicians for leadership and influence but rather to civic and economic leaders. The earliest leaders included Catholic Church workers and small businessmen. Even in the late 1950s and early 1960s Puerto Ricans did not seek an indigenous politician; rather the Commonwealth Office was used for community leadership. The political power and strength of the urban machine first required development of the ethnic "intermediaries," and then ethnic machine "subleaders," and eventually, machine leaders. The urban machine controlled the rewards and benefits that a lower socio-economic ethnic group needed to survive in the city.

Traditionally, party leaders provided patronage rewards to the local neighborhood political leaders who would then distribute it to the loyal voters and the ethnic community. The rewards depended on whether the party was in power and on the cultural and economic demands and needs of the particular ethnic community, as well as on the number of votes cast in previous elections. In return for the downward flow of rewards, there was an upward flow of support from the community to the gatekeepers, to the city's top political leaders. The top political leaders would get rewards and patronage to distribute from the city administration which in turn needed the support of the political leaders. The modern urban government process would show major types of socio-economic services and benefits going directly from the city administration sector to the ethnic community sector, thereby weakening the link between the party apparatus and the administration and the party apparatus and the ethnic community.

This scheme did not work for Puerto Ricans. For a very long time the Puerto Rican community lacked any political power or electoral representation. Though ethnic intermediaries or gate-keepers were many times mere mouthpieces for the machine's policy, as Ira Katznelson contends,[18] they were very important in developing a community's political and economic influence — however limited — which then made it possible for many members of the particular ethnic group to move up on the socio-economic ladder. These gate-keepers may have been more effective in the development of political influence than were the anti-poverty program leaders in the 1960s.

The "poverty-crats" could never play the same political role of developing ethnic power as the traditional gate-keepers in other communities for two reasons. First, federal law and state and city regulations limited the political role that employees in the various poverty programs could play. As state and federal employees, some Puerto Ricans may have been seriously weakened in the political role they might have been able to play only a few years earlier. The Puerto Rican leader involved with a poverty program, for example, cannot represent Puerto Ricans "more" than other groups in his or her jurisdiction. Under the old system the Italian ethnic leader represented the interests of the Italians, the Irish leader, the Irish, and so forth, and this was because the basic political organizing unit was the ward which was organized around the ethnic neighborhoods. The ward system corresponded to a general pattern of ethnic group settlement which allowed for stable communities. This was the case for the Italians, Jews, and the Irish—and to a lesser extent for blacks also. The pattern for Puerto Ricans has been characterized by their settlements on the fringes of Italian and black neighborhoods, as in places like East Harlem and Bedford-Stuyvesant, which presented a great political disadvantage for Puerto Ricans.[19] Today, however, Puerto Rican community leaders who work in the city's various federal, state, and city community programs are told that they must represent all the people in their area, that it is illegal to "discriminate." Unlike yesterday's gate-keepers, Puerto Rican poverty-crats, as federal employees, must only administer social programs—they are placed in positions that call for the implementation of federal programs with federal guidelines, presumably without any politicking. The gate-keeper of the Italian, Irish, Jewish, and some black communities was in a bargaining position for the community (even if personal purposes were ulterior).

One might look at socio-economic characteristics of Puerto Ricans in New York City as an explanation of the historical lack of electoral activity among Puerto Ricans. Though the economic status of this group does not impact the level of politicalization, two factors refute this explanation as the major one. The first is historical—early immigrants had similar socio-economic characteristics as Puerto Ricans and were active in the local and city-wide political scene. But in addition, as Robert Lane writes,

> Rates of electoral assimilation (achieving a rate of turn-out similar to that of matched established groups) vary more with the participation norms of the migrant's place of origin than with the education, sex, or (urban) occupation of the migrants. Therefore, the lower the

participation norms of the migrants' place of origin, the lower the rate of electoral assimilation.[20]

Puerto Ricans, in Puerto Rico, have a much higher turnout rate for elections than is the case for all voters in the United States. Between 80 and 90 percent of Puerto Ricans vote in Puerto Rican elections, while in New York City some important elections have experienced less than 20 percent turnout from this group. According to Lane's thesis Puerto Ricans should have one of the highest turnout rates in New York City—but this is not the case.[21] The relative absence of sophisticated electoral organizations, as are found in Puerto Rico, and high electoral turnouts in communities in Puerto Rico bring into question Lane's thesis when applied to the Puerto Rican community in New York City. Puerto Ricans living in Puerto Rico are avid voters. The 80 to 90 percent figure is a cross class figure, that is, lower-income Puerto Ricans vote as frequently as higher-income Puerto Ricans in Puerto Rico. Rafael Ramirez stated that:

> In the case of Puerto Rico we find that, contrary to the situation of other Latin American countries, there exists a high level of electoral participation. . . . This level shows that there is not a significant difference in abstention between the very poor zones of slums and "public housing" and other residential areas.[22]

Most Puerto Ricans of voting age in Puerto Rico know who the governor is, who the mayor and local electoral officials are.[23] It seems that in New York City, however, these same Puerto Ricans hardly vote.

There are a number of other explanations for the historical lack of electoral politicking in the Puerto Rican community which are related to differences with early immigrant groups. There seems to have been a greater political effort to redesign, or restructure the neighborhoods immigrants lived in. Parenti writes that "since early colonial times, nearly every group arriving in America has attempted to reconstruct communities that were replications of the old world societies from which they had emerged."[24] Perhaps the Irish, Italians, and Jews who found themselves in New York City were thinking in terms of making their communities as socially and politically "cozy" as possible; many Puerto Ricans, on the other hand, thought they would be returning to Puerto Rico in a relatively short time— there was not a need to reconstruct the neighborhoods where they lived. The relative ease of return to Puerto Rico encouraged this attitude. Even today, younger Puerto Ricans still may hear parents talk incessantly of returning to the Island once "the children are grown." This made the Puerto Rican settlement experience substantially different than those of other immigrant groups as Gordon K. Lewis points out;

For the first time in a long history of American immigration there is a two-way movement: the working class migrant may decide, after an almost casual decision to make the trip north, to return home instead of remaining permanently. Since the cost of the northward trip today represents about two weeks pay for the average islander as against some three months earnings in the pre-war period, it is evident that this is a new phenomenon in the historic migration movement and the promised land.[25]

And thus, why should one put time and effort into such a cold city like New York only to give it up one day and return home?

Unlike the black migrant from the South, Puerto Ricans never saw New York as the place to enhance one's social mobility. The Puerto Rican, therefore, perhaps could not be frustrated like the black migrant who was disillusioned when confronting the cruelty of the big city. This disillusionment, however, may have helped to politicize black migrants. Ted Gurr in *Why Men Rebel* writes that a group's sense of "relative deprivation" is a psychological condition in which a people's value expectations dramatically increase without satisfaction.[26] Applying this analysis to Puerto Ricans, we may say that the migrant of the first generation realistically did not think that the city government would satisfy his needs before satisfying the wants and needs of its "bona-fide" citizens. The Puerto Rican migrant never accepted fully American citizenship and its implications for equal treatment. This migrant was more a worker in someone else's country. The political expectations of the Puerto Rican were low. The Puerto Rican would not feel slighted upon seeing other groups favored by the government—all governments were supposed to protect its own citizens before protecting "strangers." This is Marvick's argument explaining the political passivity of earlier blacks in contrast to the younger, more militant blacks. He writes,

> The argument here is not that Negroes were passive, apathetic, and for generations unable to protest effectively because they had become disenchanted with the American Creed—alienated from American Society. Probably more commonly, Negro adults had never allowed themselves to become enchanted with democracy in the first place, so far as their own community and private lives were concerned.[27]

Alienation could have led to political organization or passivity—in the Puerto Rican case, however, this concept cannot be turned to for an explanation of the particular state of the group's political developments.

Manuel Maldonado-Denis writes that Puerto Ricans were different than prior immigrants to the United States:

Of all the ethnic groups that migrated to the U.S., Puerto Ricans are the only ones that never completely cut their ties with their fatherland. They never did like Cortes in Vera Cruz, whose determination to keep himself and his men from returning to Spain was symbolized by his burning of the ships. They continually go back to their island, to their homeland. Unlike the Blacks, for whom Africa is not truly a home, Puerto Ricans do have a place, a nation, a culture that they can look to.[28]

It was the proximity of the island, along with the strong cultural ties of the first generation Puerto Ricans to Puerto Rico which might have delayed the politicalization of the Puerto Rican community. Joseph Fitzpatrick voices the idea that

> the proximity of the island and the ease of return seem to prompt the Puerto Ricans to find in the island the sense of strength, support and identity that formed immigrant communities of American cities. . . . There is a great deal of truth in the comment that this is not a Puerto Rican migration, but a process of Puerto Rican commuting.[29]

The continual touch with Puerto Rico could perhaps explain the comparatively slow acculturation to the politics of New York City. One person interviewed for this study, Joseph Erazo, referred to this as "umbilicalism." But socially, the process of acculturation was also very slow as Oscar Lewis states in *La Vida:*

> Our survey indicated that there was little important change in customs and language among lower-income Puerto Ricans in New York. They formed small islands in the city and perpetuated their culture. Contacts with North Americans were few and often limited to landlords, government officials and other functionaries. The process of adjustment and assimilation to North American culture was slow and different.[30]

Though there were distinct "Puerto Rican" parts of neighborhoods to be found in New York City, the residential and "generational" mobility level was always extremely high. At a much earlier date Ivan Illich writes,

> Considering this dispersal and the tendency to commute to the Island, it is no wonder that there are hardly any Puerto Rican national neighborhoods in the traditional sense. One result is that it is difficult for Puerto Ricans to develop local grassroots leadership within their own group; either this concentration per city block is too thin, or the intention to stick to the neighborhood is absent, or the necessity to organize with their own is weak because all are citizens who at least

understand some English and have official "protection" from the government labor office—the first instance of something like a Consulate for American Nationals.[31]

Puerto Ricans were constantly moving to and from Puerto Rico and thus the intention to "stick" was very weak. The mobility rate of Puerto Ricans between Puerto Rico and New York City is still high.[32] Unlike other ethnic groups that experience one "first generation" stage, Puerto Ricans may be experiencing several due to the new arrivals to the city every year.

The fact that many Puerto Ricans return to Puerto Rico (although not the majority, and it is difficult to establish precisely how many), at the same time that many arrive here from Puerto Rico, establishes a constant replanting of the resident Puerto Rican population in the United States, there is a constant flow of 'first generation' which maintains the links of nationality alive. For example, in 1960, 92.3% of all Puerto Ricans older than 14 years residing in the United States were born in Puerto Rico. In 1970, 93% of all heads of families over 16 years residing in the United States were born in Puerto Rico.[33]

It is difficult for the Puerto Rican community to move beyond the first generation stage when a constant, self-replenishing influx keeps providing an ample supply of "first generation-ers."

The effect of mobility on the political development of the Puerto Rican community might be especially detrimental when one considers that not only constant 'to and from' movement of the same migrants might be occurring between Puerto Rico and the United States, but also the internal mobility rate of this community is very high compared to blacks and the general population. Of approximately 740,000 Puerto Ricans surveyed in 1970 by the Bureau of the Census for example, only about 330,000 or 44 percent were living in the same household as in 1965. Of approximately 1,600,000 blacks surveyed, 900,000 or 50 percent were living in the same household, and of 10,600,000 whites, roughly 7,000,000 or 67 percent were living in the same household.[34] James Wilson alludes to this factor when he says that a high level of mobility has been a major reason why certain municipalities in California never developed a sophisticated political organization that could mobilize grassroots supporters:

Given the rapid growth and high mobility of California's population, it is questionable whether an effective precinct organization could have been constructed even if the formal party machinery had been legally strong and patronage plentiful. It has been estimated that about a fourth of the persons in the state did not live at their present addresses one year ago. Organizing the grassroots when the population turnover is so high would be exceptionally difficult under the best circumstances.[35]

The model described here can also be seen in the case of temporary workers — and Puerto Ricans can be viewed as such. As Edna Bonaich says, "temporary workers have very little reason to join the organizations and unions of a permanent work force, and tend not to do so . . . in addition to the general depressing effects on wages of being temporary, this motive leads to a fairly rapid turnover in personnel making organization more difficult and hindering the development of valuable skills which could be used for bargaining."[36] Bonaich is speaking of labor organizations and labor bargaining skills — but this model can be used for explaining the effect of temporary citizens on political organizations and political bargaining skills in the Puerto Rican community.

Walter Gene and Herbert Castner show that high mobility adversely affects the politically poor communities in urban America. They found great difficulty in organizing high mobility, poverty-area blacks in Seattle under the Central Area Motivational Program. They write:

> Approximately one out of every four persons listed as club members had moved since the listing approximately 18 months previously. The data from the community sample indicates that the overall mobility rate for persons living in the area serviced by CAMP is even higher than this: of those interviewed in the sample, 47% indicated that they had changed their residence at least once during the past two years. Such a high rate of mobility implies that almost any association which is based on the local neighborhood, as these clubs were, will experience a heavy and rapid attrition of members.[37]

This rate of mobility, then, seems to be another factor in explaining the low level of electoral activism in some Puerto Rican areas.

But there may be ecological reasons why the Puerto Rican was not initially as electorally motivated as seems to be the case for earlier immigrant groups. Physically, the city has changed from a basically horizontal city to a vertical city. Along with the higher degree of transiency in a vertical city there is also less access to people living there. Ross R. Baker says, "The high-rise ghetto is an organizer's nightmare." Though earlier immigrant groups may have been as poor as blacks and Puerto Ricans today, it was physically easier to organize the Italians, the Jews, and the Irish. Baker states:

> The tenement house of seventy years ago was a far more manageable unit of organization than the high-rise, public housing apartment house. It is not difficult to imagine how much more amenable to po-

litical organization were the Jews on Henry Street or the Italians on Mulberry Street than the Blacks on Cabrini Green in Chicago, in Sells Wright in Newark or in the Norriss Homes in Philadelphia.[38]

Because there was never a desire to settle in New York City permanently, in addition to physical barriers to grassroots-type political organizing, there has always been a low political profile exhibited by the Puerto Ricans.

Social class is another reason that explains the low level of political involvement of Puerto Ricans. While this factor should not be overly emphasized, social scientists have established that the lower a person is on a socio-economic scale the less is the tendency to become politically involved.[39] The psychological dynamic involved is that lower economic class individuals are made politically timid by their position in the social structure. Many poor people will not "demand what is theirs" because they are put in a very tenuous position economically, politically, and very important, psychologically. Poor people become confident enough to be politically aggressive only in a highly personal environment, but this is one of the least effective ways for a lower economic class to deal with a complex bureaucracy. Gideon Sjoberg writes that,

> The lower-class person stands in awe of bureaucratic regulations and frequently is unaware that he has a legal and moral claim to certain rights and privileges. More often, however, it is the lack of knowledge of the system's technicalities and backstage regions that is responsible for the lower-class person's inability to manipulate the bureaucratic system to his advantage.[40]

The Puerto Rican community, as primarily a low-income one, may have been discouraged from achieving a threatening level of organization vital in fighting urban bureaucracies and in gaining power in an ethnic political setting. This is similar to C. V. Hamilton's concept of "functional anonymity."[41] The Puerto Rican will not become politically involved because some services are automatically provided to the recipient, and the bureaucratic regulations that go along with these services discourages electoral involvement. Michael Royko explains that in machine Chicago, in the poorer parts of the city, precinct captains threatened people who didn't vote with sanctions: "Don't vote, and you might be cut off welfare. Don't vote, and you might have building inspectors poking around the house."[42] "Functional anonymity" is the result of the converse of this relationship between party and potential voters; the warning for Puerto Ricans in New York City might be "participate too actively and you might lose your public housing apartment or you might be cut off welfare."

These are some reasons why the Puerto Rican community has not experienced the same history of electoral involvement as other ethnic groups in New York City. It will be interesting to find out whether in the 1980s, Puerto Ricans begin to become involved electorally, despite continuing social, demographic, and cultural differences with other groups.

NOTES

1. U.S. Department of Commerce, Bureau of the Census, "Persons of Spanish Origin in the U.S." Series No. 259, March 1973, p. 20.

2. See *Puerto Rico: Leyes Fundamentales* (Rio Piedras, Puerto Rico: Editorial Edil, Inc., 1973).

3. C. W. Mills, *The Puerto Rican Journey* (New York: Russell and Russell Co., 1967), esp. his chapter, "The Journey."

4. See also Harvey S. Perloff, *Puerto Rico's Economic Future* (Chicago: University of Chicago Press, 1946). For a more recent and in depth study of the relationship between the economy of Puerto Rico and migration movements to the United States, see H. C. Barton, Jr. "The Employment Situation in Puerto Rico and Migratory Movements Between Puerto Rico and the United States," in *Summary of Proceedings: Workshops on Employment Problems of Puerto Ricans*, Center for the Study of the Unemployed, School of Social Work, New York University, 1968.

5. *La alternativa socialista*, Puerto Rican Socialist Party (Puerto Rico: Impresora Nacional Inc., 1974), p. 61.

6. Oscar Handlin, *The Newcomers* (New York: Anchor Books, 1962), p. 22.

7. Professor Luis Nieves Falcon has written on the sociology of Puerto Rican immigrants and he suggests other differences between this group and European immigrants: 1) Other (non-Puerto Rican) migratory movements have been characterized by their individual tendencies. That of the Puerto Rican has tended to be a familial movement. 2) For the foreign immigrant cultural assimilation was justified by the pursuit of citizenship. This is not the case with the Puerto Rican who, before migration, is a United States citizen. 3) Unlike the European immigrants, the Puerto Rican migrant had not any intentions of permanently leaving Puerto Rico. See *Diagnostico de Puerto Rico* (Rio Piedras, Puerto Rico: Editorial Edil, 1971), p. 246.

8. Falcon, *Diagnostico de Puerto Rico*.

9. From 1951 to 1964 the Mexican Farm Labor Act permitted the Secretary of Labor to authorize the importation of farm workers for temporary employment in the United States.

10. Manuel Maldonado-Denis, *Puerto Rico: A Socio-Historic Interpretation* (New York: Random House, 1972), p. 312.

11. Ibid., p. 312.

12. Constance M. Green, *The Rise of Urban America* (New York: Harper and Row, 1965), p. 98. This was also the case with southern blacks and some

northern cities. Dr. C. V. Hamilton pointed out to the author how a black newspaper, the *Chicago Defender,* recruited blacks from the South to work in Chicago in the 1910s and 1920s. See also Paul Baran and Paul Sweezy, *Monopoly Capital: An Essay on the American Economic and Social Orders* (London, 1968).

13. Rudolph J. Vecoli, "European Americans: From Immigrants to Ethnics, *International Migration Review* 6 (Winter 1972): 411.

14. Humbert S. Nelli, "Ethnic Group Assimilation: The Italian Experience," in *Cities in American History,* ed. Kenneth T. Jackson and Stanley K. Schultz (New York: Alfred A. Knopf, 1972), p. 205.

15. Ibid., p. 202.

16. Patricia C. Sexton, *Harlem Español* (Mexico: Editorial Diana, 1966), p. 133.

17. Robert Dahl, *Who Governs?* (New Haven, Conn.: Yale University Press, 1961), see chap. 4, "The Ex-Plebes."

18. Ira Katznelson, *Black Men, White Cities: Race, Politics, and Migration in the United States, 1900–1930, and Britain, 1948–1968* (London: Oxford University Press, 1973), see especially chap. 6.

19. Joseph P. Fitzpatrick, in *Puerto Rican Americans: The meaning of migration to the mainland* (Englewood Cliffs, N.J.: Prentice-Hall, 1971), writes on this point, "Although Puerto Ricans are scattered widely throughout the City, and are concentrated in some areas, it is doubtful whether they have established those geographical concentrations which were so important to the strong communities of earlier immigrant groups. One key to the strength of the earlier immigrants was the pattern of housing. At the point of second settlement, the earlier immigrants began to establish these tightly knit, strong communities. . . . These dense concentrations gave rise to large areas which became Little Dublins, the Little Italies, the Little Germanies, the larger concentrations of Jewish people, or others. They became stable, settled communities where a particular style of life was established and maintained."

20. Robert E. Lane, *Political Life: Why and How People Get Involved in Politics* (New York: Free Press, 1959), p. 269.

21. This can be shown by comparing local Assembly District elections in different ethnic neighborhoods in New York City. The latter can be identified with census tracts. But also see Mark R. Levy and Michael S. Kramer, *The Ethnic Factor: How America's Minorities Decide Elections* (New York: Simon and Schuster, 1973), pp. 89–93 and *New York Times,* August 26, 1969 and October 15, 1970.

22. Rafael Ramirez, "Marginalidad, dependencia, y participacion politica en el arrabal," *Problemas de Desigualdad Social en Puerto Rico,* ed. Rafael Ramirez, Carlos Buitrago, Barry Levine (España: Ediciones Libreria Internacional, 1972), p. 108.

23. Puerto Rico has one million registered voters of which 80 percent continually vote in elections. This figure is highlighted by the awkward system of primary voting found in Puerto Rico. See Kal Wagenheim, *Puerto Rico: A Profile* (New York: Praeger Publishers, 1970), p. 149. Also see Luis Nieves Falcon, *La Opinion Publica y las Aspiraciones de las Puertoriqueñas* (Puerto Rico: Editorial Universatoria, 1972.)

24. Michael Parenti, "The Persistence of Ethnic Identification" *American Political Science Review* 61 (September 1967): 719.

25. Gordon K. Lewis, *Puerto Rico: Freedom and Power in the Caribbean* (New York, Monthly Review Press, 1963), p. 7.

26. Ted Robert Gurr, *Why Men Rebel* (Princeton, N.J.: Center of International Studies, Princeton University Press, 1970).

27. Dwaine Marvick, "The Political Socialization of the American Negro, in *American Ethnic Politics,* ed. Lawrence Fuchs (New York: Harper and Row, 1968), p. 265.

28. Maldonado-Denis, *Puerto Rico,* p. 323.

29. *New York Times,* September 12, 1971.

30. Oscar Lewis, *La Vida* (New York: Random House, 1966).

31. Ivan Illich, "Puerto Ricans in New York," *The Commonwealth* (June 22, 1956), p. 294.

32. A study conducted by City University and funded by the Health Services Administration in the late 1960s found that "Puerto Ricans were ethnically the most mobile—71.6% of Puerto Rican families moved in the five-year period, compared with 59.7% of non-whites and 44.1% of whites," *New York Times,* August 1, 1968.

33. *La alternativa socialista,* p. 65. See the following data and discussion on Puerto Rican migration: Joseph Fitzpatrick, *Puerto Rican Americans: The Meaning of Migration;* U.S. Department of Labor, "A Socio-Economic Profile of Puerto Rican New Yorkers" (July 1975), and *Labor Migration under Capitalism: The Puerto Rican Experience,* Centro de Estudios Puertorriquenos (New York: Monthly Review Press, 1979).

34. See U.S. Bureau of the Census, Census of Population and Housing: 1970, Final Report PHC(1)-145, parts 1, 2, and 3. These figures are the author's interpretations based on reported figures.

35. James Q. Wilson, *Amateur Democrats: Club Politics in Three Cities,* (Chicago: The Free Press, 1966), p. 104.

36. Edna Bonaich, "A Theory of Ethnic Antagonism: The Split Labor Market" *American Sociological Review* 37 (October 1972): 551.

37. Walter Gene and Herbert Castner, "Organizing the Poor: An Evaluation of a Strategy" *Social Science Quarterly* 50 (December 1969): 464.

38. Ross R. Baker, "The Ghetto Writ Large: The Future of American Cities," *Social Policy* (January-February, 1974): 28.

39. See, for example, Robert Lane, *Political Life: Why and How People Get Involved in Politics,* and Angus Campbell, Warren E. Miller, and Donald E. Stokes, eds., *The American Voter* (New York: Wiley and Sons, 1960).

40. Gideon Sjoberg, "Bureaucracy—The Lower Class," *Sociology and Social Research* (April 1966): 330.

41. C. V. Hamilton, "Public Policy and Some Political Consequences" in *Public Policy,* ed. Margarite Ross Barnett and James A. Hefner (Port Washington, N.Y.: Alfred Press, 1976).

42. Michael Royko, *Boss: Richard Daley of Chicago* (New York: Signet Books, 1971), p. 69.

4. From Exiles to Minorities: The Politics of Cuban-Americans

Maria de los Angeles Torres

SINCE THE 1800s, THE United States has attempted to influence Cuban politics, but it was not until the 1959 Cuban revolution that the government began to implement these efforts through Cubans who lived in the United States. As early as 1960, the United States government recruited, trained, and armed Cubans to overthrow the revolutionary government. Throughout the rest of the decade, Cubans were the foot soldiers for U.S. policies in Latin America.[1] In the early 1970s, the Republican Party under Richard Nixon began to use Cubans for a new set of domestic functions typified by the Watergate break-in. A more liberal Democratic administration of Jimmy Carter approached Latin America, and particularly Cuba, with a new perspective.[2] His human rights approach did not favor Cubans who advocated hardline policies toward Cuba but rather Cubans who favored a dialogue with the Cuban government. In 1981, within his first weeks of power, Ronald Reagan reversed this brief moment of improved U.S.–Cuba relations, and the role of Cubans in the United States changed again.

The political activities of Cubans in the United States have been concentrated in the realm of foreign policy. In the 1980s, Cubans have also played an important role in domestic policies, especially vis-à-vis other Latinos. This is primarily because the major political parties have an awakened interest in courting the Latino vote. In the past, both Mexicans and Puerto Ricans, the two largest groups, have voted with the Democratic Party. On the other hand, Cubans have tended to support the Republican Party. Therefore the Republicans have projected Cubans as their Latinos.

In the last twenty-five years, Cubans in the United States have realized that they are here to stay. Therefore, the community's politics are now focusing on the United States. While this new role represents a well-articulated plan by the Republicans, it also reflects the maturing of an economic and political base within the Cuban community itself. As such, it signals the transition from an exile group to a minority community.

HISTORY

Cubans have long been politically active in the United States. Exile politics have either supported or opposed the United States' policies toward Cuba, depending on the moment. In the early 1800s, groups of Cubans fought alongside Southern slaveowners against Spain, hoping to annex Cuba to the South and thus preserve slavery on the island.[3] In the late 1800s, Cuban tobacco workers migrated to the United States in search of employment. Eventually they formed the backbone of the Cuban movement for independence against Spain. Interestingly, they also organized the most radical wing of the American Federation of Labor.[4]

Throughout the 1930s, Cuban political emigres sought refuge in the United States from the Machado dictatorship. Together with progressive North Americans and other political emigres, they published an opposition newspaper in New York that they smuggled into Cuba.[5] During the 1950s, Fulgencio Batista's repressive regime again forced many Cubans to the United States. With support from Cubans living throughout the country, they formed committees sympathetic to the 26th of July Revolutionary Movement headed by Fidel Castro.[6] In 1959 after the defeat of Batista by the revolutionary forces, Cubans migrated to the United States in great numbers. This time it was not immigrants of working-class background, but rather the middle and upper classes.

After the 1959 revolution, the tradition of the progressive Cuban immigrant changed radically. Since the initial post-revolutionary immigrants from Cuba were those most adversely affected by the programs of the revolution, most tended to be politically reactionary. They did not intend to make the United States their permanent home. The first Cubans to leave the island clung to the belief that the revolutionary government would be toppled and they would return to Cuba. In 1961, after the failure of the U.S. sponsored Bay of Pigs invasion, those hopes began to fade.[7] Up to 1965, the year that the Cuban government defeated the internal counterrevolution, several groups led raids on the Cuban coast, smuggled arms and newspapers into Cuba, and maintained an active fundraising drive among Cubans in the United States. Many times fundraising was done through extortion and threats of being fired if a worker did not contribute to the weekly drives.[8]

While Cuban emigres have come to the United States with a political and personal history, the policies of the particular administration in power have significantly influenced the unfolding of events in their settlements. At times, this influence commenced with immigration policies developed especially for them. Special visa waivers and resettlement programs for the post-revolutionary immigration were part of the strategy to use Cuban immigrants to discredit the Cuban revolution. In 1961, the United States brought more than 15,000 Cuban children to this country through the State Department–sponsored "Peter Pan Operation."[9] The Catholic Church and the U.S. Chamber of Commerce in Havana convinced Cuban parents that if they did not send their children to the United States, the revolutionary government would send them to the Soviet Union. Once in the United States, children could legally claim their parents.

The government also set up special resettlement programs which included food, clothing, medical care, and cash benefits. Later on, the Department of Health, Education, and Welfare administered a scholarship fund to help Cubans pay for college education.[10] Unlike that of other Latin American immigrants, the entry and settlement of Cubans into North American society was greatly facilitated by the United States government.

National security apparatus and policies had a dominant influence on the politics of the post-revolutionary Cuban community. The U.S. intelligence network gave life to the first political organizations and actors in the Cuban community. In fact, it was agents from the Central Intelligence Agency who hand picked the members of the 'government in exile' that was supposed to take over the government in Cuba after the Bay of Pigs invasion.[11] Foreign policies aimed at overthrowing and discrediting the Cuban revolution were in part implemented through Cuban emigres.[12] These policies have been both covert and, in later years, more public.

This development has not only been a function of the federal government's influence on the community. The Cuban community in the United States is also a product of the fragmented national elite that was overthrown. Most of this sector of Cuban society left after the revolution bringing with them experience, knowledge, habits, and, in many cases, relationships that over time have been replicated within North American society. As this sector has matured, it has realigned in some instances and developed its own economic and political interests.

In general, Cubans are highly politicized.[13] Most have lived through a revolutionary period in their homeland where crucial political decisions were common. Not all Cubans left Cuba because they were disaffected with the revolution, but it was a deciding factor for the initial wave of immigrants in the early 1960s. As such, Cuba thus remained the central concern of emigre politics for many years.

The concern for homeland and the broader context of United States–Cuba relations have invariably drawn Cubans into the foreign policy arena.

Cubans have provided both the human resources for U.S. projects toward Cuba and the legitimacy to carry these projects out. For many years the political activities of Cubans have unfolded in the realm of foreign policies, a realm in which the interests of the United States determined the rhythm and sequence of events.

Increasingly, however, Cuban-Americans are developing their own interests. While for the first wave of immigrants there has been a net downshift in their economic and social positioning in the United States compared to where they were in Cuban society, Cubans have built an impressive economic base in Miami and other cities.[14] The maturation of this base demanded political avenues by which these new interests could be articulated and defended. Politically, this has signaled the transition of an exile community focused on returning to Cuba to a minority community concerned about making the society in which they live to be more responsive.

This process occurs at a time when Latinos as a group are emerging as a political force in the United States. The relationship between Latinos and U.S. society is generally marked by a historical and cultural conflict.[15] So while Cubans have played a role in the foreign policy arena which generally coincides with the views of the United States government, in the ongoing struggles of Latinos for affirmative action programs, bilingual education and services, and political representation, not all sectors of the Cuban community are guaranteed allies of the state, but rather potential allies to minority communities.

CUBANS IN THE 1970s: PLURALIZATION AND DIALOGUE

In the two and a half decades since the Bay of Pigs, the Cuban community has increasingly participated in electoral activities to influence U.S. political structures. As life in the United States created new needs and interests in such political activities, entrance into the political system was predictable.

Unexpectedly, Cuban political activities were highly diversified, not monolithic as the popularly held image suggests.[16] During the first years of exile, political activity focused on returning to Cuba and defeating the revolution. As time passed, the revolution consolidated, and political activities increasingly became related to emerging social issues. Community organizations in Miami began demanding more and better social services for the needy sectors such as the elderly and the youth.[17] Those working with the elderly joined forces with Miami Beach–based senior citizens to advocate for quality medical care for their members. A University of Miami group of psychologists was one of the first to participate in national Latino social service advocacy organizations.[18]

Those groups which did not focus on toppling the Cuban revolution were met with hostility from those which were. The Cuban right felt threatened by organized activities that could be interpreted as abandonment of the exile cause. Yet the community as a whole was less concerned with returning to Cuba than with making it in the United States. This reformist tendency continued to grow.

While in the social service sectors, normalization of relations was not a concern, the lack of concern with overthrowing the revolution placed these groups on the more liberal side of the political spectrum. Their demands for more government-supported services for the needy was evidence that Cubans were facing problems in the United States.

In questioning the inefficiencies of the United States, some individuals involved in social service organization did begin to question whether or not the revolution in their homeland had resulted in gains for the poor. The social service movement was not generally concerned with foreign policy, yet its activities tended to ally it with those that were, since both sectors were challenging the monolithic control held by Cuban conservatives who were primarily interested in overthrowing the Cuban revolution and either ignored or denied the social and economic problems facing the community in the United States.

The process of pluralization of the exile community,[19] as the diversification of politics has been called, was especially evident among young people. Confronted with the civil rights and anti-war movements, a significant number of Cuban students on North American campuses experienced a radicalization process that was to have surprising political implications in the long run.

The first signs of this movement were in publications such as *Nueva Generacion* and the more politically defined efforts of *Areito* and *Joven Cuba*. *Joven Cuba* called on Cubans to become part of the civil rights struggles of the black and Latino communities. *Areito,* first published in Miami, was more concerned with building bridges between Cubans in the United States and in Cuba. An organization called "Jovenes Cubanos Socialistas" emerged in Puerto Rico.[20] Their radical stance of calling for a normalization of relations with Cuba was echoed by other sectors of the community as well. In the early 1970s a debate ensued as to whether or not Cubans should hold a dialogue with the government they had left.

Young Cubans interested in returning to Cuba clustered around these various groups and publications. After intense lobbying efforts, the Cuban government started granting a small number of visas. In 1977, the Cuban government shifted its policy and granted the Areito group fifty-five visas.

From this initial group, the Antonio Maceo Brigade was organized.[21]

The visit of these young Cubans to Cuba had a tremendous impact on the government and people of Cuba who had not been willing previously to open communications with Cubans who had left the revolution.[22] The trip of the Antonio Maceo Brigade paved the way for future dealings with the Cuban government and the Cuban communities abroad. Both in Cuba and the United States, the myth of a monolithic Cuban community had been shattered.

Cubans Abroad in Dialogue with the Cuban Government

The Cuban community which in the 1970s had appeared unchanging to most observers was in fact increasingly polarized in regard to its vision of relations with the revolution. Although most Cubans outside the island did not support the revolution,[23] they nevertheless had various concerns which necessitated at least some conversations with the Cuban government. These concerns included travelling to Cuba to visit relatives, reunifying families, and releasing political prisoners.

In September 1978, President Fidel Castro announced that he would hold conversations with representatives of the Cuban communities abroad.[24] The "Dialogue" as these conversations were named, occurred for several reasons. There was a climate of rapprochement between the United States and Cuba. The United States had lifted the travel ban it had imposed on its residents. The Cuban government and the United States had traded "Interests Sections," a sort of embassy through third countries, as a step toward reestablishing full diplomatic relations.[25] Also, the Cuban government had consolidated its power and thus was in a better position to deal with people who had left the country. Finally, there were Cubans abroad ready to hold a dialogue with the Cuban government.[26]

The impact that the easings of tension between the United States and Cuba had on this process cannot be underestimated. As part of a new human rights strategy toward Latin America, the Carter administration's willingness to explore the development of relations with Cuba created the political space for those Cuban-Americans who had been lobbying both governments to establish relations. Although the tendency for rapprochement with the revolution had already developed in the Cuban community, it did not consolidate until relations between Cuba and the United States became a political probability. The larger context of U.S.–Cuba relations defined the political possibilities.

The Dialogue was held in two sessions, one in November, the other in December of 1978. The agenda included the release of political prisoners, permission to leave the island for those prisoners and former political prisoners and their families, the reunification of divided families and the right of Cubans living abroad to visit their relatives on the island. One hundred forty participants representing the religious, labor, youth, professional, and business sectors of the Cuban community attended the meetings.

The Antonio Maceo Brigade presented the Cuban government with a more radical agenda which included the right of repatriation, the right to study in Cuba, the creation of an institute within the Cuban government to represent the interests of the Cuban communities abroad, the opportunity to participate in social and professional organizations within Cuba, and the establishment of exchanges between Cubans on the island and abroad.[27]

In January 1979, the Cuban government started releasing 400 political prisoners a month. This lasted approximately one year. The United States accepted jailed prisoners and their families, but refused to grant visas to former political prisoners and their families. They were told that they had to apply through the regular Latin America quota. For most people, this represented a wait of anywhere from three to eight years. In 1965 under similar circumstances, the Cuban government opened up the port of Camarioca to those wishing to pick up their relatives. This time another "Camarioca" solution was discussed as a possibility if the United States did not grant visas.

Another agreement between the Cuban government and Cubans abroad resulted in the visit to Cuba of over 120,000 Cubans. It was clear that while Cubans abroad had broken with the revolution, they were interested in being able to visit their families and their homeland. Committees to defend and implement the accords of the Dialogue sprung up throughout the United States, and in Puerto Rico, Venezuela, Mexico, and Spain.[28]

The willingness of the U.S. and Cuban governments to negotiate changed the political climate between the two countries. Cuban-American organizations calling for normalizing relations between the two countries found that their demands were now politically acceptable and therefore carried a level of legitimacy. In these new conditions, Cuban-American organizations working toward reestablishing relations with their homeland flourished.[29] The increased contact with Cuba also spurred professional and cultural interest among Cubans inside and outside of Cuba. For a time, the tendency for rapprochement became important outside the initial youth sector which prompted it.

Perhaps the most significant political development was the formation of the Cuban-American Committee. This group composed of a broad

cross section of professionals was the first official Cuban-American lobbying group in Washington. They circulated petitions, met with political representatives, and held press conferences. Unlike past political organizations
of the Cuban community, the Cuban-American Committee was involved
in "politicas a la Americana."

In 1979, the Committee presented the State Department with a peti-
tion signed by over 10,000 Cubans asking for a speedy normalization of
relations between the United States and Cuba.[30] But as a significant number of Cubans welcomed the relaxation of relations with Cuba, groups
who were still trying to overthrow the revolution felt more and more isolated. Their promises of invasions and return to the island were no longer
relevant. The Cuban community had come to understand that the revolution was an irreversible process.

The counterrevolutionary groups reacted violently to these developments. Their first point of attack was on the participants of the Dialogue.
In 1979, Omega 7, one of the most active terrorist organizations, claimed
credit for over twenty bombings aimed at Dialogue participants' homes
and businesses. They sent communiques to the Miami offices of the Associated Press and United Press International vowing to kill any Cuban who
traveled to Cuba. In April 1979, Omega 7 claimed credit for the assassination of Carlos Muniz Varela, a twenty-six year old member of the Antonio
Maceo Brigade who coordinated the offices of Viajes Varaderos in Puerto
Rico, an agency involved in arranging travel to Cuba. In November of the
same year, in Union City, New Jersey, they killed another participant of
the Dialogue, Eulalio Negrin.[31] Although these groups were successful in
intimidating many Cuban-Americans, their reliance on terrorism clearly
demonstrated that they were isolated.

In response to these threats, more liberal minded Cuban-Americans
launched an unprecedented national campaign against terrorism which
demonstrated that they had learned how to use the political system. Cuban-
Americans successfully lobbied several Congressmen to set up special Congressional hearings on Cuban-American right wing terrorism. They had
Mel King introduce a resolution in the Massachusetts House of Commons
condemning terrorism. They were also instrumental in assuring that the
Rutgers University's Constitutional Legal Clinic document cases of intimidation and assassinations.[32] Because of this campaign, the White House
eventually set up a special F.B.I. task force and named Omega 7 the most
dangerous group in the United States.[33]

The political legitimacy received by those calling for a rapprochement with the revolution contributed to shifting the political spectrum in
the Cuban community. Supporters of the Dialogue had successfully organized a base of support in the Cuban community that expanded the politi-

cal spectrum. The demand of normalizing relations with Cuba at least recognized that there was a government with which Cuban-Americans had to negotiate. It also recognized that Cuban-Americans were in the United States to stay. Since the political space in the community had expanded, organizations that were advocating for the needs of Cuban-Americans were no longer susceptible to the charges that they were abandoning the cause of toppling the Cuban government. They were no longer targets for the right.

Within this expanded political space, new issues emerged. For one, the Cuban community became a vocal supporter of bilingual programs in Dade County, a clear departure from mainstream North American opinions. There was even support from the Miami community for bilingual voting materials. Further, an unprecedented number of Cubans became naturalized citizens of the United States, a necessary requirement for voting.

Within the Democratic Party, a new organization, Hispanic American Democrats, formed in 1979.[34] It attempted to unify Latinos under the same banner. Traditional Cuban-American Democrats as well as representatives from the Dialogue movement played a key role. No longer did conservative Cubans monopolize the contacts with the political structures.

The political developments in the Cuban community were accompanied by parallel ideological currents. Especially significant was the change in self-definition from an exile people to a community.[35] In some sectors, the definition went further and included a conception of Cubans as a minority group within the United States. Few Cubans continued to refer to themselves as exiles. This reflected the changing international relations as well as the changing political focus for Cuban-Americans.

Cuba was still very much at the center of political debate and life in the Cuban community. New forms of political participation emerged, however, which related to the status of Cuban-Americans as U.S. citizens. New political concerns such as the defense of First Amendment rights grew. Perhaps most significantly, the use of electoral and pressure group methods of political participation by Cuban-American progressives in the 1970s, changed the rules of politics in the community. These activities proved to be effective and set a new standard on how to conduct the political business of the Cuban community.

CUBAN-AMERICANS IN THE 1980s: ENTERING MAINSTREAM POLITICS

Cuban-Americans entered the 1980s in the limelight of the Mariel immigration. The immigration of 120,000 Cubans and the rise of a conservative president combined to reverse the liberalizing trend which had developed during the Carter administration. For the first time in years many

Cuban-Americans perceived that the Cuban revolutionary government could fall. This fueled the traditional right wing groups, who quickly organized paramilitary camps.[36] This counterrevolutionary tendency combined with the consolidation of the New Right in the White House.[37] The result was to halt the new diplomacy which had developed in the Cuban community during Jimmy Carter's term. The groups that emerged in the Reagan era can be called the anti-Dialogue.

The Reagan administration developed more sophisticated plans for Cuban-Americans. While allowing Cuban-Americans and Nicaraguans to fight a covert war in Nicaragua, they also actively promoted Cuban-Americans to key positions throughout government and the Party.[38] The general trend of the 1970s toward electoral political participation coincided with the Republican strategy for making Cuban-Americans key actors in the administration. In the 1980s, Cuban-American political participation in lobbying, partisan, and electoral activities proliferated. For the right, it was done with the legitimacy of the Republicans, for progressives it has been done in coalition with other minority groups.

As early as the fall of 1980, key Republicans had their eyes on Cuban-Americans. This was especially evident in operatives of the New Right whose ideology had coincided with that of conservative Cuban-Americans in past political relations. Roger Fontaine, former Latin American advisor to the National Security Council, had stated that what was needed in Washington was a strong conservative Cuban-American lobby group.[39] A few months after the 1980 presidential election, a group of Cuban-American businessmen and ideologues formed the Cuban-American National Foundation.

The board of directors of the Foundation consisted of male leaders of Miami's financial and import-export sector. Directors and trustees of the board each made sizeable contributions to fund the Foundation's budget.[40] Many of the companies represented on the board benefitted from trade and investments in Latin America. They also benefit from Reagan's policies toward Latin America that explicitly aim to protect investments abroad.

Jorge Mas Canosa, president of Church and Tower Construction Company, was the first president of the board. The board named Frank Calzon as its first executive director. He had been the former director of "On Human Rights," a Washington-based group that had been dedicated to publishing materials and lobbying Congress on human rights violations in Cuba. Roger Fontaine had also been on its board of directors.

During its first year of operations, the Cuban-American National Foundation spawned two other organizations: the National Coalition for a Free Cuba, a political action committee first headed by Frank Hernandez, president of Agro-Tech International which was involved in agro-business with Latin America; and, the Cuban-American Public Affairs Council, a lobbying group.

Although the Foundation claims to be non-partisan, the projects it has lobbied for closely resemble many of Reagan's. Perhaps most indicative of the Foundation's links to the administration and to the New Right were its activities related to the passage of Radio José Marti, the administration's radio station beamed at Cuba. While the idea of the project first appeared in a report on Latin America by the Santa Fe Group,[41] a conservative ad hoc think tank group that surfaced during the 1980s presidential elections to elaborate policy recommendations for Ronald Reagan and subsequently for the National Security Council, the White House initiated the radio project and Paula Hawkins, the former Republican Senator from Florida, introduced it in the Senate. As a means of developing support for the project, the President formed a Commission on Broadcasting to Cuba. He named two Cuban-Americans to the Commission, Tirso de Junco and Jorge Mas Canosa.

Even though the bill initially faced opposition, especially from North American broadcasters, a final version authorized the Voice of the Americas to establish the Radio Marti program. The Foundation had played a key role for the administration in gathering nationwide support for the bill. After its passage, the President named Ernesto Betancourt, a member of the Foundation's speakers bureau, as its director.[42]

The Cuban-American Committee had lobbied against the bill. This time they were not met with terrorists but with an organized lobbying group. Unfortunately for the Cuban-American groups that had lobbied for an easing of tensions between the two governments, the President's project had the effect of worsening relations. The Cuban government responded by suspending agreements it had previously reached with the Reagan administration on the return of Mariel prisoners and on exit visas for political prisoners. More surprisingly the Cuban government suspended the accords of the Dialogue and for a year did not allow Cuban-Americans to visit the island. Although in part, this was meant to be a message to the Cuban community, it showed that the Cuban government had not fully developed a coherent policy toward the Cuban communities outside of Cuba. Their action surprised supporters of the Dialogue for in effect it aligned the Cuban government with the most reactionary forces in the Cuban community who had consistently fought against the travel of Cuban-Americans to Cuba.[43] The Cuban government's suspension of the accords of the Dialogue forced the Cuban-Americans who supported it to refocus their political activities.

The Cuban-American National Foundation also helped the President lobby for a variety of other foreign policy projects. These included aid to the Contras, support for the Grenadian invasion, and funds for anti-government rebels in Angola. They were also instrumental in helping the President pass his Caribbean Basin Tax Plan, which directly benefitted the businessmen on the board. Clearly, the Foundation was a product of a maturing economic base in Miami and its merger to Cuban-American conservative ideologues.[44]

The Republicans not only accepted Cuban-Americans as lobbying supporters, they also actively promoted many of them to key policy positions within the government and the Party hierarchy. The highest level appointments included José Sorzano, the second president of the Board of Directors of the Foundation, as Ambassador to the Economic and Social Council of the United Nations and Otto Reich to various diplomatic posts. Not all appointments have been concentrated in the realm of foreign policy — others have been in institutions that have domestic policy functions.[45]

Within the Republican Party, Cubans have also been placed in key positions. The powerful Republican Finance Committee invited Carlos Benitez, also on the board of the Foundation, to join its other nine members. In many states, Cubans direct the Republicans' Hispanic Assemblies. In fact, in 1983, the Party replaced the president of the National Hispanic Assembly, Fernando C. de Baca, a Mexican from New Mexico, with Tirso de Junco, a Cuban from California. Cubans in Florida have provided the Republican Party with a base with which to attempt to establish itself in Democratic Party–controlled states. The electoral strategies have generally relied on fielding numerous Cuban-American candidates against Democrats. In 1982, this included running Manuel Yglesias against Claude Pepper.[46]

With these Cuban appointments and candidates, the Republicans have been able to build the image that they have Latino support. Cuban-Americans have thus been very valuable to a Party that since the 1960s has had a serious problem with minorities. Their relationship with the Republicans have signaled the changing function of Cuban-Americans from merely foreign policy actors to domestic policy actors as well.

Despite all the political successes of the Reagan-aligned Cuban-Americans, this group was not able to elect a mayor in Miami. In 1985, Xavier Suarez became the first Cuban-born mayor of Miami. In the first round of the elections, Maurice Ferre, a national Democrat and Puerto Rican incumbent, came in third. The run-off was between Raul Masvidal, a vocal supporter of Reagan and member of the Board of Directors of the Cuban-American National Foundation, and Xavier Suarez. Miami voters turned down the more ideological candidate for the more technocratic candidate.

While the Republicans did garner more than 90 percent of the Miami

Cuban-American vote in the 1984 Presidential elections, they did not fare as well with Cuban-Americans in northern and midwestern cities. Percentages for the Republicans ranged from 65 percent in New York to 68 percent in Chicago.[47] In part, these regional differences are due to the role that Cubans who support domestic programs which better distribute the goods of society as well as foreign policies that are less interventionist have played vis-à-vis other minorities in the electoral arena. This has been possible in cities outside Miami where the right wing is less dominant and where there are fewer acts of political repression against progressive activists.[48] Cubans in these cities are a minority of other Latinos. Thus, Cuban-Americans have had a shared experience with other Latino communities that has impacted on their political world view. Cuban-Americans in urban areas have also suffered the severe cutbacks of federal services and are less likely to be supportive of the Reagan administration. This has resulted in a diversity of political opinions and organizations.

In the 1984 Presidential elections, progressive Cubans formed an unprecedented Cuban-American Democrats Committee. They lobbied the Party with a document produced by the Cuban-American Committee outlining a series of policy issues which affected Cuban-Americans as well as other Latinos.[49] These included high school drop out rates, better services for the elderly, day care needs, and bilingual educational opportunities for the young. It outlined concerns over immigration policy. In a section on foreign policy, they also supported peaceful solutions to the crisis in Central America and the Caribbean.

The lack of opportunity to develop a more humane and less interventionist foreign policy based on the rights of Latin American countries to choose their destiny forced Cuban Americans interested in relations with Cuba to concentrate on local issues which in turn have provided the basis for them to build coalitions with other minorities. Many progressive Cubans were radicalized in minority community movements—these past political relations have eased the process of building bridges with these other communities. In cities outside of Miami, progressive Cubans have participated in building minority electoral coalitions. In Chicago, a small but significant group of Cuban-American Democrats participated in the 1983 mayoral elections. Over 50 percent of Cubans voted for Harold Washington despite a well-organized campaign by the Cuban right in support of the Republican candidate, Bernard Epton.[50] In Boston, Cubans also played an important role in Mel King's campaign for mayor. In Philadelphia and in Atlanta, progressive Cubans are a part of the largely minority urban coalitions which control those municipal governments. To date the most impressive documentation of this trend is the results of the 1987 Chicago Mayoral elections. Both in the primary and in the general elections, the

Cuban-American community was the Latino community that gave Harold Washington the highest proportion of their vote.[51] In the 1980s, progressive Cubans are playing an important part in unifying Hispanics and blacks. The 1970s polarization of the Cuban community is being played out in a broader political arena in the 1980s.

THE COMING DECADES

The transition from being exclusively foreign policy actors to being domestic policy actors as well signals the change from an exile community to a minority community, that is, a community whose political concerns are focused on the country in which they now live. In the coming decades, it is likely that there will be increasing liberalizing trends in Cuban-American politics especially in regard to local issues. While this will probably first occur outside of Miami, even there, it will become more evident as time passes. Yet perhaps the greatest polarization will surface as Cubans who are not members of the new elite face the realities of being a minority in the United States. While the more reactionary political forces have tended to control, a more progressive tendency has unfolded in the heart of a once perceived monolithically anti-communist community. And this has created the possibility of defining a political agenda that will bring important sectors of the Cuban community closer to other Latinos and blacks.

NOTES

1. For a detailed account of Cuban-American covert activities in Latin America, see W. Hinckley and William Fuller, *The Fish is Red* (New York: Harper and Row, 1981). Also, J. Dinges and S. Landau, *Assassination on Embassy Row* (New York: Panther Books, 1980).

2. Wayne Smith, *The Closest of Enemies: A Personal and Diplomatic Account of U.S.–Cuban Relations since 1957* (New York: W. W. Norton, 1987).

3. P. Foner, *A History of Cuba and Its Relation to the United States* (New York: International Publisher, 1983), vol. 2, p. 9; and J. A. Saco, *Contra al anexion* (La Habana, Cuba: Editorial de Ciencias Sociales, 1987).

4. G. Poyo, "Cuban Revolutionaries and Monroe County Reconstruction Politics: 1868–1876," *Florida Historical Quarterly,* 60, no. 4 (1977): 407–422; G. Poyo, "Key West and the Cuban Ten Years War," *Florida Historical Quarterly* 57 (1979): 289–307; and L. Perez, "Cubans in Tampa: From Exiles to Immigrants," *Florida Historical Quarterly* 62, no. 2 (1978): 129–140.

5. Personal interview with Jaime Zaiger, San Antonio, Texas, May 1978. He participated in the publishing of newspapers which were then smuggled into Cuba.

6. *Organo del Movimiento 26 de julio* (Miami and New York: 1957–1959), and a personal interview with Julio Bauta, Executive Committee Member of the Chicago 26th of July committee, November 1984.

7. R. Fagen, R. Brody, and T. O'Leary, *Cubans in Exile: Disaffection and Revolution* (Stanford, Calif.: Stanford University Press, 1968).

8. L. Arguelles, "El Miami Cubano," *Arieto* 7, no. 28 (1980): 4–15. See also, A. Portes, and R. Bach, *Latin Journey: Cuban and Mexican Immigrants* (Berkeley, Calif.: University of California Press, 1985), pp. 200–238.

9. R. Hernandez, "La politica imigratoria de Estados Unidos y la revolucion cubana," *Centro de Estudios Sobre America,* La Habana, Cuba, March 1980; and Esther Bravo, dir., *Los que se fueron,* Cuban and Canadian co-production, 1983.

10. L. Casal, Y. Prieto, and R. Prohias, "The Cuban Migration of the Sixties in its Historical Context: Cubans in the United States," unpublished paper, 1979; L. Casal, "Cubans in the United States: Their Impact on U.S.," in *Revolutionary Cuba in the World,* ed. M. Weinstein (Philadelphia: ISPH Press 1979); and A. Portes, "Dilemmas of a Golden Exile: Integration of Cuban Refugee Families in Milwaukee," *American Sociological Review* 34 (August 1969): 505–518. Sociologist Lourdes Casal contributed to the scholarship on the Cuban community in the United States, as well as the organizing of various Cuban-American organizations which called for normalizing relations between Cuba and the United States. Also see A. Portes and R. Bach, *Latin Journey,* pp. 85–87.

11. Peter Wyden, *Bay of Pigs: The Untold Story* (New York: Simon and Schuster, 1979), p. 114.

12. L. Arguelles, "Cuban Miami: The Roots, Development, and Everyday Life of an Emigre Enclave in the National Security State," *Comtemporary Marxism 5* (Summer 1982): 27–44. Also see L. Arguelles, "Studies in the Political Economy of the U.S. National Security State: The CIA and the Origins of Cuban Exile Terrorism," Joint Meeting of the Latin American Studies Association and the Midwest Association of Latin American Studies, Indiana University, Bloomington, Indiana, 17–19 October 1980; and Carlos Forment, "Caribbean Geopolitics and Foreign State Sponsored Social Movements: The Case of Cuban Exile Military, 1959–1979," in *Cubans in the United States,* ed. M. Uriarte-Gaston and Jorge Canas-Martínez (Boston, Mass.: Center for the Study of the Cuban Community, 1984), pp. 65–102.

13. Max Azicri, "The Politics of Exile: Trends and Dynamics of Political Change Among Cuban Americans," *Cuban Studies/Estudios Cubanos* (July 1981–Jan. 1982): 53–73; and S. Nazario, "Yanqui Si: After a Long Holdout, Cubans in Miami Take a Role in U.S. Politics," *The Wall Street Journal,* 7 June 1983, p. 1. See also A. Portes and R. Moza, "Naturalization, Registration and Voting Patterns of Cubans and Other Ethnic Minorities: A Preliminary Analysis," paper presented at a Conference on Citizenship and the Hispanic Community, National Association of Latino Elected Officials, Washington, D.C., May 1984; and, A. Portes, "Dilemmas of a Golden Exile," pp. 505–518.

14. The group of economists at Florida International University has published extensively on the waste of human resources present in the Cuban com-

munity. For a sampling of their work, see A. Jorge and R. Moncarz, *A Case of Subutilization and Dislocation of Human Capital Resources: The Cubans in the United States,* Working Paper, Human Resources and Development Program, College of Business at the University of Texas, San Antonio, November 1981; and Jorge and Moncarz, International Factor Movement and Complementary Growth and Entrepreneurship under Conditions of the Cultural Variation and J. Valdes Paz and R. Hernandez, "La estructura social de la comunidad cubana en Estados Unidos," in Uriarte-Gaston and Canas-Martínez, *Cubans in the U.S.,* pp. 186–217.

15. R. de la Garza, interview with National Public Radio, July 1983. The Southwest Voter Registration and Education Project and Cuban-American Committee 1984 Presidential Election Exit Poll 1984 clearly show differences among Latino communities and regional differences in the case of Cuban Communities.

16. A. Portes and N. Amaro, "Una sociologia del exilio: situacion de los grupos cubanos en los Estados Unidos," *Aportes,* 23 (Jan. 1972): 9–15.

17. L. Casal and R. Prohias, *The Cuban Minority in the U.S.: Preliminary Report on Need Identification and Program Evaluation* (Boca Raton, Fla.: Florida Atlantic University, 1973); and A. Hernandez, ed., *The Cuban Minority in the U.S.: A Final Report on Need Identification and Progress Evaluation* (Washington, D.C.: Cuban National Planning Council, 1974).

18. This group set up "Spanish Family Guidance Clinic in Miami." Among their publications is included José Szapocznick, Javeir Lasaga, and Priscella Perry, "Outreach in the Delivery of Mental Health Services to Hispanic Elders," *Hispanic Journal of Behavioral Sciences* 1, no. 1 (1979): 21–40.

19. G. Diaz, "El proceso de pluralizacion del exilio cubano," *Nueva Genarcion* (Nov. 1970).

20. Grupo Areito, *Contra viento y marea* (La Habana, Cuba: Casa de las Americas, 1979); and J. Diaz, *Del exilio a la partia* (Havana: UNEAC, 1979). The first few issues of *Arieto* dealt with the identity of Cuban youth in the United States but focused much more on the relationship with Cuba. In the last issues, *Arieto* has expanded to include more writings on Latin America in general. *Joven Cuba* focused on the problematic position of Cubans as a national minority in the United States and was much more concerned with the relationship with other groups such as Puertoriquenos and Mexicanos. *Nuevos Rumbos,* published by a Cuban student group at the University of Florida at Gainesville, was closer to the *Arieto* perspective.

21. *Arieto* 4, no. 3–4 (Spring 1978). This is a special issue on the Antonio Maceo Brigade. Since 1978, the author has interviewed numerous young Cubans who travelled in the early trips to Cuba.

22. Jesus Diaz, dir., *55 Hermanos.* ICAIC. 1978. A documentary of the first trip home by Cubans living abroad.

23. R. Fagen, et al., *Cubans in Exile.*

24. "Interview with President Fidel Castro," *Arieto* 6 (Sept. 1979).

25. Wayne Smith, *The Closest of Enemies.*

26. L. Casal, "Invitacion al dialogo," *Arieto* 5, no. 17 (1978): 5–9.

27. *Baragua* 1, no. 1 (Spring 1979): 2.

28. M. Azicri, Un analysis pragamatico del Dialogo entre la Cuba del interior y del exterior," *Arieto* 5, no. 19–20 (1979): 4.

29. Manolo Gomez, "El exilio pide relaciones con Cuba," *Arieto* 5, nos. 19–20 (1979): 7–9.

30. *U.S.–Cuba Bulletin,* the official newsletter of the Committee, has an excellent review of the Committee's activities.

31. J. Stein, "Inside Omega 7," *Village Voice,* 10 March 1980, pp. 1–5; and J. Stein, "Army in Exile," *New Yorker,* 10 Sept. 1979, pp. 42–49.

32. E. Schneider, "The Basis of and Need for a Coordinated Federal and State Investigation and Prosecution of Cuban Exile Terrorism," Rutgers Law School, Constitutional Litigation Clinic, May 1979.

33. In 1980, the FBI reported that Omega 7 was the most dangerous terrorist group in the United States. P. Herman, "Highest Priority Given by U.S. to Capture Anti-Castro Group," *The New York Times,* 3 March 1980, pp. 1–3.

34. Interview with Franklin Garcia, summer 1980.

35. Alicia Torres, "U.S. Network Evening News of Cuba: 1972–1981," Master's Thesis, University of Texas, 1984.

36. S. Taylor, "Latins Training in U.S. Raise Questions of Criminal and International Law," *New York Times,* 24 December 1981, p. 14; and R. Lindsey, "Foes of Nicaragua Regime Training California," *New York Times,* 18 January 1982. For a background on the Mariel immigration, see R. Bach, "The New Cuban Immigrants; Their Background and Prospects," *Monthly Labor Review* 1 (October 1980): 39–46; "The New Cuban Exodus: Political and Economic Motivations," *Caribbean Review* 11, no. 1 (1982): 22–26; R. Bach and L. Triplett, "The Flotilla Entrants: Latest and Most Controversial," *Cuban Studies/Estudios Cubanos* 11, no. 2, and 12, no. 1 (July 1981–Jan. 1982); and Peter Winn, "After the Exodus; Is the Cuban Revolution in Trouble?" *The Nation* 7 (June 1980).

37. U.S. Department of State, Bureau of Public Affairs, *Cuba's Renewed Support for Violence in Latin America,* Special Report No. 90, 14 December 1981; and *Communist Interference in El Salvador,* Special Report No. 80, 23 February 1980.

38. Personal interview with Bob Bailon, Republican National Committee, May 1983, and personal interview with Bernie Sweeney, Coordinator of Ethnic Liaison Office, May 1983.

39. L. Arguelles reported interview with Roger Fontaine, Nov. 1980.

40. *Financial Reports of the Cuban-American National Foundation* filed with the Federal Election Commission, Quarterly Reports 1982 to 1984. Also, L. Lagnado, "Anti-Castro Pac in Washington," *The Nation* 15 (Oct. 1983); and personal interview with F. Calzon, former Executive Director, Cuban-American National Foundation, May 1983. For an in-depth analysis of the Miami financial sector, see P. Lernoux, *In Banks We Trust* (New York: Doubleday/Anchor Press, 1984), chaps. 5–9; for a brief description, see P. Lernoux, "The Miami Connection: Mafia, CIA, Cubans, Banks and Drugs," *The Nation* 18 (February 1984): 186, 198; and G. Martinez, "Cuban Exiles Pour Money Into Congressional Races," *Miami Herald,* 27 Sept. 1982, p. 1.

41. *A New Inter-American Policy for the Eighties,* ed. R. Tambs (Washington, D.C.: Council on Inter-American Security, 1980).

42. U.S. Cong., House, *Statement to the Committee on Foreign Affairs,* by T. Enders, 97th Cong., 2nd Sess., H. Dept. 5427, March 3, 4, and 24, 1982. "The Subject is Cuba," Speaker's Bureau, Cuban American National Foundation. For a comprehensive analysis of the issues involved and a list of the Board of Directors, see N. Serafina, N. Smith, and D. Siddal, *Radio Jose Marti,* Senate Committee on Foreign Relations, 28 June 1982.

43. M. Perez-Stable, "Diversidad y politica de cubanos," *El Miami Herald,* 7 Oct. 1985, p. 5.

44. R. A. Zaldivar, "Cuban Lobby Courts Allies, Reaps Clout," *Miami Herald,* Monday, Aug. 11, 1986, p. 1.

45. *A Directory of Hispanic Appointees in the Reagan Administration* (Washington, D.C., March 1983).

46. Personal interview with Don Hayes, Campaign Manager for Manuel Yglesias, June 1982.

47. Southwest Voter Registration and Education Project, *Analysis of the Hispanic Vote in 1984 Presidential Elections,* 1984; and M. Gomez, "The Hispanic Vote in the Election," *U.S.–Cuba Bulletin* 3, no. 1 (Feb. 1985): 1–6.

48. For a historical documentation of acts of terrorism against Cuban-Americans, see M. Torres, "From Exiles to Minorities: The Politics of the Cuban Community in the United States," chapter III, Part 3, University of Michigan dissertation, 1987.

49. M. Gomez, "Cuban-Americans, Hispanics and the 1984 Elections: A Memorandum to the Democratic Party, its Presidential Candidate," *Cuban-American Committee,* 1984.

50. Midwest Voter Registration and Education Project, *Exit Poll, 1983, Chicago Mayor Elections Report.* 52 percent of Cubans voted for Harold Washington.

51. Midwest Voter Registration and Education Project, Chicago, 1987 Mayoral Primary and General Elections, 1987. In the primary elections 68 percent of Cubans interviewed supported Harold Washington; in the general election this increased to 72 percent. This percentage was higher than Mexican, Puerto Rican, Central and South American percentages for Harold Washington.

5. Latino Politics in the Midwestern United States: 1915–1986[1]

Richard Santillan

THE CONVENTIONAL STUDY OF Latino politics in the United States, and Mexican-American politics in particular, has been based largely on popular fallacies rather than historical facts.[2] These outdated assumptions have often promoted the narrow view that Latinos themselves are primarily responsible for their own powerlessness. A lack of political sophistication and an unwillingness to culturally assimilate are frequently cited as the principal internal factors for Mexican-American and Puerto Rican invisibility within the political arena. Latino political scientists, however, are academically challenging and rapidly negating many of these old-fashioned ideas. They offer instead original interpretations defining Latino political history as well as present alternative external factors which contribute to the shortage of political representation among Latinos.[3]

Some of these old myths, unfortunately, continue to linger on without much interruption, including the widespread opinion that Mexican-American political activities are limited solely to the southwestern United States, where the majority of Mexican-Americans reside. A closer investigation of Latino political history, however, reveals that Mexican-Americans have been politically active in the Midwest for four generations and, more importantly, are currently involved with Puerto Rican and Cuban-American groups in reshaping the political landscape of this important region.

This historical oversight can be attributed in major part to the fact that a number of southwestern Mexican-American leaders and scholars have unintentionally overlooked the reality that nearly two million Mexican-Americans, Puerto Ricans, and Cuban-Americans live in the ten states that comprise the Midwest, nearly 16 percent of the total Latino population in the United States.[4] In 1985 there were 450 elected and appointed midwestern Latino officials, and these numbers are rapidly increasing with each election year.[5] The Midwest Voter Registration Education Project, for ex-

99

ample, estimates that midwestern Latinos could hold a thousand elected and appointed positions by 1990.[6]

Between 1981 and 1986, I traveled extensively throughout the Midwest interviewing approximately 500 Mexican-American, Puerto Rican, and Cuban-American political and community activists in order to gain a greater understanding of both the historical and contemporary factors contributing to this growing political mobilization. I also reviewed numerous governmental reports, newspaper articles, campaign materials, and scholarly studies which provide further testimony about the Latino experience in the Midwest. These interviews and documents, when pieced together, unveil a new and extraordinary chapter which speaks favorably of Latino politics in the United States.

The study of midwestern Latino political behavior is critical for two important reasons. First, this new political evidence presents fresh insight regarding the subject of the social and economic conditions which, regardless of region, largely determine the ideology and strategies of Latino organizations. Mexican-Americans, for example, in both the Midwest and the Southwest, have encountered similar historical experiences, and, as a consequence of this common bond, they have established several corresponding types of organizations vital to their respective communities. These include mutual aid societies, veterans' groups, political associations, "Viva" clubs, La Raza Unida, and caucuses inside both major parties.

Second, and more importantly, it appears that a number of Latino strategies being advanced in the Midwest may provide far-reaching clues for enhancing Latino political clout elsewhere in the United States. Midwestern Latino organizational efforts, for instance, cannot rely solely on large Latino populations to elect Latino candidates, which is the general case in the Southwest, New York, and Florida. Therefore, the Latino leadership in the Midwest has been compelled to be more politically creative in seeking political offices and securing a fair share of economic resources and social services for its people. Midwestern Latinos, as a result of their innovative politics, have tended to advocate stronger alliances with non-Latino groups, foster closer ties between Latino Democrats and Republicans, work carefully inside both the church and union structures, and encourage and promote Latinos to leadership positions.

This article is divided into three major parts. Section 1 is a brief overview of the Spanish/Mexican influence in the Midwest prior to the twentieth century. Section 2 surveys the roots of midwestern Mexican-American and Puerto Rican organizations between 1915 and 1959, and section 3 examines the factors that have helped escalate Latino midwestern political visibility between 1960 and 1986.

This article will focus primarily on the Mexican-American political experience in the Midwest for three main reasons: first, Mexican-Americans arrived in the region nearly sixty or seventy years prior to significant Puerto Rican and Cuban immigration, respectively; next, Mexican-Americans are generally located throughout the Midwest, whereas the settlement of Puerto Ricans (in the Great Lakes region) and Cubans (in Chicago, Cincinnati, and Indianapolis) took place in very specific geographical areas; and finally, Mexican-Americans are by far the largest of any of the Latino groups now residing in the Midwest. This study, nevertheless, will discuss the post–World War II political relationship among these three Latino groups.

I

Latino roots in the Midwest can be traced back for several centuries. In the spring of 1541, Spanish soldiers under the command of Francisco Vasquez de Coronado became the first Europeans to enter present-day Oklahoma and Kansas in their quest for gold.[7] By 1763, the Spanish Empire encompassed all of the Midwest, including what is now the state of Minnesota.[8]

The Spanish government, in addition to seeking gold, was occupied in economic trade with the city of St. Louis, Missouri, and as a consequence, it established several trading posts along the Mississippi River. The Spanish government eventually abandoned these lands because of economic hardships in Spain, hostile Indians, unfriendly weather conditions, rebellions within its colonies, and military threats from newly arrived European nations. Spain negotiated these midwestern lands over to France in 1801, which in turn sold them to the United States in 1803 as part of the Louisiana Purchase. A diplomatic dispute regarding the ownership of Texas in the aftermath of these international transitions ultimately led to the bitter war between the United States and Mexico in 1846.

The Spanish and Mexican legacy in the Midwest is still manifested today in the historical names of several cities, including Toledo, Ohio; Mexico, Missouri; Montevideo, Minnesota; El Dorado, Kansas; Cuba and Tampico, Illinois; Peru, Indiana; Alma, Michigan; and Montezuma, Iowa. Moreover two of Iowa's counties are named Cerro Gordo and Buena Vista, in honor of U.S. military victories during the war against Mexico.

By the late nineteenth and early twentieth centuries, large numbers of Mexicans were recruited for work in a variety of midwestern industries.[9] The push and pull factors responsible for this massive northern migration included the harsh economic and political conditions under the Diaz regime, the expanding American economy, tighter immigration laws prohibiting cheap labor from Eastern Europe, the attractiveness of higher wages,

the geographical proximity of Texas to the Midwest (San Antonio, for example, is closer to Kansas City and Chicago than to Los Angeles), and
relatively easy access by railroad.

The last factor regarding railroad travel was a powerful incentive that
navigated thousands of Mexicans to the Midwest. Mexicans who worked
for the railroad companies were allowed free transportation throughout
the United States, and many workers took advantage of this complimentary benefit by repeatedly traveling back and forth between the Midwest
and the Texas-Mexico borders.[10] As a result of this cyclical process, many
Mexican railroad workers returned for work to the Midwest with family
members and friends who were merely charged a minimal fee for riding
the trains. This long-term labor demand also helps explain why the Mexican culture and language have been preserved inside many of these midwestern Mexican-American outposts to this day. Furthermore, railroad
workers and their families were provided free housing that consisted of
old boxcars stretched along the railroad tracks. These dreadful conditions
were nevertheless preferable to the jobs in the Southwest, where travel expenses and high rents were deducted from already low wages.[11]

In addition to the railroads, Mexican workers were employed in a
wide range of midwestern occupations, including coal and steel plants, auto
manufacturing, lumber mills, packinghouses, tanneries, sugar refineries,
oil and nitrate plants, textiles, farm and construction equipment, ice houses,
grain farms, and agriculture (cotton, sugar beets, asparagus, apples, toma-
toes, cherries, pickles, onions, and cucumbers). Mexican-American migrants continue to comprise the bulk of field workers in the Midwest today. By the 1920s, the largest employers of Mexican labor anywhere in
the United States were located in the Great Lakes Region.[12]

II

When these newly arrived Mexican immigrants reached the Midwest, they encountered varying degrees of racial discrimination and prejudice.[13] These levels of public resentment were principally determined by
two key factors: first, the proportion of the Mexican community to the
overall Anglo group, and second, the economic stability of the community. The higher the ratio of the Mexican population and accompanying
job competition, the greater the intensity of social segregation and racial
hostility toward the Mexican immigrant.

One common experience shared by nearly all these Mexican immigrants was crowded and segregated housing: "By 1925, most of the major
cities in the Midwest had colonies in the rundown areas. As the need for

cheap labor became more intensive in the northern industries, the colonies increased in size."[14]

The impoverished Mexican communities were likely to be cloistered near the industries of employment, and the living conditions were often harsh. People still vividly recount the social hardships, including the lack of hot running water, the discomforts of outdoor bathrooms, the inadequate housing space to accommodate their large families, unpaved and unlighted streets, and the frigid cold during the winter months.[15] These marginal Mexican communities were often physically disassociated from the rest of the main city either by railroad tracks or rivers.

Many of these original midwestern Mexican-American neighborhoods have been physically demolished as a result of federal and local urban renewal programs initiated during the 1960s and 1970s. The remnants of other long-time Mexican-American communities, however, can be located today in southeast Scottsbluff, Nebraska; southwest Detroit, Michigan; west Des Moines, Iowa; west St. Paul, Minnesota; south Milwaukee, Wisconsin; south Chicago, Illinois; south Toledo, Ohio; west Kansas City, Kansas; and west Gary, Indiana.

The emerging leadership of these new Mexican communities saw the immediate need for establishing grassroots associations in order to combat racial bias and for safeguarding the Mexican culture from total assimilation. These "sociedades mexicanas" were started as early as 1915 in the Midwest by self-employed Mexican businessmen and gradually took on an assortment of charitable duties, including job referrals, legal services, providing life insurance, and encouraging naturalization and voting.[16] By the early 1920s, these Mexican benevolent associations could be found throughout the Midwest. They include Sociedad Mutualista National (Oklahoma); Sociedad Mutualista Mexicana (Ohio); Circulo Mutualista Mexicano (Michigan); Sociedad Funeraria Miguel Hidalgo (Kansas); Sociedad Benito Juarez (Illinois); Sociedad Mutualista Mexicana (Nebraska); and the Anahuac Society (Minnesota). The city of Gary, Indiana alone had eleven mutual societies, and the city of Chicago had twenty-three groups.[17] There were several attempts to coordinate joint cultural activities between many of these various Mexican fraternities.

By the late 1920s, these midwestern Mexican communities had evolved into permanent settlements replete with churches, small businesses, cultural centers, Spanish language newspapers, union halls, schools, and organized sports programs.[18] Many Mexicans, now endowed with a new sense of social stability, became naturalized U.S. citizens and in doing so were quickly recognized by some politicians as a potential voting bloc. The Latin-American Political Club, for example, was organized in 1929 for the sole purpose of political participation, including hosting forums for candidates seeking the Mexican vote in Indiana.[19] In addition, a Mexican-American, William Emilio Rodriguez, was elected to the Chicago City Council in 1915 under the banner of the Socialist Party.[20]

This newly discovered political voice was, however, unexpectedly extinguished as a consequence of the Great Depression and the implementation by the Hoover Administration of the Repatriation Program, which systematically deported thousands of Mexicans (many of them American citizens) back to Mexico during the 1930s.[21] The U.S. government's official explanation for this unprecedented action was that this expulsion plan would considerably reduce unemployment and save taxpayers money by eliminating social services for aliens. In reality, these massive deportations, especially in the Midwest, were primarily triggered by deep-rooted racial discrimination and selfish economic considerations, led by such groups as the American Legion and labor unions with a self-vested interest in eliminating "foreigners" from competition with Anglo workers for scarce jobs.[22]

These repatriation efforts, unlike those in the Southwest, inflicted serious social damage upon the entire Mexican community in the Midwest.[23] Furthermore, this drastic reduction in the Mexican population during the 1930s severely crippled the midwestern Mexican political agenda set in motion during the 1920s. Thus, the natural growth of Mexican-American political development in the Midwest was disrupted for at least one entire generation and consequently placed Mexican-Americans in a disadvantaged position behind other midwestern ethnic groups competing for the same political resources.

The Mexican-American community in the Midwest, nevertheless, has displayed a rare ability for continuously overcoming these social pressures of racial isolation, physical displacement, and repeated accusations of un-American behavior. The midwestern Mexican-American leadership made it quite evident during the 1940s and 1950s that it would renew its determination for both social integration and political representation, regardless of the harmful impediments placed in its path.[24] The dynamic leadership during this time period was comprised mainly of American-born war veterans who had distinguished themselves with impressive combat credentials in both World War II and Korea.:

> Besides being from the well-known neighborhoods of towns in the Southwest, many of the Mexican-Americans in the induction centers hailed from such rarely mentioned places as North Platte, Nebraska; Garden City, Kansas; Cheyenne, Wyoming; Missoula, Montana; Ogden, Utah; Chester, Pennsylvania, and other far away places like Gary, Indiana; Detroit, Michigan; Lorain, Ohio; St. Louis, Missouri; and Oklahoma City, Oklahoma.[25]

Mexican-Americans in the Midwest have won at least five Congressional Medals of Honor, and several others have been awarded citations for valor.[26] The most celebrated case of Mexican-American patriotism is represented by the small town of Silvis, Illinois, where nearly 130 of its young Mexican-American men have fought in World War II, Korea, and Vietnam.[27] A street in the heart of this close-knit Mexican-American community has been renamed "Hero Street" in memory of these young men, including eight who were killed in action. Today many elected officials from both major parties visit Hero Street each year to pay special tribute to the prominent contributions of Mexican-Americans in the defense of the nation.

This formal recognition, however, has not always been the case for the Mexican-American serviceman. As Mexican-Americans slowly returned from these global conflicts, especially World War II, they were immediately confronted again with visible reminders of their second-class status in both the Southwest and the Midwest.[28] Many Mexican-American veterans were refused membership in their local VFW chapters and denied services by some of the local business establishments. These overt acts of racial discrimination were not isolated cases, but were commonplace throughout the Midwest.[29]

Many of these returning Mexican-American soldiers were now more cognizant of these clear forms of discrimination, than they had been prior to their military enlistments. They became increasingly indignant with the constant reminders of blatant social inequality as represented by unpaved streets, segregated housing, lack of adequate sewage, and restriction to certain sections of movie houses, restaurants, parks, and churches. These vocal groups of second-generation Mexican-Americans strongly felt that they should be considered first-class citizens in light of the fact that they had fought side by side with Anglos on the battlefields:

> We fought for the American ideals that our parents had taught us as children and we believed that our misfortune was merely a way of life. After the war, we clearly realized that these deplorable conditions only existed because of racial discrimination. We were no longer afraid like our parents to confront the local officials regarding these terrible problems. Our battle for eliminating social discrimination was less frightening when compared to the horrors of war we had recently experienced overseas.[30]

In deference to their elders, these Mexican-American veterans brought these serious grievances to the immediate attention of the Mexican leadership representing the old, established mutual aid societies. These midwestern war veterans, however, became quickly frustrated because these sympathetic associations had primarily limited themselves to promoting cultural activities and were too socially inflexible to meet these new political challenges against the local authorities. These strong-minded veterans brought their complaints directly to the city councils who, in turn, dismissed their pressing concerns.[31] It became quite evident to these impatient veterans that, while they had undergone a political transformation, these local officials, on the other hand, had continued to stereotypically view the Mexican-American community as submissive migrant workers.

The midwestern Mexican-American veterans (as a result of these official rebukes) formed several advocacy organizations, including the adoption of the G.I. Forum, which overlapped in Ohio (1954), Kansas (1955), Nebraska (1955), Missouri (1956), Michigan (1956), Illinois (1957), Indiana (1957), Iowa (1958), Minnesota (1958), Oklahoma (1958), and Wisconsin (1958).[32]

LULAC, a pre–World War II organization, was also organized in the Midwest during the 1950s. The establishment of these post–World War II organizations signaled a new era in Midwest Mexican-American politics, and as a result, the mutual aid leadership reluctantly relinquished its community influence to the management of the G.I. generation. LULAC, G.I. Forum, and other similar types of nationwide organizations were primarily instrumental in skillfully abolishing overt forms of legal discrimination, including the unfair poll tax, exclusion of Mexican-Americans from juries, educational and social segregation, and the termination of the dreaded bracero program.[33] Furthermore, these groups demonstrated an unyielding belief in cultural immersion into the American mainstream and a fierce loyalty for American patriotism:

> If LULAC sought to soften its image through the use of the phrase "Latin American," the Forum erased any obvious reference to ethnicity altogether. While it is probably true that even the aggressive demands which the organization made for its rights as "Americans" may have been a militant action for its time, it is perhaps equally true that its exaggerated conformity and overly dramatized patriotic posture did serious damage to the consciousness of the organization's membership. This is especially true for the chapters in the Midwest.[34]

These groups ironically exhibited a strong inclination to exclude themselves from participating directly with partisan politics despite the fact that some of the leadership had been politically appointed to serve in both the Kennedy and Johnson administrations.[35] The eventual outcome of this controversial policy of political restraint was the inevitable emergence of a new set of Mexican-American organizations in the late 1950s and early 1960s which encouraged direct involvement in electoral politics.

Finally, the post–World War II period also witnessed the large-scale migration of Puerto Ricans to the U.S. mainland both for employment and for educational opportunities. The city of New York became the home for thousands of Puerto Ricans in the early 1950s, with smaller communities located jn Chicago, Cleveland, Lorain, Gary, East Chicago, Milwaukee, and Detroit.[36]

In the early 1950s, the midwestern Puerto Rican community, like its Mexican predecessors, established several mutual aid associations in order to assist Puerto Ricans in making the social and economic transition into American society. These newly founded groups included the First Puertorrican Club, Asociacion Benefica Hijos de Borinquen, and Los Caballeros de San Juan.[37]

At first, the older Mexican-American community and newly arriving Puerto Ricans did not socially embrace each other, largely due to cultural, language, and physical distinctions which produced initial suspicion on both sides.

Moreover, the midwestern Mexican-American leadership, as a rule, resented sharing the political spotlight with a new Spanish-speaking group who, according to some Mexican-Americans, had not yet paid their political dues. Puerto Ricans are American citizens at birth, and consequently, the Democratic Party made mild political overtures to these incoming Puerto Ricans. This scant attention by the Democrats toward Puerto Ricans caused many Mexican-Americans to label Puerto Ricans as political rivals who were encroaching upon their political territory, rather than as electoral partners.[38]

The economic issue of job competition between Mexican-Americans and Puerto Ricans was never a divisive factor since there was plenty of work for everyone. Many of the early cultural and political misunderstandings have gradually faded away with each subsequent Mexican-American and Puerto Rican generation, and more importantly, by the 1970s the political circumstances would become ripe for both groups to work cooperatively on common issues and candidates.

III

The decade of the 1950s closed with a new shift of political gears among third-generation Mexican-Americans. This particular breed of Mexican-Americans, unlike the G.I. generation, openly expressed a high opinion of their Mexican culture and, more importantly, firmly believed that ethnic pride could serve as a binding element for politically unifying Mexican-Americans in the Southwest and the Midwest.[39]

Several midwestern organizations which wholeheartedly embraced this philosophy of ethnic politics were soon formed in several states, including the Political Association for Spanish-Speaking Organizations (PASSO), Mexican-American Political Association (MAPA), Mexican-American Clubs, Mexican-American Political Action Committee (MAPAC), and Latin-Americans for Political Action (LAPA).[40] These newly founded groups officially endorsed candidates, promoted voter registration drives, sponsored political forums, and encouraged naturalization: "Our future is to play the role of the conscience of the liberal movements in the Democratic and Republican parties; and address ourselves to the task of eliminating the evils of discrimination."[41] These political activities were clearly instrumental in the immediate election of a handful of midwestern Mexican-American and Puerto Rican candidates during the late 1950s and early 1960s.[42]

Furthermore, the 1960 "Viva Kennedy" campaign served as the special catalyst that helped consolidate these generic groups into a national united task force. The Kennedy effort is often described as a southwestern political phenomenon, which is historically incorrect since similar "Viva Kennedy" activities were conducted in the states of Illinois, Indiana, Michigan, Nebraska, and Iowa.[43] Moreover, midwestern Mexican-American "Viva" organizations were directly involved in the presidential campaigns for Johnson (1964), Rockefeller (1964), Humphrey (1968), Robert Kennedy (1968), McCarthy (1968), and Nixon (1968).[44]

The 1960s grape and lettuce boycotts also had a profound role in advancing the political aspirations of midwestern Mexican-Americans, especially cooperation between the Mexican-American union membership, migrant workers, and Chicano college students.[45] Boycott committees were established on several college campuses and in key cities such as Detroit, Chicago, St. Louis, Milwaukee, St. Paul, Gary, and Cleveland. The United Farmworkers' Union, as it had done in the Southwest, provided many midwestern Latinos the opportunity to learn the art of organizing. This included utilizing telephone banks, hosting press conferences, publishing newsletters, conducting house meetings, picketing, and learning how to pressure and negotiate agreements with supermarket executives and public officials. Many of these organizational skills would eventually be applied to midwestern voter registration programs and political campaigns during the 1960s and 1970s.[46]

The 1960s, likewise, witnessed the expanding popularity of the Chicano movement in the Midwest. This southwestern ripple effect included the establishment of Brown Beret chapters, the creation of Chicano studies programs, student walk-outs and protests, the formation of MECHA and other student groups, and federal and state funding for community-based organizations.[47] Furthermore, individuals including Jose Angel Gutierrez, Reies Lopez Tijerina, Corky Gonzales, and Cesar Chavez spoke countless times before enthusiastic midwestern audiences during this passionate period.

Similarly the concept of the La Raza Unida Party spilled over into the Midwest, with LRU chapters located in Michigan, Ohio, Wisconsin, Nebraska, Indiana, and Illinois.[48] The Midwest La Raza Unida, however, took on a different form and strategy, primarily because of the small Latino population in the Midwest:

> Unlike its southwestern counterpart, La Raza Unida in the Midwest developed as an organized pressure group rather than a political party. Chicano leadership in the Midwest felt La Raza Unida would be more effective in obtaining reforms and benefits as an organization rather than a political party. A party, they felt, would risk exposing voter weakness among Chicanos.[49]

Last, the period between 1961 and 1971 saw the midwestern resettlement of Cubans from Florida and Cuba. The Cuban population, when compared to Mexican-Americans and Puerto Ricans at this time, was politically insignificant. Cubans settled in Illinois (21,957), Ohio (2,342), Michigan (2,767), Indiana (1,673), and Missouri (1,272).[50]

The midwestern Cuban community, unlike the earlier Mexican-American and Puerto Rican immigrants, did not form mutual aid associations or Latino political alliances, largely because Cubans perceived themselves as temporary political refugees anxiously awaiting their expeditious return to Cuba. Furthermore, these politically conservative Cubans were extremely aggravated with the militant wing of the midwestern Mexican-American and Puerto Rican Civil Rights Movements of the 1960s (the Brown Berets and the Young Lords) who publicly applauded and admired both the Cuban Revolution and Fidel Castro.[51]

The conclusion of the 1960s clearly revealed the unfolding multiplicity of strategies evolving inside the Mexican-American political leadership in the Midwest. The outspoken components of this organizational spectrum consisted of the old established groups represented by the mutualistas and the seasoned G.I. generation, the Mexican-American political associations, and the Chicano movement organizations. All three sides shared the common conviction that social equality was achievable within the existing framework of electoral politics, but disagreed among themselves regarding the principal method of both acquiring political influence and tackling social problems, i.e., cultural assimilation, the ballot box, or confrontation.

The establishment of the Midwest Council of La Raza in 1970 was a primary mechanism in reconciling this delicate trinity of viewpoints, and one which served to strengthen the political partnership among Latino leaders for the upcoming 1970s.[52] The major aim of the MWCLR was to:

give greater cohesion to the efforts of Spanish-speaking groups to advocate their own interest and to focus attention on the presence of Spanish-speaking people in the Midwest. Its activities included conferences, community development, communications, education, research, and training.[53]

The MWCLR was a key force which eloquently persuaded most of the midwestern Mexican-American leadership to view itself primarily as a larger community of intermutual interests rather than merely as isolated local communities with particular issues. This regional sentiment was further reinforced by demographic data presented in the 1970 census, which reported that the Spanish origin populations of Illinois, Indiana, Michigan, and Ohio were approximately equal to those of Colorado, Arizona, and New Mexico.[54] The midwestern Mexican-American political leadership, now collectively armed with this broader geographical perspective and the new population statistics, swiftly expanded the scope of its political crusade. First, in order to take immediate advantage of these new numbers, the Mexican-American leadership cooperatively launched several ambitious voter registration efforts sponsored by such groups as the United Mexican-American Voters of Kansas, the Alianza Latina Political de Iowa, the Wisconsin Voter Education Project, and the Mexican-American Voters of Nebraska.[55]

Second, the 1970s saw the profusion of Mexican-American and Puerto Rican candidates seeking elected and appointed offices for all levels of government, including state legislatures.[56] The vigorous and effective legislative campaign of Paul Rojas reflected the uniform theme of many of these campaigns:

> The Paul Rojas campaign is more than an effort to elect a new councilman. It is a call for unity in the Mexican-American community. For too long, this area [West Kansas City] has been victimized by unconcerned bosses who are alien to the community and depend on the work of "vendidos" to do their bidding.[57]

Third, Mexican-Americans formed numerous "Viva" clubs on behalf of several liberal and moderate Anglo Democratic and Republican candidates seeking elected offices.[58] Some of these victorious candidates did respond positively after their campaigns by appointing Latino liaisons to their staffs and by hosting regular community meetings with the Latino leadership which provided Mexican-Americans modest access to elected officials for the first time.

Fourth, the Latino leadership was remarkably successful in convincing state legislatures to establish Mexican-American state commissions in each of the midwestern states. These unique commissions were initially designed to provide guidance to elected and appointed officials regarding favorable policies and legislation to help address the special problems faced by Mexican-Americans and Puerto Ricans.[59] The unprecedented establishment of these state agencies was a tremendous political breakthrough for the Latino leadership because these state-sponsored commissions formally recognized Latinos as a legitimate public constituency with specific issues and problems.[60] More importantly, these commissions have provided the Latino leadership with indispensable benefits, including a valuable outlet for disseminating information, direct entrance to the governor's office, official ties with the media, service as an intermediary in introducing and monitoring pending legislation, a way to secure closer networking among Latino groups, greater accessibility to state documents and files, and a valuable training ground for cultivating community leadership.

Last, the cumulative effect of all these political initiatives during the 1970s pushed both the reluctant Democratic and Republican parties into taking some remedial steps to incorporate a few Latino interests within both parties. These partial improvements included sending Mexican-American and Puerto Rican delegates to local, state, and national conventions, obtaining minority representation on steering committees, and integrating a number of Latino issues during campaigns.[61] These mild concessions, however, were clearly token in nature, and mainly a superficial attempt by both parties to diffuse the growing popularity of La Raza Unida and the Midwest Council of La Raza.

Many of the political strategies introduced in the 1970s have been carried over into the 1980s, and more significantly, are currently being largely supplemented as a result of the following new projects and information. First and uppermost in the 1980 U.S. census data report, which revealed a significant increase in the Latino midwestern population between 1970 and 1980, with several midwestern cities reporting considerable increases in the Latino populations, including Milwaukee, St. Paul, Kansas City, Detroit, Des Moines, and Chicago.[62] This census information also suggested that this midwestern Latino growth would continue uninterrupted beyond the year 2000.

The city of Chicago is a dramatic example of this demographic prosperity. Here it is estimated that Latinos will comprise 25 percent of the city's population in fifteen years.[63] These new midwestern figures are intensifying the political enthusiasm among Latino groups, which confidently view these growing numbers as a powerful voting bloc with the potential to extract greater concessions from the political system during the 1990s.

Second, the Midwest Voter Registration and Education Project (MVREP) was established in 1982 as a vehicle for converting these new numbers into eligible voters.[64] The MVREP, which is modeled after the Southwest Voter Registration and Education Project and reminiscent of the MWCLR, provides both technical and financial assistance to local Latino groups openly engaged in voter registration and political education. Furthermore, the MVREP routinely sponsors numerous state and regional conferences which provide vital information regarding the critical essentials for organizing successful campaign efforts.[65]

These MVREP seminars have significantly promoted the unusual success of several Latino candidates elected and appointed to offices in Hutchinson, Kansas; East Chicago, Indiana; Racine, Wisconsin; Cleveland and Youngstown, Ohio; Chicago, Illinois; and St. Paul, Minnesota. The affirmative impact of these local victories is, in turn, inspiring midwestern Latinos to actively seek state and congressional offices, with positive results already evident in Illinois, Minnesota, Kansas, and Indiana.[66]

Third, midwestern Latinos are challenging longtime voting rights abuses which have historically restrained Latinos from winning their fair share of elected positions. Latinos in the Midwest, like their southwestern counterparts, are victims of such adverse electoral mistreatment as racial gerrymandering, at-large district election systems, voting roll purges, denial of bilingual staff and campaign materials, physical intimidation, last-minute changes in polling places, and racially polarized voting.[67]

The midwestern offices of MALDEF, the Puerto Rican Legal Defense and Educational Fund, along with local Latino community groups, were in the forefront of the bitter redistricting battles during the early 1980s. These local and state reapportionment efforts took place in Detroit, Milwaukee, and Chicago.[68] The Latino communities were successful in convincing the judicial system that both the Milwaukee and Chicago reapportionment plans violated their civil rights by diluting their voting power. The courts, therefore, ordered both the redrawing of new district boundaries and special elections. The historical outcome in Chicago was the stunning election of two Latino candidates favored heavily by Mayor Harold Washington, a black, which literally broke the political stalemate between Mayor Washington and the former majority on the Chicago City Council.[69] Mayor Washington, clearly aware of the political importance of the Latino vote in his 1987 reelection bid, added several key Latino appointments to his administration.[70] More importantly, Chicago Latinos have, in pragmatic terms, demonstrated their sophistication in playing the much sought-after role of the "swing vote" in the largest city in the Midwest and the third largest city in the nation, and this is more so than the Latinos in Los Angeles, San Antonio, and New York City.

Fourth, the 1980s have witnessed the steady stream of new Latino midwestern professional associations in the fields of law, business, social services, education, public administration, the media, and women's issues.[71] These newly established middle-class organizations are providing the solid economic and political foundations in some midwestern cities necessary to advance the Latino political agenda at all levels of government.

The 1980s is also experiencing the first significant electoral involvement of Cuban-Americans in the Midwest. This second-generation offspring, unlike their elders who formed business associations for wielding political influence, are actively participating in voter registration programs, campaigns, and working inside both major parties.[72]

This new pragmatic approach among some midwestern Cuban-Americans also appears to be tied to liberal politics, influenced by several interrelated factors, including the middle- and working-class nature of the original midwestern Cuban exiles, geographical and political isolation from Florida, ethnic acculturation, growing discrimination against Cuban-Americans, and the political influence of both the Mexican-American and Puerto Rican Civil Rights Movements in the Midwest.[73]

Several Cuban-Americans, for example, worked hard along with Puerto Ricans and Mexican-Americans for the election of Mayor Washington in 1983, with a Cuban-American presently heading the Latino Affairs Office in Chicago. Moreover, these progressive Cuban-Americans are currently taking steps in Chicago to form a permanent political committee for future political campaigns. This political pattern among younger Cuban-Americans appears to be taking place also in Ohio, Missouri, and Indiana.[74]

Finally, the Midwest Latino leadership continues to exert heavy pressure on both major parties for increased appointments and financial support for Latino candidates. Both the Democrats and the Republicans are slowly opening their political doors wider in order to accommodate a number of Latino concerns.[75] Latinos are predicting that both political parties will gradually offer better proposals prior to the 1988 local, state, and national elections in the Midwest.[76]

Notes

1. This article is a summary of a chapter from a forthcoming book entitled *Latino Politics in the United States: A Comparative Study of Styles and Strategies*. I would like to thank Duane Matthew Dodson for his excellent editing and California State University at Pomona for its generous support of my research project. Also, my heartfelt appreciation to all the Latino men and women in the Midwest who have generously opened both their hearts and homes for this study.

2. Miguel David Tirado, "Mexican-American Community Political Organizations: The Key to Chicano Political Power," *Aztlan* 1 (Spring 1970); and Salva-

dor Alvarez, "Mexican-American Community Organizations," in *Voices: Readings from El Grito,* ed. Octavio Romano (Berkeley, Calif.: Quinto Sol, 1971).

    3. F. Chris Garcia, *La Causa Politica: A Chicano Politics Reader* (Notre Dame, Ind.: University of Notre Dame Press, 1974); F. Chris Garcia and Rodolpho de la Garza, *The Chicano Political Experience: Three Perspectives* (North Scituate, Mass.: Duxbury Press, 1977); Joan Moore and Harry Pachon, *Hispanics in the United States,* (Englewood Cliffs, N.J.: Prentice-Hall, Inc., 1985); and Chicano Studies Center, *Politics and the Chicano,* (Los Angeles: University of California at Los Angeles, 1974).

    4. Leobardo F. Estrada, "A Demographic Comparison of the Mexican Origin Population in the Midwest and Southwest," *Aztlan* 7, no. 2 (1974). These ten states are Kansas, Nebraska, Missouri, Iowa, Minnesota, Wisconsin, Illinois, Indiana, Michigan, and Ohio.

    5. Interview with Juan Andrade, Executive Director of the Midwest Voter Registration Education Project (MVREP), September 2, 1985, Toledo, Ohio. Also, *A Directory of Hispanic Elected and Appointed Officials in the Midwest,* MVREP (No date).

    6. Interview with Luis Gonzales, former field director for the MVREP, East Chicago, Indiana, August 2, 1986.

    7. Michael M. Smith, *The Mexican in Oklahoma* (Norman, Okla.: University of Oklahoma Press, 1980).

    8. John Francis Bannon, *The Spanish Borderlands 1513–1821* (New York: Holt, Rinehart, and Winston, 1974).

    9. Dennis Nodin Valdez, *El Pueblo Mexicano en Detroit y Michigan: A Social History* (Detroit: Wayne State University, 1982); Minnesota Historical Society, *Mexican-Americans in Minnesota* (St. Paul, Minn.: Minnesota Historical Society, 1977); John Caro Russell, Jr., and Walter D. Broadway, *Minorities in Kansas: A Quest for Equal Opportunity,* (Topeka, Kan.: Office of the Governor, 1968); Ralph F. Grajeda, "Chicanos: The Mestizo Heritage," *Broken Hoops and Plain People,* (Nebraska Curriculum Development Center, 1976); Gilbert Cardenas, "Los Desarraigados: Chicanos in the Midwestern Region of the United States," *Aztlan* 7, no. 2 (1974); also, Francisco A. Rosales, "Mexicans in Indiana Harbor During the 1920's: Prosperity and Depression," *Revista Chicano-Riquena* 4 (October 1970).

    10. Interview with Sebastian Alvarez, June 19, 1986, Fort Madison, Iowa. Mr. Alvarez and his brother, Manuel, worked forty and fifty years, respectively, with the railroads, beginning in the early 1920s.

    11. Interviews with Joe Romero, June 11, 1986, Scottsbluff, Nebraska; Benjamin Castinado, June 14, 1986, Scottsbluff, Nebraska; Miguel Teran, June 18, 1986, Des Moines, Iowa; and Gilbert Sierra, June 21, 1986, Davenport, Iowa.

    12. Interview with Ricardo Parra, August 12, 1986, South Bend, Indiana.

    13. Interviews with Peter Macias, June 24, 1986, Davenport, Iowa, and Rosendo M. Terronez, June 21, 1986, Silvis, Illinois. Both men are collecting historical documents and conducting interviews regarding the social experiences of Mexicans in the Quad Cities during the 1920s and 1930s.

    14. Ciro Sepulveda, "The Origins of the Urban Colonies in the Midwest— 1910–1930," *Revista Chicano-Riquena* 4 (October 1976): 99.

15. Interviews with Anthony and Rita Navarro, Davenport, Iowa, June 20, 1986.

16. Interviews with Sebastian Alvarez, June 19, 1986, Fort Madison, Iowa; Frederico Herrera, July 11, 1986, Milwaukee, Wisconsin; Ben Navarro, August 20, 1986, Racine, Wisconsin; and Jose Anquino, August 8, 1986, East Chicago, Indiana. All four men were very active with the Midwest mutual aid associations during the 1920s and 1930s.

17. Jose Amaro Hernandez, *Mutual Aid for Survival: The Case of the Mexican-American* (Florida: Krieger Publishing Company, 1983), p. 75; and Felix M. Padilla, *Latino Ethnic Consciousness: The Case of Mexican-Americans and Puerto Ricans in Chicago,* (Notre Dame, Ind.: University of Notre Dame Press, 1985).

18. Edward Adam S. Kendzel, *Detroit's Pioneer Mexicans* (Grand Rapids, Mich.: Littlefield Press, 1980); Susan M. Diebold, "The Mexicans," *They Chose Minnesota* (Minnesota Historical Society); Alicia Florez, Carmen Garcia and Eva Pierra, *Historia Mexicana: Topeka, Kansas* (Historia Mexicana, Inc., 1984); Chas. M. Meyers, "The Mexican Problem in Mason City," *The Iowa Journal of History and Politics* (Iowa City, Iowa: The State Historical Society of Iowa, April 1929); and Kathleen Eberdt, *Special People: Ethnic Contributions to the Bettendorf Community* (Iowa: Bettendorf Museum, 1983).

19. Interview with Abe Morales, June 21, 1986, Gary, Indiana.

20. Interview with Ray Romero, October 10, 1986, Chicago, Illinois.

21. Abraham Hoffman, *Unwanted Mexican-Americans in the Great Depression: Repatriation Pressures, 1929–1939* (Tucson, Ariz.: University of Arizona Press, 1974).

22. Interviews with Abe and Rita Morales, June 21, 1986, Gary, Indiana; Filiberto Murguia, June 10, 1986, Milwaukee, Wisconsin; and Jesse Villalpando, June 21, 1986, Griffith, Indiana. The Morales were eyewitnesses to these repatriation efforts in both Gary and East Chicago, Indiana in the early 1930s. Mr. Murguia returned to Mexico with his family, which had been deported in 1931, whereas Mr. Villalpando's family refused to leave because his mother continued to insist that her children were U.S. citizens and should remain in the country. Also see Neil Betten and Raymond A. Mohl, "From Discrimination to Repatriation: Mexican Life in Gary, Indiana, During the Great Depression" *Pacific Historical Review* 42 (August 1973).

23. Daniel T. Simon, "Mexican Repatriation in East Chicago, Indiana," *The Journal of Ethnic Studies* 2 (Summer 1974).

24. Interviews with I. C. Plaza, June 16, 1986, Omaha, Nebraska, and Lando Velandez, June 17, 1986, Des Moines, Iowa. Both men were very active in organizing Mexican-American veteran organizations after World War II. In addition, Mr. Velandez was awarded the Silver Star for his heroics against Nazi forces in Europe.

25. Raul Orin, *Among the Valiant: Mexican-Americans in World War II and Korea* (Alhambra, Calif.: Borden, 1966), p. 28.

26. Sgt. Veto R. Bertoledo, Decatur, Illinois (World War II); Private Manuel Perez, Chicago, Illinois (World War II); Private Edward Gomez, Omaha, Nebraska (Korea); Emilio de la Garza, East Chicago, Indiana (Vietnam); and Miguel Keith-Hernandez, Omaha, Nebraska (Vietnam).

27. Interviews with Joe Terronez, June 21, 1986, Silvis, Illinois; and Charles Sandoval, East Moline, Illinois, June 22, 1986. Mr. Terronez, a Silvis city councilman since 1962, was the driving force for establishing Hero Street Park. Mr. Sandoval, who served in World War II, lost two older brothers in action.

28. Carl Allsup, *The American G.I. Forum: Origins and Evolution* (Austin, Texas: The University of Texas Press, 1982).

29. Interviews with Abe Morales, July 21, 1986, Gary, Indiana; Ben Franco, August 18, 1985, Omaha, Nebraska; and Lupe Flores, September 2, 1985, Toledo, Ohio.

30. Interview with Anthony Navarro, June 20, 1986, Davenport, Iowa.

31. Interview with I. C. Plaza, June 16, 1986, Omaha, Nebraska.

32. Henry A. J. Ramos, *A People Forgotten, A Dream Pursued: The History of the G.I. Forum—1948-1972* (American G.I. Forum of the U.S., 1983).

33. Ibid.

34. Ricardo Parra, Victor Rios, and Armando Gutiérrez, "Chicano Organizations in the Midwest: Past, Present and Possibilities," *Aztlan* 7, no. 2 (1974).

35. Interview with Abe Morales, June 21, 1986, Gary, Indiana.

36. Joseph P. Fitzpatrick, *Puerto Rican Americans: The Meaning of Migration to the Mainland* (Englewood Cliffs, N.J.: Prentice-Hall, Inc., 1971).

37. Interview with Eugene Rivera, September 2, 1985, Lorain, Ohio. Mr. Rivera, who serves on the Lorain School Board, is currently writing a book on the Puerto Rican history in Lorain, Ohio. Also interviews with Mario Palacios and Louis Pena, August 8, 1986, East Chicago, Indiana.

38. Interviews with Tony Baez, July 11, 1986, Milwaukee, Wisconsin; Dagoberto Ibarra, July 11, 1986, Waukesha, Wisconsin; and Jose Álvarez, July 31, 1986, East Chicago, Indiana. These individuals are currently attempting to unify the Puerto Rican and Mexican-American leadership.

39. Interviews with Oscar Sanchez, August 5, 1986, East Chicago, Indiana; Ben Navarro, August 20, 1986, Racine, Wisconsin; Ricardo Parra, August 30, 1985, South Bend, Indiana; and Robert Ramirez, August 19, 1985, Des Moines, Iowa.

40. Interview with Richard Parra, August 12, 1986, South Bend, Indiana.

41. Author's personal files.

42. Joe Terronez, Silvis City Council (1962); Jesse Gomez, East Chicago City Council (1959); Jane Gonzales, Saginaw City Council (1962); and Evelio Rosario, Lorain City Council (1961).

43. Interviews with Joseph Ramirez, June 16, 1986, Omaha, Nebraska; Dante Navarro, August 27, 1986, Milwaukee, Wisconsin; and Jesse Villalpando, July 21, 1986, Griffith, Indiana. All three men were active in the 1960 "Viva Kennedy" campaign in the Midwest.

44. Interview with Dante Navarro, August 27, 1986, Milwaukee, Wisconsin.

45. Interview with Baldimar Velasquez, Executive Director of the Farm Labor Organizing Committee (FLOC), September 2, 1985, Toledo, Ohio.

46. Interviews with Perry Garcia, June 21, 1986, Davenport, Iowa; John "Buck" Serrano, June 23, 1986, Davenport, Iowa; and Eva Zavala, June 25, 1986, East Moline, Illinois.

47. Patrick Velasquez-McKee, June 16, 1986, Omaha, Nebraska. Mr. Velasquez has been active in Chicano activities for many years in the Midwest and presently serves as the executive director of the Chicano Resource Center in Omaha.

48. Ricardo Parra, Victor Rios and Armando Gutierrez, "Chicano Organizations in the Midwest: Past, Present and Possibilities," *Aztlan* 7, no. 2 (1974).

49. Ibid, p. 240. Also see the report entitled, *La Raza Unida,* University of Notre Dame Archives, MWCLR Collection. The study details the history of La Raza Unida in the Midwest.

50. Rafael J. Prohias and Lourdes Casal, *The Cuban Minority in the U.S.: Vol. I* (New York: Arno Press, New York Times Company, 1980), p. 20.

51. Interview with Maria Torres, October 10, 1986, Chicago, Illinois.

52. Interview with Ricardo Parra, August 30, 1985, South Bend, Indiana.

53. Parra et al., "Chicano Organizations," p. 242.

54. Estrada, "Demographic Comparison," p. 205.

55. Interviews with Rudy Perales, August 17, 1985, Lincoln, Nebraska; Miguel Teran, July 18, 1986, Des Moines, Iowa; and Robert A. Ruiz, August 14, 1985, Kansas City, Kansas.

56. A sample of candidates includes Demetrio Saerez (Council at Large, Lansing, Michigan); Martin Morales (Mayor, Grand Rapids, Michigan); Maria Elena Castellanos (Saginaw School Board); John "Al" Rodriguez (Kansas City Board of Education); Jesse Mora (Kansas State Representative); Ness Flores (Circuit Court Judge, Waukesha County, Wisconsin); Dante Navarro (Wisconsin State Representative); and Irene C. Hernandez (Cook County Board of Commissions, Chicago, Illinois). Not all of these candidates won their elections; however, these campaigns reflected the growing political participation of Latinos during this time period.

57. *Venceremos,* vol. I, no. 7, February 1971. *Venceremos* was a community newspaper published in Kansas City, Missouri during the early 1970s.

58. Interviews with Jose Juarez, August 13, 1986, South Bend, Indiana; Jesse Gomez, July 31, 1986, East Chicago, Indiana; Jose Arrendondo, August 6, 1986, East Chicago, Indiana; Albert Miera, July 3, 1986, St. Paul, Minnesota; Ricardo Diaz, July 10, 1986, Milwaukee, Wisconsin; and David Ramirez, August 22, 1985, Minneapolis, Minnesota.

59. Interviews with Leticia Patino, September 1, 1985, Columbus, Ohio; Jose Trejo, July 1, 1986, St. Paul, Minnesota; Francisco Rodriguez, July 7, 1986, Madison, Wisconsin; Miguel Teran, July 18, 1986, Des Moines, Iowa; and Rudy Perales, August 17, 1985, Lincoln, Nebraska. All five individuals are or were executive directors of these commissions in each of their respective states.

60. Ibid.

61. Interviews with Mary Campos, August 20, 1985, Des Moines, Iowa; Todd Lefko, August 21, 1985, St. Paul, Minnesota; Ignacio Salazar, September 5, 1985, Detroit, Michigan; David Vega, August 29, 1985, Chicago, Illinois; and Olga Villa-Parra, August 30, 1985, South Bend, Indiana.

62. Interview with Juan Andrade, September 2, 1985, Toledo, Ohio.

63. Jorge Casuso and Eduardo Camacho, "Hispanics in Chicago," *The Chicago Reporter* (series of articles published between 1984 and 1985).

64. Interview with Juan Andrade, September 2, 1985, Toledo, Ohio.

65. Interview with Luis Gonzales, former field director of the MVREP, August 2, 1986, East Chicago, Indiana.

66. Interviews with Jesse M. Villalpando, Indiana State Representative, July 21, 1986, Griffith, Indiana, and Conrad Vega, Minnesota State Representative, August 23, 1985, St. Paul, Minnesota.

67. Interviews with Joe Romero, June 11, 1986, Scottsbluff, Nebraska; Ray Romero, July 17, 1983, Chicago, Illinois; Jane Garcia, October 21, 1981, Detroit, Michigan; and Oscar Mireles, August 19, 1986, Milwaukee, Wisconsin.

68. Interviews with Laura Reyes Kopack, October 21, 1981, Detroit, Michigan; Juna Mireles, August 19, 1986, Milwaukee, Wisconsin; and Ricardo Tostado, August 27, 1985, Chicago, Illinois.

69. Interview with Luis Gonzales, August 2, 1986, East Chicago, Indiana.

70. Interview with Maria Torres, Chicago Director of the Latino Affairs Office, October 9, 1986, Chicago, Illinois.

71. Interview with Laura Reyes Kopack, Detroit, Michigan, March 16, 1983.

72. Interview wtih Enrique Serra, August 23, 1985, St. Paul, Minnesota. Also see Miren Ariarte-Gaston and Jorge Canas Martinez, *Cubans in the United States* (Boston: Center for the Study of the Cuban Community, Inc., 1984).

73. Interview with María Torres, October 10, 1986, Chicago, Illinois. Also see Rafael J. Prohias and Lourdes Casal, *The Cuban Minority in the U.S.*, 2 vols. (New York: Arno Press, 1980).

74. Interview with Miriam C. Delgado, October 11, 1986, Indianapolis, Indiana. Also see Maria de Los Angeles Torres, *From Exiles to Minorities: The Politics of the Cuban Community in the United States,* University of Michigan, Ph.D. dissertation, 1986.

75. Interviews with Roy de la Rosa, Hispanic liaison for the mayor of Milwaukee, August 26, 1985, Milwaukee, Wisconsin; Lupe Flores, delegate to 1984 state GOP convention, September 2, 1985, Toledo, Ohio; Teodosio Feliciano, September 3, 1985, Cleveland, Ohio; Elizabeth Balli Sandoval, 1984 Iowa State Latino Coordinator for Mondale, August 20, 1985, Des Moines, Iowa; Robert C. Hernández, Kansas City, Missouri councilman, September 3, 1986; Richard A. Ruiz, Kansas City, Kansas councilman, August 14, 1985; Simon Sierra, longtime Republican official, Silvis, Illinois; Enrique Serra, Vice-Chair of the Minnesota State Republican Party, August 23, 1985, St. Paul, Minnesota; Enrique Rodriquez, Assistant to Detroit Mayor Coleman Young, Detroit, Michigan, September 5, 1985; Raynae Lagunas, delegate to 1984 National Democratic Convention, August 19, 1985, Des Moines, Iowa; Gloria Rocha, Michigan State Chair of the Republican National Hispanic Assembly (RNHA), Detroit, Michigan, March 19, 1984; Frances García, Mayor, Hutchinson, Kansas, August 15, 1985.

76. Interviews with Jesse Villalpando, July 21, 1986, Griffith, Indiana, and Gregory J. Sanchez, June 28, 1986, East Chicago, Indiana. Villalpando has been active in Democratic politics nearly thirty years; Sanchez is involved with GOP politics.

PART II

Input to the Political
System: Participation

IN ORDER TO AFFECT THE political system, Latinos must have effective input to governmental decision makers. Latino interests and needs must somehow be aggregated and effectively communicated to governments. In the American political system, this is often done through many various kinds of actions and organizations. In the activist decade of the late 1960s and early 1970s, the most publicized means were those such as marches, boycotts, sit-ins, strikes, walkouts, demonstrations, and other unconventional tactics. More traditional means include electoral activities such as campaigns, elections, and other activities of political parties; interest group activities such as lobbying; and direct individual communication. These occur at all levels—local, state, and national—and involve all branches of government—legislative, executive-bureaucratic and judicial.

During the decade of the Hispanics in the 1980s, most Latino political energy and attention have been focused on electoral activities. This direction has emphasized the fact that a great deal remains unknown about the voting behavior and related political activities of Latinos. Over the past fifteen years there have been a few good studies of Hispanic electoral participation; however, these are still too few in number to support very many conclusive generalizations and hypotheses. However, some general patterns have emerged. For example, Latinos, with the exception of Cubans, generally are registered to vote in lower proportions than are majority culture citizens. There is some dispute about whether or not, once registered, Hispanics vote in the same proportions as do non-Hispanics.

There have been very few scientific surveys which focus on the political attitudes, values, and beliefs of Hispanic adults, and only one, comprehensive, in-depth survey of a large sample of Latinos to this point. The article by Garcia and Arce takes some political information contained in the 1979 National Chicano Survey and applies this to what we know about Hispanic activity in the electoral arena, including political organizations.

119

The authors first review the extant literature on the subject and then add the results of their own research. They find that one of the major reasons for the low rate of Hispanic voting is the significant proportion of Mexican-Americans who are not citizens, approximately one-third. About 40 percent of eligible Hispanics are in fact registered, and they generally are as likely to vote as are non-Hispanics. The voting preferences of this sample mirror those of Hispanics surveyed in less comprehensive studies in their basically Democratic partisan tendencies. The rate of Chicano electoral participation has increased substantially through the 1970s and the first half of the 1980s.

Organizational membership has been low among Chicanos, as it is for the general population. Activity in strictly political associations is minimal. Politically relevant attitudes among Chicanos in this survey were found to be supportive of electoral norms. However, demographic variables, such as comparatively lower education, lower occupational status, and lower age, combine to have a depressing effect on participation. Both positive civic attitudes and collective action orientations seem to exist in significant proportions among the Chicano respondents. Yet, these orientations do not seem to be directly translated into a very high level of actual political participation. Much more research is needed to elucidate the existence and distribution of particular political orientations in order to relate these more closely to the actual political behavior of Latino Americans.

The study by Portes and Mozo focusing on the political participation of Cuban-Americans finds that noncitizenship is not a major factor in political participation among that group since the Cubans are among those Latinos with the highest rate of naturalization. Cuban-Americans participate in the electoral process at a rate as high or higher than the Hispanic population nationwide and probably as high as any other ethnic group. In comparison to other Hispanic groups, Cubans tend to vote less for Democratic candidates and more for Republicans. The conservative candidate orientation of Cuban-Americans is in marked contrast to those of other Latinos. The history of the Cuban immigrant to the United States reflects a strong antipathy toward communism and socialism. Another factor contributing to this conservative position may be the higher socioeconomic status of the Cubans. A statistical test of the latter hypothesis in the Miami–Dade County area revealed that income did not significantly raise voter turnout but did have a significant effect on voting preferences, i.e., party and ideology. However, the effect of income was secondary to that of Cuban ethnicity.

There may be an increased possibility of Cubans' social and political participation becoming more like those of other Latinos as time and distance from the Castro takeover increases. Cubans in the United States are becoming less concerned with issues on the homeland and more concerned with domestic U.S. issues. Moreover, they are experiencing a heightened sensitivity to discrimination against them by the majority culture.

An examination of political participation, particularly in elections, by the third major Latino group, Puerto Ricans, is provided by Angelo Falcón. In his article, he addresses the similarities and differences in Latino and black politics in New York City and the possibility of coalition politics between these two ethnic groups. An analogy is drawn between the emerging "majority-minority" politics in New York City and that which is occurring or will occur in many of the major metropolitan areas in the United States and perhaps even nationally as distinctive, ethnic, colored minorities become an increasingly larger proportion of the population. The cultural, demographic, and socioeconomic features of each of the groups is examined as well as each group's political history. Issue differences between blacks and Latinos are surveyed, including the role of government in society, bilingual education, and immigration policy. Statistics are presented as to the comparative representation of each group in New York government as well as on electoral participation patterns and levels. Finally, the reasons for black and Latino differences are listed, and Falcón points out how these differences would have to be reconciled in order to have a political coalition.

The midwestern United States is an important and interesting area in which to examine Latino political electoral participation. Its Latino or "Spanish" population in the Chicago area, for example, is composed of Puerto Ricans, Mexican-Americans, Cubans, and other Spanish Americans. The Greater Chicago area has a significant number of Spanish Americans, perhaps as large as 30 percent. They are not concentrated in any one part of the city. There is also a substantial black population in the area. Another salient fact about the area was the existence of a long-known and well-established political machine, the Daley organization. The demographic situation in the midwestern U.S. is a microcosm of the nation in terms of the nationality groups' relationships to major parties and the consequent possibilities for coalitional and organizational activity.

In their article, Salces and Colby relate many of the obstacles which have worked against Spanish Americans in Chicago in their bid to gain political power proportionate to their numbers. The relatively low rate of political participation there is attributed to lack of education, geographic dispersion, nationality fragmentation, and a generally unresponsive local Democratic Party organization. Other factors militating against political participation are the relatively large number of noncitizens, particularly among the Mexican-Americans and Cubans as well as their relatively recent residency in that area. As the socioeconomic resources of Spanish

Americans increase, as the population grows, and as the party structure becomes more competitive and open, it is possible that political opportunities for Spanish Americans will increase.

Much more survey research is needed to elucidate the existence and distribution of particular Latino political orientations in order to understand the parameters of the Latino political community and to relate political attitudes to the actual political behavior of Latino Americans.

One example of such research at the municipal level is the article by McManus and Cassel. Based largely on a local opinion survey, the authors hypothesize that Spanish language usage is an obstacle to Hispanics' participation in local politics. They also found low involvement in organizations except for a strong relationship with the Democratic Party. The geographical dispersion of Hispanics in Houston also makes it difficult for Mexican-Americans to coalesce in an effective way. The possibilities of a liberal alliance with blacks and/or liberal whites are explored. An examination of public policy preference revealed distinct differences between the Mexican-American community and the rest of the community, as Mexican-Americans are considerably more interested in public education, immigration policies, and employment issues. Since local politics and local issues probably are at the forefront of Hispanic political efforts, these observations on policy preferences, the potential for local political alliances, rates of local participation and awareness, and the implications of geographical residential patterns for political districting involve some basic and enduring political considerations of the Mexican-American community.

Although the traditional affiliation of major Hispanic groups has been with the Democratic Party for the last half century, there was a period in the middle and later 1960s during which much Latino attention was focused on the activities of a "third," Latino party, *El Partido La Raza Unida*. The functions of American political parties are multiple, but some of their most important electoral functions are to aggregate effectively the interests of a large number of people and, while presenting these to the general public, to put together a coalition of voters and leaders which can promote that ideology. Above all, a party aims to put its supporters into office through successful campaigns which win elections.

In their article Muñoz and Barrera trace briefly the history of La Raza Unida Party and posit their ideas about the problems of ideology and strategies which led to the party's virtual demise. Students played major roles in the formation and activities of La Raza Unida. Students have major advantages as well as serious disadvantages in their positions within the party, and even these roles themselves are very ambiguous. The difficulties of a minor party, particularly one based on culture and national origin, are exemplified by the development and demise of La Raza Unida. Problems in overcoming the impetus of the major Democratic and Republican parties, overriding generations of partisan attachment, garnering the resources necessary to compete with the major parties, meeting state requirements for certification as a party—all of these were encountered as serious obstacles. In addition, in the case of La Raza Unida, there was the additional stigma of being a "radical" party as well as the existence of major ideological differences within the Chicano population concerning the strategies and objectives of the party. Major ideological thrusts that often were in conflict with one another were the Marxist philosophy and that of cultural nationalism. As the more militant and activist student-based Chicano movement declined in the mid-1970s, so did the fortunes of La Raza Unida. The successes and failures of the party have implications for subsequent Chicano politics, both in their impact on former members and as a broader lesson on political input strategies within the American political system.

In addition to viewing from another perspective one of the seminal chapters of La Raza Unida Party, that in Crystal City, Valdez also looks at two other political "input" organizations within the Chicano movement. Discussed in turn are an *ad hoc* pressure group, the East Los Angeles Educational Issues Coordinating Committee (EICC), and a midwestern cross-ethnic coalitional organization, the Latin American Union for Civil Rights (LAUCR). The latter was broad based in its objectives, seeking control of community social service agencies as well as advocating changes in local governmental institutions. Any organization will be affected by the negative perceptions of its members by the larger social community. Negative perceptions toward LRUP in Crystal City served as a cohesive force and a protective mechanism for the group. In the case of the EICC, it had a different impact, changing the ideological composition of the group to one which was more acceptable. The LAUCR was not perceived particularly negatively, and the rather neutral attitude was a factor in its demise. The author postulates that more important than the effect of the larger society's attitudes and actions upon the organization were the organizations' responses, the exclusiveness of the membership, and the incentives used to recruit members.

The primary value of this study for those wishing to understand the factors which lead to success or failure in Latino politics is that organizational characteristics are as important as ideology and cultural features. The focus of those interested in politics is not so much on the organization *qua* organization, but on organization as a means toward an end, the end being effective and successful political input.

Along with electoral activity, including voting and involvement with political parties, the involvement of interest groups as major agencies of political input is particularly important. Both *ad hoc* and coalitional interest groups were examined in the article by Valdez. Those interest groups were primarily concerned with affecting the decisions of legislators and executives, but interest group activity also is directed at judicial decision makers. In fact, interest group litigation has been one of the major tactics used with some success by such disadvantaged groups as ethnic minorities. The resources needed for successful action in the judicial arena are somewhat fewer and of a different nature than those needed in the larger legislative/bureaucratic political arena. O'Connor and Epstein hypothesize that three factors — the recruitment of expert counsel, the use of a test case strategy, and cooperation with other groups — maximize the chances for success of relatively powerless groups going before the bar. They apply these criteria to the activities of the Mexican-American Legal Defense and Education Fund (MALDEF), and they find that these are helpful in explaining MALDEF's successes, particularly since 1973 when the group's operations and objectives were somewhat modified. Successes in the area of educational benefits, and later in gerrymandering and districting cases, reaffirmed the advantages of this kind of strategy.

6. Political Orientations and Behaviors of Chicanos: Trying to Make Sense Out of Attitudes and Participation

John A. Garcia and Carlos H. Arce

INCREASED NATIONAL MEDIA COVERAGE and more aggressive leadership have given widespread credence to the belief that the 1980s is the decade of the Hispanics. As the largest and longest-established Hispanic group, Chicanos or Mexican-Americans provide an ideal case for examining the Hispanic political advance in the United States. Despite considerable population growth, modest economic and educational gains, and dramatic political successes in the early 1980s, the political activity by Chicanos on the American national scene is still in its developmental and adaptive phases. A rise in the political stock of Chicanos can be easily predictable with the growth and continual maturation of indigenous civil rights and advocacy organizations and the salience in the U.S. of Hispanic policy concerns (i.e., immigration reform, bilingual education, voting rights, U.S.–Mexico relations, Central America). These factors provide some excellent opportunities for observers trying to attain a clearer understanding of the participatory orientations and participation among Chicanos surveyed in the 1979 Chicano Survey.

More specifically, we will look at Chicanos' beliefs in active political participation and in getting involved politically on behalf of the Chicano community's interests. In terms of political participation, we examined voting and belonging to organizations. To assess electoral participation, we examined not only voting, but registration and naturalization of the sizeable foreign-born adult Chicano population. In addition to electoral participation, individuals also become involved in organizations, and this type of associational behavior provides valuable insights into the proclivity of Chicano individuals to exercise their rights and privileges of this society.

Before a fuller understanding of individual political participation is possible, one also needs to explore critical political orientations of Chicanos. We are particularly interested in identifying those political attitudes, values, and related opinions which are thought to impact on the likelihood of Chicanos being politically active. Since current Chicano political activity is on a dramatic rise, fueled by successes in large city mayoral elections and increases in congressional representation, we are particularly concerned with identifying those factors that specifically tap the Chicano political experience. Ethnicity and its various dimensions, along with relevant socioeconomic characteristics, should prove to be very important in explaining the extent of Chicano political participation. As a result, a central focus of this research includes those cultural and socioeconomic characteristics which are highly salient to Chicanos. Among these, we are particularly interested in nativity and generational distance from Mexico, language use, and educational attainment.

This article will then address the following questions: (1) Given specific participation modes and orientations, how are Chicanos distributed along these dimensions? (2) What are the relationships between socioeconomic characteristics and organizational membership? (3) What is the association of electoral participation with socioeconomic variables? (4) Are there positive linkages between political orientations and the two participation modes—voting and organizational membership?

Mexican-Americans and Political Activity

The Chicano presence in the southwestern United States predates the acquisition of the region by the United States after the War with Mexico in the 1840s. Since their incorporation into the United States, the Chicano political experience has undergone several notable stages (Alvarez 1973; Cuellar 1971). Characteristic of this experience is a wide variety of adaptive strategies which have been influenced by historical conditions, regional variations, structural arrangements (such as labor market and related economic patterns), increased immigration from Mexico, and concentration in urban areas. In reviewing the literature on Chicano political participation and civic orientations, it is important to recognize the impact of the aforementioned factors which can be determinants of individual patterns of participation in the political world. This literature review covers research on electoral participation, communal organizational activity, and political orientations.

Organizations and the Chicano Community

Much of the research on Chicano organizations has focused on historical documentation of the long-standing presence of organizations in the Chicano community and the development of taxonomies of Chicano organizations. In an important early effort, Tirado (1970) illustrated the variety of organizations that have addressed the Chicano community's needs (i.e., economic adjustment, social services, advocacy, cultural maintenance, etc.). Other researchers have examined the wide regional variations among Chicanos (Rosales 1979), community organizations (Acuña 1981; Briegal 1970), political organizations (Vigil 1974; Gutierrez and Hirsch 1973), and patterns and levels of associational membership (Grebler et al., 1970; Teske and Nelson 1976). Certainly the success of any organization depends on the types and amount of resources that are available. Members' economic well-being, educational levels, organizational size, geographic concentration, social cohesiveness, prestige, and effective leadership are significant resources. The relatively low availability of these resources has resulted in low levels of organizational membership in the Chicano population. That is, prior to the 1970s many Chicano organizations were local in scope, small scale in membership, and primarily servicing the internal needs of the community. Some exceptions to locally based organizations were groups like LULAC, American G.I. Forum, and Alianza Hispanamericana. The absence of a significant professional and middle-class segment within the Chicano community (Sheldon 1965; Garcia and de la Garza 1977) until the 1970s also limited the expertise pool from which to draw. More recently, Chicano organizations have been able to generate more economic and human resources for their national and local efforts, while the base of their effectiveness still remains a strong appeal to ethnic loyalty. This serves as a natural basis for organizations.

In the UCLA Mexican-American Study Project (Grebler et al. 1970), Chicanos in Los Angeles had relatively low levels of awareness of politically oriented organizations. For example, fewer than 10 percent of Los Angeles Chicanos were very familiar with organizations related to politics (i.e., MAPA, LULAC, Democratic party, etc.). Ranges of basic Chicano awareness (having heard of any of these organizations) were 4 to 42 percent. In a similar study conducted in Texas (Teske and Nelson 1973), the researchers found Chicano membership in organizations to range from 1 to 15 percent. Low levels of organizational membership are common patterns for most Americans, and it seems to be an even more pervasive phenomenon among Chicanos. About one-third (32 percent) of all citizens participate in organizational activities working with some local group on a community problem. A similar number have worked through formal organizations (Verba and Nie 1972).

Mexican-Americans' low levels of organizational awareness and membership have placed Chicanos some distance from the mainstream political system. On the one hand, the limited opportunity structure available to Chicanos plays a major role in their tendency not to join and maintain organizational membership at rates comparable to other groups. Time constraints, organizational skills, educational levels, and English language proficiency, all serve to influence levels of involvement. On the other hand, another series of explanations has been utilized to explain low levels of organizational membership among the Mexican origin population — their cultural background. Concepts like traditional culture, primary kinship systems, fatalism, religious traditionalism, and present-time orientations (Tirado 1970) have been proposed as factors which depress Chicano organizational involvement. One continuing debate among researchers is the differentiation between culture and class. Some of the previously identified items can be classified as cultural; while other researchers may argue that a culture of poverty has class ramification. Apart from issues of conceptual clarification, these issues also pose some measurement issues.

Finally, the political climate for organizational involvement (i.e., having models of successful and active organizations, lack of fear or repression) can create an atmosphere conducive to joining organizations, and when such factors are not available Chicanos' associational tendencies are predictably low.

Electoral Participation

As a result of research efforts on voting behavior of Chicanos, several patterns have been identified. The more consistent findings have been significantly lower rates of voter registration and turnout than Anglo and black voters (Levy and Kramer 1972), primarily Democratic party affiliation (J. Garcia 1979; de la Garza and Cottrell 1976), and moderately high patterns of bloc voting (Lovrich and Marenin 1976; J. Garcia 1979). It has also been noted that ecological factors, such as relative size and concentration of Chicano community, status, legal enforcement of voting requirements, and extent of societal tolerance for protecting and increasing minority electoral participation are significant influences on Chicano voting.

In recent years, major efforts by Chicano advocacy groups, including the Southwest Voter Registration Education Project (SVREP) and the Mexican-American Legal Defense and Educational Fund (MALDEF), and many local organizing activities have increased Chicano levels of electoral participation. Through vigorous voter registration campaigns (particularly in Texas) and litigation challenges of redistricting plans and at-large elections, SVREP and MALDEF have produced increases in registered voters, thus contributing to the victories of many recently elected Chicano public officials (J. Garcia 1986). For example, both MALDEF and SVREP were co-counsels in the 1980 State of Texas reapportionment case as well as lead counsels in the State of New Mexico reapportionment lawsuit. In addition, MALDEF engaged in class action suits in Texas, California, and other states with Hispanic concentrations that challenged at-large election systems. It was argued that this form of election system seriously diminished the chances of minority representation and accentuated racial/ethnic polarized voting (Garcia and de la Garza 1977). As far as voter registration efforts, SVREP alone has conducted 517 registration campaigns since 1975. Between 1976 and 1980, a 30 percent increase in Hispanic registered voters (SVREP 1983) was reported.

In spite of these recent improvements, the gap between Chicano and Anglo voter participation has only been slightly closed. For example, in the 1982 Texas general election, 38.3 percent of the Mexican-American registered voters turned out to vote for governor, compared to 49.7 percent of all voters (SVREP 1982). Yet Chicano voter participation was 80 percent greater than their previous level in the past gubernatorial election. Works by McClesky and Merrill (1973) and Levy and Kramer (1972) have illustrated this pattern for the early seventies. Research reports by the SVREP (1976, 1980, 1982) continue to show persistent gaps of 10 to 25 percentage points between Chicano registration and Anglo registration levels. Similar patterns exist for turnout levels of Chicanos. Consistently, Chicanos tend to vote 10–20 percent less than their Anglo counterparts. However, it should be noted that many important state and local variations do occur. For example, in areas of northern New Mexico, Southern Colorado, Southern Arizona, and parts of south Texas, Chicanos have levels of turnout similar to that of Anglos, and at times slightly higher. In these locations, situational factors such as local personalities and ethnically defined political races, local issues compelling to Chicanos, historical patterns, and sophisticated organizational activities increase awareness and participation.

Another long-standing characteristic of the Chicano electorate since the 1960s has been its predominant affiliation with the Democratic party (J. Garcia 1979; de la Garza 1974). In recent elections (1976, 1980, 1982), this pattern of over 70 percent Democratic affiliation and 70 percent plus vote for Democratic presidential candidates has been reinforced by strong organizational activity within the Chicano community (SVREP 1980, 1982). The range of Chicano support for Democratic presidential candidates from 1960 to 1980 was 70 to 90 percent. In fact President Carter received 70 percent compared to Ronald Reagan's 25 percent in 1980, while Carter had received 81 percent of the Chicano vote in 1976. The 1984 Presidential election featured a slight shift of Chicanos toward the Republican incumbent. President Reagan received approximately 30 percent of the Chicano votes, while support for Walter Mondale ranged from 50 to 80 percent among Mexican-American voters in southwestern states. Yet one dimension of party affiliation, strength of partisanship, has not been as pervasive. Habits, generational transmission of partisanship, and the Republican party's "benign neglect" may affect the continuance of affiliation, but not necessarily a vigorous attachment (Mindiola and Gutierrez 1983).

Another characteristic identified with Chicanos' electoral patterns is voter polarization. In many communities and regions, Chicano voters tend to support Chicano candidates, while non-Chicano voters vote for non-Chicano candidates (J. Garcia 1979; de la Garza 1974). This pattern resembles urban blacks' bloc voting (Lovrich and Marenin 1976; Antunes and Gaitz 1975); however, Chicano bloc voting is not as polarized as that of blacks.

INFLUENCES ON ELECTORAL PARTICIPATION

Explanations about the comparatively low levels of electoral participation have centered on cultural and sociodemographic factors and on structural conditions. Language (Arce 1982), cultural loyalty and knowledge, and nativity (J. Garcia 1981b and 1982) have been suggested as critical factors affecting electoral participation. Strong cultural attachments have been found to be associated with either political isolation and distance, or heightened ethnic group consciousness and politicalization (J. Garcia 1981b; Arce 1978). That is, a stronger cultural attachment to "things Mexican" can have the effect of placing one's reference point toward the mother country rather than the U.S. In this way, one takes less interest and involvement in the "host" political system. On the other hand, ethnic group consciousness can make one more critical of group treatment and stimulate one to get involved politically. The adaptations of Chicanos are varied. While these seemingly contradictory cultural influences have been identified, current research efforts are still sorting out their directional effects.

The principal explanatory model regarding participation has been the socioeconomic status model (Verba and Nie 1972). According to this model, individual participation is influenced largely by one's educational attainment, occupational status, and income level. These factors affect the motivation, skills, resources, and opportunities for participation. Individuals with higher socioeconomic status will demonstrate greater electoral participation, as exhibited through registration, voting, and involvement in campaigns. Additional demographic factors, particularly age and gender, have been added to the model, introducing a life cycle dimension and a concomitant structural/socialization influence for both males and females.

Other types of explanations concentrate on structural/legal conditions and psychological orientations. Structural/legal conditions such as literacy tests, poll taxes, annual registration systems (with purging), designated office locations for voter registration, gerrymandering, multi-member districts, and political intimidation have served to severely inhibit active electoral participation by Chicanos (Garcia and de la Garza 1977). Federal government policies, especially the Civil Rights Acts of 1964 and 1965, the Voting Rights Act of 1975, and numerous judicial decisions, have attenuated the negative structural factors.

On the other hand, the manner with which one develops political orientations (i.e., political trust, cynicism, efficacy, citizenship roles, etc.) is important in determining how an individual becomes attached to the political system and its components, as well as the type of evaluative feelings toward government the individual adopts (Fraser 1971; Carmines 1978; Clausen 1968). Studies of Chicano political socialization (F. C. Garcia 1973; Stevens 1977) suggest that Chicano children have inculcated the basic norms and values of the American ethos, yet display higher levels of political cynicism and lower efficacy than their non-minority counterparts. Research (Clarke 1972) has demonstrated that levels of efficacy and trust play an important role in defining participation roles. Finally, the concept of political consciousness (Gurin et al 1980; Verba and Nie 1972) has been introduced to the socioeconomic status model to explain higher-than-expected levels of political participation for minorities under particular conditions. For Chicanos, the presence of ethnic group consciousness (J. Garcia 1982) has been associated with a more critical view of the American political system and its effects on levels of political participation.

This brief discussion of Chicano electoral participation and its determinants indicates an improving level of activity, but significant gaps between Chicano voting and other groups persist. In addition, a variety of factors seem to influence individual electoral activities. The most utilized model has focused on socioeconomic status, with several refinements appropriate to Chicanos. In this preliminary research effort, we utilize both sociodemographic and cultural factors and we inquire further into the relationship of Chicano organizational affiliation and involvement to electoral activity.

ANALYTIC STRATEGY

Using responses from a personal interview survey of a sample of Mexican origin adults, we have selected a strategy that provides both a descriptive profile of Chicano political reality and an assessment of the factors and conditions which lead individuals to opt for different alternatives in becoming politically active actors in American society. More specifically, we have identified four dependent variables to be part of the political dimensions of Chicanos. They are: civic orientations (i.e., range of civic political activities); collectivist orientations (i.e., sense of group identity oriented toward political action); electoral participation; and organizational membership. The more detailed description of these variables and our sample's distribution on them will be presented later. In addition, we have incorporated six sociodemographic variables in order to exercise the extent of association between these factors and the dependent variables. For example, in the population at large, middle-aged and older persons are more likely to be members of organizations than young persons. Does this general pattern also apply to Chicanos? Finally, following our analysis of these associations, we will look at the extent of interrelationships between the political orientations of Chicanos with their political behavior.

The Data: Chicano Survey

The data for this analysis came from the 1979 Chicano Survey by the Survey Research Center of the University of Michigan. Interviews were conducted on a probability sample of Mexican-ancestry households in the southwestern United States (California, New Mexico, Arizona, Texas, and Colorado), and in the Chicago metropolitan area. Mexican-ancestry households were defined as those in which the primary provider and/or other adults living in the household were of at least half Mexican ancestry. If more than one adult in the household was eligible on the ethnic origin criterion, then the respondent was randomly chosen from those eligible. For example, in a married couple when both spouses were of Mexican ancestry, the respondent was randomly selected, but in an intermarried couple, only the Mexican origin spouse was eligible and that person was interviewed. Nearly 11,000 households were screened for ancestry, and, of these, 1,300 were of Mexican descent; 991 interviews were completed. In its final composition, the sample is statistically representative of between 88 and 90 percent of the total United States population of Mexican ancestry, as identified by the U.S. Bureau of Census. The interviews, which lasted an average of 3 hours and 20 minutes per respondent, were fully bilingual, and the Spanish and English versions of the questionnaire were printed in side-by-side format. The final distribution of language of interview was almost equal between English and Spanish respondents, with slightly more interviews having been conducted in Spanish than in English. The interview covered numerous topics, including language use, culture, social identity, political consciousness, mental health and personal well-being, work and labor force histories, and family life.

Compared to Bureau of Census estimates for the Mexican origin population (derived from the Current Population Survey [CPS] for March, 1979), Chicanos in our sampled households are very slightly younger (median age of 20 versus 21 years), and have less school completed (for 14-year-olds and older, 9.4 years versus 9.8 years). Households in this sample have an average of 4.4 persons compared to 4.1 in the CPS, and they are more likely to be husband-wife households (82 versus 80 percent). These differences, however, are for the most part negligible. Other sample characteristics relevant to the substance analysis reported here are: 38 percent of the respondents were born in Mexico; 59 percent are female; 83 percent of the males and 70 percent of the females are currently married.

PARTICIPATION AND ORIENTATIONS: A PROFILE

Our discussion of the literature on participation (electoral and organizational) rests on the key role of political orientations which individuals develop toward the political system. How one assesses the political system, the expectations of a person regarding responsiveness from the system, and the acceptability of various political activities should serve as major influences on the decision to vote and/or join organizations. It is anticipated that these political orientations define the political climate from which Chicanos draw the motivation to join organizations and participate in the electoral process. One can describe this as a multi-stage process. That is, external or structural factors, as well as individual socialization experiences, influence the kinds of political orientations one develops. These, in turn, serve as the motivation to become politically involved. If positive motivations are present, then we would expect the Chicano to engage in specific political activities (i.e., voting, joining organizations, etc.).

Participation Measures

Since we are primarily concerned with actual participation, we asked respondents to indicate whether they belonged to any organization(s) and what their voting record was in 1976 (i.e., registrant and voter). As has been the case with the limited studies of Chicano organizational membership, we found that only a small percentage (15.6 percent) belonged to *any* organization at all (see table 1). It should be noted that the item made no reference to any type of organization. When we restrict the type of organization to only civic and/or political groups, then the level of organizational involvement is significantly reduced (i.e., less than 5 percent overall).

Examining the electoral arena, two-fifths of the eligible respondents (citizens) were registered to vote in 1979. However, nearly one-third of the 991 Mexican-Americans interviewed were ineligible to register because of non-U.S. citizenship. This sizeable percentage represents a major attrition of potential voters for the Mexican-origin community. As noted elsewhere, low rates of naturalization (J. Garcia 1981a) persist for the Mexican-born population. Finally, slightly more than one-fourth of the total sample (26.7 percent) actually voted in the 1970 presidential election. This factor can be visualized as a prominent juncture along an electoral pipeline, from which the "leakage or loss" of potential voters is quite pronounced.

To illustrate this electoral pipeline, let us begin with the total sample (n = 991). A total of 309 persons were not eligible to vote because they were not citizens. This leaves 682 Chicanos who could vote if they were registered. Yet only slightly more than one half (58.5 percent) of this remaining group is actually registered to vote. Of the eligible voters, a total of 264 persons voted in the 1976 general election which represents two-thirds (i.e., 66.2 percent) of the registered Chicanos. The only comparable data is the SVREP report on the Latino vote in 1976. They reported a 68.9 percent voter turnout among registered voters.

In order to explore further, we created an electoral participation index, as well as differentiating members and non-members of organizations. The electoral participation index was constructed by differentiating the critical stages of electoral participation (see table 1). The first level includes the non-eligibles or non-citizens (32.2 percent). As noted previously, this constitutes a major component of our sample and of the Mexican-American adult population. The second group are those eligible to register or citizens that have not registered to vote (26.3 percent). These first two categories of non-voters represent almost three-fifths of the sample. The smallest group includes those Chicanos who are registered to vote, but did not

TABLE 1

*Political Participation Modes
for Chicano Survey Respondents*

POLITICAL PARTICIPATION MODES	% POSITIVE RESPONSES
Belong to an Organization	15.6
Registered to vote in 1979[a]	40.3
Voted in 1976 Presidential election	26.7
N = 991	

a. The item reflects the percentage of all respondents who were currently registered at the time of the interview. A total of 309 respondents (31.2%) were ineligible to register to vote since they were not citizens.

vote (7.3 percent). As suggested by the size of the last group, the voters (34.2 percent), once registered to vote, Chicanos do exercise their vote. Again, two critical junctures are evident in the Chicano electoral participation process. The first is attaining citizenship, and the second is activating eligible voters to register.

Certainly, distinctions between voting age population, eligible citizens, and registered voters are critical in determining the extent of electoral participation. Overcoming the impediments to registration would be a major factor positively affecting Chicanos to vote. This aspect will be elaborated more extensively in a subsequent section.

Our levels of organizational membership reflect similar findings in previous studies. Slightly less than one-sixth belong to any type of organizations (15.6 percent). The type of organizations most frequently mentioned were religious (Cursillos and Guadalupanos) or work-related groups (unions and professional organizations). Since organizational membership usually results in better political skills and opportunities for individuals and communities, Chicanos still demonstrate a real need to increase and expand their organizational experiences.

Political Orientations

Having identified the two participation variables (i.e., electoral and organizational), the next step is to construct indices of political orienta-

TABLE 2

Orientations toward Political Participation
Modes among Chicano Respondents

Orientations for Participation Modes (by rank order)	% Positive Responses
Express opinions by voting	94.5
Support bilingual education or pressure school officials to adopt it	92.7
Organize Mexican descent to bloc vote	87.8
Pressure employers to hire more persons of Mexican descent	79.8
Participate in a demonstration to change law or policy	77.6
Shop at stores owned by Mexicans	75.8
Boycott goods that Mexican-American organizations oppose	51.6
N* = 947	

*Represents mean average number of responses for the seven items. Responses were 935–952.

tions. Respondents were asked to express the extent of their approval or support of various political activities that are usually carried out by persons and groups in American politics. The items ranged from the value of voting to engaging in direct action such as demonstrations or economic boycotts (see table 3). For each type of activity, the respondent indicated whether she/he felt it was a good thing to do or not. Overwhelming support was given to the importance of voting as a means to express opinions (94.5 percent), utilizing bloc voting (87.8 percent), and supporting bilingual education (92.7 percent). A second cluster of support (75–80 percent) was found for collective activities specifically aimed to improve the Mexican origin community (i.e., pressuring employers, economic boycotts, and participation in demonstrations). We separate all of these responses as a two-tier distribution because less overwhelming consensus existed for the second set of activities. It seems quite evident that identifiable tendencies toward political action are pervasive among the Chicano respondents.

A factor analysis with all seven types of political activities (i.e. boycotting, demonstrating, voting, petitioning, etc.) produced two factors. We have designated these two clusters as "civic orientation" and "collectivist orientation" (see table 4). The civic orientation measure represents a cluster of three attitudes that focus on a number of political activities that an active member of the political system pursues. Such activities include: voting as an individual expression; getting people of Mexican descent to vote;

TABLE 3

*Political Orientation Measures — Civic and
Collectivists — among Chicano Respondents*

POLITICAL ORIENTATIONS	PERCENTAGE	NUMBER OF RESPONDENTS
Civic Orientation[a]		
Low	7.9	76
Medium	22.4	215
High	69.7	670
Collectivist Orientation[b]		
Low	12.8	123
Medium	23.2	223
High	64.0	615

a. The civic orientation represents a cluster of attitudes that focus on a number of political activities that many citizens pursue. The specific items were the following: getting people of Mexican descent to vote, voting as an individual expression, and supporting demonstrations to change unfair laws.

b. The collectivist orientation represents a sense of ethnic community in a policy setting. The specific items were: shop at Mexican-owned stores, support bilingual education, and pressure employers to hire persons of Mexican descent. A factor analysis with the seven items divided into those two factors.

and supporting demonstrations to change unfair laws. The collectivist orientation includes items which reflect a sense of ethnic group identification in a specific policy setting. In this case a sense of ethnic community exists across the areas of employment opportunities for Chicanos, bilingual education, and supporting ethnic businesses.

Examination of the distribution of respondents on the two political orientation scales indicates that most Chicanos are in the higher or more politicized levels. That is, over two-thirds (69.7 percent) of our sample scored at high levels of civic orientations, defined as support for at least two of the three political activities. Similarly, almost two-thirds (64.0 percent) fell into the high level of collectivist orientation, defined in a similar fashion. It would seem that Chicanos have developed strong predispositions to active political participation in a group manner. With this pattern of political orientations, one might expect active levels of political participation. As we noted before, participatory attitudes are conducive to actual political behavior. Yet as we evidenced in tables 1 and 2 the participation rates are rather low.

POLITICAL ORIENTATIONS, PARTICIPATION, AND SOCIODEMOGRAPHIC TRAITS

After describing the basic patterns of Chicano political orientations and participation modes, we will try to identify and assess some relevant demographic characteristics to serve as important explanatory factors as-

TABLE 4

Voting and Organizational Participation Modes Among Chicano Respondents

POLITICAL PARTICIPATION MODES	PERCENT	NUMBER
Electoral Participation Index[a]		
Non-eligibles	32.2	309
Low	26.3	252
Moderate	7.3	70
High	34.2	328
Organizational Membership		
Yes	15.6	151
No	84.4	821

a. The electoral participation index was constructed by differentiating stages of electoral activities. Therefore the four categories were: ineligible registrants (non-citizens); eligible registrants but not registered; eligible, registered voters, but non-voters; and registrants who voted.

sociated with these political orientations and participation modes. Based on the literature on political participation of Chicanos and of other groups, we have selected six sociodemographic variables to examine: age; gender; educational attainment; occupational status; nativity; and generational distance. These variables represent well-established demographic factors relevant to all populations, as well as a mother country linkage which is particularly important to understand Chicano political behavior.

First, we examine the extent of association of these sociodemographic variables with the two political orientation variables (see table 5). For civic orientation variables, nativity, education, occupational prestige, and generational distance prove to be statistically significant. For the Mexican-born, higher levels of civic orientations were evident than for native-born Chicanos. This could represent some degree of internalization of civic duty norms and an immigrant perspective. This pattern is reinforced when examining generational distance. That is, Mexican-born respondents with Mexican-born parents also have higher levels of civic orientations than respondents who are more generationally close to the U.S. The socioeconomic variables of education and occupational prestige produced some unanticipated results. Higher levels of civic orientations occur among respondents with lower occupational prestige as well as with lower educational attainment. Previous socialization literature (F. C. Garcia 1973) suggests that persons with lower income and education levels take on a subject citizenship role.

For the collectivist orientation, the same demographic variables proved to be statistically significant, with the addition of the age variable. That is, being older, Mexican-born, and closer generationally to Mexico are all associated with high levels of collectivist orientations (sense of ethnic community). Similarly, lower occupational prestige scores and educational attainment are associated with higher collectivist orientations. Clearly, a sense of ethnic community is more prevalent among the more "Mexican" and the working class (categories which are of course not mutually exclusive). Our findings produce results different from the other works on political participation. Usually, higher levels of socioeconomic status are associated with participatory orientations; yet that was not the case for these Chicanos. This finding is a significant one, warranting closer examination. One preliminary explanation could be the distinction between immigrant vs. minority group perspectives. That is, contrasts between the host and mother country suggest a figure of reference that may put the U.S. in a positive light. On the other hand, with more generations in the U.S., native Chicanos compare their status with other native groups and may be more cynical about participation. Overall, the participation orientations of Chicanos are very positive. With such predispositions to participation, we might expect high levels of political participation.

TABLE 5

*Political Orientation Measures
and Sociodemographic Traits
of Chicano Respondents*

| | POLITICAL ORIENTATIONS | | | | | |
| | Civic | | | Collectivists | | |
SOCIODEMOGRAPHIC TRAITS	Low	Med. %	High	Low	Med. %	High
Age						
17–30	8.6	21.4	70.1	11.8	26.9	61.3
31–50	7.8	23.6	68.6	15.1	24.3	60.5
51 and over	7.1	21.8	71.1	9.3	16.0	74.7
		(–)			(*)	
Nativity						
U.S. born	8.6	26.3	65.2	16.2	25.3	58.6
Mexican born	6.8	16.1	77.2	7.4	19.9	72.8
		(*)			(*)	
Gender						
Male	8.0	20.7	71.2	13.4	25.4	61.1
Female	7.8	23.5	68.7	12.3	21.7	65.9
		(–)			(–)	
Educational Attainment						
0–5 yrs.	4.8	15.9	79.4	3.9	13.4	52.7
6–11 yrs.	9.4	21.8	68.8	12.5	23.2	64.3
High school	9.2	29.6	61.2	19.2	30.5	50.3
Post-secondary	8.4	27.7	63.9	20.5	31.3	48.2
		(*)			(*)	
Occupational Prestige Score						
Low	6.7	20.3	73.0	8.2	19.9	71.9
Medium	10.6	22.7	66.7	18.9	24.0	57.1
High	10.5	29.5	60.0	20.6	31.2	48.1
		(*)			(*)	
Generational Distance						
Mexican born R and parent(s)	6.9	16.1	77.0	7.2	19.9	72.9
U.S. born R and Mexican born parents	8.0	24.0	68.1	13.9	23.3	62.8
U.S. born R and parents	9.0	28.2	62.8	18.3	26.9	54.8
		(*)			(*)	
			**N = 961			

(–)   Chi-square statistic not significant

(*)   Chi-square significant at ≤ .03 level

(**)   The total N's for each of the variables is 961, with the exception of educational attainment (n = 955)
and occupational prestige score (n = 883)

Our earlier examination of organizational membership revealed modest levels of participation by the Chicano respondents (see table 6). Since organizational membership can vary from religious groups to neighborhood associations to Chicano activist organizations, our respondents were asked which organizations were most important in their community. We divided the mentioned organizations into general organizations and those whose focus and membership were specifically Chicano-oriented (i.e., Brown Berets, LULAC, COPS). As noted in table 6, Chicanos who are members of any organization tend to be more aware of Chicano organizations and their activities. Certainly, more secondary associations enable an individual to have more information and awareness of other organized activities in the community. Ironically, being a member of a Chicano organization does not significantly increase one's levels of awareness of other Chicano organizations. It would seem that being a member of an organization is a rather mixed and limited experience in which participation is difficult to interpret.

Organizational Membership

As with the political orientation variables, we utilized the same sociodemographic items to assess the extent of association with organizational membership. As with the orientation variables, five of the sociodemographic variables were statistically significant (see table 7). U.S.-born respondents are more likely to join organizations than their Mexican-born counter-

TABLE 6

Organizational Membership Among Chicano
Respondents and Awareness of Chicano Organizations

| | AWARENESS OF CHICANO ORGANIZATIONS[a] (number of times mentioned) | | |
	None	One	Two or More
Organizational Membership*			
No	539(65.9)	230(28.1)	49(6.0)
Yes	71(47.3)	55(36.7)	24(16.0)
Type of Organization			
Chicano organization	12(50.0)	7(29.2)	5(20.8)
Non-Chicano organization	54(46.6)	45(38.8)	17(14.8)

*Significant Chi-square at the .01 level.
a. The respondents were asked to identify local groups or organizations of Mexican descent with influence, if any.

parts. This relationship is also supported by the generational distance variable. That is, individuals who were second or third generation Chicanos in the U.S. were more likely to belong to an organization. Middle-aged and older adults are more likely to join organizations; while no difference occurred between males and females. The two sociodemographic variables — occupation and education — are positively associated with organizational membership. This pattern is most noticeable as higher occupational prestige respondents (35.7 percent) belong to an organization.

The results of this examination confirm findings of previous research. That is, higher levels of socioeconomic status serve as a motivator to and provide a better opportunity structure for organizational involvement. Organizational membership appears to have a cumulative effect. Persons with

TABLE 7

*Organizational Membership and Sociodemographic
Traits of Chicano Respondents*

	ORGANIZATIONAL MEMBERSHIP	
SOCIODEMOGRAPHIC TRAITS	Yes	No
Nativity*		
U.S. born (n = 601)	18.3	81.7
Mexican born (n = 369)	10.8	89.2
Age*		
17–30 (n = 310)	9.8	90.2
31–50 (n = 438)	18.4	81.6
51–highest (n = 230)	17.6	82.4
Gender		
Male (n = 395)	16.4	83.6
Female (596)	14.8	85.2
Educational Attainment* (n = 964)		
0–5 years (n = 259)	11.2	88.8
6–11 years (386)	10.6	89.4
High school graduate (152)	17.8	82.2
Post-secondary (169)	30.5	69.5
Generational Distance*		
R and parents born in Mexico (n = 363)	10.7	89.3
R born in U.S., parents in Mexico (292)	16.8	83.2
Both R and parents born in U.S. (315)	19.7	80.3
Occupational Prestige Score*		
Low (n = 482)	11.0	89.0
Medium (n = 219)	16.9	83.1
High (n = 190)	35.7	64.3

*Indicates Chi-square was significant at ≤ .05 level.

a higher socioeconomic status have greater chances to become involved in organizations and the skills important to participate in them. Also, those who belong to an organization show more political competence than those who do not belong to any organization (Almond and Verba 1963). The cumulative feature is amplified even more among persons who are members of more than one organization than among single member persons. On the other hand, a longer exposure to U.S. society serves to facilitate higher levels of organizational membership. This raises some questions which we will address below about the degree of political integration of Mexican-born and first-generation Mexican-origin persons within the U.S. political system.

Voting Behavior

The second behavioral variable was voting. Since the data were collected in 1979, respondents were asked about their participation in the 1976 Presidential elections. The results in table 8 indicated the variety of reasons why Chicano non-voters did not exercise their vote. It should be noted that the respondent was asked to give the primary reason she/he did not vote. Therefore, it becomes possible for a non-registered Chicano to cite a lack of interest in voting as his/her primary reason. Not surprisingly, the most prevalent reason for not voting was non-citizenship (50.6 per-

TABLE 8

Reasons for Not Voting in 1976
Presidential Election Among Chicanos

Major Reasons	N(%)	N/R*
Not a U.S. citizen	309(50.6)	—
No interest in voting	66(10.8)	21.9%
Not registered to vote	46(7.5)	15.3
Dislike politics in general	40(6.5)	13.3
Did not like any of the candidates	30(4.9)	10.0
Physical limitations to get to polls	22(3.6)	7.3
Unable to take time off from work	16(2.6)	5.3
Voting does not matter	16(2.6)	5.0
Politics too complicated	15(2.5)	5.0
Too young to vote in 1976	14(2.3)	4.7
Unaware of elections	8(1.3)	2.7
Other reasons	28(4.6)	9.3
	N = 610	

*N/R represents percentages for those respondents who were eligible to vote as citizens for each of the stated reasons.

cent). The results are presented in two different ways in table 8. The first column reflects the percentages based on the total number of non-voters, the second column removes the non-citizens from the totals. For citizens, the most common reasons for not voting were lack of interest in voting and non-registered status. It would seem that the former attitude might affect the latter condition (not registered to vote).

Two other frequently cited reasons for not voting were a dislike for politics in general and dissatisfaction with the candidates. These reasons strongly suggest a distance between the Chicano potential electorate and elections. They help explain why, despite there being a strong political orientation to support the value of voting, there is a major drop-off in the actual exercise of the vote.

When asked about their presidential preference and partisan affiliation, those Chicano registered voters showed overwhelming support for Jimmy Carter and the Democratic party (see table 9). Over four-fifths of the voters cast their ballots for Jimmy Carter (83.1 percent), while incumbent President Gerald Ford received 15.4 percent. Our sample results compare favorably with the electoral analysis of SVREP's study of the Latino vote in 1976. Their study indicates that Latinos cast 81 percent of their votes for Jimmy Carter. The traditional pattern of Chicano support of the Democrats remained in force in 1976 (75.6 percent). The number of Chicanos who express no party preference or are independents exceeds the number who support the Republican party (15.1 vs. 8.8 percent). Obviously, the base of Democratic affiliation remains strong, but potential for change is definitely evident, as the percentage of Latino votes for Ronald

TABLE 9

Presidential Choice and Partisan Preference
Among Chicano Respondents

	N	%
1976 Presidential Choice[a]		
Jimmy Carter	281	83.1
Gerald Ford	52	15.4
Others	4	1.2
Which Party do you support?		
No party preference	76	11.9
Democrats	475	75.6
Republicans	55	8.8
Independent	20	3.2
Other	3	.5

a. Only those individuals who were registered to vote and voted in the 1976 Presidential election were asked this question.

Reagan in 1980 was 25 percent (SVREP 1980). Republican party support depends more on the party's efforts, particularly its national leadership, to penetrate the Chicano community rather than on any inherent conservative ideology among Chicano voters.

As with the other participation variables, our electoral participation index was examined with the six sociodemographic variables. It should be noted that only those who are citizens were included in this analysis (see table 10). Four of the six variables were statistically significant. For naturalized Mexican-origin respondents, higher levels of electoral participation were evident than for native-born Chicanos. It would seem that the act of naturalizing serves as a conversion experience in which one is more

TABLE 10

Electoral Participation Index and Sociodemographic Traits
of Mexican-Origin U.S. Citizens[a]

	ELECTORAL PARTICIPATION INDEX		
SOCIODEMOGRAPHIC TRAITS	Low	Medium	High
Nativity**			
U.S. born	39.6	10.7	49.7
Mexican born	29.6	11.1	59.3
Age*			
17–30	55.2	14.2	30.6
31–50	34.1	8.7	57.1
51–93	27.3	10.9	61.8
Gender			
Male	34.2	10.3	55.6
Female	41.3	11.1	47.6
Generational Distance			
R & parents born in Mexico	30.6	10.2	59.2
R born in U.S., and parents born in Mexico	35.9	11.5	52.6
R & parents born in U.S.	42.7	10.2	47.1
Educational attainment*			
0–5 yrs.	39.3	12.1	47.7
6–11 yrs.	46.0	10.3	43.7
High school graduate	42.8	8.0	49.3
Post-secondary	27.7	12.7	64.7
Occupational Prestige Index*			
Low	47.8	12.3	39.9
Medium	35.5	8.4	56.0
High	26.5	9.9	63.6
N = 650			

a. The respondents in this analysis represent only those who are citizens and therefore eligible to vote.
*Significant Chi-square at ≤ .01
**Significant Chi-square at ≤ .03

mindful of citizenship obligations (i.e., voting). Not surprisingly, older individuals are more likely to vote. This is consistent with most voting studies that older persons develop more "stakes" in the system and voting becomes a way in which to express their opinions. Clearly, higher socioeconomic status—education and occupational prestige—are also positively associated with voting. This is also consistent with patterns reported in other studies. Since we excluded non-citizens from this analysis, the generational distance variable does not prove to be a significant factor. In all of our analyses, gender does not prove to be statistically significant. Although there are modest differences in extent of organizational membership, voting, and even in participatory orientations, these differences do not seem to require that we distinguish the Chicano community by gender in terms of voting behavior. However, this does not preclude the possibility that on particular issues or for subgroups of Chicanas (e.g., marital status groupings), gender may be an important variable. We have not explored the gamut of political issues that could separate our sample based on gender. For example, positions on abortion, ERA, military conscription, etc., could produce differences by gender.

Political Orientations and Participation

To the point that our analysis has focused on two participation modes and also on participatory orientations, it was anticipated that these would be highly associated. That is, if an individual displayed positive or high levels of participatory orientations, this should be associated positively with voting and belonging to organizations. A further analysis of the relationship between actual participation modes and participatory orientations is shown in table 11. These results are both interesting and puzzling. For electoral participation, both civic and collectivist orientations are statistically significant. Yet the pattern is such that higher levels of civic orientations (agreement with the importance of voting and expressing policy views) are more prevalent among Chicanos at the lower end of the electoral participation index. Similarly, those individuals with a sense of ethnic community (collectivist orientation) are also less likely to participate in the electoral process. For those Chicanos with collectivist orientations, the electoral arena may not be viewed as an effective mechanism for change.

For organizational membership, the pattern is in a similar direction, but not statistically significant. Non-members have stronger dispositions for civic and collectivist orientations than members of organizations. Certainly one dimension of the political experience of the Chicano is the loss of impetus from the participatory orientations to specific participation activities.

It may well be that other predispositions and/or experiences mediate

TABLE 11

Associations between Political Orientations
and Participations Modes Among
Chicano Respondents

| | POLITICAL ORIENTATIONS | | | | | |
| | Civic | | | Collectivists | | |
PARTICIPATION MODES	Low	Medium	High	Low	Medium	High
Electoral Participation						
Low	7.7	23.9	68.4	14.2	25.1	60.7
Medium	7.1	22.9	70.0	12.9	31.4	55.7
High	9.2	28.5	62.3	16.9	25.2	57.8
		(*)			(*)	
Membership in Organization						
No	8.0	21.7	70.2	12.3	22.2	65.4
Yes	7.4	26.2	66.4	15.4	28.2	56.4
			N = 970			

*Statistically significant at ≤ .05

what should logically be positive cues to participate. For example, it is possible that patterns of political cynicism or alienation, as well as negative experiences with governmental actors and institutions, separate the general societal ethos of participation from the actual limitations of participation. For example, Buzan's study (1980) of political cynicism and its relationship with local control by Chicanos or bicoalitional groups suggests that negative experiences with regime institutions, norms, and non-Chicano political actors increase levels of political cynicism and conflict. Therefore, how agents of the dominant political system react and relate to Mexican-origin residents may color their assessment of the societal norms for "democratic" participation and how they may carry out those participatory expectations. It could be that Chicanos have internalized these values, but do not practice them due to inconsistencies as to how the system works. The linkage between political attitudes and orientations with political behavior still remains a complex process in which the conversion of attitudes to predicted behavior is not very easily understood.

THE POLITICAL ORIENTATIONS AND BEHAVIOR OF CHICANOS:
SOME CONCLUSIONS

This article has dealt only partially with aspects of the political attitudes and behavior of Chicanos. Specifically, the analysis has focused on two dimensions of political participation—electoral activity and associational behavior—and on two political orientations which tap beliefs and attitudes related to actual political behavior. Several general observations can be made from the findings reported here. First, although the gap between Chicano and non-Chicano voting rates persists, the level of electoral participation is somewhat higher than what had been reported in the early 1970s. This increase over the past decade is supported by other recent data. For example, results of the 1980 presidential election (SVREP, 1983) indicated that 63.4 percent of Hispanics in the nine states with greatest Hispanic concentration voted compared to 67 percent for the general electorate. Regionally, Chicano voter turnout levels were highest in Illinois and Colorado and lowest in Texas in the 1980 Presidential election. Such regional variations further reflect the structural and historical differences from state to state.

Second, Chicanos once registered are very likely to vote and, in this respect are similar to other population groups. Third, the potential Chicano electorate tends to be significantly diminished by the extremely high proportion of non-naturalized Mexican-born persons. This sizeable segment (approximately one-third) of the voting age population reflects one critical feature of the potential growth of the Chicano electorate. Naturalization of Mexican-born residents will warrant more attention, especially in regard to the contributing factors and the role civic organizations may play. It should be noted that ineligibility from voting does not totally remove the Mexican-born from the electoral process. They can, and may undoubtedly do, participate in campaigns, voice political opinions with family and friends, and contribute to campaigns. However, the nature and extent of their involvement with the electoral process is relatively unexplored.

In addition, another critical area for Chicano electoral participation is activating the non-registered citizen, native-born or naturalized, to register. Organizations like SVREP have conducted numerous campaigns throughout Chicano communities with success. It would seem that increasing Chicano registration would virtually assure many more Chicanos voting. Continuing that effort seems critical if Chicanos are to vote in proportion to their population.

Our inquiry of organizational membership produced less clear results. Organizational affiliation is still relatively low among Chicanos. Involvement in organizations tends to be related principally to religious or work-related groups. The lack of civic organizational membership, or involvement in distinctly politically oriented activities, may be an important missing ingredient for Chicanos. One clear factor affecting organizational involvement is an obvious socioeconomic bias. Higher socioeconomic status and longer exposure to U.S. society significantly differentiates joiners from non-joiners. This parallels the pattern of socioeconomic influences on electoral participation. The opportunity structure and social skills may be greater for the higher status group, allowing them to engage to a greater extent in such participatory behaviors than less educated and working-class Chicanos.

In addition to the two participation modes, political orientations or predispositions were also examined. Individuals develop attitudes and expectations about the political system, its actors, and its processes. In this analysis, positive civic and collectivist orientations were found to be prevalent among the Chicano respondents. They believe in the value of "active citizenship" in terms of voting and making their opinions known. They also exhibited a sense of ethnic community in defining relevant issues and demands on the political system. These predispositions seem to be more evident among the lower socioeconomic component of the community, as well as among the Mexican-born.

Yet despite these strong orientations toward active participation, a major drop-off occurs when examining political participation. Somehow these orientations do not translate into higher rates of participation. For voting and registering, this attrition is largely accounted for by the high rates of non-naturalization. The incentives to pursue citizenship may not be viewed as sufficient to motivate persons to undertake this civic act. Alternatively, or in addition, it is possible that institutional and experiential factors (i.e., intergroup hostility, political exclusion) mitigate these positive orientations. Certainly, the linkage between political attitudes and behavior for Chicanos is a complex process in which our research effort only scratches the surface. It also points out that the political integration process among the Chicano community is both an uneven and diverse one. That is, by political integration we are referring to the cohesiveness of the members in the U.S. political community. For Chicanos, this can entail positive identification with the political system, internalizing prevailing norms, and involving oneself with the major organs of political participation.

A study of Chicano leaders (de la Garza 1984), indicated a belief that we are now in the decade of the Hispanic, and their political world is still undergoing continuous political development and growth. The past decade provided many opportunities for developing greater political sophistication and skills. In many respects, Chicano politics can be portrayed as playing "catch-up" politics. Gains in organizational development, political representation, and policy advocacy have occurred. Yet the Chicano community is one that still needs to expand the political relevance of participation to broader segments and to directly link participatory orientations with political behavior.

Research support for this project was made available by NIMH (NIMH-3024491) and the National Chicano Research Network.

REFERENCES

Acuña, Rodolfo, 1981. *Occupied America: A History of Chicanos* (Second edition). New York: Harper and Row.

Alvarez, Rodolfo, 1973. "The Psycho-Historical and Socioeconomic Development of the Chicano Community in the United States," *Social Science Quarterly* 53(4): 920–942.

Almond, Gabriel, and S. Verba, 1963. *Civic Culture*. Princeton: Princeton University Press.

Antunes, G. and C. M. Gaitz, 1975. "Ethnicity and Participation: A Study of Mexican Americans, Blacks, and Whites," *American Journal of Sociology* 80: 1192–1211.

Arce, Carlos H., 1978. *National Study of Chicano Identity and Mental Health: A Proposal for Research.* Ann Arbor, Michigan: Survey Research Center.

———— 1982. "Language Proficiency and Other Correlates of Voting by Mexican Origin Citizens," unpublished manuscript, Institute for Social Research, Ann Arbor, Michigan.

Briegal, Kaye, 1970. "The Development of Mexican-American Organizations," in Manuel Servin, ed., *Mexican Americans: An Awakening Minority.* Beverly Hills: Sage Publications.

Buzan, Bert, 1980. "Chicano Community Control, Political Cynicism and Validity of Political Trust Measures," *Western Political Quarterly* 32 (March, No. 1): 108–120.

Carmines, Edward, 1978. "Psychological Origins of Adolescent Political Attitudes," *American Politics Quarterly* 6(2): 167–186.

Clarke, J. W., 1972. "Race and Political Behavior," in K. S. Miller and R. M. Dreger, eds., *Comparative Studies of Blacks and Whites in the United States.* New York: Academic Press.

Clausen, John A., ed. 1968. *Socialization and Society.* Boston: Little, Brown and Company.

Cuellar, Alfredo, 1971. "Perspective in Politics," in Joan Moore, ed., *Mexican Americans.* Englewood Cliffs, N.J.: Prentice-Hall.

de la Garza, Rodolfo, 1974. "Voting Patterns in Bicultural El Paso: A Contextual Analysis of Mexican-American Voting Behavior," *Aztlan* 5 (Spring/Fall, Nos. 1 and 2): 235–260.

———— 1984. "And Then There Were Some: The Role of Chicanos as National Political Actors, 1967–1980," *Aztlan* 15 (Spring, No. 1): 1–24.

de la Garza, Rodolfo, and C. Cottrell, 1976. "Chicanos and Internal Colonialism: A Reconceptualization," paper presented at the International Studies Association Annual Meeting, Toronto, Canada.

Fraser, J., 1971. "Personal and Political Meaning Correlates of Political Cynicism," *Midwest Journal of Political Science* 15:347–364.

Garcia, F. Chris, 1973. *The Political Socialization of Chicano Children.* New York: Praeger.

Garcia, F. Chris, and R. de la Garza, 1977. *The Chicano Political Experience.* N. Scituate, Mass.: Duxbury Press.

Garcia, John A., 1979. "Analysis of Chicano and Anglo Voting Patterns in School Board Elections," *Ethnicity* (June): 168–183.

——— 1981a. "Political Integration of Mexican Immigrants: Explorations into the Naturalization Process," *International Migration Review* 17 (Winter): 1–24.

——— 1986. "The VRA and Hispanic Political Representation," *Publius* 16 (Fall): 49–66.

——— 1981b. "Ethnic Identification and Political Consciousness: Unraveling the Effects among Chicanos," paper presented at Western Political Science Association (Denver, Colorado).

——— 1982. "Ethnicity and Chicanos: Explorations into the Measurement of Ethnic Identification, Identity, and Consciousness," *Hispanic Journal of Behavioral Sciences* 4(3): 295–314.

Grebler, Leo, J. Moore, and R. Guzman, 1970. *The Mexican-American People.* New York: The Free Press.

Gurin, Pat, A. Miller, and G. Gurin, 1980. "Stratum Identification and Consciousness," *Journal of Social Psychology,* 40:30–47.

Gutierrez, Armando and H. Hirsch, 1973. "The Militant Challenge to the American Ethos: 'Chicanos' and 'Mexican Americans'," *Social Science Quarterly* 53 (March, No. 4): 830–845.

Levy, Mark, and M. Kramer, 1972. *The Ethnic Factor: How Minorities Decide Elections.* New York: Simon and Schuster.

Lovrich, N. P., and O. Marenin, 1976. "A Comparison of Black and Mexican-American Voters in Denver: Assertive Versus Acquiescent Political Orientations and Voting Behavior in an Urban Electorate," *Western Political Quarterly* 29(2): 284–294.

McClesky, Clifton and B. Merrill, 1973. "Mexican-American Political Behavior in Texas," *Social Science Quarterly* 53(4): 785–798.

Mindiola, T., and A. Gutierrez, 1983. "Voters and Non-Voters: A Case Study of Mexican-American Voters in Houston" (Preliminary Report). Houston, Texas: Mexican-American Studies Program and Research Institute for Mexican-American Studies.

Rosales, Francesco Arturo, 1979. "Mexicans in Indiana Harbor during the 1920s: Prosperity and Depression," *Revista Chicana—Riqueña* (Año cuatro, 4) Otoño, 88–100.

Sheldon, Paul M., 1966. "Community Participation and the Emerging Middle Class," in Julian Samora, ed., *La Raza: Forgotten Americans.* Notre Dame, Ind.: University of Notre Dame Press.

Southwest Voter Registration and Education Project, 1976. *The Latino Vote in the 1976 Presidential Election.* San Antonio, Texas: SVREP.

———— 1980. *The Latino Vote in the 1980 Presidential Election.* San Antonio, Texas: SVREP.

———— 1982. *The Latino Vote in the 1982 Presidential Election.* San Antonio, Texas: SVREP.

———— 1983. *National Hispanic Voter Registration Campaign.* San Antonio, Texas: SVREP.

Stevens, A. Jay, 1975. "The Acquisition of Participatory Norms: The Case of Japanese and Mexican-American Children," *Western Political Quarterly* 28 (June): 281–295.

Teske, R., and B. H. Nelson, 1973. "Two Sides for the Measurement of Mexican-American Identity," *International Review of Modern Sociology* (3): 192–203.

———— 1976. "An Analysis of Differential Assimilation Rates among Middle-Class Mexican Americans," *Sociological Quarterly* 17(2): 218–235.

Tirado, Miguel David, 1970. "Mexican-American Community Political Organizations: The Key to Chicano Political Power," *Aztlan* (Spring): 53–78.

Verba, S., and N. Nie, 1972. *Participation in America.* New York: Harper and Row.

Vigil, Maurilio, 1974. "Ethnic Organizations Among Mexican Americans of New Mexico: A Political Perspective," unpublished Ph.D. dissertation, University of New Mexico.

7. The Political Adaptation Process of Cubans and Other Ethnic Minorities in the United States: A Preliminary Analysis[1]

Alejandro Portes and Rafael Mozo

SINCE THE ARRIVAL OF FIDEL CASTRO to power in January 1959, close to 800,000 Cubans have left their country for the United States. The latest wave, the Mariel Boatlift brought 125,000 new refugees between April and October of 1980 (Diaz-Briquets and Perez 1981). As a result, the Cuban population in the United States, a relatively insignificant group in pre-Castro days, has grown to become the second largest foreign-born minority in the country and the third-largest Hispanic group. Between 1970 and 1979, approximately 280,000 Cubans were admitted to legal permanent residence in the United States; this figure represented 6.4 percent of legal immigration during the decade and ranked Cuba as the third-largest source of immigration, behind Mexico and the Philippines. By 1980, the Cuban-origin population had reached 803,000 or 5.5 percent of the total Hispanic population (U.S. Bureau of the Census 1982).

Although Cubans represent only one-tenth of the Mexican-origin population—the largest Hispanic minority in the country—they have had a significant local impact due to their high level of concentration in a few geographic areas. Approximately one-fifth of the Cuban population lives in the New York Metropolitan Area and its environs, and half is concentrated in the Miami Metropolitan Area.

NATURALIZATION PATTERNS

The rate at which an immigrant group acquires citizenship is important, first, as an indicator of its collective desire to become integrated in

From *International Migration Review* 19 (March 1985): 35–63. Reprinted with permission of the authors and *International Migration Review,* 209 Flagg Place, Staten Island, N.Y. 10304-1148.

the host society and, second, as a measure of its potential political power through electoral participation. As political refugees, many Cubans appear to have resisted initially the idea of surrendering their citizenship. There is a popular and journalistic lore about the fierce patriotism of the earlier exile waves and their commitment to overthrow the Castro regime and return to Cuba (Thomas and Huyck 1967; *Time* 1978). Whatever the factual accuracy of these statements, the trend in recent years has been toward a rapid rate of naturalization, exceeding that of other immigrant groups and contributing significantly to the increasing political influence of this group in South Florida.

Data show that more than 178,000 Cubans acquired U.S. citizenship during the seventies. This figure represents 12 percent of all naturalizations during the decade. By comparison, Mexican naturalizations amounted to only 6 percent, despite the much larger size of the legal immigrant cohorts from that country. Canadian naturalizations represented only 3 percent, despite the large pool of eligible individuals accumulated during many years of legal immigration. Finally, all of Western Europe combined barely doubled the number of naturalizations from Cuba. The relative weight of Cubans in the yearly totals was significantly greater during the early 1970s and tended to decline during subsequent years. This pattern can be attributed to the large pools of individuals eligible for naturalization created by the earlier waves of Cuban migration during the early and mid-1960s and their subsequent decline. It also suggests that, contrary to popular lore, many early exiles were quite willing to accept U.S. citizenship soon after becoming eligible.

The absolute and relative contribution of an immigrant group to total naturalizations must be distinguished from its rate of citizenship change. Clearly, the numbers changing nationality in a given year are a function both of the collective propensity to do so and the size of the pool of eligible individuals. To isolate the former, one must compare the number of naturalizations for different groups controlling for their size. Following Warren (1979), we analyze naturalization rates by comparing the numbers changing nationality for different immigrant groups over a period of ten years. Cuban naturalizations are compared with those of immigrants from Mexico, the single largest national group, with the rest of Latin America, Canada, all of Western Europe, and Asia. Separate series are presented for each year in order to examine variation across years, as well as nationalities.

There are a number of results which are consistent across the three cohorts:

a) The Mexican naturalization rate is the lowest, representing one-seventh of the average for all countries. The Canadian rate is also very low, oscillating between one-fourth and one-fifth of the average.

b) Cuban naturalization rates are high. They consistently exceed the rate for all countries and those for individual countries and regions, except Asia. In 1970 and again in 1971, Cuban naturalizations more than doubled the rate for the rest of Latin America, as well as for Western Europe.

c) The number of immigrants from all countries changing nationality peaks after seven years in the United States. This trend is consistent across all cohorts and is repeated in individual series for Asia, Western Europe, and (with one exception) Canada.

d) All Latin American naturalizations tend to peak later than the average. The Mexican is the slowest, reaching its mode in the ninth or tenth year. The Cuban series followed the seventh-year trend in the 1969 cohort; in the two subsequent ones, however, they peaked in the eighth year. The series corresponding to the rest of Latin America follow an intermediate course reaching their modal value in the eighth, ninth, or tenth years.

We hypothesize that national differences found in these data are due to a combination of three factors; (1) geographical distance from places of emigration; (2) reasons for departure; and (3) educational and occupational background of each immigrant group. The countries and regions analyzed above can be divided accordingly in three categories:

1) Lowest rates of naturalization correspond to the two nations contiguous to the United States—Mexico and Canada. Neither flow is politically motivated. In addition, proximity to the home country gives to the move abroad a certain lack of finality. The pattern of cyclical, back-and-forth migration reported by a number of studies of Mexican immigration seems to be a powerful force discouraging a shift of allegiance toward the host country (Cornelius 1981; Reichert 1981).

2) Intermediate rates correspond to Western Europe and Central and South America. Again, neither flow is primarily due to political reasons. Unlike Mexico and Canada, however, the sending countries are at a considerable distance from that of destination, making cyclical migration more expensive and difficult. Distance from places of origin and the costs of return may encourage permanent settlement in the receiving country and an eventual shift of citizenship. However, the fact that the move is anything but final is demonstrated by naturalization rates among South Americans and Europeans which are, in most cohorts, lower than average.

3) Highest rates are found among Cuban and Asian immigrants. Although Cuba does not have a land border with the United States,

it is the third closest country of any size, next to Mexico and Canada. Physical proximity is counteracted in this case by the political character of emigration. For most Cubans, leaving their country represented a decision of nearly irreversible consequences. In the absence of a credible chance of return, contingent on the overthrow of the Castro government, Cuban refugees faced the prospect of permanent resettlement in the United States. In all appearance, this prospect weighed more heavily than the lingering hopes of return, leading to high rates of naturalization among early exile cohorts. Asian immigrants are, however, the group that shifts citizenship most frequently, and the reasons for this propensity are not apparently political. Vietnamese refugees were not present among the cohorts analyzed here which were composed overwhelmingly of citizens of countries friendly to the United States. The long distance journey of Asians does not provide a sufficient explanation either since many Latin Americans and Europeans come from equally far away lands without exhibiting the same inclination to change national allegiance.

The third causal factor listed above comes into play here, namely the distinct educational and occupational composition of this immigrant group. The annual reports of the Immigration and Naturalization Service do not tabulate data on education by country, but they do provide information on occupational categories. In addition, there are data for the Eastern Hemisphere on the number of immigrants coming under the third preference category, reserved for professionals. There is little question that Asian immigrants surpass all others in their average occupational background. The proportion of professionals among this group more than doubles the corresponding figure for all countries, regardless of whether total or economically active immigration is considered. Professionals are more numerous among Asian immigrants than among any other individual country or region; they are also far more likely to make use of the third preference category than those from any other region in the Eastern Hemisphere.

REGISTRATION AND TURNOUT

Registration to vote and actual participation in elections are the most immediate indicators of integration into the American political system. This statement applies to both naturalized foreigners and the native-born. The available census data for the presidential election of 1980 and the congressional election of 1982 are presented in table 1. The data indicate that the

TABLE 1

Voting Registration and Turnout in U.S. Elections—1980–1982

	I Number Reported Registered (000s)	II Percent Registered, All Persons 18 yrs. and over	III Percent Registered, Excluding Non-Citizens	IV Number Reported Voting (000s)	V Percent Voting, All Persons 18 yrs. and over	VI Percent· Voting, Excluding Non-Citizens	VII Percent of those Registered Who Voted
Presidential Election—1980							
Total	105,090	66.9	69.7	92,994	59.2	61.7	88.6
White	94,170	68.4	70.8	83,845	60.9	63.1	89.1
Black	9,854	60.0	61.7	8,293	50.5	52.0	84.1
Spanish Origin	2,980	36.3	53.6	2,455	29.9	44.1	82.2
Congressional Election—1982							
Total	106,074	64.1	66.9	80,259	48.5	50.7	75.8
White	94,206	65.6	67.9	71,660	49.9	51.6	76.1
Black	10,416	59.1	61.1	7,578	43.0	44.5	72.7
Spanish Origin	3,094	35.3	51.7	2,217	25.3	37.1	71.7

Spanish-origin population of voting age has much lower registration and voting rates than the U.S. population as a whole. The Spanish rates are about one-half the figures for the white population. This immense gap is partially explained by the large number of Hispanic adults who are non-naturalized foreigners. Columns III and VI of the table present adjusted figures, after excluding non-citizens. The distance narrows considerably, but there is still a significant disadvantage for the minority: in both 1980 and 1982, the Spanish adjusted registration rate was 15 percent below the national average; the gap separating it from the white population was even greater. In the 1980 presidential election, Hispanic citizens trailed the voting of blacks by 8 percentage points and that of whites by almost 20 points.

Unfortunately, the Bureau of the Census does not disaggregate the data by national origin and hence it is impossible to analyze inter-group differences in registration and turnout. It is likely, however, that significant differences exist between the various Hispanic groups. In particular, it can be hypothesized that the propensity to naturalize among the Cuban-born population will be followed by higher levels of political participation once citizenship is acquired.

In the absence of national-level data, we turn to an analysis of registration and turnout in the Miami Metropolitan Area where, as seen above, over half of the Cuban-origin population concentrates. Table 2 presents electoral data for the Miami SMSA as reported by the Census. It shows that the proportion of registration and voting among the Spanish-origin adult population again falls significantly below the average while that among black adults tends to be somewhat higher. The Census does not adjust SMSA electoral data by citizenship. In the case of Miami, this adjustment should be significant because of the large number of recent Cuban and other Latin American immigrants who are not yet eligible for citizenship.

We estimated the Spanish-origin population eighteen years of age or over who are U.S. citizens for the Miami SMSA on the basis of Census publications and certain simplifying assumptions about the age structure of this population. The resulting figure can be used to adjust the above rates of registration and turnout.[2] Adjusted rates are presented in the bottom rows of both panels of table 2. The new figures exceed the registration and voting rates in both elections for the total metropolitan population and for white voters. The adjusted rates also come very close to the high levels of electoral participation among blacks in the area and exceed them in one instance. Although tentative, the assumptions on which these estimates are based appear reasonable. Results suggest that Spanish-origin citizens in Miami take a more active role in electoral politics than that reported nationwide and that their rates of participation are not significantly inferior to those of other major ethnic groups in the local population.

TABLE 2

Voting Registration and Turnout in the Miami SMSA—
Elections of 1980 and 1982

	NUMBER REPORTED REGISTERED	PERCENT REGISTERED, ALL PERSONS 18 YRS. & OVER	NUMBER REPORTED VOTING	PERCENT VOTING, ALL PERSONS 18 YRS. & OVER
I. Presidential Election—1980				
Total	612,360	54.0	531,846	46.9
White	436,590	50.0	377,704	43.2
Black	170,695	66.9	151,304	59.3
Spanish-origin[a]	136,216	31.2	121,809	27.9
Spanish-origin, citizens only[b]	136,216	65.1	121,809	58.2
II. Congressional Election—1982				
Total	679,896	53.2	460,080	36.0
White	515,029	51.6	373,296	37.4
Black	160,849	62.0	85,873	33.1
Spanish-origin[a]	125,837	27.2	89,751	19.4
Spanish-origin, citizens only[b]	125,837	60.2	89,751	42.9

a. Persons of Spanish origin may be of any race.
b. Estimates. note 2.
Sources: U.S. Bureau of the Census, *Population Characteristics Series P-20 #370*, April 1982, Table 6 and *#383*, November 1983, Table 17, U.S. Bureau of the Census, *Detailed Population Characteristics— 1980, Florida*. Table 194 and *General Social and Economic Characteristics, Miami SMSA*, Tables 59, 116.

This conclusion is supported by local county data on voting turn-out among citizens registered to vote. Table 3 presents the relevant figures which include data for all of Dade County, and for areas of "high" black and Hispanic concentration. Black voters represent 99 percent on the average of those registered in black areas; Spanish-origin voters, however, represent between 38 and 73 percent in areas designated as Hispanic. This introduces a degree of ambiguity in the results since "Spanish" rates include an unknown number of non-Spanish voters. This kind of data does not warrant inferences about individual political behavior, but can only be used to establish aggregate-level trends. With this caveat in mind, the data indicate a consistently higher-than-average turnout in areas where the Spanish-origin electorate concentrates. This result again supports, albeit less directly, the notion that rates of electoral participation among this minority are higher in South Florida than in the nation as a whole.

It is not possible with the data at hand to disaggregate these results for the various Hispanic groups. Cubans represent, however, 70 percent

TABLE 3

Turnout Among Registered Voters—Miami SMSA
Percent Registered Voters Who Actually Voted

	ELECTION		
	Presidential, 1976	Gubernatorial, 1978	Presidential, 1980
Dade County Total	72.5	59.5	74.0
Hispanic Precincts[a]	75.7	60.0	78.2
Black Precincts[b]	—	42.7	72.3

Source: Metro-Dade Elections Department, Election Summaries, Miami, 1983 (Special Tabulations).
a. Contiguous precincts in areas where the proportion of Spanish-origin registered voters averages 38 percent or higher.
b. Contiguous precincts in areas where the proportion of black registered voters averages 99 percent.

of the Spanish-origin population of the Miami metropolitan area, 86 percent of its foreign born, and 91 percent of its naturalized citizens. Hence, whatever is distinct about Hispanic political participation in Miami must be due, in large part, to the Cuban presence and its electoral behavior. The incompleteness of the available data makes it impossible to reach conclusions as firm as those on the subject of naturalization. Yet, it can be tentatively concluded that Cubans not only naturalize at a higher rate than other immigrant groups, but that the level of electoral participation in the areas where they concentrate is higher than for the Hispanic population nation-wide and at least not inferior to those of other ethnic components of the local population.

VOTING PREFERENCES

Ethnic minorities, especially those of recent arrival, have traditionally supported more progressive candidates and parties with more egalitarian platforms. These political preferences follow quite logically from the collective self-interest of these groups in abandoning the bottom of the social pyramid and finding avenues of economic and social mobility (Parenti 1967; Alba and Chamlin 1983).

Most Hispanic groups in the United States presently follow a similar pattern. Both Mexican-American and Puerto Rican voters tend to lean strongly toward the Democratic Party and support the more progressive candidates as a reflection of their socioeconomic situation (Nelson and Tienda 1984). The Cuban voting pattern, however, stands in stark contrast to those of other major Hispanic groups since it continues to have a strong conservative bent.

Table 4 illustrates this orientation with data from recent elections in Dade County. As in the preceding section, the categories of comparison are average voting figures for Dade County as a whole and for areas of high black and Hispanic concentration. As in the previous analysis, these comparisons do not provide an exact estimate of Cuban voting preferences since not all voters in areas designated as Hispanic are themselves of Spanish origin and not everyone among the latter is Cuban. Thus, results must be interpreted, in a strict sense, at the ecological rather than individual levels.

In 1976, Hispanic precincts in Dade County were significantly less likely to vote Democratic and to support the Carter presidential candidacy or the incumbent Democratic congressman, Dante Fascell. In 1978, support for the Democratic gubernatorial candidate was significantly lower than the average in the Hispanic areas and significantly higher in the black ones. The same trend was apparent in the vote on an anti-racial discrimination referendum that year: Hispanic and black areas again fell at opposite ends of the continuum, their difference exceeding 20 percentage points.

The gap actually expanded in the 1980 presidential elections. As before, areas of high Hispanic concentration showed a marked preference for conservative candidates and weak support for liberal ones; the black pattern was exactly the opposite. County-wide, Reagan received slightly over half of the vote, but in the Spanish precincts he captured almost three-fourths; Carter received only 40 percent of the total vote, but an overwhelming 95 percent in the black areas. The Cuban vote in areas of Hispanic concentration is diluted to an unknown extent by other Hispanic and non-Hispanic voters; it is not likely that the latter possess as uniform a conservative orientation as the refugees. Thus, these aggregate trends probably minimize actual differences in political preferences between Cubans and other segments of the local electorate.

The most plausible interpretation of the well-known political conservatism among Cuban exiles must be found in the history of this minority and its reasons for emigration. Experiences under the Revolution, which prompted many Cubans to leave their country, were translated for many into a fervent anti-communism which permeated subsequent perceptions of U.S. domestic issues. Even mildly progressive ideas and groups are viewed with suspicion in the Miami Cuban community; while candidates of the right profit from the militant opposition of the refugees to anything reminiscent of their socialist past.

This interpretation can be challenged, however, by pointing to the vaunted economic success of Cubans in South Florida. Higher income

TABLE 4

Voting Preferences in Dade County

DADE COUNTY	Nov. 1976 GENERAL ELECTION			Nov. 1978 GUBERNATORIAL ELECTION		Nov. 1980 GENERAL ELECTION			
	Democrats %	For Carter %	For Fascell %	For Graham %	For Non-Discrimination Ordinance %	For Carter %	For Reagan %	For Hawkins %	For Fascell %
TOTAL	74.2	58.1	70.8	70.0	42.0	40.2	50.4	48.2	65.3
Hispanic Precincts[a]	65.0	45.6	64.2	57.3	34.1	23.8	70.9	62.8	57.1
Black Precincts[b]	—	—	—	87.9	66.7	94.8	3.8	16.2	93.4

Source: Metro-Dade Elections Department, *Election Summaries*, Miami, 1983 (Special Tabulations).

a. Contiguous precincts in areas where the proportion of Spanish-origin registered voters averages 38 percent or higher.
b. Contiguous precincts in areas where the proportion of black registered voters averages 99 percent.

groups have traditionally voted at higher rates than the average and also tended to support more conservative candidates and platforms (Orum 1983: chap. 9). It is possible that the apparent electoral behavior of Cuban-born citizens—high participation and a strong conservative bent—reflect their newly acquired wealth rather than their lingering resentment against the Cuban Revolution. The electoral behavior of the refugees could thus simply be attributed to their high economic status.

As seen above, average levels of income among Cubans in the United States are higher than those of Hispanics as a whole, but they do not exceed those of the total U.S. population. It is possible with the data at hand to go further and test systematically the above conflicting interpretations of political behavior. Table 5 presents the results of regressing variables tapping both electoral participation and political orientations on average income and ethnic composition of the thirty-six electoral districts in which Dade County is divided. Dependent variables are electoral turnout in the presidential elections of 1976 and 1980 and percent voting for Carter in each. Independent variables are median income of the district, total number of registered voters, percent of Hispanic voters, and percent of black voters.

Ordinary least squares (OLS) coefficients presented in table 5 are unbiased, although they may not be most efficient. This is because the nature of the data makes it likely that error variances are heteroskedastic. For this reason, we replicated the analysis with a generalized least squares (GLS) regression procedure (Hanushek and Jackson 1977: chap. 6). The new estimates restated OLS figures, including size of effects and approximate significance levels. Given the robustness of OLS results and their greater ease of interpretation, we opted for presenting them here.

As seen in table 5, voting turnout is primarily determined by district size and ethnic composition of the electorate. The latter is the most important predictor, although the group that makes the difference varied from 1976 to 1980. In both years, however, percent of black voters had a negative effect on turnout while percent of Hispanic voters had a positive one. In 1980, in particular, the effect of Hispanic concentration, net of median income and district size, almost tripled its standard error. In substantive terms, each point growth in the Hispanic voting population produced a net increase of one-tenth of one percent in district turnout. Contrary to expectations, average income levels did not have a significant effect in either year after controlling for population size and ethnic composition.

Income did have a significant effect on voting preferences, as indicated in the bottom rows of table 5. This effect does not eliminate, however, the sizable impact of ethnic composition. In 1976 and again in 1980, greater income and greater concentration of Hispanics decreased the pro-

TABLE 5

Effects of Median Income and Ethnic Composition on Aggregate Voting Turnout and Electoral Preferences—Dade County Districts 1976, 1980[a]

	INDEPENDENT VARIABLES					R² Minus Ethnic Variables	Significance of Difference
DEPENDENT VARIABLES	Number of Registered Voters	Median Income	Percent Black Voters	Percent Hispanic Voters	R²		
Voting Turnout, 1976	.325* (2.48)	.159 (1.14)	-.404** (2.83)	.239 (1.73)	.485	.139	.001
Voting Turnout, 1980	.318* (2.30)	.261 (1.76)	-.116 (.77)	.411** (2.81)	.423	.180	.01
Percent for Carter, 1976	.177* (1.99)	-.292** (3.09)	.661*** (6.83)	-.256** (2.72)	.763	.093	.001
Percent for Carter, 1980	.129** (2.55)	-.163** (3.02)	.828*** (15.00)	-.226*** (4.22)	.923	.035	.001

a. Figures are standardized regression coefficients; those in parentheses are t-values.

*p < .05
**p < .01
***p < .001

portion of Carter votes, while number of black voters increased them. Both ethnic effects are strong. In 1980, the Hispanic coefficient tripled its standard error and the black coefficient was fifteen times as large. Net of income, each percent of black voting population produced an increase of three-fifths of one percent in the Carter vote; each additional percent of Hispanic population decreased it by one-fourth of one percent.

We can readily conclude that the positive associations between Hispanic (Cuban) concentration and higher electoral participation and conservative voting preferences are not spurious. Effects of income levels run in the predicted directions, but they do not account for the distinct voting patterns in areas of Hispanic or black concentration in Miami, nor for the remarkable differences between the two. This conclusion is poignantly illustrated by the last three columns of table 5: explained variance in both electoral turnout and voting preferences is reduced to insignificance once the ethnic composition variables are removed.

Areas of high Cuban concentration in South Florida thus vote more frequently and more conservatively than the average, offering a marked contrast with the political behavior patterns of Hispanic districts elsewhere in the United States. Reasons for this unique trend are not found in the defense of a privileged economic situation; although the data cannot support a definite conclusion, they point again in the direction of the unique history of this minority and the attitudes rooted in its home country experience as the prime determinants of its current behavior.

FUTURE TRENDS

Conservatism seems to be a consistent and enduring trait of Cuban political behavior. Still there are some signs which suggest a possible convergence with national voting preferences and perhaps with those of other Spanish-origin groups in the future. The signs are admittedly faint, but they are worth a brief review.

To examine different aspects of their process of adaptation to American society, a longitudinal study of adult male Cuban refugees was conducted between 1973 and 1979. A sample of 590, approximately equal to the universe of refugees in the study's target categories arriving in Miami during the second half of 1973 were interviewed. Slightly over 70 percent of this sample was traced and re-interviewed in 1976 and again in 1979. A series of tests for bias due to sample mortality yielded uniformly negative results, indicating that sub-sample follow-ups were representative of the original and, hence, of the universe of original refugees. These tests and other details of data collection have been discussed extensively elsewhere (Portes and Bach 1985; Wilson and Portes 1980; Portes, Clark, and Lopez 1982).

Table 6 presents responses of this sample to a series of questions tapping the issues of political integration and ethnic identity over time. By 1973, the Castro government had been thirteen years in power and realistic expectations of overthrowing it were dim. Still, almost half of the refugees indicated that they did not intend to settle in the United States and 60 percent reported plans to return if the Castro regime fell. In the same year, almost no one perceived discrimination against Cubans and one-fourth

TABLE 6

Plans and Perceptions of Cuban Refugees
During Their First Six Years in the United States

	1973	1976	1979
	(N = 590) %	(N = 427) %	(N = 413) %
I. Plans to resettle in the U.S. permanently?			
Yes	53.7	88.5	95.9
No	31.7	4.7	2.4
Doesn't know	14.6	6.8	1.7
II. Would return to Cuba if Castro government fell?			
Yes	60.6	50.5	22.6
No	10.1	27.9	51.7
Doesn't know	29.3	21.6	25.7
III. Plans to become U.S. citizen?			
Yes		77.2	85.7
No		7.3	4.9
Doesn't know		15.5	9.5
IV. Is there discrimination against Cubans in the U.S.?			
Yes	4.6	26.8	26.4
No	69.1	69.8	62.5
Doesn't know	26.3	3.4	11.1
V. Are Anglo/Cuban relations close or distant?			
Close		69.4	63.7
Distant		24.7	25.5
Doesn't know		5.9	10.8
VI. How do Anglos see themselves in relation to Cubans?			
Inferior		0.2	1.5
Equal		56.4	47.3
Superior		43.4	50.8

Frequencies based on full samples each year; percentages based on respondents interviewed at all three
points in time parallel these results too closely to merit reproduction.
Sources: Portes (1984).

of respondents said that they did not know whether discrimination existed. These early perceptions and plans fit quite well the image of a political exile community oriented toward return and relatively indifferent to events in the host society.

After three and, especially after six years, the situation had changed dramatically. This is illustrated in table 6 by questions on permanent settlement and perceptions of discrimination. Plans to remain in the United States increased significantly comprising, by 1979, almost the entire sample. Intentions to return after the overthrow of the Castro government declined from over half to less than one-fourth of the refugees. By 1976, already three-fourths of the respondents planned to become U.S. citizens; three years later, the figure climbed to 86 percent, including twenty-four who had already acquired citizenship. These trends clearly signaled a move away from the original return goals and correspond to the high propensity to naturalize detected above.

This shift in settlement plans was accomplished by an equally significant change in ethnic perceptions. Perceptions of discrimination against Cubans in the United States increased from almost zero in 1973 to over 25 percent three years later; "don't know" responses declined accordingly. Other perceptual questions included in the 1976 and 1979 surveys yielded similar distributions: majorities continued to give positive responses, but a substantial one-fourth of the sample described Anglo-Cuban relations as "distant" or "hostile." When asked how Anglos perceived themselves in relation to Cubans, much larger proportions indicated awareness of social distance; by 1979, half of the respondents believed that Anglos saw themselves as superior to Cubans.

These data have been analyzed in greater detail elsewhere (Portes 1984). The basic conclusion is that the shift from return expectations toward permanent settlement have run parallel to a significant rise of perceptions associated with ethnic awareness. To the extent that this trend continues, it may be expected to affect political behavior in the direction of shifting the focus of attention from issues relating to Cuba and global political struggles toward the emerging problems and interests of Cubans as a domestic minority. Given the many adaptation difficulties still faced by this group, such a shift may result in a significant move toward the center of the political spectrum.

There are other indicators that point in the same direction. Despite their avowed conservatism, 47 percent of registered Cuban voters are affiliated with the Democratic party and most have supported government aid for the elderly and students and health benefits for pregnant women (Nazario 1983). More to the point are voting results of a 1980 Dade County referendum to prohibit the use of public monies for programs in a language other than English. Contrary to the usual pattern, Hispanic precincts voted more "liberally" than the average in this instance: close to 70 percent of voters in areas of high Spanish concentration supported continuation of bilingualism, as opposed to 40 percent overall (Elections Department 1983). This obvious display of collective self-interest suggests the beginnings of a shift in attitudes and increasing awareness of the problems and needs of Cubans as an ethnic minority.

In synthesis, the Cuban experience of naturalization and electoral participation contrasts markedly with those of other immigrant groups and, in particular, those of other Hispanic minorities. Despite an earlier attachment to the goal of returning to their country, Cubans naturalize more frequently than anyone else, except Asian immigrants. In their area of principal concentration, Cubans who have acquired U.S. citizenship are estimated to participate in electoral politics at least as actively as other groups, a pattern markedly different from that of Hispanics elsewhere in the country. However, Cuban voting preferences appear guided less by immediate economic and social interests than by values and orientations rooted in political experiences prior to emigration. The consistently conservative preferences found in areas where this minority concentrates cannot be explained by higher-than-average income levels. There are some signs, however, that the process of transformation from a political exile community into an ethnic group is advancing rapidly. As it progresses, the current gap in voting preferences between Cubans and other voters, especially other Hispanics, may well narrow.

More generally, this analysis suggests several aspects of the political adaptation process not commonly stressed in the immigration literature. First, there are significant differences in the rates at which various immigrant minorities naturalize and the propensity to do so is determined by a plurality of factors, ranging from geographic considerations of place to status origins. Second, the extent of political participation also varies significantly even among groups sharing the same general cultural origins. More importantly, determinants of differential participation can be far removed from immediate material considerations and depend primarily on beliefs acquired prior to emigration. Finally, the process of political adaptation is highly dynamic and can register significant changes even in the course of a single generation. Research on this aspect of immigrant adaptation thus requires a non-static methodology able to capture major shifts over time and establish the temporal order of their determinants.

NOTES

1. This article represents a revised version of a paper originally prepared for the Conference on Citizenship and the Hispanic Community, National Associa-

tion of Latin Elected Officials, Washington, D.C., May 5, 1984 and for the Conference on Cuban-American Studies sponsored by the Center for the Study of the Cuban Community at M.I.T. We wish to thank Joseph Malone of the Department of Elections, Dade County, Florida for his help in the data collection for this paper. Data analysis was supported by grant #SES-8215567 from the National Science Foundation and by a graduate fellowship from the Organization of American States.

   2. The estimating equation is as follows:

$$C = (O - F + N)\,(1 - Ch)$$

Where:

   C — Spanish-origin citizens, 18 years of age or over
   O — Spanish-origin persons
   F — Foreign-born persons of Spanish origin
   N — Naturalized citizens of Spanish origin
   Ch — Citizens of Spanish Origin, 17 years or younger

All figures are for the Miami SMSA in 1980.

From Census data, we have:
   O — 580,025
   F — 423,542 (Bureau of the Census, 1983b, Tables 59, 116)

Data on naturalized citizens of Spanish-origin are reported only at the state level. We assume that the same proportions apply at the local (Miami) level since two-thirds (67.6 percent) of the Spanish-origin population of Florida concentrates in this metropolitan area and since there is no reason to expect a differential naturalization rate for those living elsewhere. Thirty-nine percent of Spanish-origin foreign-born persons in Florida had become citizens by 1980 (U.S. Bureau of Census, 1983c, Table 194). Hence: $N = F(.39) \cong 165,181$

   Age breakdowns for the Spanish-origin population are also reported at the state level only. An additional complication is that the data do not differentiate the population of voting age unambiguously; the nearest bracket includes persons between 15 and 19 years of age. To estimate Ch, we assumed: 1) That the state proportion of Spanish-origin citizens, 17 years of age or younger is the same as in the Miami SMSA. This assumption is justified for the same reasons given above. The state proportion after performing the relevant age bracket adjustment is .35. Hence:

$$C \cong 209,082$$

REFERENCES

Alba, R. D., and M. B. Chamlin. 1983. "Ethnic Identification among Whites." *American Sociological Review* 48:240–247. April.
Bach, R. L., 1984. "Socialist Construction and Cuban Emigration: Explorations into Mariel." Paper presented at the conference on Cuban-American Studies: Status and Future, M.I.T., May 26.

Bach R. L., J. B. Bach and T. Triplett. 1981. "The Flotilla 'Entrants': Latest and most Controversial." Cuban Studies II:29–48. July.

Clark, J. M., J. I. Lasaga and R. S. Reque. 1981. "The 1980 Mariel Exodus: An Assessment and Prospect." Special Report. Washington, D.C.: Council for Inter-American Security.

Cornelius, W. A. 1981. "Immigration, Mexican Development Policy, and the Future of U.S.-Mexican Relations." In American Assembly of Mexico and the United States. Edited by R. H. McBride, Englewood Cliffs, N.J.: Prentice Hall, Pp. 104–27.

Diaz-Briquets, S., and L. Perez. 1981. "Cuba: The Demography of Revolution," Population Bulletin 36:2–41. April.

Elections Department. 1983. "Elections Summaries." Miami: Metro-Dade Government, Special Tabulations.

Hanushek, E., and J. E. Jackson. 1977. Statistical Methods for Social Scientists. New York: Academic Press.

Nazario, S. 1983. "After a Long Holdout, Cubans in Miami Take a Role in Politics." Wall Street Journal. June 7.

Nelson, C., and M. Tienda. 1984. "The Structuring of Hispanic Ethnicity: Historical and Contemporary Perspectives." Department of Rural Sociology, University of Wisconsin–Madison. Manuscript.

Orum, A. 1983. Political Sociology, 2nd Edition. Englewood Cliffs, N.J.: Prentice-Hall.

Parenti, M. 1967. "Ethnic Politics and the Persistence of Ethnic Identification." American Political Review 61:717–26. Sept.

Pedraza-Bailey, S. 1984. Political and Economic Migrants in America: Cubans and Mexicans. Austin: University of Texas Press.

Peterson, M. F. 1984. "Work Attitudes of Mariel Boatlift Refugees." Cuban Studies, 14:1–19. Summer.

Portes, A. 1984. "The Rise of Ethnicity." American Sociological Review 49:383–97. June.

Portes, A., and R. L. Bach. 1985. Latin Journey: Cuban and Mexican Immigrants in the United States. Berkeley: University of California Press.

Portes, A., J. M. Clark and R. L. Bach. 1977. "The New Wave: A Statistical Profile of Recent Cuban Exiles in the United States." Cuban Studies 7:1–32. Jan.

Portes, A., J. M. Clark and M. M. Lopez. 1982. "Six Years Later: The Process of Incorporation of Cuban Exiles in the United States." Cuban Studies 11/12: 1–24. Jan.

Reichert, J. S. 1981. "The Migrant Syndrome: Seasonal U.S. Wage Labor and Rural Development in Central Mexico." Human Organization 40:59–66. Spring.

Thomas, J. F., and E. E. Huyck. 1967. "Resettlement of Cuban Refugees in the United States." Paper presented at the Meetings of the American Sociological Association, San Francisco.

Time. 1978. "Hispanic Americans: Soon the Biggest Minority." Oct. 16.

U.S. Bureau of the Census. 1982. Statistical Abstract of the United States, 1982. Washington, D.C.: U.S. Government Printing Office.

————. 1983a. 1980 Census of Population, General Population Characteristics, United States Summary. Washington, D.C.: U.S. Government Printing Office.

————. 1983b. 1980 Census of Population, General Social and Economic Characteristics, United States Summary. Washington, D.C.: U.S. Government Printing Office.

————. 1983c. 1980 Census of Population, Detailed Population Characteristics, State of Florida. Washington, D.C.: U.S. Government Printing Office.

Warren, R. 1979. "Status Report on Naturalization Rates." Washington, D.C.: Bureau of the Census, Working Paper #CO 1326, 6/C.

Wilson, K. L., and A. Portes. 1980. "Immigrant Enclaves: An Analysis of the Labor Market Experiences of Cubans in Miami." *American Journal of Sociology* 86:295–331. Sept.

8. Black and Latino Politics in New York City: Race and Ethnicity in a Changing Urban Context

Angelo Falcón

WITH RACIAL-ETHNIC MINORITIES expected to increase from 48 percent of New York City's population in 1980 to close to 60 percent in 1990, the political consequences of this development are, surprisingly, not well understood. An important reason for this is that the dramatic growth and increasing diversity of the city's population is a subject that is not being adequately addressed by researchers or policymakers. While, on the one hand, there is a tendency to ignore or oversimplify the role of minorities in the city's political process, there appears to be, on the other, problems in how minority politics are conceptualized in such rapidly changing circumstances.[1]

This study will begin by arguing that black and Latino politics in New York City can be expected to enter a potentially new phase of development in the late 1980s. This will be the result of demographic changes occurring not only in New York, but in most of the country's larger cities. However, it will also be argued here that developments in the last two decades in New York have put strains on how minority politics has been defined and that these developments call for a basic reassessment of prevailing theories and concepts in this area. In order to illustrate this, the second part of this analysis will concentrate on the problem of the increasingly limited meaning of the term "minority" in contemporary New York City politics. This will be done by presenting a comparative analysis of the black and Latino political experiences in the city. Some conclusions will be presented on the implications of this both for research and minority political strategies in New York and other urban centers.

Original released as an Institute for Puerto Rican Policy discussion paper, December 1985. Reprinted with permission of the author.

171

FROM MINORITY TO MAJORITY: THE NEW CONTEXT
OF MINORITY POLITICS IN NEW YORK CITY

As New York City moves from being majority white to majority non-white in the 1980s, it is confronted with some old issues in new ways. Being no different than many other cities that are going or have gone through this experience, its position as an international corporate and finance center makes its response to this growing minority presence of very broad interest.

Despite a two-decade old decline in total population, New York remains the country's largest city and with this comes the continuing distinctiveness of its size. To point out that more than half of its population is nonwhite is, therefore, a significant development since the more than 3.5 million blacks, Latinos and other minorities this represents are greater, for example, than the total population of the second largest city in the United States in 1985, Los Angeles, as well as equal to or greater in population than close to one-fourth of all the nations in the world.[2] The political potential of such huge numbers of people in one city is enormous, and impossible, one would imagine, to ignore politically.

In 1980, New York City's population, according to the Census, was 52 percent white, 24 percent black, 20 percent Latino and 4 percent Asian and other minority. By 1990, it is estimated that with a total population projected to be 2 percent smaller, this will change to 41 percent white, 28 percent black, 24 percent Latino, and 7 percent Asian and other minority (or 59 percent nonwhite).[3] (See table 1.) These changes will be the result of the continuing decline of the city's white population (expected to decrease by 22 percent in the 1980s) and increases in all its nonwhite population groups (+ 14 percent for blacks, + 17 percent for Latinos, and + 69 percent for Asians and other minorities).[4]

The significance of this transformation of New York into a "majority minority" city in the late 1980s takes on an even greater significance when compared to similar developments nationally. (See table 2.) In 1980 only two of the country's ten largest cities, Detroit and Baltimore, were majority nonwhite (overwhelmingly black). By 1990, given current population trends, it can be reasonably projected that perhaps as many as eight of these ten cities will be predominantly black and Latino.

Consequently, New York will be facing this minority political challenge within a national context it shares. The development of black and Latino politics in New York will, no doubt, be buttressed by these broader trends, which have the potential to push it to a new level of activity and importance to the city as a whole, as well as nationally.

These major changes in the racial-ethnic makeup of New York come

TABLE 1

New York City Population by Race and Ethnicity
1970, 1980 and 1990 (Projected)

| | POPULATION (000s) | | | | | | PERCENT CHANGE | |
| | 1970 | | 1980 | | 1990 | | | |
GROUP	Total	%	Total	%	Total	%	1970–80	1980–90
Whites	4,997	63.3%	3,668	51.9%	2,871	41.3%	– 27%	– 22%
Blacks	1,514	19.2%	1,695	24.0%	1,929	27.7%	+ 12%	+ 14%
Latinos	1,201	15.2%	1,406	19.9%	1,646	23.7%	+ 17%	+ 17%
Other Minority	185	2.3%	303	4.3%	511	7.3%	+ 64%	+ 69%
Total	7,897	100%	7,072	100%	6,957	100%	– 10%	– 2%

Source: Adapted from: Emanuel Tobier, *The Changing Face of Poverty* (New York: Community Service Society, 1984), p. 104; and U.S. Bureau of Census, 1980 Census of Population, vol. 1. Characteristics of Population, chap. B. *General Population Characteristics. Part 34. New York.* PC80–1–B34 (Washington, D.C.: U.S. Government Printing Office, 1982), Table 31, pp. 195–196.

TABLE 2

Black and Latino Composition of
Ten Largest U.S. Cities, 1980

CITY	POPULATION (000s)	% BLACK	% LATINO[a]
New York, NY	7,072	25.2	19.9
Chicago, IL	3,005	39.8	14.0
Los Angeles, CA	2,967	17.0	27.5
Philadelphia, PA	1,688	37.8	3.8
Houston, TX	1,595	27.6	17.6
Detroit, MI	1,203	63.1	2.4
Dallas, TX	904	29.4	12.3
San Diego, CA	876	8.9	14.9
Phoenix, AZ	790	4.8	14.8
Baltimore, MD	787	54.8	1.0

a. Latinos may be of any race and are included in the black category.
Source: U.S. Bureau of the Census, *1984 Statistical Abstract of the United States* (Washington, D.C.: U.S. Government Printing Office, 1984), Table 29, pp. 28–30.

at a time when local and national political responsiveness to minority and urban concerns has not only been low, but antagonistic as well. Since the late 1970s, but particularly under the Reagan Administration in the 1980s, government efforts to help minorities and the poor, such as social welfare programs, affirmative action, and civil rights enforcement, have come under attack.[5] The dramatic growth of immigration from Third World countries, mainly Latin America and Asia, has, in part, helped fuel a "new patriotism" in the United States that has led to punitive immigration reform proposals, attacks on bilingualism that have taken the form nationally of a movement to formally make English the official language of the United States, and a general increase in scapegoating and violence against non-whites.

In New York City, blacks and Latinos, who make up 90 percent of its minority population, share a common subordinate position in the city's social and political systems, perhaps more so than in other parts of the country. For example, in 1982 the poverty rate for the city as a whole was estimated to have been about 24 percent, while for blacks it was 35 percent and for Latinos, 45 percent.[6] As a consequence of these high poverty rates, although blacks and Latinos combined were about 44 percent of New York City's population in 1980, each represented 36 percent (and, thus together, close to three-quarters) of the city's population living below the federal poverty level that year. Projected poverty rates and changes in the population would indicate that blacks and Latinos comprise an even larger portion of the city's poor people today.

In addition, blacks and Latinos not only live in the poorest and most deteriorated sections in the city, but unlike many other cities where they live in virtually isolated neighborhoods of their own, there is much greater black-Latino residential proximity and interaction in New York. This is particularly the case between blacks, Puerto Ricans, and Dominicans, while other Latino groups in the city exhibit lower rates of segregation from nonminority whites.[7] Coupled with the African roots of the Spanish-speaking (as well as English and French Creole) Caribbean, from where most new black and Latino groups in New York originate, this situation helps reinforce the continuities between the experiences of the two groups in the city.[8]

The social problems faced by both blacks and Latinos in New York are strikingly similar. These include very high unemployment rates, segmentation in the weakest sectors of the city's economy, extremely high dropout rates from the schools, and intense residential displacement due to factors such as disinvestment and gentrification.[9] Along with these problems is the persistent one of the lack of representation of blacks and Latinos in the city's major decision-making centers as well as significant underrepresentation in its secondary political institutions, primarily in the ward-based legislative bodies on the local and state levels.

THE POLITICAL RELEVANCE OF THE TERM "MINORITY" IN THE 1980s

Despite the common circumstances that blacks and Latinos in New York City find themselves in, differences between them are important to understand. The overgeneralized use of the term "minority" has more often than not served to confuse rather than aid analyses of black and Latino politics. Many Latinos complain that blacks use the term to increase their political leverage while excluding Latinos from the benefits that ensue from this strategy. There are blacks who view the use of the term as a way of diluting their claims on American society by allowing other groups to piggy-back on the black struggle.[10] On another level, evaluating demographic changes in New York City from 1974–1983, Salins has gone as far as to propose that the "entire minority/non-minority typology should probably be scraped in a city where we have such a large scale continuing immigration of citizens from every corner of the globe."[11]

One of the major difficulties that the use of the term "minority" creates is the tendency to uncritically collapse the experiences of black and Latinos into one global category that could be meaningless or misleading in certain contexts. The problems with this are many, as an analysis of black-Latino differences in a number of areas will illustrate. Those to be examined here include black and Latino views on race and minority status, their differences in approaching issues such as bilingualism and immigration, the differential access to government between them, and their respective patterns and levels of electoral participation.

Race and Minority Status

A variety of factors contribute to the significantly different ways in which blacks and Latinos view the race question. American blacks have emerged from an experience of slavery in the United States in which race has historically been viewed as a genetic attribute, a context which served to define their people racially.[12] Latinos, on the other hand, have a wider variation in skin color, a legacy of a Spanish colonial past which in the Caribbean, from which most of those in New York came, entailed greater interracial mixing of Spanish, other European, African, and indigenous Indian peoples. As a result, there is more of a tendency for Latinos to view race from a physiological perspective. In this sense Latinos entered a society which perceives race differently than they have historically, leading to a greater ambiguity on this question by Latinos than by American blacks today.[13]

The potential divisiveness of this issue between blacks and Latinos should not be underestimated. While there are large numbers of Latinos that reject the bi-polar racial assumptions of the United States and prefer to identify more along national-origin lines (that is, as Puerto Ricans, Dominicans, Colombians, etc.), there is the longstanding suspicion by American blacks that Puerto Ricans and other Latinos really consider themselves to be white.[14] Interestingly enough, within the black community itself this issue has been a recurrent one in terms of its West Indian components, many of whom also appear to identify primarily along national-origin rather than racial lines.[15]

These differences in self-identification have also carried over into how blacks and Latinos perceive their minority status in the United States. While American blacks have developed a distinctive heritage after close to four hundred years in the United States, Latinos in New York come from culturally and/or politically foreign countries. Compared to the black rootedness in the U.S. experience, albeit in a subordinate relationship, Latinos, particularly in the Northeast, have a more tenuous relationship.

There are many Latinos who, as a consequence, do not quite see themselves as a minority group in the United States in the way American blacks do. There is among Latinos a widespread belief that they are temporary immigrants with the ultimate aim of returning to their countries of origin. This belief is reinforced by three factors: (1) the high degree of circular migration to and from their countries of origin[16]; (2) the strong influence and visibility of home country politics, issues, and traditions in their U.S. communities[17]; and (3) the significantly lower naturalization rates of Latino groups that predominate in New York City compared to most other immigrant groups.[18]

Politically, of course, this creates a certain ambivalence toward life in the U.S. and its political institutions.[19] However, at the same time, groups like Puerto Ricans, who have a larger portion of its members with a longer history in New York than other Latinos and that, as a result, are more multigenerational, have on the whole developed views closer to American blacks on their minority status in the United States.[20] There is evidence as well that other Latino groups, particularly Dominicans, are moving in the Puerto Rican direction and becoming more involved in New York politics.[21] For example, on the Upper West Side of Manhattan, which is largely Dominican, a Dominican was elected Democratic Party district leader and one also unsuccessfully, ran for City Council against a white incumbent, signalling a growing involvement in electoral politics.

The issue inevitably arises whether the European immigrant model of political and social adaptation is an appropriate one for Latinos, if not blacks. While in the black case the relevance of this model has been effectively refuted, its applicability in terms of Latinos has been more persistently invoked.[22] "A common political analogy," Barnett explains, "likens blacks to white ethnic groups and is followed by arguments that even if blacks are not precisely like white ethnic groups, their usages of group power can produce similar results. This model," she finds, "is troublesome because it distorts white ethnic group history (most significantly the way they really used politics) and the sociology of both the black experience and the white ethnic experience."[23] Browning, Marshall, and Tabb observe, "Though there are undeniable parallels between blacks and Hispanics and the earlier immigrant groups, there are also clear differences . . . in the cultures, in the circumstances in which they came to the United States, in the times they arrived, in the economic opportunities available, in the attitudes of dominant groups towards them, and in the structure and operation of governments."[24] They find that, as a consequence, the "process of mobilization, incorporation, and responsiveness is problematic rather than automatic."

The critical dimension in relationship to the European immigrant model's usefulness in explaining the Latino experience in the U.S. is that of social class as it interacts with race and ethnicity, what Barnet refers to as "structural differentiation."[25] In New York City, the relevance of this model to Latinos of lower class backgrounds, Puerto Ricans and Dominicans, is highly doubtful, while for those with higher class backgrounds, such as Cubans and Colombians, it appears more appropriate.[26] However, as the impact of the large influx of lower class and darker skinned Cubans from the 1980 Mariel boatlift has shown, such models are extremely fragile guides within today's American sociopolitical context: from being the model Latino group to be emulated in the 1960s and 1970s, after the boatlift a 1982 Roper survey found that Americans in general viewed Cubans as the least desirable group in the country, ranking them below blacks, Puerto Ricans and Mexican-Americans.[27]

On both the questions of race and minority status in the U.S., blacks and Latinos exhibited differences. These differences are not all that clear-cut but rather involve differences of degree. The reason for this is that among Latinos there are sectors that respond to these questions in much the same way blacks do, and among blacks there are foreign-born elements with views more similar to Latinos in this respect. Group perceptions of race and their minority status are clearly key in how the term "minority" is defined, making our lack of understanding of the form they have taken and can take a needed focus for greater attention.

Issue Differences

How blacks and Latinos each view their status in the United States would, of course, have important implications for their respective stances on a wide range of social issues. Perhaps most illustrative of this is the issue of bilingual education, which is identified as primarily being a Latino concern. Blacks in general have not been receptive to the introduction of this approach for a variety of reasons. One that is most frequently aired is that bilingual programs in the schools would divert scarce funds away from much-needed compensatory programs for black children, a fear reinforced by teacher unions that perceive a threat to the jobs of their mostly non-bilingual members. In Boston in the mid-1970s and other places where there were legal battles over school desegregation and busing, and that had significant Latino populations, blacks also found themselves in conflict with demands for bilingual education that requires, by definition, a high degree of segregation of non-English speaking students.[28] The growing presence of non-English speakers, primarily Haitians, in the black population of New York, however, raises the bilingual issue within their own ranks, and is beginning to force American blacks to deal with this issue in a different way.[29] Despite this development in selected local areas, the fact remains that nationally and in New York generally, the black community's support of bilingual education is low and, at times, negative.

Another area of a significant divergence in views between blacks and Latinos is over the role of government in society. The black experience in the U.S., especially evident during the civil rights movement, is one that has come to see government, particularly at the national level, as socially activist. Many Latinos came to the U.S. with very different backgrounds thus creating less of a consensus on this question. These range from Latinos that are in the U.S. as non-citizens (legally and illegally) and those that left countries with politically repressive governments who would be suspicious or uncomfortable with government to those, like Puerto Ricans, who are U.S. citizens from birth and come from countries formally under the American political system.[30] The selectivity of some of the Latino migrations to the U.S. of people of higher social class backgrounds, such as was evident among pre-Mariel Cubans and many Central and South Americans, places economic concerns over political ones in their migratory calculus, which along with the influence of the views of many contemporary migrants in the U.S., reinforces an expectation of a very limited role of government in their lives. Among Latinos, therefore, a continuum of opinion on government is evident that, in large part, appears to be primarily generational and affected by social class background, indicating that it is a fluid area of opinion. While, once again, in the black community in New

York a similar spectrum of views exists as its foreign-born sectors grow, it seems to be a stronger influence among Latinos given their more peripheral involvement in the U.S. civil rights movement.

A third issue area which is extremely controversial today is immigration policy. An important aspect of the debate over this issue is the degree to which newcomers, both legal and illegal, are taking jobs away from U.S. citizens.[31] As the Liberty City riot in Miami in 1980 highlighted, blacks can come to see Latinos, in that case Cubans, as "foreigners" illegitimately taking jobs away from "natives."[32] While this issue does not always emerge as starkly as this, it does loom as an unresolved tension in black-Latino relations throughout the country. Again, in New York City such a situation is being increasingly replicated, although to a smaller degree, within the black community itself with its growing foreign-born elements.

Government Access

A critical area of concern for minority politics in New York City is the sharply divergent access to government that blacks have in contrast to Latinos. This section will briefly examine three areas in which this is the situation: representation among elected government officials, participation in the local government work forces, and the distribution of government expenditures on the poor.

Although blacks and Latinos currently make up over half of New York City's population, they were not represented in any elective government posts above the ward level (such as Mayor, City Council President, Borough President, etc.) up to 1985 when a black was once again elected Manhattan borough president since 1977, and were underrepresented in ward-level offices. In 1985, blacks and Latinos made up only 25 percent of the city's officeholders in the State Senate, 26 percent of those on the City Council, and 30 percent of those in the State Assembly.[33] The only citywide ward-based bodies where blacks and Latinos approached population parity are the thirty-two Community School Boards, which are themselves subordinate to a seven-member central Board of Education that is appointed by the Mayor and the Borough Presidents. Since 1975, the number of blacks and Latinos in these elected offices, excluding the School Boards, has remained fairly static, increasing from 35 to 38. On the School Boards, the number of blacks and Latinos has increased between 1973 and 1983 from 109 (37 percent of the total) to 129 (45 percent of the total).

However, when we compare the level of black with Latino political representation, large differences are revealed. Latinos, despite representing about 45 percent of the total black and Latino population in the city, held only 10 (or 26 percent of the 38 elected government posts held by these two groups combined in 1985 that were mentioned above. On the Community School Boards, Latinos held only 48 (or 37 percent of the 129 positions held by both blacks and Latinos after the 1983 election.

To an even larger degree, these differences in black and Latino levels of representation exist in city and state government employment. In 1983, blacks and Latinos combined comprised 40 percent of the total New York City government work force and 26 percent of its top executives.[34] When compared to the 32 percent of the total city government workers that were black, only 8 percent were Latino. Of the top city government executives, only 7 percent of the total were Latino in contrast to the 19 percent that were black. At the state government level, blacks and Latinos together account for 20 percent of the statewide government work force and 10 percent of the Governor's appointments to policy-level and other positions.[35] Even with smaller percentages in the state population (in 1980 Latinos accounted for 10 percent and blacks 13 percent of the state's population), Latinos held a miniscule 3 percent of state government jobs compared to 17 percent that were held by blacks. Of total gubernatorial appointments as of 1984, Latinos made up less than 4 percent of the total, while blacks made up 6 percent.

A recent study on government expenditures on the poor found that although blacks and Latinos made up 71 percent of the city's poor people in 1980, they received only an estimated 65 percent of what it termed its "poverty budget," which it put at a total of $14.8 billion in 1983.[36] Due to a variety of factors, a major one having to do with age and the effect of the more expensive services the elderly, who are mostly whites, receive, this analysis found that Latinos received less in grants and services than either black or whites. To the per capita poverty budget expenditure on whites in 1983 of $6,786, blacks were allocated $5,412 and Latinos $4,517.

The significantly less access that Latinos have than blacks or whites to political and public bureaucracy representation, as well as to budgetary resources, would indicate that this would be a more salient issue to Latinos than to blacks who are in a better position to entertain "post-access" concerns. Politically, therefore, this Latino lag behind blacks has important implications and is the source for the greater emphasis Latinos seem to give to questions of basic group visibility, including symbolic recognition.

Electoral Participation Patterns and Levels

Many of the differences between blacks and Latinos that have been discussed here also impact on the electoral participation patterns and levels of these two groups and the type of issues this raises. An area where the importance of these differences in the electoral arena has become most

pronounced in the last couple of years has been that of candidate preference, particularly in terms of the Jesse Jackson and Ronald Reagan campaigns for President in 1984, and the reelection campaign of New York
Mayor Edward I. Koch in 1985. These, above all, have proven to be critical tests for the state of minority coalition politics in New York City.

The Jackson campaign, with its Rainbow Coalition strategy to unite
all political "outsider" groups, was a clear opportunity to forge a black-
Latino coalition. The results, however, were very mixed in New York. In
the April 3, 1984 Democratic Presidential Primary in New York State,
only 33 percent of Latinos voted for Jackson compared to 76 percent of
Blacks.[37] While on the surface this difference between black and Latino
voters would dispell any notion that they voted as a block, the fact is that
this appeared to be by far the greatest degree of support that Jackson received from Latinos than anywhere else in the country.[38]

In the 1984 Presidential election, compared to only 10 percent of black
voters in New York City who cast their ballots for Reagan's reelection,
over 30 percent of Latinos did so.[39] This occurred despite 80 percent of
Latinos being registered in the Democratic Party, as are blacks. Therefore,
even in terms of an election where it was widely perceived that black and
Latino interests, particularly in New York City, were equally being threatened, the response of each group was significantly different.

A more recent example of this political divergence is the New York
Mayoralty campaign of 1985. An important part of the opposition to the
incumbent, Ed Koch, was thought by many to be the equally intense ani-
mosity shared by black and Latinos to what has been generally perceived
as his insensitivity to minority concerns and his pandering to the white
backlash element against black and Latinos.[40] It was felt by the anti-Koch
forces that the momentum of the Jesse Jackson Rainbow Coalition strategy,
which locally was antagonistic to Koch, would carry over into the Mayoral race.

The only problem with this strategy was that it glossed over large
differences that existed between blacks and Latinos in their opposition to
Koch's reelection. As early as 1984, polls showed that although 72 percent
of blacks opposed his reelection, only 54 percent of Latinos did, with 46
percent supporting Koch compared to only 17 percent of blacks.[41] A more
recent poll, taken in April-May 1985, found that 66 percent of Latino
Democrats planned to vote for Koch in the September 1985 primary compared to only 22 percent of blacks.[42] The results of this primary was that
an estimated 62 percent of Latinos voted for Koch compared to 42 percent
of blacks and 71 percent of whites.[43]

By assuming that as "minorities" blacks and Latinos automatically
held the same political preferences, the anti-Koch forces assumed a unity

that did not exist naturally and, as a result, developed a flawed political strategy that seems to have further divided blacks and Latinos, at least in terms of Koch's reelection. This situation became further aggravated when the black organization most prominent among the anti-Koch movement at the time, the Coalition for a Just New York, endorsed a marginal black candidate for Mayor at the last moment on February 8, 1985 at the expense of a much more viable Puerto Rican politician that they were expected to endorse.[44] This controversial decision, the outcome of political strategies and competition specific to black leadership politics in the city, illustrated the dangers of an overgeneralized and naive "minority" or "Rainbow" political strategy.

Such black-Latino voter divergences have not always characterized the political relationship between these two groups in the city. It was perhaps in 1966, in the vote over the retention of the Civilian Review Board in the Police Department, that the issue of race came to the fore politically in New York City with its greatest force.[45] In that election, which was seen as a critical election in this regard, blacks and Latinos voted to retain the Board by a large margin in contrast to whites who opposed it as overwhelmingly, with the outcome being its abolishment. From that point on blacks and Latinos were widely viewed throughout the city as forming a minority voting block as distinct from whites. This perception began to change in the 1970s and is clearly now a candidate for a major reassessment in light of the more recent developments discussed earlier.

Finally, even in terms of levels of voting there are important differences between blacks and Latinos. Latinos have consistently had lower registration and turnout rates than blacks in New York City: in the November 1984 Presidential election, 52 percent of voting age Latinos were registered to vote compared to 56 percent of blacks and 60 percent of whites.[46] (See table 3.) However, despite equivalent turnout rates among those registered, 70 percent for blacks as well as Latinos, a lower percentage of Latinos than blacks entering the voting booth cast a vote for President: 11 percent of Latino voters did not vote for any of the Presidential candidates (they cast what the Board of Elections terms a "blank vote"), compared to 7 percent of blacks and 5 percent of whites who did the same. A more extreme example of this problem was the 1983 New York State referendum on ten propositions. In that election, headed by a transportation bond issue question, over 44 percent of Latino voters in New York City entered the voting booth but did not cast any vote on the main proposition, compared to 30 percent of blacks and 13 percent of whites.[47]

In terms of party loyalty and voter participation trends, there are significant differences as well between blacks and Latinos. Although 80 percent of registered voters in both groups were, as already mentioned, en-

TABLE 3

*Voter Participation Rates by Racial-Ethnic Group for New York City
1982 and 1984 (in percentages)*

	LATINOS		BLACKS		WHITES		TOTAL	
	1982	1984	1982	1984	1982	1984	1982	1984
Registration Rate[a]	35.1	51.8	39.4	56.1	48.7	60.2	44.7	57.8
Party Enrollment								
% Democrats	81.7	80.4	78.7	80.4	66.6	64.6	70.4	70.2
% Republicans	6.6	6.2	7.5	5.8	16.8	16.6	14.0	13.0
% Independents	9.4	11.1	10.9	11.4	12.9	15.5	12.2	14.1
% Other Parties	2.3	2.3	2.9	2.4	3.7	3.0	3.4	2.7
Gender of Those Registered								
% Men	40.2	41.0	54.4	41.0	43.9	44.3	45.6	43.3
% Female	59.8	59.0	45.6	59.0	56.1	55.7	54.4	56.7
Voter Turnout Rate[b]	63.3	69.6	64.2	70.0	71.8	81.7	69.8	77.6
Party Receiving Vote[c]								
Democrats	70.6	61.3	77.9	73.7	54.9	47.9	60.5	54.6
Republicans	14.1	22.2	10.8	13.6	31.7	40.8	26.1	33.3
Other Parties	7.0	5.9	5.2	5.9	9.7	6.5	8.8	6.3
Blank Votes	8.3	10.6	6.1	6.8	3.7	4.8	4.6	5.8

a. As percent of total voting age population for the group.
b. As percent of total registration for group.
c. Political party turnout breakdown for votes cast on particular party's line for top office on the ballot,
   not just for the candidate.
Sources: Calculated from data from the New York City Board of Elections, New York State Legislative
   Task Force on Reapportionment, and the U.S. Census Bureau.

rolled in the Democratic Party, only 61 percent of Latinos compared to
74 percent of blacks voted on that party's line for President that year. Compared to the 1982 gubernatorial elections, the increase in registration rates
was much higher among blacks and Latinos (each increased by 17 percentage points) than whites (who had an 11 percentage point increase). But
the increase in voter turnout rates was lower for Latinos (a 4 percentage
point increase) between 1982 and 1984 than for blacks (6 percentage points)
and whites (10 percentage points), offsetting gains made in registration increases in this period by minorities. During the Jesse Jackson campaign,
the differential impact of the increase in "group consciousness" on participation levels between blacks and Latinos became evident: in New York
City, Jackson's campaign and appeal for a Rainbow Coalition served to
dramatically motivate blacks to have the highest turnout rate in recent
memory in a primary held in the city, with 52 percent of registered black
Democrats turning out to vote compared to only 38–39 percent of whites
and Latinos on April 3, 1984.[48] Absent the Jackson candidacy in the gen-

eral election that year, black turnout once again fell to previous low levels, but it apparently had little or no effect on Latino voters either way.

Reasons for Black-Latino Differences

Having outlined black-Latino differences in a number of important areas, it might now be appropriate to present some reasons for them. There are at least six underlying factors that require further analysis and research:

1. Historical Differences. As already mentioned, the effects of the black experience with slavery in the United States compared to the Latino colonial experience are critical to any understanding of many of the current values and perceptions of each group. The specific black history in the U.S. has produced a set of institutions, such as an indigenous black church and national civil rights organizations, that do not have equivalents in the Latino communities in the Northeast.[49] The deep moral dilemma that the "peculiar institution" of slavery has posed for the United States historically has elicited a significant level of white support both locally and nationally that does not have a counterpart, either in depth or length of time, in the Latino community, particularly in the Northeast.[50] This has important consequences for the type of resources and political support that blacks have available in contrast to Latinos.

2. Class and Occupational Patterns. While both the black and Latino communities in New York City are overwhelmingly poor and working class, there are important differences of degree in their respective class compositions and economic locations. For example, a recent study has found that in 1982 in New York City, out of 61 professional specialties analyzed, Latinos were represented on a par with their representation in the city's labor force (18 percent) in only one, athletes, compared to 11 in which blacks had at least labor force parity (25 percent or above).[51] There are other areas, already discussed, that are also indicative of these class/occupational differences, namely the greater representation of blacks in government jobs and the role that the black church has played in the development of an important black religious professional stratum. Latinos are also located in weaker sectors of the city's economy, particularly manufacturing, to a greater extent than blacks.[52] Such differences, subtle although they may appear, have important impacts on the resources and political interests of each group.

3. National versus Local Networks. In contrast to blacks, who have developed a fairly elaborate national network of institutions and influentials that include sectors of the country's white power structure to some extent, Latinos are organized in a more local fashion. While Mexican-Americans in the Southwest come the closest among Latinos to blacks in

this regard, although on a more regional basis, Latinos in the Northeast are projected much more locally. Therefore, Latinos in New York City do not have an equivalent to a National Association for the Advancement of Colored People (NAACP), National Urban League, or national network of black churches to help "frame" their local issues and agendas in a more national context in quite the same way that blacks do.[53]

4. Residential Factors. In New York City, as has been observed elsewhere, Latinos appear to have different residential patterns than blacks, affecting how these communities organize themselves and even their degree of political representation. One feature of both black and Latino communities in New York that appears to be unique is the multiplicity of local neighborhood power structures that exist. Instead of there being one major area of the city that is predominantly black or Latino, there are many, each of which has its own history, political leadership, institutions, and specific issues and problems. Most recently in the black community, for example, there has emerged an internal power struggle for dominance between the politicians in Manhattan's Central Harlem with those of Brooklyn's Bedford-Stuyvesant neighborhoods.[54] The dynamics of these neighborhood interactions and their overall political impacts are not well understood and have generally been downplayed or ignored in the literature.

One of the most noted differences to emerge from the few existing black-Latino comparative studies is that blacks are more residentially segregated than Latinos, and the political consequences of this in terms of electoral representation and reapportionment issues.[55] In New York City, for example, of the total 60 State Assembly Districts, only three have Latinos majorities up to 54 percent, while there are seven that have black majorities over 75 percent.[56] Some have argued that Latinos are, therefore, more integrated into the city's population than blacks and point to this as an indicator of greater assimilation. However, the data and reality appear to indicate that rather than integration, what Latinos are experiencing in New York, particularly Puerto Ricans and Dominicans, is a more *detailed* residential segregation pattern than that of blacks due to a number of specific historical and political factors.[57] In other words, Latinos in New York City are highly segregated in smaller geographic areas than blacks, giving the *appearance* of greater residential integration as well as diluting their political strength in the city's relatively large political divisions.

5. Cultural Factors. There are a number of cultural factors that affect how blacks and Latinos approach New York City politics. These flow primarily from their points of origin. The much larger foreign-born segment of the Latino population brings with it views toward race, nationalism, language, the role of government, and so on that have not been

developed within a specifically U.S. context. These affect how each community defines issues, what symbols it responds to, styles of leadership, and their commitment to life and institutions in the U.S. The foreign-born factor, therefore, becomes a critical one to explore, not only in understanding black-Latino differences, but differences within each one of these two groupings.

6. Societal Responses. While most of this discussion has concentrated on the internal characteristics of these two minority communities, it is also important to examine the role of their social context in the development of these characteristics.[58] Above all, there are the economic functions that blacks and Latinos have adopted in New York City and how these have changed over time. The relationship between the economic role and status of a particular group and its political influence is striking, as is the case with Puerto Ricans who are in a widely acknowledged weak political position at a time when their role in the New York economy is at its most dubious.

Government has also responded quite differently to blacks than it has to Latinos. For example, while it appears to have played a more direct role with blacks to counter unacceptable unemployment levels by providing them with low-level public sector jobs, its response in the Latino case has primarily been the provision of welfare.[59]

CONCLUSIONS

At a certain level, it can be argued that such an emphasis on black-Latino differences belies the more important commonalities between these groups and that to compare two such poor communities in this way is a distortion of a more important reality. The problem with such an argument is that recent developments in New York City have revealed a greater potential for black-Latino political devisiveness at a point when they, together, have reached majority population status and should instead be poised to spearhead a new period in minority politics in the city. It, thus, becomes critical, from both theoretical and practical perspectives, to realistically assess those forces that underlie these tensions rather than to continue to ignore or downplay them.

What does such a black-Latino comparative analysis tell us? First of all, it highlights some of the conceptual strains in the term "minority." This points to the need for a more restrictive use of the term. Convenient as it may appear, it is analytically weak and its overgeneralized use has had the effect of inaccurately homogenizing the experiences of racial-ethnic groups, or of being a shorthand device for subsuming the situation of

Latinos and other groups under that of American blacks, no matter how inappropriate this may be.

There is a need, therefore, to get a better understanding of the "minority" category and how the groups it covers see themselves in relation to it.[60] By definition, it is a secondary identification for blacks and Latinos and in this sense points to the need for a much greater appreciation of the use of such terminology at different levels of abstraction. Historically, its meaning and salience as a form of group identification have changed and will continue to do so. The problem has been that the meaning of the term has been primarily determined by non-minorities rather than "minorities" themselves. In this conjuncture, the argument presented here is that this situation needs to be reversed.

More attention also needs to be given to the specificities of the racial-ethnic groups that fall under the minority category. Along with this is the growing need for comparative studies between these various groups.[61] This would go some way to counter the tendency to only do comparisons between minorities and whites, which do not necessarily appear to be the most important, particularly in terms of minority community mobilization issues.

These considerations not only have an academic relevance, but a very practical one as well. For those interested in mobilizing minority political power, the issues raised in this study can hopefully provide the basis for a more realistic assessment of the opportunities and problems involved in such coalition-building. Thus, although the level of abstraction chosen here has been to compare black with Latinos, it should also be clear at this point that difficult coalition-building issues exist *within* each of these communities themselves on a number of levels.[62]

This analysis opened with the observation that New York City's shift to a "majority minority" city in the 1980s indicated that minority politics will be thrust into a potentially new level of activity and importance. This, however, is not assured and is contingent on a number of factors. One is whether blacks and Latinos will be able to forge the types of coalitions that are necessary or will continue the current process of fragmentation.[63] An important aspect of this will be the nature and future direction of black and Latino political leadership in the city, which has been in a state of crisis, not only locally but nationally, for some time now.[64]

A second factor that is vital in defining the nature of minority politics in New York City is the response of dominant institutions and elites in the city and nationally. Will the continued growth of its minority population mean that white elites will seek to find ways to fairly incorporate nonwhites into the city's political system, continue to exclude them, or find more effective ways to coopt them?[65] New York, more so than many other cities, has been able to postpone confronting the issue of minority political empowerment and has found ways to displace minority demands for even symbolic representation. The reasons for this resistance and the mechanisms used need to be better understood and analyzed.[66] However, the point is that minority politics is not something that is simply defined internally, but develops within a broader context that plays a critical role in shaping it as well.

A third factor affecting the impact of minority politics in New York City is how blacks and Latinos define the issues that they will be advocating. Since the late 1970s, when in the black community nationally electoral politics was embraced as the most viable strategy to pursue by most black leaders, the notion of a "New Black Politics" began to emerge.[67] What advocates of this approach pointed to was that black electoral politics carried with it a different set of values and issues than traditional interest or ethnic group politics did. Nelson describes this new thrust by pointing out that a "central premise of this approach to black political life is the notion that genuine progress can only be made if the pursuit of community goals is placed ahead of individual goals as an organizing priority. Proponents," he continues, "of the new black politics believe very strongly that the most potent form of power available to black America is power that emanates from the collective action of the community. . . . At bottom the new black politics is a politics of social and economic transformation based on the mobilization of community power."[68]

In New York City, the prevailing policies of promoting economic growth and restructuring its economy at the expense of its poor people, who are overwhelmingly black and Latino, offer a critical test for the emergence of a "New Minority Politics" that is able to produce viable alternatives and a different political consensus in the city.[69] To only have black and Latino faces replace whites in the political system without major changes in policy, as appears to be currently occurring, would simply be a continuation of politics as usual to the detriment of black and Latino interests in New York City. In this regard, and in light of the many challenges outlined in this study, minorities in New York City find themselves at a major crossroads today.

NOTES

1. Recent examples of this problem can be found in the following: Robert W. Bailey, *The Crisis Regime: The MAC, the EFCB and the Political Impact of the New York Financial Crisis* (Albany, N.Y.: State University of New York Press, 1984); Michael N. Danielson and Jameson W. Doig, *New York: The Politics of Re-*

gional Development (Berkeley, Calif.: University of California Press, 1982); Peter W. Colby, ed., *New York State Today: Politics, Government, Public Policy* (Albany, N.Y.: State University of New York Press, 1985); Paul E. Peterson, ed., *The New Urban Reality* (Washington, DC: Brookings, 1985), especially the editor's generalizations about Latinos which clearly contradict the New York case (p. 22); and, except for Tobier's contribution, Charles Brecher and Raymond D. Horton, eds., *Setting Municipal Priorities: American Cities and the New York Experience* (New York: New York University Press, 1984).

2. International data taken from: *World Development Report, 1980* (Washington, DC: The World Bank, 1980), pp. 110–111.

3. Emanuel Tobier, *The Changing Face of Poverty: Trends in New York City's Population in Poverty: 1960–1990* (New York: Community Service Society, 1984), pp. 103–105.

4. Ibid. Also see: Emanuel Tobier, "Population" in Brecher and Horton, eds., *Setting Municipal Priorities*, pp. 38–42; and Peter D. Salins, "New York in the Year 2000 Revisited," *New York Affairs* 7:4 (1983).

5. Leslie W. Dunbar, ed., *Minority Report: What Has Happened to Blacks, Hispanics, American Indians and Other Minorities in the Eighties* (New York: Pantheon, 1984).

6. Tobier, *The Changing Face of Poverty*.

7. See the following articles by Douglas S. Massey: "Residential Segregation of Spanish Americans in United States Urbanized Areas," *Demography* 16:4 (November 1979): 553–563; and "A Research Note on Residential Succession: The Hispanic Case," *Social Forces* 61:3 (March 1983): 825–833.

8. See various articles in Sidney W. Mintz, ed., *Slavery, Colonialism, and Racism* (New York: W. W. Norton, 1974).

9. Compare the following two reports: *Status of Black New York Report 1984* (New York: New York Urban League, 1984); and *The First Step Toward Equality: Hispanic Population Statistics, New York State/New York City* (New York: National Puerto Rican Forum, 1979). For an excellent case study see: Richard Schaffer and Neil Smith, "The Gentrification of Harlem," paper presented to the Annual Conference of the American Association for the Advancement of Science, New York, May 24–29, 1984.

10. For examples of this see: Robert Rheingold, "Government 'Minority' Category Growing to Include More Groups," *The New York Times* (July 20, 1978), p. 1; and Thomas A. Johnson, "Term 'Minority' Shunned by Black Social Workers," *The New York Times* (April 22, 1979), p. 26.

11. Salins, "New York in the Year 2000 Revisited," p. 18.

12. David Musick, *Oppression: A Socio-History of Black-White Relations in America* (Chicago: Nelson-Hall, 1984).

13. Clara Rodriguez, "Puerto Ricans: Between Black and White," *New York Affairs* 1:4 (Summer 1974).

14. "The colored immigrant understood quickly," Ottley and Weatherby observed in 1940 about Puerto Ricans in New York City, "that most white Americans regarded anyone who spoke a foreign tongue, particularly Spanish, as being white, and therefore the immigrant called himself 'white'." Roi Ottley and Wil-

liam J. Weatherby, eds., *The Negro in New York: An Informal Social History,* *1626–1941* (New York: Praeger, 1967), p. 191.

15. Roy Simon Bryce-Laporte, "New York City and the New Caribbean Immigration: A Contextual Statement," *International Migration Review* 13:2 (Summer 1979): 214–234.

16. Frank Bonilla, "Ethnic Orbits: The Circulation of Capitals and Peoples," *Contemporary Marxism* 10 (1985): 148–167.

17. For a discussion of these "expressions of presence," see José Hernandez, "A Research Strategy for New Immigrants" in Lionel Maldonado and Joan Moore, eds., *New Immigrants and Old Minorities: The Urban Scene* (Beverly Hills, Calif.: Sage Urban Affairs Annual Review 28, forthcoming).

18. The Census Bureau found naturalization rates for 1980 of 25.5 percent for Dominicans, 24.9 percent for Colombians and 24.7 percent for Ecuadoreans compared to a 50.5 percent rate for total immigrants nationally. See United States Bureau of the Census, *Statistical Profile of the Foreign-Born Population: 1980 Census of Population* (October 1984), Table 1. These Latino groups are the largest in New York City. For discussions on the political and social implications of these low naturalization rates, see National Association of Latino Elected and Appointed Officials (NALEO), *Proceedings of the First National Conference on Citizenship in the Hispanic Community* (Washington, DC: NALEO Educational Fund, 1984).

19. Discussed in: James Jennings, *Puerto Rican Politics in New York City* (Washington DC: University Press of America, 1977), pp. 59–63. More generally, see Joan M. Nelson, *Temporary Versus permanent Cityward Migration: Causes and Consequences* (Cambridge, Mass.: MIT Center for International Studies, 1976).

20. Adalberto Lopez, "The Puerto Rican Diaspora: A Survey" in his *The Puerto Ricans: Their History, Culture, and Society* (Cambridge, Mass.: Schenkman, 1980), pp. 323–343. For an alternative view, see J. M. Blaut, "Are Puerto Ricans A National Minority?" *Monthly Review* 29:1 (May 1977): 35–55; and Edna Acosta-Belen. "The Literature of the Puerto Rican National Minority in the United States," *The Bilingual Review* V:1–2 (January-August 1978): 107–116.

21. Eugenia Georges, "New Immigrants and the Political Process: Dominicans in New York" (Occasional Paper 45: Center for Latin American and Caribbean Studies, New York University, April 1984); and Philip M. Kayal, "The Dominicans in N.Y.," *Migration Today,* 2 Parts (June 1978): 16–23 and (October 1978): 10–15.

22. In the black case see: Marguerite Ross Barnett, "The Congressional Black Caucus: Illusions and Realities of Power" in Michael B. Preston, Lenneal J. Henderson, Jr. and Paul Puryear, eds., *The New Black Politics: The Search for Political Power* (New York: Longman, 1982), pp. 48–53 for a recent, but brief, critique of the immigrant analogy; Robert Blauner, *Racial Oppression in America* (New York: Harper & Row, 1972), pp. 53–81; Stanley Lieberson, *A Piece of the Pie: Blacks and White Immigrants Since 1880* (Berkeley, Calif.: University of California Press, 1980); and Steven P. Erie, "The Two Faces of Irish Power: Lessons for Blacks," paper presented at the Annual Meeting of the American Political Science Association, New York, August 31–September 3, 1978.

23. Barnett, "The Congressional Black Caucus," p. 48.

24. Rufus Browning, Dale Rogers Marshall, and David H. Tabb, *Protest Is Not Enough: The Struggle of Blacks and Hispanics for Equality in Urban Politics* (Berkeley, Calif.: University of California Press, 1984), p. 244.

25. Barnett, "The Congressional Black Caucus."

26. Jennings, *Puerto Rican Politics,* pp. 44–53, in contrast to Joseph P. Fitzpatrick and Lourdes Travieso Parker, "Hispanic-Americans in the Eastern United States," *The Annals of the American Academy of Political and Social Science* 451 (March 1981): 98–110; and Nathan Glazer and Daniel P. Moynihan, *Beyond the Melting Pot: The Negroes, Puerto Ricans, Jews, Italians, and Irish of New York City* (Cambridge, Mass.: MIT Press, 1971), pp. lxix–lxx.

27. "Opinion Roundup," *Public Opinion* (June/July 1982), p. 34.

28. For a general discussion of this problem, see Manuel del Valle, Ruben Franco, and Camille Rodriguez Garcia, "Law and Bilingual Education: An Examination of the Litigation Strategy" in Raymond V. Padilla, ed., *Ethnoperspectives in Bilingual Education Research: Bilingual Education and Public Policy in the United States* (Ypsilanti, Mich.: Eastern Michigan University, 1979), pp. 73–76.

29. Susan Huelsebusch Buchanon, "Language and Ethnicity: Haitians in New York City," *International Migration Review* 13:2 (Summer 1979): 298–313.

30. See special issue on "The New Immigration" of *Society* (September/October 1977); Glazer and Moynihan, *Beyond the Melting Pot,* pp. 108–110; Joan Moore and Harry Pachon, *Hispanics in the United States* (Englewood Cliffs, N.J.: Prentice-Hall, 1985), esp. chaps. 8–10; and, on a more general level, Colin Greer, "The Ethnic Question" in Sohnya Sayres et al., eds., *The 60s Without Apology* (Minneapolis: University of Minnesota Press, 1984), pp. 119–136.

31. Discussed in: Colin Greer and Josh DeWind, "A Labor-Oriented Perspective on Immigration Policy" in Alan Gartner, Colin Greer, and Frank Reissman, eds., *Beyond Reagan: Alternatives for the '80s* (New York: Harper & Row, 1984), pp. 193–208; and George Borjas and Marta Tienda, eds., *Hispanics in the U.S. Economy* (Orlando, Fla.: Academic Press, 1985).

32. "Blacks: Resentment Tinged with Envy," *Time* (July 8, 1985), pp. 56–57.

33. George Hallett, "Tables: Percentage of Elected Officials in New York City That Are Black or Hispanic (1985)" (New York: Citizens Union Foundation, 1985).

34. "New York City Full-Time Work Force Statistics as Reported in the EEO-4 Report on Fiscal Year-End Payroll for June 1983" and "Summary of Top 135 Executive Positions in Mayoral Agencies," both cited in: Segundo Mercado Llorens, "Interview: Koch on Hispanic Issues," *U.S. Hispanic Affairs* (August/September 1984): 39.

35. William G. Blair, "Study Says Hispanic Workers Don't Get Enough State Jobs," *The New York Times* (October 31, 1982); Wayne Barrett, "Cuomo Rigs Race Record," *The Village Voice* (March 27, 1984); and Josh Barbanel, "Figure on State's Hispanic Hirings Disputed," *The New York Times* (May 6, 1984).

36. David A. Grossman and Geraldine Smolka, *New York City's Poverty Budget: An Analysis of the Public and Private Expenditures Intended to Benefit the City's Low Income Population in Fiscal 1983* (New York: Community Service Society, 1984), p. 48.

37. *The Puerto Rican and Latino Vote in the 1984 NYS Democratic Presidential Primary* (New York: Institute for Puerto Rican Policy, 1984), p. 2.

38. Ibid.

39. Calculated from data from the New York City Board of Elections, New York State Legislative Task Force on Reapportionment, and the U.S. Bureau of the Census.

40. Arthur Browne, Dan Collins, and Michael Goodwin, *I, Koch: A Decidedly Unauthorized Biography of the Mayor of New York City, Edward I. Koch* (New York: Dodd, Mead, 1985), esp. chap. 13.

41. *The 1985 Mayoral Race and the Puerto Rican-Latino Community in New York City: A Challenge to Current Discussions* (New York: Institute for Puerto Rican Policy, 1984).

42. New York Times/WCBS-TV, "New York City Race Relations Survey" (April 27–May 3, 1985), Ques. 2.

43. These are preliminary estimates calculated from 99 percent counts of returns reported in newspapers.

44. Utrice C. Leid, "Mayoral Race '85: The Big Surprise," *The City Sun* (February 13–19, 1985), p. 1ff; and Jeffrey Schmalz, "Endorsement of Farrell Splits Minority Caucus," *The New York Times* (February 18, 1985), p. 81.

45. Edward T. Rogowske, Louis H. Gold, and David W. Abbott, "Police: The Civilian Review Board Controversy" in Jewell Bellush and Stephen M. David, eds., *Race and Politics in New York City: Five Studies in Policy-Making* (New York: Praeger, 1971), pp. 59–97.

46. See note 32. Asians, it appears, have an even lower voter registration rate than Latinos: in Manhattan's Chinatown, for example, the estimated registration rate was only 16 percent among its voting age population. In this estimate and those of other groups, no attempt has been made to factor in the ineligibility factor of noncitizenship, since the Census undercount combined with the uncertainty of estimates on the number of undocumented persons are difficult, if not impossible, to reasonably control for.

47. See note 32.

48. *The Puerto Rican and Latino Vote in the 1984 Democratic Presidential Primary.*

49. Lynn Walker, *Civil Rights, Social Justice, and Black America* (Working Paper 433: The Ford Foundation, New York, N.Y., 1984).

50. Robert L. Allen, with Pamela P. Allen, *Reluctant Reformers: Racism and Social Reform Movements in the United States* (Garden City, N.Y.: Anchor, 1975).

51. Walter W. Stafford, *Closed Labor Markets: Underrepresentation of Blacks, Hispanics and Women in New York City's Core Industries and Jobs* (New York: Community Service Society, 1985), Table 1E.

52. Ibid. Also see Borjas and Tienda, eds., *Hispanics in the U.S. Economy*, esp. chaps. 10 and 11.

53. There have been some efforts in recent years to address this problem in the Puerto Rican community with the establishment of organizations such as the National Puerto Rican Coalition, the National Conference of Puerto Rican

Women, the National Congress for Puerto Rican Rights, and the National Puerto Rican/Hispanic Voter Participation Project.

54. John F. Davis, "Anti-Koch Strategy: Divide and Lose," *The Village Voice* (February 19, 1985), pp. 8ff.

55. See, for example: E. J. Dionne, Jr., "Integration Lies At Heart of Dispute on Primary," *The New York Times* (September 14, 1981). Also see Terry J. Rosenberg and Robert W. Lake, "Toward a Revised Model of Residential Segregation and Succession: Puerto Ricans in New York City, 1960–70," *American Journal of Sociology* 81 (March 1976): 1142–1150; and Delbert Taebel, "Minority Representation on City Councils: The Impact of Structure on Blacks and Hispanics," *Social Science Quarterly* 59:1 (June 1978): 142–152.

56. Figures from New York State Legislative Task Force on Reapportionment.

57. See: Angelo Falcón, "Puerto Rican Political Participation: New York City and Puerto Rico" in Jorge Heine, ed., *Time for Decision: The United States and Puerto Rico* (Lanham, Md.: North-South Publishing, 1983), p. 31; Rosa Estades, *Patterns of Political Participation of Puerto Ricans in New York City* (Hato Rey: University of Puerto Rico Press, 1978), p. 82; and José Ramon Sanchez, "Some Reflections on the Housing of Puerto Rican Labor in New York City From 1950 to 1980" (Unpublished paper: SUNY College at Old Westbury, 1983).

58. A point made by John Walton and Luis M. Salces, "Structural Origins of Urban Social Movements: The Case of Latinos in Chicago," *International Journal of Urban and Regional Research* 3:2 (June 1979): 235–249.

59. Clara E. Rodriguez, "Economic Factors Affecting Puerto Ricans in New York" in History Task Force, Centro de Estudios Puertorriqueños, *Labor Migration Under Capitalism: The Puerto Rican Experience* (New York: Monthly Review Press, 1979), pp. 211–212.

60. For example, see Felix M. Padilla, *Latino Ethnic Consciousness: The Case of Mexican-Americans and Puerto Ricans in Chicago* (Notre Dame, Ind.: University of Notre Dame Press, 1985).

61. A model of this approach is the recent study of California urban politics by Browning, Marshall, and Tabb, *Protest is Not Enough*. This point is also made by John Hope Franklin and Joan W. Moore in articles in an issue on "American Indians, Blacks, Chicanos, and Puerto Ricans" of *Daedalus* 110:2 (Summer 1981): 1–12 and 275–299, respectively.

62. Douglas T. Gursk and Lloyd H. Rogler, "The Hispanics," *New York University Education Quarterly* 11:4 (Summer 1980): 20–24.

63. Angelo Falcón, "Puerto Rican and Black Electoral Politics in NYC in the 'Decade of the Hispanic'," *Newsletter: Centro de Estudios Puertorriqueños/ Hunter College* (June 1985), pp. 8ff.

64. Sam Roberts, "Residents Are Hard Pressed to Name Leaders: City's Minority Politicians Face a Recognition Problem," *The New York Times* (May 19, 1985), p. 6E.

65. Martin Shefter, *Political Crisis/Fiscal Crisis: The Collapse and Revival of New York City* (New York: Basic Books, 1985) provides an excellent historical analysis of these relationships. For a recent journalistic look at the city's power

structure, see Sam Roberts, "Who Runs New York Now?" *The New York Times Magazine,* part 2 (April 28, 1985), p. 89.

66. Useful starting points are provided in Ira Katznelson, *City Trenches: Urban Politics and the Patterning of Class in the United States* (New York: Pantheon, 1981); and Jack Newfield and Paul DuBrul, *The Abuse of Power: The Permanent Government and the Fall of New York* (New York: Viking, 1977).

67. See, for example, the following: Preston, Henderson, Jr. and Puryear, eds., *The New Black Politics;* Charles V. Hamilton, "Political Access, Minority Participation, and the New Normalcy" in Dunbar, ed., *Minority Report,* pp. 3–25; Rod Bush, ed., *The New Black Vote: Politics and Power in Four American Cities* (San Francisco: Synthesis Publications, 1984); and James Jennings and Monte Rivera, eds., *Puerto Rican Politics in Urban America* (Westport, Conn.: Greenwood Press, 1984).

68. William E. Nelson, "Cleveland: The Rise and Fall of the New Black Politics" in Preston, Henderson and Puryear, eds., *The New Black Politics,* pp. 187–188.

69. Outlines of such alternatives are provided in William K. Tabb, *The Long Default: New York City and the Urban Fiscal Crisis* (New York: Monthly Review Press, 1982); and John Mollenkopf, *The Contested City* (Princeton, N.J.: Princeton University Press, 1983).

9. Mañana Will Be Better:
Spanish-American Politics in Chicago

Luis M. Salces and Peter W. Colby

THE SPANISH-AMERICAN POPULATION of Chicago is estimated to be 450,000 to 870,000, or 15 to 28 percent of the city's residents. Yet, there are no Spanish-American ward committeemen, aldermen, or state legislators and few city employees. A 1974 *Chicago Reporter* study revealed that only 1.7 percent of full-time city employees and only 1.2 percent of city officials were Hispanics. In fact, the only elected Spanish-American officials from Chicago are Cook County Commissioner Irene Hernandez, University of Illinois Trustee Arturo Velazquez, Jr., and Circuit Court Judges David Cerda and Jose Vazquez. What accounts for the present powerlessness of Hispanics in electoral politics, and what does the future hold for this very sizable portion of Chicago's population?

NONPARTICIPATION

The primary reason for the political weakness of Spanish Americans in Chicago is that so few of them participate in elections. There are a number of reasons for this. Most Spanish Americans are very recent immigrants to the city, having arrived in the 1960s and 1970s. Like other immigrant groups in American history, they are going through the process of learning about politics and how it can benefit them. Their difficulties are compounded by a language problem and the fact that many of them are not citizens and, therefore, are not eligible to vote. Puerto Ricans are citizens by law, but a recent study indicated that about 70 percent of Mexican-Americans and Cubans in Chicago are foreign citizens. Not surprisingly,

Puerto Ricans have much higher rates of electoral participation than Mexicans or Cubans. The Hispanic population has a lower average age than either the black or white population of Chicago, which means that fewer Spanish Americans are old enough to vote while many others fall into the young adult category, a group which tends to vote in lower numbers. Spanish Americans are less educated and work mainly in lower paying jobs. The net result is that Spanish Americans account for only about 5.1 percent of the registered voters in Chicago. Approximately 80,000 of the city's 1,400,000 registered voters are Hispanic.

Spanish Americans are not concentrated in any one part of the city. Mexican-Americans are most prominent in the Near West Side, Lower West Side (Pilsen), South Lawndale (Little Village), Brighton Park, McKinley Park, Bridgeport and New City (Back of the Yards), and South Chicago community areas. Puerto Ricans have generally settled north of the Mexican neighborhoods in West Town, Humboldt Park, Logan Square, Lincoln Park, and Lake View. Cubans live north of the Puerto Ricans in areas like Uptown, Rogers Park, and Albany Park. In sum, these three nationalities and other Central and South American peoples are scattered throughout the city.

Perhaps the most interesting feature of this residential pattern is that Spanish Americans are much more integrated with whites than are blacks. Furthermore, Mexican-Americans, Puerto Ricans, and Cubans are about equally or better integrated with whites than they are with each other.

The political geography of Spanish-American voters in Chicago shows the wide dispersion of Spanish surnamed voters. They constitute 5 percent or more of the electorate in 17 wards. In these 17 wards, there are nine wards where Spanish surnamed voters are at least 10 percent of the ward, and in these nine, there are only two wards where they number over 30 percent of the voters. Hispanics do not comprise a majority of the electorate in any ward, although their percentage of registered voters is growing rapidly in most of the nine wards where they have at least 10 percent of the voting population (see table 1).

The chief reasons why there are no wards with a majority of Spanish surnamed voters are 1) the small number of such voters and 2) their dispersed residential pattern. It should be noted, however, that ward boundaries have been altered on occasion in a manner that served to further divide the Hispanic population. For instance, Mexican-Americans residing in the 10th Ward prior to 1971 were split into the 7th, 8th and 10th wards after redistricting. At the same time, the 31st Ward western boundary was moved to include an area not yet populated by Puerto Ricans while a heavily Puerto Rican section was shifted from the 31st to the 26th Ward.

TABLE 1

Spanish Surnamed Registed Voters in Nine Leading Spanish-American Wards
(1979)

WARD	PERCENT OF WARD VOTERS	NUMBER	PERCENT INCREASE 1972–1979
31	41.8%	8,883[a]	17%
33	29.9	7,077[a]	136
26	27.5	5,495[a]	– 9
32	24.5	5,143[a]	30
22	22.4	4,492[b]	58
25	20.8	3,598[b]	40
30	17.2	4,695[a]	290
1	15.5	3,377[b]	17
7	11.8	3,121[b]	66

a. Predominantly Puerto Rican
b. Predominantly Mexican American

MOBILIZATION

To be effective in politics, organized effort is crucial. Spanish Americans face two major obstacles in their efforts to mobilize politically: their internal heterogeneity and the split focus of their organizations. What are sometimes lumped together as Spanish-American organizations are in reality separate organizations serving different national groups: Mexicans, Puerto Ricans, and Cubans. The other problem is that most groups are more concerned with service, social, and recreational needs than with forging political power. A study of 130 Spanish-American organizations sponsored by the Center for Urban Affairs at Northwestern University found that the typical organization in Chicago had been in existence for less than five years, had 48 members, was staffed by volunteers and had an annual budget of $2,500. Lack of participation and money weakens many of these groups. The combination of limited resources and division along national lines has prevented the growth of strong, citywide political organizations representing the interests of Spanish Americans.

Spanish Americans have hardly had a chance to gain anything from the regular Democratic organization in Chicago. The high centralization attained by the Democratic organization under the late Mayor Richard J. Daley not only reduced interparty competition, it also stifled the development of new political groups which might eventually challenge the party's hegemony. Under Daley, the Democratic Organization had a particularly debilitating effect on Spanish-American as well as black political activities because the organization had its greatest strength in the very wards where these minorities were the strongest. Therefore, the chances of Spanish-American candidates seeking election as independent Democrats or Republicans has been very slim. Every successful Hispanic candidate has been endorsed by the Democratic organization. In contrast, not one of the 13 Hispanics who have run for alderman as independent Democrats since 1963 has won.

The centralization attained by the Democratic party under Daley also reduced intraparty competition. Without true competition, the political clout of minorities such as Spanish Americans is limited because the small number of votes that a minority contributes rarely makes a difference in a monopolistic situation. If there were several competing political groups, a small number of votes could make the difference between winning and losing. The result is that regular Democrats often pursue the cautious strategy of registering Hispanic voters only when they are sure of their loyalty to the organization.

Recent election returns show little evidence of change (see table 2). In the nine wards with the largest concentration of Spanish-American registrants, there were only two contests in the last election for committeemen. If we look at the percentage of the vote obtained by the winning candidate, we must conclude that in only one ward was there evidence of real intraparty competition. In the 33rd Ward, Alderman Richard Mell achieved the rare distinction of defeating the incumbent committeeman, John B. Brandt. These nine wards had low turnouts, probably due

TABLE 2

*Regular Democratic Organization Strength
in Leading Spanish-American Wards*

| | | | | PERCENTAGE FOR REGULAR CANDIDATE IN MOST RECENT MAYORAL PRIMARIES | | |
| | 1976 ELECTION FOR WARD COMMITTEEMAN | | | | | |
Ward	Winner	Percent	Rank by turnout among 50 wards	Daley 1975	Bilandic 1977	Bilandic 1979
31	Nedza	100%	22	66%	70%	60%
33	Mell	60	26	58	50	54
26	Bieszczat	100	30	66	58	65
32	Rostenkowski	100	31	64	50	54
22	Stembark	100	38	63	55	51
25	Marzullo	100	44	72	70	69
30	Lechowicz	89	21	55	44	48
1	D'Arco	100	43	69	69	67
7	Bertrand	100	35	46	36	35

in large measure to low registration and low voting among the Spanish population.

Results of the last three mayoral primary elections affirm the strong support that these nine wards have given the regular organization. For instance, Michael A. Bilandic carried seven of the nine wards even while losing to Jane M. Byrne in 1979. Because Hispanics comprise only a minority of the voters in these wards, it cannot be directly inferred that they support the regular organization. Survey evidence confirms, however, that most Hispanics are Democrats and tend to vote for candidates of the regular organization. But it seems obvious that Spanish Americans have few options in seeking their political fortunes in Chicago. They can try in the nine wards where the regular Democratic organization has very strong control or in the other 41 wards in which the Spanish Americans are less than 10 percent of the voters.

The Democratic organization is in the business of winning elections, and the 50 party leaders in the wards are in the business of retaining their power. Consequently, the political mobilization of Spanish Americans will occur only if it can help achieve these goals. But the aftermath of Jane Byrne's election and her controversial first months in office make the future of the party uncertain.

If the Democratic organization becomes less centralized, there will be an increase in intraparty competition. Decentralization of the party structure should produce two related, and important, changes in Spanish-American political power in Chicago. First, it will produce an increase in Spanish-American political participation, and second, it should accelerate the incorporation of Spanish Americans into the party's decision-making structure. Decentralization may also improve the success of "independent" or "quasi-independent" Democrats, giving minorities like Spanish Americans a strong political voice.

To the extent that the organization reduces its present turmoil by reestablishing the same, or a similar, organizational structure as the one developed under Daley, the next ten years will be the same as the previous twenty. That is, the party will give ground very slowly in those areas of public policy which are important to Spanish Americans and will gradually reallocate jobs and favors to the Hispanic community as its size and loyalty to the Democratic organization grows.

As long as the party or any of its leaders do not need to turn out the Hispanic voters in large numbers in order to win, anything beyond incremental improvements for them is unlikely. And there's not much hope that other political organizations will help much. At the present moment, independent and Republican organizations are either weak or nonexistent in Chicago's wards.

FRAGMENTATION

In summary, our analysis of the political situation of Spanish Americans shows a group new to the city, lacking the numbers, the language, the citizenship status, and the educational and economic resources of other groups. It is a picture of a group fragmented along nationality lines and so dispersed that it makes up a minority in many wards rather than a majority in a few wards. Yet, the picture could change. For example, the rapid population growth of Spanish Americans makes it a larger group every day. Even if the pattern of residential dispersion continues, voter majorities could be built in wards such as the 31st and 33rd. Reapportionment after the 1980 census may speed or retard this process, depending on how ward boundaries change. As for education, evidence of rising achievements is already present. It will take time for this exceptionally youthful group, recently arrived in the city, to mature and sort out its political options, but the future looks considerably brighter than the present.

10. Mexican-Americans in City Politics: Participation, Representation, and Policy Preferences

Susan A. MacManus and Carol A. Cassel

HISPANICS ARE THE COUNTRY'S FASTEST GROWING minority. Of all Hispanic groups, Mexican-Americans, residentially concentrated in the American Southwest, are the largest (60 percent). The sheer growth in the Mexican-American population, and their coverage under the 1975 Amendment to the Voting Rights Act of 1965, mandate close attention to Mexican-American representation and political opinions. The purpose of this study is to examine these aspects of Mexican-American politics at the municipal level.

This article reports the results of a survey which explores the political attitudes of Mexican-American registered voters which relate to municipal government. We presume that previous findings that Mexican-Americans (Browning, Marshall, and Tabb 1979; Karnig and Welch 1979) and Hispanics (MacManus 1978; Taebel 1978) are underrepresented on U.S. city councils are true. This study examines *why* it is difficult to elect Mexican-Americans and makes several suggestions about how Mexican-American representation might be optimized.

In addition, we present information about policy preferences of Mexican-Americans on issues which may be addressed by local officials. Representation involves aggregation of common interests as well as election of representatives from a specific ethnic community. It is important to understand policy preferences when contemplating representation of common interests and, sometimes necessarily, choosing between districting schemes to elect Mexican-Americans and districting schemes to represent common interests through minority alliances. Aggregation of com-

From *Urban Interest* 4 (Spring 1982): 57–69. Reprinted with permission.

mon interests and election of Mexican-Americans to city offices are both means by which the Mexican-American community can gain influence in city politics.

THE SURVEY

This study reports the results of a 1980 survey of Spanish-surnamed registered voters conducted in Houston, Texas—the largest city in the Southwest.[1] The population of Houston is approximately 15 percent Mexican-American, 24 percent black, and 61 percent Anglo (and others).[2] This makes Houston ethnically representative of many cities in the Southwest which have significant minority populations of both Mexican-Americans and blacks (Lopez 1981).

For this study, 262 names were selected randomly from a complete listing of Spanish-surnamed registered voters. The sample was stratified by geographical location to ensure that the sample contained a cross-section of Houston's geographically dispersed Mexican-Americans. From the sample of 262 names, 200 telephone interviews, averaging 15 minutes each, were completed. Twenty-nine of the 262 refused to be interviewed and 33 were not home. Bilingual interviewers offered respondents the option of being interviewed in either Spanish or English. Nineteen of the 200 persons interviewed (9.5 percent) chose to be interviewed in Spanish.[3]

Data from two additional Houston surveys were used to supplement the Spanish-surnamed survey. These surveys, one of 399 and one of 647 registered voters, provided data by which to compare Houston's Mexican-American population with its black and Anglo populations.[4] Both of these surveys were conducted within the same one-year period as the Spanish-surname survey. Both were also telephone interviews of registered voters chosen in a stratified random sample. These samples were stratified geographically to obtain a representative sample of Houston's residentially concentrated black population.[5]

Self-Identity. We begin by reporting the results of a survey item which asked Spanish-surnamed respondents which ethnic label they prefer— Mexican, Mexican-American, Chicano, Latin, Hispanic, American, or other? The vast majority (81 percent) prefer Mexican-American, American, or Mexican. Only a small percentage (3.5 percent) prefer the Chicano label.[6] We therefore refer to our Spanish-surnamed respondents as Mexican-American throughout this article.

Participation. This study examines political interest as one indicator of a group's potential for political participation. Previous studies have found that Mexican-American participation is lower than participation of Anglos or blacks (Grebler, Moore, and Guzman 1970; Antunes and Gaitz 1975; and Welch 1977) even when socioeconomic status is controlled (Antunes and Gaitz 1975). Since this study is based on registered voters, unlike the studies cited above, it is uncertain whether this study will find Mexican-Americans to be less politically interested than Anglos or blacks. The fact that political interest motivates people to register as well as vote may mean that differences in the level of interest among the three ethnic communities are relatively small.

Levels of interest in politics among registered Mexican-Americans, Anglos, and blacks are compared in table 1. The data show that even among registered voters, Mexican-Americans are less interested in politics than Anglos or blacks. This is one of several factors which explain why it is more difficult for Mexican-Americans than Anglos or blacks to elect members of their community to municipal offices.

One hypothesis which could explain why interest among Mexican-American registered voters is relatively low is that a portion of Mexican-Americans rely on Spanish rather than English, and use of the Spanish language reduces one's level of political awareness. We test this hypothesis because use of the Spanish language is perhaps the major feature which distinguishes Mexican-Americans from blacks. One study (Lamare 1974) found that an important explanation for the level of political awareness among Mexican-American children is use of the Spanish or English language. English-oriented children were more politically aware than Spanish-oriented children, and children who used both English and Spanish fell between the two extremes.

TABLE 1

Level of Interest in Politics by Ethnicity

| | LEVEL OF INTEREST | | | |
ETHNIC GROUP	Very Interested	Somewhat Interested	A Little Interested	Not Interested
Mexican-American (n = 196)[1]	34%	33%	20%	13%
Black (n = 101)[2]	37	41	15	7
Anglo (n = 273)[2]	42	44	11	3

Sources:

1. Survey of 200 Spanish-surnamed registered voters in Houston, Texas, June 6–July 9, 1980.
2. Survey of 399 registered voters in Houston, Texas, September, 1979.

NOTE: Respondents were asked: "In talking with citizens, we've found that people's interest in politics and government differ a lot. Thinking about yourself, would you say you were very interested, somewhat interested, only a little interested, or not at all interested in government and politics?"

Mexican-American interest is significantly lower than black interest at the .05 level.

Spanish-oriented respondents (9.5 percent of our survey respondents) were identified as those who preferred to have the interview conducted in Spanish. These respondents were significantly less interested in politics than respondents whose interviews were conducted in English (see table 2). Data in table 2, of course, cannot prove that Spanish language orientation causes lower political interest. Other factors, such as length of residence in the United States, may affect both language orientation and level of political interest. But since most Americans rely on television and newspapers — which are overwhelmingly English — for political information, Spanish language orientation is a logical explanation for the lower politicization of Mexican-Americans compared with blacks. Language may also be a barrier to registration. Low registration is another factor which makes it more difficult to mobilize Mexican-Americans than Anglos or blacks in city politics.

Another indicator of the level of politicization of an ethnic group is the group's participation in political organizations. According to studies cited above, such group activity is low in the Mexican-American community. Some of the reasons given for their low level of organized participation are the "newness" of Mexican-American political organizations (LULAC, La Raza Unida) relative to black political organizations (NAACP, Urban League), and the lack of an ethnic-based movement with goals shared by all Mexican-Americans, such as the civil rights movement for blacks.

Since most studies of Mexican-American participation were conducted in the early 1970s, we were interested in determining whether low organizational participation rates still characterize Mexican-Americans in 1980. Awareness of, and membership in, political and social organizations among these registered voters is low. Only 9 percent of the survey respondents report they belong to a Mexican-American community organization.[7] Only

TABLE 2

Level of Interest in Politics by Language Preference

	LEVEL OF INTEREST[b]	
LANGUAGE PREFERENCE[a]	Very/Somewhat Interested	Little/Not at All Interested
Spanish (n = 18)	44%	56%
English (n = 178)	70	30

Source: Survey of 200 Spanish-surnamed registered voters in Houston, Texas, June 6–July 9, 1980.
a. Respondents were given the choice of having the interview conducted in either Spanish or English.
b. See Note, Table 1.
Significant at .02 level.

50 percent can recall the name of even one such organization (see table 3). The fact that the League of United Latin-American Citizens (LULAC), the oldest organization, is the best known suggests that the "newness" theory of Antunes and Gaitz (1975) may be correct.

Minority Alliances. Garcia and de la Garza (1977) found Mexican-Americans, like blacks, have identified strongly with the Democratic Party ever since the New Deal when the Democratic Party's economic policies were aimed at helping lower socioeconomic groups. Comparison of the party affiliations of Mexican-Americans, blacks, and Anglos in Houston shows that Mexican-Americans and blacks remain overwhelmingly Democratic (see table 3). On the basis of partisan preference, Mexican-Americans appear to be natural allies of blacks in community politics. Browning, Marshall, and Tabb state that "for minorities, alliance with liberal Democratic coalitions has been the most important vehicle for representation," even in nonpartisan municipal elections (1979:211).

Only 6 percent of Mexican-American voters express an affiliation with La Raza Unida, the Mexican-American third party. Instead, it appears that Mexican-Americans—like other Americans—have developed ties to a traditional party based on preference for Democratic Party policies and the transmission of party identification from parents to their children. Rejection of the third party alternative would seem to enhance the ability of Mexican-Americans to align themselves in liberal coalitions.

Liberal alliances are critical for Mexican-Americans because they are a population minority in almost all southwestern cities. Such alliances are

TABLE 3

Political Party Affiliation by Ethnicity

	ETHNIC GROUP		
POLITICAL PARTY	Mexican-American[a]	Black[b]	Anglo[b]
Democrat	68%	70%	32%
Independent	9	25	38
Republican	17	5	29
La Raza Unida	6	NA	NA
	100%	100%	100%
	(n = 193)	(n = 99)	(n = 263)

Sources:

a. Survey of 200 Spanish-surnamed registered voters in Houston, Texas, June 6–July 9, 1980.

b. Survey of 399 registered voters in Houston, Texas, September, 1979.

Note: Respondents were asked: "In party terms, do you generally think of yourself as a Democrat, Republican, Independent, La Raza Unida (Mexican-Americans only), or none of the above?"

also important because Mexican-Americans tend to be more geographically dispersed in local communities than blacks, making the election of Mexican-Americans to city councils more difficult, even when districting schemes are designed to encourage the election of minorities through single-member districts.[8] In addition, because of low levels of registration and large numbers of noncitizens who are included in population totals for districting purposes, Mexican-Americans are likely to remain an *electoral* minority in single-member districts where they make up a majority of the population. For example, in Houston—a city with nine single-member district seats and five at-large seats on the council—Mexican-Americans comprise 63 percent of the population of the district affirmatively gerrymandered for them but only 42 percent of the total registered voters in the district. In each of the eight other single member districts, Mexican-Americans make up between 4 and 20 percent of the total population of the district but only 3 to 7 percent of the registered voters.

Since Mexican-Americans and blacks are both overwhelmingly Democratic, it would seem natural that the two groups would form a coalition. Yet, at the local level, there may be difficulties as well as advantages in attempting to form such an alliance. Some studies (Grebler, Moore, and Guzman 1970; Ambrecht and Pachon 1974; Henry 1980) have asserted that Mexican-Americans sometimes do not favor such coalitions. Henry (1980:8) speculates that the reason may be "a very real fear on the part of many [Mexican-Americans] that black organizations and leaders are too strong to permit an equal partnership in any alliance [with Mexican-Americans]."

Data in tables 4 and 5 provide empirical evidence that Mexican-Americans do feel that blacks are stronger politically. Less than half (45 percent) of Mexican-American voters believe they have at least some political influence, whereas nearly three-fourths (72 percent) believe that the black community has at least some political influence (see table 4).

Mexican-Americans also feel that blacks are making greater political progress. They feel that blacks are more aided by affirmative action by a ratio of five to one and that blacks are "getting ahead faster" by a ratio of four to one (see table 5). These feelings of competition may make cooperation between Mexican-Americans and blacks difficult in municipal politics. The common interest both groups have in city jobs, services, and neighborhood facilities ironically often divides the two communities.

Because of the tenuousness of minority alliances, some have even suggested that single-member districting schemes may be more favorable to Mexican-Americans when Mexican-Americans are included in districts which also include Anglos rather than blacks (Garcia and de la Garza 1979; Lopez 1981). This approach is justified on the basis of both geographical

TABLE 4

Mexican-American Perceptions of their Political Influence
Relative to the Political Influence of Blacks

LEVEL OF INFLUENCE	% RATING OF INFLUENCE OF MEXICAN-AMERICANS	% RATING OF INFLUENCE OF BLACKS
A Lot of Influence	8%	31%
Some Influence	37	41
Little Influence	40	24
No Influence	15	4
	100%	100%
	(n = 191)	(n = 190)

Source: Survey of 200 Spanish-surnamed registered voters in Houston, Texas, June 6–July 9, 1980.
Note: Respondents were given the following instructions: "With regard to groups having an influence on *local* governmental decisions, I'd like to read you a list of several groups in the community and ask whether you think they have a *lot* of influence, *some* influence, only a *little* influence, or *no* influence at all in the making of government decisions. First of all . . . the black community; the Mexican-American community."

TABLE 5

Mexican-American Perceptions of Minority Group Achievement

MINORITY GROUP	GROUP RATINGS: MOST AIDED BY AFFIRMATIVE ACTION[a]	GROUP RATINGS: GETTING AHEAD FASTEST[b]
Blacks	55%	70%
Anglos	11	NA
Mexican-Americans	6	17
Women	8	NA
All Groups Aided Equally	16	10
No Groups Aided	4	3
	100%	100%
	(n = 132)	(n = 186)

Source: Survey of 200 Spanish-surnamed registered voters in Houston, Texas, June 6–July 9, 1980.
a. Respondents were given the following instruction: "One of Houston city government's programs is designed to aid minorities in gaining employment opportunities inside City Hall. The program is called Affirmative Action Program. In your opinion, which of the following minority groups has been aided *most* by this program?"
b. Respondents were asked: "Overall, which group do you think is getting ahead faster in Houston, the Mexican-Americans or the blacks?"

proximity and shared political attitudes. Lopez's study of interethnic residential segregation in the urban Southwest finds that Mexican-American residential patterns vis-à-vis blacks have become more like that of Anglos (1981:59). He asserts that "the trend in Mexican-American attitudes is away from an association with blacks and toward an alignment with Anglos" and that Anglos are much more accepting of Mexican-Americans than they are of blacks (Lopez 1981:60).

Another approach, where geographically possible, is to create districts which combine all three ethnic groups, in which Mexican-Americans are a plurality. This would make Mexican-Americans less dependent on alliances with either Anglos or blacks. Such affirmative gerrymandering might be justified by the fact that Anglos and blacks comprise pluralities of other districts.

Policy Preferences. Mexican-American voters were asked what they perceived to be the major problems facing Mexican-Americans and the community at large in the City of Houston. Major problems are listed in table 6. Schools, immigration policies, and employment are rated as the most important problems facing the Mexican-American community. These data support Garcia and de la Garza's assertion that "the issue on which there is most agreement [among Mexican-Americans] is the need for better education of [Mexican-American] children" (1977:4).

Public transportation and law enforcement are considered to be the most important problems facing the community at large. Differences between perceived concerns of the Mexican-American community and the community at large suggest that while there may be no single overwhelming political issue which mobilizes the Mexican-American community, such as the civil rights issue mobilizes blacks, there are several policy priorities (schools, immigration, employment) which make Mexican-Americans politically distinctive in local politics.

DISCUSSION

Because of their population growth and recent (since redistricting in the 1970s) recognition under the Voting Rights Act as an ethnic minority whose representation is protected by the federal government, Mexican-American political participation, representation, and policy attitudes are important aspects of municipal politics in the American Southwest. This study finds that compared to the black minority, Mexican-Americans are less likely to participate in politics and less likely to achieve representation in city governments. Since language may be a barrier to politics, it is possible that Mexican-Americans will remain less politicized than blacks for

TABLE 6

*A Comparison of Mexican-Americans' Ratings of the Major Problem
Facing their Ethnic Community and the Community-at-Large*

MEXICAN-AMERICAN COMMUNITY		COMMUNITY-AT-LARGE	
Problem Area[a]	% Rating Problem Most Important	Problem Area[b]	% Rating Problem Most Important
Public education (schools)	20%	Public transportation	26%
Immigration policies	14	Law enforcement	17
Employment	14	Maintenance of local streets	9
Lack of Mexican-American		Public education (schools)	8
unity	12	Planning and growth	
Discrimination	7	management	5
Language and cultural		Garbage	4
barriers	6	Inflation	4
Law enforcement	5	Employment	4
Lack of Mexican-Americans		Immigration	3
in city government	4	Federal programs	3
Housing	4	Pollution control	2
Quality of local officials	3	Taxes	2
Inflation	3	Discrimination	2
Garbage	2	Housing	2
Planning and growth		Lack of zoning	2
management	1	Drainage and flood control	2
Other	4	Youth	1
	99%	Other	3
(n = 162)			99%
		(n = 184)	

Source: Survey of 200 Spanish-surnamed registered voters in Houston, Texas, June 6–July 9, 1980.
a. Respondents were asked the following open-ended question: "What do you feel are the major problems facing the Mexican-American community in Houston today?"
b. Respondents were asked the following open-ended question: "What do you think are the one or two major problems facing the Houston area today that you would like to see government do something about?"

some time to come. The greater geographical dispersion of this group, and the inclusion of noncitizens in population totals used for districting purposes also make it harder for Mexican-Americans to elect members from their community, even in single-member districts.

We have several suggestions for optimizing the election of Mexican-American representatives. One, mentioned above, is the creation, where possible, of districts which are ethnically mixed, but where Mexican-Americans comprise a plurality. A second is the use of mixed rather than single-member or at-large districting schemes.[9] In mixed systems, Mexican-Americans might have a chance to obtain seats of both types—single member district seats in areas where they are geographically concentrated, and at-large seats where they can unite and coalesce with liberal allies. Further empirical research is needed to determine whether, in fact, these suggestions would maximize the election of Mexican-Americans to city councils.

Representation and influence in city politics can also be obtained by Mexican-Americans through liberal alliances. The most obvious alliance in cities with substantial Mexican-American and black populations would appear to be a Mexican-American-black coalition. Both are largely working class populations with needs for employment, government services, and better schools for their children. Yet as our study shows, Mexican-Americans and blacks also find themselves in competition for these things in city governments. Mexican-Americans, as politically the weaker of the two minorities, may prefer to maximize their influence through election of members of their ethnic community rather than through coalitions with blacks.

Whatever the case, this will be a reappearing issue in city politics in the Southwest in areas where the two minorities are significant parts of the population (especially Texas and California) and in other parts of the country which contain other Hispanic minorities and blacks. The tremendous growth in their population and their official minority status under the Voting Rights Act make Hispanic representation a topic of considerable interest.

NOTES

1. The survey instrument was designed by Susan A. MacManus but administered by a professional polling agency, Telesurveys of Texas, Houston, Texas. Richard D. Jaffe and Rosie Zamora Cope of Telesurveys of Texas compiled the list of Houston's Spanish-surnamed registered voters from the official 1979 Texas voter registration list and the U.S. Census Bureau's Hispanic surname tape. The sample used in this study was drawn from that list.

2. These figures are 1979 population estimates calculated by demographers for use by the City of Houston in drawing its council district boundaries following a vote by the citizens to adopt a mixed system of electing council members (Smolka 1979).

3. The percentage of the respondents who chose to be interviewed in Spanish (9.5 percent) is somewhat less than the percentage of monolingual Spanish-speaking respondents (15.2 percent) Garcia found in his survey of 5,404 Mexican-Americans in five southwestern states (1981:90). This is to be expected since our sample is of registered voters.

4. The University of Houston Office of Research and Development provided Susan MacManus with a limited grant-in-aid which was used to collect the data included in the survey of 399 registered voters. We thank Richard Murray and Robert Thomas for use of their survey of 647 registered voters in Harris County, Texas.

5. The 95 percent confidence interval for the sample of 200 registered Mexican-Americans is ± 8 percent. The 95 percent confidence interval of the combined sample of 599 (200 + 399 is ± 6 percent; and the 95 percent confidence interval of the combined sample of 847 (647 + 200) is ± 4 percent (Roll and Cantril 1972:78). (These figures will vary with the number and distributions of categories in survey items). Subnational surveys of individuals are usually based on sample sizes of 200–1000 (Sudman 1976:87).

6. These findings are consistent with those of Garcia (1981:90) in his study of 5,404 persons age 14 and older of Mexican origin in five southwestern states. Garcia found that when given the choice of labeling themselves as Mexican-American, Chicano, Mexican, Mexicano, or Other Spanish, Mexican-American was selected by 50.7 percent; Other Spanish by 20.7 percent; Mexican by 20.7 percent; Mexicano by 4.4 percent; and Chicano by 4.0 percent.

7. Lower Mexican-American participation in political and social organizations relative to blacks and Anglos has been documented by others as well. In their study of Houstonians' membership in voluntary associations, Antunes and Gaitz found that "blacks participate most, whites are the next most active group, and Mexican-Americans rank third" (1975:1202). In a study of the political power structure in Houston, Smyser (1977) also found that Mexican-Americans "have been . . . less powerful, less involved in politics as a rule, than have blacks." He attributes this to a lower organizational participation rate among Mexican-Americans, especially the older, business community members: "For years, Mexican-American businessmen have been less powerful, less involved in politics as a rule, than have blacks. The strength of the Mexican-American political organization rests with eager young volunteers, many of them not yet 20."

8. Sixty percent of Houston's Mexican-American registered voters live outside the district affirmatively gerrymandered for them.

9. The degree of underrepresentation of Hispanics was found to be less in mixed electoral systems (– 1.5 percent) than in a single-member district systems (– 2.6 percent) or in various at-large systems (ranging from – 2.6 percent in those with residency requirements for all seats to – 10.5 percent in at-large, non-geographically-based positional systems) (MacManus 1978:157).

REFERENCES

Ambrecht, B. C. S. and H. P. Panchon. 1974. "Ethnic mobilization in a Mexican-American community: an exploratory study of East Los Angeles, 1965–1972." Western Political Quarterly (September): 500–519.
Antunes, G. and C. M. Gaitz. 1975. "Ethnicity and participation: a study of Mexican-Americans, blacks, and whites." American Journal of Sociology 80 (March): 1192–1211.
Browning, R. P., D. R. Marshall, and D. H. Tabb. 1979. "Minorities and urban electoral change." Urban Affairs Quarterly 15 (December): 206–228.
Garcia, F. C. and R. O. de la Garza. 1977. The Chicano Political Experience: Three Perspectives. North Scituate, Mass.: Duxbury Press.

Garcia, J. A. 1981. "Yo Soy Mexicano . . . : Self-identity and sociodemographic correlates." Social Science Quarterly 62 (March): 88–98.

Grebler, L., J. W. Moore, and R. C. Guzman. 1970. The Mexican-American People. New York: The Free Press.

Henry, C. P. 1980. "Black-Chicano coalitions: possibilities and problems." Paper presented at the Annual Meeting of the Midwest Political Science Association, Chicago, April 24–26.

Karnig, K. and S. Welch. 1979. "Sex and ethnic differences in municipal representation." Social Science Quarterly 60 (December): 465–481.

Lamare, J. W. 1974. "Language, environment and political socialization of Mexican-American children," in R. Niemi (ed.) The Politics of Future Citizens. San Francisco: Jossy Bass.

Lopez, M. M. 1981. "Patterns of interethnic residential segregation in the urban Southwest, 1960 and 1970." Social Science Quarterly 62 (March): 50–63.

MacManus, S. A. 1978. "City council election procedures and minority representation: are they related?" Social Science Quarterly 59 (June): 153–161.

Roll, C. W., Jr., and A. H. Cantril. 1972. Polls: Their Use and Misuse in Politics. New York: Basic Books.

Smolka, R. G. (ed.). 1979. "Justice Department approves computer-based realignment of Houston voting districts." Election Administration Reports 9 (October 10).

Smyser, C. 1977. "Houston's power: taking a share." Houston Chronicle (June 30): 6.

Sudman, S. 1976. Applied Sampling. New York: Academic Press.

Taebel, D. 1978. "Minority representation on city councils: the impact of structure on blacks and Hispanics." Social Science Quarterly 59 (June): 142–152.

Welch, S. 1977. "Identity in the ethnic political community and political behavior." Ethnicity 4 (September): 216–225.

11. La Raza Unida Party and the Chicano Student Movement in California

Carlos Muñoz, Jr., and Mario Barrera

THE ORIGINS OF LA RAZA UNIDA PARTY

YOUTH OF MEXICAN DESCENT IN the United States were deeply affected by the politics of the times during the turbulent decade of the 1960s.[1] Those who were college and university students during that time were exposed to the civil rights movement, the farm worker struggles for unionization, and the protest movement against the war in Vietnam. They were also strongly influenced by the Black Power movement that stressed pride in black culture and black control of community institutions.

During this time Chicano student activists became involved in the organization and implementation of electoral campaigns for local candidates and in the development of new grassroots community organizations, as well as in the revitalization of traditional ones. As their level of political consciousness and militancy grew, however, they became more and more critical of the old guard Chicano political leadership and organizations. They began to perceive the need for alternative institutions and organizations and to call for a new and more radical direction of Chicano politics.

Many of the student activists who participated in community politics came to be influenced by the symbolism and teachings of Rodolfo "Corky" Gonzales, leader of Denver's Crusade for Justice. Gonzales became the leading exponent of a Chicano nationalist ideology, and in 1969 his organization hosted the first annual Chicano National Liberation Youth Conference that brought together thousands of activist youth and students from all over the country to discuss, debate and develop a plan for action for the fast rising Chicano Power movement in the United States. It was

From *Social Science Journal* 19 (April 1982): 101–119. Reprinted by permission of *Social Science Journal*.

at that conference that the concept of an independent Chicano political party was first raised.

Among the dominant themes of the Chicano Youth Liberation Conference were the necessity for community control of institutions and the creation of alternative institutions. The two major political parties had been denounced as not responding to the needs and aspirations of the Chicano community. The new political party was first launched in Texas, where it grew out of a student-based organization called MAYO (Mexican-American Youth Organization).

MAYO had been formed in San Antonio by five young Chicanos who were graduate and undergraduate students at Saint Mary's University. Among them was Jose Angel Gutierrez, who was later to initiate La Raza Unida Party in the south Texas town of Crystal City.[2] MAYO was conceived by these young activists as an organization of organizers rather than one based on mass membership. It was youth oriented, looking both on and off campus for its recruits. The MAYO organizers were critical of traditional Mexican-American organizations, such as the GI Forum, the League of Latin American Citizens (LULAC), and others. They were antiracist, in favor of Chicano cultural preservation, and radical in their rhetoric.[3] They engaged in a number of activities focused on antipoverty efforts and other social issues. In spite of some of their more radical-sounding pronouncements, they were strongly influenced by Saul Alinsky's organizing methods and his "pragmatic," anti-ideological approach.[4]

In May of 1969, a MAYO statewide meeting in Texas resulted in a decision to concentrate the organization's activities on the Winter Garden area of south Texas, an area of small agricultural communities and a heavy Mexican concentration. It was felt by the MAYO activists that working exclusively on separate local issues failed to provide the continuity and the depth of impact which they wanted to achieve, and they therefore placed the focus on *community control* of institutions.[5] The young MAYO organizers felt that the Winter Garden area would be ideal for developing a model which could serve Chicano organizers in other parts of the state and in the Southwest.

Jose Angel Guiterrez was elected as the chief "implementor" of the Winter Garden Project since he had grown up in the town of Crystal City, a community of some 10,000 people, 80 percent of them Mexican, and the self-designated "Spinach Capital of the World."[6] His efforts, and those of his wife and a few other organizers, resulted in the formation of La Raza Unida Party and the eventual takeover of the city school board and city council by party candidates.

The takeover of Crystal City stimulated interest in the concept of La Raza Unida Party in other areas. A MAYO national conference in Mission, Texas, in December of 1969 put top priority on the formation of the party, and MAYO chapters became active in the organization of party chapters throughout the state in the ensuing years. By 1971, La Raza Unida had largely supplanted MAYO as the student activist organization and focus of activities.[7] Organizational work for the party also began in other areas, particularly in Colorado and in California.

Although the greatest concentrations of Chicanos in California are in the southern part of the state, it was in the north that the first La Raza Unida chapters were formed. The Oakland-Berkeley Chapter had its first organizational meeting on November 22, 1970, a few days after the state-wide elections which had featured a campaign for governor by a Chicano running on the ticket and platform of the Peace and Freedom Party. A motion was passed at this meeting which read:

> La Raza Unida Party will not support any candidate of the Democratic or Republican Party or any individual who supports these parties.[8]

The founding document of the chapter, published soon afterwards, went on to state:

> We, the people of La Raza, have decided to reject the existing political parties of our oppressors and take it upon ourselves to form LA RAZA UNIDA PARTY which will serve as a unifying force in our struggle for self-determination.
>
> We understand that our real liberation and freedom will only come about through independent political action on our part. Independent political action, of which electoral activity is but one aspect, means involving La Raza Unida Party at all levels of struggle, in action which will serve to involve and educate our people. We recognize that self-determination can only come about through the full and total participation of La Raza in the struggle.[9]

Both the striking successes of the Texas model and the call for an independent Chicano party at the Denver Youth Conference had served as stimuli for the formation of this first California chapter. One of the organizers of the Oakland-Berkeley Chapter had served as chairman of the workshop on racism at the Denver Conference.[10] By the end of 1971, chapters of *La Raza Unida* had been formed throughout the state, at the initiative of local organizers rather than as part of a coordinated, centralized effort. The resulting organizational fragmentation was to characterize the party during its brief but intense existence.

The organizers of the California branch of the party threw themselves into a variety of political activities during 1971. Regional conferences were held in both northern and southern California in order to discuss platform and strategy and to stimulate the formation of new chapters. A major effort was launched to register voters with La Raza Unida. According to state law, a minimum of 66,334 persons would have had to register as La Raza Unida members for the party to gain official ballot status. A number of local elections were contested by candidates of La Raza Unida, although the official designation could not appear on the ballot.

The most highly publicized electoral campaigns were those of Raul Ruiz in Los Angeles. The first of these took place in the Forty-eighth State Assembly in 1971, a heavily Democratic district with some 18 percent Spanish-surnamed voters.[11] Ruiz, publisher of La Raza magazine, former student activist, and one of the original organizers of the City Terrace chapter of La Raza Unida, ran against the heavily favored Democratic candidate Richard Alatorre and the Republican Bill Brophy. The candidacy of Ruiz forced a runoff election between Alatorre and Brophy, which the latter won with 46 percent of the vote to Alatorre's 42 percent, with Ruiz polling 7 percent and a Peace and Freedom Candidate 3 percent. Since Ruiz's votes would almost surely have been Democratic votes in a normal election, La Raza Unida received wide-spread publicity for having played a "spoiler" role and demonstrating that the Democratic Party could no longer rely so confidently on Chicano voter support.[12] The second Ruiz campaign was in 1972, in the Fortieth State Assembly District in East Los Angeles. He ran against incumbent Democratic Assemblyman Alex Garcia and received 13 percent of the votes this time around, a higher percentage than he had received before, but disappointing to his supporters in that this district was more heavily Chicano and expectations had been higher.[13]

In the February 1973 issue of La Raza magazine, Raul Ruiz analyzed the election and its results in a remarkably candid commentary that pointed out some of the California party's problems and unresolved issues. In it he stated:

> No matter how we rationalized, it was a disappointment not to receive more votes — especially from the Chicano community. There was not a single precinct that actually came close to giving us a majority. As a matter of fact, Garcia established a pattern of overwhelming superiority throughout the district — this, also, unfortunately, and frankly quite surprisingly, was also true in the Chicano community.
>
> Garcia certainly was not a strong incumbent. As a matter of fact, he was probably the weakest. . . . Garcia had also established the worst record of attendance in the history of the State of California. . . . Garcia does not speak good Spanish and says little or nothing substantial in English. . . . Then why did he win and why did he win so big, especially in the barrios? Another question we have

to ask ourselves is 'If we did not win, did we actually succeed in politicizing or educating the community of their sociopolitical condition?'

Now this does not mean that we are wrong in the establishment of a new political concept and structure. But it does mean that we have a difficult road ahead. We cannot expect to do away with a political party that has been using and confusing our people for many years, for over half a century, with a few months of campaign activity. I think it presumptuous, and as a matter of fact, insulting that we should consider our people's beliefs so lightly.

The people might be wrong in their assessment of the Democratic Party but they nevertheless believe in it and support it with their votes. Our people have formed a traditional voting pattern as strong as their religious pattern. One could say that a Mexican is born a Catholic and a Democrat, neither of those institutions really serves him but he strongly defends and supports them.

It is true that winning the office for the sake of winning is not the all-consuming reason for our political existence because we believe that the political consciousness that the people receive from our contact with them is more important. This, though, cannot be employed so loosely as to imply that anything we do in our political activity in fact increases the awareness of the people politically. . . . The fact of the matter is that we not only lost but we failed to politicize the people to any meaningful depth. . . .

We failed to recognize that new registrations, whether young or old do not necessarily create a dependable block of potential votes. . . . Many will register because it's different, others because of emotionalism, others because you happen to ask them, and others because they were confused. A very small fraction registered into the party because of a definite political consciousness to create social change.

Our partido is not as our name states but rather, it is a goal that all of us should strive to attain.

La Raza Unida is still a dream.[14]

The themes that were sounded in this short article were to be heard again and again in the increasingly acrimonious debate over the proper role of La Raza Unida Party that was already beginning to take place.

The year 1972 was also important for La Raza Unida because of the statewide and national conferences that took place then. A statewide meeting was held in San Jose in April of 1972, at which a wide variety of issues were discussed. The creation of a statewide organization aimed at eliminating regional antagonisms was discussed, but it was eventually decided to remain with the existing three-part regional organization, divided into northern, central, and southern parts of California. In July of the same year, some five hundred persons gathered for a second statewide meeting in Los Angeles. Ideological tensions within the party were clearly evident, with debates taking place as to the proper amount of emphasis to place on electoral activity, and also as to whether the party would be exclusively Chicano in composition or should aim at a broader Latino and Third World constituency.[15] The second issue was resolved in favor of remaining focused on the Chicano community, but the first issue was to continue plaguing the party in the future.

In September of 1972, a climactic event took place in the history of La Raza Unida Party, not only for California but for the organization as a whole. The first national convention of the party was held in El Paso that month in order to try to create a national organization, and to determine the role of La Raza Unida in the 1972 election. Much of the activity of the convention was overshadowed, however, by the struggle for the national leadership of the party that took place between Jose Angel Gutierrez and Rodolfo "Corky" Gonzales, the leader of the party in Colorado.

The tension between the two men had surfaced during the debates on what emphasis to place on electoral activity that occurred prior to the convention. Those favoring a more radical politics tended to support Gonzales because of his emphasis on ideology as opposed to electoral activity, while those who tended to support Gutierrez did so largely because of his nonideological approach, more in line with the electoral politics orientation that had succeeded in South Texas. This debate had resulted in the early departure of the Southern California Regional Delegation from the party meeting in Los Angeles in July. It also resulted in the distribution of a position paper that, among other things, addressed the issue of the Gonzales-Gutierrez struggle in the following terms:

> We in the Southern Region are aware of the differences that exist between el Partido in Denver and the party in Texas. It is our understanding that the "Denver Perspective" is that we should strive only to develop a revolutionary vanguard party that aims to conduct "political education campaigns." The "Texas Perspective" is being interpreted by some as one holding to the view that the Partido must strive to win elections and be willing to engage in hardnosed negotiations with non-Partido politicians for purposes of ripping off valuable resources needed to organize the Partido in some areas. . . . In the final analysis the perspective of the vanguard party and that of the successful electoral party are not mutually exclusive. . . . We believe that the local situation must dictate the . . . orientation of the Partido . . . where there are small Chicano populations and no real chance of winning elections, the vanguard perspective can perhaps be the best

tool. . . . In those areas where there is a majority or near majority of Chicanos, then the effort must be made to win.[16]

On the surface the national convention was a huge success, with hundreds of delegates in attendance from throughout the Southwest and Midwest. Underneath the activity and enthusiasm, however, lurked seemingly irreconcilable divisions that were to loom larger and larger as time went on. The struggle for leadership between Gutierrez and Gonzales represented several different things at the same time. It was certainly a personal struggle between two charismatic leaders, each with a devoted following and a strong feeling for power. The contest also represented a certain amount of regionalism, with the delegates from Texas and Colorado equally desirous of having the party's leadership vested in their home states. At a more fundamental level, however, the choice between the two men reflected a divergence in ideological and strategic thinking that was becoming more evident throughout the party. "Corky" Gonzales, a dramatic figure with his all-black outfit and his coterie of ever-present bodyguards, had been moving away from the narrowly cultural Chicano nationalism of which he had originally been the high priest. His ideological statements now were interspersed with themes of internationalism and class conflict, and at least lip service to the women's movement and the struggle against sexism.

Jose Angel Gutierrez, on the other hand, remained steadfast in his orientation. He favored a focus on local issues specific to the Chicano community and argued against diffusing the thrust of the movement by emphasizing international issues. His style remained pragmatic and largely nonideological, at least in the sense of lacking a structured and broadly encompassing ideology. His appeals were still largely nationalistic, and he paid little attention to issues of class or sexual oppression.

In the contest for selection of a national chairman, Gutierrez had an advantage in that he had been the inventor of the model that others were attempting to copy elsewhere, and in the end he was selected by the convention and Gonzales was named vice-chairman. The show of unity which followed the election was only show, however, and the national organizational structure that was formed at the convention, *El Congreso de Aztlan,* failed to materialize because of the continuing personal and ideological divisions within the party.

The convention also voted to pursue a completely independent path, refusing to endorse the presidential or other candidates of either major party. Gutierrez had come to the convention prepared to espouse a strategy of supporting whichever presidential candidate offered Chicanos the better deal, and thus attempting to function as a "swing" vote. However, the sentiment for remaining independent was so much in evidence at the convention that he never actually formally proposed the idea to the delegates.

The California delegation to the national convention was divided in its loyalties. The division between Gutierrez and Gonzales was reflected within its ranks, with the San Francisco Bay Area delegates and part of the Los Angeles delegation supporting Gonzales, and southern California and the rest of the Los Angeles delegates going to Gutierrez.

The saga of La Raza Unida in California had largely played itself out by the end of 1973. The frustrations of the electoral campaigns, the ideological divisions within the party, and other factors analyzed in a later section of this article, had combined to undermine many of the state's chapters and to seriously weaken the others. The state party's newly formed Central Committee held its first meeting in October of 1973, but it came at a time when the party had already substantially declined.[17] The last significant involvement of the party came in 1973 when it initiated an attempt to incorporate municipally an unincorporated area of East Los Angeles, a predominately Chicano area. Raul Ruiz and a slate of La Raza Unida candidates led the voting for the proposed city council, but since the incorporation proposal was defeated, the campaign was in vain.

THE STUDENT ROLE IN LA RAZA UNIDA

The full extent of student participation in California's version of La Raza Unida Party has generally not been fully appreciated. It would not be an exaggeration to say that La Raza Unida in this state was largely an outgrowth of the Chicano student movement and that its internal workings were for the most part shaped by students, friends of students, and faculty.

The Los Angeles City Terrace Chapter, to which Raul Ruiz belonged, had a membership which was about 30 percent student.[18] Many of the members who were not students at the time either had been recently or were connected with colleges in some way. Raul Ruiz, their most prominent member, was a college instructor, and his campaign manager was a student.[19] The East Los Angeles Chapter, also among the most active, was formed out of an independent studies class at California State University at Los Angeles and was originally overwhelmingly student in composition.[20] Later on, more community people were to join, but the tone continued to be set by students. About half of the Oakland Chapter's members were students, and some of the other members were college instructors.[21] In Orange County the membership was about 80 percent student.[22] In the San Jose Chapter, another important chapter in a major urban area of Chicano concentration, the proportion of students was also about 80 percent.[23] The Riverside–San Bernardino Chapter was approximately 30 percent student, and the majority of its original organizers were students.[24] A heavy student representation thus characterized most La Raza Unida chapters in California with some exceptions, such as Union City and La Puente. It should be kept in mind that many of these students were not exclusively student, in the sense that some of them held part-time jobs to support themselves. Nevertheless, it was usually their connection with the campus that led them to participate in La Raza Unida.

Interviews with former activists of La Raza Unida bear out the contention that the Chicano student movement was largely working class in its origin. Respondents were virtually unanimous in characterizing most student activists in La Raza Unida as having come from working-class backgrounds, with a smaller group coming from middle-class families, usually lower middle-class. Thus, there was not a big gap between the class background of most students and the class of most of the community people to whom La Raza Unida reached out. Nevertheless, the particular status of students as students tended to separate them from the community at large in ways that will be described below in more detail.

Students were significant in La Raza Unida chapters not only in terms of their proportion of the membership, but in terms of the kinds of roles they occupied within the organization. In most of the chapters mentioned above, students dominated in the leadership roles, in part because they had more time than non-students to devote to the work of the party.[25] Students, then, were located in organizational positions that allowed them to play a directing role in *La Raza Unida* and to influence decisively the ideological orientation and the strategies and tactics of the various chapters. Students were the ones who were also involved in the work of the chapters in a relatively continuous manner. During periods of intense activity, as when a publicized political campaign was taking place, larger numbers of non-student, community people were likely to get involved. With the passing of the elections, however, their participation would decline in relation to that of students.

Students who participated in La Raza Unida were often students who had had previous political experience or who were simultaneously involved in other types of political and student organizations. A large proportion of the students had been or were involved with MEChA or other student organizations on their respective campuses. Among other organizations in which La Raza Unida student activists had participated were the United Farmworkers Union, the Brown Berets, the Junior LULACS, Parents Involvement in Community Action (East Los Angeles Chapter), CASA, various anti-war organizations, *Catolicos por La Raza, Quinto Sol* (Oakland Chapter), the Socialist Workers Party, the Community Services Organization, Community Alert Patrol (San Jose Chapter), the Angela Davis Defense Committee (San Jose Chapter), and the Communist Party. The students who had had previous political experience tended to be the stronger activists within the chapter. They also tended to be more progressive, more militant, more likely to have a global perspective, and more idealistic.

Why is it that students were so heavily represented in the formation of La Raza Unida Party in California? The answer to this question is closely tied to the existence of a strong and vigorous Chicano student movement at the time. Through their involvement in campus politics students had been in a certain sense put in motion, and the very dynamics of that motion tended to propel them beyond the confines of the campus, not only in La Raza Unida but into other organizations as well. The student movement, in other words, had served as an agent of mobilization. The urge to become involved in off-campus politics was strong in Chicano students precisely because many had ambivalent feelings about being *on* campus in the first place. Chicano students could not help but be aware that they were a small and relatively privileged group as compared to most of their friends and acquaintances from the barrio and from high school. Although they still identified strongly with the Chicano communities from which most of them came, being on campuses where they formed a small proportion of the student body and where they were usually physically removed from the barrios produced feelings of guilt and isolation. "The community" and people who were active in the community were idealized, and the feeling that Chicano students should be working in the communities was perennially expressed at MEChA meetings and in Chicano Studies classes. La Raza Unida was one avenue for realizing these objectives, and its nationalistic thrust provided an almost tailor-made vehicle for feelings of integration and solidarity with the community.

The existence of the Chicano student movement and of Chicano Studies classes also acted as conduits for ideas whose origins lay elsewhere, as in Texas and Colorado. Chicano students were more likely than nonstudents to hear of the development of La Raza Unida in those states through their participation in classes and attendance at student conferences. Gonzales and Gutierrez were frequent speakers at campuses throughout the state as part of Chicano Cultural Week, *Cinco de Mayo,* or other special festivities. The Chicano student movement and its by-products, such as Chicano Studies, also served as channels for information about other off-campus Chicano political movements.

In some cases the relationship between Chicano Studies and La Raza Unida was very direct. In both the City Terrace and the East Los Angeles chapters, for example, some students received credit for field work courses through their participation in La Raza Unida.[26] In Oakland, Chicano Studies programs at Laney and Merrit community colleges were centers of La Raza Unida activity, although students did not receive course credit for such work.[27] At San Jose, the first wave of students in La Raza Unida were from Chicano Studies classes.[28] In Orange County, a number of students received credit through a course in community organization for their organizing work in La Raza Unida Party. Through Chicano Studies, then, students were at least partially able to synthesize their academic role and their activist role.

The large proportion of students in the California version of La Raza Unida Party had important consequences for the workings of the party. Certain characteristics of students were clearly assets to the party, while others were liabilities; and most of the respondents were keenly aware of both. Typically, the evaluation of student participation in La Raza Unida tends to be ambivalent. On the positive side there is agreement that the party benefited from the energy that students were able to put into organizational work. Given that their schedules were generally more flexible than those of working people, and that they usually had few family obligations, students were able to devote more of their time to party work. They were also relatively mobile, and thus able to attend out-of-town conferences and workshops. Students had a great deal of enthusiasm, at least in the early stages, and this was important for developing a new organization. Students also had certain types of skills to contribute. They had greater writing skill than most community people, an ability helpful in drafting resolutions, publicity, and announcements. Many of them were also articulate and could function as spokespersons for the party. Often they were knowledgeable about national and international issues; their knowledge broadened the information base of chapters.

On the other side of the question, a number of disadvantages of having such heavy student representation have also been noted by respondents from the different chapters. While some students were or had recently been active in other political organizations, generally they lacked experience and in-depth knowledge of the local political system in which they tried to operate.[29] Students tended to be more rhetorical and theoretical in their statements; at times community people felt that students were talking down to them. Some were perceived as participating in La Raza Unida only for the college credit they could receive. There was also a generation gap that made it difficult for college students to communicate with older people in the community. In some chapters many of the students were not from the local communities and had difficulty establishing ties and feelings of rapport with local residents. Students were often perceived by community people as transient and somewhat unreliable. This tended to be more true for University of California students, who often came from other parts of the state, than for students at the community or state colleges. A state-

ment from a respondent who had herself been a student while active in
La Raza Unida illustrates many of these feelings:

> Students had no prior experience in a political party. They didn't know
> how one functioned or how to organize. They were very young and
> lacked maturity. We needed a mature leadership to do something with
> the energy. We spun our wheels a lot and didn't think through posi-
> tions we made as to the consequences of what we said or did. . . .
> Contradictions were never dealt with and we often took on more than
> we could handle. They were full of ideals without experience. . . .
> We needed more working people to balance us and keep us from go-
> ing off the deep end which was a tendency we had. In the long run
> it hurt us because we got a lot of students, but as soon as they dropped
> out, there went the chapter.
>
> In an abstract sense students were committed to the commu-
> nity, but they were not personally committed. They would show up
> at meetings but didn't show up to do hard work. They never related
> face-to-face with the community like going door-to-door to convince
> people to register in the partido. They had an idealized conception
> of what the community was, but never met anyone that they imag-
> ined from the community. They refused to see that the community
> wanted what most American middle class people have and want, such
> as material possessions, a car, a good education for their children,
> a vacation, enough food. They thought the community wanted some-
> thing other, such as a political philosophy. . . . They very much ideal-
> ized and romanticized the community, much like they do the *vato
> loco* today.[30]

Student participation, then, posed somewhat of a dilemma. Indispensable
to the formation of the party, students also brought with them a host of
characteristics which, if not sufficiently counterbalanced, created weaknesses within the organization.

Sexism within the party also posed a dilemma for party unity. Women
were an important component of most La Raza Unida chapters in California. In the San Jose and City Terrace chapters, for example, half or more
of the members were women. In the Oakland and Riverside–San Bernardino chapters the proportion of women was about one third, and it was
about one fourth in the East Los Angeles and Orange County chapters.
Interviews with women members of La Raza Unida indicate that important problems existed in dealing with the role of women in the party, just
as they did in the Chicano student movement as a whole. Women were
generally assigned to handle routine tasks within the organization, and in
most chapters it appears that few efforts were made to encourage women

to assume leadership positions. Men tended to dominate ideological discussion within the meetings of the chapters in a manner that many women found difficult to deal with.[31]

Women within the party began to organize as women relatively late in the life of the party after it had drastically declined. In 1975, a women's group called *La Federacion de Mujeres del Partido Raza Unida* was formed in southern California to take up the concerns of women in the party. Some of the tone of the organization can be seen in the following statement:

> La Federacion de Mujeres del Partido Raza Unida does not view the men as the enemy but the system as being the oppressor. Our struggle is not a battle of the sexes but a common struggle for the true liberation alongside the men. The purpose of the Federacion is to develop La Mujer into the leadership positions at A-1 levels of the Partido. . . . La Federacion shall not be limited to only women but shall make every effort to involve men as well as educate them to the issues and needs of La Mujer. La Raza Unida Party is opposed to the domination of one sex by another and recognizes no distinction between men and women in the common leadership. Both women and men of La Raza must provide leadership.[32]

IDEOLOGY AND STRATEGY

The model that was developed in Texas was that of a third party based on ethnic identification and cutting across class lines. The concept of "La Raza" was intended as a broad designation that could bring together those people whose origins could be traced to the blending of Indian and European peoples in Mexico and other Latin American countries. Within the Texas context "La Raza" is a common term of self-designation among the Spanish-speaking people, virtually all of whom are Mexican in origin. The concept of a party called La Raza Unida was thus in essence that of a party based on identification as a national minority, and the ideology was thus broadly nationalistic in tone. Self-determination was an important part of the concept, self-determination interpreted not as secession from the United States but as the gaining of control of existing institutions and the creation of new ones where necessary.

In California the ideological currents then flowing in the Chicano student movement blended in well with this ideological thrust. The student movement was basically nationalist in its orientation, and the idea of forming an alternative political party based on the Chicano community had broad appeal to students. In terms of ethnic identification most of the chapters of La Raza Unida in California unambiguously identified as Chicano, with the partial exception of some Bay Area chapters such as Oakland, where a broader Latino identification responded to the large numbers of persons from Central America in the area.

When it came to translating the concept of an ethnically based party into a working reality, however, some very fundamental problems were immediately uncovered. The Texas model was based on a region of the country where Chicanos were the overwhelming majority of the population and where the takeover of local political power by mobilizing the vote was a real possibility. In California, however, there are few analogous situations, particularly in the urban areas in which La Raza Unida was strongest, due in part to the concentrations of Chicano college students there. In spite of this situation, a considerable part of the energy of most party chapters went into registering people to vote under the Raza Unida party label and to campaigning for local office. A strategy based on such an approach soon encountered frustration. The drive to place La Raza Unida on the statewide ballot never came close to realization. By January of 1974, only slightly more than 20,000 registrations had taken place, with over 66,000 needed to qualify for official party status. The campaigns for statewide office also came to little, as typified in the highly publicized races of Raul Ruiz for the State Assembly. The possibility still remained that Raza Unida candidates could play the "spoiler" role and shake up the Democratic party to some degree, but this in itself was not enough to sustain interest and commitment.

Given this situation, other strategic orientations emerged within the party and led to open conflicts over strategy within chapters and at regional conferences. The major school of thought opposing the emphasis on registration and campaigns had several components. One was that the chief focus of effort should be on increasing the levels of information and awareness of political issues on the part of the Chicano population, that is, "raising the level of political consciousness." The Lincoln–Boyle Heights Chapter and the Labor Committee Chapter of La Raza Unida, both from the Los Angeles area, championed this approach.

Defenders of this position felt that the party chapters should concentrate their work on specific community issues rather than electoral campaigns and should carry on their work the year around. Campaigns, it was argued, were too diffuse and led to peaks of activity followed by extended periods of inactivity. Tactically, proponents of this view also supported the increased use of such militant and highly visible events as marches, rallies, picketings, and demonstrations. Registration drives and electoral campaigns, including that for the incorporation of East Los Angeles, were dismissed as "reformist." The true goal of La Raza political activity, it was felt, should be educational, with winning political campaigns a secondary goal, if that.

This approach also presented some important problems. One had to do with the level of resources available to the party. Carrying on political work based on community issues during the entire year called for resources which were not available to Raza Unida chapters, particularly since some of this work involved the providing of services to the underserved. Such work could be carried out on a volunteer basis for a certain period of time, but it was difficult to sustain over an extended period. Moreover, work of this nature could as well be done through existing groups that, though political in outlook, were not necessarily organized as political parties *per se.*

Behind these strategic differences lay even more fundamental divisions on basic political ideology. At one level it could be said that the ideological orientation of La Raza Unida activists was quite eclectic. The 1960s and early 1970s were periods of considerable intellectual and political ferment, and bits and pieces of various ideologies often found their way into the political debates and pronouncements within La Raza Unida and the Chicano student movements as a whole. Among the political-ideological influences cited by the respondents as having made some impact on their thinking and on that of other party activists were Franz Fanon, Malcolm X, Saul Alinsky, Cesar Chavez, "Corky" Gonzales, Fidel Castro, Huey Newton, and Karl Marx. The Black Power and anti-war movements clearly had an effect, and feminism was beginning to have its impact as well. For the most part, however, the influence of these various thinkers and movements was fragmentary and unsystematic. The most common bases of agreement among La Raza Unida activists were, on the one hand, the perception of Chicanos as an oppressed people, and, on the other, a dissatisfaction with the two traditional parties and a conviction that they had not responded to the needs of Chicanos.

Beyond those very broad bases of agreement, the most common ideological orientation by far was that of nationalism, with a heavy emphasis on cultural identification and cultural issues. It was not entirely cultural in its thrust, of course, since there was also an emphasis on the control and creation of institutions. Still, anti-assimilation and the preservation of a different cultural identity continued to lie at the heart of La Raza Unida's appeal. Some excerpts from a position paper presented at a conference by Armando Navarro, the main organizer of the Riverside–San Bernardino–Upland Chapter of La Raza Unida and a graduate student at the time, can serve to illustrate the tone of much of the California party:

La Raza Unida marks the emergence of a new way of life for Chicanos throughout the United States. Its appearance signifies a major Chicano commitment to terminating the more than a century of oppression of Mexican people in the U.S., and a full Chicano realization that to end this oppression, Chicanos must seek new concepts, new strategies, and new organization. . . .

To achieve this, La Raza Unida must become more than a political organization. It must symbolize the creation of a nation within a nation, a spiritual unification for effective action of all persons of Mexican descent in the United States. One principle dominates La Raza Unida thought—that the destiny of each Chicano is linked immutably to the destinies of every other Chicano. . . .

Unity will only be achieved by the formation of an evolutionary doctrine which is compatible with the philosophy, culture, and life style of la Raza. This doctrine will seek to synthesize the diverse perspectives of La Raza so that ultimately one dominant perspective will prevail. . . .

The evolutionary doctrine must be buttressed by nationalism. This nationalism will be predicated on the beauty and strength of the culture of La Raza. Cultural nationalism will act as a stimulus for the unification of La Raza. Cultural nationalism will be defined for the purpose of identifying the cultural values held in common by La Raza as a people . . . cultural nationalism will provide the foundation, strength, and unity which is needed in engendering La Raza Unida's evolutionary doctrine. . . .

La Raza Unida will use the culture as a common bond to bring about the unification of La Raza Cosmica.[33]

Side by side with the dominant nationalist ideology existed a more radical, Marxist-oriented ideological tendency, unevenly represented in the different chapters. The Riverside–San Bernardino–Upland Chapter had little or no Marxist influence, as was generally true of the "inland" chapters, those away from the large coastal cities. The Oakland Chapter, on the other hand, had a fairly strong left orientation, including some independent socialists and several members of the Socialist Workers Party. The San Jose Chapter had a minority of Marxists, with the students more inclined towards left ideology than the nonstudents.[34] The Labor Committee of the Los Angeles area, a chapter which was not confined to a small geographical area but which recruited from the entire Los Angeles region, was the only predominantly Marxist chapter in the state.

During the period in which La Raza Unida was most dynamic, the Marxist tendency remained relatively small, and for the most part was not openly expressed. As time went on there was more of a trend toward a Marxist analysis in some chapters, but the trend was generally resisted by other chapters. This was true, for example, in the City Terrace chapter, where by 1975 some chapter members were joining Marxist groups such as the Community Labor Party, the Socialist Workers Party, the October League, and the Communist Party USA.[35] This move to the left on the part of some Raza Unida activists heightened the ideological conflict within the party but usually resulted in the more radical members becoming dissatisfied and leaving the organization. The Labor Committee Chapter, for example, eventually left the party to form the Marxist-Leninist oriented August Twenty-ninth Movement (ATM).

Ideological debate between the more Marxist and more nationalistic party members tended to center upon several key issues. The more radical members were more often in favor of broadening the scope of the party to include non-Chicanos. At the 1972 statewide conference in Los Angeles, for example, some of the members proposed that La Raza Unida be converted into a multiracial "people's party," but this motion was rejected.[36] Marxists also argued for more attention to international issues, and particularly to antiimperialist struggles in other countries, such as Vietnam. The original platform of the Oakland chapter, one of the more progressive in the state, called for immediate withdrawal of U.S. forces from Southeast Asia, the granting of independence to Puerto Rico, and the release of political prisoners in Latin American countries.[37] Nationalists, on the other hand, wanted to maintain a narrower focus on local issues. Where a close connection could be demonstrated between an international issue and the Chicano community, however, the more internationally minded orientation was able to exert an important influence. The war in Vietnam, for example, became an important Chicano issue and the target of a major Chicano march in Los Angeles because of the high proportion of Chicanos who were being recruited into the armed forces and dying overseas. The march became known as the Chicano Moratorium Against the War and reflected a desire to remain separate from the Anglo dominated antiwar movement.

Radical members of the party also tended to favor the more consciousness-raising approach to political work and to deemphasize the winning of electoral contests. The more radical members were more inclined to drag their feet on the registration drive, which all chapters were supposed to push, and to feel that the political campaigns were "reformist" and "unrevolutionary."

The Marxist tendency added one other component which the nationalist orientation lacked. It provided a fundamental critique of American capitalism and insisted that the problems of Chicanos addressed by

Raza Unida, such as poverty, political powerlessness, racism, and cultural intolerance, were unlikely to find solutions within the existing structure of society. The nationalist tendency never tied its analysis of Chicano problems to the broad workings of the American political economy and never called for a fundamental restructuring of society. By attributing the problems of Raza to diffuse attitudes such as prejudice, the party implied that solutions to racial problems could be found within the existing framework of society. Thus it failed to challenge the presuppositions of liberal capitalist ideology at its roots and, in effect, left unchallenged the hegemony which those assumptions exercise over the minds of most members of the society, including Chicanos.

THE DECLINE OF LA RAZA UNIDA

By 1973, La Raza Unida Party was already in a state of decline. Some chapters, particularly in Los Angeles, maintained some level of activity through 1975 but were much reduced in numbers. After 1975, the few chapters which still claimed to be in existence were essentially skeleton chapters. The decline of the party in California can be traced to several powerful trends which combined in a disastrous way.

One reason for the decline clearly lay in the failure to achieve statewide ballot status, a difficult task given California's tough requirements for new parties. The party had invested a considerable proportion of its resources in the registration drive, and its failure could not help but have a profound demoralizing effect. This demoralization was compounded by the emotional letdown after the frantic activities of 1972, a presidential election year.

An even more fundamental factor in the decline of the party was the division which had taken place at the 1972 national conference in El Paso. The struggle between the backers of Jose Angel Gutierrez and "Corky" Gonzales had resulted in some very basic antagonisms within the party, and the California delegation had been split in its loyalties. That split was carried back to its home state by the delegation. When the conflict prevented the formation of the national steering and policy-making body which had been projected at the conference, the future of the party looked bleak indeed to Californians as well as others. The fact that the Gutierrez-Gonzales conflict paralleled to a substantial degree the California split between the nationalistic and the radical ideological tendencies further aggravated the situation.

The failure of the electoral campaigns which various Raza Unida chapters mounted in 1971 and 1972 also contributed to demoralization, especially for the dominant nationalistic sector of the party. The disappointing showings in most of the campaigns left that sector with no viable or even plausible strategy. The failure on the part of La Raza Unida leadership to evaluate the "Texas model" critically left the California party casting about in confusion. In order to sustain a high level of commitment and activity, some kind of return had to be produced, and the leadership was unable to suggest what it might be. The fragmentation and localism of the California party, which characterized it throughout its existence, made it impossible even to deal with the strategic question in a systematic manner at the state-wide level.

A related factor was the cooptative response of the Democratic Party leadership, some of whom had become concerned about La Raza Unida incursions into the traditionally Democratic Chicano vote. The Raul Ruiz campaigns in Los Angeles had attracted more attention, and it was no coincidence that in 1972 the Democratic Party elected five Chicanos to State Assembly seats, up from two in the previous election. This had the effect of defusing La Raza Unida's most potent appeal to Democratic voters, the lack of representation of Chicanos in high elective office.[38]

Another basic cause for the decline of La Raza Unida has been completely missed by analysts of the party. The fact, little appreciated to this day, that La Raza Unida in California was fundamentally a product of the Chicano student movement meant that its fortunes were closely tied to the campus-based movement. The overall decline of the student movement inevitably meant a decline in its off-campus extension. As students turned their attention elsewhere, the party lost its most dynamic component and entered its precipitous decline.

Finally, the possible effect of government counterintelligence activities on California's La Raza Unida Party is difficult to assess. While there exists considerable evidence of such activities with respect to the party in Texas and in Colorado, this is not true for California.[39] La Raza Unida in California, was, of course, less significant politically than in Texas, and it is reasonable to assume that it attracted a correspondingly lower level of concern among agents of the intelligence community.

The Aftermath

Raza Unida student activists who remained in college generally went on to enter professional careers, often in the public sector. Among them one finds college faculty members, high school counselors, outreach specialists and organizers for community-oriented public agencies, teachers, lawyers, health workers, counselors, and public administrators. Most of them seem to have entered careers in which they could pursue their goal of serving the community and making some social changes in at least a marginal way.

Politically, former La Raza Unida student activists have gone in several different directions. Some have remained in the Marxist organizations with which they were already affiliated, or toward which they moved while still in La Raza Unida, such as the Socialist Workers Party or CASA. Former members of the City Terrace chapter, according to two respondents, went into the August Twenty-ninth Movement, the Communist Labor Party, the October League, the Communist Party of the United States of America, and the Socialist Workers Party.[40] Some of the more disillusioned members have dropped out of the political scene altogether. The most common paths, however, have taken ex-members either back into the Democratic Party or into a variety of locally based issue-oriented organizations which carry on struggles around criminal justice, health, education, employment, immigration, and other matters of concern to Chicano communities. They provide a reservoir of experienced activists who may at some future time be attracted back into a broader, more programmatic political organization, given the right political situation and a more coherent strategy than La Raza Unida was able to provide.

On balance, the evaluation of former activists tends to be favorable towards their experience in La Raza Unida. Many feel that their participation in the party sharpened their awareness of social issues and gave them valuable political experience that they have applied in other organizations. For some it led to a broader political consciousness and a sensitivity to international issues, as well as to other issues which are not always directly connected to the Chicano community but which nevertheless have repercussions there. Friendships and personal networks were established through party work which have continued since then and which have facilitated other political work. It also led to a realization that a more thorough and in-depth analysis of racial problems and of strategies for overcoming them is needed. While not fundamentally breaking the ideological hegemony that exists in the United States, the Partido de la Raza Unida did provide for some of its members experiences that could eventually contribute to that end.

CONCLUSION

Historically, third parties in the United States have had a difficult time. The winner-take-all nature of United States elections and the cooptative skills of the two major parties have combined to make most alternative party ventures short-lived affairs. Typically, those parties which gain some following find their more appealing planks taken over by one of the major parties, and soon thereafter it is business as usual.

The California version of La Raza Unida had some additional difficulties besides these systemic ones. One was its largely student base. The advantages which students brought to the party building effort were offset by predispositions which one La Raza Unida organizer has described as "quixotic."[41] When student energies turned in other directions, the party's major support was effectively kicked out from under it.

Perhaps the major stumbling blocks in the party's path, however, were ideological in nature. The original version of La Raza Unida had been developed in Texas, where local majorities made the gaining of community control a realistic strategy. The California organizers attempted to transfer the model but were unable to adapt it to that state's very different circumstances. The failure of the electoral effort left the party floundering in confusion, and alternative strategies, such as coalition building, were never explored.

At a deeper level, it is also true that the party's ultimate goals remained vague. "Self-determination" was the organization's overall goal, but the concrete meaning of that term was never spelled out. Did self-determination mean the taking over of existing economic and social institutions, or the creation of new ones based on different principles? In the absence of an alternative vision of society, change-oriented political organizations inevitably fall back into some version of liberal ideology, and apparently La Raza Unida was no exception. The failure to develop a true alternative is surely a testament to the strength of the prevailing ideology and to the tenacious hold that its basic assumptions have on most political actors.

Despite these limitations, the experience of La Raza Unida in California was valuable in providing concrete political experience to many new activists. Significant networks developed from it, and skills gained in party work have been applied in many other contexts. La Raza Unida Party should thus be seen as part of a long tradition of Chicano political activism and resistance dating back to the mid-nineteenth century. This tradition has encompassed forms of political struggle ranging from electoral politics to union organizing to armed uprisings. Hopefully the continued study and analysis of such experiences will contribute to building political movements that can more effectively break through the limitations with which we have become so familiar, and point the way to more fundamental solutions to our seemingly intractable social problems.

NOTES

The authors gratefully acknowledge the assistance of Elena Flores in interviewing several former La Raza Unida Party members.

1. A broader view of the Chicano student movement is provided in Carlos Munoz, Jr., *Youth and Political Struggle: The Chicano Student Generation.*

2. Armando Navarro, "El Partido de La Raza Unida in Crystal City: A Peaceful Revolution," Ph.D. dissertation, University of California, Riverside, 1974, p. 19.

3. Ibid., pp. 21, 37–39.

4. Ibid., pp. 25–26.

5. Ibid., p. 202.

6. John Schockley, *Chicano Revolt in a Texas Town* (Notre Dame, Ind.: University of Notre Dame Press, 1974), p. 14.

7. Navarro, "El Partido de La Raza Unida in Crystal City: A Peaceful Revolution," p. 381.

8. *Rasca Tripas* (Oakland, Calif.: n.d.).

9. Ibid.

10. Bernardo Garcia, interview, Oakland, Calif., January, 1979.

11. Richard Santillan, "The Politics of Cultural Nationalism: El Partido de La Raza Unida in Southern California, 1969–1978," Ph.D. dissertation, Claremont Graduate School, 1978, p. 204.

12. Frank Del Olmo, "Raza Unida: Barrio Power?" *Los Angeles Times,* December 13, 1971.

13. Santillan, "The Politics of Cultural Nationalism," p. 216.

14. Raul Ruiz, "La Raza Unida Party," *La Raza,* February 1978, pp. 4–5.

15. Santillan, "The Politics of Cultural Nationalism," p. 170.

16. Carlos Munoz, Jr., "On the Status of La Raza Unida Party in Califas, Aztlan: A Position Paper," personal files of Carlos Munoz, Jr.

17. Santillan, "The Politics of Cultural Nationalism," p. 182.

18. Kathy Borunda, inverview, Los Angeles, December 1978, and Raul Ruiz, interview, Los Angeles, August 1980.

19. Borunda interview.

20. Richard Santillan and Gloria Santillan, interview, Los Angeles, December 1978.

21. Garcia interview.

22. One of the authors of this article, Carlos Munoz, Jr., was an organizer of this chapter while a faculty member at the University of California, Irvine.

23. Andy Lucero interview, San Jose, January 1979, and Elena Minor, interview, San Jose, January 1979.

24. Armando Navarro, interview, San Bernardino, December 1978.

25. This was not true, however, of the City Terrace chapter where the core leadership came from the staff of *La Raza* magazine. Ruiz interview.

26. Betty Cuevas, interview, Los Angeles, December 1978; Santillan interview; Ruiz interview.

27. Garcia interview.

28. Lucero interview.

29. Rosalio Munoz, interview, Los Angeles, December 1978.

30. Minor interview.

31. Cuevas interview.

32. Minutes of September 22, 1975 meeting, quoted in Santillan, "The Politics of Cultural Nationalism," p. 189.

33. Armando Navarro, "The Concept of La Raza Unida" paper presented at a Raza Unida Party Conference, Riverside, Calif., 1972.

34. Minor interview.

35. Borunda interview.

36. Antonio Camejo, "Activists Discuss Problems of Building a Chicano Party," *The Militant,* July 21, 1972, p. 13.

37. *Rasca Tripas.*

38. Richard Santillan, personal communication.

39. Santillan, "The Politics of Cultural Nationalism," pp. 275–276.

40. Borunda, Cuevas interviews.

41. Navarro interview.

12. Selective Determinants in Maintaining Social Movement Organizations: Three Case Studies from the Chicano Community

Avelardo Valdez

THE FOCUS OF THIS RESEARCH IS THE identification of organizational factors which facilitate or impede the maintenance and goals of social movements. The following study discusses changes within three organizations that were part of the Chicano Movement during the 1960s and early 1970s. This movement was characterized by independent political and cultural activities among Mexican-American organizations struggling to overcome subordination in American society. Although recognizing the importance that ideology, class conflict, police oppression, and other factors had on the Chicano Movement, this study narrows its focus to organizational tactics and characteristics as an explanation for the changes these groups experienced.

Social movements are collective attempts to influence societal interrelationships, structures, and institutions.[1] Movements bring together divergent groups and individuals for what is perceived by participants as a common cause. A traditional assumption about social movement organizations is their inevitable institutionalization through goal transformation, organizational maintenance, and oligarchization.[2] According to this view, informal organizations begin with relatively unstructured behavior and culminate in organizations with varying degrees of interpersonal and bureaucratic relationships which tend to accommodate themselves to the larger social system. The literature is replete with case studies that support the notion of organizational transformation of social movement.[3]

More recent views challenge conventional notions about social move-

Reprinted from *Critica* 1 (Spring 1985): 30–50. Reprinted with permission.

ment transformation on the grounds that they are incomplete.[4] According to Ash and Zald, "There are a variety of other transformational processes that take place including coalitions with other organizations, organizational disappearances, factional splits, increased rather than decreased radicalism and the like."[5] In support of this view are those who argue that the emergence of oligarchization depends upon other conditions; for example, assumption of transitoriness of an organization's members' identification with a broader social movement, ideological commitments of members and elites, level of organizational egalitarianism, and regularly sanctioned processes of mutual- and self-criticism.[6]

The Chicano Movement provided an opportunity to further explore this notion of goal transformation since it encompassed a wide variety of groups and organizations manifesting diverse organizational characteristics. Within this movement some groups had characteristics which parallel formal organizations, while others resembled loosely-knit informal groups. Their political ideologies ranged from groups based on Marxist doctrines to more liberal pluralistic groups concerned with improving public services in their neighborhoods.[7] Additionally, these organizations varied in the kind of members they attracted and the kind of commitment expected of them. The political and social milieu in which each group operated also differed: while some groups were allowed to operate freely, others were actively suppressed by political opponents.

Based on the observation of organizations and groups associated with the Chicano Movement, this research presents evidence that goal transformation is not an inevitable process for social movement organizations. Rather, goal transformation seems to be conditionally based upon organizational factors that vary among groups associated with the movement. The present paper attempts to test this assumption by addressing three topics: 1) the effect of the society's perception of the group on its organizational transformation; 2) the influence of the organization's goals in the transformational process; 3) the relationship between the group's organizational transformation, the methods used to recruit members, and the kind of commitments expected from the membership.

The following case study analysis provides a means to determine the importance of each factor independently. It will demonstrate as well the combined impact of these factors on the organization.

A Case Study of Three Chicano Social Movement Organizations

The following are case studies of three Chicano organizations: the East Los Angeles Educational Issues Coordinating Committee (EICC), La

Raza Unida Party of Crystal City (RUP), and the Latin American Union
for Civil Rights (LAUCR) of Milwaukee, Wisconsin. These three organizations represent, but do not exhaust, the diversity of groups comprising the
Chicano Movement between 1968 and 1974. Many groups and organizations appeared during this peak period in almost every area of the United
States which has a substantial Chicano population. These organizations
had divergent goal structures and addressed a number of issues pertinent
to their immediate area. They functioned, nonetheless, within the loosely
knit framework of the Chicano Movement.

After 1974 the Chicano Movement experienced a significant decrease
in movement activity. This decline may be traced to several sociopolitical
factors. One is that the Chicano Movement was not an independent entity
with centrally directed organizational goals and a cohesive nationwide structure. In fact, it was part of the general social unrest of the 1960s which
ranged from civil rights to the counter-culture and antiwar movements.
By the middle of the 1970s, the idealist activism stemming from social unrest gave way to complacency, and eventually these movements faded away.
The Chicano Movement was not immune from the shift to complacency.
Similarly, many groups important to the movement began to disappear,
including the three selected for analysis in this study. Nevertheless, between
1968 and 1974, there was a variety of transformational processes that occurred among the organizations.[8]

East Los Angeles Educational Issues Coordinating Committee[9]

The core membership of the Educational Issues Coordinating Committee (EICC) was recruited from an informal group of community activists, students, clergymen, and teachers dissatisfied with the public education system in East Los Angeles during the winter of 1967–68. Previous
efforts at reform which had been mounted by independent groups of Chicano professionals, educators, and sympathetic Anglos had met with failure.

These failures, along with growing student discontent in the schools
and increasing political consciousness among Chicanos, contributed to the
formation of an *ad hoc* committee to address the issue of educational reform. It proved to be a precursor of the EICC. Two East Los Angelenos
express the sentiment of the Chicano community at that time:

> In 1967–68 there were rumblings in East Los Angeles. People were
> becoming aware of the fact that we were getting the short end of the
> stick. We, as Chicanos, were being oppressed. There was a time when
> you could see the news every day on blacks burning down ghettos,
> and it got people to thinking "We're living under the same condi-
> tions; we're going to have to initiate some type of change."[10]

After several weeks of meetings, the *ad hoc* committee presented a series of demands to the Los Angeles Board of Education. Included in the demands were improved school lunches, flexible standards of dress, together with substantive issues such as curriculum modifications.

In the spring of 1968 the Board of Education refused to meet with the group or to even consider their demands. They decided on a high school walk-out as the best way to dramatize the poor educational conditions existing in the East Los Angeles schools. In this way, the *ad hoc* committee hoped to compel the school board to negotiate. The activist tactic of a school walk-out depended on the assistance of various Chicano student groups, including the United Mexican-American Students (UMAS).[11] As the situation became increasingly tense in the East Los Angeles high schools in March of 1968, the students walked out on their own, independently of the *ad hoc* group.

It was shortly thereafter that the *ad hoc* group evolved into the EICC. Participation in the EICC was open to all "reasonable" persons interested in creating a program of selective changes in the school system necessary to meet the needs of Mexican-Americans.[12] The first organizational meeting produced the following statement of purpose:

> The purpose of the EICC is to invite all responsible opinions, including students, parents, community groups, etc., in an assertion of human dignity to create a program of suggestive changes in the school system that will enable the educational establishment to more adequately, justly, and efficiently meet the needs of the Mexican-American population.[13]

The philosophical basis for the EICC was not much different from that of previously existing Mexican-American political organizations. The main differences lay in the use of confrontational tactics as a means to accomplish essentially similar goals. Further, the EICC appealed to a nationalistic sentiment in the community by using ethnic slogans and symbols. Many of the more moderate members of the EICC advocated softening the group's radical image. They suggested the goals of EICC could be better achieved through cooperation and mediation with institutional representatives. However, there were others who viewed cooperation and mediation as cooptation and advocated even more confrontational activities and strategies. In the end, this small minority of radicals within the group was isolated from decision-making circles and eventually left the committee altogether.[14]

In the months that followed, those members who remained active in the EICC gradually transformed the organization into a formal extension of the Los Angeles Board of Education — the Mexican-American Education Commission. Within two years, it lost all of its Chicano Movement goals and became tangled in the bureaucracy of the Board of Education.

La Raza Unida Party of Crystal City[15]

La Raza Unida Party (RUP) was an organized expression of a growing political consciousness among Chicanos in south Texas during the late 1960s. The forerunner of the RUP was the Mexican-American Youth Organization (MAYO) which was one of the first politically active Chicano groups during this period to address itself to self-determination. Jose Angel Gutierrez, a leader in the MAYO organization, returned to his hometown, Crystal City, in the summer of 1969 to organize La Raza Unida.[16] This case study is restricted to the organizational development of La Raza Unida and its transformation in Crystal City.

During the 1968–1969 school year, Chicano students, parents, and school officials clashed over a list of demands and grievances growing out of school policies which many thought were discriminatory. Gutierrez and his followers began to focus these organizational efforts around school-related issues. Working primarily with students, organizers were successful in persuading them that the most crucial factor in organizing and developing strategy was the involvement of their families. They expressed the political significance of family participation in the following:

> You know civil rights are not just for those under twenty-one. They're for everybody—for grandma, for daddy and mamma, and los chamaquitos and primos and sisters and so on. We've all got to pitch in . . . You see the familia Mexicana está organizada.[17]

Throughout the fall of 1969, the Crystal City Board of Education continued refusing to recognize the grievances and demands of Chicano students. In response, the students began to boycott classes in December of 1969. The weekend following the start of the boycott, the first of a number of rallies was held in the city park. Local boycott leaders and prominent Mexican-American politicians from other areas of Texas spoke at these rallies.

The boycott served to polarize relations between Chicano and Anglo residents in this small south Texas town. Polarization had always been a tacit part of life in Crystal City; however, the school boycott brought it to the surface and Chicano leadership exploited the situation. Further, there was an appeal to a strong cultural identity and nationalism. This became an integral part of the overall strategy to overcome imbedded feelings of powerlessness and inferiority in the Chicano community. As the school walk-out proved successful and was followed by other successful political actions, the strategy seemed to be a correct one.

After the boycott, the Chicano organizers launched a massive voter registration which led to the formation of La Raza Unida Party as an organization concerned with more than educational issues. In the spring election of 1970, Raza Unida candidates appeared on the ballot for the Board of Education and the City Council in Crystal City, as well as other towns in Zavala County. The election was a bitter one, however; Raza Unida received 55 percent of the votes cast. This was principally due to the support base established during the school walk-out. Chicano candidates nominated by the party won three seats on the Board of Education, thereby constituting a controlling majority.[18] Two Chicanos were elected to the City Council of Crystal City. In 1974 Jose Angel Gutierrez was elected County Judge, thus solidifying La Raza Unida's control of Zavala County.

The success of the party in Crystal City led to its expansion into a statewide organization and to chapters in far western and midwestern states.[19] It was in Texas, however, that the organization had its greatest successes, culminating in a gubernatorial campaign where the Raza Unida candidate received 100,000 votes in 1974.[20] It is important to note that Raza Unida victories were concentrated in south Texas where Chicanos are numerically stronger and where they have not had significant political or social organization. The decline of the party began in 1974; but until that year it functioned as a sophisticated movement organization with the same goals set in 1969.[21]

The Latin American Union for Civil Rights[22]

The Chicano and Puerto Rican communities of Milwaukee were spurred to collective activism in 1968 by the discriminatory hiring practices of a local electrical components manufacturer. The company was located adjacent to the largest Chicano and Puerto Rican residential area in Milwaukee, yet it hired only a minimal number of minority employees. Through the efforts of an Anglo priest who was the director of a Catholic social service agency in this Hispanic area, Chicanos and Puerto Ricans met to discuss the issue.

The Chicanos attending these preliminary sessions were not representatives of already established organizations usually associated with advocating Mexican-American interests. These traditional groups primarily served cultural and social functions and seldom involved themselves in political issues outside of established power structures. The Chicanos who met were, however, a new breed of political leaders including returning Vietnam veterans, college students, ex-gang leaders, and new arrivals from south Texas.

The influence of the New Left and the black protest movement was clear; and these Chicanos did not believe accommodation to already existing conditions was the only alternative for change in their community.

In an effort to involve a larger part of the Hispanic community, these persons held public hearings, which became scenes of angry confrontation between the organizers and more conservative Mexican-Americans. The recognized leaders of traditional groups, e.g., Catholic priests, mutual aid society officers, Democratic Party ward leaders, and community businessmen, avoided the controversial hearings.

The organization that resulted from this initial coalition was the Latin American Union for Civil Rights (LAUCR). During its early development, the LAUCR pursued two objectives: controlling community social service agencies and implementing changes in city and county institutions. The former were means for increasing community participation in the LAUCR and resources. According to LAUCR leaders, administrators and staff workers in these agencies, through contact with clients, would be able, theoretically, to bring a political consciousness to the Chicano community. The second objective was more of a problem as it frequently involved tactics of direct confrontation with city and county institutions, such as the welfare department, food stamps office, or public schools. Media coverage of these tactics of protest and disruption aroused considerable interest in the Chicano community, particularly when the LAUCR director was arrested during a welfare demonstration. The benefits from these tactics were marginal as a rule when compared against the ends they were intended to effect. Failure to meet the primary objectives tended to erode interest throughout the community and the support base of the organization diminished.

A few years later, the LAUCR emphasis continued to advocate changes in social service agencies and institutions; however, its tactics were now less confrontational. Incrementalism became the primary goal, and the original goals of the organization became secondary. The leadership remained the same, but membership fluctuated and organizational maintenance soon became the most important preoccupation. In 1970 the LAUCR began accepting funds from government social services, on which it relied more during the next few years. Eventually it was forced to concentrate on implementing goals dictated by the funding source.[23]

ANALYSIS OF DATA

In this section, each topic area is tested against the data from the three organizations case study. In this way, the transformational processes of social movement organizations may be clarified.

Perception of Social Movement Organization by Society

The topic discussed here considers how perceptions by the wider society toward a social movement group influences its organizational transformation. The perception then dictates attitudes, actions, and responses to the movement group which has a significant effect on its longevity. Conventional wisdom on social movement suggests that organizations perceived negatively tend to exist for a shorter duration than those perceived in a more positive light. This is supported by Gillespie's[24] study on tenant unions where conservative tactics were implemented to gain wider public support and subsequent longevity. The type of reaction engendered is based upon the threat the group poses to the power structure, or the extent to which the group's values diverge from those of the larger society. This response is based on a perceived threat rather than an actual one. Alternatively, there are others who take the position that negative perceptions might create greater cohesion among groups, thus prolong its longevity.[25]

Chicanos in Crystal City, Texas, comprised 19 percent of the population in 1969.[26] Socioeconomic and political inequalities between Chicanos and Anglos had historically polarized the two communities.[27] In 1969, when the school boycott was organized, Anglos recognized its significance, but miscalculated the profound and widespread effect it would have. The largely Anglo power structure assumed that this group of Chicano dissidents, much as those before them, could be easily manipulated. This assumption flowed from a previous experience when the Chicano community elected a majority of Chicanos to the City Council in 1962. This fortuitous event in Chicano political history ended in the manipulation and cooptation of Chicano leadership by Anglos in 1968.[28] The Chicano leaders of 1969 were not ignorant of this history and were determined to avoid the same mistakes and conditions that led to a return of power to the Anglo political structure.

The Anglo reaction to the initial social protest in Crystal City was a negative one. The polarization between the two communities became more rigid as Chicano leaders deliberately used Mexican nationalistic symbols and anti-Anglo rhetoric. Chicano leaders also discouraged compromise with the Anglo community even when neutral Anglo arbitrators were proposed for negotiations. This added to the hostility between the groups. According to La Raza Unida organizers, "polarization was a deliberate method of organizing means to avoid the mistakes of 1962, when Chicanos eventually compromised away their organizational goals."[29] This strategy may have contributed to La Raza Unida successfully maintaining its organization over a six-year period, despite a generally hostile social environment in Crystal City. Data from this case indicate that negative perception alone is not always sufficient to effect organizational transformation. In the case of La Raza Unida, the negative perception was actually cultivated as an organizational goal and it served an important function as a factor in organizational maintenance. Thus, it may be said that the perception, in this case negative, contributed to the longevity of the movement organization by the fact that it became a rallying point for its membership.

The Anglo power structure of Los Angeles perceived the Educational Issues Coordinating Committee as a threat to their social and political stability, principally because of EICC's potentially widespread support base. The school walk-outs initially affected four high schools in East Los Angeles and later spread to several other high schools with significant Chicano student bodies throughout Los Angeles.

Appearing even more threatening to the power structure was the support EICC received from traditional Mexican-American political organizations in southern California. In estimating the potential support for EICC, one would calculate and include a majority of the estimated one million Spanish-surnamed residents who comprise almost 20 percent of the county population.[30] As the student walk-out and EICC gathered support and gained momentum as a social organization, the negative perception by the larger society was manifested in the application of legal force and in attempts at cooptation. Legal force was first applied when the Los Angeles Grand Jury identified and arrested thirteen persons as "conspirators" for their participation in the school walk-outs. This Grand Jury action was followed by other arrests and the harassment of EICC leaders and supporters. The result of this legal force was a schism within the EICC between those who supported more militant tactics in the defense of arrested individuals and those who advocated more moderate means to effect the same end.

Moderate EICC members gained control of the organization. Not wishing further confrontation with the police or the courts, the now controlling group changed its goals and transformed the organization into a formal extension of the Los Angeles Board of Education. This transformation took place after more radical members were isolated from the EICC and police tactics intimidated others from participation. In this case, negative perceptions by the power structure produced such hostility that the movement organization was forced to transform itself.

In 1968 the Spanish-surnamed population of Milwaukee comprised only 5 percent of the total SMSA.[31] The relatively small size of this population and the close physical proximity to other ethnic groups lessened the perceived possibility of any group arising from the community to pose a serious threat to the social and political stability of Milwaukee. As became evident during the LAUCR's initial organizational meetings, there was only a small percentage of support within the Chicano community. The political machine governing Milwaukee had long before established means of accommodating the small Mexican-American and Puerto Rican communities. The machine depended largely on the manipulation of their civic, religious, and business organizations.[32] When it became evident that the black and Chicano coalition was a temporary relationship, the power structure became only minimally interested in the activities of the LAUCR. The organizational changes which the LAUCR subsequently experienced were the results of internal factors rather than those related to the wider societies reactions.

The data gleaned from the three sample cases in this study are not sufficiently conclusive to either validate or reject the traditional notion that a negative perception by society necessarily inhibits organizational maintenance. The cases of La Raza Unida Party and the Educational Issue Coordinating Committee are instructive. Both groups were negatively perceived by the power structures in their respective communities. In the former, however, the negative response was instrumental as an organizing factor which contributed to the maintenance of La Raza Unida.[33] A similar response to EICC acted to destroy it as a movement organization.[34] The instance of the Latin American Union for Civil Rights (LAUCR) is one whose organization is perceived neutrally by the larger society. Since the LAUCR was not perceived as a threat and there was little response to it (except a benign attitude on the part of the power structure), it soon ceased to function as a movement organization. Therefore, negative perceptions did not contribute to the demise of these three movement organizations in the significant way that most theorists have predicted. This data suggests that a movement organization's reaction to the response of the dominant society is more important in considering the kind and degree of organizational transformation. In each instance, the movement organization's reaction proved to be an important determinant in the direction of the transformation.

Social Movement Goals and Organizational Longevity

The nature of a social movement's goals determine the potential conflict between it and the larger society. Social theorists argue that value-oriented social movements have greater negative impact than norm-oriented social movements.[35] The latter are predicated upon issues arising within a common consensual framework and are less controversial. Value-oriented social movements tend to generate greater hostility because the issues they confront are usually more difficult to resolve than those posed by norm-oriented movements. As mentioned previously, traditional theory on social movements forecasts that as the organization experiences increased hostility, it becomes more susceptible to organizational transformation in the form of oligarchization, goal displacement, and organizational mainte- nance. The extent of the hostility between the social movement and the larger society is predicated on the group's goals.

La Raza Unida Party was a value-oriented social movement commit- tee with goals designed to change the fundamental social, economic, and political relations between Chicanos and Anglos in south Texas. Beyond being value oriented, La Raza Unida leadership developed a multi-goal strategy. Once the issues which precipitated the initial confrontation that brought La Raza Unida to the fore were resolved, the party immediately moved to the school board and city council elections. Simultaneously, La Raza Unida began organizing efforts in the remainder of Zavala County and in south Texas. La Raza Unida achieved a series of relatively major accomplishments on behalf of Chicanos in the late 1960s and early 1970s which contributed to Chicanos experiencing a sense of self-worth and a renewed ethnic pride.

The Milwaukee and Los Angeles organizations with goals predicated upon specific material issues fell short of their stated objectives. As a re- sult, both organizations could not avoid the problems of organizational transformation and goal displacement. The initial goal of the LAUCR was the reversal of discriminatory hiring practices in a local electrical assembly plant. The goal was never achieved as a tangible victory. In an effort to maintain the organization, there was a transformation of goals. The result was a community-based organization relegating social change to a second- ary function and elevating to a primary function the delivery of social ser- vices to community residents.

The EICC goals are centered upon instituting educational reforms in predominantly Chicano high schools. To dramatize the goals, there was a spontaneous walk-out involving hundreds of Chicano students from sev- eral schools. Although the goal was educational reform, the power struc- ture perceived the EICC as a threat to its social control and stability. The EICC, however, perceived itself as a normative organization whose efforts were concentrated in changing educational policy within the framework of existing institutions. When the EICC was unable to achieve a tangible victory through protest and confrontation, it shifted its tactics to the poli- tics of accommodation, eliminating much of its social movement orienta- tion. This shift led to its incorporation as an extension of the Los Angeles Public School Administration. The potential support base remained un- changed, but the organization became more interested in maintaining it- self as a vehicle of reform.

Organizational goals appear to be significant variables in predicting organizational transformation. The case studies indicate that groups with value-oriented goals are more likely to survive than those with norm-oriented goals. That is to say, had the EICC and LAUCR been successful in achieving the goals they had for themselves, it would not have necessarily followed that they could have continued as social movement organizations due to their norm-oriented goals.

In Milwaukee, for example, a successful venture would have meant eliminating discriminatory hiring practices in a local assembly plant. In Los Angeles, it would have meant a reasonable improvement in the educational system for the Chicano community. In both instances, success in accomplishing the norm-oriented goals would have eliminated the reason for their existence. One might speculate that there was little likelihood of their survival as social movement organizations. Both challenging groups would have experienced what Gamson describes as "acceptance and new advantage"—therefore, having no real purpose to exist.[36]

In contrast, the La Raza Unida in Crystal City developed a strategy based on goals which encompassed a broad range of values. A concomitant of establishing the group as a viable third party within the political structure of Texas was the value-oriented goal of making Chicanos break away from a tradition of Anglo domination. The immediate political control of Crystal City and Zavala County was only the initial stage of the process. The organization survived despite a negative perception and outright hostility to it because the strategy which spurred the membership produced a sense of goal accomplishment. Whether the goals were actually achieved or whether they were in fact modest gains was secondary to the perception within the party of its own success. This sense of accomplishment, then, provided an "ideal perfect stable organization" during the period 1968 to 1974.[37]

Incentives Used to Recruit Members
and Kinds of Commitments Expected of Members

Organization transformation and goal maintenance are closely related to the kinds of incentives provided in recruiting members.[38] Equally as important to the longevity of a social movement group is the level of commitment required of its membership. Membership contributes significantly to a movement organization's goals, stability, or instability. In view of these factors, the incentive system used to recruit members might explain the type of membership a particular group attracts and may help determine the organization's response to both internal and external pressures.

La Raza Unida was an exclusive organization whose membership was generally restricted to individuals demonstrating a strong allegiance to organizational goals.[39] There were two kinds of membership in La Raza Unida in Crystal City. On a general level, one could support the organization through identification with goals, attendance at party functions, and by voting behavior. On a more specific level, one could become a member of La Raza Unida's Ciudadanos Unidos, which was the local decision-making body of the party. Membership in Ciudadanos Unidos was very restricted, open only to those with a clear commitment to the party and its goals. In fact, before an individual was admitted to the membership, he/she was closely scrutinized by a selection committee, which then made a recommendation to the entire body for its deliberation and vote.

The exclusive nature of La Raza Unida prevented serious splits or schisms from developing within the party—at least until 1974. Major differences within the organization were absorbed by the policy-making body of the group, Ciudadanos Unidos. For example, a conflict arose over statements certain members were making to the press regarding policy decisions within the party. This posed a serious question about the decentralized decision-making process of La Raza Unida. However, after a long afternoon of debate, the issue was settled within the structure of Ciudadanos Unidos. As was often the case in La Raza Unida, personal differences became secondary to organizational goals, and this led to a higher degree of member consensus and consistent policy. La Raza Unida was successful in avoiding serious schisms because of its ability to confront problems of internal conflict.

The success of La Raza Unida was also a reflection of the purposive incentive structure used to attract members. Purposive incentives are those that attract persons to an organization because of the intrinsic value of its goals. These values are suprapersonal in that they will not benefit members directly or in any tangible way.[40] Although a system of patronage evolved in Crystal City in the gift of Raza Unida, it was kept to a minimum and never became the primary reason for participation by the wider membership.

A group with a membership recruited by purposive incentives has a greater ability to shift tactics without transforming organizational goals. This is not always true of groups which use other kinds of incentives. Based upon its recruitment incentives, La Raza Unida easily moved from the school boycott to city and county elections without a major change in its goals.

The Educational Issues Coordinating Committee (EICC) was an inclusive social movement organization with a heterogeneous membership. That is, as an organization it was essentially a coalition of divergent interests with a central focus directed at instituting reforms in the public schools. The EICC included among its members, lawyers, educators, students, clergymen, and grass-roots persons who were recruited mainly by material and solidarist incentives. This membership was integrated into the majority society by a multiplicity of affiliations. These interconnections ranged over social status, ethnicity, and often classes.[41] The majority of EICC's membership was not committed to social change values beyond those attendant to the immediate issue of the school. Therefore, it is possible to say that the major reason for EICC's inability to survive as a movement organization was the result of the diversity of its members and the incentives used to recruit them.

Conflict surfaced within the EICC membership over the strategy to be used to defend those Chicanos indicted by the Los Angeles Grand Jury for their role in the school walk-outs. The conflict did not remain at the strategy level, but expanded to the larger question of organizational goals. Eventually, those advocating a more activist position were shunted aside. This left the organization in the control of issue-oriented individuals. Once this control was solidified, the organization was transformed into a formal extension of the Los Angeles Board of Education. The merger with the school board was approved by the EICC membership on the grounds that it was a tactic which would expand their resource base and facilitate the achievement of their goals. The EICC did not perceive an inconsistency or a contradiction in the transformation of the group to the Mexican-American Advisory Council. At this crucial juncture, the EICC failed to sustain itself as a social movement organization.

The Latin American Union for Civil Rights (LAUCR) indicates a pattern of development similar to that of the EICC. The LAUCR was an inclusive organization that employed solidarist and material incentives to recruit membership. The general objective of the LAUCR was the establishment of a mass grassroots organization with the main emphasis upon creating normative changes. When the achievement of this goal proved improbable in the foreseeable future and the organization acquired an independent financial support base, the development of a mass grassroots membership was curtailed.

The shift in organizational goals was an indirect result of the incentive system used to recruit LAUCR's initial membership. In order to maintain even the skeletal membership that remained, LAUCR leaders and organizers were compelled to satisfy the membership's material and solidarist needs. The general objective which brought LAUCR to life was discarded and in its place came the objective of controlling the social service agencies that were beginning to emerge in the community. Through control of these agencies, the LAUCR was able to satisfy its members' needs by appointing them to positions on boards of directors and to salaried jobs within the agencies. That LAUCR was able to maintain itself for the period was based on the selective incentives used to create solidarity among its membership. Similarly, Gamson, when describing two co-opted movement groups that developed close relationships with the antagonists, states:

> That they were able to do this (increase membership) at the same time they were failing to deliver any real collective benefits to their constituency may well have been due to their use of selective inducements to membership.[42]

That is, these two groups, like the LAUCR, were able to deliver incentives which encouraged participation in the organization.

The three case studies strongly support the idea that those groups with membership recruited on the basis of purposive value systems are more likely to survive than those with solidarist and material values. However, as Ash and Zald point out, there might be a point where exclusivity might engender schisms among these types of groups and contribute to the organization's transformation.[43] Therefore, there might be some medium point of exclusivity that must be reached. Another factor that may have contributed to the absense of schisms among La Raza Unida was its strong organizational structure. As Gamson states:

> Centralization of power is an organizational device for handling the problem of internal divisions and providing unity of command.[44]

In the case of La Raza Unida, and less so with LAUCR, the organization had a centralized structure that was able to absorb disputes.

CONCLUSION

This study fails to confirm the notion that goal transformation is an inevitable process for social movement groups. The present findings show that goal transformation among the three Chicano Movement groups was conditionally dependent on organizational factors that either facilitated or impeded the process. Although not exhaustive, this discussion presents examples of some of these alternatives and conditional factors which tend to influence this process. In this study, groups with value-oriented goals were more likely to be perceived as threatening to the entrenched power structure. As a result of this perception, value-oriented Chicano groups were more likely to be subjected to political repression and to legal force than were norm-oriented Chicano groups. However, the ability to survive was less dependent on the larger society's attitudes and actions than on the exclusiveness of the membership and the incentives used to recruit members. That is, those groups with an exclusive membership based on purposive incentives to recruit members, such as La Raza

Unida Party, were more likely to retain their movement characteristics. On the other hand, the EEIC and the LAUCR, which had inclusive memberships based on material or solidarist incentives to recruit members, were less resistent to pressures for change. Another factor that may have contributed to the movement group's longevity is the degree of bureaucratic arrangement and structure. La Raza Unida and LAUCR both displayed a much more developed organizational structure than the EICC; subsequently both groups were able to absorb differences internally without creating factionalisms and schisms.

The relevance of this study for understanding Chicano social movement groups is underscored when we turn to past studies on Mexican-American political organizations. The majority of these studies have a strong "personalistic" orientation, emphasizing strong kinship or familialism as an asset in building and maintaining organizations.[45] Recently, Muñoz and Barrera argue that the failure of the Chicano Movement rests with its inability to develop an overall encompassing ideology.[46] Given that both views are valid, since the former takes into consideration cultural aspects that distinguish Chicanos from those of the larger society, and the latter deals with the absence of political direction, they are insufficient for understanding the transformation of Chicano social movement groups unless consideration is given to the organizational factors addressed here.

NOTES

1. See William Kornhauser, *The Politics of Mass Society* (New York: The Free Press, 1959); Neil J. Smelser, *Theory of Collective Behavior* (New York: The Free Press, 1963); Ralph H. Turner and Lewis Killian, *Collective Behavior* (Englewood Cliffs, New Jersey: Prentice-Hall, 1972).

2. H. J. Gerth and C. W. Mills, *From Max Weber: Essays in Sociology* (New York: Oxford University Press, 1960); Reinhard Bendix, *Max Weber: An Intellectual Portrait* (New York: Doubleday, 1960); Seymour M. Lipset, Martin A. Trow, and James S. Coleman, *Union Democracy: The Internal Politics of the International Typographical Union* (New York: The Free Press, 1977); Ralph H. Turner, "The Public Perception of Protest," *American Sociological Review* 34 (December 1969).

3. See Philip Selznick, *TVA and the Grass Roots* (Berkeley: University of California Press, 1949); Joseph Gusfield, "Functional Areas of Leadership in Social Movements," in A. W. Gouldner and R. de Charms, eds., *Studies in Leadership* (New York: Harper and Row, 1962); Robert K. Merton, *Social Theory and Social Structure* (Glencoe: The Free Press, 1957).

4. Roberta Ash and Mayer N. Zald, "Social Movement Organization: Growth, Decay and Change," *Social Forces* 44 (March, 1966); Russel Curtis, Jr., and Louis Zurcher, "Social Movements: An Analytical Explanation of Organiza-

tional Forms," *Social Problems* 21 (3, 1974); William A. Gamson, *The Strategy of Social Protest* (Homewood, Illinois, Dorsey Press, 1975); Joyce Rothchild-Whitt, "Conditions Facilitating Participatory Democratic Organizations," Sociological Inquiry 46 (2, 1976); Craig J. Jenkins, "Radical Transformation of Organizational Goals," *Administrative Science Quarterly* 22 (December, 1977).

5. Ash and Zald, "Social Movement Organization."

6. Rothchild-Whitt "Conditions Facilitating"; and Jenkins, "Radical Transformation."

7. Carlos Muñoz, Jr. and Mario Barrera, "La Raza Unida Party and the Chicano Student Movement in California," *The Social Sciences Journal* 19 (April, 1982), reprinted in this volume.

8. My intent is not to prove that Chicanos have distinct sociopolitical histories and cultures in different parts of the United States, but to show that in terms of political development, there are differences within their immediate social and political environments which are more or less conducive to the development and growth of social movement organizations.

9. This analysis is gathered from various resources including Miguel Tirado's "The Mexican American Minority Participation in Voluntary Associations," Ph.D. dissertation, Claremont, 1970; Carlos Muñoz, "The Politics of Protest and Chicano Liberation," *Aztlan* 5, (no. 1 and 2, 1974), *La Raza Magazine* (Los Angeles, 1968–1969), and interviews with individuals associated with the EICC.

10. Ray Santana and Mario Esparza, "East Los Angeles Blowouts," in *Parameters of Institutional Change: Chicano Experiences in Education* (Hayward, California: Southwest Network, 1974).

11. The Chicano student enrollment in these five East Los Angeles high school was as follows: Belmont, 69 percent; Wilson, 81 percent; Roosevelt, 85.7 percent; Lincoln, 87.7 percent; and Garfield, 93.6 percent. Los Angeles School District, Division of Planning and Research, Report No. 312, Racial and Ethnic Survey, 1973.

12. David Miguel Tirado, "Mexican-American Community Political Organization," *Aztlan* 1 (Spring, 1970); Gerald Paul Rosen, *"Political Ideology and the Chicano Movement"* (San Francisco: R. and E. Research Associates, 1975).

13. Tirado, "Mexican-American Community."

14. Ibid.; Carlos Muñoz, Jr., Mario Barrera and Charles Ornelas, "The Barrio as an Internal Colony," in F. Chris Garcia, ed., *La Causa Politica* (Notre Dame, Indiana: University of Notre Dame Press, 1974).

15. This material is primarily from John Shockley's *Chicano Revolt in a Texas Town* (Notre Dame, Indiana: University of Notre Dame Press, 1974), and from personal interviews with Crystal City residents and party officials between 1969 and 1979.

16. See John Staples Shockley, *Chicano Revolt in a Texas Town.* For more information on the impact Gutierrez and MAYO were having on Texas politicians, see an article titled "Impetuous MAYO Militants Alarming to Rep. Gonzalez," in *The San Antonio Express,* June 6, 1969; also, "The Chicano Revolt—What Next?" in the *San Antonio Express and News,* January 11, 1970.

17. Maxine Baca-Zinn, "Political Familism: Toward Sex Role Equality in Chicano Families," *Aztlan* 6 (Winter, 1975): 16.

18. For a comprehensive outline of Gutierrez' political goals, see "Aztlan: Chicano Revolt in the Winter Garden Area," unpublished paper, Crystal City, 1970. Particular attention should be given to the fourth goal of Aztlan. This identifies Chicanos in south Texas as a colonized nation.

19. Muñoz and Barrera, "La Raza Unida."

20. Armando Cavada, "La Raza Unity Party and the Chicano Middle Class," (September, 1974), pp. 17–21.

21. After 1974–1975, La Raza Unida was plagued with many of the problems that other social movement groups faced. Finally, by 1979 the organization dissipated because of internal strife caused by conflicts over goals and leadership.

22. This information is gathered from the researcher's personal involvement in the organization from 1968 to 1973, as well as personal interviews, newspaper accounts, and organizational reports.

23. The LAUCR initially received funds from a private religious foundation with no direct obligation to them. However, after LAUCR became more established they began to receive funds from a federally sponsored agency which demanded more strict adherence to program guidelines.

24. David P. Gillespie, "Conservative Tactics in Social Movement Organizations," in Jo Freeman, ed., *Social Movements of the Sixties* (New York: Longman, 1983).

25. See Rothchild-Whitt, "Conditions Facilitating."

26. Characteristics of the Spanish-Surnamed Population by Census Tract for SMSA's in Texas: 1970 Census of Population, Department of Commerce, Bureau of the Census, May 1974; Supplementary Report.

27. In Crystal City, Texas, Chicanos were politically and economically dominated by agricultural Anglo power interests. The majority of Chicanos in this area are employed as seasonal workers and migrate to the Midwest during the summer months. Economically, this general area of south Texas, identified as the Winter Garden region, is one of the poorest in the nation. Chicanos are politically subordinate to Anglo power interests despite the fact that they comprise 90 percent of the city's ten thousand total population. Located forty sparsely populated miles from the Mexican border, this Chicano community is provided with a continuous exposure to Mexican culture. This close proximity accounts for their comparatively high identity as a separate ethnic group and retention of Mexican cultural characteristics. This strong identity as an ethnic group was accompanied by restricting social interaction among their own subculture. These social factors, along with the political and economic variables, created hostile sentiments between the Anglo and Chicano communities. This made acculturation and assimilation difficult, if not impossible — even for those Chicanos desiring it. See Shockley, *Chicano Revolt in a Texas Town,* and Gutierrez, "Aztlan: Chicano Revolt in the Winter Garden Area."

28. Shockley, *Chicano Revolt.*

29. Richard Santillan, *La Raza Unida* (Los Angeles: Tlanquilo Publications, 1973).

30. Characteristics of the Spanish-Surnamed Population by Census Tract for SMSA's in California: 1970 Census of Population, Department of Commerce, Bureau of the Census, May 1974, Supplementary Report.

31. U.S. Census of Population and Housing, 1970; Census Tracts, Milwaukee, Wisconsin, SMSA, U.S. Department of Commerce Publication.

32. Avelardo Valdez, "A Narrative of the Latin Community since 1968–1974," unpublished paper. University of Wisconsin, Milwaukee, 1974.

33. This was the case in the 1963 Crystal City elections where Chicano politicians were eventually displaced. Traditionally, this had been the method Anglos used to manipulate Chicano political movements in this region of Texas.

34. This process is clearly indicated by Muñoz, "Politics of Protest" in "The Politics of Protest and Chicano Liberation." The process of cooptation is responsible for the disintegration of the EICC as a social movement organization in East Los Angeles.

35. Smelser, *Theory of Collective Behavior,* and Turner and Killian, "Collective Behavior."

36. Gamson, *Strategy of Social Protest.*

37. Ash and Zald, "Social Movement Organization," argue that a perfect stable organization would be one which over time always seemed to be getting closer to its goals without gaining them. Value-oriented organizations, then, would generally be more apt to survive as stable organizations since their specific goals are always a means for more profound societal change.

38. Peter Clark and James Q. Wilson, "Incentive Systems: A Theory of Organizations," *Administrative Quarterly* vol. 6 (September, 1961); Ash and Zald, "Social Movement Organization."

39. Exclusive organizations are those that require from members a disciplined commitment and allegiance to organizational goals. These organizations require a greater amount of time and energy and permeate all aspects of the member's life. Inclusive organizations require minimal levels of commitment. There is usually a pledge of general support without specific duties, and a short indoctrination period or none at all.

40. Clark and Wilson, "Incentive Systems" briefly describe three types of incentives that are offered by organizations to harness individuals to organizational tasks—material (money and goods), solidarist, and purposive incentives. They state that any organization may be able to offer all three; different types of organizations have more of one than the others to offer.

41. Gusfield, "Functional Areas of Leadership," identified such structures as "linked pluralism." These types of structures, he states, are easily susceptible to social control mechanisms.

42. Gamson, *Strategy of Social Protest,* p. 69.

43. Ash and Zald, "Social Movement Organizations."

44. Gamson, *Strategy of Social Protest,* p. 108.

45. See Tirado, "Mexican-American Community," for an exhaustive discussion of this issue.

46. Muñoz and Barrera, "La Raza Unida."

13. A Legal Voice for the Chicano Community: The Activities of the Mexican-American Legal Defense and Educational Fund, 1968–1982[1]

Karen O'Connor and Lee Epstein

LITIGATION LONG HAS BEEN recognized as an important political tool of disadvantaged groups (Cortner 1968). In this paper, we discuss the utility of litigation on behalf of the Chicano[2] community by the Mexican-American Legal Defense and Educational Fund (MALDEF). More specifically, after describing the historical circumstances surrounding the creation of MALDEF, we draw on previous studies of interest group litigation to formulate hypotheses concerning interest group success in the judicial arena. We then test these hypotheses through an examination of the litigation activities of MALDEF between 1968 and 1982.

LITIGATION AS A POLITICAL TOOL

Writing in 1959, Clement E. Vose was one of the first to document the importance of group use of the courts. His examination of the National Association for the Advancement of Colored People (NAACP) and its independent Legal Defense Fund's (LDF's) use of the courts to end restrictive covenants revealed that litigation was critical; as an organization litigating on behalf of a disadvantaged group, the NAACP realized that it could not attain its goals in the legislative sphere. But, as Vose's study clearly indicated, the NAACP's recognition of the utility of litigation did not automatically lead to success. In fact, Vose's examination of the

Reprinted from *Social Science Quarterly,* Vol. 65, No. 2, June 1984. Copyright © 1984 by the University of Texas Press. By permission of the authors and the publisher.

NAACP's decades-long struggle to end restrictive covenants revealed that at least three factors were critical to its ultimate success: first, after realizing that the courts were the only potentially amenable forum for the advancement of minority rights, NAACP founders recruited attorneys well schooled in the intricacies of civil rights law (Vose 1959). According to Vose, this task was facilitated by the concentration of black attorneys in several northeastern cities and by the fact that the vast majority of these lawyers had been educated at the Howard Law School in Washington, D.C. Thus, within a relatively short period of time, the NAACP was able to recruit well-trained attorneys as well as to establish a crucial network of cooperating attorneys sympathetic to its cause.

This network, coupled with the NAACP's maintenance of a national office in Washington, D.C., facilitated the development of a direct sponsorship strategy by keeping the organization abreast of potentially good test cases, a second factor noted as critical to its success by Vose. While soon after its creation in 1909 the NAACP filed an amicus curiae brief in *Guinn v. United States* (1915), a challenge to Louisiana's grandfather clause, its leaders shortly thereafter realized that direct sponsorship would be the most effective way to achieve its goals. In fact, as Vose has noted, control over the course of litigation at the trial court level where a record could be established for later appeal was particularly critical to the NAACP's ability to obtain judicial invalidation of restrictive covenants.[3]

A third factor noted as critical to the LDF's success was its ability to garner support from other litigators. The assistance and support of the U.S. government in court, for example, lent legitimacy to the NAACP's claims and led to an almost one-sided presentation of race cases, thereby increasing the likelihood of success. Thus, according to Vose, the NAACP's simple recognition of the utility of litigation was only the first step in achieving invalidation of restrictive covenants. Additionally, expert counsel, the use of a test case strategy, and cooperation with other litigators contributed to its ultimate success in *Shelley v. Kraemer* (1948).

The importance of these factors was further substantiated in subsequent studies of the NAACP LDF's litigation activities. Both Jack Greenberg's (1974, 1977) and Richard Kluger's (1976) analyses of the LDF's role in the school desegregation cases that culminated in *Brown v. Board of Education* (1954) note the importance of each of these factors. For example, LDF general counsel Thurgood Marshall's decision to initiate a series of cases at the trial court level to whittle away at adverse precedent was pointed to by both authors as critical to the LDF's success. This series of cases allowed the LDF to establish itself as an expert litigator in the area of school segregation. Additionally, during the course of this litigation campaign, the LDF facilitated creation of a receptive judicial environment through securing the publication of several law review articles authored by well-respected constitutional scholars and enlisting the assistance and support of the U.S. government as amicus curiae. According to Greenberg and Kluger, these factors helped to explain the LDF's landmark victory in 1954 (see also Hahn 1973; Barker 1967).

Not only is there agreement among those who have studied the NAACP LDF concerning factors critical to its success, but those who have analyzed other disadvantaged groups have reached the same conclusions. For example, Manwaring's (1962) study of the Jehovah's Witnesses found that frequent participation by committed attorneys in cooperation with the American Civil Liberties Union (ACLU) facilitated its efforts to persuade the Supreme Court to invalidate compulsory flag salute requirements.

Another disadvantaged group—women—also has relied heavily on litigation to attain greater rights. However, as O'Connor (1980) has noted, women's rights organizations, unlike the LDF and the Jehovah's Witnesses, have had but mixed success because of the absence of one organization to represent their interests in court. Instead, the involvement of several groups including the National Organization for Women (NOW), the Women's Rights Project of the ACLU, and the Women's Equity Action League has made use of a test case strategy difficult. Additionally, the large number of women's rights litigators has strained foundation funds, which has reduced the ability of many of the groups to afford the often high costs incurred through direct sponsorship of litigation. Thus, women's rights groups have been unable to pursue a truly coordinated test case strategy, a factor considered critical to success.

A Formulation and Test of a Hypothesis of Interest Group Litigation: An Examination of MALDEF's Activities

As the preceding discussion suggests, studies of the litigation activities of a variety of organizations representing disadvantaged groups provide the basis for theoretical generalizations concerning interest group use of the courts to achieve rights unavailable in other forums. The findings of these and other studies (Burke 1981; Cortner 1975; Rubin 1982; Shattuck and Norgren 1979; Sorauf 1976; Stewart and Heck 1982; Wasby 1981), which have thoroughly examined groups that have succeeded or obtained only limited success in court, allow us to formulate the following hypothesis: If interest groups (1) recruit expert counsel, (2) use a test case strategy, and (3) cooperate with other groups, then they will maximize their chances of success, at least at the level of the U.S. Supreme Court.

To investigate the continuing importance of the elements enumerated in this hypothesis, we examine the activities of MALDEF, the major representative of Chicano interests in court. The significance of such an examination is twofold: first, Chicanos, like blacks, the Jehovah's Witnesses, and women, can be classified as a "disadvantaged group," but litigation efforts on their behalf never have been fully examined. Second, an analysis of this sort is timely because MALDEF's victories have just begun to make a major impact on the law. Thus, a study of its activities, like those conducted of other groups that have resorted to litigation, may help to explain not only the relevance of the factors perceived as critical to litigation success, but also to provide a fuller understanding of the evolution of an interest group litigator.

THE ESTABLISHMENT AND LITIGATION ACTIVITIES OF MALDEF

Like many other disadvantaged groups, Chicanos early on recognized their inability to seek rights through traditional political avenues and thus sporadically resorted to litigation (Vigil 1978:125). It was not until the 1960s, however, that the need for organized, sustained litigation activity on behalf of Chicanos became apparent. For example, in the course of litigating a common tort claim, Pete Tijerina, a League of United Latin American Citizens (LULAC) leader, was confronted with a jury panel of no Chicano surnamed individuals, but his client could not afford the high cost of a challenge to its discriminatory composition. Because Tijerina believed that this case symbolized the plight of Chicanos in court, he sent another LULAC member to attend a 1967 NAACP LDF conference to explore the possibility of establishing an organization to litigate on behalf of Chicanos. Tijerina's representative met with Jack Greenberg, the executive director of the NAACP LDF, who then set up a meeting between Tijerina and Ford Foundation representatives (Markham 1983). Within a year of that meeting, MALDEF was incorporated with the assistance of a $2.2 million start-up grant from the Ford Foundation (Teltsch 1968).

In addition to Ford's financial support, MALDEF received practical information and guidance from the NAACP LDF. In fact, LDF attorney Vilma Martinez, who later was to become the executive director of MALDEF, had not only helped prepare the initial Ford grant application but also served as a liaison between the two organizations ("San Antonio Native" 1973). Additionally, Greenberg was named to its first board of directors.

Not only was MALDEF assisted by LDF staff members, it was specifically modeled after the LDF. In fact, in announcing the Ford grant, the foundation's president McGeorge Bundy drew the following parallel: "In terms of legal enforcement of civil rights, American citizens of Mexican descent are now where the Negro community was a quarter-century ago" (Teltsch 1968:38). Thus, at least from Ford's perspective, MALDEF was to function for Chicanos in the same way that the LDF historically had assisted blacks.

To facilitate and to direct its initial efforts, MALDEF, like the LDF, quickly acted to draw upon the expertise of prominent Mexican-American attorneys to staff its headquarters in San Antonio and its Los Angeles affiliate office. Tijerina was installed as its first executive director, and Mario Obledo, a Texas assistant attorney general and former state director of LULAC, was hired as general counsel. MALDEF, however, quickly was confronted with a paucity of experienced litigators. In fact, in announcing Ford funding of MALDEF, Bundy had underscored the need for such an organization, noting that there were "not nearly enough Mexican-American lawyers and most of them have neither the income or experience to do civil rights work" (Teltsch 1968:38). To remedy this situation, the Ford grant included provisions for scholarships for 35 Mexican-American law students with the goal of increasing the number of Chicano attorneys.[4] Nevertheless, this was a long-term solution to a problem that immediately confronted MALDEF. Thus, four of the nine attorneys intially "hired" by MALDEF were non-Chicano Vista volunteers (MALDEF n.d.). Additionally, in establishing its own network of cooperating attorneys, MALDEF was forced to rely heavily on non-Chicano lawyers.

Thus, while MALDEF was modeled after the LDF, from the start it was faced with problems unlike those experienced by the LDF. It had difficulty in recruiting experienced Chicano attorneys and in dealing with the Mexican-American community at large, which from some accounts misunderstood MALDEF's objectives. For example, immediately after MALDEF established its offices in San Antonio and Los Angeles, both were inundated with claims. Many of these claims, however, involved routine "legal aid" type cases that were best settled out of court and did not necessarily present issues upon which important constitutional cases could be made.

These sorts of problems, coupled with the militancy of some of MALDEF's personnel[5] (Diehl 1970), prompted the Ford Foundation to send in outside evaluators to examine MALDEF's day-to-day activities in 1970 ("Mexican Aid Fund" 1970:48). These evaluators made several "recommendations" that were aimed at increasing MALDEF's national presence and reputation in the LDF model. More specifically, according to Tijerina, Ford threatened to terminate MALDEF's funding if it did not move its headquarters out of Texas and relocate in a more "neutral" city such as Washington, D.C., or New York ("Ford Group" 1970). Cognizant of the

importance of a presence in the West, however, MALDEF chose instead
to relocate its headquarters to San Francisco while retaining its two other
offices and only later opening up a D.C. office (Grover 1970). MALDEF,
however, followed other Ford suggestions; not only was Tijerina replaced
as executive director as requested by Ford (Murphy 1970), but MALDEF
also combined the positions of executive director and general counsel, its
board selecting Mario Obledo to fill this new position ("Mexican Aid
Fund" 1970:48).

As executive director, Obledo immediately sought to increase
MALDEF's national visibility as recommended by the Ford Foundation
and to strengthen ties with other established civil rights groups. For example, during Obledo's tenure, MALDEF established a New Mexico branch
office in conjunction with the New Mexico Law School, the New Mexico
Legal Rights Project, and the Albuquerque Legal Aid Society. A Denver
office also was opened under Obledo's leadership. Additionally, MALDEF
moved to increase its national presence through association with the LDF
and NOW, among others, to pressure the federal government for enforcement of fair employment practices legislation (Shanahan 1972; Cowan
1972).

Perhaps most important, however, aware of the problems of functioning as a quasi legal aid clinic, Obledo moved to have MALDEF bring
more cases to the U.S. Supreme Court. Thus, as early as 1973, the Court
handed down decisions in eight cases in which MALDEF had participated,
five of which were amicus curiae briefs filed alone or in conjunction with
other organizations. In the remaining three cases sponsored by MALDEF,
only one, *White v. Regester* (1973), which involved the constitutionality
of at-large election districts, resulted in a favorable decision. In contrast,
in *Logue v. U.S.* (1973), MALDEF was unable to convince the Court that
the U.S. government should be liable for the negligence of city jail employees. Far more devastating, however, was its loss in *San Antonio v. Rodriguez* (1973). In its first appearance before the Court,[6] MALDEF (1972)
argued that:

> in Texas, the poor receive one type of education by every measure,
> while the affluent are afforded a quite different and superior educa-
> tional opportunity. This Court should not allow Texas to impose
> upon a minority what is obviously unacceptable to the majority.
> (p. 56)

This argument, however, failed to convince the Court to find that education was a fundamental right protected by the Fourteenth Amendment.
Instead, the justices held that Texas would not be required to subsidize
poorer school districts, where there were often large concentrations of

Chicanos. Thus, *San Antonio* resulted in a devastating loss, creating additional legal barriers instead of favorable precedent upon which MALDEF could build a test case strategy.

In sum, under Obledo's leadership, MALDEF attempted to implement the Ford Foundation's suggestions through a variety of different strategies. It successfully established new offices and attempted to build ties with other groups. But, as its loss in *San Antonio* revealed, MALDEF acted too quickly and did not sufficiently "prime" the Supreme Court either through frequent appearances as amicus curiae or the use of test cases. Thus, although by 1973 MALDEF had accomplished a number of its objectives, in the wake of its losses during 1973 Obledo resigned to return to private practice ("Vilma Martinez" 1973). In September 1973, Vilma Martinez was selected to replace Obledo after MALDEF's board considered several candidates including Juan Rocha, who had recently been hired to head the new MALDEF D.C. office ("San Antonio Native" 1973).

Martinez immediately set into motion a series of changes: first, having always been interested in fund raising (Markham 1983) and in fact, having played a major role in MALDEF fund raising from the beginning, Martinez restaffed the D.C. office with the objectives of improving MALDEF's government relations, funding sources, and its national visibility. Second, MALDEF began to create specialized litigation and educational projects to meet its growing needs and to afford its attorneys an opportunity to develop greater expertise. For example, in 1974 a Chicana Rights Project was created to fight sex discrimination faced by Mexican-American women. Other projects established by MALDEF handled education, employment, and voting rights. A year later, it also created a legal intern/extern program to help train and later assist Chicano attorneys to set up practices in local communities. Finally, and perhaps most important, MALDEF became more selective about its involvement in cases as Ford had earlier urged. Generally, it began to limit its participation to important test cases that were considered to have "broad implications" (MALDEF n.d.:30). This selectivity allowed MALDEF, like the LDF, not only to maximize its resources but to avoid adverse precedent such as that established in San Antonio.

To accomplish this goal, MALDEF began to concentrate in a number of legal issue areas but continued to be particularly interested in education. In the wake of *San Antonio,* however, MALDEF's leaders reevaluated their strategy in that area. Building upon arguments set forth in the first article about undocumented aliens ever to appear in the *American Bar Journal* and written by a MALDEF attorney (Ortega 1972), MALDEF lawyers began to devise a strategy to create favorable precedent by which to improve the legal status of all Chicanos. Thus, under the directorship of Peter Roos, who had previously worked at the Harvard Center for Law and Education and at the Western Center of Law and Poverty, MALDEF's Education Litigation Project filed several lawsuits challenging the constitutionality of actions of many school districts that refused to enroll the children of undocumented aliens, unless tuition was paid.

After several years of litigation, one of these cases, *Plyler v. Doe* (1982), resulted in a major, landmark ruling from the U.S. Supreme Court. MALDEF attorneys including Martinez and Roos had argued that the Texas code, which allowed school districts to exclude some children, violated the Fourteenth Amendment. According to MALDEF (1981):

> When public schooling is available to all but the children of one excluded class, the members of that class are inexorably relegated to a low station in life, subject to exploitation and removed from the meaningful discourse of the day. As one is properly and regularly reminded, "A mind is a terrible thing to waste."

In adopting MALDEF's reasoning, the Supreme Court, for the first time, directly held that the children of undocumented, illegal aliens were protected by the equal protection clause. Writing for the Court, Justice Brennan noted that:

> it is difficult to understand precisely what the State hopes to achieve by promoting the creation and perpetuation of a subclass of illiterates within our boundaries, surely adding to the problems and costs of unemployment, welfare and crime. . . . If the State is to deny a discrete group of innocent children the free public education that it offers to other children residing within its borders, that denial must be justified by a showing that it furthers some substantial state interest. No such showing was made here. (102 S. Ct. 2382, 2402)

Thus, *Plyler* provided MALDEF's "best victory" to date (MALDEF 1982:4) and has presented MALDEF with a major precedent upon which to build.

APPLICATION OF HYPOTHESIS TO MALDEF's LITIGATION ACTIVITIES

Based on other studies of interest group litigation, we hypothesized that (1) the recruitment of expert counsel, (2) the use of a test case strategy, and (3) cooperation with other groups would maximize a group's chances of success.

From the preceding discussion of MALDEF's activities, we can now attempt to investigate the importance of the three factors commonly assumed to be critical to the success of interest group litigation.

Expert Attorneys

When MALDEF was established, its founders recognized the importance of recruiting highly skilled attorneys who would be sensitive to the pervasive discrimination suffered by Chicanos. Unlike the LDF, which could draw on a large number of black attorneys schooled in civil rights law, there were few Chicano attorneys experienced in civil rights litigation, which initially forced MALDEF to rely on non-Chicano attorneys to supplement its staff. Thus, many of the first programs initiated by MALDEF were designed to increase the number of Chicano attorneys, train them in civil rights law, and then help establish them in practice within the Chicano community and not necessarily toward developing legal expertise *within* MALDEF.

When Martinez replaced Obledo, however, she immediately recognized this organizational deficiency, and she actively recruited several attorneys with strong civil rights backgrounds (Markham 1983). For example, Morris J. Baller, who was made head of the Developmental Litigation Project, had formerly served, like Martinez, as an LDF staff attorney. And, Joel G. Contreras, who was hired to be the director of the Employment Litigation Project, had served in a similar capacity with the Lawyer's Committee for Civil Rights Under Law (LCCRUL). He also had previously worked at the EEOC. Both Martinez and the staff that she hired, therefore, interjected an increased level of expertise in civil rights litigation that neither Obledo nor Tijerina possessed. Interestingly, almost all of the attorneys added to MALDEF's staff were Chicanos,[7] and in fact, some had been trained in the legal extern program or assisted by MALDEF scholarships.

Thus, unlike the LDF, MALDEF faced initial difficulties because of the absence of Chicano attorneys trained in civil rights law. This problem, which translated into major legal defeats, losses of scarce time and resources, and some internal dissension, was substantially reduced through MALDEF's programs, specialized projects, and by Martinez's recruitment efforts.

Test Case Strategy

Until the Ford Foundation report, MALDEF largely functioned as a legal aid society, albeit one that met the particular needs of the Chicano community. After 1970, however, MALDEF initiated several diverse kinds of suits that ultimately reached the Supreme Court. But, in only one of the three cases it argued during the 1972 term was it victorious. Its victory in *White* can be largely attributed to its initial emphasis on voting rights and attention to the development of a strong record at the trial court level. Conversely, its losses in *Logue v. U.S.* and *San Antonio* may be explained by its pursuit of Supreme Court resolution of issues that the Court had not yet been "primed" to address; MALDEF's 1972 term appearances were its first before the Supreme Court. Thus, unlike many other groups, which generally file amicus curiae briefs prior to bringing test cases before the Court, in 1972 MALDEF did not have any of the advantages of traditional repeat players (Galanter 1974). And, perhaps more important, MALDEF's failure to "test the waters" in the education area produced disastrous precedent that stood as an additional legal stumbling block for litigation of other claims.

Recognizing these problems, MALDEF, under the leadership of Martinez, actively sought to increase its visibility as an amicus curiae in the Supreme Court while simultaneously developing a litigation strategy to whittle away at the adverse precedent established in *San Antonio,* in particular, and against aliens, in general. To accomplish this latter task, MALDEF closely modeled its activities after those followed by the LDF prior to *Brown.* Recognizing that the plight of children denied access to education by the state presented facts to evoke the sympathy of the Court, MALDEF initiated a series of "test cases" that culminated in *Plyler.* While *Plyler,* like the LDF's victories prior to *Brown,* is a victory standing alone, it also provided MALDEF with a major precedent upon which to build. In fact, since *Plyler,* MALDEF has initiated a number of lawsuits challenging discrimination against undocumented aliens in a variety of areas (Markham 1983).

But, its victory in *Plyler,* perhaps, places MALDEF at a critical juncture in its history both in terms of its litigation activities and organizational viability. Believing that she had accomplished her objectives (Markham 1983), Vilma Martinez left MALDEF shortly before the Court's announcement of the *Plyler* decision. Whether her successor and MALDEF will take full advantage of the gains won at least in part because of her insistence upon the utilization of a test case strategy is a challenge that confronts MALDEF as it moves into the 1980s.

Cooperation

Since its creation, MALDEF has cooperated with numerous civil rights organizations. For example, from the beginning, MALDEF has enjoyed strong ties with the NAACP LDF. Members of the LDF not only helped MALDEF secure Ford funding but also sat and continue to sit on its board. In fact, one of its first board members, Vilma Martinez, ultimately became its general counsel and brought several LDF staffers with her. Additionally, ties between the two groups are evident in their support of each other's litigation efforts.

While MALDEF has regularly worked with the LDF and other like-minded groups, full cooperation has been difficult at times because MALDEF represents a class whose best interests are not always served by non-Chicano organizations. For example, in *Keyes v. Denver School District* (1973), the NAACP LDF argued that the court-ordered Denver school desegregation plan should be upheld. MALDEF, however, which was forced to participate to assure the representation of Chicano interests, urged the Court to reconsider sections of the lower court order because it did not consider minority schools to be those that contained large populations of *both* Chicano and black children.

MALDEF, to some extent, has also attempted to work with the federal and state governments. Many of its attorneys had government experience prior to coming to MALDEF; others, including Obledo, have continued to speak on behalf of MALDEF from their government positions.[8] Additionally, MALDEF's litigation efforts have been facilitated by government-supported VISTA volunteers and outright grants from the U.S. government. In fact, during fiscal years 1981 and 1982, MALDEF received nearly 1.3 million dollars from the federal government (a figure derived from MALDEF 1982:13). Thus, unlike the other factors considered critical to litigation success, MALDEF, since its establishment, has attempted to cooperate with other groups and governments. In certain types of issue areas, however, cooperation has often been difficult because of MALDEF's unique focus.

CONCLUSION

As the preceding analysis indicates, the factors considered critical to interest group litigation success are helpful in explaining the evolution of MALDEF. In general, our discussion indicates that until 1973 MALDEF functioned more as a legal aid society than as an interest group litigator. While the Ford Foundation tried to put MALDEF on course, it was not until under Martinez's leadership that MALDEF was reorganized and reoriented to pursue the kinds of activities for which it was originally created. *Plyler v. Doe*, which was (1) initiated by a specialized MALDEF Project, (2) begun as a test case, and (3) supported by amicus curiae briefs from several other groups, is illustrative of the potential impact MALDEF can have on the Supreme Court if litigation is properly pursued.

Thus, this analysis has not only reaffirmed the importance of all three factors to litigation success, but also of the utility of litigation for disadvantaged groups. As MALDEF moves into the 1980s, it, as other representatives of disadvantaged groups have done in the past, can continue to build upon important precedents that it helped to create.

NOTES

1. We would like to thank Nancy Rossman for her research assistance. We would also like to express our appreciation to Stephen Wasby and the anonymous reviewers for their very helpful comments and criticisms of an earlier draft of this manuscript. Portions of this research were funded by the Emory University Research Fund. Editor's note: Reviewers were Rodolfo Alvarez, Rodolfo de la Garza, F. Chris Garcia, and Ricardo Romo.

2. Although the terms "Mexican-American" and "Chicano" often are used interchangeably by scholars (see Garcia and de la Garza 1977:14; Grebler, Moore, and Guzman 1970:385–87), we use the term "Chicano" because it is the term most frequently used in the briefs of the Mexican-American Legal Defense and Educational Fund.

3. This recognition, in fact, partially explains why the NAACP established an independent legal defense fund in 1939 solely to litigate on behalf of black interests (Vose, 1959).

4. This program continues to be a high-priority MALDEF project.

5. One MALDEF staffer, for example, made widely reported "anti-gringo" statements causing the Ford Foundation to come under fire for its support of Chicano groups. Political activities on the part of employees of Ford-funded operations even led the House Ways and Means Committee to hold hearings to seek ways to limit this sort of activity on the part of tax-exempt foundations (Diehl 1970).

6. In 1970, however, MALDEF unsuccessfully sought review from the Supreme Court in *Jiminez v. Naff.*

7. In fact, one non-Chicano attorney, George Korbel, who had litigated *White v. Regester* and is an authority on Voting Rights Act violations ("Suit Challenges" 1972; Davidson and Korbel 1981), was fired by Martinez and later sued to regain his position (Diehl 1976; "MALDEF Attorney" 1976).

8. For example, after Obledo became California's Secretary of Health and Welfare, he continued to file briefs on MALDEF's behalf. Similarly, Ed Idar, who formerly was associated with the San Antonio office, has participated on behalf of MALDEF since becoming an assistant attorney general in Texas.

REFERENCES

Barker, Lucius. 1967. "Third Parties in Litigation: A Systematic View of Judicial Function," *Journal of Politics* 29 (February): 41–69.

Burke, Susan Olson. 1981. "The Political Evolution of Interest Group Litigation," in Richard A. L. Gambritta et al., eds., *Governing through Courts* (Beverly Hills, Calif.: Sage).

Cortner, Richard. 1968. "Strategies and Tactics of Litigants in Constitutional Cases." *Journal of Public Law* 17:287–307.

———. 1975. *The Supreme Court and Civil Liberties Policy* (Palo Alto, Calif.: Mayfield).

Cowan, Edward. 1972. "FPC Urged to Bar Bias in Gas, Electric Utilities," *New York Times,* 23 June.

Davidson, Chandler, and George Korbel. 1981. "At Large Elections and Minority-Group Representation: A Re-Examination of Historical and Contemporary Evidence," *Journal of Politics* 43 (November): 982–1005.

Diehl, Kemper. 1970. "HBG Denies Role in MALDEF Center Move Plan," *San Antonio News,* 18 March.

———. 1976. "Fired Lawyer Sues MALDEF," *San Antonio News,* 4 March.

"Ford Group Denies Fund Cut Threat." 1970. *San Antonio News,* 19 March.

Galanter, Marc. 1974. "Why the 'Haves' Come Out Ahead: Speculation on the Limits of Legal Change," *Law and Society Review* 9 (Fall): 95–160.

Garcia, F. Chris, and Rudolph O. de la Garza. 1977. *The Chicano Political Experience: Three Perspectives* (North Scituate, Mass.: Duxbury Press).

Grebler, Leo, Joan W. Moore, and Ralph C. Guzman. 1970. *The Mexican-American People* (New York: Free Press).

Greenberg, Jack. 1974. "Litigation for Social Change: Methods, Limits, and Role in Democracy." *Records of the New York City Bar Association* 29:9–63.

———. 1977. *Judicial Process and Social Change:* Constitutional Litigation (St. Paul, Minn.: West).

Grover, Nell Fenner. 1970. "MALDEF Moving to San Francisco," *San Antonio Express,* 26 June.

Hahn, Jeanne. 1973. "The NAACP Legal Defense and Education Fund: Its Judicial Strategy and Tactics," in Stephen L. Wasby, ed., *American Government and Politics* (New York: Scribner).

Kluger, Richard. 1976. *Simple Justice: The History of Brown v. Board of Education and Black Americans Struggle for Equality* (New York: Knopf).

MALDEF. N.d. *Diez Anos.*

———. 1972. Brief for Appellees submitted in *San Antonio Independent School District v. Rodriguez,* No. 71-1332.

———. 1981. Motion to Dismiss or Affirm submitted in *Plyler v. Doe,* No. 80-1538.

———. 1982. Annual Report.

"MALDEF Attorney Sues to Keep His Job." 1976. *San Antonio Express,* 5 March.

Manwaring, David. 1962. *Render unto Caesar: The Flag Salute Controversy* (Chicago: University of Chicago Press).

Markham, Roseanne. 1983. Interview with Lee Epstein at MALDEF Washington, D.C., office, 13 January.

"Mexican Aid Fund Getting New Look." 1970. *New York Times,* 5 April, p. 48.

Murphy, Alice. 1970. "Pete Tijerina Firing Requested by Ford," *San Antonio Express,* 21 March.

O'Connor, Karen. 1980. *Women's Organizations' Use of the Courts* (Lexington, Mass.: Lexington Books).

Ortega, Joe C. 1972. "The Plight of the Mexican-American Alien," *American Bar Association Journal* 58 (March): 211.

Rubin, Eva R. 1982. *Abortion, Politics, and the Courts* (Westport, Conn.: Greenwood).

"San Antonio Native to Head MALDEF." 1973. *San Antonio Express,* 25 October.

Shanahan, Eileen. 1972. "One U.S. Agency Challenges Another on Antibias Accord," *New York Times,* 30 September.

Shattuck, Petra T., and Jill Norgren. 1979. "Political Use of the Legal Process by Blacks and American Indian Minorities," *Howard Law Journal* 22:1.

Sorauf, Frank J. 1976. *The Wall of Separation: Constitutional Politics of Church and State* (Princeton, N.J.: Princeton University Press).

"Suit Challenges Precinct Boundaries." 1972. *San Antonio Express,* 24 August.

Stewart, Joseph, Jr., and Edward Heck. 1982. "Ensuring Access to Justice: The Role of Interest Group Lawyers in the 60s Campaign for Civil Rights," *Judicature* 66 (August): 84–95.

Teltsch, Kathleen. 1968. "Grant Aids Latins in the Southwest," *New York Times,* 2 May, p. 38.

Vigil, Maurilio. 1978. *Chicano Politics* (Washington, D.C.: University Press of America).

"Vilma Martinez Gets Top MALDEF Post." 1973. *San Antonio News,* 25 October.

Vose, Clement E. 1959. *Caucasians Only* (Berkeley, Calif.: University of California Press).

Wasby, Stephen L. 1981. "Interest Group Litigation in an Age of Complexity." Paper presented at the annual meeting of the Midwest Political Science Association, Cincinnati, Ohio.

Cases Cited

Brown v. Board of Education, 347 U.S. 483 (1954).

Guinn v. United States, 238 U.S. 347 (1915).

Jimenez v. Naff, 397 U.S. 1005 (1970).

Keyes v. Denver School District #1, 413 U.S. 189 (1973).

Logue v. U.S., 412 U.S. 521 (1973).

Plyler v. Doe, 102 S. Ct. 2382 (1982).

San Antonio Independent School District v. Rodriguez, 411 U.S. 1 (1973).

Shelley v. Kraemer, 334 U.S. 1 (1948).

White v. Regester, 412 U.S. 755 (1973).

## PART III

The Conversion Process: Representation and Decision Making

CONVERSION IS AT THE HEART of the policy-making process. Persons in positions of authority—legislators, executives, administrators, judges—convert the inputs which they receive from individual constituents, interest groups, political parties, and others into binding policy decisions, that is, laws and regulations. The needs, desires, and wants of the citizenry are not automatically and mechanistically converted into public policy. Decision makers are human, affected by all the pressures, indecision, and value conflicts to which all persons are subject. Public officials must take the mixture of demands and pressures directed toward them, integrate these with their own personal preferences, take into consideration the specifics of the situation as well as their place in an organizational/group system, and then somehow make the "correct" decision which will become binding public policy. Thus, it is important who or what these public authorities are. There is little doubt that their backgrounds and other personal characteristics have an impact on the kinds of decisions they make or do not make.

One of the political disadvantages of Latinos throughout U.S. history has been that they have been inadequately represented by their own co-ethnics in decision-making capacities, the assumption being that Latino representation will make more decisions which are favorable to the Hispanic community. More often than not, the system has resisted this change in its key personnel, or on some occasions it has either co-opted Latinos or appointed Latinos to "token" positions. In either of these two latter situations, the effect on policy making is minimal. In the case of co-optation, the values, objectives, and agenda of the majority power structure are accepted by the Hispanic official as the price for a position, and in the latter case, the Latino official is simply a showpiece or window dressing with little real political or governmental power. Nevertheless, the Latino community continues to push for increased Hispanic representation in the halls of government at all levels.

Throughout history, Latinos have been greatly underrepresented in the United States Congress. One of the reasons for the paucity of Latino legislative representation has been the practice of gerrymandering by the people in power. Legislative district boundaries have been drawn to eliminate or at least minimize the number of Latino congressmen. In his article, "Hispanics Gain Seats in the 98th Congress After Reapportionment: An Analysis of the Breakdown of Traditional Barriers," Vigil provides a quick review of the changes in Hispanic politics over the past two decades, observes the underrepresentation of Hispanics in the United States Congress, and details a review of the post–1980 Census reapportionments. The unfortunate outcomes of previous gerrymandering, which have resulted in the exclusion of minorities, are recounted. State-by-state reports are given of the reapportionment process in the southwestern states of California, Texas, and New Mexico, and the subsequent involvement of Hispanics in elections. In his conclusion the author notes the favorable results of recent reapportionments and subsequent elections in increasing the representation of Hispanics in Congress, bringing its Latino membership to eleven. He points out the possibilities for greater success and offers hope for favorable policy action by the now larger Hispanic congressional contingency.

An important question is whether increased representation of Hispanics in Congress necessarily would result in more favorable policies being enacted. The research by Welch and Hibbing begins to answer that question. That liberal policy representation of Hispanics can be correlated with Hispanic representation in Congress and with the proportion of Hispanics in congressional constituencies is demonstrated in their study. The authors use data on demographic representation and ideology, i.e., conservative voting patterns, in the period from 1972 to 1980 to elaborate upon the relationship between Hispanic constituencies and the voting patterns of Hispanic members of the House. Latino members of the House were elected from only half of the eight majority Hispanic congressional districts in the nation. One of the obstacles to electing Hispanic representatives was the undetermined but significant number of Hispanic noncitizens and nonvoters in these districts. The authors did find a significant correlation between the voting patterns of the Hispanic representatives on 1,740 votes over a nine-year period and liberal (or at least less conservative) positions as evidenced by roll-call voting. There was a positive correlation, although not nearly as strong, between larger populations of Hispanic voters in the congressional districts and a more liberal voting record of the *non*-Hispanic representatives from those districts.

The 1982 election, which was based on the congressional reapportionments of 1980, increased the number of Hispanic members of Congress by four. By 1984 the Hispanic caucus numbered nine full representatives and two nonvoting delegates from the territories. Along with the increase in numbers came more visibility, more attention, and a greater diversity within the group. Members of the Hispanic caucus found themselves taking different positions on issues or the same position on a topic for different reasons. The report by Wieck provides some insight into the dynamics of congressional policymaking, including considerations by the representatives of their constituents. Other factors affecting their taking positions that are illustrated by the article include partisanship, seniority in the House, public opinion as manifested in opinion surveys, interactions with a major interest group LULAC, relationships with non-Hispanic colleagues, particularly legislative leaders, evaluations of administrative agencies, in this case, the Immigration and Naturalization Service, and differing opinions on the role and importance of ethnicity *per se.* The fact that there are different perceptions as to what ought to be on the agenda of the Hispanic caucus is vividly evidenced by the concern over whether the caucus ought to engage itself in international politics, more specifically, the relationship between Spain and Israel.

While the focus of most concern over Latino representation in government seems to be on the legislative branch, some observers feel that representation of Hispanics in the executive branch is at least as important. Many people underestimate the great impact which both elective and appointed administrative officials have on the formulation as well as the implementation of public policy. In his article, Pachon asserts that the Latino communities have not been influential in the policymaking process at the national government level largely because of a lack of representation of Hispanics in the federal bureaucracy. Contrary to popular impression, the federal administration and its agencies are greatly involved in the formulation, as well as the implementation, of policy. Success in current "techno-bureaucratic" politics entails at least minimal participation in administrative agencies. Pachon also blames the lack of Latino influence on the policymaking process on the absence of major national political interest groups of Latinos and the biracial, i.e., black and white, perspective of most public policymakers. For these two reasons, he believes that Hispanic representation in the bureaucracy is particularly important. Some data is provided to show the extremely small level of membership of Hispanics in the federal bureaucracy, particularly in the higher levels of both the legislative and executive bureaucracies. Past attempts at structural reforms (i.e., creating Hispanic agencies) have met with only limited success. Pachon proposes increasing Hispanic representation in federal bureaucratic offices, perhaps through more effective affirmative action policies, and urges increased awareness among Latinos of the importance of their involvement in bureaucratic politics. The ways this can be accomplished include emphasizing government service among Latino youth and through the publication of policy-oriented literature by Hispanic scholars.

Even if Latinos are represented by co-ethnics in the legislative and executive branches, to be responsive to Hispanic needs they must perceive their role as a special one, that is, as representing the Latino community. Alternatively, they must attempt to exert influence on their colleagues on behalf of Latinos in order to impact policy favorably.

A major research project by de la Garza inquired extensively and intensively into the perceived roles of Chicano political elites during the administration of President Jimmy Carter. His hypothesis was that truly "active" representation of Hispanics in legislative as well as executive/administrative positions would help to impact public policy in a positive direction for Hispanics. Attempts were made to distinguish the representatives of each Chicano political generation from those that preceded it and, most importantly, to determine if these representatives perceive themselves as having a special responsibility to represent the interests of Hispanics. Some evidence was found of generational differences as well as expressions of a special duty to represent their ethnic group. This was especially so among Washingtonians compared to those in the states of the Southwest, and also was more evident among administrators and Hispanic organizational leaders than among elected officials. In some of his other research, de la Garza had found that not only were Chicano political elites different from their Anglo counterparts in that they were more likely to come from families of lower socioeconomic status but also that their experiences with discrimination constituted a very important political socialization experience that affected their perception of their decision-making roles and responsibilities.

One of the principal reasons for the underrepresentation of Latinos at all levels of government has been the existence of electoral districts which have made the election of Latinos very difficult. Santillan has taken an extensive look at the activities of Latinos in the politics of redistricting, both at the state and congressional level. He reviews briefly the history of ethnic gerrymandering and the negative impact of malapportionment on Latino political representation and other activities. He then sketches the historical involvement of Latinos in the reapportionment efforts of the 1970s and the period following the 1980 reapportionment. The 1981 effort and its results are reviewed for nine states in which there was significant Latino involvement in redistricting. Recommendations for exerting maximum influence on the 1991 reapportionment also are included.

There is considerable evidence that Latinos are more concerned with problems and policies at the state and local levels than with national issues.

Certainly, most of the day-to-day issues which concern socioeconomically disadvantaged people are state and local ones, such as education, transportation, employment, law enforcement, housing, and health care. Over the past two decades, most of the political successes for Latinos have occurred at the local and, to a lesser degree, at the state level. Through the 1970s, Latino representation on school boards, county commissions, city councils, and state legislatures increased dramatically. In the decade from 1974 to 1984 the number of Latino elected officials more than doubled to a total of more than three thousand. An attempt to discover the impact of increased Hispanic representation in a state legislature was conducted by Mindiola and Gutierrez for the state of Texas. Their research addresses the general question of how important it is for Latinos to have Latino legislators in representative bodies, and also the auxiliary question as to how effective Latino legislators actually are in passing the legislation which they have introduced.

Overall it seems that increased Latino representation in public policy-making bodies does have a favorable impact on policies which are helpful to the Latino political community. The exact conditions under which favorable conversions of needs and wants into positive governmental policies are not clearly delineated at this time, but additional research should elucidate further this critical process of conversion.

14. Hispanics Gain Seats in the 98th Congress after Reapportionment

Maurilio E. Vigil

Background: The Changing Face of Hispanic Politics

In the mid-1960s, after decades of seeming quiescence, Hispanic Americans added their voices of protest to those of black Americans and native Americans in the United States. This period witnessed many forms of activist protest, especially among Mexican-Americans, including mass demonstrations, marches, picketing, boycotts, civil disobedience, and even some violent confrontations. For the first time, the so-called "forgotten Americans" publicly declared their demands for equal status as American citizens. As the decade of the 1970s passed, however, the signs of activism waned, creating the impression that the movement had fizzled. Now, in the 1980s, new evidence indicates that Hispanics, like blacks, have regrouped and begun to work through conventional styles for political change within the framework of the American political system.

The 1980s have seen a shift in emphasis from activist protest politics to the politics of the ballot box. There are several manifestations of this new mood, but the most important are increases in the number of Hispanics in the U.S. Congress as a result of the 1982 congressional elections. Hispanics gained three new seats in Congress and consolidated another won earlier in the year. Other manifestations of the changing face of Hispanic politics include increasing numbers of Hispanic voter registration and voter participation, more Hispanic municipal and county office holders, and Hispanic state legislators. Probably the most important victories, however, were the election of the first Hispanic as mayor of San Antonio, the na-

From *International Social Science Review* 59 (Winter 1984): pp. 20–30. Reprinted with permission of *International Social Science Review*.

tion's tenth largest city, and the election of a Hispanic as governor in New Mexico.

In 1981, Henry Cisneros was elected mayor of San Antonio, Texas, on the strength of overwhelming support from San Antonio's Mexican-Americans, who make up 54 percent of the 785,000 population. In 1982, Toney Anaya became New Mexico's fourth Hispanic governor in history and the second in modern history.[1] He also received overwhelming support from New Mexico's Mexican-Americans, who make up 36.6 percent of the state's population. In both cases Hispanics provided evidence that they would support their own candidate, a condition which has been questioned by some social scientists in the past.[2]

HISPANICS IN CONGRESS

The 1980 U.S. census of population revealed that Hispanics now comprise a total of 14,600,000 people, making them, next to blacks, the largest ethnic minority in the United States. More importantly, the new figure reflects an increase of 67 percent over the past decade, making Hispanics the fastest growing group in the United States. Already underrepresented in the United States Congress in 1970, Hispanics were even more underrepresented by the end of the decade, when there were only five of them serving in Congress, all being members of the House of Representatives. Hispanics made up 6.6 percent of the U.S. population in 1970, but comprised only 1.3 percent of the representation in the House of Representatives. The five Hispanics serving in the U.S. House in 1981 included Henry Gonzales, a Democrat who has represented a district comprising San Antonio, Texas, since 1961; E. "Kika" de la Garza, a Democrat who has represented a district from the Corpus Christi-Brownsville, Texas, region since 1964; Edward Roybal, a Democrat who has represented a district from Los Angeles, California, since 1962; Manuel Lujan, Jr., a Republican who has represented New Mexico since 1968; and Robert Garcia, a Democrat and the only Puerto Rican in the group (the others being Mexican-Americans), who has represented a New York City district since 1978.[3] Matthew J. "Marty" Martinez became the sixth Hispanic serving in the U.S. House in July 1982, when he was elected to serve the unexpired term (the remainder of 1982) of resigning California Congressman George Danielson. Because Congressman Martinez' seat was one affected by the reapportionment, it will be included in a later discussion. There have been no Hispanics serving in the United States Senate since 1976, when New Mexico's Joseph M. Montoya was defeated for reelection.[4]

CONGRESSIONAL REAPPORTIONMENT AFTER THE 1980 CENSUS

Although the number of representatives serving in the U.S. House of Representatives is not fixed by the Constitution but is established instead by federal law, the size of the House has remained at 435 seats for the past four decades. The method used to distribute seats is as follows: every state is given, in accordance with Article I, Section 1 of the Constitution, one seat in the House. A formula based on the principle of "equal proportion" produces "priority numbers" on the basis of the state's population which yield to each state a second, third, or fourth seat and so on. The principle of "equal proportion" is an effort to conform to the Constitution and the "one person one vote" guideline established by the Supreme Court in the case of *Wesberry versus Sanders* in 1964. Further court rulings have required that a district's population not deviate more than 1 percent from the average district population of that state.[5] The priority numbers distribute seats until all 435 have been exhausted. Every ten years the decennial census, a redistribution of congressional seats is in order to compensate states which have gained population. Naturally, this is done at the expense of other states whose proportion of the population has declined.

Shortly after the 1980 census was completed, it was found that about three-fourths of the nation's 435 congressional districts had gained population. Of these, 10 districts had increases greater than 50 percent and 58 districts had increases greater than 30 percent.[6] Accordingly, a U.S. Census Bureau report released on June 10, 1981, indicated that major congressional redistricting would be required. The 1980 census produced more grumbling than normal, however, because the states which lost seats included the industrial Midwestern and Northeastern states, while those that gained seats were concentrated in the South and Western sun-belt half of the country. Figure 1 shows the complexion of American states which lost and gained seats after the 1980 census. The biggest loser was New York state, which lost five seats. Ohio, Illinois, and Pennsylvania each lost two, while Massachusetts, New Jersey, Michigan, Indiana, South Dakota, and Missouri each lost one. Florida was the biggest beneficiary, as it gained four new seats, while Texas gained three, California two, and Washington, Oregon, Nevada, Utah, Colorado, Arizona, New Mexico, and Tennessee each gained one.[7] New York, the biggest loser, filed suit in U.S. District Court challenging the census figures. Judge Henry Werker ruled that an adjustment in the congressional districts would be necessary because the Census Bureau had undercounted the population. His ruling was overturned, however, by the U.S. Court of Appeals, which said that the lower court could not order such an adjustment without considering what effect it would have on other states.

Although federal laws and court decisions have established the guidelines for congressional reapportionment, the actual determination of the composition of congressional districts is left to the states or, more specifically, to the state legislatures in most states, although some states have nonpartisan commissions which participate in the process.

The redistricting process is inherently complex because of the need to establish districts which are almost exactly equal in population size while taking into account other demographic variables of the population, such as economics and rural or urban character. The problem is further complicated by a plethora of "political" variables which invariably emerge. The most important political influence present in the redistricting process is that of political parties. Each party traditionally sees reapportionment as a way of improving its position in Congress. The party in control of the legislature will usually have an inherent advantage in the process, while the minority party will be forced to go to court to challenge inequitable practices.

In recent years, ethnic minorities have perceived reapportionment as a way to correct traditional representational imbalances. This position was enhanced by the enactment of the 1970 Voting Rights Act which prohibited the drawing of districts that have the effect of diluting minority voting strength. In 1980, minority groups were better prepared than in 1970 to challenge congressional and state reapportionment plans that dilute their representation.

The courts, because of the provisions of the Voting Rights Act and greater vigilance by the U.S. Department of Justice, American Civil Liberties Union (ACLU), and organizations representing ethnic groups, have been more wary of state redistricting proposals and have been inclined to favor minority groups when redistricting plans are blatant examples of efforts to dilute minority voting strength. In the case of *Washington versus Davis,* for example, the court was concerned that "segregative policies of the political parties might deprive minority voters of the experience or benefit of political organization."[8]

The utilization of redistricting to remedy traditional underrepresentation of minorities has not been without critics. David Wells, for example, has argued that "affirmative gerrymandering," to equalize representation of specific groups, is no better than the gerrymandering which it is designed to eliminate. Says Wells: "The most effective way to prevent gerrymandering, both affirmative and negative, is not to impose arbitrary quotas; nor is it to vest special power in some judicial umpire or even in a non-partisan authority. Rather, it is to make sure that whoever draws the district's lines cannot do so in a manner calculated to bestow special advantage to any ethnic group, any political party, any partisan faction, any favored candidate or any favored geographic area. The best way is to establish firm, explicit, politically and ethnically neutral guidelines or grand rules. Such rules would eliminate a judgment as to where district boundaries shall be placed and who will be helped, and who will be hurt, which is the very essence of gerrymandering."[9]

Notwithstanding the ongoing debate on the matter, it is evident that ethnic minorities fared more favorably from the congressional redistricting process following the 1980 census. Blacks won three more seats in the House of Representatives in the 1982 election, bringing their number to 21 in the 98th Congress, which is the highest number of blacks ever. Hispanics also gained three seats, bringing their number to nine, which is also the highest number in history. The remainder of this study will be devoted to analyzing the circumstances and processes that led to such Hispanic gains in Congress.

THE REAPPORTIONMENT PROCESS AND HISPANICS

Because the Hispanic population is most heavily concentrated in the sun-belt states where the new congressional seats were located, it was natural to expect that they might benefit. However, as the following state by state descriptions will show, the process for Hispanics was less than simple, as they had to employ sophisticated legal and political maneuvering to overcome traditional barriers.

California

In California, the 4,500,000 Hispanics who make up 19.2 percent of the population also comprise one-third of the total Hispanic population in the United States. Most of these, or 80 percent, are Mexican-Americans. Despite high population numbers, Hispanics have traditionally been underrepresented in elective office. In 1982, for example, they held three State Senate and four State Assembly positions.

California qualified for two more congressional seats as a result of the 1980 census, and the resultant redistricting created two "open" districts with no incumbent congressman, and restructured several others which forced at least one incumbent congressman to relocate. A third vacancy was created when an incumbent congressman did not seek reelection. Because Hispanics were heavily concentrated in two of the above districts, they gained two of the three seats.

The redistricting process in California was specifically designed to increase Democratic Party representation in Congress, but also had the effect of helping Hispanics. In 1982, Democrats held 22 of California's U.S. House positions to 21 for Republicans, but despite population shifts to the suburbs (traditionally Republican strongholds) and already underpopulated Democratic urban districts, the state legislature, controlled by the Democrats, reapportioned the legislature in a way to enhance Democratic strength.[10]

Democratic U.S. Representative Phillip Burton, a close ally of California State Assembly Speaker Willie L. Brown, Jr., assumed the leadership role of liaison with the state legislature in congressional redistricting. Representative Burton produced the plan which was designed to secure as many as five new seats for the Democrats. The plan was structured so that at least eight incumbent Republican congressmen were placed in competition with one another. Representatives Barry Goldwater and Robert Dorman avoided an intraparty fight for their respective districts by running instead for the U.S. Senate. Representative David Dreier defeated fellow incumbent Wayne Grisham in the June primary and John M. Rousselot chose to run in a new district rather than face another incumbent, Carlos Moorhead. The Burton plan was adopted by the California legislature on September 15, 1981.

Because of its clear partisan gerrymandering nature, Republicans employed a two-pronged attack in challenging the plan, including a court suit to challenge the law and a statewide referendum asking voters to nullify it.[11] Despite their efforts, however, the plan was carried out.

A. *30th Congressional District.* California's 30th congressional district, represented by Democrat George Danielson for most of the 1970s, was changed considerably by the 1981 redistricting. The new district encompasses such suburban Los Angeles cities as El Monte, Alhambra, Monterey Park, San Gabriel, Montebello, Maywood, and Cudahy. Although once a rich agricultural area of orange, lemon, and walnut groves, the district is now heavily industrialized with major manufacturing in rocket motors, automobile parts, and electronic components.[12]

On June 8, 1982, a special election to fill the old 30th district seat vacated by Representative Danielson was held coinciding with the primary election for the new 30th seat. Matthew "Marty" Martinez, 53, a state assemblyman from Monterey Park (who was just completing his first term), was supported by the Waxman-Berman political machine and benefited from the heavy concentration of Hispanics, who make up 54 percent of the district's population. Martinez won the primary in a close race over Dennis Kazarian, who had been an aide to Representative Danielson. Martinez also won the special election with 32.4 percent of the votes over Kazarian, who received 29.1 percent, and Ralph Ramirez (a Republican), who received 15.9 percent, and two other opponents. Martinez won a special election runoff on July 13, 1982, with 51 percent of the vote over Ramirez, who received 40 percent. Martinez immediately flew to Washington and was sworn in on July 15 to serve the remaining 5.5 months of Representative Danielson's term and become the sixth voting member of the congressional Hispanic Caucus.[13] The victory gave Martinez the important advantage of incumbency in the district when he faced Republican Congressman John Rousselot, who had moved from the 26th district when the redistricting had placed him against another Republican. Martinez won the November 2 general election with 54 percent of the vote over Rousselot, who received 46 percent, a margin of 8,975 votes.

B. *34th Congressional District.* One of California's new districts, the 34th, is made up of suburban Los Angeles communities. The two largest cities in the district are located at different ends and contain about 80,000 people each. In the south is Norwalk, an older community made up of working-class people, about 40 percent of whom are Hispanics. On the other end is West Covina, a newer, still growing, and more affluent community. Also located in the district—whose population is 47 percent Hispanic—are Pico Rivera, La Puente, and South El Monte.[14]

Although the district was structured to provide a congressional base for one of several local Hispanic Democratic politicians, none entered the race. Initially, the only candidate was former three-time Congressman Jim Lloyd from West Covina, who received endorsement from the U.S. Chamber of Commerce and several Hispanic political leaders, including the mayors of Pico Rivera and La Puente. Eventually, Esteban Torres, a former White House official under Jimmy Carter and U.S. representative to UNESCO, entered the race. Although Torres's ties to East Los Angeles politicians concerned some Hispanic leaders in the suburban district who viewed his entry in the race as an attempt by the Los Angeles "Taco Mafia" to take over the 34th district, the issue soon died down when many prominent Hispanics endorsed his candidacy. Torres drew support from organized labor, national Hispanic leaders and organizations, and other national Democratic leaders. Helped by such support and a vigorous campaign, Torres defeated Lloyd and a third candidate, Fred Anderson, in the June primary.[15] Torres won convincingly in the November 2 general election, receiving 57 percent of the vote to 43 percent for Paul Jackson, his Republican opponent, a margin of 17,500 votes.

Texas

Texas, where Hispanics number 2,900,000, or 21 percent of the state population, was the only state in 1982 with more than one Hispanic congressman. Texas received three new seats as a result of the 1980 census, and the Texas state legislature adopted a new congressional district map incorporating the three new seats on August 10, 1981. In this case the plan, recommended by Republican Governor William Clements and conservative Democrat House Speaker Billy Clayton, was pushed through the legislature by a coalition of of conservative Democrats and Republicans.

On August 14, a group of blacks and Hispanics filed suit in U.S. District Court claiming that the reapportionment plan discriminated against the voting rights of the two groups. Specifically, at issue was the shaping of districts in South Texas, Dallas–Fort Worth, and Houston areas. Texas is one state where election law changes must conform to guidelines established by the 1965 Voting Rights Act. Thus, the federal court deferred action on the suit, pending review by the U.S. Department of Justice.

On January 29, the Justice Department issued a ruling that the new reapportionment improperly divided the Hispanic population in two South Texas districts—the 15th and the 27th. The legislature-approved plan made the 15th district 52 percent Hispanic. The Justice Department maintained that the plan packed the 15th with Hispanics, while diluting their strength in the 27th.

When Governor Clements refused to call the legislature into special session to remedy the problem, the three-judge federal panel rearranged the two South Texas districts on February, virtually assuring that Hispanics would win both seats.[16] Since popular Hispanic Congressman E. "Kika" de la Garza was the incumbent in the 15th district, the court's redistricting plan only helped assure his reelection.

The 27th district, one of the three new Texas districts, is comprised of a strip of five counties lined up in the southeastern tip of Texas, stretching north and south along the coast of the Gulf of Mexico. At the northern tip is Corpus Christi and at the southern tip is Brownsville, the two largest cities in the district. The people of Brownsville were not too satisfied with the composition of the district as established by the court. There, residents have regarded the larger Corpus Christi as a traditional competitor for tourists and trade and worried that their interests would take second place to those of Corpus Christi. Corpus Christi is the second largest (next to Houston) Texas seaport and has large petrochemical and aluminum plants and seafood processing. Brownsville, on the other hand, is more of a Mexican-style city with a larger proportion of Hispanics. Export-import trade with Mexico is basic to the economy and it is a major agricultural producer of fruits and vegetables. Nueces (Corpus Christi) and Cameron (Brownsville) counties have traditionally been supporters of the Democratic Party and, since the new district was two-thirds Hispanic, it was tailor-made for a Hispanic congressman.[17]

In this district, Solomon P. Ortiz, the Nueces (Corpus Christi) County sheriff, a veteran of eighteen years of public officeholding in Nueces County, entered the race, and as in the past the working-class Hispanics provided the support needed for electoral victory. In the primary, Ortiz faced a crowded field of candidates which included four Hispanics. Ortiz, who got 25.6 percent of the vote, narrowly defeated former State Representative Joe Salem, a popular Lebanese jeweler who speaks Spanish and is quite popular with Hispanics, by only 653 votes. Salem got 24.8 percent of the vote. Jorge Rangel, a young Harvard-educated attorney from Corpus Christi, ran an aggressive well-financed media campaign, but ended up a distant third in the race with 18.5 percent. He was followed by State Representative Gerald Gonzales (17.3 percent) and Ruben Torres, a former state representative and chairman of the Texas Pardons and Parole Board, who got 13.8 percent.

In the run-off election, Ortiz received the endorsement of Torres, the only candidate from Cameron County, and, by thus consolidating the Hispanic vote in the district, defeated Salem by almost 6,000 votes (Ortiz 56.2 to Salem 43.8 percent).[18]

In the general election Ortiz went on to defeat the Republican nominee Jason Luby, a former mayor of Corpus Christi, in a landslide. Ortiz received 65 percent to 35 percent for Luby, a margin of 31,350 votes.

New Mexico

In New Mexico, Hispanics make up 36.6 percent of the state population, which is the largest percentage of any state. The New Mexico population increased by 28.1 percent since the 1970 census. Thus, New Mexico also qualified for a new seat in the 98th Congress.

New Mexico is the state which has maintained the most continuous Hispanic representation in the U.S. House of Representatives and the only U.S. senator. The first Hispanic U.S. senator was O. A. Larrazolo, a Republican, who was elected in 1929 to fill the unexpired term of Senator A. A. Jones, who died in office. Larrazolo, who had served as the third New Mexico governor (1919–1920), attended only the 1929 session of Congress. In 1934, Dennis Chavez, then a Democratic congressman, sought to restore Hispanic control of one of New Mexico's U.S. Senate seats, but he was defeated by Republican Senator Bronson Cutting in a close race. When Cutting was killed in a plane crash in 1935, Democratic Governor Clyde Tingley appointed Chavez to the vacancy. Chavez was reelected five times, and died in office in 1962, after serving 28 years, longer than any other person in New Mexico history. Joseph M. Montoya, then a U.S. representative, ran for Chavez' seat in 1964 and defeated Edwin L. Mechem, who had been appointed to the position. Senator Montoya served until 1976, when he was defeated by Harrison Schmitt.

When New Mexico became a state in 1912, it was entitled to only one member of the U.S. House of Representatives. The first Hispanic to serve in that position and the first Hispanic to serve as a regular voting member of Congress was Benigno "B.C." Hernandez, who served from 1915 to 1916 and from 1919 to 1920. Other Hispanics to serve in the single position were Nestor Montoya (1921–1922) and Dennis Chávez (1931–1934). New Mexico was allotted a second seat in Congress in 1942 and Antonio M. Fernandez was elected to the new seat. Fernandez served until 1956, when he died in office. He was succeeded by Joseph M. Montoya, in 1957, who served until 1962.[19] Republican Manuel Lujan, Jr., restored Hispanic parity in 1968, when he was elected to the first congressional district. Lujan, who has been reelected seven times, and is now in his 15th year in Congress, was elected from the new congressional district encompassing Bernalillo, Torrance, Guadalupe, and De Baca Counties.

Third Congressional District. Because the greatest population growth in New Mexico has been in the Albuquerque metropolitan area included in the old first congressional district, represented by Manuel Lujan, it was apparent to political demographers that one of the three new districts New Mexico was entitled to would be a metropolitan district which would serve the Albuquerque metropolitan area (Bernalillo County). Congressman Lujan, as a resident of Albuquerque, promptly announced that he would run from the metropolitan district. The only question that emerged during the reapportionment process regarding this district was which of the smaller counties near Bernalillo would be added to this central district to bring its population to approximately one third of the state population. Torrance County was proposed in the original plan, but eventually De Baca and Guadalupe Counties were also included.

The boundary lines for the remaining two districts became a matter of controversy in the legislature. Although the historical political and economic patterns of the state seemed to suggest that a northern district and a southern district were the most logical alternative, some conservative leaders in the legislature saw otherwise.

To understand the ensuing reapportionment struggle, it is necessary to profile the regional diversity of the state. New Mexico has not only been characterized by its large Hispanic and Indian populations (Indians make up 8.1 percent of the population), but also because both populations are concentrated in the northern half of the state. These groups have also been characterized by low per capita income, higher unemployment, and greater dependence on social programs—welfare and food stamps—than other groups in the state. The north has also had a large corps of skilled and unskilled labor and small farmers.

The southern half of the state, especially "Little Texas" in southeastern New Mexico, has been characterized by a greater Anglo concentration, and a more conservative orientation representative of large and medium-scale farming-ranching interests.

These traditional socioeconomic differences between the northern and southern half of the state have been reflected in political voting patterns. The north has supported liberal and moderate Democrats in national and state elections, while the south has supported conservatives and Republicans.[20]

With such clearly identifiable regional differences along ethnic, economic, and political lines, the redistricting process seemed to point to a north-south-central congressional district configuration. Predictably, however, the redistricting process was influenced by special and ideological interests.

Although Governor Bruce King had indicated in 1980 that the issue of congressional and state legislative reapportionment would be undertaken by a special session of the legislature sometime in late 1981 or early 1982 and after the final census figures were available, the first congressional redistricting bills were introduced in the 1981 session of the legislature. Although the legislature did not adopt any measure, it foreshadowed the reapportionment conflict which would emerge later. Two bills were introduced in the state House of Representatives. One bill called for the division of the state into north-south-central congressional districts. Another bill called for the division of the state into east-west-central congressional districts. This latter bill was introduced by Representative Dan Berry, a leading member of the coalition of conservative Democrats and Republicans, who controlled the House of Representatives. This Berry bill, which would have had the effect of splitting in two the heavy concentration of Hispanics in northern New Mexico, was adopted by the House voters and Election Committee and passed by the House of Representatives. The state Senate, recognizing the controversial nature of the bill and the probability that it would be challenged in court by minorities (both because of dilution of Hispanic votes and because census results were not yet complete), refused to take any action on the House-passed measure. Thus, the bill died when the legislature adjourned.

In January 1982, Governor King called the legislature into special session ten days prior to the regular session in order to consider congressional and state legislative reapportionment. Although Governor King had earlier indicated that he would leave the matter of reapportionment to the legislature, he was clearly concerned that he might get a congressional reapportionment bill similar to the Berry plan, which had passed the House the year before. Signaling that he would probably veto such a proposal, and indicating his own preference for a plan which respected traditional economic, social, and political patterns, King presented his own reapportionment plan to the legislature.

The King plan was essentially a variation of the north-south-central district form, except that it divided the state almost diagonally, with boundaries for the two districts beginning near the northeast corner and running diagonally (along county lines) to the southwest corner of the state. This plan, probably more than any other proposed, recognized the regional differences in New Mexico. The Hispanic and Indian concentrations were in the proposed northwest district and the Anglo-farming-ranching conservative interests fell in the southeast district. The King plan also proposed that the central district would consist of Bernalillo County, Torrance County, and the "bedroom communities" of Corrales (in Sandoval County) and Bosque Farms (in Valencia County), since the latter were really part of the Albuquerque metropolitan area. This proposal to split counties is probably what made this plan unpopular, as the legislature seemed determined to respect county lines in reapportionment.[21]

Although at least five different plans were given serious consideration by the legislature, the basic contention was between the north-south-central district structure and the east-west-central district structure. Four of the plans were variations of the north-south-central plan, while the fifth was the Berry plan, which was reintroduced.

The debate on the measures, especially in the House of Representatives, was quite heated and bitter, with liberal Democrats condemning the Berry plan as discriminatory and a deliberate attempt to dilute Hispanic votes.[22] Representative Berry retorted, with candid irony, that Hispanics were one third of the state population and that his proposal gave them one third of the population in every district. Such reasoning, when publicly stated, would surely have been material for a court hearing on the matter if it had become necessary.

The debate on the measures reached a climax in the closing days of the special session when the Senate adopted a last-minute compromise bill prepared by Senator John Pinto (the only Indian in the Senate). The Pinto Bill, essentially a variation of the north-south-central district plan, offered a new twist in that it consolidated all the most Indian and Hispanic counties in the northern district, and it also placed Lincoln County in the northern district. Lincoln County was the home county of U.S. Congressman Joe Skeen, a Republican who had announced intentions of seeking reelection and had actively lobbied Republican state legislators to reject the Berry plan in favor of a north-south-central alternative. Alarmed at this new development, Skeen undoubtedly made known his displeasure to Republican legislators.

The House of Representatives meanwhile had adopted a slightly modified version of the Berry plan, which still retained one Hispanic county—San Miguel—in the southern district. When it became clear that neither house would accede to the other's vision, a Joint House-Senate Conference Committee was created to iron out the differences in the bills. The conference committee arrived at a predictable compromise in which a trade-off of San Miguel and Lincoln Counties occurred. The Hispanic San Miguel County, along with Harding County, went to the northern district, while Lincoln County and Grant County were restored to the southern district, thus satisfying the concerns of Congressman Skeen.

The compromise version of the bill was probably as satisfactory as could be expected for Hispanics, since only one county—Guadalupe—which had traditionally been part of the Hispanic coalition, was detached in the new districting map, which sacrificed it in the central metropolitan district.

The plan could not have been more ideally tailored for Bill Richardson, a political newcomer to New Mexico, who had established his credibility as a viable congressional candidate by running a very close race against Congressman Lujan in the 1980 election. Even before the new district boundaries were arrived at, Richardson had announced that he would be a candidate. Roberto Mondragon, the popular two-term lieutenant governor, also announced his candidacy along with District Judge George Perez and Santa Fe Attorney Tom Udall, a political novice in New Mexico, who was trying to capitalize on his father Stuart and uncle Morris Udall's name recognition.

Although a newcomer to New Mexico, Bill Richardson assumed the lead in public opinion polls and built on it with an extensive media and personal campaign. Richardson, a Hispanic by virtue of his mother's Mexican background, made his ethnicity clearly known in Spanish-language television and radio announcements. An extremely outgoing personality, Richardson devoted full time to the campaign and for the first six months of 1982 was literally everywhere in the district. Richardson received over 60 percent of the delegate votes in the preprimary convention and top position on the ballot. Lieutenant Governor Mondragon, although the better known candidate, was hampered by lack of finances for a strong media campaign, and his duties as lieutenant governor, which prevented him from devoting more time to the campaign. The result was that Richardson received the nomination over Mondragon by 3,488 votes. Richardson received 36.3 percent, Mondragon 30.1 percent, Perez 19.2 percent, and Udall 13.7 percent of the vote.

Having won the most important Democratic primary, Richardson was able to run a more low-key campaign for the general election against the little known Republican candidate, Marjorie Bell Chambers. He won the November general election overwhelmingly, receiving 64 percent of the vote to Chambers' 36 percent, a margin of almost 38,000 votes.

CONCLUSION

The convening of the 98th Congress saw the greatest number of new Hispanic congressmen than ever in American history, and the greatest numbers of Hispanic members of Congress ever. A total of 11 Hispanics (counting the two nonvoting members from Puerto Rico and the Virgin Islands) now belong to the Congressional Hispanic Caucus, the coalition of congressmen who represented Hispanic interests.

Although the reapportionment process which enabled the four new Hispanics to achieve their seats in Congress was an obstacle course that presented formidable barriers, their ultimate success indicates that Hispanics have begun to move forward in the American political arena.

Assisted by significant legislation, such as the 1965 Voting Rights Act (and its revisions), the more responsive posture of the federal courts, and a more sympathetic and responsive Democratic Party, along with the growing interest, involvement, and bloc-voting by Hispanic voters, Hispanics have made impressive gains in the 98th Congress.

There is little doubt that there is room for improvement. Texas' 44th congressional district, including El Paso, with a Hispanic population of 60 percent; California's 44th congressional district, including central San Diego; Colorado's third district, including Pueblo and the San Luis Valley; and Arizona's Pima County (Tucson) district; and, of course, the greater Miami area are examples where substantial Hispanic concentrations of population might be targeted by Hispanic candidates in the future.

Ultimately, the number of Hispanics in Congress will only be as viable as the political influence they can wield individually and collectively (as the Hispanic Caucus) in pursuit of public policies favorable to Hispanics. Fortunately, the five veteran Hispanics have reached a level of seniority which yields to each substantial political influence — Representative Garza as chairman of the House Commerce Committee, Representative Lujan as the ranking Republican on the Interior Committee, Representative Gonzales as a ranking member of the Banking and Small Business Committees, and Representative Roybal as a member of the Appropriations Committee — and are among the highest ranking members of the House of Representatives. What remains is for these congressmen to act individually and collectively in pursuit of public policies that will begin to pave the way for social, economic, and political opportunities for all Hispanic Americans.

NOTES

This paper was supported by a grant from the Institute of Research, New Mexico Highlands University.

1. Jerry Apodaca was elected governor of New Mexico in 1974 and served from 1975 to 1978. Prior to Apodaca, Ezequiel C. de Baca, elected in 1914, served in 1915 (but died in office) and Octaviano A. Larrazolo, elected in 1916, served in 1917 and 1918.

2. Mark Levy and Michael Cramer, "Patterns of Chicano Voting Behavior," in *La Causa Politica: A Chicano Politics Reader,* F. C. Garcia, editor (Notre Dame, Ind.: University of Notre Dame Press, 1974) pp. 241–249.

3. Two other Hispanics serve as nonvoting members of Congress. They are Baltasar Corrada, who represents Puerto Rico, and Ron De Lugo, who represents the Virgin Islands.

4. Senator Joseph M. Montoya had served in the U.S. Senate from 1964 to 1976. Before Montoya, Dennis Chavez represented New Mexico in the Senate from 1935 until his death in 1962.

5. *Kirkpatrick versus Preisler,* 394 U.S. 526, which says: "Equal representation for equal numbers of people is a principle designed to prevent debasement of voting power and diminution of access to elected representatives. Toleration of even small deviations detracts from these purposes."

6. Alan Murray, "Redistricting Still Plagued by Confusion," *Congressional Quarterly Weekly Report,* January 19, 1981, pp. 69–72.

7. Ibid.

8. "Racial Dilution in Multimember Districts," *Michigan Law Review,* March 1978, p. 694.

9. David Wells, "Affirmative Gerrymandering Compounds Districting Problems," *National Civic Review,* January 1978, p. 17.

10. "*Congressional Quarterly and Weekly Report,* May 30, 1981, pp. 941–942.

11. Phil Duncan, "Burton Stuns GOP with California District Map," *Congressional Quarterly,* September 19, 1981, p. 1797. The court suit failed, but voters approved the Republican-sponsored referendum, which overturned the legislature's reapportionment. The legislature will have to rewrite the law.

12. Ibid., April 24, 1982, pp. 937–938.

13. Congressional Hispanic Caucus, *ADVANCE,* August 1982, p. 1.

14. *Congressional Quarterly,* April 24, 1982, pp. 939–940.

15. Ibid., June 12, 1982, p. 1416.

16. Phil Duncan, "Courts at Odds Over Texas Redistricting," ibid., April 3, 1982, p. 752.

17. Ibid., p. 762.

18. Ibid., April 17, 1982, p. 885; June 12, 1982, p. 1429.

19. For a discussion of these prominent Hispanic congressmen, see Maurilio Vigil, *Los Patrones: Profiles of Hispanic Political Leaders in New Mexico History* (Washington, D.C.: University Press of America, 1980).

20. For a discussion of New Mexico politics and voting patterns, see Maurilio

Vigil, *Chicano Politics* (Washington, D.C.: University Press of America, 1978), chap. 7; "Jerry Apodaca and the 1974 Gubernatorial Election in New Mexico," *AZTLAN* 9 (1978): 133–150.

21. David Steinberg, "King Unveils Alternative Plan for Congressional Redistricting" *Albuquerque Journal,* January 8, 1981.

22. Representative Raymond Sanchez, House majority floor leader and the remaining leader of the liberal Democratic Mama Lucy Faction, which controlled the House until 1978, was the most vehement critic. For more on the Mama Lucy Faction, see Maurilio Vigil, "The Mama Lucy Faction in the New Mexico Legislature: A study of Chicanos in Legislative Politics," *New Mexico Highlands University Journal,* July 1980:50–59.

15. Hispanic Representation in the U.S. Congress

Susan Welch and John R. Hibbing

WHILE POLITICAL SCIENTISTS ARE beginning to analyze the extent, nature, and consequences of Hispanic political representation at the local level (Taebel 1978; Dye and Renick 1981; Karnig and Welch 1979; Welch, Karnig, and Eribes 1983), no systematic attention has been given to their representation in Congress. This omission is both curious and unfortunate in that 1 of every 16 people in the United States is of Hispanic ancestry. Perhaps the explanation for the lack of attention to Hispanic representation in Congress is that Hispanics make up a disproportionately small percentage of the population of Congress. As of 1980, only 1 out of every 87 members of the House of Representatives (5 out of 435) was Hispanic.[1] But we believe this fact is all the more reason to study Hispanic representation.

REPRESENTATION: DESCRIPTIVE AND SUBSTANTIVE

We approach this subject by using Pitkin's (1967) definitions of two types of representation.[2] The first, descriptive representation, simply refers to the ability of groups to elect representatives with similar traits — in this case, being of Hispanic ancestry. John Adams, for example, hoped the Congress would become an exact miniature of the entire populace in terms of relevant demographic characteristics. While this desire has not come to fruition, it is of interest to examine the degree to which Hispanic constituents are able to elect one of their own to the U.S. House.[3]

What factors facilitate the ability of a group to achieve descriptive

Reprinted from *Social Science Quarterly,* Vol. 65, No. 2, June 1984. Copyright © 1984 by the University of Texas Press. By permission of the authors and the publishers.

representation? Their numerical strength, no doubt, is a primary consideration. Assuming voters usually vote for someone of their own group if possible (Karnig and Welch 1981), the only way for a minority group to have a chance of securing adequate representation in a single-member district system is for that minority group to be heavily concentrated in some districts. This is why district elections to city councils provide nearly equitable representation for blacks in white majority cities, but at-large elections do not (Karnig and Welch 1981; Engstrom and McDonald 1982). In Congress, too, black majority districts in recent years have normally sent black representatives to Congress. In the 97th Congress (1981–82), only two black majority districts had white representatives, while in only three districts where blacks were a minority were blacks elected.

The numerical strength of the Hispanic population in electing representatives is diluted by the fact that many Hispanics are not citizens. About one-fourth of the Hispanics counted in the Census were foreign-born. While many of these are citizens, many are not. This situation has implications for descriptive representation. It means that a minority of the Hispanic population have no voice in choosing their representatives. Thus the potential for equitable descriptive representation is likely to reflect not the total population but the smaller citizen population. We have not seen data on Hispanic noncitizens by congressional district. However, it is very likely that the highest proportions of noncitizens are in those districts with the largest Hispanic populations, those we might expect to be most likely to elect Hispanic representatives.

In addition to descriptive representation, one can also be represented substantively, that is by having a representative with congruent policy views (Pitkin 1967) acting as an advocate. This means that a group can be represented without having its own members in representative roles, but rather by having its representatives act and vote in accordance with its policy preferences. If a group consensus is strong on a set of policy issues, we can say that the group is being represented in a substantive sense if representatives vote in accord with this consensus.

The problem in measuring substantive representation is that it is often difficult to determine whether or not a consensus exists on policy issues. Hispanics are not a homogenous group; unlike blacks, for example, they do not vote uniformly for Democrats. However, with the possible exception of Florida's Cuban population and some well-established groups in the Southwest, we would expect Hispanics, on the whole, to be more liberal than Anglos, more likely to favor government intervention in the marketplace and in protecting individual rights.

Again, the large noncitizen component of the Hispanic population complicates our understanding. One might expect that substantive representation would refer to representation of the whole population and not just its citizen subset. Yet representatives might feel little obligation to provide substantive representation for noncitizens, especially when their interests conflict with those of constituents who are permitted to vote. In our examination of substantive representation, we explored the effect of the total Hispanic population as measured in the decennial Census.

In this analysis we examined the following questions:

1. How many of the districts with significant Hispanic populations elect Hispanic representatives?

2. Do Hispanic representatives adopt a distinctive pattern of roll call voting?

3. Do large Hispanic populations have an effect on the voting behavior of their representatives?

To conduct this analysis, we employed data on the personal traits and voting records of U.S. representatives as well as information on the nature of the various congressional districts, particularly the percentage of the district's population that is of Hispanic descent. Our study covers the period 1972–1980 (the 93d through the 96th congresses).[4]

FINDINGS

The distribution throughout the nation of the Hispanic population can help explain why Hispanics are descriptively underrepresented. Only 6 percent of the nation's congressional districts (27) have constituencies that are over one-fourth Hispanic, and only eight districts are over 50 percent Hispanic—six in the Southwest (defined as Texas, California, New Mexico, Arizona, and Colorado), and one each in the New Jersey–New York area and in Florida. Clearly, then, while the Hispanic presence is a significant one, the distribution is highly skewed with the great majority of congressional districts (308) containing Hispanic populations that are 5 percent or less of the total district population.

A majority Hispanic population in the district is no guarantee that the district will be represented by a Hispanic, although it certainly does improve the odds. In 1980, for example, only four of the eight majority Hispanic districts had Hispanic representatives.[5] Some of these eight districts undoubtedly did not have a majority of Hispanics who were citizens, much less voters. Of all the districts without Hispanic majorities, only one (the 1st District of New Mexico, with 43 percent Hispanic) had a Hispanic representative. The fact that districts with 26–49 percent Hispanic populations could muster only one Hispanic representative is not surprising in light of the similar pattern for blacks noted earlier. Further, the fact that some portion of this Hispanic population was not enfranchised means that their actual political clout was even less than their sheer numbers indicated.

Descriptive representation may not mean substantive representation at all. Cynics may argue that members of minority groups who are in high positions have been coopted by the majority elites and that the value of such a representative to the minority community is symbolic only. To determine if Hispanics vote differently, we focused on the conservative coalition support scores compiled by all representatives in four recent congresses.[6] We attempted to explain variations in this score by whether or not the representative compiling the voting record was Hispanic. Since there were only a few Hispanic representatives, our findings are tentative, but our expectation was that the roll call behavior of Hispanics would be significantly different from that of non-Hispanics. If the relationship operated as expected, Hispanic representatives, other things being equal, should build more liberal voting records than their non-Hispanic counterparts. This assumption was based on the lower socioeconomic status of Hispanics and the commitment of Mexican-Americans and Puerto Ricans to the Democratic party (Grebler, Moore, and Guzman 1970; Levy and Kramer 1973).

One could also examine Hispanic voting patterns by using votes on specific legislation as dependent variables. While this might have the advantage of allowing a focus on legislation more particularly of relevance to Hispanics (such as immigration law) rather than a wide array of legislation, the narrower approach also has limitations. What votes should be chosen? How many roll call votes deal specifically with Hispanic interests? In spite of the appeal of a case study approach, using a narrow definition of "Hispanic interest" votes might result in so few votes as to capture idiosyncratic voting patterns rather than larger underlying predispositions. Thus, while future researchers may want to fine-tune our analysis by examining individual issues, this "first pass" will be more beneficial if it provides a broad view.

We regressed conservative coalition support scores on whether or not the representative was a Hispanic. We also included in the regression the party identification of the representative, as well as other variables generally believed to affect the voting behavior of representatives: the percent urban population in the district, the percent black in the district, and the percentage of the district's population with incomes ranking below the poverty line. Because these variables have known relationships with roll call voting, they are necessary in order to specify properly the equation. With them included, we were better able to isolate the true influence of being a Hispanic on roll call behavior.

Table 1 provides both the standardized and unstandardized coeffi-

TABLE 1

Hispanic Representatives and Conservative Coalition Support Scores

	PEARSON'S r	BETA	b (STANDARD ERROR)		N
All districts with 5 percent or more Hispanics	.04[a]	-0.07[*b]	-12.6	(6.0)	501
Southwest	.05	-0.15*	-23.2	(9.1)	304
New York–New Jersey area	$-.16$*	-0.02	-3.1	(10.0)	214

a. Correlation of whether or not representative is a Hispanic with conservative coalition support scores.
b. Relationship of conservative coalition support scores to being a Hispanic, controlling for constituency and personal characteristics described in text.
$p \le .05$.

cients as well as tests of significance. By concentrating on the unstandardized coefficients we see that, other things being equal, a Hispanic representative would be predicted to have a voting record that is nearly 13 points less conservative than a non-Hispanic representative. Table 1 also provides separate results for the two regions with Hispanic representatives in the 1970s—the Southwest and the New York–New Jersey area. When this division is made, we see that the strength of the overall relationship derives almost exclusively from the Southwest. For New York and New Jersey, the relationship was not significant and the size of the coefficient was quite small. For the Southwest, however, the coefficient was quite large, indicating that Hispanic representatives, on average, compiled voting records over 23 points less conservative than non-Hispanic representatives in the Southwest. This relationship easily achieved traditional levels of significance. Despite the small number of Hispanic representatives, we can say with some certainty that Hispanic representatives were more liberal than their non-Hispanic counterparts, controlling for party and constituency factors. Thus, from the perspective of the typical Hispanic constituent, residing in a district with a Hispanic representative did make a difference.

Of course, it is possible for the concerns of Hispanics to be represented by non-Hispanics. Substantive representation may occur despite the lack of descriptive representation. In fact, given the small number of Hispanic representatives, this would appear to be the major way Hispanics are currently represented in the U.S. Congress. We hypothesized that substantive representation would have taken place to the extent that the more Hispanics there were in a congressional district, the more likely the representative would vote in a liberal manner.

Again using the roll call records from four recent congresses, we regressed conservative coalition voting scores on the percent Hispanic in the district. We used the same controls as in our earlier regression plus a dummy variable indicating whether or not the representative was a Hispanic. We limited the analysis to only those districts with at least a 5 percent Hispanic population. This restriction seems appropriate since there is no basis for an expectation that an extremely small Hispanic constituency will have a discernible impact on the roll call voting of representatives.[7]

As the top line of table 2 demonstrates, the relationship was in the hypothesized direction (the more Hispanics in a district, the less conservative the roll call voting of the representative), and was significant at the .05 level. Though the R^2 was a respectable .67, meaning all the independent variables accounted for about two-thirds of the variance in the conservative coalition support scores, the size of the coefficient for percent Hispanic was not large. Since the unstandardized coefficient (b) was 0.19, an increase of about 5 percent in Hispanic population would lead to a decrease in the level of conservative voting by the pertinent representative of only about one point, *ceterius paribus*. So, while the relationship is significant and in the expected direction, it is not extremely powerful.[8]

When we performed separate analyses for the three areas of the country with major Hispanic concentrations—the Southwest, Florida, and the New York–New Jersey area—the relationship was in the predicted direction in all three regions (see table 2). However, the coefficient fell short of significance in the Southwest even though there were more cases in this region than the others. In the New York and New Jersey area and especially in Florida the relationship was easily significant and the coefficients were much larger. In fact, in Florida every 5 percent increase in percent Hispanic in a congressional district would lead to a 6 point drop in conservative voting on the part of the representative, other things being equal. This finding might seem surprising in light of accepted wisdom about His-

TABLE 2

Relationship of Percent Hispanic to Conservative Coalition Support Scores

	MEAN PERCENT HISPANIC	BETA[a]	b	(STANDARD ERROR)	R^2, ALL VARIABLES	N
All districts with 5 percent or more Hispanics	18.2	− 0.08*	− 0.19	(0.09)	.67	501
Southwest	20.0	− 0.09	− 0.19	(0.12)	.52	304
New York–New Jersey area	9.6	− 0.23*	− 0.58	(0.16)	.75	214
Florida	9.5	− 0.60*	− 1.20	(0.13)	.81	60

a. Controlling for percent urban, percent below poverty line, party, percent black, region (in national equations), and Hispanic representative.

panics in the Southwest being more liberal than other Hispanics. However, in Florida, many districts are very conservative.[9] Thus, representatives from Florida districts with larger Hispanic populations are more liberal than those from other Florida districts, but not necessarily more liberal than non-Florida representatives with large Hispanic constituencies.

IMPLICATIONS

Though Hispanics are not heard in the U.S. Congress as clearly as their numbers imply they should be, their concerns and desires are not ignored completely. We have found that the number of Hispanics in a district is important in explaining the type of representation the district will receive. Not surprisingly, increased numbers of Hispanics improve the chances a district will elect a Hispanic. But given the paltry number of Hispanics in the House—an increase of only three Hispanics in the 98th Congress amounted to a 50 percent increase over the 97th Congress—the major implication of our research, and the most realistic immediate hope for most Hispanics, is that non-Hispanic representatives will be somewhat responsive to the needs of Hispanic constituents.

Here we find that increases in the number of Hispanics produce representatives whose voting records indicate greater support for the liberal programs favored by the majority of Hispanic voters. In two districts that were identical in number of blacks, percentage of the district's population living in central cities, race and party of the representatives, and percentage of the constituency living below the poverty line, identical in just about every way except that one district had a 5 percent Hispanic population and the other had a 50 percent Hispanic population, our findings indicate that the roll call voting of the representative of the former district would have been about 8 or 9 points more conservative than the record compiled by the representative of the heavily Hispanic district. Thus, in the U.S. House, Hispanics do not lack influence; they just lack the influence their numbers warrant.

Our research on Hispanic congressional representation has been exploratory and hence rather general. We must await the election of more Hispanic representatives to draw firm conclusions about their behavior. As more Hispanics are elected, we will need to examine their achievement of leadership positions and important relevant committee assignments. Other possible fruitful research directions include testing generalizations about conservative voting on legislation specifically concerning Hispanics, such as politics on immigration, farm labor, bilingual education, and those directed toward low-income populations. And, of course, scholars interested in Hispanic politics will need to monitor carefully patterns of apportionment as they relate to Hispanic representation.

NOTES

1. Since 1980, some changes have occurred. One Hispanic was appointed to the House in 1980 and three more were elected in 1982. Two more Hispanics — from Puerto Rico and the Virgin Islands — serve but do not vote in the House, so they have not been included in the analysis. All but one of the Hispanics — Robert Garcia of New York — are from the Southwest.

2. Others have drawn contrasts similar to those of Pitkin's. Alvarez (1979), for example, contrasts "representativeness" with "representation." Representation is defined as advocacy on behalf of a group, with representativeness describing the equity of location of members of the group within an organization. These terms, then, are roughly analogous to Pitkin's substantive and descriptive representation.

3. The House of Representatives is used because of the special status it was and is accorded as a representative body. With smaller constituencies and more frequent elections, members of the House should be attuned to their constituents if anyone at the federal level is.

4. Though it would have been useful to include the 98th Congress in our analysis, detailed information about the demographic characteristics of the newly redrawn districts is not available at thie writing. (Neither are scales of roll call voting since the Congress is still in progress.) Our primary sources of data are the *Congressional Quarterly Almanac* (1972–80, various volumes) and the *Almanac of American Politics* (Barone et al., 1972–82, various editions). Since members of Congress build distinct voting records in every Congress, we have treated each representative's record in each of these two-year periods as a unique case. Thus, the total possible N for the project was 1,740 (4 × 435), even though the total number of individuals serving during these eight years was much lower. A few of these 1,740 voting records had to be removed because they were not compiled over the course of an entire Congress.

5. The others: California's 30th District, 62 percent Hispanic, represented by George Danielson; Florida's 14th District, 55 percent Hispanic, represented by Claude Pepper; Texas's 16th District, 57 percent Hispanic, represented by Richard White; Texas's 23d District, 53 percent Hispanic, represented by Abraham Kazen.

6. These scores are altered by failure to vote, so we have undertaken the standard correction procedures. See Poole 1981. The use of adjusted conservative coalition support scores as a measure of ideological voting is made attractive by Poole's finding that this measure correlates more strongly than any other with an overall conservative-liberal dimension.

7. Even with this restriction the N is still over 500, indicating there were approximately 125 districts in each of these 4 congresses with 5 percent or more Hispanic population.

8. Unlike the situation with the translation of black demands into roll call

votes, there appears to be no curvilinearity in the relationship between number of Hispanics in a district and roll call voting (see Bullock 1981; Black 1978).

9. Mean conservative coalition score for each region:

Florida	67.9
Southwest	54.9
New York–New Jersey	33.7

REFERENCES

Alvarez, Rodolfo. 1979. "Institutional Discrimination in Organizations and Their Environment," in Rodolfo Alvarez, Kenneth G. Lutterman, and Associates, eds., *Discrimination in Organizations* (San Francisco: Jossey-Bass).

Barone, Michael, et al. 1972–82. *The Almanac of American Politics*. Various editions (New York: Dutton).

Black, Merle. 1978. "Racial Composition of Congressional Districts and Support for Federal Voting Rights in the American South," *Social Science Quarterly* 59 (December): 435–450.

Bullock, Charles. 1981. "Congressional Voting and the Mobilization of a Black Electorate in the South." *Journal of Politics* 43 (August): 662–682.

Congressional Quarterly Almanac. 1972–80. Various volumes (Washington, D.C.: Congressional Quarterly, Inc.).

Dye, Thomas, and James Renick. 1981. "Political Power and City Jobs: Determinants of Minority Employment," *Social Science Quarterly* 62 (September): 475–486.

Engstrom, Richard L., and Michael D. McDonald. 1982. "The Underrepresentation of Blacks on City Councils: Comparing the Structural and Socioeconomic Explanations for South/Non-South Differences," *Journal of Politics* 44 (November): 1088–1099.

Grebler, Leo, Joan W. Moore, and Ralph C. Guzman. 1970. *The Mexican-American People* (New York: Free Press).

Karnig, Albert K., and Susan Welch. 1979. "Sex and Ethnicity in Municipal Representation," *Social Science Quarterly* 60 (December): 465–481.

———. 1981. *Black Representation and Urban Policy* (Chicago: University of Chicago Press).

Levy, Mark, and Michael S. Kramer. 1973. *The Ethnic Factor* (New York: Simon & Schuster).

Pitkin, Hanna. 1967. *The Concept of Representation* (Berkeley, Calif.: University of California Press).

Poole, Keith T. 1981. "Dimensions of Interest Group Evaluation of the U.S. Senate: 1969–1978," *American Journal of Political Science* 25 (February): 49–67.

Taebel, Delbert. 1978. "Minority Representation on City Councils," *Social Science Quarterly* 59 (June): 142–152.

Welch, Susan, Albert K. Karnig, and Richard Eribes. 1983. "Changes in Hispanic Local Public Employment in the Southwest," *Western Political Quarterly*.

16. Different Interests, Personalities Hurt Unity of Hispanic Caucus

Paul R. Wieck

ON MAY 5, REP. BILL Richardson, D-N.M., one of the four freshmen Hispanics in Congress, took charge of a special order on the House floor honoring El Cinco de Mayo, a Mexican holiday celebrating the victory Mexican troops won by holding off the invading French at Puebla in 1862.

Several of Richardson's colleagues, both Anglo and Hispanic, joined in the floor tributes but Richardson, seen by some as the most aggressive of the Hispanic newcomers, wanted to leave a special mark.

That day, he did it by speaking in Spanish—claiming later that it was a first on the House floor—after Chairman Eligio de la Garza, D-Texas, of the House Agriculture Committee had spoken.

Unlike Richardson, de la Garza is of the old order, a man devoted to the seniority system which has rewarded him with his chairmanship,

a man who gets upset when anyone rocks the boat. He didn't like it when Richardson spoke in Spanish.

"De la Garza jumped all over me," Richardson said later, adding that "he told me I was pushing too hard."

The story of the pushy freshman upsetting the hidebound senior isn't new to politics or any other endeavor. However, it does illustrate the strains within the 11-member Hispanic caucus (two are non-voting delegates from the territories) at a time when that diverse group is trying to find enough common ground to become an effective force.

Until redistricting gave the caucus four new members (two from California, one each from New Mexico and Texas), the caucus was made up of a handful of independently minded members who'd been around for a long time and had worked in tandem only when it was convenient. The freshmen have changed things.

"They're terrific," says Caucus Chairman Robert Garcia, D-N.Y., going on to say "they're one breath of magnificent fresh air. They've doubled our numbers. It's just terrific."

They've also made it necessary for a caucus which was more of an informal arrangement than an organized group to think about its agenda.

Events dictated the first item on the agenda—immigration reform.

It happened exactly five months after Richardson spoke in Spanish on the House floor. That day, Oct. 5, word leaked out that House Speaker Thomas P. "Tip" O'Neill, D-Mass., had pulled the Simpson-Mazzoli immigration bill off the House calendar after several weeks of intense lobbying by several members of the Hispanic caucus led by Rep. Edward Roybal, D-Calif., one of the senior members.

Five caucus members gathered at a hastily called press conference to claim what Garcia called a "major victory" and the "first cohesive win" for their diverse group.

It brought the caucus the first serious attention it had received from the media.

To caucus members, the results were disappointing. Instead of being applauded for stopping a bad bill, they opened their morning papers over the next week to find a rash of anti-O'Neill cartoons on editorial pages and a new perception of the Hispanic Caucus as, to quote Garcia, "an obstacle" to immigration reform. They were accused of vetoing the only solution being offered to what many regard as a major national problem—the waves of illegal aliens crossing our borders.

At the Oct. 5 press conference, Garcia declared it the intention of the caucus to draft a bill to deal with the problem.

Late in November, Speaker O'Neill called their hand by telling a *Boston Globe* reporter that he plans to bring up the Simpson-Mazzoli bill shortly after the Congress convenes in January, a move Garcia said "took us by some surprise."

The problem of drafting a bill the caucus can unite behind was summed up by Rep. Manuel Lujan Jr., R-N.M., when he explained that "everyone (in the caucus) is opposed to the Simpson-Mazzoli bill but each one of us has different reasons."

Lujan, a conservative Republican who comes out of the oldest Hispanic community in the country, will support only limited amnesty. Garcia, a Puerto Rican who represents the barrios of the South Bronx and embodies the liberal ethic of the urban Northeast, favors blanket amnesty for everyone illegally in this country.

Lujan and Garcia unite in opposition to the employer sanctions. Rep. Henry Gonzalez, D-Tex., the senior member of the caucus, wants sanctions as the only way to stop the "coyotes," as the smugglers are called. Says Gonzalez: "I tend to sup-

port sanctions as a way of controlling the smugglers. No smuggler
brings illegals in without an employer waiting."

Even before O'Neill called their
hand, work was under way on an
alternative.

The approach that has the best
chance of uniting the caucus is a bill
that simply beefs up the Immigration and Naturalization Service so,
to quote Roybal, "it can do its job."
Roybal would accomplish this by
giving it more money and personnel.

With more money, Roybal hopes
the INS can do a better job along the
border and clear up the backlog of
requests for legal status, thus eliminating some of the need for amnesty.

He also wants changes in the law
to clean up what he considers minor areas of discrimination in the
law.

At the League of United Latin
American Citizens, Arnoldo Torres,
the most visible of the Hispanic lobbyists in Washington, is putting together a similar bill. Torres leaves
out Roybal's accent on "legalization"
(he says it can be taken up later),
but stresses the need to give INS the
computer capability to keep track of
students and visitors who overstay
their visas and have become one of
the largest groups of illegals in the
country. He would also beef up enforcement of labor laws.

"Everybody agrees on enforcement of the present law on control
of the border," says Garcia, adding
"our focus will be on enforcement.
We come out now as obstacles to a
bill."

But will the public, including the
rapidly growing Hispanic minority,
be satisfied with such a bill?

A recent poll in de la Garza's
south Texas border district shows
that an overwhelming majority of
both Mexican-Americans and Anglos think the flow of illegal aliens
not only depresses wages but costs
jobs. The same poll shows strong
backing for strict enforcement of immigration laws.

A clear majority in that poll,
done by three Pan American University professors, supports employer
sanctions.

Two top pollsters—Peter Hart, a
Democrat, and Lance Tarrance, a
Republican—did a nationwide poll
for FAIR, a group that wants to seal
the borders, and found that big majorities of both Hispanics and blacks
believe that illegal aliens take jobs
and depress wages. And, by even
wider margins, those polled support
employer sanctions.

Taken together, the two polls suggest that the Roybal approach isn't
strong enough to satisfy the constituency of the caucus.

It remains to be seen if anyone
will exploit that gap.

If the caucus is to have an agenda
that deals with the problems of the
more than 15 million Hispanics,
many of them at the bottom of the
economic and social ladder, it will
have to go far beyond the problems
of immigration.

It will also have to decide where
to draw the line.

Early last summer, Garcia, acting
as caucus chairman, drafted a letter

to Prime Minister Felipe Gonzales of Spain asking, on behalf of the caucus, that he "review" the fact that Spain does not have diplomatic relations with Israel. Citing what he called the special relationship between Israel and the United States, Garcia wrote that "it does not seem unreasonable to hope that your government would seriously consider having formal diplomatic relations with Israel."

Garcia passed the letter around and 10 of the 11 members of the caucus, including Lujan and Richardson, signed it.

Garcia's letter raises an important question, namely: Should the Hispanic caucus (or any other caucus, for that matter) involve itself in the internal politics of another country?

San Antonio's Gonzalez, a loner in the caucus whose only priorities are the needs of his own district, was the only caucus member who didn't sign Garcia's letter. When asked whether the caucus should involve itself in another country's internal affairs, he answers "no" without hesitation. "I don't think we should be involved in Spain's internal politics."

Garcia, who says he couldn't find Gonzalez when he was circulating the letter, says "Henry doesn't go off on any tangents."

But some of those who signed are having second thoughts.

Richardson, whose name appears next to Garcia's on the first page of the letter, said he didn't recall Garcia asking him about it but said that now he would say no to the letter.

Lujan, when asked if he thought the letter he signed was proper, said: "No, I don't think so. I think we ought to deal in legislative issues. The only connection with Spain is that we all speak Spanish."

Meanwhile, Spain's Gonzales sent word to Garcia that he was making progress on the Israeli matter.

The caucus members also tend to agree that the White House shouldn't have to clear its Latin American policies with them even though they're convinced they have some expertise in that area which would be valuable.

"Our caucus should demonstrate more interest and concern with Latin America, but that doesn't mean we have the right to veto foreign-policy decisions or make them," Richardson said.

Another big question is how partisan the predominantly Democratic group should be.

Lujan, who didn't join the caucus until 1980 (he was elected in 1968), is the only Republican among the 11 members and he says it's too oriented toward Democratic programs.

"I didn't join for many years because every single position the caucus took would be the most liberal it could take. It was when Herman Badillo (Garcia's predecessor from the South Bronx who founded the caucus) was running it."

Now he says the causus has a rule that says "unless all members agree, it isn't a caucus position."

Despite this, Lujan says he complained to Garcia last fall that the annual fund-raising dinner had become "completely politicized" with O'Neill as the speaker this year and AFL-CIO President Lane Kirtland as the speaker last year. "I told him if it happened again next year, I would resign from the caucus and write the corporations who support it that they wouldn't be well-served in continuing to support it."

This outrages Garcia, who says "every year we have tried to get a Republican speaker. I've always invited the president, the vice president, the majority leader, the minority leader in writing. They've never accepted. I've already sent letters to both parties to speak at our September dinner."

San Antonio's Gonzalez has another problem with the fund-raising dinner.

Gonzalez has been in Congress for more than 20 years and he's never accepted contributions from people outside his district. So, a few years back, he was astounded to get a phone call from a lobbyist who wanted him to know he was going to buy 10 tickets to the annual fund-raising dinner.

He immediately called Roybal, who was chairman then, and complained. The result—Gonzalez chuckled as he told it—was that Roybal "drew a black line through my name on the letterhead."

Gonzalez sees a need for written caucus rules, lest the chairman "report stands or makes moves in the name of the caucus." This worries Gonzalez who is quick to point out, "I've never confused my role in Con-

gress. I'm not a regional or a state spokesman. I don't hold myself beyond my scope."

The Hispanic caucus isn't the only one which taps corporate sources for funds; indeed, it is the major source of funds for some caucuses.

The caucus has set up a separate corporation to handle the dinner because the proceeds have been used to buy a building on Capitol Hill to house its operation.

If Garcia has his way, the agenda of urban liberals—federal money for housing, education, jobs and other programs—will be the Hispanic caucus agenda.

Garcia is convinced that is the agenda the country's 15 million-plus Hispanics need, explaining that "they're hard-working people who have the same needs as everyone else."

During the days when the voting members of the caucus (delegates do not have a vote in Congress) were Gonzalez, Roybal, de la Garza, Lujan, and Garcia, it didn't make much sense for Garcia to push his urban agenda as the caucus program since at least two members—Lujan and de la Garza—couldn't be counted on to support it on the floor. The four freshmen, though they're as individualistic as their seniors, are a different breed in the sense that they are apt to go along with Garcia.

While Richardson is described as the "most aggressive of the lot" by those who watch the caucus on a daily basis, California's Esteban Torres, a Democrat who is a former United Nations official and labor leader, works quietly but commands great respect from his fellow members.

Torres' fellow Californian, Democratic Rep. Matt Martinez, worked long and hard in the party vineyards before coming to Congress and is seen as a spunky fighter for the same kind of programs Garcia is pushing.

But Rep. Solomon Ortiz, D-Texas, who comes from a rural district in South Texas, is seen as giving the caucus a perspective that is conservative in some respects but not when it comes to supporting the bread-and-butter items on Garcia's agenda.

That kind of agenda may split the caucus from time to time but it won't make them a target.

It's when the caucus is seen as frustrating immigration reform or sticking its nose into foreign policy or pushing for the kinds of programs that set them apart that they become a target.

That may be what worried de la Garza when he jumped all over Richardson for speaking in Spanish on the House floor.

Again, the issue isn't the language itself but a residue of fear in the Anglo community that ethnic politicians in the Hispanic community have a kind of separatism in mind.

But the insistence of Hispanic leaders that Spanish-speaking children in the public schools be taught in their own language until they're proficient enough in English has led to a lot of misunderstanding.

So has the bitter opposition of Hispanics like LULAC's Torres to efforts to have English declared the country's official language.

But Torres, perhaps the most aggressive of the ethnic politicians who prod the caucus, denies any ulterior motives. "Spanish as a second language in this country has never been our interest. We're committed to learning English."

Torres blames FAIR, an immigration reform group, for inflaming public opinion on that issue at this time.

Because the needs of the Hispanic community are so great and they so often find themselves defending unpopular positions on issues like immigration reform, some caucus members share de la Garza's concern over Richardson's ploy in speaking Spanish on the House floor when members gathered to honor the Mexican holiday, El Cinco de Mayo.

It was, in their minds, the wrong issue to push at a time when the caucus is trying to define its role.

17. Hispanic Underrepresentation in the Federal Bureaucracy: The Missing Link in the Policy Process

Harry P. Pachon

DESPITE THE UNPRECEDENTED ADVANCES that have been made by Chicano, Puerto Rican, and other Hispanic groups in articulating the policy concerns of the Hispanic community at the national level, Hispanic input into the federal domestic policy-making process continues to be minimal or missing altogether. Groups such as the Forum of National Hispanic Organizations, the National Council of La Raza (NCLR), the National Association of Latino Elected and Appointed Officials (NALEO), the Congressional Hispanic Caucus, League of United Latin American Citizens (LULAC), Mexican American Legal Defense and Education Fund (MALDEF) and others have made Hispanic concerns known in specific public policy areas such as the census, bilingual education, the voting rights act, immigration, and other high visibility issues that are most commonly associated with this community. Yet, the issues that are most closely identified with the Hispanic community are few when compared to the myriad number of policy issues that Congress and the federal executive consider every year—year in and year out.[1] What about these other issues? How is the Hispanic community faring in regard to them? Let us consider some examples:

1. While details of the 1984 budget are now known, as of this date very little is known on how this budget (outside of bilingual education) will affect the Hispanic community.

From *The State of Chicano Research in Family, Labor, and Migration Studies* (Stanford, Calif.: Stanford Center for Chicano Research, 1983), pp. 209–219. Reprinted with permission of the author.

2. In the development of new legislation affecting AFDC families, Hispanic input has been nil in the present administration.

3. When the past administration proposed its national urban policy initiative to Congress, Hispanic input was almost totally absent throughout the entire policy development process.

4. When welfare reform was being considered in the late 1970s, there was no Hispanic representation in the Bureau that was mainly responsible for its development. (Income Security Policy, Assistant Secretary for Planning and Evaluation, Department of HEW.) This occurred in spite of the fact that 12 percent of the low-income families in the U.S. that would have been affected by this proposal were Hispanic.

A commonly cited reason on the lack of Hispanic input in these cases is the relative recentness of arrival of Hispanic interest groups at the national level. Most political observers would agree that it was not until the late 1960s that a handful of individuals began articulating national Hispanic concerns. From this period to today, the number and breadth of Hispanic organizations at the national level has grown impressively. However, their numbers are still few and their resources limited. Those organizations which are active in attempting to influence the policy process, e.g., LULAC, NALEO, NCLR, have either one or two person operations in Washington, or are able to allocate only portions of their resources to the time-consuming task of legislative and executive lobbying. In contrast, other ethnic organizations such as the Urban League, the NAACP, the American Jewish Committee, with their million dollar budgets, their large staffs, and their decades of history, indicate the relative disparity of organizational development and political influence of the Hispanic community vis-à-vis other ethnic groups.

Besides the lack of organized political influence, another factor accounting for the lack of Hispanic input — and frequently less cited — is that, for many federal policy makers, "minority" still means black. "Race" means either black or white. Chicanos, Puerto Ricans, and other Hispanics who do not fit into this biracial perspective are either ignored or assumed to be the same as black Americans. The result quite often is an attempt to meet the needs of all minority groups with the same remedy, or, to assume that Hispanic needs have been met because other minority communities' needs have been addressed.

This biracial perspective and lack of awareness of the Hispanic community among public policy makers are due not only to the community's lack of political influence, but also the fact that Hispanics are absent from the standing bureaucracies that are so responsible for setting the parameters for domestic public policy. It is the thesis of this presentation that Hispanic underrepresentation in the federal bureaucracies is the critical missing link that is often overlooked in attempting to explain this community's lack of impact on the policy process.

This is understandable, however, since acknowledging that the standing bureaucracies are significantly involved in the political side of the policy process is a concept that most Americans shy away from. There is still the Wilsonian notion that American public bureaucracies—at the federal, state, and local levels—are non-political organizations that administer policies passed by politicians. Thus, while the media and the public give great attention to the passage of public laws by Congress, much less attention is paid to a *Notice of Proposed Rulemaking* or final promulgation of regulations in the *Federal Register*. Yet, policy analysts and administrators in the various domestic departments, and of course in the Office of Management and Budget, are critically involved in making decisions that affect all Americans. Several reasons are acknowledged[2] as accounting for the importance of the bureaucracy in the policy process. When public policy is legislated by Congress, policy goals are set forth in the most general of terms. Interpretation and operationalizing of such terms as the "needy," "a household," and "the family," are left in the hands of agency bureaucrats. The very characteristics that the public negatively associates with governmental bureaucracies—knowledge of routine, expert specialization, in-depth understanding of obscure regulations—are the factors that enable members of the bureaucracy to be in such commanding positions in determining the parameters of public policy. Development of this type of expert knowledge is critical when one considers that many domestic policy issues are "techno-bureaucratic" in nature. Specifically, techno-bureaucratic issues are ones involving complex policy and implementation considerations that are not subject to quick and easy solutions (or understanding). For example:

1. Where should a "cap" on benefits be placed on welfare families and their children? Should a ceiling on benefits be placed after a certain number of children? If so, how many?
2. What should the formula be for determining a state's allocation of emergency energy relief funds? Should frost belt states be treated differently than sunbelt states? If so, to what degree?

Techno-bureaucratic questions like these are ones that federal agency officials wrestle with every day. Yet, these same officials have a startling lack of information on the Hispanic community. Historically, they have failed to ask the question, "How does policy X impact on the Hispanic community?" Currently, they are still continuing to overlook the Hispanic community's characteristics of large extended families, bilingualism, and biculturalism, and the implications of these factors to federal policies and programs.

How does one measure this lack of representation in the bureaucratic policy process? A simple percentage of Hispanic employment in government, or in any agency, is not a valid statistic of the group's representation — or its lack thereof — in the policy-making process.[3] The Social Security Administration, for example, has one of the highest percentages of Hispanics in any governmental agency, yet, a great number of them are concentrated at the case or street worker level. A more accurate statistic would be to determine what numbers or percentages of Hispanics are at present significant policy-making levels within a department or within key agencies in a department.[4] Adopting this approach makes one focus on the highest level of the federal bureaucracy, the Senior Executive Service (SES). The SES, formed during the Carter Administration, is the highest level of career government employment. Although there are over three and one half million government employees, there are, by legislative mandate, less than 7,500 SES positions. Typically, SES positions are considered the elite, top management and policy-related positions in any agency. Hispanics comprise 7.8 percent of the population, yet according to the U.S. Office of Personnel Management, the community's representation in this corps of bureaucrats is 1.7 percent. Out of the 6,736 SES positions, less than 70 were held by Hispanics in 1982.

Other key positions in the federal bureaucracy — most notably in the domestic departments — are social science analytic and program evaluation positions. These slots are ones designated as analytic positions within a department or an agency and are ones charged for conceptualizing and analyzing agency programs and utilizing applied social science research for determining program effectiveness. Out of 16,064 such positions in the government, only 440 (2.7 percent) are held by Hispanics. Thus, the previously stated question, "How does program X affect the Hispanic community," may not be foremost in many analytic agendas.

Underrepresentation by occupational category, however, is but one measure of the Hispanic presence in the bureaucracy. One could argue that it is as important to have Hispanics in key governmental agencies, regardless of their position, as it is to have them in specific positions. If one examines policy and analytic units and overall policy-making agencies, such as the Office of Management and Budget, one finds a similar picture of Hispanic underrepresentation. For example, in the office of the Assistant Secretary for Planning and Evaluation, Department of Health and Human Services, out of 150 employees, one is Hispanic. In similar counterpart agencies, the record is much the same. In the Office of Planning, Budgeting, and Evaluation, Department of Education, there are no Hispanics. In the Office for Policy Development and Research, Department of Housing and Urban Development, there are no Hispanics. Finally, in the Office of Management and Budget, the office most closely associated with the President, there are four Hispanics out of 950 staff members.

If one looks at the legislative bureaucracy, Hispanic underrepresentation is also the rule. For example, on the House Appropriations Sub-Committees for the Department of Health, Human Services, Education, Labor, and Housing and Urban Development, there are no Hispanics. In the counterpart authorization committees, there are also no Hispanics. In Congress as a whole, there are 70 (0.3 percent) out of 20,000 staff members.

What has been the response from the federal government in attempting to increase Hispanic presence in the policy process? In the 1960s and 1970s, the first response (besides affirmative action) was to meet the needs of Hispanic representation through structural reform. Specifically, this took the response of instituting offices or agencies whose purpose was to articulate the needs and concerns of the Hispanic community. The Cabinet Committee on Opportunities for Spanish-Speaking Americans exemplified this response on a government-wide basis. At the departmental level, its counterparts were the Hispanic Concerns offices, such as the ones established in the Departments of Education and Housing and Urban Development. The attempt to overcome the problem of Hispanic underrepresentation in the policy process by establishing these advocacy offices was, in hindsight, doomed to failure. Although the personnel in these offices often did a tremendous job in articulating the Hispanic concerns (for example, note the record of the Division of Spanish-Surnamed Americans within the office of the Assistant Secretary for Planning and Evaluation, Department of Health, Education and Welfare), these offices never became established actors in the policy process. Many factors worked against them (e.g., inadequate staffing, placement outside the regular stream of departmental decision making, being looked down upon by personnel from other offices), which contributed to their ineffectiveness in meeting their objectives.[5]

Besides structural reforms, another response in meeting the need for Hispanic representation at the federal level has been every administration's attempt, since John F. Kennedy, to appoint highly visible Hispanic political appointees. Beginning with Kennedy, reaching a highpoint with President Carter, and continuing with President Reagan, administrations have played the traditional ethnic political game of publicizing Hispanic appointees. These appointees (some more than others) have labored to do the double job of serving as a political appointees with a specific responsibility, e.g., Assistant Secretary, and also serving as the policy access points for Hispanic community concerns. Many individuals, such as Fernando Oaxaca during President Ford, William Medina and Bambi Cardenas under President Carter, and many current Hispanic appointees in the present Administration, have all tried to fulfill these dual functions. Yet, political appointees, as a group, face certain problems. Endemic to appointees is the length of time it takes to learn the responsibilities of a new position. An old Washington dictum states that it takes weeks to simply get to know all the acronyms in an agency. Political appointees do not begin to participate in the every-day policy decisions until well into their appointments. Even then, the time they can devote to techno-bureaucratic matters is limited, given the variety of functions they have to fulfill. Finally, the nature of a political appointment means political appointees often do not remain in office long enough to become effective. In the cases where political appointees overcome these obstacles, they become highly influential. For example, there is no doubt that the initial push for implementing the Roybal Act (P.L. 94-311, "Better Social Statistics for Hispanics") came, in part, from Fernando Oaxaca's leadership at OMB. It is also not a coincidence that the national Hispanic Housing Coalition began at HUD when Dr. William Medina was HUD's Assistant Secretary for Management. Yet, these are exceptions.

While political appointees come and go, the permanent bureaucracy remains, continuing to develop its institutional memory and often being the only actor that has the expertise to critically outline all policy options and their past history.

The shortcomings of federal responses to institutionalized Hispanic input in the policy process highlights a central theme of this paper. The long-range solution to institutionalizing Hispanic concerns in the policy process of federal agencies is to increase Hispanic representation in these offices. One realizes that this policy representation raises the spectre of resurrecting the "quota" or an affirmative action system which has been so unpopular in this country. Yet, it is highly suspect that all of these bureaucracies have not been able to recruit or retain qualified Hispanic employees. Given this dismal record, one can argue that the burden of proof falls upon these agencies in documenting how they have been, and continue to be, responsive to the Hispanic community, lacking any Hispanic representation themselves.

What can Chicano, Puerto Rican, and other Hispanic academics do about this situation? It is first necessary to realize that Hispanic academics are in a critical position to have some impact on the present situation. If one acknowledges that the experiential knowledge of the policy process is valuable, then it should follow that Hispanic students and academics who are interested in politics and the policy process be encouraged for internships and participatory experiences in state capitals and in Washington, D.C. The Congressional Hispanic Caucus, for example, has a semester fellowship where graduate students are placed in standing committees of the House of Representatives, such as the Appropriations Committee, the Housing Committee, and Committee on Agriculture. Hispanic organizations such as the National Council of La Raza have, in the past, had federal internships. Other organizations such as the American Political Science Association (APSA) and the Institute for Educational Leadership (IEL), have established fellowship programs for academics. Aside from experiential opportunities, government service needs to be emphasized as a potential career for Hispanic students. Despite present budgetary cutbacks, the continued growth of the federal and state governments has been a fact of life for the past quarter of a century. Hispanic undergraduate and graduate students need to be aware that government service offers rewarding and challenging careers for them to consider. Hispanic faculty are in a key position to encourage students to become aware of public service opportunities.

Finally, Hispanic academics need to realize that there is a lack of Hispanic perspectives on the policy process at the national level. Academics need to creatively address the issue of how to overcome current problems that exist by not having representation in the bureaucratic policy processes. For example, there are other means of having an impact on the technobureaucratic policy issues. Publishing policy-oriented literature, for example, is still an appropriate means of having such impact. Popular articles, such as Op-Ed columns in national and major metropolitan newspapers (which, unfortunately, do not earn points in the tenure process) are critical in shaping public policy.

Hispanic underrepresentation in the federal government will continue — most likely through the upcoming decade. Until the Hispanic community fully addresses this issue, it will too often be the case that the Hispanic community will be in a reactive position on major domestic policy issues instead of being an active participant in the domestic policy process that is so relevant to our communities.

NOTES

1. For example, in the 96th Congress, 613 Public Laws were passed encompassing 3,000 pages of legislation. The House of Representatives alone considered and passed 1,167 bills. Source: Congressional Reference Service.

2. See Laurence Lynn, *Managing the Public's Business* (New York: Basic Books, 1981), and Kenneth Meier, *Politics and the Bureaucracy* (North Scituate, Mass.: Duxbury Press, 1979).

3. Hispanic employment increased 0.8 percent from the years 1969 to 1979. At this rate of increase it will take to the year 2025 before Hispanic employment in the federal government reaches parity in correspondence to the present proportion of Hispanics in the nation.

4. This measure represents the *potential* for Hispanic representation in the policy process. Of course there are cases where ethnic bureaucrats refuse (consciously or unconsciously) to identify with their community. Conversely, there are majority bureaucrats who have done exemplary jobs in addressing minority concerns. The literature on this subject, i.e., representative bureaucracy, strongly indicates that minority representation in the civil service fulfills both the normative democratic goal of group representation in the political system as well as the utilitarian goal of minority input in the policy process. See David Rosenbloom, "Representative Bureaucracy: Still Controversial After All These Years?" a paper presented at the panel of the American Political Science Association annual meeting, Washington, D.C., August, 1979. See also, Meier and Nigro, "Representative Bureaucracy and Policy Preferences," *Public Administration Review* 69 (July/August 1976): 458–469.

5. The author is indebted to Victor Vasquez, former director of the Division of Spanish-Surnamed Americans, Assistant Secretary for Planning and Evaluation, Department of Health, Education, and Welfare, for having so freely shared his insights into the history of these offices.

18. Chicano Elites and National Policy-making, 1977–1980: Passive or Active Representatives

Rodolfo O. de la Garza

THIS STUDY ANALYZES HOW Chicano elites in Washington, D.C. defined and performed their roles during the Carter administration. The analysis combines the literature on political generations with the theory of representative bureaucracy to generate and test hypotheses regarding the attitudes and behavior of these elites. Specifically the study seeks to determine if these elites share and actively represent Chicano interests, and if so, what the results of those efforts are.

The paper is divided into three sections. The first reviews the literature on political generations and representative bureaucracy and integrates the two approaches to generate hypotheses regarding Chicano elite attitudes and behavior. The second reviews the argument for the rise of a new Chicano political generation and shows that as a group these elites are members of that generation. In the third section, the paper describes the role perceptions and policy orientations of these elites, the tactics they use in pursuit of their objectives, and the results of their efforts.

The data presented here are taken from a larger study of Chicano political elites conducted between 1978–1980. The specific data used for this study are taken from fifty-eight interviews conducted with forty-one political appointees in the Carter Administration, four congressmen, and thirteen community leaders and representatives of national organizations based in Washington, D.C. The respondents constitute more than a sample; they represent almost the entire population of Washington-based elites in office between 1978–1979. Only three individuals, one congressman and two appointees, refused to be interviewed. Of the organizations and community leaders identified, only one could not be contacted.

314

I. Political Generations and Representative Bureaucracy

A political generation is a group of individuals that shares formative political socialization experiences and, as a consequence, also shares political attitudes and behavior (Rintala 1979). Often it includes more than one biological generation, and members of the generation usually but not necessarily recognize that they are a distinctive group and frequently interact and reinforce their bonds (Huntington 1977; Rintala 1979).

It is also important to note that a new political generation represents a break with the past. Its members will share many values with the former generation(s), but they will be distinct in key areas. The development of a political generation, thus, often accompanies major societal disruptions because these disruptions usually lead to the reevaluation of societal norms and values.

The theory of representative bureaucracy is based on two premises. First, the role of the bureaucracy is equal to or greater than the role of the legislature in policymaking (Long 1979; Kranz 1976; Krislov 1974). Second, legislators are increasingly incapable of representing the numerous class and ethnic interests that characterize almost all national populations (Kingsley 1944; Krislov 1974; Kranz 1976). The composition of the U.S. Congress illustrates the validity of this premise.

> If one were to set forth in law the facts of life of the American Congress, it would appear that, to be eligible, overwhelmingly a candidate had first to be in the upper-income bracket or second, either personally or through his associates, to be able to command substantial sums of money. Expressed as custom, such conditions are passed over save for carping criticism of Marxists; yet if they were expressed in law, they would clearly characterize our constitution as oligarchic (Long 1952).

Therefore, advocates of representative bureaucracy argue that all major class, ethnic, and cultural interests must be included within the bureaucracy if they are to be served and societal cohesion developed.

Initially it was assumed that such representation was achieved merely by including in the bureaucracy individuals who shared the principal demographic or cultural characteristic of the group in need of representation (Krislov 1974). F. C. Mosher (1968) challenged this assumption and distinguished between passive and active representation. Passive representation occurs when bureaucrats have demographic characteristics comparable to those of the total population. Active representation refers to those situations where administrators articulate the interests of the specific group which it is assumed they represent because of shared demographic attributes (Mosher 1968; Thompson 1976).

Although there is no necessary relationship between passive and active representation, it is widely assumed that passive and active representation are linked and that minorities will better represent their group than will non-minorities (Thompson 1976, 202; Krislov 1974, 73). Moreover, because the public has few mechanisms for holding administrators accountable, a group may only hope that the administrators "representing" it share its attitudes and values. Thompson argues, however, that even shared values do not guarantee representation. For representative bureaucracy to exist, he insists that administrators must act to increase the advantages of the group (Thompson 1976, 202–203).

Efforts to define the existence and effect of representative bureaucracy in the United States have produced mixed results. First, there is disagreement as to whether the United States has a representative bureaucracy by any definition. One study concludes that a representative bureaucracy does indeed exist because the bureaucracy reflects the middle-class nature of American society and "the general American consensus transcending class barriers and covering a wide field of political and social values" (Subramaniam 1967, 1018–1019). A subsequent study challenges this conclusion and argues that American bureaucracy is not representative even by minimal, that is passive, standards (Meier 1975, 541–542). This finding is supported by studies of black representation in state bureaucracies where only "extremely mild" support for existence of passive bureaucracy was found (Sigelman and Karnig 1976, 242). A general study of ethnic minorities and women also rejects the conclusion that the United States has even a passive representative bureaucracy (Kranz 1976, 193–197).

Efforts to determine if there is a linkage between passive and active representation also yield mixed conclusions. Meier and Nigro point out that although representative bureaucracy theory posits a sequential relationship between social origins, socialization experiences, and attitudes and behavior, few studies actually attempt to examine empirically the linkages among these variables. Furthermore, the theory does not take into account the socialization experiences individuals undergo once they become members of organizations (Meier and Nigro 1976, 459–460). Their test of the theory also proved inconclusive. They conclude that "knowing the origins of the supergrades tells us little about their attitude and correspondingly less about their policymaking behavior." Nonetheless, they did find that of eleven demographic variables, the one which had the greatest impact on the attitudes of the supergrades was race. It had a direct effect on eight of twelve variables, though the impact was "statistically unimpressive" (Meier and Nigro 1975, 465–466). They also suggest that social origins and attitudes are most highly correlated in issues related to the social conditions of minorities, but even here the impact of professional socialization within particular agencies is as significant as ethnic origins. They conclude, therefore, that the principal value of representative bureaucracy is that it provides a "symbolic affirmation" of the nation's democratic values but that it has "little real policy impact" (Meier and Nigro 1976, 466–467).

Thompson's findings more strongly support the theory. Although historically minority administrators were often less supportive or sensitive to minority clients than were non-minority administrators, he cites recent studies to show minority professionals to be significantly more positively oriented to minority clients than are non-minority professionals. He concludes that passive and active representation may be linked and that socialization in an agency does not necessarily supersede prior socialization (Thompson 1976, 205–208). Furthermore, he found that minority clients respond differently to minority professionals than to white professionals (Thompson 1976, 208–210). This is a significant finding given that the ultimate test of representative bureaucracy is "functional effectiveness" (Krislov 1974, 129).

Thompson draws on his findings to identify the conditions under which a passive-active representational linkage is most likely to exist. Linkage is more likely when:

1. Institutions and groups in society articulate an ideology of minority pride and press for the advancement of minority interests.
2. Minority officials deal with issues which have patent ramifications for the well-being of their race.
3. Minority employee associations exist in an agency.
4. Minorities occupy discretionary jobs, especially if those jobs are in the lower echelons.
5. Members of a minority group work in close proximity to one another (Thompson 1976, 212–217).

When combined with the literature on political generations, Thompson's findings increase in significance. In the past, passive and active representation were apparently unconnected, and this probably reflected the efforts of minority officials to adapt to general societal conditions. Until the Civil Rights Movement, and surely for several years afterward, it may be argued that minority officials self-consciously attempted to prove their "objectivity and competence." Behaviorally, this meant that they had to prove themselves to be neutral and professional, that is, they had to behave like non-minorities and could not openly act as ethnic advocates. Sometimes this led to over-compensation and anti-minority behavior by minority officials, as the reputations of many black and Chicano cops, judges, and teachers in the past attest. The Civil Rights Movement, however, appears to have contributed to developing a new political generation, and Thompson's findings regarding recent changes in the behavior of minority officials suggests that these new officials are recruited from this new generation.

Thus, there is a relationship between representative bureaucracy theory and the literature on political generations. Specifically, in the American context, the relationship between the two may be stated in the following proposition: If civil rights activities led to the creation of a new political generation among minorities, then officials who are members of that generation may be expected to be active representatives. As Thompson indicates, however, minority officials constitute but one part of a larger group or political generation which is characterized by common attitudes and objectives. Thus, the existence, activities, and success of these officials is directly linked to groups beyond themselves.

Based on this formulation, then, if contemporary Washington-based Chicano elites are members of a new political generation, they will be active representatives. The next section of this paper reviews the development of this new Chicano generation and shows that the respondents included here are indeed members of that new political generation.

II. The New Political Generation and the Chicano National Elites

Contemporary Chicano elites are members of a new political generation that differs from previous generations in several key aspects (de la Garza and Vaughan 1984). They are the first group since the late nineteenth century to hold significant numbers of high level public offices and to be in a position to influence public decisions (de la Garza 1984; Garcia and de la Garza 1977). This generation also experienced the civil rights and antiwar movements of the 1960s and early 1970s, and they came to office with different orientations and commitments from previous political generations (Moore and Cuellar 1970). Finally, this new generation draws from all the southwestern states, and its membership is primarily characterized by a heightened sensitivity to Chicano issues and a commitment to using the political system to redress historical wrongs. De la Garza and Vaughan (1984) conclude that "discriminatory experiences . . . are the best predictor of the participatory motivations of this generation of Chicano elites. . . . Not only did the majority of respondents share in these (discriminatory) experiences, but these experiences are a primary factor in their decision to become politically active. . . . They became oriented toward and involved in politics primarily as a result of discriminatory experiences associated with their class background."

By the late 1970s, there were three groups of Chicano elites: congressmen, political appointees, and organizational leaders. Of these, the latter two are hypothesized to be members of the new political generation and thus to be "active representatives." As a group, they average slightly more than 35 years of age and the great majority are from working-class homes. Only eight report their father as having been a professional of any type. They are well educated; only four are not college graduates, and 64 percent were attorneys. Thus, like other elites in this generation, they are the direct beneficiaries of the newly created opportunities that only recently began to be made available to the Chicano community. Nonetheless, they also shared in the discrimination experienced by Mexican-Americans at large. Almost 95 percent report that they have been discriminated against, and 68 percent state that those experiences were the primary or a major factor influencing their decision to become politically active.

Comparing national level elites with elites in the Southwest indicates that there are no important statistical differences between the two. As table 1 shows, the two populations differ only in educational attainment. Given the greater visibility and more rigorous screening procedures employed when recruiting for national compared to state appointments, this difference is to be expected. With that exception, it is clear that the Washington-based political appointees and organizational leaders resemble the state elites along each of the dimensions used to define the existence of a new Chicano generation. Thus, membership in these Washington-based groups was not restricted to individuals who by background or orientation were different from other members of this new generation. Instead, these elites share all the major characteristics of the new generation and therefore should be considered members of that group.

However, there is a sense in which the Washington political appointees and organization leaders differ significantly from Chicano elites elsewhere. Although they have had little influence in shaping policy, Chicano elites have participated in decision making, if only sporadically, across the Southwest. Occasionally, Chicanos have served in local and state agencies; areas with high population concentrations such as southern Arizona, South Texas, southern Colorado, and northern New Mexico have a long history of Chicano legislative representation. Moreover, some spokesmen and organizations throughout the region have intermittently protested against discrimination in labor education and social service delivery (Acuna 1981; Allsup 1982). Thus, even though Chicanos were greatly unrepresented in local and state decision-making circles, public officials were regularly reminded of their presence.

At the national level, however, officials were only beginning to be-

TABLE 1

Demographic and Socio-Political Characteristics of
State[a] vs. National Level Chicano[b] Elites

	Age	Sex	Education	Father's Occupation	Politics Discussed at Home[c]	Family Members in Politics
Wash. v. state elites	N.S.[d]	N.S.	Sig. < .005	N.S.	N.S.	N.S.

	Personal Discriminatory Experiences	Discrimination As a Motivating Factor	Evaluation of Current Chicano-white Relations	Initial Interest in Politics
Wash. v. state elites	N.S.	N.S.	N.S.	N.S.

a. Includes Arizona, California, New Mexico, and Colorado. New Mexican elites are excluded because they are so numerous and because they constitute a distinct group with characteristics that reflect the unique history of New Mexico (see Acuna 1981; de la Garza and Vaughan 1984). Including them would thus yield biased results.

b. For analytical purposes, all respondents are considered Chicanos even though the sample included less than 3 percent non-Chicano Hispanics.

c. For response categories within each of these variables, see de la Garza and Vaughan (1984).

d. N.S. = X^2 not significant at < .05.

come aware of Chicano concerns by the mid-1970s (de la Garza 1984). In 1967, President Johnson's creation of the Cabinet Committee on Mexican-American Affairs indicated national leaders were developing an awareness of Chicano issues. In 1969, however, labor legislation specifically designed to assist Mexican-Americans was lost in Congress because it was routed to a committee concerned with U.S.–Mexican relations. When it was finally retrieved and passed, President Nixon vetoed it (Rankin 1971). The extension of the Voting Rights Act to the Southwest in 1975 suggests that national leaders had finally developed at least some awareness of the issues that had historically affected the Mexican-American community.

The physical presence of Chicanos in Washington closely paralleled the changing perceptions of national leaders of Chicano concerns. Prior to 1967, Chicanos had virtually no presence in the nation's capital. With the establishment of the Cabinet Committee, Chicanos were assured of having some role as political appointees in all subsequent administrations even though the specifics of that role have varied with each administration. Under President Nixon, for example, Mexican-American appointees were little more than window dressing used to attract Mexican-American votes (de la Isla 1976). While President Carter publicized his appointees so as to increase his share of the Chicano vote, he also appointed a few Chicanos and Puerto Ricans to serve as directors of major agencies such as the Immigration and Naturalization Service and as assistant secretaries with substantive responsibilities in the Departments of Housing and Urban Development, Health, Education and Welfare, and Interior. The great majority, however, filled lower level positions with significantly less decision-making authority. Thus, even though their numbers were increasing and their responsibilities expanding, as of 1978–79 Chicano administrators as a group had not yet established themselves as permanent powerful actors in national politics.

By the late 1970s, organizational leaders were also contributing to the development of a national Chicano presence. Some of these represented recently established organizations like the National Council de la Raza that were evolving from regional to national organizations. Others represented organizations like the League of United Latin American Citizens that were of long standing but had only recently established a Washington presence. Some individuals represented new organizations designed to represent specific constituencies such as Chicano government employees or business-men and professionals. A fourth type included representatives of the Chicano and Latino offices of established national organizations such as labor unions and the Roman Catholic Church. They totaled less than fifteen, however, and, like their administrative colleagues, they were new to the national political arena.

Chicano legislators comprise the third group of actors that contributed to creating a Chicano presence by the late 1970s in Washington, D.C. They were the first set of Chicano actors to arrive in Washington. Of the five in office in 1978–79, four had been elected in the mid-1960s, and one began his freshman term in 1978. The first four include two Texas Democrates, one Democrat from Los Angeles, and a New Mexican Republican. The newest member of the group, Roberto Garcia, is a New York Democrat who is Puerto Rican by ethnicity but Mexican-American and Puerto Rican by self-identification. Except for Congressman Garcia, all began their careers and achieved their current positions prior to the Chicano Movement. As a group, therefore, the Chicano congressional delegation should not be considered part of this new generation and thus should not be expected to be "active representatives" of Chicano interests.

By 1978, then, Chicanos were beginning to establish themselves as actors on the national political stage. For the first time, they were present in sufficient numbers within the executive branch and as lobbyists within agencies and Congress. Furthermore, the activities of these two groups may also have enhanced the visibility and political clout of the Chicano legislative delegation. In sum, the conditions seem to have been present for Chicano elites, particularly appointees and organizational leaders, to begin influencing national policy for the benefit of the Chicano community —in short, to begin functioning as active representatives.

III. Role Perceptions, Policy Attitudes, Behavior, and Effectiveness of Chicano Elites

As members of this new political generation, Chicano appointees would be expected to define themselves as representatives of the Chicano community. The following respondents' descriptions of their jobs and constituencies indicates that, to a significant degree, they do.

When asked to describe the "most important aspect of their job," 83 percent of the administrators answered in formal professional terms describing the specific responsibilities of their office, that is, "I administer a housing program," or "I advise the head of this agency on employment needs of Mexican-Americans and Puerto Ricans." Seven percent defined their tasks as "helping people," whatever form that takes, and 10 percent specifically indicated that they functioned primarily as advocates for the Mexican-American community.

When asked to define their constituencies, that is, "to whom do you feel your primary responsibility," 56 percent (23) answered in organizational terms, that is, "to my agency," "to my superior"; 22 percent (9) answered in class terms, such as, to the poor or needy; and 22 percent answered in ethnic specific or ethno-class terms, that is, "the Chicanos community," "poor Chicanos," "the poor, but since Chicanos are overwhelmingly poor, that means Chicanos."

Combining the responses to these two items suggests that a sizeable minority of these appointees define themselves as expected of active representatives. In view of the presumed neutrality that governs bureaucratic behavior, it is noteworthy that four (10 percent) openly state that their primary task is to be a Chicano advocate. Combining that with the nine (22 percent) who define their constituencies in class terms which also would specifically include Chicanos, indicates that a significant proportion of these elites define their roles as predicted, that is, they see themselves as serving Chicano interests within their respective agencies.

It is also important to note that other officials who define their roles in formal, non-ethnic terms, may nonetheless regularly and self-consciously advocate in behalf of the Chicano community. Indeed, some of the most important achievements described below resulted from efforts by senior administrators and congressmen who do not define their roles ethnically but who, in their own views, regularly act in defense of Chicano interests. Furthermore, some of the officials indicate that the best way to defend Chicano interests is to not be identified as a Chicano advocate. Combining, then, those who see themselves as Chicano advocates with those who act in defense of Chicano interests without so identifying suggests that a sizeable proportion of this group functions as active representatives of the Chicano community.

If these elites act as community advocates, they are expected to share the concerns of their consituencies. Unfortunately, there are no studies examining the policy preferences of the Chicano community in the years studied here, and thus it is difficult to compare Chicano elite and mass views for that time period. A 1982 survey of Chicanos in East Los Angeles and San Antonio does offer some basis for comparison, however (de la Garza and Brischetto 1983). While the Washington appointees and organization leaders considered economic issues, political apathy, racism, and educational problems to be the key issues affecting Mexican-Americans (de la Garza 1982), the respondents in East Los Angeles and San Antonio indicated that the issues of greatest concern in their respective cities were crime, inadequate social services, education, discrimination, and unemployment. Both groups expressed overwhelming support for bilingual education, with 90 percent of the East Los Angeles–San Antonio sample and 92 percent of Chicano elites in Washington, D.C. supporting it. It is also significant that, given the national concern over immigration then and now, neither the East Los Angeles–San Antonio sample nor the respondents in this study identified immigration as an issue affecting the Chicano community.

It seems these elites share the concerns of the Chicano community. Except for the saliency of crime at the local level and for the elites' concern for increased Chicano political involvement, there is little difference in the major issues each identified. The broad economic categories concerning elites would seem to encompass the public's more specific concerns regarding unemployment and inadequate social services. Both evaluate racism/ discrimination as a continuing problem, both strongly support bilingual education, and neither is concerned about illegal immigration.

As Thompson has argued, however, minorities must do more than share the values of their constituencies if they are to represent them; they must explicitly act to benefit the group (Thompson 1976, 202–203). This section will review the behavior of these elites to determine if they act to advance Chicano interests and describe the consequences of that behavior.

Overall, as hypothesized, Chicano congressmen as a group did not champion Chicano issues. Instead of forming a cohesive group actively representing Chicano interests, by and large they functioned as individual legislators pursuing their own interests. Their lack of cohesion may reflect the partisan, ideological, and rural-urban differences that characterize the group (de la Garza 1984) as well as patterns of political socialization that differ from those of this new generation. This may partially explain why only Congressmen Garcia (the youngest member of the group) and Roybal see themselves as having a "special obligation" to serve Chicanos, while the remaining three do not, and one has long been openly antagonistic to Chicano activism (Dugger 1980). Despite these differences, in 1976, under the leadership of Congressman Roybal the group did establish the Congressional Hispanic Caucus and, subsequently, the National Association of Latino Elected Officials, organizations intended to enhance the role that Chicano elites have in national policymaking.

Individually, two have already and openly influenced policies directly affecting Chicanos. As a member of the Appropriations Committee, Congressman Roybal directly influenced funds allocated to bilingual education and minority health services and Congressman Garcia was very active in insuring that the Bureau of the Census listened and responded to Chicano and Latino concerns in the design and implementation of the 1980 census (de la Garza 1984).

The remaining three legislators serve Chicano constituents but do not systematically address Chicano interests. That is, while they devote considerable time and energy to responding to individual requests from constituents and are praised by Chicano elites in their respective states for those services, none identifies himself or is identified by Chicano elites across the Southwest with any programmatically related activities that specifically addresses Chicano concerns.

The political appointees as a group represented Chicano interests more aggressively than congressmen. Indeed, they were more likely to recognize a "special obligation to serve Chicanos," and the need to be an "ethnic advocate" than were Chicano elected and appointed officials in any southwestern state. Their behavior reflected those attitudes. Early in 1977 they attempted to establish a caucus to unify the group and mobilize it toward common objectives. While it did not achieve its overall objectives, the caucus did facilitate the development of communications networks which were essential in helping the appointees influence policy. Several senior-level appointees, furthermore, quickly demonstrated their commitment to Chicano interests and their willingness to act as Chicano advocates. Community leaders in Washington, D.C., and the Southwest soon recognized and praised these officials for the impact they were having. Lower-level officials, lacking the authority to make or influence decisions directly, assisted each other, higher-level Chicanos in Washington, and state and local officials and activists by providing "inside" information regarding activities within their respective agencies that was otherwise unavailable. These appointees, thus, were instrumental in providing Mexican-American political actors from southwestern states access to bureaucratic arenas from which they had been traditionally excluded. Furthermore, many of these appointees articulated Chicano concerns during policy-making sessions, and senior level appointees made decisions that clearly benefitted Chicano constituents (de la Garza 1984).

Chicano organizational leaders also actively articulated Chicano concerns during these years. They were particularly involved in lobbying legislators and administrators on economic development issues, bilingual education, immigration, and civil rights. It is unclear, however, the degree to which spokesmen for these organizations were articulating community interests or their own institutional concerns. Many of these organizations were conduits through which federal programs for Chicanos were implemented, and they therefore had a vested interest in having federal programs continue and expand. While Chicano officials did not always agree with or approve of the activities of these organizational spokesmen (de la Garza 1984), they recognized that these spokesmen were, in fact, involving themselves in and affecting the policy process in the name of the Chicano population.

Conclusion

The objective of this paper has been to determine if Chicano elites in Washington, D.C. during the Carter Administration "actively" represented Chicano interests. It has shown that political appointees and organizational leaders did indeed serve in this capacity, but that congressmen as a group did not. Furthermore, while collectively these elites did not effect any major long-term policy changes directly benefitting the Chicano population as a whole, there is no doubt that many, including two congressmen, regularly articulated Chicano concerns and directly benefitted specific segments of the Chicano population by influencing how policies were interpreted, implemented, and funded.

These appointees and organizational leaders, then, should be considered as members of the new generation of Chicano elites. As such, they behaved in accordance with the theory of representative bureaucracy.

The Chicano legislators, on the other hand, as a group are not part of that new generation. Except for Representative Garcia, all began their careers within another political context, and they attained their current positions prior to the development of this political generation. Their formative political experiences and professional socialization thus differs significantly from that of this new generation. It is not surprising, therefore, that the legislators did not see themselves as having particular obligations to Chicanos, or that the appointees and organization leaders reported that they were able to work closely with only two members of the Chicano congressional delegation.

In conclusion, the Washington-based members of the Chicano generation successfully endeavored to serve Chicano interests. That they did not accomplish more may be explained to a large extent by their lack of numbers, experience, cohesion, and independent economic and political resources (de la Garza 1984). Congressman Roybal succinctly summarized the problems facing these elites.

> There are four Mexican-Americans in Washington, while Jews have twenty-seven seats and Arab-Americans have six. The black community is far better organized than we are. When they speak to a congressional committee, they do it with one voice, like the NAACP or the Urban League. What we need is a united political front like the blacks have had for fifteen years. We're at least fifteen years behind them.

The Chicano community will be well served if future national elites increase their resources while maintaining the attitudes and commitments that characterized these appointees and organizational leaders. Even under those conditions, however, the Chicano community will not derive maximum benefits from its national elites until its congressional delegation as a group works with these other elites to create a cohesive group that continuously functions as an "active representative" of Chicano interests.

BIBLIOGRAPHY

Acuna, Rodolfo. 1981. *Occupied America: A History of Chicanos*. New York: Harper and Row, Second edition.

Allsup, Carl. 1982. *The American G.I. Forum: Origins and Evolution*. Austin: Center for Mexican-American Studies: The University of Texas at Austin.

De la Garza, Rodolfo O. 1982. *Public Policy Priorities of Chicano Political Elites*. U.S.–Mexico Project Series: Working Papers #7. Washington, D.C.: Overseas Development Council.

———. 1984. "And Then There Were Some: The Role of Chicanos as National Political Actors, 1967–1980," *Aztlan* 15 (Spring): 1–24.

De la Garza, Rodolfo O., and Robert Brischetto. 1983. *The Mexican American*

Electorate: Information Sources and Policy Orientations. San Antonio: Southwest Voter Registration Education Project.

De la Garza, Rodolfo O., and Davis Vaughan. 1984. "The Political Socialization of Chicano Elites: A Generational Approach," *Social Science Quarterly* 65 (June): 290–307.

De la Isla, José. 1976. "The Politics of Reelection: Se Habla Espanol," *Aztlan* 7 (Fall): 427–452.

Dugger, Ronnie. 1980. "Gonzales of San Antonio, Part V: The Politics of Fratricide," in the *Texas Observer.*

Garcia, F. Chris, and Rudolph O. de la Garza. 1977. *The Chicano Political Experience: Three Perspectives.* North Scituate, Mass.: Duxbury Press.

Huntington, Samuel P. 1977. "Generations, Cycles, and Their Role in American Political Development," in Richard J. Samuels, ed., *Political Generations and Political Development.* Lexington, Mass.: Lexington Books, pp. 9–27.

Kingsley, J. Donald. 1944. *Representative Bureaucracy: An Interpretation of the British Civil Service.* Yellow Springs, Ohio: Antioch Press.

Kranz, Harry. 1976. *The Participatory Bureaucracy.* Lexington, Mass.: D.C. Heath and Company, 1976.

Krislov, Samuel. 1974. *Representative Bureaucracy.* Englewood Cliffs, N.J.: Prentice Hall.

Long, Norton E. 1952. "Bureaucracy and Constitutionalism," *American Political Science Review* 46 (Sept.): 808–818.

————. 1979. "Bureaucracy, Pluralism, and the Public Interest," paper presented at the *American Political Science Review* Annual Meeting.

Meier, Kenneth John. 1975. "Representative Bureaucracy: An Empirical Analysis," *American Political Science Review* 69 (June): 526–542.

Meier, Kenneth John, and Lloyd G. Nigro. 1976. "Representative Bureaucracy and Policy Preference: A Study in the Attitudes of Federal Executives," *Public Administration Review* 36 (July-August): 458–469.

Moore, Joan, and Alfredo Cuellar. 1970. *Mexican Americans.* Englewood Cliffs, N.J.: Prentice Hall.

Mosher, Frederick. 1968. *Democracy and the Public Service.* New York: Oxford University Press.

Rankin, Jerry. 1971. *Mexican American and Manpower Policy.* Unpublished dissertation, University of Arizona.

Rintala, Marvin. 1979. *The Constitution of Silence.* Westport, Conn.: Greenwood Press.

Sigelman, Lee, and Albert K. Karnig. 1976. "Black Representation in the American States: A Comparison of Bureaucracies and Legislatures," *American Politics Quarterly* 4 (April): 237–246.

Subramaniam, V. 1967. "Representative Bureaucracy: A Reassessment," *American Political Science Review* 61, (Dec.): 1010–1019.

Thompson, Frank J. 1976. "Minority Groups in Public Bureaucracies," *Administration and Society* 8 (Aug.): 201–226.

19. The Latino Community in State and Congressional Redistricting: 1961–1985[1]

Richard Santillan

THE ACTIVE PARTICIPATION OF ETHNIC and racial minorities in the American political system has been a major development of the past three decades. This increasing political visibility can be attributed largely to minority efforts in challenging and eliminating discriminatory election laws and practices which have historically limited minority participation in politics and the mustering of political resources.

As a direct consequence of the voting rights struggles, much progress in election reform has been achieved — as is evidenced by the existence of multilingual ballots; the elimination of filing fees, literacy, and language requirements; the termination of the dreaded poll tax; the shortening of residency requirements; and minor accommodations to third parties and independent candidates.[2]

Most minority gains were made by utilizing both the legislative and judicial branches of government. The Voting Rights Acts of 1965, 1975, and 1982 are some of the most important pieces of legislation enacted to protect the voting rights of ethnic and racial minorities in the United States. Prior to these reforms, one widely accepted view regarding the lack of minority political power was that minorities themselves were responsible for their own powerlessness.[3] This "explanation" often cited such factors as voter apathy, refusal to speak English, the poverty cycle, and lack of minority understanding of how government operated. However, as each impediment to political participation was either removed or modified, the political involvement of minorities slowly increased, as measured by traditional electoral criteria (i.e. participation in campaigns, voter registration drives, political appointments of minorities, and serious recognition by both major parties).

From the *Journal of Hispanic Politics,* vol. 1 (1985): 52–66. Reprinted with permission.

The Latino community is an excellent example of a constituency of common interests which has taken full advantage of hard-won voting opportunities to insure its rightful place in the decision-making process at all levels of government. The recent elections of Latino mayors in Denver and San Antonio, and of a Latino governor in New Mexico, as well as the establishment of national Latino voter registration programs, dispel popular myths of the "mañana" syndrome and the Latino political leadership.

Latino organizations have discovered over the years that the legislative branch of government has often been slow in removing archaic election laws and practices. For that reason, Latinos have often turned their attention to the courts for judicial remedies. The Latino community has been partly successful in persuading the courts to remove old-fashioned election procedures which have stifled the political voice of 15 million Latinos in the United States.

A recent example of Latino strategy is the legal actions initiated by both the Mexican-American Legal Defense and Educational Fund (MALDEF) and the Southwest Voter Registration Project (SWVRP) aimed at replacing the at-large district election system with single-member districts.[4] Both MALDEF and SWVRP have been highly successful in convincing the courts to replace the old system of at-large election with single-member elections in Texas. In addition, MALDEF and SWVRP are presently challenging at-large district election systems in New Mexico and California, and it is likely that they will prevail in their actions.

The transition from at-large to single-member districts will further enhance Latino influence on local issues, including social services. More importantly, the winning of local office by Latino political candidates has often served as a springboard to higher state and congressional positions. Many Latino state and federal legislators have received their political baptism in local politics. For example, in California, such individuals include U.S. Congressmen Edward R. Roybal (the only Latino to serve on the Los Angeles City Council in this century) and Matthew Martinez (former mayor of Monterey Park), California State Senators Joseph Montoya (former mayor of La Puente) and Ruben Ayala (a former member of the Chino School Board), and Assemblyman Chuck Calderon (formerly, a member of the Montebello School Board).

Nevertheless, Latinos continue to be victimized by ethnic gerrymandering despite these other encouraging signs of political progress. Redistricting is not a familiar process to the general population largely because it occurs only once every ten years and often has been conducted in an atmosphere of secrecy by state legislators. Yet redistricting is perhaps the most important political issue that state legislators and reapportionment commissions undertake at the beginning of each decade. Redistricting battles have been primarily limited to those between Democrats and Republicans over the issues of incumbent protection and promotion of partisan advantage. However, in the 1980 redistricting efforts, Latinos were active participants, and as a consequence expanded the scope of the reapportionment conflict.[5]

This article will be divided into four parts. The first part provides a general description of the redistricting process and its detrimental impact on the political social growth of the Latino community. The second part reviews the redistricting activities by Latinos in 1971. The third section examines the role Latinos played in the 1981 redistricting proceedings in nine different states. And the last part gives policy recommendations for the upcoming 1991 redistricting.

Latino efforts to eliminate ethnic gerrymandering span nearly twenty-five years, and include three distinct periods of redistricting activities (the redistrictings of 1961, 1971, and 1981). These three periods cannot be viewed as being divorced from one another, but must be seen as parts of an ongoing reform process that has been gradually overcoming the political fragmentation of Latino communities in the United States. Each period of Latino participation in redistricting has seen significant headway made, preparing the next generation for promoting further the fair and equitable representation of Latinos in American politics. Thus, the redistricting achievements of Latinos in 1981 can be partly attributed to the groundwork laid by Latino activists in two previous redistricting ventures, in the 1960s and the 1970s.

I

Following the release of each decade's Census Bureau data, each state is required to revise its legislative boundaries in order to achieve political districts of equal population. This standard of one person–one vote is in compliance with the guidelines set by the United States Supreme Court. This was not always the case, however. Prior to the 1960s, both state and federal courts viewed malapportionment as an issue to be resolved by state legislatures, and not in the judicial arena.

However, under the Warren Court, this position changed so dramatically that it is often referred to as the "reapportionment revolution."[6] In 1962, the United States Supreme Court held in *Baker v. Carr* that the reapportionment of the Tennessee state legislature was a justiciable issue. In 1964, in *Reynolds v. Sims,* the Supreme Court passed the one man–one vote ruling, which the Court itself later upheld in *Oregon v. Mitchell.*

As a result of these landmark decisions, many state legislatures were called into special session and found themselves immediately lost in mass confusion and partisan bickering. Many of the new state redistricting plans were found unacceptable by the courts and were returned to the legislatures for further revisions.

In these legislative deliberations of the early 1960s, the Latino community did participate, but only minimally. For example, in 1961, Edward Roybal, then a Los Angeles city councilman, testified before the Reapportionment and Election Committees of the California State Senate and Assembly, requesting fairer district lines which would enhance Latino political power.[7] Also, the Mexican-American Political Association of California passed a conference resolution urging the state legislature to draw district lines in such a manner as to increase Latino opportunities for winning elective office.[8] Except in California, Texas, and New Mexico, however, there appears to have been no other organized Latino redistricting activities in the 1960s.

This lack of Latino visibility during the 1960s redistricting process cannot be interpreted as reflecting a deficiency of Latino interest in politics. During this time, the Latino political leadership was heavily involved in the "Viva Kennedy" campaign, in organizing political associations, in conducting massive voter registration drives, and in fielding candidates for local and state offices. It appears that redistricting merely took a back seat to these more immediate concerns in the 1960s.

The court-approved redistricting plans of the 1960s helped increase Latino political representation in the American Southwest. For example, at the time of the 1961 California redistricting, there were no Chicanos in the California State Senate or Assembly, or in the California congressional delegation. The intensity of discrimination can be measured by the fact that between 1912 and 1961, no Latino served in either the state legislature or in the congressional delegation.[9] By the end of the 1960s, however, four Latinos had been elected to the California Assembly, and another to the U.S. House of Representatives.

In Arizona, total Latino legislative representation increased from three in 1962 to five in 1970. In Colorado, at the time of the 1962 redistricting, no Chicano was serving in the state legislature; however, by 1970, three Latinos were serving in the state House and one in the state Senate.[10] In Texas, the legacy of racial discrimination against Mexican-Americans minimized their political participation in state and federal politics, even after the Supreme Court's redistricting decisions; unlike the other states, Texas' 1960s redistricting plans were not approved until after 1970. As for New Mexico, Chicano representation had always been excellent, and remained that way.

According to Fernando Padilla, Chicano representation in Southwest legislatures increased from 35 in 1962 to 59 in 1970.[11] Padilla adds that not all of these new seats can be directly attributed to court action, although the courts were for the most part responsible for these gains. Other scholars, however, have expressed a different perspective regarding Latino dependency on the courts for increasing Latino representation:

> Reliance on judicial protection of representation rights could well stifle the emerging legitimacy of Chicano political action. It could well weaken Chicano involvement in the to-and-fro of political struggle and make Chicanos wards of the courts, rather than contenders in the market-place of politics.[12]

Since the redistricting battles of the 1960s, Latino political leaders have come to realize that ethnic gerrymandering is a major detriment to the Latino community, for the following reasons:

1. Underrepresentation has denied Latinos a full opportunity to contribute to the process of government which establishes the rules by which we all live.
2. It has excluded Latinos from significant participation in forming state policies, and has therefore led to policies which have provided Hispanics with an inferior education, denied them equal economic opportunities, called into question the state's commitment to equal justice, and generally worked to keep Latinos in the status of second-class citizens.
3. Underrepresentation has closed off certain political avenues through which Hispanics could otherwise voice their problems and grievances.
4. Underrepresentation has limited the ability of Hispanics to introduce and support critical legislation to alleviate immediate social and economic problems which plague the *barrios*.
5. Underrepresentation has softened the Latino voice on how state and federal funds are distributed to communities for human and social services, including health services, education, housing, and transportation.
6. The low political visibility of Latinos at the local and state levels has hindered their upward political mobility to higher offices of increased influence—especially national offices.
7. The shortage of Hispanic political representatives tends to limit Hispanic access to the mass media, which might otherwise serve as the means to articulate the aspirations and problems of the nation's Spanish-speaking communities.
8. The shortage of Latino political leaders denies the Latino com-

munity the powerful personalities around whom the community might rally to work on issues of importance to Chicanos and other Hispanics.[13]

This new awareness of the negative impact of ethnic malapportionment encouraged Latinos in the 1960s to prepare and organize for the upcoming 1971 redistricting activities.

II

Latino redistricting efforts in the 1970s were largely overshadowed by other Latino political activities during this period.

Nevertheless, some of these other actions would later play a role in the redistricting proceedings. First of all, there was the emergence of La Raza Unida Party, a third political party which represented the political arm of the Chicano movement and whose philosophy advocated cultural nationalism and independent political action:

We accept the framework of constitutional democracy and freedom within which to establish our own independent organizations among our people in the pursuit of justice and equality and redress of grievances. La Raza Unida pledges to join with our courageous people organizing in the fields and in the *barrios*. We commit ourselves to La Raza, at whatever cost.[14]

In perspective, La Raza Unida Party contributed significantly to advancing the political agenda for greater representation and to rekindling the idea of community control. The *partido* was partly responsible for reforming election codes which historically discriminated against third parties and independent candidates. Also, as a result of its success in local elections in Texas and New Mexico, La Raza Unida increased the pressure on both parties, especially the Democrats, to support Latino candidates in order to maintain a certain degree of credibility. Then again, La Raza Unida Party afforded Latinos the opportunity to develop skills in campaigning, organizing voter registration drives, lobbying, and hosting political conferences. Thus, party activities lessened Chicano dependence on non-Chicano political groups. And finally, the *partido* represented the first serious attempt to organize a national Hispanic political movement, as opposed to state and regional political organizations with narrower perspectives.[15]

Elsewhere in American politics at this time, the Republican Party was implementing its "Southwest Strategy" for the upcoming 1972 presidential campaign.[16] The GOP had come to accept some hard political realities. First, the population of the nation was shifting from the Northeast to the Southwest. It was thought that this demographic trend might continue for decades, and thus enormously increase the political importance of the Sunbelt because of the addition of congressional seats and electoral votes after reapportionment. Second, the largest ethnic minority in this region (and in fast-growing Florida) was Latinos. Thirdly, the growing appeal of La Raza Unida Party provided the GOP with evidence of Latino dissatisfaction with the traditionally paternalistic behavior of the Democratic Party—and thus with evidence of opportunities in the future for GOP gains among Latino voters. And finally, Republicans came to realize that a minor shift of Latino voters toward Republican candidates could result in the defeat of several Democratic candidates who relied heavily on the loyal support of Latino voters.

Unlike La Raza Unida Party, which attempted to attract the working class in the Latino community, the Republican Party decided to target the small but flourishing Latino middle class by stressing traditional Republican values such as strong family bonds, prayer in school, patriotism, the work ethic, and respect for law and order.

On November 7, 1972, President Richard Nixon received 30 percent of the Latino vote in his landslide victory over Democratic hopeful George McGovern.[17] While Nixon did well in middle-class Latino areas (as was expected), a pleasant surprise for the GOP was the strong showing by the president in the *barrios,* especially in East Los Angeles and South Texas. Latino Democratic leaders, however, refused to concede major Republican and La Raza Unida gains in the Latino community, and dismissed the notion of a new realignment:

> Just before the election we realized the President could get 27–30 percent of the Spanish-speaking vote. But my feeling then, as now, was that it would not come so much from defections to the Republicans and to La Raza Unida as from general apathy and unwillingness to vote.[18]

However, behind the scenes, Latino Democratic leaders were urging the Democratic Party either to institute meaningful reforms or to face the possibility of further erosion of Latino support for Democratic candidates and policies. The Democratic Party responded by establishing a Latino caucus within the party structure, by making some Latino appointments at all levels of the party, and by offering technical and financial support to Latino Democratic political candidates.

In summary, it may be said that Latino participation in both the GOP and La Raza Unida Party in the 1970s was politically healthy as well as necessary. Historically, the Democratic Party had taken the Latino vote for granted, whereas the Republicans had simply ignored Latinos. As a consequence, Latinos had never been in a position of power where they could bargain for appointments and favorable policies. Latino involvement in three different parties now altered this harmful relationship and placed Latinos in a better position to negotiate politically regarding Latino interests and concerns. One issue of immediate concern to Latinos clearly was the 1971 redistricting process.

Regardless of the fact that Latino leaders in the Democratic Party, the GOP, and La Raza Unida differed radically in philosophy and strategy, all Latino leaders agreed in principle to the need for fair representation to be gained by eliminating ethnic gerrymandering. And in the 1970s, the Latino leadership was better prepared than ever before to confront the redistricting issue head on.

Latinos established redistricting organizations and/or testified before legislative committees concerning equitable redistricting in several states, including California, Illinois, New York, Michigan, New Mexico, and Arizona.[19] Some of the organizations active in the 1971 redistricting battle were Chicanos for Fair Representation, the Mexican-American Political Association, the Mexican-American Legal Defense and Educational Fund, the Latino Legislative Caucus, the League of United Latin American Citizens, the American G.I. Forum, and La Raza Unida Party. In some states, such Latino organizations offered their own specific redistricting plans aimed at helping increase Latino representation.

On most issues, the political interests of Latinos and the Democratic Party have usually coincided, but redistricting was one issue which strained this delicate partnership. As was the case in 1961, Latino demands for more favorable districts to elect Latinos tended to threaten Anglo Democratic incumbents whose districts included Latino communities. These Democratic incumbents refused to surrender their seats in order to satisfy lofty ideas concerning "good government."

The Republican Party, recognizing this inherent conflict, saw a golden opportunity to take advantage of the situation by making friendly overtures to the Latino leadership regarding the possibility of a joint effort to extract concessions from the Democratic leadership. However, GOP offers to provide technical and financial assistance were rejected by the Latino leadership, which opted to go it alone. The GOP proposal for an alliance with Latinos might have been based on two political calculations: First, GOP support of Latinos might be viewed as good public relations, forwarding the "Southwest Strategy"; and second, GOP redistricting aims might be achieved indirectly in the future through the success of possible Latino lawsuits.

Latinos involved in redistricting understood that both Democratic and Republican redistricting strategies worked against the political aspirations of the Latino community. The traditional Democratic practice during redistricting was to fragment the Latino community into many districts in order to insure that there would be loyal Democratic Latino votes for many Democratic Anglo incumbents. On the other hand, the traditional Republican tactic was to "pack" or concentrate Latinos into a small number of districts, which guaranteed the election of a few Latinos but undermined their ability to influence the electoral outcome in surrounding districts (this gave the GOP a better chance to defeat Democratic incumbents). In either case, the result was that Latinos did not have political influence in proportion to their overall population.

Latino Democrats, who found themselves in an awkward position, warned the Democratic leadership that another gerrymander of the *barrios* in 1971 would lead Chicanos to seek refuge with La Raza Unida Party and the GOP:

> The Democratic Party can continue to frustrate the Mexican-American community, the Mexican-American voter, and can turn him off by denying us representation through the creation of seats. And in doing so they will, in effect, be pushing the Mexican-American toward La Raza Unida.[20]

One Latino Democratic legislator from California even threatened to switch his affiliation to the GOP if his party continued to slice up the Latino community for the selfish purposes of Anglo Democrats.[21]

Despite their pleas, the Latino communities in several states were again victimized by ethnic gerrymandering. For example, in Chicago and Detroit, the Latino communities were divided among several congressional and legislative districts, while the Puerto Rican and Chicano communities in the South Bronx, Philadelphia, East Los Angeles, and San Antonio were divided among the districts of several Democratic incumbents.

The only viable option open for Latinos was to seek relief in the courts. After several months of legal maneuvering, the state courts rendered their decisions, which resulted in a few modest gains but fell far short of the original objectives set by the Latino leadership. Nevertheless, the Latino leadership took advantage of those few new opportunities and supported Latino candidates in several states. Between 1972 and 1978, Chicano state legislative representation in the Southwest increased from 59 to 81, a net gain of 22 seats.[22] Ironically, one of the factors which contributed to the decline of La Raza Unida Party was its partial success in forcing the Democratic Party to support more Latino candidates; this, in turn, removed a key reason for the continued existence of La Raza Unida.

In addition to legislative gains, other Latino political milestones during the 1970s included the election of Chicanos to the governorships of New Mexico and Arizona in 1974, attempted incorporation of East Los Angeles in the same year, birth of the Southwest Voter Registration Education Project in 1972, establishment of the Republican National Hispanic Assembly and the Hispanic American Democrats, increased visibility and participation of Hispanic women in the electoral process, election of a Latino mayor in Miami, election of New York Puerto Ricans to both the state and the federal legislatures, and inclusion of Latinos in the Voting Rights Act of 1975. In his passionate speech for passage of this act, U.S. Congressman Edward Roybal of California summarized the challenges for the 1980s:

> We are involved today in a fundamental constitutional issue, one that goes to the very democratic roots of this country. That issue relates to the right of people to cast a meaningful and effective vote. The preservation of this right is important to the vitality of this country's political system. Its denial, its enfeeblement can only jeopardize our commitment to democratic principles. In my own state of California, the more than three million Mexican-Americans continue to experience serious impediments to registration and voting participation. The discriminatory practices include at-large board elections; redistricting, registration and voting irregularities; changes in polling places and lack of bilingual registrars and election officials. The total effect of these practices has been a negligible level of representation for Mexican-Americans. For them the bicentennial will, to a great extent, represent a critical point in history—a decision between renewed faith in our Constitution and system of government, or further disillusionment. It is my hope that we act positively in taking up that historical and political challenge—and affirming the Constitution as a living document for Spanish-speaking Americans.[23]

III

The active participation of Latinos in the 1981 redistricting process was not unexpected, considering their involvement in both 1961 and 1971. Several on-going political developments practically guaranteed that the Latino community in the 1980s would try to insure that its redistricting concerns were heard and, more important, that its growing political power was reflected in the final redistricting plans.

The factors which contributed to this political maturity included the expanding role of Latinos in politics; continued efforts by the Republican

Party to recruit Latinos; an emerging Latino middle class; introduction of computer technology to Latino politics; the growing presence of Latino professionals in the areas of law, business, education, the mass media, and politics; Latino voter registration programs; and the emergence of a national political consciousness among Latinos.

Although Latinos in the early 1980s were active across the country in redistricting, there existed an absence of cooperation among Latinos in the various states to share technical resources, legal assistance, and organizational strategies to maximize their collective effort. But in spite of this lack of coordination and communication, when the redistricting effort is viewed in its totality, Latinos seem to have shared several common redistricting experiences:

1. The Latino community was probably the most vocal and active group in redistricting. Their degree of involvement can be measured by their testimony before legislative redistricting committees and commissions, their development of model redistricting plans, their lobbying and court actions, and by the media coverage which all of these activities received.

2. Hispanics followed a strategy of utilizing coalition-building among various Hispanic groups as a means of maximizing their influence upon the redistricting process. The alliance of a diversity of Hispanic groups proved to be an effective political tool.

3. The Republican Party made overtures to the Latino political leadership to form a partnership to gain reapportionment concessions from the Democrats. The purpose of this GOP strategy was to increase the number of minority districts, in hopes that the Republican Party would then have a better chance to defeat Democrats who depended on Latino and black voters to stay in office.

4. The Democratic Party, as in the past, tended to hinder the Latino community regarding redistricting. However, most of the gains made by Latinos actually came from Democratic plans.

5. Latinos made significant gains in the congressional redistricting plans and elected four new Hispanic congresspersons in November of 1982. Latinos also made significant gains in the lower houses of the state legislatures, but fared very poorly in the state Senates.

6. Latino legislators often served as members of legislative redistricting committees and commissions. In California, the chairman of the Assembly reapportionment committee was an Hispanic.

7. Reapportionment commissions, when compared with legislative redistricting, were more detrimental to the Latino community, especially in the states of Michigan and Pennsylvania.
8. The introduction of computer technology helped Latinos develop their own redistricting plans, and also to analyze plans of the legislatures to detect possible racial gerrymandering.
9. Latinos effectively utilized the media to publicize the redistricting goals of their community.
10. As in the 1960s and 1970s, Latinos in several states, as a last resort, sought court action to overturn plans which diluted the political influence of the Latino community. In some cases, Latinos were successful in overturning malapportionment plans.

The following is a summary of Latino redistricting activities in nine states during the 1980s.[24]

Arizona[25]

A Joint Select Committee on Redistricting was responsible for drawing new district lines in Arizona. The 19 member committee included two Latino legislators. Public hearings were held throughout the state, but with little public input except from the Latino and Native-American communities.

The aims of the Latino leadership were two: first, to maintain the current number of Latino legislative seats, and second, to push for a new congressional district for Latinos. The demand for this new congressional district went along with GOP plans, whereas Latinos were in conflict with Democrats over this issue. Latinos were concerned about dilution of minority voting strength and requested review by the United States Department of Justice.

In summary, the Latino community maintained its representation in Arizona but lost an opportunity to elect the first Latino congressperson from Arizona. However, such a new seat may still come into being before 1990.

California[26]

Californios For Fair Representation (CFR) was a statewide coalition of Latino groups which headed the redistricting push in California. CFR representatives testified before the Assembly and Senate redistricting committees, calling for more Latino districts. Latino legislators served on both committees, and one was Chair of the Assembly committee.

The Latino community comprises nearly 25 percent of the state population in California, but the number of Latino elected officials in the state legislature and the California congressional delegations has traditionally been extremely low. For example, prior to the 1981 reapportionment, Latinos held only one congressional seat out of 43, and a mere eight state legislative seats in the 120 member body.

As a result of some very hard work, Latinos captured the two new congressional districts given to California in 1981, and had a decisive influence in increasing the number of heavily Latino Assembly seats outside of Los Angeles County. The Latino community has filed a suit which is presently pending before both the federal courts and the U.S. Justice Department.

Colorado[27]

The 1980 Colorado Reapportionment Commission (CRC) was comprised of eleven members, including two Latinos. The Mexican-American Legal Defense and Educational Fund (MALDEF) spearheaded Latino redistricting efforts in Colorado, presenting model redistricting plans and sending representatives to testify before the CRC.

Latino representation in Denver was a major problem for Latinos, because the Colorado population boom had occured outside of Denver— and, therefore, some Denver seats would have to be transferred to other parts of the state. Therefore, Latino legislative incumbents were pitted against one another in two districts, and this resulted in a net loss of two Latino legislators.

It must be pointed out, however, that the Colorado Latino leadership is confident that these two losses will eventually be recovered in Latino communities outside of Denver. In addition, the election of Frederico Peña (a Mexican-American) as mayor of Denver in 1983 softened the setback suffered in the 1981 state redistricting.

Illinois[28]

The two major groups in the Latino redistricting effort in Illinois were the Puerto Rican Legal Defense and Educational Fund (PRLDEF) and MALDEF. Both these groups provided testimony and presented model redistricting plans to the Illinois Reapportionment Commission. The plans called for two Latino Senate seats and an Assembly district in the southwest and northwest parts of Chicago.

The Illinois commission ignored these recommendations, however, and instead divided Latino areas among four Senate districts—none of which had more than 47 percent Latino population. Also, both MALDEF and PRLDEF were opposed to the two proposed Latino Assembly districts, which had 62 percent and 53 percent Latino populations. Both organizations filed suit in federal court, charging racial discrimination. In January of 1983, a settlement was reached between the state and the plaintiffs. Under the new agreement, three Assembly districts, with Latino populations of 63 percent, 50 percent, and 71 percent, were drawn, along with two Senate districts with Latino populations of 56 percent and 38 percent.

Following the implementation of these new boundaries, Chicago's Latino community elected its first Latino representative in history to the Illinois Assembly. Because the Latino community in Chicago is the fastest growing minority group in the state, the prospects for additional legislative seats in Illinois seem promising for the near future.

Michigan[29]

In 1980, the Hispanic Political Coalition (HPC) was formed to lobby the Michigan Reapportionment Commission to create two Detroit state House seats where Latinos could maximize their political clout. As more Latino organizations and non-Hispanic groups joined HPC, the name of the organization changed to the Southwest Detroit Committee For Fair Representation (SCFR).

Part of the SCFR strategy was to prevent a repeat of the 1970 Michigan redistricting scheme, which carved the Latino community in southwest Detroit into four districts, thus denying Latinos any real opportunity to elect one of their own to the Michigan legislature. SCFR testified before the Reapportionment Commission in both Lansing and Detroit. In Detroit, over one hundred supporters attended the hearings to demonstrate their backing for the SCFR model redistricting plans. In early March 1982, the Michigan Supreme Court took control of state redistricting when the Reapportionment Commission became deadlocked as a consequence of bitter partisan politics. The SCFR submitted a brief to the court requesting that its recommendations be incorporated into the final plans. However, the Latino community was divided in such a manner as to foreclose any chance of winning a legislative seat. Surprisingly, a Latino candidate did run in one of the new districts and lost by a mere 130 votes, giving Latinos a political boost for the next election.

New Mexico[30]

Redistricting is conducted in New Mexico by the Legislative Council Service, and in 1981 Latino legislators served on the council. New Mexico is unique because Latinos there enjoy real political clout at all levels of government, holding presently the governorship and two of the three congressional seats.

Yet, New Mexico Latinos and Native-Americans were displeased in 1981 by the gerrymandering of several districts. The Southwest Voter Registration Project filed suit on behalf of 27 Latinos and Native-Americans on the grounds of dilution in the redistricting plans of minority voting strength. Another lawsuit was filed by some Latino Democratic legislators whose districts were merged together.

In 1982, the New Mexico plans were found unconstitutional by a federal court, and New Mexico was ordered to draw new plans. But the second set of plans was discovered to violate minority voting rights also, and as a result of court action and intervention by the U.S. Justice Department, Latinos and Native-American communities won additional seats.

New York[31]

The Puerto Rican Legal Defense and Educational Fund (PRLDEF) and other Puerto Rican groups presented testimony in New York, along with model redistricting plans which could have increased Puerto Rican numbers in the state legislature and the New York congressional delegation. The New York legislature, on the other hand, wanted to wait until after the 1982 election, and even possibly after 1986, to draw new districts.

The PRLDEF, in conjunction with the Black Legislative Caucus, brought suit in order to have new districts drawn prior to the 1982 general elections. The courts ordered new district lines to be drawn before April 16, 1983.

The strategy of the Puerto Rican community was first to protect its two state senators and five assemblypersons, and then to capture an additional congressional seat and a state Senate seat. However, the legislature refused to incorporate these suggestions into the final plans.

Pennsylvania[32]

The Puerto Rican community formed two groups which were instrumental in redistricting—the Ad Hoc Committee on Hispanic Legislative Districts and the Hispanic Coalition on Reapportionment. These two groups concentrated their efforts on the north-central section of Philadelphia, a Puerto Rican community for forty years. In 1981, there were no Latino elected representatives in the Pennsylvania state legislature.

The aim of the Puerto Rican leadership was to push for one or possibly two strong Puerto Rican districts, but the Legislative Redistricting

Commission responded with a tentative plan for dividing the Puerto Rican community among seven House districts, none of which would have a Latino population in excess of 15 percent.

Latinos testified against the commission proposal and supported a plan to create a district with 53 percent Latinos. In the final outcome, however, the 180th district had only 40 percent Latinos. Latinos filed a lawsuit, but in December of 1981, the Pennsylvania Supreme Court denied review and upheld the state plans.

Texas[33]

The groups spearheading the Latino redistricting activities in Texas were MALDEF, the Southwest Voter Registration Project, Texas Rural Legal Assistance, and the League of United Latin American Citizens. As in other states, Latino legislators served on the state's redistricting committees.

The redistricting actions for the state Senate, Assembly, and congressional districts followed similar patterns. First, the Latino community gave testimony and presented model plans to the legislative committees; second, the legislature ignored these recommendations and diluted Latino political strength; and finally, Latinos filed suit and generally did well in the courts.

In the final Texas plans, five congressional districts had Latino majorities (three of those were actually represented by Latinos); twenty House districts had 60 percent or more Latino populations (fifteen of these were represented by Latino House members); and five Senate districts were majority Latino (four of these were represented by Latinos).

IV

The 1980s have witnessed a continued growth in the number of Latinos serving in state legislatures and the U.S. Congress. Presently, Hispanic representation in state stands at 34, with 86 in state houses and assemblies.[34] Furthermore, the size of the Latino congressional delegation has nearly doubled, from five to nine, in the past two elections.

These improved Latino political fortunes can be attributed in large part to the Latino redistricting efforts of the past twenty-five years. Reapportionment gains, however, must be placed in their proper perspective. While it is true that the Latino community has been able to secure certain districts in which Latino candidates could run successfully for political office, Latinos still do not control anything resembling their fair share of political districts, based upon their proportion of the total population. Accordingly, the following are the author's recommendations for strengthening the hand of the Latino community as regards the 1991 redistricting:

1. The Latino community must be informed as soon as possible on the process and timetable for the 1991 reapportionment.
2. A cooperative relationship must be developed between the Latino community and the U.S. Census Bureau. Census information will be critical for testimony and for drawing district plans.
3. A national Latino conference on the subject of redistricting should be held between 1987 and 1988. The purpose of the meeting would be to bring together participants to discuss future redistricting strategies and cooperation.
4. A national Latino redistricting clearinghouse should be established, to be responsible for newsletters, publicity, and research reports, and for providing technical assistance to Latino groups. A possible funding source for such a "think tank" could be Latino national organizations.
5. There must be a full-time staff both at the national and state levels to coordinate redistricting activities.
6. A national redistricting legal committee should be established, to be comprised of attorneys and law students who will share legal information and ideas on strategies. The Latino legal community has played an important role in redistricting including the work of MALDEF, PRLDEF, Latino bar associations, and Latino law student groups. Such organizations should assign one or more staff people to coordinate the legal groundwork for the upcoming reapportionment battles, which most likely will be resolved again in the courts.
7. Political alliances should be formed with other minority groups whose desire for more "ethnic districts" coincides with the aims of Latino redistricting activists.
8. The Latino leadership must open wider the political opportunities for the full and active participation of women in the upcoming redistricting activities. Latinas were major contributors in both the California and the Michigan reapportionments, and demonstrated effective leadership. The continued exclusion of women from Latino politics can only serve to retard the political growth of the community.
9. The mass media must be utilized at every opportunity in order to articulate the views of Latinos on the topic of redistricting.
10. The Latino community must take a stand independent from both parties, and *cannot* afford to align itself with only one party.

Previous redistricting experiences have seen both parties claiming to represent the redistricting interests of Latinos, when, in
reality, both were only promoting their own agendas.

11. Latino groups involved with the upcoming redistricting should
work closely with Latino legislators to share information and
coordinate activities in order to maximize pressure from both
the "inside" and the "outside." However, a word of caution: Latino legislators are no different from other public officials during redistricting, and have often aligned themselves first with the
interests of their party at the expense of the Latino community.
Latino legislators in 1991 must be held accountable for their redistricting actions.

12. Latinos must incorporate as part of their strategy the new advances in computer technology. Latinos in California and Texas
in 1981 had access to computers, which proved to be critical for
developing redistricting plans and detecting possible legislative
gerrymandering.

13. The Latino community must be careful in supporting special
reapportionment commissions rather than the legislatures to conduct redistricting. Reapportionment commissions have not been
effective alternatives for increasing Latino representation in the
state legislatures and Congress. In fact, special commissions have
been the greater of the two evils, because commissioners are appointed and therefore are neither accountable nor susceptible
to pressure from the Latino community.[35]

CONCLUSION

The redistricting journey for Latinos has been filled with numerous
legislative and judicial detours and roadblocks. Yet, Latinos managed to
overcome many of those obstacles between 1961 and 1981, and are now
prepared to dismantle the remaining barriers in 1991.

This article has focused on state and congressional redistricting, but
it should be mentioned that during this same time frame, Latinos were
also involved with local and county reapportionments to increase Latino
membership on city councils and on school and county boards. The juris-
dictions involved have included New York, Chicago, Los Angeles, Austin,
Houston, San Antonio, El Paso, San Francisco, Oakland, Phoenix, and
Milwaukee.

Reapportionment will certainly be a key issue determining whether
the Latino community in the future is truly to have significant political

power and influence in the American political decision-making process. As a result of population growth in the 1980s, California, Texas, and Florida are already almost guaranteed at least one additional congressional seat each in 1991. The creation of legislative districts which will elect Latinos to office is not, however, by any means the magical solution which will bring an end to all the social problems that plague the Latino community. But certainly a louder political voice for Latinos is a factor which will be helpful in the gradual attainment of social and political equality.

For the future, two things are certain. Both major parties will continue to try and manipulate the political rules to protect themselves at the expense of Latinos, and the Latino community will be in the forefront of those challenging these power brokers to meet their democratic responsibilities. Both the Democratic and Republican parties are now on notice that Latinos will continue to press their claims for fair and equitable representation in the upcoming 1991 reapportionment.

NOTES

1. The author would like to thank both Donna Dannan, Secretary in the Ethnic and Women's Studies Department, and Stuart Anderson for their valuable assistance in typing and editing my article. Also, a special tribute to all the women and men who have participated in Hispanic redistricting activities since the 1960s. It is these women and men whose dedication and commitment created the inspiration for this publication.

2. United States Commission on Civil Rights, *The Voting Rights Act: Unfulfilled Goals* (Washington, D.C., 1981).

3. F. Chris Garcia and Rudolph O. de La Garza, *The Chicano Political Experience: Three Perspectives* (Boston: Duxbury Press, 1977).

4. F. A. Cervantes, "Polarized Voting: Concepts and the Politics of Voting Rights Litigation in Corpus Christi, Austin and Other Texas Cities." Paper prepared for the Conference on Contemporary Issues in Chicano Politics, February 28, 1985, at the University of Houston. Also, interview with Rigaberto Vasquez, SWVRP representative in California, May 4, 1985.

5. Richard Santillan (ed.), *The Hispanic Community and Redistricting: Volume II* (Rose Institute of State and Local Government, Claremont McKenna College, 1984).

6. Alan Heslop, *Redistricting: Shaping Government For A Decade,* (Rose Institute of State and Local Government, Claremont McKenna College, 1981).

7. Interview with Congressman Edward Roybal, August 26, 1980, Washington, D.C.

8. Kenneth C. Burt, *The History of the Mexican-American Political Association and Chicano Politics in California* (Honors Thesis, University of California, Berkeley, 1982), p. 43.

9. Fernando V. Padilla and Carlos B. Ramirez, "Patterns of Chicano Representation in California, Colorado and Nuevo Mexico," *Aztlan: Chicano Journal of the Social Sciences and the Arts* (Spring and Fall 1974): 189–234.

10. Fernando V. Padilla, "Chicano Representation by Court Order: Impact of Reapportionment," in Richard Santillan (ed.), *The Chicano Community and California Redistricting: Volume I* (Rose Institute of State and Local Government, Claremont McKenna College, 1980), pp. 83–101.

11. Ibid.

12. Jay Rosenlieb, "Racial Politics and Representation: Chicanos and Redistricting," *Claremont Journal of Public Affairs* 7 (Summer 1980): 44.

13. Richard Santillan, *California Reapportionment and the Chicano Community: An Historical Overview 1960–1980*, (Rose Institute of State and Local Government, Claremont McKenna College, 1980), pp. 40–41.

14. Armando Rendon, *Chicano Manifesto: The History and Aspirations of the Second Largest Minority in America* (New York: Collier Books, 1971), p. 331.

15. Richard Santillan, *The Politics of Cultural Nationalism: El Partido de La Raza Unida in Southern California, 1969–1978* (Ph.D. Dissertation, Claremont Graduate School, 1978). Also see John Staples Shockley, *Chicano Revolt in a Texas Town* (Notre Dame, Ind.: Notre Dame University Press, 1974); Tony Castro, *Chicano Power: The Emergence of Mexican America* (New York: Saturday Review Press, 1974); and Alberto Juarez, "The Emergence of El Partido de La Raza Unida: California's New Chicano Party." *Aztlan* 3, (no. 2 Fall 1972).

16. Richard Santillan, "Latinos and Republican Presidential Campaigns: From Eisenhower to Reagan," Paper prepared for the Conference on Contemporary Issues in Chicano Politics, February 28, 1985, at the University of Houston.

17. Interview with Alex Armandariz, National Hispanic Coordinator for Nixon in 1972, September 6, 1984, Washington, D.C.

18. Frank del Olmo, "Growing Latin Political Power Reflected in Election Results," *Los Angeles Times,* November 14, 1972.

19. Leroy Hardy, Alan Heslop, and Stuart Anderson (eds.), *Reapportionment Politics: The History of Redistricting in the Fifty States,* (Beverly Hills, Calif.: Sage Publications, 1981).

20. Statement by Richard Calderon before the California Civil Rights Commission, Sacramento, California, January 22, 1971. Also, interview with Calderon, October 16, 1980, Los Angeles, California.

21. Interview with former California State Senator Alex P. Garcia, July 23, 1980, Sacramento, California.

22. Padilla, "Chicano Representation by Court Order."

23. Statement of Congressman Roybal before the Subcommittee on Constitutional Rights of the Senate Committee on the Judiciary, April 22, 1975.

24. The following summaries are from articles published in Santillan (ed.) *The Hispanic Community and Redistricting: Volume II.*

25. John A. Garcia, "Reapportionment in the Eighties: The Case of Arizona and Chicanos."

26. Carlos Navarro and Richard Santillan, "California Redistricting in the 1980s: Californios For Fair Representation."

27. Richard Castro, "Colorado General Assembly Redistricting Plans."

28. Juan Cartagena, "The Role of the Puerto Rican Community in the Reapportionment of Legislative Bodies in the 1980s."

29. Laura Reyes Kopack, Edward and Gloria Rocha, Jeff Stansbury, and Steve Walker, "The Hispanic Fight for Fair Representation in Michigan."

30. Paul L. Hain, F. Chris Garcia, and Robert U. Anderson, "New Mexico Reapportionment, 1982."

31. Cartagena, "The Role of the Puerto Rican Community."

32. Ibid.

33. Dionisio S. Salazar, "Texas Redistricting: Mexican-American Participation and Influence."

34. *Hispanic Link Weekly Report* Vol. 2, No. 47 (November 19, 1984): 1.

35. Project Participar, *The California Latino Position on a State Reapportionment Commission* (San Francisco, 1984), and California Advisory Committee to the U.S. Commission on Civil Rights, *Statement on the California Initiative to Establish a Reapportionment Commission* (Washington, D.C., 1982).

20. Chicanos and the Legislative Process: Reality and Illusion in the Politics of Change

Tatcho Mindiola, Jr., and Armando Gutierrez

WITHIN THE AMERICAN POLITICAL system, a great degree of emphasis is placed on the electoral process as the vehicle for social and economic change. Groups as varied as labor unions, church organizations, and chambers of commerce are continually pointed in the direction of elections in seeking promotion of their interests. In particular, groups with grievances are exhorted to forego the path of demonstrations, strikes, and such in favor of supporting the candidacies of individuals who will represent their views in the halls of government decision making. Perhaps no group has heard this view more often and more consistently than Chicanos. Both liberals and conservatives have joined in a chorus calling on Chicanos to register, organize, run candidates, vote, attend precinct caucuses, and myriad other activities defined as "legitimate" forms of political participation. The reward for adhering to the rules is increased representation, and increased representation is purported to lead to social and economic advancement and improvement. But is this true? Does increased political representation among Chicanos lead to an improved standard of living for the Chicano community? In South Texas, for example, Mexican-origin people have had some of the highest rates of poverty, illiteracy, hunger, and unemployment in the U.S. Yet it is also one of the regions that has the highest rate, both in absolute and relative terms, of elected and appointed Mexican-American officials. Is the community relatively better off in terms of their overall social and economic status, and if they are, can the improvement be traced to the power and actions of elected officials?

Our point is that a positive relationship between increased political representation and improvement in socioeconomic status should not be accepted as an axiom. The correlation, if any, is an empirical question which can only be answered through investigation.[1] This essay attempts to take one such research step by examining the legislation introduced by Chicano legislators in Texas during the 67th legislative session (1981). It will not offer the definitive word on whether the Chicano community is experiencing an increase in their status as a result of increased representation in the legislature, but it will point to generalizations and speculations as they pertain to Chicano legislators and their efforts.

THE INCREASE IN CHICANO REPRESENTATION

Although Chicanos may be voting in larger numbers than ever before, this alone does not explain the increase in the number of Chicano legislators in Texas. Rather the increase is more a function of single member districts being mandated by the courts. In 1964, the U.S. Supreme court ruled that each legislator in a state's legislative body should represent an equal number of people.[2] Lawsuits were subsequently filed in Texas forcing the legislature to comply with the ruling by creating single member districts.[3] The system of single-member districts is not without its flaws but it nevertheless guarantees that some Chicanos will be elected to the legislature since some districts are now comprised primarily of Mexican-Americans.[4] Among the twenty-two districts in Texas in 1981 with a Chicano representative, only seven did not have a majority Chicano population registered to vote. Of these seven districts, however, four have a registered Chicano population of at least 40 percent, thus giving them a major voice in who gets elected. The increase in the number of Chicano representatives and state senators, therefore, is a result of the creation of single member districts.

THE EXTENT OF REPRESENTATION

In order to gauge fairness in representation, it is common practice to compare the relative size of the Chicano population with the relative number of elected Chicano officials, the assumption being that fairness or parity is achieved when the relative numbers are in congruence. In 1980, the U.S. Census Bureau reports that Mexican-origin people made up 19 percent of Texas' population.[5] In 1981 during the 67th legislative session, the 22 Chicano legislators (18 representatives and 4 senators) comprised 12 percent of the total number of 181 legislators. Thus, despite the gains of the last two decades, Chicano representation still lags behind their relative proportion in the state. Parity dictates there should have been 34 instead of 22 Chicano legislators in the 67th session. To the extent that Chicano interests tend to be identified as "liberal," this minority status within the larger, more conservative legislative body also suggests that Chicano legislators are likely to have difficulty getting their legislation passed.

THE FUNCTION OF LEGISLATORS

Legislators have a variety of functions. One function is to formulate and introduce legislation, including resolutions and amendments. It is important to note that while getting legislation passed is the ultimate goal of its introduction, some legislators will use the process of bill introduction for the purpose of creating public awareness. For example, it has been understood that the Texas legislature as presently constituted would never pass a bill granting collective bargaining rights to farmworkers. Some would argue that without such failures, legislation to outlaw the use of the short handle hoe by farmworkers would not have been successful in the session under consideration. Also, many legislators will piecemeal their intent through the introduction of several bills over several sessions. The creation of a commission, for example, may become law in one session, but the funding to support the commission's work may be deliberately left out and attempted in the next session.

A second legislative function is to vote on legislation which moves through the process. Legislation which is deemed favorable to minorities can be supported while legislation which is detrimental can be lobbied and voted against. A skilled legislator can utilize this part of the process to water down legislation which is particularly harmful to minority interests.

Third, legislators are the people's representation in government, and paying attention to and servicing the myriad needs of people is one of the key responsibilities of legislators. In many instances this service to constituents has little to do with the "official" power of elective office. Hence, such activities as writing letters of recommendation to colleges, providing information on available scholarships, or helping find employment, often are acts for which elected officials are repaid with constituent loyalty.

Another more amorphous, yet not unimportant, function of legislators is a symbolic one. They serve as a psychological link between the public and their government. For minorities this function is probably more important than for the general population given that, historically, minorities have not had substantial representation in terms of numbers. It may also explain why Mexican-Americans are often regarded as less than demanding of their representatives. It may be enough that they simply *have* a representative.

This cursory glance at the basic functions of legislators is hardly complete. The focus of this paper, however, is only upon the legislation which Chicanos introduced. An assessment of how effective the legislators are should not be drawn solely upon the information presented herein. A more comprehensive analysis of the effectiveness of legislators would include an investigation of *all* of their functions and for the duration of their service as representatives.

Legislation Introduced by Chicanos

There were 3,696 pieces of legislation introduced during the 67th legislative session in Texas. Chicanos introduced 349, or 9 percent, of the bills. Since they comprise 12 percent of all legislators, this means that Chicanos do not introduce legislation at a volume consonant with their relative size. The difference, however, is relatively small.

What kinds of issues do Chicanos address through their legislation, and do their concerns differ from other legislators? Chicanos addressed 53 separate topics, while the legislation introduced by Anglo legislators dealt with 73 different topics. Assuming that the number of bills a particular area receives reflects legislative priorities, the top five concerns among Chicanos in rank order are education, the courts, criminal procedure, elections, and parks and wildlife. Among Anglo legislators the top five priorities are education, taxation, courts, crimes, and elections.

How successful are Chicanos in getting their legislation through the intricate legislative process? There are over two hundred separate actions which can be taken on a piece of legislation as it moves through the legislature on the way to becoming a law. For ease of interpretation these actions are classified into nine broad steps as shown in table 1.

The data shows that 32.2 percent of the legislation (66 bills) introduced by the Chicano representatives and 25.7 percent of the legislation (489 bills) introduced by non-minorities never made it beyond the first step of introduction and committee assignment. At the second step an additional 48.8 percent of Chicano legislation (100 bills) died in committee in comparison to 40.9 (779 bills) percent for other members. If the first two steps are added together, 87 percent of the Chicano-sponsored legislation and 66.6 percent of the bills introduced by non-minority members never went beyond the first two steps. In other words, a large majority of the legislation introduced by all legislators never went beyond the second step, but this is more the case for legislation introduced by Chicanos. The investigation also found that only 22 bills, or 10.7 percent, of Chicano legislation became law. This is in comparison to 452 bills, or 23.6 percent, of the legislation introduced by Anglo legislators.

TABLE 1

How Legislation Fared Through the Process By Ethnic Group
House of Representatives 67th Legislative Session, Texas, 1981

	CHICANO REPRESENTATIVES									
Steps	1	2	3	4	5	6	7	8	9	Total
Number	66	100	3	6	5	1	—	22	2	205
Percent	32.2	48.8	1.5	2.9	2.4	.5	—	10.7	1.0	100

	OTHER REPRESENTATIVES									
Steps	1	2	3	4	5	6	7	8	9	Total
Number	489	779	12	65	77	9	2	452	18	1903
Percent	25.7	40.9	.6	3.4	4.1	.5	.1	23.6	1.0	100

Code:

1 = Bill Introduction and Assignment to Committee
2 = Committee Action
3 = Floor Action
4 = Bill Introduction and Assignment to Committee (Opposite House)
5 = Committee Action
6 = Floor Action
7 = Conference Committee
8 = Effective
9 = Ineffective

Generally speaking senators have more success than representatives in moving their legislation through the process, but there are still disparities within the Senate between Chicano and non-Chicano senators, especially in the number of bills which actually become law. If the first two steps are added together, the statistics actually favor Chicano-sponsored legislation: 45.6 percent never got beyond the second step in comparison to 54.1 percent of the legislation introduced by non-Chicano senators. From the third step forward, however, a larger proportion of bills introduced by Chicanos die at each step and a smaller proportion become law: 24.3 percent of the legislation sponsored by Chicanos, and 30.5 percent of the legislation introduced by non-Chicano senators became law. In sum, although Chicano senators are more successful than Chicano representatives, they are not as successful as non-Chicano senators.

CHICANO-RELATED LEGISLATION

The significance of having Chicano legislators lies in the assumption that they will address the problems and issues facing the Chicano community. As legislators, of course, their point of attack on these problems should be to introduce legislation which offers solutions to these problems. While no absolutes can be offered, it is doubtless the case that few non-minority legislators will place high priority on introducing minority-related legislation. The question, therefore, is how much of the legislation introduced by Chicano legislators deals with a Chicano issue or problem. Answering this question involves analyzing each piece of legislation introduced and making a judgment as to its importance and relevance for the Chicano community. Identifying legislation which is exclusively concerned with a Chicano issue is not difficult. Bills, for example, which deal with bilingual education clearly have implications for the Mexican-American population. Nor is it usually difficult to identify some bills as not addressing a Chicano issue. Legislation which extends the dove season, for example, does not deal with an issue which primarily affects Chicanos. In between these two groups of legislation, however, are bills which are not easily classified.

Several Chicanos, for example, introduced legislation which calls for new courts in areas of the state were Chicanos reside in large numbers, such as in the Rio Grande Valley, El Paso, and the Corpus Christi area. This raises the possibilities of a Chicano being appointed and/or elected judge. But how much impact will this ultimately have upon the Chicano community? Do Chicanos receive more justice under a Chicano judge? The assumption, of course, is that they should, but the matter has not been properly researched in order to make a valid judgment. In fact some would argue that minorities who attain positions of power, such as a judge, are more harsh in their treatment of their own group in order to demonstrate to non-minorities their impartiality. The point is that assessing legislation for its impact and relevance for minorities involves making value judgments. With this in mind the legislation introduced in the 67th session was classified into one of four groups, as follow:

1. Legislation which does not deal with a Chicano-related concern.
2. Legislation which does not deal with a Chicano concern but which has minor relevance for minorities because of the topic addressed.
3. Legislation which does not deal with a Chicano concern but which has major relevance for minorities because of the topic addressed.
4. Legislation which addresses a Chicano concern.

An example of legislation which is considered to have no relevance to minority affairs is HB 1189 introduced by State Representative Froy Salinas of Lubbock. This bill exempts fish and wildlife from the endangered species list in Texas if the fish or wildlife are lawfully taken in another state.

An example of legislation which was judged to have minor impact upon minority communities is HB 1737 introduced by State Representative Frank Media of San Antonio. This bill increases longevity pay for state employees. Since some Mexican-Americans and other minorities are employed by the state this would affect them. The increase in pay, however, is minimal and thus the bill was placed in this category.

Examples of legislation which do not address a specific Chicano issue but which have major relevance for Chicanos and other minorities are HB 393 introduced by State Representative Joe Hernandez of San Antonio and HB 1946 introduced by State Representative Juan Hinojosa of McAllen. Hernandez's bill calls for prisoners to earn $1.80 per hour while incarcerated by the Texas Department of Corrections, provided they are performing meaningful labor. One half of a prisoner's monthly salary would be given to a compensation fund. Each inmate would have the option of contributing more to the fund, and the additional contribution would be considered as one of the factors in justifying parole. The bill would affect Chicanos and blacks because a disproportionate number of inmates in the Texas Department of Corrections are minority. But since many Anglos are also incarcerated the bill does not exclusively affect minorities. Hence, it was placed in the third category.

An example of legislation which addresses a Chicano issue is HB 886 introduced by State Representative Matt Garcia of San Antonio. Representative Garcia's bill deals with bilingual education and expands the program to students in the middle and high schools. This bill asks that students with no or limited proficiency in English be instructed in their primary language for the purpose of teaching them basic English language skills. Theoretically, the bill applies to all students who do not speak English, but it was aimed at Spanish-speaking Mexican and Chicano populations.

These examples illustrate the guidelines used in classifying the legislation. At a very general level of reasoning it could be argued that all legislation affects minorities in some respect. Our intent here, however, was not necessarily to take exception to the generality, but rather to apply a more exacting standard for analytical purposes. Others, of course, are invited to assess and refine our efforts.

The information presented below in table 2, shows that out of a total of 349 individual bills introduced by Chicano Representatives and Senators, only 19, or 5.4 percent, had major or exclusive relevance for Chicanos.

It would appear that Chicano legislators are not introducing a great deal of legislation which impacts primarily on this community.

If all the Chicano-related legislation had passed into law, the Chicano legislators in the 67th Legislature would have accomplished the following:

TABLE 2

Chicano-Sponsored Legislation Classified
by Relevance for the Chicano Community

| | INTRODUCED | | | |
Steps	1	2	3	4	Total
Number	217	89	23	19	349
Percent	62.2	25.5	6.6	5.4	100.0

Code:

1 = Legislation which does not deal with a Chicano-related concern.
2 = Legislation which does not deal with a Chicano concern but which has minor relevance for minorities
   because of the topic addressed.
3 = Legislation which does not deal with a Chicano concern but which has major relevance for minorities
   because of the topic addressed.
4 = Legislation which addresses a Chicano concern.

— Mexican-American culture in the state would have been strength-
   ened through the implementation of bilingual education through
   high school.
— The right to speak, write, and publish in Spanish would also be
   codified.
— An attack upon the use of inhalants by Chicano youth would have
   been launched by tightening the regulations governing the manu-
   facture and sale of chemicals which are used as inhalants.
— Pan American University located in the Rio Grande Valley would
   have received a special appropriation to repair hurricane damage,
   and a branch of Pan American would have opened in Brownsville
   as an upper division institution.
— School districts which have large numbers of children of undocumented immigrant parents and large numbers of educationally disadvantaged students would have received more money from the
   legislature.
— It would be against the law to deny someone emergency medical
   care because of their inability to pay, and it would be a state crime
   to commit an offense against someone because of race or ethnicity.
— Agricultural workers would be entitled to unemployment and worker's compensation, the use of short handle hoes in agricultural work
   would be against the law, and the agricultural industry would come
   under the jurisdiction of a state Agricultural Labor Relations Board.
   The legislation if passed would represent noticeable and significant
gains. But how much of the Chicano-related legislation actually became

TABLE 3

Chicano-Sponsored Legislation Which Passed into Law
Classified by Relevance for the Chicano Community

	PASSED				
Steps	1	2	3	4	Total
Number	41	8	4	4	57
Percent	71.9	14.0	7.0	7.0	100.0

Code:

1 = Legislation which does not deal with a Chicano-related concern.
2 = Legislation which does not deal with a Chicano concern but which has minor relevance for minorities because of the topic addressed.
3 = Legislation which does not deal with a Chicano concern but which has major relevance for minorities because of the topic addressed.
4 = Legislation which addresses a Chicano concern.

law during the 67th session? The information in table 3 shows that of 19 such bills introduced by Chicanos, only 4 or 21.1 percent became law. The four bills which passed establish bilingual education through the 6th grade, require certain chemicals to contain additives to discourage inhalant abuse, outlaw the use of short handle hoes for agricultural work, and grant a special appropriation for Pan American University.

INTERPRETATION

Most of the legislation introduced by Chicano legislators in the 67th session did not pertain to a minority issue. How is this to be interpreted? One interpretation is that Chicanos are failing their primary constituencies by not introducing more minority-related legislation. This view assumes that ethnic and racial issues should be the prime consideration of at least a significant portion of the legislation which is introduced by Chicano legislators. Given the longstanding nature of the problems facing Chicanos, perhaps this should be the case. There are, however, several factors which must temper this interpretation.

First, we must consider the composition of each of the legislators' districts. Although most of the districts represented by Chicano legislators have a majority of Chicanos, there are, nevertheless, Anglos living in the districts. This is especially true in those districts where Chicanos do not comprise a majority of the constituency. This means that if a legislator is truly to represent his or her district in regard to introducing legislation some of the legislation will be non-minority related.[6] Parenthetically, it should be recognized that the same holds for non-minority legislators. That is, to the extent that Chicanos reside in their districts, they too should introduce minority-related legislation.

Second, it is likely that some of the legislation which the Chicano community wishes to see introduced may not be related to a "minority" issue. It is simplistic to assume that all of the desires and concerns of Chicanos are restricted to what we identified as minority issues.

Third, legislators sponsor bills for interest groups which do not necessarily reside in their own district. Interest groups often write their own legislation and then seek someone to introduce it. This kind of legislation will usually not address a minority issue, even though it may have been introduced by a minority legislator. Some legislators perform this function out of a sense of duty, for financial and research support, or because they believe in the issue addressed by the legislation.[7] Additionally, they may believe that legislation benefitting a particular industry will have an indirect benefit to their constituents. A bill that benefits the petrochemical industry, for example, may be supported by the belief that a strong industry will employ more Chicano workers.

Fourth, legislators have varying perceptions regarding what their primary role is and how best to perform it. Some legislators, for example, do not believe that introducing legislation is the most important function of a legislator and hence do not place a high priority on drafting and sponsoring legislation. This is particularly the case for minority legislators since many recognize that in the white, conservative context of the Texas legislature, the passage of legislation introduced by and relating to minorities is an uphill battle. This works to keep the number of minority-related bills introduced low.

Fifth, as occurs in other institutions in American society, there may be pressures on a minority legislator to be "a legislator first, and a minority second."[8] These pressures hold that if a minority legislator spends an inordinate amount of time and energy dealing with specifically minority issues, he or she ceases to perform as a legislator "is supposed to."

Finally, related to the above, many minority legislators both consciously and subconsciously seek to please their Anglo colleagues and superiors. In some instances, this may be a calculated move to become "one of the boys" (although the behavior is not limited to men), in order to improve leverage and influence.[9] In others, it may be a psychological desire to be liked by those whom one perceives as authority figures.[10] Whatever the reason, and the above are not exhaustive nor mutually exclusive, the vast majority of legislation introduced by Chicano legislators is not related to minority issues. If this standard alone is used to assess the impact of the election of more minority legislators, Chicanos would appear to be no better off today than before the passage of the Voting Rights Act over twenty years ago. It is important to note that within the Chicano community there currently exist no organizations or mechanisms to hold public officials accountable. In a few communities, Communities Organized for Public Service (COPS) has begun to perform such a function but in the vast majority of Chicano communities elected and appointed officials operate with the realistic perception that their performance is highly unlikely to be scrutinized by a critical public. This can not help but reduce, in many instances, the levels of performance of Chicano officials.

Another finding illustrated by the information is that Chicanos are not as successful as their Anglo counterparts in passing their bills into law. There are several reasons which may explain this. One is the lack of experience. The relatively larger number of Chicanos in the 67th legislative session is a phenomenon of the last twenty-five years. This means that experience, continuity, and seniority are not as well established as among non-minority legislators.

A second reason may relate to committee assignments. Chicanos may not receive appointments in sufficient numbers to the committees which play key roles in moving legislation along. The Calendars Committee in the House, for example, is important because it schedules legislation to be debated on the floor. In the 67th session there were no Chicanos on this key committee.

A third reason involves the topics which are addressed by Chicano legislators. If, in fact, the legislation which they introduce is generally "liberal" in its orientation, there would be predictable opposition from conservative legislators and powerful interest groups. These groups tend to dominate the political process in Texas. Overcoming such opposition is often a most formidable task.

A related reason is the perceptions of non-minority legislators. According to interviews with the Chicano legislators, Anglo legislators tend to see all minority-sponsored legislation as liberal at best and radical at worst. These perceptions on the part of other legislators may hinder and even doom much of the legislation introduced by Chicanos.

A fifth reason is prejudice and institutional racism. A person does not stop being a Chicano simply because he or she is a legislator. Chicanos in Texas are still operating in a legislative system which historically has ignored or paid minimal attention to the needs of minority communities. In short, racial prejudice and discrimination is still quite operative in Texas and the legislature is not immune from its effects.

Finally, and perhaps the most obvious reason, Chicanos still constitute a numerical minority in the Texas legislature. In the 67th session,

Chicano legislators comprised 12 percent and the combined percent of blacks and Chicanos in the House and Senate was 19 percent. Even a joint effort by these two groups can not succeed without Anglo support. It appears that said support can not be counted upon very often, particularly when legislation is heavily skewed toward a "minority" interest.

How is one to judge the role of Chicano legislators and their Chicano-related legislation as instruments of social change? First, a distinction must be drawn between what is attempted and what is accomplished. In terms of what was attempted, the legislators examined have a better than average record. In terms of success, however, based on the 67th session, the record is less than impressive since only nine bills which had exclusive concern for Chicanos passed. Granted there are many reasons for this; but, the point remains that if success is to be ensured the obstacles defeating minority related legislation must be confronted and mastered. In this regard there should be close coordination between representatives and senators, with senators carrying more of the responsibility since they have been more successful in passing legislation. Also, there are issues vital to minority well-being which were not addressed. The high dropout rate among Chicano students, for example, needs special attention as does the high unemployment rates in the Rio Grande Valley. Further, there is a desperate need for an economic development plan which would improve the overall economic situation of Chicanos. Although this is probably the single most important issue facing minority communities, none of the Chicano-sponsored legislation dealt directly with economic development issues.

Accomplishing change through the legislative process is slow, deliberative, difficult, and piecemeal. Change as it generated through legislation is generally moderate and "trickle down" in nature. This is not to argue that legislative change cannot have dramatic results. The Federal Civil Rights Act of 1964 and the Voting Rights Act of 1965 most certainly are responsible for a quantitative improvement in the political status of minorities in this country. Yet, dramatic as these changes have been, the economic and social position of Chicanos relative to the Anglo community has varied little since their passage two decades ago.

This may partially explain why Chicano voter turnout remains relatively low in spite of the expenditure of vast sums of money for voter registration and education. Cynicism, apathy, and alienation may be the inevitable by-product of a process that consistently promises much more than it is able to deliver.[11]

Chicano legislators could conceivably introduce legislation which would significantly alter the social and economic position of minority communities. Under current circumstances, however, there is little likelihood that such legislation would pass. Nevertheless we must emphasize that the potential remains. If the number of Chicano legislators continues to increase; if they are emboldened by their growing numbers; and if they can engage in coalition building with their black counterparts and others who support their issues, this potential could turn into a positive reality.[12]

It should also be mentioned that as Chicano legislators achieve more seniority and experience their effectiveness should also improve. Already, the creation of a Mexican-American Legislative Caucus in Texas has provided a mechanism for a more systematic and coordinated approach to legislative and political strategy. The legislators can now create a common agenda, portray a unified front, and map out plans for priority issues and concerns. Insiders are hopeful that this caucus will greatly increase the effectiveness of Chicano legislators.

This, of course, raises a final point. As we have attempted to make clear, the present is but an initial attempt to investigate the relationship between the election of Chicano officials and governmental policies that impact the Chicano community. It is evident to these researchers that the following kinds of future research are vital: First, there needs to be continual, longitudinal research on Chicano elected officials over time in order to arrive at a more comprehensive and fair conclusion as to individual and group effectiveness. Second, similar research must be extended to all levels of decision making. From the United States Congress to city councils, school boards, and the like, research must scrutinize Chicano elected and appointed officials. Such research is vital in order to assess the performance of our representatives, map out our community's future strategies, and make the most effective and efficient use of our very limited time, energy, and resources. Chicanos must move beyond the stage wherein simply having representatives is enough. Chicanos must demand that their elected and appointed officials be accountable to the community. Only through such a process will the "best and brightest" of our community move in to fill those positions so critical to Chicanos' future well-being.

NOTES

1. An example of research which addresses this question is Rufus Browing, Dale Rogers Marshall, and David H. Taub, *Protest Is Not Enough* (Berkeley, Calif.: University of California Press, 1984).

2. *Reynolds v. Sims,* 377 U.S. 533 (1964).

3. *Graves v. Barnes,* 343 F. Supp 704 (W.D. Tex. 1972). Also see Paul W. Bonapfel, "Minority Challenges to At-Large Elections—The Dilution Problem," *Georgia Law Review* 353 (Winter 1976).

4. One criticism of single-member districts is that their boundaries must be redrawn every ten years to match population shifts and any redistricting results

in gerrymandering. Another criticism is that single-member districts polarize counties along racial lines.

5. U.S. Department of Commerce, Bureau of the Census, 1980 *General Social and Economic Characteristics,* Texas 680, Tables 56, 59.

6. For a discussion of how one Chicano state legislator in Texas gathers opinions about issues in his district, see Albert Luna III and Brian A. Quintero, "Public Opinion and the Minority Legislative Agenda," in *Ignored Voices: Public Opinion Polls and the Latino Community,* ed. Rodolfo O. de la Garza (Austin, Texas: Center for Mexican-American Studies, the University of Texas, 1987).

7. William Earl Maxwell and Ernest Cain, *Texas Politics Today* (New York: West, 1987), chap. 5, "Interest Groups and Political Conflict." Also see James E. Anderson, Richard W. Murray, and Edward H. Farley, *Texas Politics* (New York: Harper and Row, 1984), chap. 5, "The State Legislature."

8. This notion is discussed by Marguerite Ross Barnett, "The Congressional Black Caucus: Illusions and Realities of Power," in *The New Black Politics: The Search for Political Power,* ed. Michael B. Preston, Lenneal J. Henderson, Jr., and Paul Puryear (New York: Longman, 1982).

9. The quandary in which many Chicano leaders find themselves is discussed in F. Chris Garcia and Rodolfo O. de la Garza, *The Chicano Political Experience* (North Scituate, Mass.: Duxbury Press, 1977), chap. 9, "Chicano Political Leadership."

10. Minority group identification with members of the dominant group has been interpreted as either a colonized mentality or acculturation. An example of the former is Frantz Fanon, *Black Skin, White Mask* (New York: Grove Press 1967). For a discussion of the latter, see Amado M. Padilla, ed., *Acculturation* (Boulder, Col.: Westview Press, 1980).

11. The literature on political alienation and apathy is extensive. For a representative example dealing with Mexican-Americans, see Robert Brischetto and Rudolfo O. de la Garza, "The Mexican-American Electorate: Political Opinions and Behavior Across Cultures in San Antonio," The Mexican-American Electorate Series, Occasional Paper no. 5 (San Antonio, Texas: Southwest Voter Registration Education project, 1985).

12. Charles Henry, "Black-Chicano Coalitions: Possibilities and Problems," *Western Journal of Black Studies* 4 (Winter 1980): 202–232.

PART IV

Outputs of the Political System: Policies and Issues

MUCH OF THE "PAY-OFF" FOR participating in the political process comes in the form of outputs or outcomes of the political system in terms of governmental policy. Although the reasons for participating in politics are manifold, the central objective of most participants is to affect government's allocation of goods, values, and resources, that is, to have policy enacted that is favorable to an individual or group. By and large, Latinos have been the victims, rather than the beneficiaries, of governmental action through most of United States history. When governments have not been forces of oppression or discrimination, they have at best taken a posture of benign neglect toward Hispanics and Latinos. There have been on the statute books laws which have allowed or fostered ethnic and racial discrimination, rules and policies which have called for the separation of Hispanics from non-Hispanics, and actions which have excluded Latinos from their full rights of citizenship.

One way to seek redress of these problems has been through political action, as has been evidenced by the foregoing selections in this volume. Through political activities of various sorts, Latinos continue to make their needs, wants, and demands known to the authoritative decisionmakers in our system. Latinos have also attempted to put persons who are supportive of their views into positions of authority. The goals of these activities have been to wrest policies from the government that will assist and promote Latinos.

Governments inevitably operate to the advantage of some and to the disadvantage of others, and Latinos generally have been put at a disadvantage. However, the judicial branch, the least popularly controlled part of government, has been in the vanguard of protecting and promoting the rights and interests of Hispanics as well as other minorities. Judicial decisions calling for the desegregating of schools, protecting and promoting the electoral and franchise rights of minorities, and taking other pro–civil rights positions have produced favorable outcomes for Latinos. In the last thirty years, statutes passed by Congress, such as the civil rights laws, housing rights laws, and voting rights laws, have also produced positive effects. However, Latinos remain among the most disadvantaged minority groups in the country.

Latino politics are involved at all levels of government and throughout the United States in those areas where a significant number of Latinos reside. One instance of political activity that demonstrates some partially successful outcomes has been in the city of San Antonio. In that city, Mexican-Americans, although constituting a large portion of the population, were relatively powerless for many years. Through astute political organization, such as the Communities Organized for Public Service (COPS), Mexican-Americans in that city were able to win several important political battles at the local level and actually to institutionalize some political power at the municipal level, including the city commission, the school board, the mayoralty, and even in the private sector. The politics of confrontation as well as more traditional negotiation and bargaining were employed, and the importance of coalitional politics was also evidenced. In relating the history of the COPS organization, Sekul has provided us with a prime example of the entire political process, including resultant favorable policy outcomes.

Education is high on the agenda of Latino public policy issues. It is common knowledge that a good education accrues to the advantage of those who experience it. Latinos have received inferior and inappropriate educational services, and this area is one of the most important and controversial of all public policies. For example, there has been debate about the efficacy and wisdom of bilingual education for years. The representation of Latinos in positions of influence within the educational system, such as teachers, principals, administrators, and school board members, and the issues of equal access to educational opportunities and culturally relevant education have been continuing points of concern. Fraga, Meier, and England have examined the relationship between Hispanic representation on school boards and public policy outputs that affect Hispanic students. Surveying several large urban school districts, they examine the relationship between Hispanic representation on school boards and Hispanic employment as teachers and the impact that Hispanic teachers have on the educational environment of the Latino student. The representation of Hispanics on school boards is still proportionately below their number in the general population, and this discrepancy may continue to grow as many school districts are experiencing tremendous increases in their Latino school-age populations. At-large elections have been instrumental in keeping the proportion of Latino school board members down; however, successful court challenges are increasing the number of single-member elections in school districts. The authors conclude that Hispanics are in a subordinate political position and thus are unable to affect educational policy to their benefit to any significant extent. They call for increased political attention to public education, as they see successes in this arena as being extremely important to the betterment of the Latino community.

Latinos remain on the lower rungs of the economic and employment ladder. Unemployment is generally much higher in the Latino community than among the general majority population, and even when employment is at a comparable level, such as in the public service, Latinos are overrepresented in the lower-level jobs and underrepresented in the higher-paying managerial and administrative ranks. Welch, Karnig, and Eribes surveyed Hispanic public employment at the local level in the five southwestern states and found that there has been an increased representation in the level of Hispanic employment to the point where Latinos are only slightly underrepresented in overall numbers. However, a less positive finding is that Hispanic males are paid less than Anglo males at each level of employment and that Hispanics are clustered in the lower levels of the public work force. Moreover, Hispanic females are even in a more depressed position.

Another public policy issue which concerns Latinos is that of immigration. There has been considerable speculation about the effect of recent immigration into the United States, particularly that from Mexico. The debate over what U.S. policy should be toward immigration has involved many spokespersons for Latinos. Since much of the immigration to the United States is from Latin American nations, some have perceived this issue to be one in which the U.S. Latino community is intimately and consensually involved. De la Garza, Wrinkle, and Polinard have examined Mexican-American attitudes toward the immigration issue. They found few differences in the attitudes of Mexican-Americans compared to Anglos along several dimensions of the immigration issue. The differences that were found were largely attributed to varying degrees of "Mexicanness" and individual personal experiences among the Mexican-American population. Anglos tend to view immigration issues based on their own assessment of what they believe would be the general impact which undocumented workers would have on the American economy. Mexican-American positions seem more to reflect the perceived economic and political impacts of immigration, especially as it affects their own individual situations, than any kind of a general ethnic bond.

Most of the policy issues which are the subject of Latino political activity are in the domestic arena. However, there has also been some concern expressed about foreign policy issues and, most particularly, United States relations with Latin America. Rendon explains that Latinos have been mainly concerned with their own "survival" in the United States, but that as betterment is attained domestically, Latinos will increasingly turn their attention to relations with the Latin American countries. He expects that as Latinos turn their attention to foreign affairs they will play a much more important part in international relations in the western hemisphere. A closer relationship among Latinos of all national origins within the Americas is foreseen.

21. Communities Organized for Public Service: Citizen Power and Public Policy in San Antonio

Joseph D. Sekul

I SIR'D HIM TO DEATH." Sitting in her dining room on an overcast February day, Beatrice Gallego, former president of Communities Organized For Public Service (COPS), was recalling one of her first confrontations with a high city official. One evening in August of 1974, she and five hundred other members of COPS gathered in the auditorium of Kennedy High School on San Antonio's west side. They had come for a meeting with the city manager, Sam Granata. Gallego remembers the anger that filled the room. COPS members demanded to know why, for so many years, they had borne the burden of flooded streets and homes in their neighborhoods every time a severe storm hit the city; why hadn't the city built adequate drainage facilities? But Gallego also remembers the fear. COPS was new, not even a year old. And, except for some minor skirmishes with the city over its failure to clean up vacant lots, tear down abandoned houses, and the like, it was untested on the larger battlefield of San Antonio politics. Also, COPS members, like law-abiding citizens everywhere, had been brought up to have a healthy respect for authority figures. So they approached Granata with fear as well as anger. "We were all very nervous," Gallego recalls. And when she addressed Granata, it was, "'sir, this' and 'sir, that.' I sir'd him to death." After all "he was one of the power people."[1]

Less than two years later COPS itself was being counted among the ranks of the most powerful by the *San Antonio Light,* along with Congressman Henry B. Gonzalez, mayor Lila Cockrell, banker Tom Frost, and builder H. B. Zachary.[2] Other publications, including the *Wall Street Jour-*

Reprinted from *The Politics of San Antonio: Community, Progress, and Power,* edited by David R. Johnson, John A. Booth, and Richard J. Harris, by permission of University of Nebraska Press. Copyright 1983, University of Nebraska Press.

nal, were writing of COPS' rapid rise from obscurity to prominence and influence.[3] It was unprecedented in urban politics for a neighborhood citizens group to acquire the stature that COPS enjoyed.[4]

The foundation for COPS was laid in 1973 by Ernie Cortes when he trudged door-to-door through the south and west sides of San Antonio. Disillusioned with existing channels for political change in the city, Cortes had left San Antonio several months earlier for training as a community organizer at the late Saul Alinsky's Industrial Areas Foundation in Chicago. Now, upon his return, he began a search for the money, people, and issues needed to build an organization. Cortes first convinced a local Catholic pastor, Father Emundo Rodriguez, of the soundness of his organizing venture. Rodriguez in turn convinced several Protestant churchmen to provide money for Cortes's salary and other expenses to gets COPS off the ground.[5] Soon thereafter a social action arm of the Catholic Church, the Campaign for Human Development, stepped in with money to help COPS meet its expenses. This support lasted until 1977, when COPS became financially self-sustaining.

Cortes and other early leaders like Father Albert Benavides believed that for COPS to last, it had to be anchored by institutions with roots deep in the local communities. They discarded the PTAs as too caught up in school board politics, and settled instead on the Catholic parish networks. The parish networks included members of the parish advisory councils and others who run the festivals and sports programs—the hub of community activity within the parish. These networks became the building blocks of Cortes's new organization, and their leaders became the leaders of COPS.[6] From Holy Family came Andres Sarabia, the first president of COPS (1974–76); from St. James, Beatrice Gallego, the second president (1976–78); from San Martin de Porres, Carmen Badillo, the third president (1978–80); and, from St. Patrick's, Beatrice Cortez, COPS' current leader.

Finally, sticking close to the Alinsky rule of pragmatism, Cortes developed issues from the people. "Causes" like civil rights—issues that lacked immediate importance to the people in these neighborhoods—were avoided. To determine the issues that had pulling power Cortes asked the people in the neighborhoods what *their* problems were. They spoke of drainage, utility rates, traffic problems, and other mundane concerns that blighted their daily lives. Issues, in short, came from the bottom up rather than from the top down.[7]

This "bottom up" principle was later incorporated into the governing structure of COPS. Formally, the basic unit of membership is the "local" (or "area" or "community"—hence the name *Communities* Organized for Public Service). In 1982 only three of these locals were neighborhood groups not based in a church. One was in the northeast part of the city with a predominantly Anglo membership; the other two were black locals on the east side. Otherwise the locals were Catholic parishes. The issues had to come from the locals. If a particular issue did not catch fire in the locals, COPS would not adopt it. Thus COPS ignored problems common to other, more ideological Mexican-American groups. Police brutality, for example, while of concern to people in the locals, has not been pushed by them as a major issue, so COPS has not carried it into the political arena.[8]

Above the locals organizationally is the Delegates Congress. Each local sends delegates to this congress, which meets at least six times a year. Between the annual conventions—at which key officers, including the president, are elected and policies for the coming year are ratified—the Delegates Congress is the formal governing body for the organization. It, not the officers, makes final, binding decisions for COPS. Next is the Steering Committee, and after it the Executive Committee. These committees consist of various officers and committee chairpersons. They are responsible for the day-to-day running of the organization and for developing plans to implement policies. Recommendations on these matters are drawn up by the Executive Committee and submitted to the Steering Committee. The latter reviews these recommendations and submits them for approval to the Delegates Congress.[9]

COPS' agenda of public policy issues flows from its members' commitments to two closely intertwined institutions. The first is the family. COPS members want jobs that provide a decent standard of living for themselves and their children. They want a clean and healthy environment, and place great stock in quality education for their children. When their children grow up, parents want them to settle close by rather than relocating in other neighborhoods or cities in pursuit of higher incomes and more fulfilling careers. Finally, COPS members want their old people to live out their lives in dignity, with decent incomes and access to adequate medical care in their own neighborhoods. The second institution is the neighborhood. This is where the roots are—where the COPS people grew up, attended school, married, and reared their children. For San Antonio's Mexican-Americans and for the city's blacks, neighborhood is an integral part of culture. They are proud of these cultures and want to keep them; they don't want to be melted down in the melting pot. Neighborhood defines who they are; neighborhood reminds them of where they have been; neighborhood is where they want to stay.

COPS' commitment to family and neighborhood also stems from the influence of the Catholic Church. The church is a "member" of COPS, tied to it through affiliated parishes, financial contributions, and the manpower it has supplied for leadership.[10] Doctrinally, the Catholic Church in San Antonio became a part of COPS because it felt an obligation to promote social justice for the poor, a mission advocated by Archbishop Robert Lucey as early as the 1940s. Archdiocesan officials believed that the church needed to enter the secular arena in order to protect family life from the ravages of poverty.[11] More recently, this local tradition has been reinforced within the church by liberation theology, which argues that the Christian virtues of love and charity dictate a quest for social justice. Accordingly, churches have a legitimate role to play in the secular world to try to bring about a more equitable distribution of material wealth.[12]

The second reason the church in San Antonio aligned with COPS was to help preserve itself as a truly neighborhood institution. Residential flight from the older parishes threatened the institution of the neighborhood church. As people moved out of the older, central city areas parishes began to lose their financial base. Zoning changes often made this loss permanent, as residential areas were rezoned for light industry. While the church as a whole continued to receive financial support from people after they moved to their new parishes, it suffered a net financial loss in many cases by having to build completely new parishes. The construction of new churches, new rectories, and new schools greatly increased church debt. The church believed that COPS might help to correct this situation by bringing better streets, drainage, and schools into the old neighborhoods, thus stemming the exodus of people from the old parishes.[13]

COPS AND PUBLIC POLICY IN SAN ANTONIO

Family and neighborhood may seem to be innocuous issues, but in fact the struggle to preserve and protect them has proven both difficult and controversial in inner-city San Antonio. By working for the well-being of their families in the old neighborhoods COPS members challenged prevailing patterns of private profit and public power.

The private market has usually shaped the contours of American cities. Since profits have recently been greater in the suburban fringes, this is where business and population have gone.[14] By and large San Antonio has mirrored national trends. Its suburban periphery has grown considerably, the result of both a movement of people out of its core and of the Sunbelt migration that has given southern cities so many new residents from northern cities. A major difference between San Antonio's suburban growth and suburban growth in many northern cities is that expansion in the San Antonio suburbs has not meant a decline in the city's population and tax base. San Antonio, like other Texas cities, has enjoyed liberal annexation powers, permitting it to capture suburban growth by expanding its boundaries.[15] Thus the 92 percent population growth that occurred between 1950 and 1980 was accompanied by a 280 percent growth in land area.[16]

This difference aside, economic and demographic growth in San Antonio has followed the usual course of moving away from the older, inner city and into the new suburban area, mainly on the city's north side. In recent years between 60 and 70 percent of the growth in commercial employment has taken place in the north. While census tracts in other parts of the city have been losing population or registering only small increases, population has been surging ahead in the north. The three northern series of census tracts accounted for virtually all—96 percent—of the net population growth that took place in the country between 1970 and 1976.

Without any government intervention the north side growth probably would have come sooner or later. But the business-dominated Good Government League (GGL) stepped in to see that it came sooner. It expanded key streets and highways to channel growth northward, and it placed such important growth generators as the South Texas Medical Center and the University of Texas at San Antonio northwest of Loop 410, thereby providing magnets to pull people and investment away from the city's heart. Thus the invisible hand of the market got a helping hand from the government.

When COPS stepped forward in 1974 as an advocate of inner city interests, it was thus placing itself in the path of forces that had considerable weight and momentum. This remained so even though the GGL splintered. The GGL's 1975 breakup did weaken the business community's hold on the city council, but business influence in the public sector did not vanish. And the bulk of private sector growth was still earmarked for the north.

COPS did not oppose growth *per se*. To the contrary, its constituency has a vested interest in the social change that growth could bring. But COPS did want to redirect some of that growth into the older areas of the city. To the extent that northward expansion was to continue, COPS was determined to see that residents of its own neighborhoods did not subsidize it through utility rates that rose to cover the costs of extending service to the north side. Finally, if government was to subsidize growth, COPS wanted subsidies for inner-city as well as for suburban development.[17] The issue for COPS was thus not the fact of growth but its direction and terms. More than any other single factor, this tension between inner-city and suburban development has been at the heart of policy debate in San Antonio since 1974.

COPS' POLICY IMPACT

COPS has shaped policies in both the public and private sectors, both positively and negatively in each sphere. On the one hand it has helped enhance the quality of life in its sectors of the city; on the other hand, COPS has blocked policies that it deemed destructive of the well-being of its communities.

In the public sector COPS has targeted its resources and made its weight felt most on the city council, city utility boards, and school boards. Only occasionally has COPS sought to influence county or state level policy, and then with mixed results. On even rarer occasions, such as when it successfully challenged a city council attempt to use urban blight money to buy a golf course, COPS has lobbied the federal government.[18]

COPS' efforts have been concentrated at the municipal level because this is where its power base is most concentrated—and therefore most effective. One extremely significant political victory for COPS was the 1977 adoption of the district-based city council system. (COPS heavily and successfully backed council districting in a close referendum that pitted the group against the Alliance For A Better City, a regrouping of GGL remnants.[19]) Lines for the district system were drawn so as to give Mexican-Americans a majority or near majority in five of the ten districts. This fact has, in turn, become a key to increased policy influence by COPS, exercised through the city council. Since 1977, in three elections, these five districts have elected the candidates most in accord with COPS' positions on issues in thirteen of fifteen races. Further, in return for COPS' support of his projects, COPS has been consistently able to win the vote of councilman Joe Webb, representative of the largely black District 2 on the east side.

COPS' influence with the city council is most clearly evident in the distribution of federal funds for neighborhood improvements. It has obtained an impressive amount of money for capital improvements (streets and sidewalks, drainage, and parks) and for housing rehabilitation. The single biggest source of such money has been the Community Development Block Grant (CDBG) program. Instituted in 1974, CDBG consolidated separate federal programs aimed at fighting urban blight in low- and moderate-income areas.[20] Since CDBG began, San Antonio has received annual allotments totaling $138.7 million.[21] Some 62 percent of this money ($86.3 million) has gone to COPS districts (Districts 1, 4, 5, 6, and 7) and been used to fund the type of capital improvement projects COPS has favored. One might argue that such funds would have gone into these districts anyway, regardless of COPS' efforts, because they contain mostly low- and moderate-income persons. Yet, a comparison of lists of projects submitted by COPS to the city with city records on projects granted funding reveals that 91 percent of the $86.3 million, or $78.2 million, went for projects that COPS had specifically requested. Thus, over half, or 56 percent, of the CDBG money allotted to San Antonio has gone to COPS-endorsed projects.[22] A city official knowledgeable about the CDBG program pointed out that no other single citizens' group in the city has come close to garnering this portion of funds for projects that it favors.[23]

COPS's leverage over the CDBG program has stemmed, first, from its several friendly votes on the city council, which must approve the list of projects to be submitted to the federal government. Second, COPS has paved the way for favorable council votes by generating impressive turnouts at CDBG public hearings. Required by the federal government to solicit citizen opinion, the hearings are normally sparsely attended. COPS, however, has regularly been able to mobilize hundreds and, occasionally, a thousand persons for the hearings. Television news coverage is not uncommon. Aiding in the size of these turnouts has been the fact that a certain portion of them are held in schools or parish halls in COPS areas—a concession the organization won from the city early on in the program.[24] All this yields a lesson politicians ignore at their peril: COPS can mobilize voters.

COPS has also been influential in the use of the Urban Development Action Grant program (UDAG). Established in 1977 by the Carter Administration, UDAG was designed to combine public funds with private investment to help revitalize inner-city neighborhoods.[25] In San Antonio, UDAG has provided $20.6 million to underwrite a neighborhood redevelopment program on the near west side, the Vista Verde project. Vista Verde was a victory for COPS not only because the project was approved, but because COPS' version of the project—and not the city manager's—was adopted. COPS preferred Vista Verde to be a combined residential-commercial complex; Tom Huebner, the city manager, wanted it to be commercial only. When at first Huebner refused to discuss the matter with COPS, a delegation of COPS people, led by president Carmen Badillo, paid Huebner a "visit" in his office. They demanded, with TV cameras present, that Huebner meet with them. Eventually a meeting was held, but Huebner stood firm for his business-only plan.[26] Frustrated, COPS changed tactics. To offset Huebner's opposition the organization mobilized an impressive coalition of backers for its version of the project. They included then-councilman Henry Cisneros; labor leaders; state representatives; Robert McDermott, head of the Economic Development Foundation and USAA insurance; and Robert West, president of Tesoro Petroleum. Shortly thereafter, over Huebner's continued objections, Vista Verde was approved by the city council as a residential-commercial venture.

The third major source of federal funds for the city has been general revenue sharing, a relatively flexible program whose funds may be used for any legitimate government expense, including such operating expenses as salaries.[27] Since revenue sharing's inauguration in 1970, it has brought San Antonio an average of about $9 million per year.[28] Because San Antonio, like other cities, forestalled tax increases by using revenue sharing for operating expenses, COPS has not received a major portion of it for capital improvement projects. Thus far only about 13 percent of the revenue sharing money has gone to COPS-endorsed projects.[29]

In the summer of 1978, however, the group did score a striking victory on revenue sharing. Following the defeat of a $98.4 million bond issue that it had strongly favored, COPS set out to obtain revenue sharing money for projects that had fallen in the bond election.[30] It seemed unlikely that COPS would be able to do this because in prior years there had evolved a clear pattern of increasingly using revenue sharing for operating expenses rather than for capital improvements: from spending a high in 1970 of 74 percent of the revenue sharing allotment on capital projects, the city had dropped to alloting only 11 percent for capital projects by 1977.[31] Nevertheless, led by president Beatrice Gallego, COPS mounted an intense lobbying effort on councilmen from its districts. And, despite bitter denunciations from other council members, a council majority voted to allocate 100 percent of the revenue sharing money to capital projects favored by COPS in 1978.[32]

After the CDBG program, the largest source of money for COPS has been city bonds. Apart from the 1978 bond issue defeat, COPS has successfully campaigned for the passage of the two other bond issues since its founding in 1974, the first in 1974 and the second in 1980. As with the CDBG program, COPS' influence is reflected not so much in the portion of money allotted to its districts—bond money of late is being parceled out evenly with about 10 percent going to each district—but in its capacity to select which projects are funded. Combining the 1974 and 1980 bonds, approximately 72 percent of the $60.8 million that has gone into COPS' districts has gone for projects for which it lobbied. In addition a COPS-backed project in District 2 worth $2.1 million was passed in the 1974 bond. Although COPS had only a minimal presence in District 2 in 1974, by 1980 it had established three locals there. In 1980, 49 percent of the $8.2 million in bonds allotted to District 2 went for a COPS-endorsed drainage project. In all, 32 percent of the $145.9 million raised by these bond elections went for COPS-endorsed projects.[33]

Occasionally COPS has moved to the county and state level to procure money. Its biggest county project through early 1982 has been a still unsuccessful attempt to get three neighborhood clinics for the west side.[34] The organization is likely to persist in this venture because members remain bitter that they must travel to the far northwestern corner of the city for affordable medical care. The need for such travel came about in 1968 when the Bexar County Hospital was moved from its central city location. At the state level COPS has successfully lobbied local legislators for increases in state funds for school districts in its areas.[35] These efforts are continuing. As part of a new overall strategy of enlarging its influence at the state level, COPS, during the 1982 gubernatorial campaign, extracted pledges of increased state funding for local school districts from both major party candidates. After the opening of the Texas legislature in January 1983, the new governor, Mark White, renewed his earlier pledge of support for COPS' proposals. Similar promises were obtained from Gib Lewis, the speaker of the Texas House of Representatives, and Lieutenant Governor Bill Hobby, who presides over the state Senate. All three, in fact, agreed to make education their top priority. The final outcome of this campaign awaits the deliberations of the legislature, but COPS could at least claim to have taken some impressive first steps by enlisting key state officials in its cause.

Indeed, improved education for its children has been prominent on COPS' agendas over the years because the organization represents constituencies in some of Bexar County's poorer school districts—San Antonio, Harlandale, Edgewood, and South San Antonio. COPS has sought to lure new business into its west and south side districts and thereby expand the property tax base. It has also tried to shape the budget priorities in the Harlandale, Edgewood, and San Antonio independent school districts.

At first school board members proved unresponsive. COPS' initial demand to several boards in the mid-1970s was merely to see a copy of the districts' budgets. They were refused, being told in one case that extra copies were unavailable. COPS persisted by staging confrontations with school board members at the board meetings: on cue from leaders, COPS members walked out *en masse,* ignored the agendas and speaker sign-up sheets, cheered friendly speakers, and congregated at the front of the room. Security guards were called to restore order on occasion.

Ultimately COPS began to win influence over budget priorities. It obtained copies of the school budgets—once by threatening to send a delegation of parents to the office of the bank where the school board did business.[36] In the case of the San Antonio Independent School District influence grew after a row over the construction of a new $1.6 million administration building. COPS regarded the proposed building as unnecessary because of more pressing needs. When SAISD board president Grace Durr pressed on with plans for the building, she and other board members were defeated in the 1976 election by candidates who agreed with COPS' positions. Plans for the building were dropped by the new board.[37]

In 1980 COPS helped to alter the composition of another school board—the board of trustees of the San Antonio Junior College District. The board had been rocked by scandal involving allegations of contractor kickbacks to school officials, misuse of employee services, and the firing of maintenance workers.[38] Vowing to seek an investigation of these allegations and to reinstate the dismissed workers, dissident board member George Ozuna sought COPS' help in his upcoming electoral battle to unseat board chairman Walter McAllister, Jr. (son of former mayor and GGL head Walter McAllister, Sr.) with a promise to enlarge junior college facilities on the west side. After McAllister blocked COPS' access to a board meeting and took positions hostile to COPS, the organization, under the leadership of Carmen Badillo, sent its workers into the streets on election day with leaflets advertising McAllister's views. McAllister and his running mates racked up large north side majorities but lost the election because of even larger majorities for the Ozuna slate on the south and west sides.[39] Ozuna telephoned his thanks to COPS for its support on election night, and Carmen Badillo was one of the main speakers at the next board meeting chaired by Ozuna.

THE VETO POWER

The preceding pages have explored some of what COPS has been able to do. But much of COPS' impact in the public arena has been in terms of policy that it has been able to stop. Within its own neighborhoods COPS has, for example, forced the city to end the proliferation of vacant lots that became a dumping ground for refuse,[40] successfully opposed the construction of the proposed Bandera Freeway,[41] and ended the spread of junkyards.[42] COPS leaders cite junkyards as just one example of a larger pattern whereby industries with undesirable side effects, such as air pollution, have been located in inner-city areas, while "clean industries," such as office complexes and medical centers, have gone to the north side. In this connection in 1980 COPS, in an effort spearheaded by local leader Virginia Zamora, fought the south side construction by Barrett Industries of a cement plant. As COPS had expected, Barrett won a permit to build from the Texas Air Control Board. But, demonstrating a capacity to adapt to new forums, COPS' leaders presented its case before an administrative judge and fought the plant through a long series of hearings. The intent was to force costly delays upon Barrett, as well as to fire a shot across the bow of other potentially polluting industries looking at west or south side locations.[43]

In terms of dollars involved, COPS' veto power has been most felt on policies of citywide scope and import, particularly those relating to growth. Intent on the betterment of their own neighborhoods, COPS members are determined to see that the financial resources they believe are due their communities are not siphoned off for the betterment of other neighborhoods. COPS' first major development-related battle was to block construction of a large shopping mall over the Edwards Aquifer, the city's sole source of drinking water. COPS feared that pollution of the aquifer's recharge zone would require building water purification facilities which would be funded through higher water rates to consumers. In the end the developers got their way in the courts, but COPS' impressive showing in turning out voters for a referendum against the mall had seized the attention of city decision makers. It proved that COPS could affect the outcome of a citywide election—a point worth making at a time when city council candidates ran under the at-large system that forced them to solicit votes from all sectors of the city.

Through a long series of Planning Commission and council hearings from 1977 to 1979, COPS fought the city's proposed master plan. The principal dispute was over how much encouragement the city would give to suburban versus central city development. Neither COPS nor the city's major suburban developers liked the final version of the master plan (albeit for different reasons). After years of wrangling the plan was tabled by the city council in 1979.[44]

COPS has also opposed the City Water Board's (CWB) rate policies and other practices as biased toward north side growth—a view given credibility by the fact that John Schaefer, chairman of the CWB from 1975 to 1982, was a major area home builder. Confrontations with Schaefer have been bitter: Schaefer on occasion has called the police to quell boisterous CWB meetings with large COPS delegations.[45]

By applying pressure to both the CWB and to the city council, which must approve board rates and practices, COPS has thwarted the CWB's will several times: In 1975, led by president Andres Sarabia, COPS forced a rollback on a proposed rate hike from 39 percent to 19 percent. Under pressure from COPS in 1976 the Water Board abandoned its practice of giving developers free materials to build water mains in new suburban subdivisions. At COPS' insistence the CWB was forced to scuttle a contract with a regional river authority for the purchase of surface water. COPS also successfully lobbied against the CWB purchase of a private water company from developer Cliff Morton. After the board's long refusal, it bowed to COPS' long-standing demand to replace old water mains in inner-city areas, allocating $11 million for that purpose.[46] This commitment was reaffirmed just recently when, in the wake of COPS pressure on the city council, the CWB made the replacement of old mains its top priority after earlier omitting reference to it in a master plan designating future needs.[47] As part of the same decision, another long-standing goal of COPS was achieved when the CWB abolished the Community Water Development Fund (CWDF).[48] Over the years COPS has attacked the fund as an unfair subsidy to home builders. In 1976 COPS advocated doing away with the fund but had to settle for a council decision to disburse it only to projects within San Antonio's city limits.[49]

COPS has also clashed with the city-owned power authority, the City Public Service Board (CPSB), over utility rates and charges for extending service to new customers. COPS has consistently lobbied against rate increases, and it forced CPSB to increase charges to developers and new customers for extending service.[50]

COPS' most significant battle with CPSB has been over the South Texas Nuclear Project (STNP). The business community and others have backed the project as the cheapest available source of power for the future, given all the alternate power sources, such as coal. However, as the cost of the project rose severalfold through the 1970s, so did COPS' anxiety about it. In 1980, after astronomical cost overruns had pushed the price of the project from $933 million to $4.8 billion—with promises of yet more increases—COPS called for the city to limit its share to 14 percent of the project, or half its original 28 percent investment.[51]

The late 1981 firing of Brown and Root as both designer and builder of the STNP, combined with cost overruns and concerns over the project's safety, could eventually force San Antonio out of the project. (Austin voters have already approved a referendum to sell that city's share.) Or, as Mayor Cisneros has suggested, the project might be scaled down from two plants to one.[52] While COPS cannot take full credit for either one of these new reservations about the project, the organization did push the issue to center stage months before the project's fall 1981 crisis. By some two years of queries and pressure applied to the city council demanding justification of the STNP, and in the face of intense business community support for it, COPS placed a pullback from the project on the city's agenda.[53]

COPS AND THE PRIVATE SECTOR

In a free enterprise economy, government has limited potential to effect fundamental economic change because control over the economy rests largely in the hands of business leaders. They make most of the strategic decisions on investment that determine the level and distribution of wealth.[54] In their drive to improve their lives and the lives of their children COPS members inevitably encountered the limits of government-induced change. From its inception, the organization had always seen higher-paying jobs as a prerequisite for real material progress. But up until 1977 it had never seen a way to make headway on that issue. Its power base was tailored to put pressure on politicians and their appointees. But, as former COPS president Carmen Badillo recalled, COPS' inquiries around town revealed that the key decisions on recruiting new and potentially higher paying industries were in the hands of the business community and, in particular, in the hands of the Economic Development Foundation (EDF).[55] This was an organization of San Antonio business leaders formed to attract new industries set up mainly because of dissatisfaction with the industrial recruitment efforts of the Greater San Antonio Chamber of Commerce.

Since COPS wished to influence industrial growth, the question for COPS became how to influence the EDF. One answer came when COPS obtained a report of the Fantus Company, an industrial relocation consulting firm, on San Antonio, commissioned by the EDF. The study analyzed the strengths and weaknesses of San Antonio as a location for new business. To COPS's outrage, the Fantus report cited San Antonio's low wage structure as one of the city's strong points and recommended that industries that might upset that structure not be wooed by the EDF.[56] After reading these recommendations COPS, led by president Beatrice Gallego, attacked the EDF for attempting to perpetuate poverty in San Antonio by limiting its recruiting efforts to low-wage industries.

With the media giving it extensive coverage, a bitter battle ensued. The EDF denied COPS' charges and countered that COPS was scaring away new businesses with its demand that new firms pay a minimum annual salary of $15,000 as a prerequisite for settling in San Antonio. COPS countered that the $15,000 figure was a goal, not a prerequisite.

At first the EDF refused to meet with COPS, citing an earlier stormy meeting as the reason. But the glaring media publicity frightened other sectors of the community interested in growth, and probably the EDF as well. A number of meetings finally did take place, beginning in March of 1978. On May 30, 1978, COPS and the EDF ostensibly patched up their differences, signing an historic agreement to, among other things, work together to recruit high-paying industries. In addition, a committee was set up to promote higher skill levels among San Antonio workers.[57]

This dispute showed that political instability was the Achilles heel of business. If COPS could not use its political resources directly to influence business decisions, it could indirectly pressure business by creating an unsettled climate that frightened new investors. COPS did not realize this at first, but as the conflict wore on, COPS' leaders recognized the source of their leverage—the potential role of spoiler to the city's economic

growth. COPS agreed to work with the EDF not because it was interested
in the role of the spoiler for its own sake, but rather because it sought to
promote more and better jobs. To the extent that the EDF and other members of the business community were frightened by the prospect of future
turmoil, COPS had accomplished its objective. It had called attention to
the problem of the low wage structure of the city and had given the business community an incentive to change that structure.

COPS had kicked open the door to the private sector, but to what
avail? Would the private sector concede to COPS permanent participation
in setting business policy? Or would business leaders somehow try to keep
COPS quiet? For over a year after the agreement with the EDF was signed
little came of it. COPS suspended its confrontation tactics and waited to
see if the pact would bring better jobs. It didn't; only a handful of new
jobs came into the city. And the ad hoc committee for raising worker skill
levels met only once or twice.[58] Then, in the summer of 1979, prospects
for cooperation with the business community brightened after the EDF
supported COPS on the Vista Verde project. Encouraged, COPS seriously
considered a permanent alliance with the city's economic elites. Ultimately,
COPS dropped the permanent alliance idea. Its leaders were uncomfortable with a general shift in tactics from confrontation to negotiation. And
they were fearful of the impression that closed-door bargaining sessions
might give to the grass-roots leaders in the locals.[59] But before the organization could develop other strategies, Robert McDermott confronted
COPS with his version of citizen influence in the private sector—United
San Antonio.

Formed in January of 1980, United San Antonio (USA) is a trisector
alliance ostensibly designed to involve business, government, and the public in economic development. At the same time, it is intended to demonstrate that the city is united in its resolve to bring economic growth. In
an obvious reference to his battle with COPS, McDermott said that he had
formed USA because past experience had taught him that industrial recruitment could not be viewed as the exclusive province of business.[60]

COPS declined to join USA because it saw it, at best, as a public
relations body, and at worst, as a sinister attempt to coopt dissenting groups.
At the end of 1980, however, still convinced of the need for private sector
backing in realizing significant social change, COPS put aside its earlier
misgivings on negotiating with business. It called for meetings between
COPS and key business leaders to enlist their support in solving such problems as drainage and the ever-diminishing tax base of its communities. This
call was coupled with a warning that if COPS was rebuffed, it would go
back to being the old COPS that disrupted meetings, browbeat business
leaders in parish halls, and made those unseemly headlines.

At first the reaction to its invitation was frustrating. While key business leaders such as Glenn Biggs and McDermott met with them, COPS leaders were repeatedly told to work through USA rather than dealing directly with them. COPS refused, reaffirming its position of working only with the real power brokers.[61] In November of 1981, this impasse was broken when thirty-five key business leaders consented to sit down with COPS in what the group styled a community-level summit conference.

The proposed conference is part of a recently adopted broader COPS policy to seek direct involvement in key decisions that affect its members. Three recent events indicate that this policy is working thus far. First, the EDF has complied with COPS' request that representatives of industries considering a San Antonio location be sent to COPS so that it can discuss with them the advantages of locating in its communities. Representatives of Sprague Electric met with Beatrice Cortez in August of 1981, and in January of 1982 Sprague broke ground for a plant in the Edgewood area.[62] Second, COPS accompanied Mayor Henry Cisneros on his recent trip to Mexico to discuss alternate energy sources with President Lopez Portillo and other Mexican officials. Finally, COPS recently met with the president of Houston Power and Light, Don Jordan, to discuss the STNP. Jordan had come to San Antonio to attend a meeting of all the partners in the nuclear power project, and briefed COPS on that meeting.[63]

CONCLUSION

Only time will tell how far COPS will be able to go in shaping private sector policy or in winning business cooperation. But one thing is clear: COPS has come a long way since that night in Kennedy High School when its members diffidently approached city manager Sam Granata. It has evolved into a force to be reckoned with in city politics. In the years since its founding tens of millions of dollars have flowed into its communities, most of it in accord with COPS' priorities. Numerous government policies that threatened the vitality of its neighborhoods have been checked. Even if USA is a sham intended only to give the illusion of community influence, its creation shows that COPS has made its point: private policies have public consequences. Thus, business leaders now recognize a need to seek approval for growth policies from persons outside corporate boardrooms.

Such changes may not reverse completely the tide of suburban growth that has threatened COPS' communities, but it has slowed and shaped this growth. It has also convinced at least a few companies to locate in inner-city San Antonio. Finally, COPS has taken giant steps toward raising the quality of life in older neighborhoods, some of which may now become places where people can stay if they choose, rather than leave because they must.

NOTES

1. Beatrice Gallego, former president of COPS, interviews, San Antonio, February 1980 and September 29, 1981. For additional information on the meeting with Granata, see Paul Burka, "The Second Battle of the Alamo," *Texas Monthly,* December 1977, p. 222; see also Jan Jarboe, "Building a Movement," *Civil Rights Digest,* Spring 1977, p. 43.

2. *San Antonio Light,* June 20, 1976, p. 2-B.

3. See, for example, "Uprising in Texas: Control of San Antonio Is Slowly Being Won by Mexican-Americans," *Wall Street Journal,* July 13, 1977, p. 1; Calvin Trillin, "U.S. Journal: San Antonio, Some Elements of Power," *The New Yorker,* May 2, 1977, pp. 92–100; Jarboe, "Building a Movement," pp. 39–46; Burka, "Second Battle," p. 139; E. D. Joes, Jr., "COPS Comes to San Antonio," *The Progressive,* May 1977, p. 33–36; "COPS Beginning to Reach Their Goals," *San Antonio Express,* November 16, 1975, p. 2-B.

4. See, for example, Robert L. Lineberry and Ira Sharkansky, *Urban Politics and Public Policy,* 2nd ed. (New York: Harper and Row, 1974); and Charles R. Adrian and Charles Press, *Governing Urban America,* 4th ed. (New York: McGraw-Hill, 1972).

5. Information on Cortes's early organizational activities has been pieced together from written accounts such as Burka, "Second Battle," and Jarboe, "Building a Movement," and from various interviews and conversations with COPS leaders.

6. Father Albert Benavides, former executive vice president of COPS, interview, San Antonio, November 3, 1981.

7. A few years later in Los Angeles, where Cortes was involved in organizing another community group, he found an even more easily overlooked problem at the top of people's lists of grievances: car insurance rates. *Los Angeles Times,* May 17, 1979, Part II, p. 7.

8. Gallego interview, September 29, 1981.

9. Constitution of Communities Organized for Public Service, adopted November 23, 1975.

10. Each church is assessed annual membership dues based on the size of its budget. Members of the clergy are eligible for election as officers in COPS, although thus far a cleric has never been elected president. Also COPS' constitution requires that two clerics (a priest and a nun) be elected each year to represent the clergy. Finally, the current chief organizer and staff director of COPS, Christine Stephens, is a nun.

11. Benavides interview, November 3, 1981.

12. For one of the authoritative texts on liberation theology see Gustavo Gutierrez, *A Theology of Liberation* (Maryknoll, N.Y.: Orbis Books, 1973).

13. Benavides interview, November 3, 1981.

14. On business relocation see Edgar M. Hoover and Raymond Vernon, *Anatomy of a Metropolis*, (Cambridge, Mass.: Harvard University Press, 1959; Anchor Books, 1962), chap. 2. Census figures as of 1970 show that 54.2 percent of the residents of metropolitan areas lived beyond the boundaries of the central cities. Dennis R. Judd, *The Politics of American Cities* (Boston: Little, Brown, 1979), p. 159.

15. Arnold Fleischmann, "Sunbelt Boosterism: The Politics of Postwar Growth and Annexation in San Antonio," in David C. Perry and Alfred J. Watkins, eds., *The Rise of the Sunbelt Cities* (Beverly Hills, Calif.: Sage, 1977), p. 159.

16. Between 1950 and 1980 San Antonio's population grew from 408,442 to 788,002; its land area increased from 70 square miles to 267 square miles. *San Antonio Light*, April 12, 1981, p. 1-D.

17. For a concise history of major government subsidies to business see H. H. Liebhafsky, *American Government and Business* (New York: John Wiley and Sons, 1971), chap. 8.

18. *San Antonio Light*, May 25, 1976, p. 1-A.

19. *San Antonio Express*, January 11, 1977, p. 5-H.

20. Michael D. Reagan and John G. Sanzone, *The New Federalism*, 2nd ed. (New York: Oxford University Press, 1981), chap. 5.

21. Office of Budget and Research, City of San Antonio, "CDBG Status Report" (October 1981), p. 1.

22. "CDBG Status Report" and various request sheets submitted at public hearings by COPS.

23. Confidential interview, San Antonio.

24. Memorandum submitted by Roy E. Robbins, principal planner of the Office of Planning and Community Development, City of San Antonio, to Roy Montez, assistant director of the Office of Community Planning and Development, December 4, 1975.

25. For a brief history and analysis of the UDAG program, see Jerry A. Webman, "UDAG: Targeting Urban Economic Development," *Political Science Quarterly* 96 (Summer 1981): 189–96.

26. *San Antonio Light*, June 27, 1979, p. 8-C.

27. Reagan and Sanzone, *The New Federalism*, chap. 4.

28. City of San Antonio, "Annual Report of Grant-In-Aid Funds of San Antonio for the Fiscal Year Ended July 31, 1980," pp. 314–62.

29. San Antonio, "Annual Report" and various request sheets submitted at public hearings by COPS.

30. *The News*, April 20, 1978, p. 1-A. See also *Southside Sun*, July 6, 1978, p. 1.

31. San Antonio, "Annual Report," pp. 314–62.

32. *San Antonio Light*, July 28, 1978, p. 1-A.

33. Computed from an untitled document drawn up at the author's request by John Rinehard, capital program manager, Department of Public Works, City of San Antonio, and from "The City of San Antonio, Proposed Capital Budget (1981–1982)—Capital Improvement Program (1982–1987)," pp. 42–172.

34. *San Antonio Express*, November 25, 1981, p. 2-A.

35. Ibid., July 12, 1977, p. 1-A.

36. Beatrice Cortez, president of COPS from 1980 to 1982, interview, San Antonio, December 9, 1981.

37. *San Antonio Light,* August 28, 1977, p. 1-A.

38. For an in-depth discussion of the scandal, see Rich Casey, "Scandal at SAC," *SA Magazine,* March 1980, pp. 50–57.

39. *San Antonio Light,* April 4, 1980, p. 2-A.

40. Ibid., July 29, 1977, p. 6-A.

41. Carmen Badillo, former president of COPS, interview, San Antonio, September 24, 1981.

42. *San Antonio Express,* April 9, 1976, p. 1-A.

43. *San Antonio Light,* May 5, 1980, p. 19-A. Oddly, the plant has yet to be built. COPS leaders speculate that their challenge to the permit forced some expensive antipollution equipment on Barrett that made the cost of constructing the plant prohibitive.

44. *San Antonio Express,* July 20, 1979, p. 1-A.

45. *San Antonio Light,* January 16, 1977, p. 5-H.

46. Ibid.

47. Ibid., February 17, 1982, p. 1-A.

48. Ibid. The CWDF is a revolving fund whereby the city advances the developers money for approach water mains and the developers reimburse the city from the proceeds of the sale of the houses.

49. Ibid., January 16, 1977, p. 5-H.

50. *San Antonio Express,* July 31, 1977, p. 3-B.

51. Ibid., May 20, 1981, p. 1-A.

52. Ibid., January 23, 1982, p. 2-A.

53. Ibid.

54. Charles E. Lindbloom, *Politics and Markets* (New York: Basic Books, 1977), pp. 173–74.

55. Badillo interview, September 24, 1981.

56. *National Catholic Reporter,* December 16, 1977, p. 2.

57. "Joint Statement of San Antonio Communities Organized for Public Service (C.O.P.S.) and the San Antonio Economic Development Foundation (E.D.F.)," May 30, 1978.

58. Gallego interview, September 29, 1981.

59. Benavides interview, November 3, 1981 and Cortez interview, December 9, 1981.

60. Robert McDermott, "United San Antonio" (Personal papers of Beatrice Gallego, November 11, 1979), p. 2. This document is a proposal for the establishment of United San Antonio submitted to COPS and various other persons and groups in San Antonio.

61. Andres Sarabia, former president of COPS, interview, San Antonio, September 19, 1981 and Cortez interview, September 22, 1981.

62. *San Antonio Express,* January 21, 1982, p. 1-B.

63. Ibid., January 22, 1982, p. 2-A.

22. Hispanic Americans and Educational Policy: Limits to Equal Access

Luis Ricardo Fraga, Kenneth J. Meier, and Robert E. England

ALTHOUGH HISPANIC AMERICANS are the nation's second largest and fastest growing minority, they have received little attention in the political science literature. Hispanics have many of the same political and economic disadvantages that blacks do; but compared to blacks, we know little about their access to political power and the effect of public policies on them. This research examines the access of Hispanics to equal educational opportunity in U.S. urban school districts. We will first establish education's crucial role in determining economic and social opportunities for Hispanics and link these to political representation. We will then test several hypotheses. First, the level of Hispanic representation on urban school boards will be assessed, including a look at the relationship between selection plans, population, and representation. Second, one form of bureaucratic representation, Hispanic access to teaching positions, will be related to school board representation and Hispanic population. Third, educational policy will be linked to school board representation, teacher representation, Hispanic political resources, and social cleavages in the school district. Specifically, this paper will examine the determinants of second-generation educational discrimination—the post-desegregation acts that limit equal access to education. In most cases data on Hispanics will be contrasted with data on blacks and Anglos.[1]

HISPANICS AND EDUCATION

The history of Hispanics in America is replete with numerous instances of discrimination. Mexican-Americans have been denied rightful

From the *Journal of Politics* 48 (November 1986), pp. 850–876. Reprinted with permission of *Journal of Politics* and the authors.

title to their land (Acuña, 1981), pp. 2–120; Barrera, 1979, pp. 1–30). Immigration policies often have been designed to aid Anglo landowners at the expense of Hispanic workers (Gamio, 1971; Samora, 1971; Bustamante, 1976; Cárdenas, 1975). Efforts of workers to unionize have been discouraged (Galarza, 1977; Gómez-Quinoñes, 1972; García, 1975). To prevent remedial action in these areas by government, the right to vote has been restricted by legislation, English-only ballots, gerrymandering, at-large elections, and exclusionary slating practices (U.S. Commission on Civil Rights, 1975; Carrión, 1983, pp. 129–307; Davidson and Fraga, 1984; Fraga, 1984; Schaeffer, 1984, pp. 321–3, 331–2).

Nowhere has public policy been more detrimental to the development of Hispanics, however, than in education. Education in America is viewed as the key to upward political, social, and economic mobility (McPartland and Braddock, 1981). If individuals are denied access to quality education, then access to political power, social status, and good jobs is also limited. Despite the American ideal of equal educational opportunity, access to public education has historically been limited on the basis of race and ethnicity (Weinberg, 1977).

Both educational history and current policy clearly demonstrate that Hispanics have been denied equal access to education. Segregation of Hispanic students, particularly in California and Texas, began in the late 1800s (Fernández and Guskin, 1981, p. 112). The quality of education in these segregated schools was far below that in mainstream Anglo schools (Weinberg, 1977, pp. 144–6; San Miguel, 1982, p. 702). Although *de jure* segregation of Hispanics was outlawed when federal courts in the late 1940s declared that Hispanics were "whites," (San Miguel, 1982, p. 708; Alcalá and Rangel, 1972), *de facto* segregation has continued.

De facto segregation was furthered by two methods. Assignment systems based on assessments of language deficiencies or other individual needs, which were on their face not based exclusively upon race or ethnicity, were used to separate Hispanics from Anglos. In addition, desegregation plans often paired Hispanic and black schools but allowed Anglo students to remain in all-Anglo schools (San Miguel, 1982, p. 710). In *Cisneros v. Corpus Christi Independent School District* (324 F. Supp. 599, S.D. Tex., 1970), the courts recognized Hispanics as a separate ethnic group. This recognition allowed Hispanics to seek legal relief from segregated school systems. Because legal and policy processes move slowly, however, most Hispanics still attend segregated schools (Brown et al., 1980, p. 48; see also Orfield, 1981, p. 190; Bullock, 1980, p. 599).[2]

Equally detrimental to Hispanic students is inequitable school financing. State funding formulas often used factors such as teacher qualifications which restricted funds allocated to predominantly Hispanic districts

(Weinberg, 1977, p. 163). In addition, the largest source of locally generated revenues for public school expenditures comes from the property tax. Predominantly Hispanic school districts tend to be large central city school districts which, on a per capita basis, have a lower property tax base (see *San Antonio Independent School District v. Rodríguez*, 411 U.S. 1, 1973).

Segregation and funding decisions together can create an overall pattern of educational inequity for many Hispanic students. Other educational policy practices, however, can have as severe an impact on quality education for Hispanics. These practices are termed "second-generation school discrimination." In general, second-generation school discrimination concerns those efforts to keep educational opportunities racially separate within schools (see Rodgers and Bullock, 1972; Stewart and Bullock, 1981). Three practices have been specifically identified by the Office of Civil Rights as potentially discriminatory: ability grouping, suspensions, and tracking. These practices may appear on the surface to be normal, good educational practices; but on closer examination, they can have a deleterious impact on minority students.

Ability Grouping

Ability grouping is using intellectual ability as a criterion to assign students to different classes or different groups within a class. Ability grouping includes assignment of students to advanced, enriched, or honors classes as well as the assignment of students to special education or remedial education classes. Although ability grouping has a long tradition in education that predates efforts to desegregate schools, it has two similarities with efforts to segregate students. First, students are grouped with those racially similar to themselves and separated from those who are different. Second, status is accorded to some groups; advanced placement classes are perceived as better than regular classes; regular classes are perceived to be better than special education classes, etc. These actions, even if taken for valid educational reasons, can counteract the intent of integration, equal educational opportunity for all groups (McConahay, 1981).

Ability grouping has been criticized by a variety of desegregation scholars because it separates minority students from Anglos (see Smith and Dziuban, 1977, p. 54; McConahay, 1981, p. 47; Epps, 1981, p. 103). Rather than teaching the minority student, he or she is diagnosed as having intellectual or linguistic problems and shunted off to a special education, EMR, or in the case of Hispanics, bilingual class (Fernández and Guskin, 1981). Such criticism is reinforced by the empirical findings concerning ability grouping. The U.S. Commission on Civil Rights (1976, p. 129) reviewed a series of studies and concluded that *ability grouping actually had nega-*

tive effects on low-ability groups and that the results on high-ability groups were inconclusive. Because minority students were generally segregated into the lower-ability groups (Eyler, et al., 1981, p. 221), grouping reduced the self-esteem of minority students, produced resentment among racial groups, contributed to discipline problems and dropouts, and resulted in inferior education due to the low teacher expectations (Rosenbaum, 1976; U.S. Commission on Civil Rights, 1976). In short, ability grouping provided few of the benefits claimed by its proponents and resulted in racial resegregation harmful to minority students.

Suspensions

Suspensions are a second tactic that can be used to resegregate school systems. By disciplining minority students more severely and more frequently than Anglo students, school systems can push students out of school (Children's Defense Fund, 1974, p. 130). The literature reveals a clear pattern of disproportionate suspensions for many minority students (U.S. Commission on Civil Rights, 1976; Arnez, 1978; Kaeser, 1979). According to Eyler, Cook, and Ward (1983, p. 42), research results concerning Hispanic suspensions are mixed. In some districts Hispanics are disproportionately suspended; but in school districts with large Hispanic enrollments, the Hispanic suspensions ratio tends to be slightly lower than the Anglo ratio.

Tracking and Educational Attainment

Differences in ability grouping and discipline often coexist with differences in tracking. Children in high-ability groups generally choose or are counseled to choose a college preparatory track. Students in low-ability groups select or are counseled into vocational or general tracks (Eyler et al., 1981, p. 222). Because minority students are disproportionately placed in low-ability groups, they are less likely to be prepared for further education after high school.

A separate manifestation of the tracking phenomenon for Hispanics can be bilingual education programs. While bilingual programs are in theory a form of ability grouping, Hispanics may be pulled out of regular classes and placed exclusively in a bilingual education program. Such one-way maintenance programs can be equivalent to the establishment of a dual education system (Eyler et al., 1983, p. 137). Research also suggests (1) that children are placed in bilingual education programs based on their ethnicity rather than their English proficiency and (2) that transfers out of bilingual programs are rare, thus creating a "Hispanic track" in the school (Eyler et al., 1983, pp. 139–140).[3]

The end result of racial differences in ability grouping, suspensions, and tracking can be differentials in educational attainment (Eyler et al., 1983; Fernández and Guskin, 1981). Students assigned to lower-ability groups are more likely to perceive that education is futile (U.S. Commission on Civil Rights, 1976). Students disciplined disproportionately are likely to leave school (Children's Defense Fund, 1974). Students placed in vocational tracks are less likely to receive the best education the district can offer (Eyler et al., 1981). If minorities are discriminated against in ability grouping, discipline, and tracking, then they will be more likely to drop out of school or if they finish school will be less likely to go on to postsecondary education (McPartland and Braddock, 1981).

Because segregation, funding decisions, and second generation discrimination create an overall pattern of educational inequity, many Hispanic students do not receive the same quality education that Anglo students do. The purpose of this research is to investigate why. The history of Hispanic Americans suggests that educational inequities may be linked to political inequities between Anglos and Hispanics. Educational policy is a direct product of the political process (Weinberg, 1977). At the school district level, elected or appointed public officials set the major parameters of educational policy. Teachers, in turn, are the primary implementors of these educational policies. As such they serve as bureaucrats within the educational system who daily exercise substantial discretion in the application of educational policy to students. A lack of representation among political decision makers and subsequent access to the education bureaucracy may well be the reasons why educational policies do not benefit Hispanics. To the linkage between political representation, access to the bureaucracy, and policy impact, we now turn.

Hypotheses and Methods

We hypothesize that the number of Hispanic school board representatives in a district is due to the nature of the board election/selection plan and the Hispanic population in the district. School boards that elect members from single-member districts are more likely to have more Hispanic representatives than will school districts with at-large elections or appointive selection. We also hypothesize that increased levels of Hispanic school board representation and large Hispanic populations enhance the number of Hispanic teachers who are employed in a district. Lastly, we hypothesize that the combination of Hispanic school board representation and Hispanic teachers works to limit the second-generation school discrimination faced by Hispanic students. We also anticipate that Hispanic social and political resources and the social class differentiation between Hispanics and Anglos can serve to limit such discrimination. Theoretical justifications for these hypotheses are presented below.

The Sample

To assess these relationships, an elaborate data set was constructed from several sources. Data on school board representation were merged with data on Hispanic teachers, data on educational policy outputs, and census data for the school district.[4] The data requirements limited this study to major urban districts with a minimum of 25,000 students. Because many urban school districts have few Hispanic students, the study was further limited to those districts with 5 percent or more Hispanic enrollment. A total of 35 urban school districts met these criteria and had available data (see appendix A). We are confident that these school districts are fairly representative of the Hispanic educational experience; these districts contain 35 percent of all Hispanics residing in the U.S. in 1980. Unlike most research on Hispanics, our sample includes districts populated by Puerto Ricans, Cuban Americans, and other Hispanics as well as those populated by Chicanos.

REPRESENTATION

Although black representation in political institutions has been well studied, similar research on Hispanics is meager. Representation in most studies generally is defined in simple descriptive terms; a group is "adequately represented" if that group's percentage composition of the city council, bureaucracy, or other institution is the same as its population percentage. By this definition, blacks are underrepresented on city councils (Robinson and Dye, 1978; Karnig, 1976) and overrepresented on central city school boards (Welch and Karnig, 1978; Robinson and England, 1981).

Representation levels for Hispanics are generally lower than those for Blacks. Both Taebel (1978, p. 145) and Karnig and Welch (1979, p. 469) found that Hispanics held approximately 44 percent of the city council seats that would be expected given their population percentage. Welch and Hibbing (1984, p. 328) found an even lower level of Hispanic representation in the U.S. Congress. Most minority representation studies rely solely on this proportionality view of representation, a view that Pitkin (1967) calls descriptive representation (for exceptions see Meier and England, 1984; Welch and Hibbing, 1984; Harmel, Hamm and Thomspon, 1983; Bullock and MacManus, 1981). Proportionality is essentially a passive form of representation because someone is considered representative merely by being something (black, Hispanic, Anglo) rather than by doing something. Pitkin argues that representation should be viewed as an activity, as "acting in the interests of the represented." Many other scholars of representation have attempted to link active and passive representation by advocating a variety of representation definitions (see Eulau and Karps, 1977).

The linkage between passive representation (minority access to elected positions) and active representation (public policies that favor minority interests), has been made infrequently for black representatives and hardly at all for Hispanics. Much research on black representation uses expenditures or employment as indicators of public policy (Welch and Karnig, 1980; Dye and Renick, 1981; Eisinger, 1982a, 1982b). Expenditure measures are difficult to link to minority interests. A wealth of case-study literature avoids this difficulty but has problems of generalizability (see Keller, 1978; Levine, 1974; Nelson, 1972; Poinsett, 1979; Stone, 1971; Keech, 1968). The only empirical studies of active representation for blacks using neither expenditure nor employment data are Meier and England's (1984) analysis of second-generation discrimination against black students and Browning, Marshall and Tabb's (1984) assessment of ten California cities. The single nonemployment study of Hispanic representation and public policy finds that congressional districts with more Hispanics have members of Congress who vote less conservatively (Welch and Hibbing, 1984).

REPRESENTATION LEVELS

Engstrom and McDonald (1981) demonstrate that under certain conditions an effective way to measure passive representation is to regress the proportion of seats held by a group on the group's share of the total population. If the intercept of this regression is fairly close to zero, then the slope can be interpreted as a measure of representational equity.[5] Perfect proportional representation exists when the slope is 1.0.

The linkage between population and representation is also affected by the method of selection. Much litigation and substantial research have addressed the relationship between at-large elections and minority representation. At-large elections force minority candidates to run citywide races so that minorities must often run in an electorate with an Anglo majority. In elections with substantial racial vote polarization, minority candidates are at a clear structural disadvantage. At-large races further limit minority candidates because they require greater campaign resources than smaller district elections do.

A massive literature has shown that at-large elections result in lower levels of black representation (for a summary, see Karnig and Welch, 1982; Davidson and Korbel, 1981). Only three studies have failed to show the detrimental impact of at-large elections (Cole, 1974; MacManus, 1978; and Welch and Karnig, 1978; but see Engstrom and McDonald, 1981). Only two studies examine the impact of at-large city council elections on Hispanics. Taebel (1978, p. 151) found that at-large elections hindered Hispanic representation, but Karnig and Welch (1979, p. 474) did not. The different results may be a function of different samples (Karnig and Welch, 1979).

The seats-population regression for Hispanic school board members is shown in table 1.[6] The population slope can be interpreted as follows: for every increase of one percent in Hispanic population, Hispanics attain .774 percent more school board seats when selection plan is held constant. In other words, Hispanics hold 77 percent of the school board seats that one would expect given their school district population.[7]

Because the selection plan variables were entered as dummy variables, they have a unique interpretation. The slopes show the difference in representation between at-large and ward elections, and appointive and ward selections. At-large election plans reduce Hispanic representation on school boards by 2.6 percent relative to single-member district election. Similarly an appointive plan reduces Hispanic representation by 6.3 percent relative to the level of representation with single-member districts. Although the small number of districts with ward and appointive plans limits the statistical significance of our findings,[8] they are in the anticipated direction. At-large elections and appointive selection plans reduce levels of Hispanic representation on school boards even when one controls for the size of the Hispanic population.

The modest negative impact of at-large elections on Hispanics compared to the larger impact on blacks can be explained. Hispanics are not as residentially segregated as blacks; Lopez (1981, p. 54) found a residen-

TABLE 1

The Determinants of Hispanic School Board Representation

Independent Variable	Slope	Beta	T-Score
% Hispanic Population	.774	.82	7.91
At-Large Election Plan	− 2.635	− .10	.78
Appointed Selection	− 6.316	− .19	1.51
Intercept = 1.6 R² = .69 F = 23.0			
n = 35			

tial segregation index of 70.7 percent for blacks and 42.9 percent for Hispanics in fifty-eight southwestern cities. The greater dispersion of Hispanics mitigates some of the impact of at-large elections because they are not as concentrated in only some sections of the city. Nonetheless at-large elections do limit Hispanic representation.

ACCESS TO THE BUREAUCRACY: TEACHERS

One indirect policy output of minority access to elected positions is minority access to government employment. Dye and Renick (1981, p. 484) found that city council representation was associated with greater Hispanic employment in administrative, professional, and protective jobs. Representation had no impact on lower level government jobs. Welch, Karnig, and Eribes (1983, p. 669), on the other hand, discovered no relationship between city employment and Hispanic representation on the city council.

Greater minority employment in a school district may also result from greater minority representation on the school board. Bureaucratic positions, however, are more important than just as a source of jobs. Bureaucrats can also perform representative functions and advocate the interests of Hispanics in day-to-day policy decisions (see the vast literature on representative bureaucracy, Meier and Nigro, 1976; Saltzstein, 1979). In terms of educational policy, perhaps the most important bureaucrats are teachers. Teachers serve as role models for Hispanic students, and make day-to-day decisions that affect them (Thomas and Brown, 1982, p. 168); some scholars rate the teacher as the most important variable in the student's school environment (Smith and June, 1982, p. 232).

Table 2 shows the relationship between the proportion of Hispanic teachers and both Hispanic population and Hispanic representation on the school board. Both measures are significantly related to the number of Hispanic teachers. For each additional one percent of Hispanic population the percentage of Hispanic teachers increases by .27; in other words, Hispanics have only slightly more than one-fourth the number of teachers one would expect based on population alone. Equally important in table 2 is that Hispanic school board representation also has a positive impact. A one percent increase in Hispanic school board representation results in a .096 percent increase in teachers. No other variables including Hispanic community education or income are significantly related to the proportion of Hispanic teachers.[9]

The low level of Hispanic representation among teachers is surprising when compared to the proportion of black teachers. Blacks were over-

TABLE 2

The Determinants of the Percent Hispanic Teachers

Independent Variable	Slope	Beta	T-Score
% Hispanic Population	.274	.72	5.96
% Hispanic on School Board	.096	.23	1.98
Intercept = −.759 R^2 = .85 F = 86.6			
n = 34			

represented by 16 percent. In raw numbers, the average school district in this study has 4.2 percent Hispanic teachers and 15 percent black teachers even though the minorities' population figures are fairly equal. Why blacks are more successful in gaining access to teaching positions is not clear. Blacks have better representation on school boards (107 percent versus 77 percent), but this difference is minor compared to the difference in teachers (116 percent versus 27 percent, data not shown). The potential labor pool for black teachers might be slightly larger; the median education level for blacks in these school districts is 10.7 years compared to 9.3 for Hispanics. Again this difference is not nearly large enough to explain the huge difference in teachers. One other factor that may explain the lack of Hispanic teachers is the absence of Hispanic institutions of higher education. When blacks were denied access to white educational institutions, they could become teachers (normally in black schools) by attending black educational institutions such as Fisk, Morehouse, and Grambling. Hispanics have no similar institutions (Olivas, 1983, p. 116).

POLICY IMPACT: SECOND-GENERATION DISCRIMINATION

Although Hispanic access to school board seats and teaching positions (passive representation) is important in and of itself, such access is more important if it has policy implications (active representation). If Hispanic school board members and teachers act in the interests of the Hispanic community, then educational policies should be more beneficial to Hispanic students. We need to know if it matters to the Hispanic student whether or not he/she attends school in a district where Hispanics are represented in policy-making and policy-implementing positions. This study uses several indicators of second-generation educational discrimination as policy outcome measures.[10]

Three separate measures of ability grouping for students are available: number of students assigned to advanced classes, number of students assigned to special education classes, and number of students assigned to classes for the educable mentally retarded (EMR classes).[11] For each grouping, a "representation ratio" is calculated. For example, for the students assigned to advanced classes, the ratio is the proportion of Hispanic students in advanced classes divided by the proportion of Hispanic students in the school district. This ratio equals 1.0 when Hispanics have access to these classes in exact proportion to their numbers. When Hispanics are assigned to proportionately fewer advanced classes, the ratio is less than one. When Hispanics are assigned to more advanced classes than their students proportions, the ratio is greater than one.

To indicate discipline differentials, a ratio is created using the number of students suspended for one or more days. Similar to the ability grouping ratios, the proportion of suspended students who are Hispanic is divided by the proportion of Hispanic students in the district. Finally, three indicators of educational attainment are used based on the number of students who drop out of school, the number of students who go to college, and the number of students who attend vocational schools.[12] A representation ratio is created for each of these measures.

If second-generation educational discrimination is used against Hispanic students as it is against black students (see Meier and England, 1984), then we would expect the ratios to be less than one for advanced classes, college attendance, and post-secondary vocational enrollments. The ratios should be greater than one for special education, EMR classes, suspensions, and dropouts.

Table 3 displays the mean policy ratios for Hispanics, blacks, and Anglos. Similar to blacks, Hispanics are significantly underrepresented in advanced classes, post-secondary vocational school enrollment, and college attendance. Both blacks and Hispanics are also overrepresented in EMR

TABLE 3

Mean Educational Policy Ratios by Race of Student

Policy Ratio	Hispanics	Blacks	Anglos
Advanced Classes	.49*	.53*	1.50
Special Education	.90	1.24*	.93
EMR Classes	1.06*	2.12*	.59
Suspensions	.98	1.81*	.93
Vocational School	.31*	.89*	1.52
Attending College	.36*	.40*	2.01
Dropouts	2.02*	1.42*	.77
Teacher Ratio	.27*	.98	1.19

*Significantly different from Anglos at .01 or less.

classes and in dropouts. Unlike blacks, however, Hispanics are not over-represented in special education classes or in suspensions.

Although both blacks and Hispanics faced similar educational in-equities, the patterns are different. Blacks are clearly affected more by abil-ity grouping than Hispanics. They are overrepresented by 24 percent in special education classes, overrepresented by 112 percent in EMR classes, and underrepresented by 47 percent in advanced classes. Hispanics have severe problems only in access to advanced classes.[13]

The striking numbers in table 3, however, are for the educational attainment indicators. The Hispanic dropout rate is 60 percent worse than the black dropout rate and almost three times as high as the Anglo rate. Hispanics are less likely to attend college and significantly less likely than blacks to attend post-secondary vocational schools.

The results of table 3 suggest different patterns of second-generation discrimination for Hispanic and black students. Black students are more likely to be punished by negative ability grouping and disproportionate discipline. The result is a lower educational attainment. The process for Hispanics is more subtle. Hispanics are similarly denied access to advanced classes and funneled into EMR classes, but they are not subjected to greater discipline. Their educational attainment, however, suffers even more than blacks.

Discrimination is only one possible explanation for the ratios pre-sented in table 3. One could make an argument, though not an easy one, that these figures represent differences in educational potential. One strong argument against this view is the interrelationship of the indicators. School districts that disproportionately group black students in lower-ability groups also do this to Hispanic groups. The correlation between the Hispanic and black indices is .48 for EMR classes, .64 for special education classes, and .25 for advanced classes, and .26 for suspensions. In addition, the indices are internally consistent with each other. EMR classes, special education classes, suspensions, and dropouts are positively correlated for both His-panics and blacks. Similarly, advanced classes, college attendance, and voca-tional school enrollments are also positively correlated.[14]

SECOND-GENERATION DISCRIMINATION: AN EXPLANATION

Even though second-generation discrimination against Hispanic stu-dents is fairly prevalent, it varies substantially from district to district. School dropout rates range from a low of 1.16 to a high of 5.42; similarly college attendance rates range from .03 to 1.08. In some school districts, therefore, Hispanic students achieve equity in educational opportunity.

The important question is, why do some school districts provide greater educational equity to Hispanics than others?

Representation

One explanation for the treatment of Hispanic students concerns our earlier discussion of the relationship between passive and active representation. If school board members and teachers are effective advocates for Hispanic students, then second-generation discrimination should be lower in school districts with greater Hispanic representation in policy-making and policy-implementing positions. Two measures of representation are used: the percentage of the school board controlled by Hispanics and the percentage of Hispanic teachers. We hypothesize that a greater percentage of Hispanic school board members and a greater percentage of Hispanic teachers will result in lower levels of second generation discrimination.

The raw percentage rather than a representation ratio is used for two reasons. First, influence on the school board is a function of votes, not representation ratios. Hispanic board members should be better able to attain their goals if they have 40 percent of the seats in a district 60 percent Hispanic than if they have 10 percent of the seats in a district that is 5 percent Hispanic. Similarly the percentage of Hispanic teachers increases the probability that a Hispanic student will come into contact with a Hispanic teacher. Second, each of our policy measures already contains the proportion of the Hispanic student body as a denominator. Using a similar measure for school board members and teachers, therefore, would divide both the independent and dependent variables by essentially the same number. Such a procedure can create relationships as an artifact of the division process (Uslander, 1976).

Resources

Representation is not the only determinant of public policy. The ability to affect policies issued by the school board or implemented by the school system should be a function of Hispanic political resources. Compared to blacks, Hispanics have not developed as strong a political, economic and organizational infrastructure (see Karnig, 1979; Fernández and Guskin, 1981). Traditional measures for political resources such as other elected officials, businesses owned, social organizations founded, etc. are difficult to find for Hispanics and generally show few resources.[15] Two potential resources measures will be used — education and income (on the importance of education, see Sigelman and Karnig, 1977). Since education and income levels may be directly related to some of the policy indicators, both measures were turned into ratios that compared Hispanics to Anglos (see Karnig, 1979). The measures are the ratio of Hispanic median education to Anglo median education and the ratio of Hispanic median income to Anglo median income.

These two measures not only reflect the relative potential resources of the Hispanic and Anglo communities, but they also reflect the potential social differences between the two groups. Giles and Evans (1985; 1986) have argued that if a minority is similar to the majority, the majority will be less threatened by the demands of the minority and more likely to grant the minority access to majority institutions. Giles and Evans (1986) contend that discrimination is less likely against middle-class blacks than against lower-class blacks because middle-class blacks share many of the values of middle-class whites. They imply that class has much to do with discrimination. Feagin (1980) presents a similar argument.

The argument of Giles, Evans, and Feagin is directly applicable to Hispanics. Hispanics, especially those who physically resemble Anglos, can be assimilated into Anglo institutions easier than blacks because they may be able to "pass" for Anglos. Hispanic students with higher incomes and from families with high education levels, under the Giles-Evans-Feagin hypothesis, are less likely to be perceived as a threat to the Anglo community. We hypothesize, therefore, that the higher the ratio of Hispanic income and education to Anglo income and education, the lower the resistance of the Anglo community and the education establishment to equal treatment for Hispanic students.

Social Class

The final political explanation for second-generation discrimination is also related to the Giles-Evans-Feagin power thesis. If the school district as a whole is fairly wealthy and the Hispanic community is fairly poor, then the standardized tests used to classify students will racially differentiate between Anglos and Hispanics. In such a community, these tests may also be accorded more legitimacy. In combination the tests provide teachers and administrators with "objective" reasons for separating Hispanic students from Anglos.

If the school district itself, however, has a large proportion of poor Anglos, then use of such standardized criteria will funnel a great many Anglos into similar programs. If discrimination is an explanation for the differences in Hispanic educational equity, then we would expect such measures as special education to be used less for Hispanics when the district poverty level for Anglos is high.[16]

Second-generation discrimination in this view is based both on race and class. Given a homogeneous middle-class Anglo community, Hispanics are differentiated from Anglos by both race and class. Discrimination might be a function of either. If the Anglo community is heterogeneous, then educational policy may be used to limit opportunities of poor whites also.

Findings

The relationships between the five independent variables and the seven policy ratios are shown in table 4. For the ability grouping indicators, the regression equation predicts fairly well for special education ($R^2 = .35$) and EMR classes (.52) but not for advanced classes (.17). For EMR classes two significant relationships exist. Strong negative relationships exist between EMR placement of Hispanics and both Anglo poverty and the Hispanic/Anglo income ratio. As predicted, school districts with higher levels of Anglo poverty funnel fewer Hispanics into EMR classes; in addition, in school districts where Hispanic income is closer to Anglo income, Hispanics are less likely to be placed in EMR classes.

For special education, the only significant relationship is for the Hispanic/Anglo education ratio, but the interpretation is the same as for EMR classes. In school districts where Hispanic education levels approach Anglo levels, Hispanics are less likely to be placed in special education classes. For advanced classes, the single significant relationship is poverty. As predicted, as poverty increases, the proportion of Hispanic students who are admitted to advanced placement classes increases.

The relationship between the independent variables and suspensions is disappointing. Only one variable is significantly related to the suspension ratio, and the overall level of explanation is low ($R^2 = .17$). As predicted, the proportion of Hispanics suspended decreases in school districts with higher levels of Anglo poverty.

TABLE 4

Impact of Hispanic Representation on Educational Policy

HISPANIC POLICY RATIO	BOARD MEMBERS	HISPANIC TEACHERS	EDUCATION RATIO	INCOME RATIO	POVERTY	R^2	F
Special Education	.22	.08	− .40*	− .18	− .23	.35	2.7
EMR Classes	.22	.34	− .10	− .47*	− .70	.52	5.5
Advanced Classes	.03	− .03	.02	.13	.45*	.17	1.1
Suspensions	− .31	.41	− .19	− .09	− .41*	.17	1.8
College Attendance	− .25	.45*	.30*	.51*	.05	.61	7.7
Dropouts	.10	− .47*	− .35*	− .45*	− .16	.61	8.0
Vocational Training	− .20	.14	− .05	.35	.03	.14	.7

*p < .05
n = 31
All coefficients are standardized regression coefficients.

The most striking findings are for educational attainment. The proportion of Hispanic teachers is positively related to Hispanics going on to college and negatively related to dropouts. Both relationships are significant; for dropouts, the teacher measure has the greatest impact of any variable and for college attendance, the second greatest impact. Both the education and income ratios are also significant in these regressions. The closer that Hispanic income and education levels are to those of the Anglo community, the more likely Hispanic students are to go to college and the less likely they are to drop out. In both cases the five variables explain over three-fifths of the variation. Vocational school enrollments are unrelated to any of the independent variables.

The results of table 4 offer some promise for improving the educational experience of Hispanic students. Of the seven indicators of educational equity, clearly college enrollments and dropout rates are the most important. Both represent policy outcomes, the end result of the policy process, rather than outputs, a preliminary impact. If Hispanic students can be kept in school, they are better off even if ability grouping and disciplinary practices are discriminatory. Both these measures are significantly related to the proportions of Hispanic teachers.

The promising nature of these findings is that the number of Hispanic teachers is a variable that can be manipulated by other policy actors in the short run, whereas income and education levels probably cannot. By instituting special recruitment programs or reliance on special scholarship programs, more Hispanics can be encouraged to become teachers. Hispanic activists can focus public attention on the equity of the teacher recruitment process. The net result should be improved educational opportunities for Hispanic students. Affirmative action in this context can have a double benefit, first by providing more opportunities for Hispanic teachers and second by improving the educational environment for Hispanic students.

The relationship between Hispanic representation and educational policy toward Hispanics is significantly different from the relationship for Blacks. Meier and England (1984, p. 399) found that school board membership had a significant impact on black enrollments in EMR classes and advanced classes. The proportion of black teachers similarly had strong simple correlations with ability grouping and discipline (Meier, 1984, p. 257). Neither variable was significantly related to the educational attainment of black students.

This raises the question of why Hispanic representation on school boards appears to be unrelated to educational policy toward Hispanics. Three reasons can be suggested. First, even though ten percent of the school board seats in these districts are held by Hispanics, in many districts Hispanics lack representation. In 17 of the 35 districts, not a single Hispanic serves on the school board. Although the proportion of Hispanic teachers may be less than the proportion of school board members in the average school district, every school district in the sample has some Hispanic teachers. Second, Hispanic school board members are not without a role in the educational process examined in this article. Hispanic school board members were significantly related to the proportion of Hispanic teachers. If Hispanic school board members do nothing more than assist in gaining additional teaching positions for Hispanics (e.g., by promoting affirmative action plans), they will play a role in limiting educational inequities for Hispanic students. Third, all Hispanic school board members might not be equally effective in representing the needs of the Hispanic community. Six of the school districts in the sample have appointive school boards; in such cases Hispanic board members are appointed by non-Hispanic politicians. In addition, in at-large cities, Hispanic school board members must be acceptable to a majority of the city. In such circumstances the Anglo power structure has been known to select and run a token Hispanic candidate (Davidson and Fraga, 1984; Fraga, 1984) or to prevent Hispanic candidates from running (Fuentes, 1984, p. 132).

An indirect assessment of the quality of Hispanic school board representation under different types of selection plans can be made by examining the policy indicators for districts using each selection plan. These figures are shown in table 5. Although the small number of school districts with other than at-large selection plans limits generalizations, an interesting pattern results. For five of the seven policy indicators Hispanic students in school districts with ward or mixed election systems are better off than Hispanics in districts with at-large elections.

Although definitive conclusions are impossible with the present data, the results suggest that perhaps the type of Hispanic school board member selected in an at-large system is less effective in representing Hispanic

TABLE 5

Educational Policy Measures Under Different School Board Plans

Hispanic Policy Ratio	SELECTION PLAN		
	At Large	Ward/Mixed	Appointive
Advanced Classes	.46	.47	.64
Special Education	.91	.92	.83
EMR Classes	1.15	.92	.83
Suspensions	1.01	1.24	.61
Vocational Training	.30	.45	.22
Attending College	.38	.46	.20
Dropouts	2.09	1.82	1.96

interests. District and mixed selection plans appear to produce Hispanic school board members that can better represent the Hispanic community. The findings for appointive members are inconclusive. Given the limited number of school districts in our data set, these speculations about the quality of representation should be considered as hypotheses rather than firm conclusions (see Wald and Sutherland, 1982). Nonetheless, they are consistent with the findings of Meier and England (1984) regarding the effectiveness of black representation.

CONCLUSION

This study allows us to draw several conclusions regarding Hispanics and educational policy. Hispanics have been unable to elect school board members in numbers anywhere near their percentage in the population. This is partly due to the use of at-large elections in many school districts. Because the proportion of Hispanic teachers is related to both Hispanic population and Hispanic school board members, Hispanics are significantly underrepresented among teachers also. The findings suggest that Hispanics are in a subordinate political position and are thus unable to affect educational policy to their benefit.

One impact of educational policy, second-generation discrimination, was investigated in depth. Although some evidence of ability grouping exists, the data reveal much lower levels of educational attainment for Hispanics. Consistent with the above conclusion, we found that these differences in educational attainment are related to the lack of Hispanic political influence, particularly as translated through the lack of Hispanic teachers. Denial of equal educational opportunities, therefore, is substantially a function of unequal political resources.

All our findings, however, are not pessimistic. Two important institutional characteristics, structures of school board representation and levels of bureaucratic representation, can be manipulated to improve Hispanic access to educational opportunities. More Hispanic school board members can increase the number of Hispanic teachers, and more Hispanic teachers can contribute to higher educational achievement for Hispanic students. We do not mean to imply that these elements of public education in the United States can be changed easily. Historical evidence supports the view that subordinate racial minority group access to educational opportunities have always required a level of political influence at legislative, executive, and judicial levels which itself is inhibited by the educational process. Our study suggests, however, that minority group leaders would do well to concentrate a large part of their efforts on making such substantive changes within the educational system of the United States. The enhanced position in America of Hispanics and other subordinate racial minority groups may well depend on such successful efforts.

APPENDIX A

School Districts Included in the Analysis

COMPOSITION OF STUDENT BODY

District	% Hispanic	% Black	% Anglo
Amarillo	8	8	84[a]
Austin	24	17	59
Boston	12	44	40
Chicago	15	60	23
Corpus Christi	60	6	34
Dade County (Miami)	32	29	39
Dallas	12	44	44
Denver	30	21	47
El Paso	60	3	37
Ft. Worth	14	34	52
Fresno	30	10	60
Gary	8	80	12
Hartford	30	50	20
Houston	23	44	33
Lansing	10	18	70
Las Vegas	5	12	80
Los Angeles	35	25	34
Lubbock	28	12	60
Milwaukee	5	42	51
Newark	21	68	11
New York	30	40	30
Oklahoma City	5	31	59
Orange County (Orlando)	5	25	70
Paterson	29	52	17
Philadelphia	6	62	31
Pueblo	40	2	57
Racine	8	17	75
Salt Lake City	18	1	80
San Antonio	67	16	12
San Bernadino	24	16	58
San Diego	15	15	64
San Jose	24	2	72
Stockton	12	3	82
Tucson	33	5	61
Worchester	7	5	88
Mean all Districts	22.4	26.2	49.8
Standard Deviation	16.1	21.4	22.4

Mean Population Residing in all Districts   786,094
Mean Percent Hispanic Population   14.5
Mean Percent Black Population   15.3

a. Percentages may not add up to 100 because district contains significant numbers of other racial groups.

Notes

*We would like to thank F. Chris Garcia, Susan Welch, Joseph Stewart, Michael Olivas, Lee Sigelman, Chandler Davidson, and Charles Bullock for comments on an earlier draft of this manuscript.

1. This research uses the term "Anglo" to denote non-Hispanic whites. This Southwestern term is more precise than the commonly used term "whites," in that Hispanics are clearly excluded from the group.

2. For the 35 school districts in our sample, the segregation of blacks and Hispanics is relatively equal. For blacks 52.9 percent of students would need to be moved so that all schools had an equal racial balance; for Hispanics, the percentage is 50.5.

3. We do not imply that a properly designed bilingual education program has no benefit for Hispanic or Anglo students. A well-designed program that is intended to provide a transition to learning in English and also emphasizes the qualities of Hispanic culture would benefit both Hispanic and Anglo students. If a bilingual education program is used to eliminate Hispanics from the regular classroom, however, it has little value.

4. The data on Hispanic teachers are from the U.S. Office of Civil Rights, "Student Trend Data," and were supplied by Professor Franklin Wilson of the University of Wisconsin. School board representation data are from a survey conducted in 1978; see Robinson and England (1981). Hispanics were identified by school administrators; we assume individuals were identified by Spanish surname. Other data sources are listed in notes 11 and 12.

5. The sample size must be fairly large so that a few extreme cases do not distort the regression. An intercept different from zero has substantive implications. An intercept significantly less than zero indicates a threshold effect below which Hispanics would receive no representation. A positive intercept would indicate a bias in favor of Hispanic representation. In our case, the intercept was not statistically different from zero.

6. Engstrom and McDonald (1981) argue that selection plans are interactive with population, not additive as we present them here. We disagree with Engstrom and McDonald. Engstrom and McDonald (1981, p. 348) do not operationalize a true interactive model but rather calculate three separate regressions between black population and city council seats, one for each type of selection plan. This process forces an interactive interpretation without determining if the additive model is superior. The correct procedure would be to estimate the following equation:

$Y = a + b_1x_1 + b_2X_2 + b_3X_3 + b_4X_1X_2 + b_5X_1X_3$

where X_1 is the percent minority population, X_2 is a dummy variable for at large selection plans, and X_3 is a dummy variable for appointive selection plans, and the b's are regression coefficients.

The relationship is interactive only if b_4 and b_5 are significant. We operationalized this model, and these slopes were not significant; the model added no additional explained variation to that found in table 1. Collinearity in this regression, in fact, makes all five coefficients unstable. In a subsequent work, Engstrom and McDonald

(1982, note 6) admit that the interactive model is not superior empirically to the additive model.

7. Since these 35 school districts have large Hispanic populations, one would expect that representation is better in these districts than in other school districts. Using a sample of 168 school districts associated with the SMSAs as of 1970, the corresponding slope was .679. We also ran additional analysis to determine if the slope for this equation was too low because Hispanic voters have lower levels of turnout. Although no registration figures by race are available for these districts, we tried two surrogates, native-born Hispanics and Hispanics over the age of 18. In both cases the level of explanation was significantly worse. In addition, the regression coefficient declined rather than increased.

8. Our "sample" includes 22 at-large districts, six appointive districts, and seven districts with ward or mixed election. All school board members elected in mixed systems were elected from a ward, not at-large.

9. We also ran this equation using the percent of Hispanics with four or more years of college. This variable was not significant when entered into the equation in table 2.

10. Good policy indicators for assessing the relationship between passive and active representation must have two characteristics. First, they must be phenomena the school board members and teachers can affect. Second, they must be directly linked to the Hispanic community so that board members and teachers recognize decisions that are in the interests of the Hispanic community. Expenditure figures that are normally used (see Welch and Karnig, 1980, for the best of this analysis) fail to meet either criteria. School system expenditures are often limited by property values, state appropriations, and federal aid formulas—forces largely outside the control of the local school district. In addition, if the focus is educational equity within a school district, then the level of expenditures is often irrelevant; the distribution of expenditures is far more important.

11. The data on special education, EMR classes, and advanced classes are taken from the U.S. Office of Civil Rights, *Elementary and Secondary School Civil Rights Survey: School Year 1976–77* (Washington, D.C.) These data were provided by Professor Joseph Stewart, Jr., of West Virginia University. The data for advanced classes were a combination of data for advanced placement classes and classes for the gifted. The suspensions data are from the same source.

12. The data on dropouts, college attendance, and vocational training were taken from the National Center for Education Statistics, *Social and Economic Characteristics of U.S. School Districts,* 1970 (Washington, D.C., 1975). All data are for the school district, not the city in which the school district is located.

13. Although we have no conclusive evidence, we speculate that this pattern occurs for two reasons. First, even large districts have only limited resources available for EMR and special education classes. The large ratios for blacks indicate that many of the classroom slots are filled by black students (43 percent of the total). Given that some Anglo students must also be placed in these classes on objective criteria, this leaves fewer positions that Hispanics can fill. A second reason why Hispanics might not fare as poorly as blacks on these measures is that a discriminatory school district has another option for segregating Hispanic stu-

dents; they can be placed in bilingual education programs. The correlation between Hispanic assignment to bilingual education programs and the ability grouping measures are $-.28$ for special education and $-.23$ for EMR classes. The negative relationships indicate that bilingual education is used more when other disadvantaged classes are used less. This finding is consistent with the hypothesis that special education classes, EMR classes, and bilingual education classes can be used as substitutes for each other.

14. For Hispanics 16 of the 21 policy intercorrelations are in the correct direction. Such a pattern could occur by chance only four times in 1000 tries. For blacks, 18 of the 21 correlations are in the correct direction; the probability of this result is less than 1 in 1000.

15. We attempted to measure Hispanic resources in other ways including the number of Hispanic elected officials and the number of Hispanic-owned businesses. In the case of elected officials, too few other elected officials were identified to provide a meaningful measure. In terms of businesses, the Census Bureau does not report the number of Hispanic-owned businesses if there are fewer than 100 such establishments within a city. For ten of our cities this was the case.

16. In such programs were nondiscriminatory, then the level of Anglo poverty should not affect the proportion of Hispanics assigned to these programs. Objective need for placement of Hispanics in such programs cannot in any logical way be linked to Anglo poverty. Such a relationship suggests discrimination even if all persons assigned to special education programs objectively belong in them because it would imply that Hispanics who need to be in these classes are shut out of them so that Anglos can receive the benefits of this instruction.

REFERENCES

Acuña, Rodolfo. 1981. *Occupied America: A History of Chicanos,* 2d ed. New York: Harper and Row.

Alcalá, Carlos M., and Jorge C. Rangel. 1972. Project Report: De Jure Segregation of Chicanos in the Texas Public Schools. *Harvard Civil Rights–Civil Liberties Law Review* 7:307–391.

Arnez, Nancy L. 1978. Implementation of Desegation as a Discriminatory Process. *Journal of Negro Education* 47:28–45.

Barrera, Mario, 1979. *Race and Class in the Southwest: A Theory of Racial Inequality.* Notre Dame, Ind.: University of Notre Dame Press.

Brown, George H., Nancy L. Rosen, S. T. Hill, and Michael A. Olivas. 1980. *The Condition of Education for Hispanic Americans.* Washington: National Center for Education Statistics.

Browning, Rufus P., Dale R. Marshall, and David H. Tabb. 1984. *Protest Is Not Enough: The Struggle of Blacks and Hispanics for Equality in Urban Politics.* Berkeley, Calif.: University of California Press.

Bullock, Charles S., III. 1980. The Office of Civil Rights and Implementation of Desegregation Programs in the Public Schools. *Policy Studies Journal,* 8: 597–615.

Bullock, Charles S., III, and Susan A. MacManus. 1981. Policy Responsiveness to the Black Electorate. *American Politics Quarterly* 9:357–368.

Bustamante, Jorge. 1976. Structural and Ideological Conditions of the Mexican Undocumented Immigration to the United States. *American Behavioral Scientist* 19:364–376.

Cárdenas, Gil. 1975. United States Immigration Policy Toward Mexico: An Historical Perspective. *Chicano Law Review* 2:66–89.

Carrión, A.M. 1983. *Puerto Ricans: A Political and Cultural History.* New York: Norton.

Children's Defense Fund. 1974. *Children Out of School in America.* Washington, D.C.: Children's Defense Fund of the Washington Research Project.

Cole, Leonard A. 1974. Electing Blacks to Municipal Office: Structural and Social Determinants. *Urban Affairs Quarterly* 10:17–39.

Davidson, Chandler, and Luis Ricardo Fraga. 1984. Nonpartisan Slating Groups in an At-large Setting. Pp. 119–144 in Chandler Davidson, *Minority Vote Dilution.* Washington, D.C.: Howard University Press.

Davidson, Chandler, and George Korbel. 1981. At-large Elections and Minority-Group Representation. *Journal of Politics* 43:982–1005.

Dye, Thomas R., and James Renick. 1981. Political Power and City Jobs: Determinants of Minority Employment. *Social Science Quarterly* 62:475–486.

Eisinger, Peter K. 1982a. Black Employment in Municipal Jobs. *American Political Science Review* 76:330–392.

———. 1982b. The Economic Conditions of Black Employment in Municipal Bureaucracies. *American Journal of Political Science* 26:754–771.

Engstrom, Richard L., and Michael D. McDonald. 1981. The Election of Blacks to City Councils. *American Political Science Review* 75:344–354.

———. 1982. The Underrepresentation of Blacks on City Councils. *Journal of Politics* 44:1088–1105.

Epps, Edgar G. 1981. Minority Children: Desegregation, Self-evaluation, and Achievement Orientation, Pp. 85–106 in Willis D. Hawley, *Effective School Desegregation: Equity, Quality, and Feasibility.* Beverly Hills, Calif.: Sage.

Eulau, Heinz, and Paul D. Karps. 1977. The Puzzle of Representation: Specifying Components of Responsiveness. *Legislative Studies Quarterly* 2:233–254.

Eyler, Janet, Valerie Cook, Rachel Thompkins, William Trent, and Leslie Ward. 1981. Resegregation: Segregation Within Desegrated Schools. Pp. 210–329 in Christine Rossell et al., *Assessment of Current Knowledge About the Effectiveness of School Desegregation Strategies.* Nashville, Tenn.: Vanderbilt University, Institute of Public Policy.

Eyler, Janet, Valerie Cook, and Leslie Ward. 1983. Resegregation: Segregation Within Desegregated Schools. Pp. 126–162 in Christine H. Rossell and Willis D. Hawley, eds., *Consequences of School Desegregation.* Philadelphia: Temple University Press.

Feagin, Joe R. 1980. School Desegregation: A Political-Economic Perspective. Pp. 25–50 in W. G. Stephan and Joe R. Feagin, *School Desegregation: Past, Present and Future.* New York: Plenum Press.

Fernández, Ricardo, and Judith T. Guskin. 1981. Hispanic Students and School Desegregation. Pp. 107–140 in *Effective School Desegregation. See* Epps, 1981.

Fraga, Luis Ricardo. 1984. *Nonpartisan Slating Groups: The Role of 'Reformed' Parties in City Electoral Politics.* Ph.D. dissertation, Rice University.

Fuentes, Luis. 1984. Puerto Ricans and New York City School Board Elections: Apathy or Obstructionism? Pp. 127–138 in James Jennings and Monte Rivera, *Puerto Rican Politics in Urban America.* Westport, Conn.: Greenwood Press.

Galarza, Ernesto. 1977. *Farm Workers and Agri-business in California.* Notre Dame, Ind.: University of Notre Dame Press.

Gamio, Mario. 1971. *Mexican Immigration to the United States.* New York: Dover.

García, Mario T. 1975. Racial Dualism in the El Paso Labor Market, 1880–1920. *Aztlán* 6:197–218.

Giles, Michael W., and Arthur S. Evans. 1985. External Threat, Perceived Threat, and Group Identity. *Social Science Quarterly* 66:50–66.

Giles, Michael W., and Arthur S. Evans. 1986. The Power Approach to Intergroup Hostility. *Journal of Conflict Resolution* 30: 469–485.

Gómez-Quiñoñes, Juan. 1972. The First Steps: Chicano Labor Conflict and Organizing, 1900–1920. *Aztlán* 3:13–49.

Harmel, Robert, Keith Hamm, and Robert Thompson. 1983. Black Voting Cohesion and Distinctiveness in Souther Legislatures. *Social Science Quarterly* 64:183–192.

Kaeser, Susan C. 1979. Suspensions in School Discipline. *Education and Urban Society* 11:465–486.

Karnig, Albert K. 1979. Black Resources and City Council Representation. *Journal of Politics* 41:134–149.

Karnig, Albert K., and Susan Welch. 1979. Sex and Ethnic Differences in Municipal Representation. *Social Science Quarterly* 60:465–481.

———. 1982. Electoral Structure and Black Representation on City Councils. *Social Science Quarterly* 63:99–114.

Keech, William R. 1968. *The Impact of Negro Voting.* Chicago: Rand McNally.

Keller, Ernest. 1973. The Impact of Black Mayors on Urban Policy. *The Annals* 439:40–52.

Levine, Charles H. 1974. *Racial Conflict and the American Mayor.* Lexington, Mass.: Lexington Books.

Lopez, Manual Mariano. 1981. Patterns of Interethnic Residential Segregation in the Urban Southwest. *Social Science Quarterly* 62:50–63.

McConahay, John B. 1981. Reducing Racial Prejudice in Desegregated Schools. Pp. 252–63 in *Effective School Desegregation. See* Epps, 1981.

MacManus, Susan A. 1978. City Council Election Procedures and Minority Representation. *Social Science Quarterly* 59:153–161.

McPartland, James M., and Jomills H. Braddock. 1981. Going to College and Getting a Good Job: The Impact of Desegregation. In *Effective School Desegregation. See* Epps, 1981.

Meier, Kenneth J. 1984. Teachers, Students, and Discrimination: The Policy Impact of Black Representation. *Journal of Politics* 46:252–263.

Meier, Kenneth J., and Robert E. England. 1984. Black Representation and Educational Policy: Are They Related? *American Political Science Review* 78: 392–403.

Meier, Kenneth J., and Lloyd G. Nigro. 1976. Representative Bureaucracy and Policy Preferences. *Public Administration Review* 36:458–470.

Nelson, William. 1972. *Black Politics in Gary*. Washington: Joint Center for Political Studies.

Olivas, Michael A. 1983. Research and Theory on Hispanic Education: Students, Finance and Governance. *Aztlán* 14:111–146.

Orfield, Gary. 1981. Housing Patterns and Desegregation Policy. Pp. 185–221 in *Effective School Desegregation*. See Epps, 1981.

Pitkin, Hannah F. 1967. *The Concept of Representation*. Berkeley, Calif.: University of California Press.

Poinsett, Alex. 1970. *Black Power Gary Style*. Chicago: Johnson.

Robinson, Theodore P., and Thomas R. Dye. 1978. Reformism and Black Representation on City Councils. *Social Science Quarterly* 59:133–141.

Robinson, Theodore P., and Robert E. England. 1981. Black Representation on Central City School Boards Revisited. *Social Science Quarterly* 62:495–502.

Rodgers, Harrell R., and Charles S. Bullock, III. 1972. *Law and Social Change*. New York: McGraw-Hill.

Rosenbaum, James E. 1976. *Making Inequality: The Hidden Curriculum of High School Tracking*. New York: John Wiley.

Saltzstein, Grace Hall. 1979. Representative Bureaucracy and Bureaucratic Responsibility. *Administration and Society* 10:465–475.

Samora, Julian. 1971. *Los Mojados: The Wetback Story*. Notre Dame, Ind.: University of Notre Dame Press.

San Miguel, Guadalupe. 1982. Mexican-American Organizations and the Changing Politics of School Desegregation in Texas, 1945–1980. *Social Science Quarterly* 63:701–715.

Schaefer, Richard T. 1984. *Racial and Ethnic Groups*. 2d ed. Boston: Little-Brown.

Sigelman, Lee, and Albert K. Karnig. 1977. Black Education and Bureaucratic Employment. *Social Science Quarterly* 57:858–863.

Smith, Elsie J., and Lee N. June. 1982. Role of the Counselor in Desegregated Schools. *Journal of Black Studies* 13:227–240.

Smith, Marzell, and Charles D. Dziuban. 1977. The Gap Between Desegregation Research and Remedy. *Integrateducation* 15:51–55.

Stewart, Joseph, and Charles S. Bullock, III. 1981. Implementing Equal Education Opportunity Policy. *Administration and Society* 12:427–446.

Stone, Chuck. 1971. *Black Political Power in America*. New York: Dell.

Taebel, Delbert 1978. Minority Representation on City Councils. *Social Science Quarterly*. 59:142–152.

Thomas, Gail E., and Frank Brown. 1982. What Does Educational Research Tell Us About School Desegregation Effects? *Journal of Black Studies* 13:155–174.

U.S. Commission on Civil Rights. 1975. *The Voting Rights Act: Ten Years After*. Washington, D.C.: U.S. Government Printing Office.

————. 1976. *Fulfilling the Letter and Spirit of the Law: Desegregation of the Nation's Schools*. Washington, D.C.: U.S. Government Printing Office.

Uslander, Eric M. 1976. The Pitfalls of Per Capita. *American Journal of Political Science* 20:125–133.

Wald, Kenneth D., and Carole Sutherland. 1982. Black Public Officials and the Dynamics of Representation. Pp. 239–253 in Laurence W. Moreland, Todd A. Baker, and Robert P. Steed, *Contemporary Southern Political Attitudes and Behavior*. New York: Praeger.

Weinberg, Meyer. 1977. *A Chance to Learn: The History of Race and Education in the United States*. London: Cambridge University Press.

Welch, Susan, and John R. Hibbing. 1984. Hispanic Representation in the U.S. Congress. *Social Science Quarterly* 65:328–335.

Welch, Susan, and Albert K. Karnig. 1978. Representation of Blacks on Big City School Boards. *Social Science Quarterly* 59:162–172.

————. 1980. *Black Representation and Urban Policy*. Chicago: University of Chicago Press.

Welch, Susan, Albert K. Karnig, and Richard Eribes. 1983. Changes in Hispanic Local Public Employment in the Southwest. *Western Political Quarterly* 36: 660–673.

23. Changes in Hispanic Local Public Employment in the Southwest

Susan Welch, Albert K. Karnig, and Richard Eribes

THIS ARTICLE EXAMINES the changing nature of Hispanic employment in Southwestern municipalities between 1973 and 1978.

Despite the size and importance of the Hispanic population — especially in the Southwest — there has been scant research on the rates of Hispanic public employment. Previous research has shown that minority public employees — black, Hispanic, women, or others — are overrepresented at the bottom rungs of the occupational ladder in local, state, and federal employment, and are underrepresented in management and higher-level posts (cf. Sigelman 1976; Hall and Saltzstein 1975, 1977; Meier 1978; Cayer and Sigelman 1980; Rose and Chia 1978; Herbert 1974; Hutchins and Sigelman 1981; see also deKrofcheck and Jackson 1974).

Cayer and Sigelman (1980) found some improvement in the status of minorities and women in the total state and local workforce between 1973 and 1975. The proportion of Anglo males in the workforce dropped in both percentage and absolute terms. As a consequence, both minorities and women improved their representation. Cayer and Sigelman also showed that Anglo males continued to have higher salaries than any other group except Asian males, with little change in the 1973 to 1975 period.

There have been three studies which specifically examined Hispanic public employee salaries and job status. Garcia, Clark, and Clark (1978) found Hispanics overrepresented in New Mexico's workforce, but underrepresented at the higher pay grades. Dye and Renick (1981), on the other hand, discovered that Hispanics were employed by forty-two local governments at merely 33 percent of their population proportions, and were least well represented in administrative jobs and considerably overrepresented

From *Western Political Quarterly* 36:4 (December 1983), pp. 660–673. Reprinted by permission of the University of Utah, copyright holder.

in service jobs. However, these cites had an average Hispanic population of only 4.5 percent, making generalizations tenuous at best. Finally, Hall and Saltzstein (1977) found that the Hispanic percent of the 1973 municipal workforce in twenty-six Texas cities over 50,000 ranged from 1.6 to 78.9 percent.[1]

CORRELATES OF HISPANIC EMPLOYMENT

Earlier work has assessed the importance of several factors that might predict Hispanic employment. Demographic characteristics of the minority community are one set of possible influences. Findings concerning the relationship of minority income and education to minority public employment are mixed. Hutchins and Sigelman (1981) and Meier (1978) found minority median income or education was strongly positively related to proportionality of public employment, while Dye and Renick (1981) discovered null and negative relationships for Hispanics. Sigelman and Karnig (1977) found that black employment was strongly related to various levels of black educational achievement in the southern states—but hardly related at all in the northern states. Finally, Hall and Saltzstein (1977) discovered that although black education was *positively* related to black employment, Hispanic education was *negatively* related to the Hispanic employment use index.

Most researchers have standardized for minority population proportions by dividing the proportion of the minority employed in the city by the proportion in the population. However, Dye and Renick (1981), using proportion minority population as an independent variable, discovered that the proportion of Hispanics in the city population was modestly related to administrative, professional, and protective service employment but strongly related to office and service employment.[2]

Minority political representation provides another possible explanation for minority hiring. A minority population that is well organized and has substantial resources may promote its aims both through encouragement of affirmative action in public employment and through support of minority candidates for office. Furthermore, minorities in public office are in a position to encourage and facilitate minority hiring (cf. Karnig and Welch, 1980). Dye and Renick's (1981) study showed that the proportion of blacks on the city council was moderately associated with black administrative, professional, and protective service employment by municipalities. The ratio of black council proportions to black population proportions was less strongly related to black employment. Similar patterns were evident for Hispanics, although these findings are merely suggestive because most of the sample cities had negligible Hispanic populations. Eisinger (1982), on the other hand, found no relationship between black council representation and employment in forty-three cities, although the presence of a black mayor was related to overall black employment and employment of blacks in professional and managerial capacities.

HYPOTHESES

This brief overview of the literature indicates the absence of clear and consistent findings. Because this literature is recent and small in size, it is not surprising that we find different indices used, different ways that minorities are aggregated, and different types of analyses. In part, we will add to this fragmentation by using a different, broader data base than preceding studies. On the other hand, we will build on the prior literature by testing further some previously suggested relationships, by examining Hispanic municipal employment more closely than have other studies, and by monitoring change over a five year period, 1973–1978. In this study we will test the general hypotheses that Hispanic municipal employment will be greater overall and in specific occupations, when:

(1) Hispanics are a larger proportion of the population.
(2) The Hispanic community has higher median educational and income levels.
(3) Hispanics have more political representation.

DATA AND METHODS

Case Base

The Equal Opportunity Act of 1972 mandated states and localities to collect information on the ethnic and sex composition of their workforces. These reports (EEO-4) have been filed annually with the Equal Employment Opportunity Commission (EEOC) since 1973. The ethnicity and sex of each employee is categorized by functional area (i.e. police, fire, general administration, and so forth); by occupation type (professional, skilled crafts, clerical, etc.); and by salary categories. Further breakdowns are made by new hires, part-time and full-time workers, and so forth, making the reports a cornucopia of detailed information about state and local employees.

The Equal Opportunity Act prohibits the EEOC from releasing individual data on individual localities. Thus, most analyses to date have

TABLE 1

Trends in Hispanic Local Employment
1973–1978

Total Workforce N = 65	Total Employees	Total Males	Total Females	HISPANIC		
				Males	Females	Total
# Employees (1973)	1213.9	1047.9	166.0	160.8	22.2	182.9
# Employees (1978)	1375.4	1140.6	234.8	201.0	37.0	238.1
# Change (1973–78)	161.5	92.7	68.8	40.3	14.9	55.1
% Change in Aggregated Workforce	.133	.088	.414	.251	.671	.301
% Change in # Emp. (Average of city averages)	.15	.11	.47	.44	1.38	.47
% Employees (1973)		.853	.147	.135	.014	.149
% Employees (1978)		.820	.180	.142	.024	.166
% Change (1973–78)		−.033	.033	.007	.010	.016
% Parity with 1970 Civilian Workforce		.618	.382	.111	.059	.170
Difference from Parity (1973)		.234	−.234	.024	−.045	−.020
Difference from Parity (1978)		.202	−.202	.031	−.035	−.004

been based on the published summaries in which state and local employment is aggregated by state (cf. Meier 1978). Researchers wishing to examine local governmental ethnic breakdowns must collect these reports directly from individual municipalities, which we did.

The cities which form our sample are the Arizona, California, Colorado, New Mexico, and Texas cities which responded to our request for data on municipal employment for 1973 and 1978. Of nearly 125 cities over 25,000 with at least 10 percent Spanish-surnamed population in 1970, 93 responded with information. However, many of the 93 had not filed EEO information in 1973 or the 1973 data were inaccessible. In our descriptive analysis, we will examine only cities with both 1973 and 1978 data (N = 83–85).[3]

The average city was approximately 188,000 in population (range 25,000–2,800,000), and 1,375 was the average number of employees in 1978 (range 73–26,102). Our analysis uses cities as the units of analysis and *not* the sum of workforces collected into a single larger total. To make our task manageable and to increase the willingness of cities to send data, we confined our analysis to six functional areas: police, fire, community development, sanitation and sewage, general administration, and streets and highways. This combination includes some functions where minority employment is great (sanitation and sewage), and some (police) where minorities have made relatively few inroads (see Herbert 1974). These six services also are those which most cities provide, and they comprise the largest city bureaucracies.

Analysis and Variables

We test our hypotheses with Pearsonian correlations and multiple regression. The independent variables of Hispanic median education, median income, and proportion of the population are specified in the hypotheses. However, median education and income are highly correlated (above .75) causing multicollinearity. Thus, only income is used in our regressions. We have 1980 data on the proportion of Hispanics, but 1980 data on the Hispanic workforce is not yet available. In 1970, however, Hispanic population and workforce proportions were correlated at over .9, so that the use of population rather than workforce data does not pose a serious problem. To measure political representation, we will employ the absolute proportion of Hispanics on the city council in 1978 (drawn from a mail survey of city clerks).[4]

We examine Hispanic employment for males and females together and separately, and for two more prestigious and highly paid occupational categories: professional and administrative (managers and officials). We also analyze the employment of Hispanics in police and fire departments.

City population size will be one control variable. In Texas cities it was found to be related to black employment though not to that of Hispanics (Hall and Saltzstein 1977). Meier (1978) found that the extent of urbanization of the state was modestly negatively related to minority employment, but Hutchins and Sigelman (1981) found it positively related to the proportionality of black employment. Dye and Renick (1981) showed that city size was positively related to black but not Hispanic municipal employment. In our study, both population size and ethnic population data are adjusted to approximate 1978 figures by calculating the average annual change between 1970 and 1980, multiplying by 8, and adding to the 1970 base. The population variable was then logged.[5]

Another control is for the state in which the municipality is located. The labor market for minority candidates, in many instances, is statewide. Discriminatory practices, and thus strategies for rectification, often are part of the state's political culture and legal structure. Therefore, we entered into our regression equation a dummy variable representing each state (less California as the omitted variable.

We also controlled for form of government. It is possible that mayor-council governments will be more responsive to minority demands for public employment than manager-council systems (Lineberry and Fowler 1967; Karnig 1979). The black proportion of the workforce is also a control. Sigelman (1976) found that minorities did best in acquiring public employment precisely where females did worst. And Hall and Saltzstein (1975) found that the proportion of Hispanics in the municipal workforce was negatively related to the proportion of blacks. Thus it is possible that improvements in the employment of one group lead to decrements in the employment status of other minority groups. Karnig and Welch (1980) found this *not* to be true in the case of elected officials; increases in black and Hispanic elected officials came largely at the expense of the Anglo males, not other minorities. However, there may be a zero-sum situation over a longer period or in bureaucracies rather than in elected positions. We used somewhat different measures of the black component of the workforce in our various equations. In the overall and male and female employment equations, we controlled for the proportions of city employees that were black males and black females. In the equations examining Hispanic police, fire, managerial, and professional employment, we used the black proportion in each of these categories and a control for percent blacks in the population.[6]

Finally, we examined the effect on Hispanic employment of the change in size of the municipal workforce between 1973 and 1978. Our expectation was that workforces that grew would be better able to accommodate increased minority employment demands than would stable or shrinking workforces. Using a measure of the percent change in the size of the workforce in this five-year period, we found no relationship with our dependent variables so the variable was dropped from the analysis in order to include the eighteen cities in the analysis that had 1978 but not 1973 data.

FINDINGS

Hispanic Employment: A Descriptive Analysis

If we sum all six types of municipal departments, the average employee change during our period was 15 percent per city, or about 160 workers. The proportion of Anglo men declined somewhat after 1973, but in 1978 they were still overutilized[7] by 12.6 percent, amounting to 126 percent of parity. Hispanic men experienced a similar situation. In 1978, they were overutilized at 3.1 percent, equivalent to 126 percent of the representation of the labor pool standard. In addition, between 1973 and 1978, Hispanic males won about 25 percent of the new positions, over twice as many new jobs as parity would dictate.

On the other hand, in 1973 Hispanic women were a mere 1.4 percent of the employees, a figure which grew to 2.4 percent in 1978. This left Chicanas underutilized by − 3.5 percent. At the beginning of the period Hispanic females had but 24 percent of their expected share of the workforce and, at the end, 41 percent. In fact, during the period, Hispanic females secured over 9 percent of the new jobs, or 1.5 times the parity level; they more than doubled their numbers among city workers. This trend signals some key advancement and, yet, in 1978, Chicanas had just over four-tenths of the parity rate that their labor pool availability would warrant. Combining males and females, Hispanics were underrepresented by just .004 percent. Anglos are also underrepresented (by .032 percent) while blacks are overrepresented by .031 (not shown).

We turn now to employment in specific functions and occupations. The "officials" category is important because Officials and Administrators are the officers who direct municipal government. Despite a reduction in the number of these positions and low turnover rates, Hispanic males increased slightly their share of the "officials" category, while Hispanic females dropped from a miniscule .5 percent to an even smaller .3 percent. Overall, Hispanic managerial employment remained constant. In the professional category, females, not males, gained in percent employment. However, Hispanic males were still slightly overrepresented with regard to parity in 1978, while Hispanic females were underrepresented.

The workforces in police and fire departments were among the fastest growing in our sample. Hispanics expanded their ratio of Police and Fire positions since 1973, yet they were left substantially underutilized in both functions by 1978. Hispanic men were at virtual parity in Fire Departments, but did less well in Police Departments. Chicanas comprised rather miniscule proportions of both Protective Services.

In general, in these four selected categories, gains have been made by both Hispanic men and women. Compared to parity benchmarks, progress has been noticeable. However, one must bear in mind the small proportions of Hispanics, especially women, comprising the available workforce by which parity is judged.

Salary Levels

The question of the proportionality of Hispanic municipal employment to Hispanic workforce availability is of great importance. But how they are treated once they are employed is critical as well. Clearly, we can draw only tentative conclusions from aggregate data. To ascertain fully whether unjustified inequalities exist, we would need individual level information on skill levels, performance, and so forth. Therefore, even if we

TABLE 2

Hispanic Employment in Selected Areas (N=65)

	OFFICIALS			PROFESSIONALS			POLICE			FIRE		
	Males	Females	Total	Males	Females	Total	Males	Females	Total	Males	Females	Total
# Employees (1973)	3.7	.2	3.9	8.2	.6	8.8	34.3	8.2	42.5	21.5	.7	22.2
# Employees (1978)	3.1	.3	3.5	12.9	2.2	15.1	45.8	12.7	58.5	33.5	1.1	34.7
# Change (1973–78)	–.6	.2	–.4	4.7	1.6	6.3	11.5	4.4	16.0	12.0	.4	12.4
% Change in # Emp.	.32	.21	.37	.54	.62	.66	.88	1.03	.87	.98	.32	1.04
% Employees (1973)	.071	.005	.076	.076	.004	.080	.076	.016	.092	.087	.010	.090
% Employees (1978)	.072	.003	.075	.073	.008	.081	.080	.024	.104	.107	.008	.11
% Change (1973–78)	.001	–.001	–.001	–.003	.004	.001	.004	.008	.012	.020	–.001	.01
% Parity with 1970 Civilian Workforce	.080	.017	.097	.066	.034	.099	.111	.059	.170	.110	.059	.100
Difference from Parity (1973)	–.010	–.012	–.022	.011	–.030	–.019	–.035	–.043	–.078	–.023	–.049	–.010
Difference from Parity (1978)	–.009	–.014	–.022	.007	–.025	–.018	–.031	–.035	–.066	–.003	–.051	–.010

find gross differences in salaries, we cannot conclude that these inequities are necessarily unwarranted. Obviously, employees within a given job classification may be undertaking widely differing tasks. More critically, perhaps, due to the late entry of minorities and women into municipal workforces, there may be salary differences which stem from seniority and job experience. Nonetheless, if large disparities do exist, then at the very least this would suggest the need for municipalities continually to review their wage distribution criteria and to enhance ongoing programs of affirmative action and equal employment opportunity.

Table 3 summarizes median salary levels obtained by six ethnic gender groups in five occupational classifications, i.e., Officials and Administrators, Professionals, Technicians, Maintenance, and Clericals. The information indicated divergent patterns in the three types of occupational classes. However, in each instance, Anglo men drew the highest salaries.

In general, Hispanic males are paid less than Anglo males in each category, although by 1978 near parity existed in the professional and clerical occupations. The official category is particularly striking, with Anglo males making six to twelve thousand dollars more than any other group, male or female. Several reasons might explain these differences. There may simply be discrimination. But it is also possible that minorities and women are paid less because they are less experienced than their male counterparts, or may be found in less senior positions — assistants to department heads rather than department heads, or junior rather than senior analysts. In their eagerness to meet affirmative action goals and trans-

TABLE 3

Median Salary Levels by Occupation

TRENDS Median Salary Total Workforce		ANGLO		BLACK		HISPANIC	
		Males	Females	Males	Females	Males	Females
Officials	1973	19,450	10,550	12,900	11,800	14,508	13,800
	1978	26,400	16,783	20,500	14,500	20,534	16,100
Professionals	1973	15,500	11,800	12,550	11,250	13,800	10,586
	1978	20,250	20,476	19,650	16,500	20,468	14,500
Technicians	1973	11,900	9,600	10,450	9,600	10,509	7,550
	1978	17,033	12,463	13,400	11,150	14,500	10,543
Clerical	1973	8,350	7,900	8,983	7,533	9,600	6,200
	1978	10,900	10,775	10,495	10,527	10,485	10,457
Service	1973	10,975	10,519	9,700	10,469	10,283	9,800
	1978	17,575	14,479	12,500	10,800	13,783	10,525

mit favorable equal employment opportunity reports, personnel officers may classify jobs held by minorities and women as Official and Administrator, though in fact the positions call for less expertise than do other Official and Administrator posts. Under such a circumstance, salary differentials would be expected. Our data does not allow us to select among these explanations, but these findings certainly suggest that cities should analyze their employment and wage practices.

Hispanic females have near parity with Anglo males and females in the clerical occupations, but lag far behind the Anglo male pacesetters in every other occupation. Female Hispanic professionals, technicians, and service workers also have much smaller median salaries than Anglo females while Chicana officials as well as clerical workers are comparable to Anglo females, though still behind Anglo males. In evaluating these salaries, it should be kept in mind that Hispanic females are a small group and thus their salary levels are subject to substantial fluctuation based on small N size.

In sum, we find Hispanic salary levels of both males and females to be lower than those of their Anglo counterparts. The nature of these aggregate data does not allow us to pinpoint the reasons, which, as we have noted, may include discrimination, experience, job classifications, and differences in locale.

Predictors of Hispanic Employment

Table 4 shows the results of our regression analysis. Only those variables with significant relationships are shown. It is clear that only a few of the independent variables significantly affect rates of Hispanic employment. The proportion of Hispanics in the city's population has a consistently strong effect, with beta values between .53 and .78 in each of the seven equations. Hispanic female employment is the least affected by Hispanic population proportions, with a gain of only .1 percent municipal employment for each 1.0 percent population increase. Hispanic employment in the other categories is more sensitive to population, with b values from .46 to .93.

Locale has a fairly consistent effect on each type of Hispanic employment except that of Chicanas. Compared with the omitted category, California, Hispanic employment in New Mexico is consistently higher, controlling for the other factors. This comports well with the common wisdom that the political status of Hispanics in New Mexico is higher than that elsewhere in the Southwest. The fact that Hispanic employment is also higher in Texas, overall, among males, and in the police departments is less expected. Colorado does not differ significantly from California, while in Arizona, overall and male employment, but not more specialized em-

TABLE 4
Predictors of Hispanic Employment

Predictor Variable (Only those significant at .05 listed)	TYPE OF EMPLOYMENT						
	All Hispanics	All Hispanic Males	All Hispanic Females	Hispanic Professionals	Hispanic Managers	Hispanic Police	Hispanic Fire
% Hispanic Population	.69(.74)[a]	.66(.63)	.59(.10)	.76(.81)	.53(.46)	.78(.74)	.76(.93)
State							
Arizona	.13(.09)	.14(.09)	—[b]	—	—	—	—
Colorado	—	—	—	—	—	—	—
New Mexico	.23(.20)	.22(.16)	—	.22(.18)	.28(.19)	.20(.15)	.29(.28)
Texas	.27(.12)	.29(.11)	—	—	—	.24(.19)	—
% Black Males in Workforce[c]	(−.20)(−.58)	−.22(−.54)	—	—	−.34(−.36)[c]	−.39(−.39)	−.24(−.26)
Government form[d]	—	—	—	−.23(−.11)	—	—	—
TOTAL R²	.83	.84	.47	.67	.42	.71	.59

a. Figures are betas with unstandardized coefficients in parentheses. Other controls not shown here were Hispanic council representation, minority status of city mayors, median Hispanic income, population size, percent females in the workforce, and black population proportions (for professional, managerial, police and fire equations only).
b. Variable not significant for this dependent variable where only a line shown.
c. For the Hispanic manager dependent variable, percent black managers used; similar black equivalents were used for Hispanic professionals, police department employees, and fire department employees.
d. 1 = mayor council, 0 = city manager.

ployment, is higher than the California base. It is, of course, possible that the lower levels of Hispanic employment in Colorado and California reflect more opportunities for Hispanics in the private sector rather than less opportunities in the public.

The proportion of black males in the workforce is consistently related to six of seven dependent variables, while the proportion of black females affects none significantly. Hispanic employment is higher when black male employment is lower. This is true for all Hispanics, Hispanic males, and the specialized categories of police, fire, managers and professionals. In the latter categories, the black comparison groups examined were black police, fire, managerial, and professional employees. Thus, there does seem to be a zero sum effect such that when black males do better, Hispanic males of all categories do worse. There is no comparable effect for females.

The only other variable significant in any of the equations is a small positive effect of city manager governments on Hispanic professional employment. While one can conceive of explanations for this phenomenon, it is difficult to propose an explanation for why only professional employment is affected. Thus the data might be interpreted as anomalous.

Despite the fact that most of our variables (including median Hispanic income, total population, mayoral and council Hispanic representation, and black population) had no effect, the overall R^2 was substantial in each case, due largely to the effect of population. Thus our variables as a group predicted levels of Hispanic employment rather well. Population, locale, and black competition were important in explaining Hispanic employment, while political representation and Hispanic income levels were not.

Conclusions

On the whole, Hispanic employment was more representative of labor pool proportions in 1978 than in 1973. This suggests movement toward a more representative system — in which every group is employed in each job category in closer proportion to its population or labor pool representation. But this goal is perhaps not only unachievable but also may be undesirable given the differences in interests, skills, and preferences of individuals in various groups. Nevertheless, movement toward more proportional representation of groups in employment is an indication that patterns of discrimination, with minorities and women at the bottom of the occupational ladder, are diminishing.

In general, there are few city characteristics beyond that of the availability of the Hispanic population that predict Hispanic municipal employment. Only hypothesis 1 (that Hispanic employment is related to Hispanic population) was confirmed. Contrary to hypotheses 2 and 3, Hispanic employment was not related to either the economic status of the Hispanic community or to Hispanic political representation (in fact, relationships with these factors were often negative).

One explanation for the findings might be that in those communities containing the best educated and most trained Hispanic populations, private employment is a desirable and available alternative to public employment. In the least economically well-off Hispanic communities, neither public nor private employment may be available. In the middle communities, public but not private jobs may have opened up. We did not have the data to examine private employment, but we did compare our public employment data to Hispanic income. We found that in medium-income Hispanic communities, Hispanics have the least, not the most, municipal employment. This suggests that private employment opportunities have opened up faster than public ones for skilled Hispanics. Perhaps affirmative action in the private sector has reversed or mitigated the pattern of greater opportunities for minorities in the public sector.

One significant finding is the generally negligible association between Hispanic employment overall and that of blacks, but the strong negative association between those groups in some types of employment. Among professionals, managers, and police officers, there was a significant negative relationship between Hispanic and black employment. These, of course, are areas of employment where there has been discrimination against minorities and a strong effort on the part of minorities to gain a foothold. Thus, competition might be expected to be intense. And Hispanic and black male employment generally is negatively associated, even controlling for black and Hispanic population percents.

One negative aspect of Hispanic employment is the status of Hispanic females. Unlike Hispanic male employment, female employment is only modestly related to population (b = .10). Hence, increases in Hispanic population at this point seem to promote Hispanic male municipal employment, but not that of Chicanas. Again, it is possible that differential opportunities exist for Hispanic males and females in the private sector, that is, Hispanic females may be welcome as secretaries in private enterprises, whereas males are not welcome as white-collar workers.

NOTES

A much earlier version of this paper, based on a smaller sample of cities, was presented at the Annual Meeting of the Midwest Political Science Association. Chicago, Illinois, April 24–26, 1980. Funding for this project was provided by the

U.S. Department of Labor. The authors would like to acknowledge the cooperation of the Personnel and Affirmative Action offices of the 93 cities responding
to our request for data.

1. Unfortunately, they did not present the ratios of workforce to population, but instead created a "use index," which combined representational ratios
with distributions across salary levels.

2. Black population proportions were moderately positively related to all
types of black public employment except black female public service employment,
which had a small negative relationship.

3. Some cities did not send *complete* data for each functional area.

4. In 1978, city clerks in all 125 Southwestern cities that had at least 25,000
population and 10 percent Hispanic were contacted for information about city council composition and other details of city governance. All 125 cities responded to
the initial survey or followup letters and calls.

5. We also wished to control for the size of the workforce in our six functional areas and for the total general expenditures in each city. However, this variable was so highly related to city size that it was dropped from the analysis.

6. Black population percent was not used in the overall male and female
equations because it is highly correlated with proportion black in the municipal
workforce. It is not as highly related to black employment in these specific occupational and functional areas.

7. Overutilization refers to a comparison with labor pool statistics. For
example, we compare the proportion of the city workforce that is Hispanic male
to the Hispanic male percent in the citywide labor pool to determine the under
or overutilization of that group. As another example, we compare the proportion
of administrators employed by the city who are Hispanic females to the proportion of Hispanic females in the administrative and managerial labor pool citywide
to determine the utilization of Hispanic females as administrators.

REFERENCES

Cayer, N. Joseph, and Lee Sigelman, 1980. "Minorities and Women in State and
    Local Government: 1973–1975." *Public Administration Review* 40 (Septem-
    ber–October): 443–450.
Davis, Charles, and J. P. West. 1978. "Analyzing Perceptions of Affirmative Action
    Issues: A Study of Mexican-American Supervisors in a Metropolitan Bureau-
    cracy." *Midwest Review of Public Administration* 12 (December): 246–256.
Davis, Lenwood, and W. Van Horne. 1975. "The City Renewed: White Dream—
    Black Nightmare." *Black Scholar* 7 (November): 2–9.
Dye, Thomas, and James Renick. 1981. "Political Power and City Jobs: Determi-
    nants of Minority Employment." *Social Science Quarterly* 62 (September):
    475–486.
deKrofcheck, Maria, and C. Jackson, "The Chicano Experience with Nativism
    in Public Administration." *Public Administration Review* 343 (November–
    December): 534–539.

Eisinger, Peter. 1982. "Black Employment in Municipal Jobs: The Impact of Black Political Power." *American Political Science Review* 76 (June): 380–392.

Garcia, Jose Z., C. Clark, and J. Clark. 1978. "Policy Impacts on Chicanos and Women: A State Case Study." *Policy Studies Journal* 7 (Winter): 251–258.

Hall, Grace, and A. Saltzstein. 1975. "Equal Employment in Urban Governments: The Potential Problem of Interminority Competition." *Public Personnel Management* (November–December): 386–393.

———. 1977. "Equal Employment Opportunity for Minorities in Municipal Government." *Social Science Quarterly* 57 (March): 865–871.

Hellriegel, Don, and L. Short. 1972. "Equal Employment Opportunity in the Federal Government: A Comparative Analysis." *Public Administration Review* 32 (November–December): 851–858.

Henderson, Lenneal. 1978. "The Impact of the Equal Employment Opportunity Act of 1972 on Employment Opportunities for Women and Minorities." *Policy Studies Journal* 7 (Winter): 234–240.

Herbert, Adam. 1974. "The Minority Administrator: Problems, Prospects, Challenges." *Public Administration Review* 343 (November–December): 556–565.

Hutchins, Matthew, and L. Sigelman. 1981. "Black Employment in State and Local Governments: A Comparative Analysis." Forthcoming in *Social Science Quarterly.*

Ippolito, Dennis, W. Donaldson, and L. Bowman. 1968. "Political Orientations among Negroes and Whites." *Social Science Quarterly* 49 (December): 548–556.

Karnig, Albert. 1979. Black Resources and City Council Representation. *Journal of Politics* 41:134–149.

Karnig, Albert, and S. Welch. 1980. *Black Representation and Urban Policy.* Chicago: University of Chicago Press, 1981.

Kronus, Sidney. 1971. *The Black Middle Class.* Columbus, Ohio: Charles Merrill.

Lineberry, Robert, and E. Fowler. 1967. "Reformism and Public Policies in American Cities." *American Political Science Review* 61 (September): 701–716.

Mann, Dale. 1974. "The Politics of Representation in Urban Administration." *Education in Urban Society* 6 (May): 297–317.

Meier, Kenneth. 1978. "Constraints on Affirmative Action." *Policy Studies Journal* 7 (Winter): 208–212.

———. 1975. "Representative Bureaucracy: An Empirical Analysis." *American Political Science Review* 69 (June): 526–542.

Nachmias, David, and D. H. Rosenbloom. 1973. "Measuring Bureaucratic Representation and Integration." *Public Administration Review* (November–December): 590–595.

Rose, Winfield, and T. P. Chia. 1978. "The Impact of the Equal Employment Opportunity Act of 1972 on Black Employment in the Federal Service: A Preliminary Analysis." *Public Administration Review* 38 (May–June): 245–251.

Sigelman, Lee. 1976. "The Curious Case of Women in State and Local Government." *Social Science Quarterly* 56 (March): 591–604.

Sigelman, Lee, and A. K. Karnig. 1977. "Black Education and Bureaucratic Employment." *Social Science Quarterly* 57 (March): 858–863.

24. Ethnicity and Policy: The Mexican-American Perspective

Rodolfo O. de la Garza, Robert D. Wrinkle, and Jerry L. Polinard

ETHNICITY AND THE ROLE it plays in the formation of attitudes and public policies have long been a matter of concern for political scientists. Dahl, Wolfinger, Parenti, and others have written extensively on the political impact of ethnicity and related ethnic behavior (Dahl 1961; Wolfinger 1965; Parenti 1967). However, this concern for the impact of ethnicity had a regional and historical bias in favor of European ethnics and, as Garcia, de la Garza, and Torres (1985) note, little attention has been paid to other ethnic groups such as Mexican-Americans even though Mexicans have been immigrating into the United States since 1849.

While it is true that there is an increasing amount of literature devoted to Mexican-Americans (de la Garza et al. 1985), the impact that ethnicity has on policy concerns of Mexican-Americans remains unclear. Some studies have found policy differences between Anglos and Mexican-Americans without accounting for the independent effect of ethnicity (Lovrich 1974; MacManus and Cassel 1982). Cain and Kiewet (1984) and Miller, Polinard, and Wrinkle (1984) found that ethnicity contributed little to explaining Mexican-American attitudes toward a wide range of policy issues. De la Garza and Weaver (1985), however, found that ethnicity had a significant independent effect on Mexican-American attitudes toward public policies which were directly related to ethnic issues. On more general policy issues, the differences between Anglos and Mexican-Americans were not primarily a function of ethnic differences. There is, then, a significant lack of coherence in the literature as to the independent effect of ethnicity on public policy concerns of Mexican-Americans. It is to this point that this paper is addressed.

This paper examines the extent to which ethnicity has an independent effect on Mexican-American attitudes toward immigration. Its results

426

will enhance our understanding of a key issue affecting Mexican-American political life and contribute to an increased understanding of the role and nature of ethnicity in American political life. It will enable us to determine the extent to which ethnicity has an independent effect on Mexican-American attitudes toward a major national policy question. The findings will also help clarify whether immigration is an "ethnic" issue for Mexican-Americans, i.e., whether it is a salient issue on which Mexican-Americans overwhelmingly agree and on which they differ in their attitudes from Anglo Americans. Policy makers assume that Mexican-Americans strongly support increased Mexican immigration because of cultural and kinship ties (Simpson 1984). While scholars acknowledge the cultural ties between Mexican-Americans and Mexican immigrants (Garcia 1981; Limon 1985), there is increasing recognition of the differences between the two groups (Browning and de la Garza 1986) and of how these differences affect Mexican-American attitudes toward immigration policy (de la Garza 1985). If Mexican immigrants and Mexican-Americans are indeed two distinct communities, as has been argued by Rodriguez and Nunez (1986) and de la Garza (1985), then immigration should not be considered an "ethnic" issue and Mexican-Americans and Anglos should not differ in how they view immigration policy. If, however, Senator Simpson and those who share his views are correct, Mexican-Americans and Anglos should differ sharply in their views toward these issues.

The basic objective of this paper, then, is to examine what, if any, differences exist in Mexican-American and Anglo attitudes toward undocumented Mexican immigration. A previous study found that Mexican-American attitudes toward immigration issues varied primarily by region, by how respondents evaluated the impact that the undocumented have on the economy and on the job market, and by their level of personal experience and familiarity with the undocumented (Polinard, Wrinkle, and de la Garza 1985). Our purpose now is to determine if the factors that influence Mexican-American attitudes on this issue are the variables that shape Anglo attitudes. Our hypothesis is that immigration is not an "ethnic" issue, and, therefore, we expect ethnicity to have little independent effect on how Mexican-Americans and Anglos view immigration issues.

METHODOLOGY

The data analyzed are from surveys conducted in two research sites — one along the Texas-Mexico border and one in central Texas some 300 miles from the border. One of the reasons for the dual research sites was to allow us to utilize region as an independent variable. Our border site is Hidalgo County. This border county is among the poorest in the nation with a traditional double digit unemployment rate. The proximity to the border virtually ensures that the influences of Mexican culture and traditions will be great. There is a continuing immigration stream which assures that immigration policies and policies relating to illegal immigration will be highly salient to county residents. Data from the 1980 Census indicate that 81.3 percent of the population of the county is Spanish surnamed and that 76.3 percent of this population is native born (Bureau of the Census, 1980). Median family income is $11,232.

The other research site is Travis County, Texas, which is located approximately 300 miles from the border and has a Mexican-American population of only 15.9 percent. This Central Texas county had a median family income in 1980 of $15,741.

As sample of household telephones in the telephone exchanges of both counties was obtained by a random digit production process. All obviously commercial telephones were eliminated from the sample by the use of a reverse telephone directory. The resultant sample totaled 400 households in Travis County, of which approximately 375 were contacted. Of those contacted, the refusal rate was approximately 20 percent.

The Hidalgo County telephone sample totaled some 325 households, of which 309 were contacted. Of those contacted, approximately 14 percent refused interviews. In conducting a telephone survey in this region a major problem emerges. While more than 90 percent of all households in the nation have telephones, only approximately 83 percent of the households in Hidalgo County have telephone service (Backstrom and Hursh-Cesar 1981; Rush 1983). As Hidalgo County is one of the poorest counties in the nation, it is likely that a significant number of poor households are without telephone service. This is especially true when one considers the fact that the *colonias* (small, rural, unincorporated areas) in the region are without any telephone service. It was thus deemed advisable to supplement the telephone survey with 75 personal interviews in those areas without access to telephone service. Of the 75 selected personal interviews, all were completed. The total number of completed interviews in Hidalgo County was 341, 75 personal and 266 phone.

Interviews were conducted by a staff trained by the authors. Two-thirds of the interviewers were bi-lingual and approximately 20 percent of the interviews were conducted in Spanish from an authenticated translation of the survey instrument. The personal interviews were conducted in 14 of the more than 40 *colonias* in Hidalgo County. Household selection was done by a two-stage cluster sample, utilizing a respondent randomizing device (Backstrom and Hursh-Cesar 1981:94).

Our usable sample includes 314 Mexican-American respondents and

322 Anglo respondents. Of these, 251 Mexican-American and 73 Anglo respondents reside in Hidalgo County while 63 Mexican-Americans and 249 Anglos reside in Travis County. These proportions accurately reflect the demographic structure of the two counties.

Among the Mexican-American sample, 55 percent are female, 26 percent hold white collar occupations, 66 percent have incomes of $25,000 or less, and 42 percent have incomes of less than $15,000. The great majority (238) of the Mexican-American population were born in the United States and the rest, with one exception, were born in Mexico. More than 50 percent of the parents of our respondents were born in Mexico.

Almost half of the Mexican-American sample (44.9 percent) have family members living in Mexico with almost 33 percent maintaining some regular contact with the Mexican relatives. Fifteen percent of the respondents have relatives who are or have been here illegally.

Fifty-four percent of the Anglo portion of the sample are female, 27 percent are in white collar occupations, almost 75 percent earn less than $25,000 a year, 93 percent were born in the United States, and 26 percent have been in the state for less than ten years.

ANALYSES

The data were analyzed from a number of perspectives. First, bivariate analyses were done examining Mexican-American and Anglo attitudes toward nine policy issues related to immigration policy, including the controversial Simpson-Mazzoli provisions. After the bivariate analyses, multiple regression analyses were done to determine if the variables that affect Mexican-American attitudes are the same variables which affect Anglo attitudes and to compare the relative order of magnitude of effect. Finally, the respondents were pooled into one sample and multiple regression analyses were done to measure the independent effect that ethnicity had on the attitudes of our respondents.

As table one illustrates, when compared by income and occupation, there is little difference in the attitudes of Mexican-Americans and Anglos toward nine dimensions of the immigration issue. There is slightly more variation among Mexican-Americans than among Anglos as a function of income, however. Conversely, Anglo attitudes vary more than Mexican-American attitudes with occupational differences. Overall, what is most noteworthy is that there is no systematic variation in the attitudes of either group associated with either income levels or occupational characteristics.

Table one also illustrates that both Mexican-American and Anglo attitudes vary as a function of region. Among Mexican-Americans, regional

TABLE 1

Attitudes by Occupation, Income, & Region

Attitude	INCOME		OCCUPATION		REGION	
	Anglo	Mex-American	Anglo	Mex-American	Anglo	Mex-American
Illegals have right to welfare	NS	NS	NS	NS	NS	NS
Illegals harm country	NS	NS	NS	NS	$X^2(9) = 4.01$ P<.05	$X^2(2) = 20.3$ P<.14
Knowledge that aliens take jobs	NS	NS	NS	NS	$x^2(.1) = 4.21$ P<.05	$x^2(1) = 8.43$ P<.01
Aliens affect the way you live	$X^2(1) = 5.87$ P<.01	$X^2(1) -3.77$ P<.05	NS	NS	NS	NS
Decrease rate of immigration	NS	NS	NS	NS	$X^2(1) = 18.27$	NS
Aliens take jobs no one wants	NS	$X^2(1) = 6.20$ P<.05	NS	$X^2(1) = 8.96$ P<.01	$X^2(1) = 4.44$ P<.05	$X^2(1) = 6.82$ P<.01
Disagree with stricter enforcement of immigration laws	NS	NS	NS	NS	$X^2(1) = 8.37$ P<.05	$X^2(1) = 14.87$ P<.01
Schools admit children of illegal aliens	NS	NS	NS	NS	$X^2(1) = 8.37$ P<.01	$X^2(1) = 14.87$ P<.01
All aliens take jobs from U.S. citizens	NS	NS	$X^2(1) = 4.62$ P<.05	NS	NS	NS
Aliens abuse welfare	NS	NS	$X^2(1) = 4.55$ P<.05	NS	$X^2(1) = 5.15$ P<.05	$X^2(1) = 13.58$ P<.01

differences are associated with attitudes toward five of the nine aspects of immigration policy examined, while region is associated with attitudinal differences on six of these measures among Anglos.

These results suggest that attitudes of Anglos and Mexican-Americans toward immigration issues do not differ because of income or occupational characteristics. Both groups, however, differ because of regional differences. That is, Anglos and Mexican-Americans in Hidalgo County differ from Anglos and Mexican-Americans in Travis County, respectively. The differential regional impact of immigration on the border may help explain some of these differences. Previous research (Miller, Polinard, and Wrinkle 1984) found that respondents distinguished the impact of immigration policy on the region and themselves, that is, immigration caused problems for the region, but not necessarily for themselves.

In response to questions regarding provisions in the proposed Simpson-Mazzoli bill, both Mexican-Americans and Anglos differ in their reported levels of knowledge about the proposed bill by income, occupation, and region. With regard to the provision concerning national identity cards, there are no differences within either sample, except for income-related differences among Mexican-Americans. Lower-income Chicanos are less likely to oppose identification cards than higher-income Chicanos. Similarly, except for differences which exist among upper- and lower-income Anglos regarding support of amnesty for the undocumented, there are no differences in the attitudes of Chicanos or Anglos associated with occupation or region. Finally, neither group evidences any differences associated with income, occupation, or region and support for employer sanctions (see table two).

Overall, these results reenforce the suggestion that Anglos and Chicanos view immigration similarly. Where there are within group differences, they exist for both groups. The only exception to this is with regard to how income differences affect Chicano attitudes toward national identification cards, and Anglo attitudes toward amnesty. These differences may reflect, on the one hand, the extent to which lower-income Chicanos perceive undocumented workers as competitors on the job market (Polinard, Wrinkle, and de la Garza 1984), and on the other, the perception of lower-income Anglos that the undocumented compete with them for jobs. If this interpretation is correct, and it is reasonable to argue that it is, it lends further support to the suggestion that both Chicanos and Anglos view immigration policy from the same perspective. In these instances, working-class Anglo and Chicano attitudes may reflect the same underlying fear that the undocumented pose an economic threat.

To further compare whether Anglos and Chicanos view immigration issues from the same perspective, the relative impact of all independent

TABLE 2

Attitudes by Occupation, Income, and Region
Toward Simpson-Mazzoli

	KNOWLEDGE OF SIMPSON-MAZZOLI	ALL AMERICANS SHOULD CARRY ID CARDS	NO SUPPORT FOR SANCTION	AMNESTY FOR ALIENS
INCOME				
Anglo	$x^2(1) = 5.63$ $P < .05$	NS	NS	$x^2(1) = 4.91$ $P < .01$
Mex-American	$x^2(1) = 25.86$ $P < .01$	$x^2(1) = 10.04$ $P = .05$	NS	NS
OCCUPATION				
Anglo	$x^2(1) = 9.65$ $P < .01$	NS	NS	NS
Mex-American	$x^2(1) = 21.23$ $P < .01$	NS	NS	NS
REGION				
Anglo	$x^2(1) = 51.82$ $P < .01$	NS	NS	NS
Mex-American	$x^2(1) = 16.72$ $P < .01$	NS	NS	NS

variables listed in Appendix A on selected immigration issues, including three key provisions of the Simpson-Mazzoli bill, were measured. The regression technique used was multiple regression with forward inclusion, utilizing all the independent variables noted in the appendix. Only those variables which entered the regression equation are reported in the following tables. It is also important to note that the independent variables include multiple indicators of ethnicity. These were designed to tap the various dimensions of cultural affinity, i.e., "Mexicanness," that might exist within the Mexican-origin population respondents. For example, some Mexican-Americans may maintain no contact with relatives in Mexico, may never visit Mexico, may have no relatives who have been illegal aliens, and may consider maintaining Mexican traditions and holidays irrelevant. Others may score differently on each of these measures. Clearly, it is reasonable to assume that the latter would feel closer ties to Mexico than the former, and that could result in different views toward Mexican immigration. Stated differently, the former may constitute a different type of "ethnic" than the latter, even though both are Mexican-Americans. Because Mexican-Americans are a heterogeneous population and vary greatly in the intensity of their relationship to Mexico, unless such multiple measures are used, it may be impossible to measure accurately how "ethnicity" affects Mexican-American attitudes on immigration and other issues.

The results of the regressions presented in table three reveal several patterns. First, with regard to general immigration issues, we are able to explain more about Mexican-American attitudes than about Anglo attitudes. It is also noteworthy that region, income, and occupation contribute relatively little to the explanation of these attitudes.

It is also clear that the variables which explain Anglo attitudes differ somewhat from those which explain Chicano attitudes. Anglo attitudes toward the issues included here are affected primarily by how respondents evaluate the impact that the undocumented have on United States society and, second, by the frequency with which they have personal contact with the undocumented. Mexican-American attitudes, on the other hand, are affected primarily by personal contact with the undocumented, various manifestations of cultural affinity, and whether Chicanos view the undocumented as an asset to the United States.

Table four presents the results of regressions analyzing attitudes toward provisions of the Simpson-Mazzoli bill. The patterns which were evident in table three are again present. The single most important variable affecting Anglo attitudes is whether they view undocumented workers as an asset to the United States. Among Mexican-Americans, levels of personal knowledge of the undocumented and cultural affinity are the principal explanatory variables. The results explain a high of 32 percent of the variance.

These results reveal two patterns. First, there are differences in the way in which Mexican-Americans and Anglos view immigration issues. Mexican-Americans evaluate immigration issues based on personal experience and the extent of their "Mexicanness." Second, these results suggest that "ethnicity" as measured by Spanish surname or any single variable is too diffuse a concept to explain Mexican-American attitudes on this policy. Stated differently, it suggests that immigration is not an "ethnic" policy in the way that bilingual education is (de la Garza and Weaver 1985).

Anglos evaluate different types of immigration issues based on their assessment of the impact that the undocumented have on American society. While that seems self-evident, it is not since, as table one shows, whether or not an Anglo holds that view is independent of income and occupational characteristics. In other words, Anglos of different backgrounds may be positive or negative toward immigration issues. While we cannot explain how they develop these attitudes, it is important to note that Anglos are not unanimous in their views, and that those who think the undocumented are an asset view immigration issues differently from those who do not.

TABLE 3

Regressions on Selected Issues

	MULTIPLE R	R²	BETA
Equation #1			
Perception of immigration as a serious problem			
Mexican-Americans (R² = .2798)			
Knowledge of Simpson-Mazzoli Bill	.3829	.1466	.3829
Age	.4502	.2027	−.2411
Region	.4962	.2462	−.2162
Occupation	.5289	.2798	.1954
Importance of Diez y Seis	.5443	.2943	.1351
Anglos (R² = .2537)			
Region	.4094	.1676	−.4094
Knowledge of Simpson-Mazzoli Bill	.4413	.1947	.1805
Aliens take jobs no one else wants	.4639	.2152	−.1442
Age	.4802	.2306	−.1286
Economic contact with aliens	.4927	.2428	.1105
Belief that illegal aliens affect one's life	.5027	.2527	−.1060
Equation #2			
Disagree that schools should admit children of illegal aliens			
Mexican-Americans (R² = .3608)			
Aliens benefit U.S.	.5591	.3126	.5591
Importance of Cinco de Mayo	.5762	.3321	.1441
Aliens take jobs no one wants	.5936	.3523	.1552
Personal knowledge that aliens take			
jobs from U.S. citizens	.6006	.3605	−.1006
Anglos (R² = .2538)			
Aliens benefit U.S.	.4735	.2242	.4735
Personal knowledge that aliens take			
jobs from U.S. citizens	.4906	.2407	−.1343
Region	.5038	.2538	.1155
Disagree with stricter enforcement of immigration laws			
Mexican-Americans			
Aliens benefit or harm	.4856	.2358	−.4856
Knowledge of Simpson-Mazzoli Bill	.5172	.2675	−.1784
Number of news stories heard on			
immigration	.5385	.2900	−.1516
Sex	.5548	.3078	.1348
Illegal aliens affect way one lives	.5690	.3238	.1308
Region	.5795	.3358	.1190
Cinco de Mayo	.5896	.3477	−.1165
Personal knowledge that illegal aliens			
take jobs	.5961	.3565	.1056
Anglos			
Belief aliens benefit U.S.	.4766	.2271	−.4766
Personal knowledge that illegal aliens			
take jobs	.4994	.2494	.1558
Illegal aliens affect life	.5214	.2719	.1578

TABLE 4

Regression on Simpson-Mazzoli Issues

	MULTIPLE R	R²	BETA
Disagree with amnesty (Mexican-Americans)			
Belief aliens benefit	.5580	.3114	.5580
Personal knowledge that illegal aliens take jobs	.5931	.3518	−.2178
Belief aliens take jobs no one wants	.6061	.3673	.1366
Region	.6179	.3818	−.1250
Diez y Seis	.6263	.3977	.1054
Disagree with amnesty (Anglos)			
Belief aliens benefit	.4642	.2155	.4642
Sex	.4860	.2314	−.1335
Income	.5015	.2515	.1243
Personal knowledge that illegal aliens take jobs	.5143	.2645	−.1208
Disagree with national identity card (Mexican-Americans)			
Knowledge of Simpson-Mazzoli Bill	.3812	.1453	.3812
Occupation	.4284	.1535	−.2086
Number of news stories heard	.4496	.2022	−.1368
Personal contact with illegals	.4682	.2192	.1328
Disagree with national identity card (Anglos)			
Belief aliens benefit	.3364	.1132	−.3364
Occupation	.3674	.1310	−.1482
Aliens take jobs no one wants	.3849	.1482	.1212
Disagree with employer sanctions (Mexican-Americans)			
Belief aliens benefit	.3830	.1467	−.3830
Personal knowledge that illegal aliens take jobs	.4261	.1815	.2021
Region	.4450	.1981	.1332
Cinco de Mayo	.4601	.2117	−.1209
Disagree with employer sanctions (Anglos)			
Belief aliens benefit	.4089	.1672	−.4089

The final question to be answered, then, is whether ethnicity has an independent effect on the attitudes examined here. The results of the regressions on the combined Anglo–Mexican-American sample are reported in tables five and six. As table six indicates, while some ethnic measures do have an independent effect on these attitudes, other variables are more significant. The most significant variables are those reflecting either personal experiences with the undocumented, knowledge of their impact on the job market, and the assessment of their impact on United States society. Ethnicity per se has little explanatory power. Indeed, even specific measures of cultural affinity add only marginally to our ability to explain the attitudes of our respondents.

The same pattern exists with regard to the provisions of the Simpson-

TABLE 5

Multiple Regression on Selected Immigration Questions
Combined Anglo and Mexican-American Samples

	MULTIPLE R	R^2	BETA
Dependent Variable: Perception of immigration as an important problem			
Independent Variables			
Region	.28	.08	−.28
Aliens take jobs no one else wants	.29	.09	−.09
Number of conversations	.31	.09	−.09
Age	.32	.10	−.08
Maintain Mexican traditions	.32	.11	.07
Dependent Variable: Stricter Enforcement of Immigration Law ($R^2 = .2963$)			
Independent Variables			
Aliens benefit U.S.	.4652	.2164	−.4652
Aliens affect life	.4908	.2409	.1599
Personal knowledge that undocumented			
take jobs	.5128	.2630	.1576
Region	.5314	.2823	.1440
Cinco de Mayo	.5398	.2914	−.0971
Ethnicity	.5443	.2963	.0825
Dependent Variable: Schools should admit undocumented children ($R^2 = .2953$)			
Independent Variables			
Aliens benefit U.S.	.4953	.2453	.4953
Personal knowledge that illegals take jobs	.5269	.2672	−.1560
Cinco de Mayo	.5275	.2783	.1071
Aliens take unwanted jobs	.5340	.2852	.0883
Region	.5390	.2905	.0741
Ethnicity	.5435	.2953	−.0829

Mazzoli bill with only slight variations. With these issues, both specific measures of ethnicity and specific measures of cultural affinity affect the overall results. However, they are not the principal explanatory variables. Also, the total variation explained in these analyses is between 10 and 32 percent. It is noteworthy that income and occupation characteristics, with the exception of attitudes toward national identity cards, contribute very little to the outcome of the analyses.

DISCUSSION

The objective of this paper was to determine if ethnicity has an independent effect on Mexican-American attitudes toward immigration and to determine if immigration is an "ethnic issue."

Our findings indicate that although there are differences in the vari-

TABLE 6

Multiple Regression of Attitudes Toward Simpson-Mazzoli Provisions:
Combined Anglo and Mexican-American Sample

	MULTIPLE R	R²	BETA
Dependent Variable: Support for Employer Sanctions			
Independent Variables			
Belief that aliens benefit U.S.	.3644	.1328	−.3644
Personal knowledge that illegal			
take jobs	.3963	.1571	.1644
Ethnicity	.4246	.1803	.1535
Knowledge of Simpson-Mazzoli	.4361	.1902	−.1007
Aliens take unwanted jobs	.4442	.1973	−.0907
Total R = .19			
Dependent Variable: National Identity Card			
Occupation	.25	.06	−.2449
Knowledge of Simpson-Mazzoli Bill	.30	.09	−.19
Aliens benefit U.S.	.34	.11	−.14
Region	.36	.13	−.13
Number of	.37	.14	−.10
Maintain Mexican	.30	.14	−.08
Diez y Seis	.39	.15	.08

ables which explain Anglo and Mexican-American attitudes toward immigration issues, these differences are not directly reflective of ethnic differences. Mexican-American attitudes are primarily forged from personal experiences with the undocumented. Sometimes this leads to positive attitudes toward certain immigration policies, and sometimes to negative attitudes toward other dimensions of this issue. It is these experiences rather than the general ethnic identification that shapes how Mexican-Americans view the issues examined here. Furthermore, it is specific measures of cultural affinity rather than merely being of Mexican-origin that distinguish the attitudes of some Mexican-Americans from those of Anglo respondents. This finding supports the theory of ethnicity which suggests that it is the social relations of ethnic groups which help define those groups (Barth 1969; Cohen 1984).

These findings have significant implications for immigration policy and Mexican-American political life generally. They clearly reveal the cultural heterogeneity of the Mexican-American population and the variations with which Mexican-Americans may view even those policies that have long been assumed to be of particular concern to them. These results also indicate the differences between Mexican-Americans and Anglos to be less than what political leaders such as Senator Simpson and others have long implied.

In effect, these findings indicate that Mexican-Americans seem to learn about immigration issues differently than do Anglos, i.e., from personal experience with the undocumented rather than from either the news media or opinion leaders. The Mexican-American attitudes are more likely to be shaped by their level of personal knowledge, while Anglo attitudes are shaped by consideration of the more abstract concept of the undocumented as a benefit or harm to the society. If they consider the undocumented a threat, they are more likely to support employer sanctions, national identity cards, and stricter controls on immigration. If they consider the undocumented an asset, they are more likely to support amnesty, fewer restrictions on immigration, and other similar measures.

Finally, the argument that Mexican-Americans will, as a population, be opposed to immigration controls because of their shared cultural traditions with Mexican immigrants finds no support here. Our results indicate that, in terms of "Mexicanness," i.e., support for maintaining Mexican traditions and the maintenance of familial ties in Mexico, Mexican-Americans are quite diverse. While a minority of our respondents score high on "Mexicanness," the great majority do not.

This adds insight into our understanding of what constitutes an ethnic issue for Mexican-Americans. It seems that ethnic issues are not those which deal with Mexico or Mexicans per se. Instead, such issues would seem to be limited to those that impact directly on the current situation of Mexican-Americans. These would include programs such as bilingual education and the provision of Spanish language public services. Because such programs reflect a maintenance of Mexican cultural practices it is easy to conclude that Mexican-Americans defend such programs because of their attachment to Mexican culture and society. Instead, as is evidenced by the results of the analysis presented here, it is more reasonable to conclude that Mexican-Americans support such programs because they derive economic and political benefits from them. An issue becomes an "ethnic issue," then, not because it has Mexican cultural content, but because it affects the collective self-interest of the Mexican-American people.

APPENDIX A

Variable Code

	0 = Travis; 1 = Hidalgo
Region knowledge of Simpson-Mazzoli Bill	0 = Familiar; 1 = Unfamiliar
Believe aliens benefit or harm	0 = Benefit; 1 = Harm
Personal contact with illegal aliens	0 = No; 1 = Yes
Personal knowledge of illegal aliens take jobs from U.S. citizens	0 = Yes; 1 = No
Believe illegal aliens have effect on way you live	0 = No; 1 = Yes
Occupational status	0 = High; 1 = Low
Sex	0 = Male; 1 = Female
Generation	0 = Foreign/Native of Foreign; 1 = Native of Native
Family in Mexico with whom still in contact	0 = No; 1 = Yes
Maintenance of Mexican traditions/Spanish language/ Mexican holidays (Diez y Seis, Cinco de Mayo)	Low = Important; High = Unimportant
Travel to Mexico	0 = Never/Seldom; 1 = Frequent
Member of family been an illegal alien	0 = No; 1 = Yes
Income	0 = Low; 1 = High
Economic contact with illegal aliens	0 = Non-economic; 1 = Economic
Number of news stories heard on undocumented workers	Actual Number
Number of conversations on immigration	Actual Number

REFERENCES

Backstrom, Charles H., and Gerald Hursh-Cesar. 1981. *Survey Research.* 2nd edition. New York: Wiley.

Barth, Fredrik, ed. 1969. *Ethnic Groups and Boundaries.* Boston: Little Brown.

Browning, Harley L., and Rodolfo de la Garza. 1986. *Mexican Immigrants and Mexican Americans: An Evolving Relation.* Austin, Texas: Center for Mexican-American Studies, The University of Texas at Austin.

Cain, Bruce E., and Roderick Kiewiet. 1984. "Ethnicity and Electoral Choice: Mexican American Voting Behavior in the California 30th Congressional District," *Social Science Quarterly* 65 (June), 315–327.

Cohen, Gary B. 1984. "Ethnic Persistence and Change: Concepts and Models for Historical Research," *Social Science Quarterly* 65 (December), 1029–1042.

Dahl, Robert. 1961. *Who Governs?* New Haven, Conn.: Yale University Press.

de la Garza, Rodolfo, et al., 1985. *The Mexican American Experience: An Interdisciplinary Anthology.* Austin, Texas: The University of Texas Press.

de la Garza, Rodolfo, and Janet Weaver. 1985. "Chicano and Anglo Public Policy Perspectives in San Antonio: Does Ethnicity Make a Difference?" *Social Science Quarterly* 66 (September), 576–586.

de la Garza, Rodolfo. 1985. "Mexican Americans, Mexican Immigrants and Immigration Reform," in Nathan Glazer, *Clamor at the Gates.* San Francisco: Institute for Contemporary Studies Press.

Garcia, F. Chris, Rodolfo de la Garza, and Donald J. Torres. 1985. "Introduction" pp. 185–200 in Rodolfo de la Garza, et al., *The Mexican American Experience: An Interdisciplinary Anthology.* Austin, Texas: University of Texas Press.

Garcia, John A. 1981. "Yo Soy Mexicano . . . Self-Identity and Sociodemographic Correlates," *Social Science Quarterly* 62 (March), 88–98.

Limon, Jose E. 1985. "Language, Mexican Immigration, and the 'Human Connection': A Perspective from the Ethnography of Communication," pp. 194–210 in Harley L. Browning and Rodolfo de la Garza, *Mexican Immigrants and Mexican Americans: An Evolving Relation.* Austin, Texas: Center for Mexican-American Studies, The University of Texas at Austin.

Loverich, Nicholas P., Jr. 1974. "Differing Priorities in an Urban Electorate: Service Priorities Among Anglo, Black and Mexican American Voters," *Social Science Quarterly* 55 (December), 704–717.

MacManus, Susan A. and Carol Cassel. 1982. "Mexican Americans in City Politics: Participation, Representation and Policy Preferences," *Urban Interest* 4 (7), 57–69.

Miller, Lawrence W., Jerry L. Polinard, and Robert D. Wrinkle. 1984. "Attitudes Toward Undocumented Workers: The Mexican American Perspective," *Social Science Quarterly* 65 (June), 482–494.

Parenti, Michael. 1967. "Ethnic Politics and the Persistence of Ethnic Identification." *American Political Science Review* 61 (September), 717–731.

Polinard, Jerry L., Robert D. Wrinkle, and Rodolfo de la Garza. 1984. "Attitudes of Mexican Americans Toward Irregular Mexican Immigration," *International Migration Review* 18 (Fall), 782–799.

Rodriguez, Nestor, and Rogelio T. Nunez. 1986. "An Exploration of the Factors that Contribute to Differentiation between Chicanos and Indocumentados," pp. 138–156 in Harley L. Browning and Rodolfo de la Garza. *Mexican Immigrants and Mexican Americans: An Evolving Relation.* (Austin, Texas: Center for Mexican-American Studies, The University of Texas at Austin).

Rush, Carl. 1983. Personal communication to the authors.

Simpson, Alan K. 1984. "The Politics of U.S. Immigration Reform," *International Migration Review* 18 (Fall), 486–504.

U.S. Bureau of the Census. 1981. *Census of Population, 1980: Texas* (Washington, D.C.: U. S. Government Printing Office).

Wolfinger, Raymond E. 1965. "The Development and Persistence of Ethnic Voting." *American Political Science Review* 59 (December), 896–908.

25. Latinos: Breaking the Cycle of Survival to Tackle Global Affairs

Armando B. Rendon

ANGLO-AMERICAN SOCIETY HAS such a perverse sense of its own ethos. Everyone knows Spanish predates English on the North American continent, yet it is labeled "foreign." Hispanic Americans, the direct descendents of the first non-natives to explore the Americas, intermarry and settle among its native peoples, but are treated as a minority group whose rights and social benefits must be doled out or hard-won.

It is no surprise then that we find that in the sphere of foreign concerns this built-in transnational people, the Hispanic, have been left out of any equations or formulas in international policy making for generations — that is, until recently. In almost direct proportion to the level of awareness of themselves as a national people, Latinos have begun to assert an increasing interest in foreign affairs. Out of an aroused nationalism has come, inevitably, a mounting interest in world politics.

By comparison to other ethnic groups in the United States, however, Latinos must be characterized as newcomers, the latest ethnic on the block, as it were, when it comes to international deliberations. The fact that we must try to comprehend the Latino dimension in foreign policy under the rubric of ethnicity underscores the paradox of a community long on history but short on political presence.

To understand where the Hispanic community in the United States stands vis-à-vis world relations and, most importantly, why it suffers that status, we must understand the role of ethnicity within the Hispanic population itself. Ordinarily, we conceive of ethnicity as a way of telling "us" from "them"; certain characteristics — of speech, dress, custom, world view — tend to delineate one group of people from another.

From *Ethnicity and U.S. Foreign Policy,* revised edition, edited by Abdul Aziz Said. Copyright 1981, Praeger Publishers. Reprinted by permission of Praeger Publishers.

Within the context of the United States, ethnicity is a patchwork quilt with the nation made up of all manner of racial/cultural types rubbing elbows and living predominantly similar life styles with a like societal perception of themselves—we are all Americans and conform to something called American society.

Yet the Latino contradicts this easy approach to group identity, mainly because the Hispanic presence in the United States is a conglomerate at best, and a hopeless tangle of sociocultural origins, at worst. In other words, viewed in one light, as a working relationship among a variety of diverse people with a few common links, the Hispano is a marvel of heterogeneity. *Juntos pero no revueltos,* we put it: Together, but not scrambled. From another standpoint, Latinos convey a *mezcla,* an intermixing of races and cultures without precedent in world history, bringing together in the racial/cultural crucible encompassing the Caribbean racial groups from the farthest flung parts of the world.[1]

This heterogeneity, in fact, lies at the heart of much of the unwillingness among Latinos to forge a single voice in foreign affairs, even though, at a different level, that same heterogeneity represents a direct link with international issues of great moment.

Before moving into specific areas of Latino involvement in international affairs, there are additional factors to bear in mind with respect to the "quality" of ethnicity among Latinos.

As with no other ethnic group in the United States, the Hispanic conscience is continually being reenforced: by immigration, that is, replenishment of first-generation forces within the community; by education, with growing attention to bilingual/bicultural studies in U.S. schools; and by political action, wherein cultural pride and identity are tied to votes, jobs, funding, and social status.

Moreover, Latinos have a sense of belonging wherever they reside in the Americas. To Mejicanos, in particular, the U.S.–Mexican border represents no more than a fiction; not until the 1930s was there any real attention paid to keeping anybody out and that was because of the Depression's impact on U.S. joblessness. Hundreds of thousands of Mexican nationals were returned to Mexico. Only a few years later, however, they were readmitted under the Bracero program by which countless Mexicans entered the United States "legally," with many never to return. Thus the so-called "illegal alien problem" of the 1970s had its roots in the 1930s.[2]

Our sense of belonging is further underscored by an even older history traceable to native American roots. *Indigenismo,* which is strongest among Chicanos but a powerful sentiment among Puerto Ricans, accounts for an added sense of pride and direction. Native to the Americas, bound to the land by blood and history, the Hispanic proponents for greater involvement in world matters resent the closed system that the Foreign Service has represented for decades, even centuries. A later discussion about hiring practices will help provide an appreciation of Latino feelings in this regard.

Hispanic Americans have become aware that they as a total population in the United States place this country fourth among the Spanish-speaking nations of the world. On the basis of this ranking and the cultural/historical bonds to the rest of the Americas, the Latino senses a certain powerfulness in these ties, a kind of internationalism that should and can be exploited for the benefit of all the Americas. Best of all, Latinos feel these linkages derive from an already established protocol that can serve as a direct political link to the Spanish-speaking world.

Every tendency of the Latino is toward a reaffirmation of the broad multicultural basis on which the transnational people we now call Latinos is founded. While on a global standard, the trend of Hispanic nationalism suggests that Latinos are simply part of the retribalization or segmentation of society, in fact, Hispanicism or Latinoism is more correctly construed as the acculturation process fighting to assert itself in spite of world tendencies. Simply put, Latinos are basically hard at work in adapting internally as well as with the outside world.

HISTORICAL NOTES

The history necessary to set the proper perspective for the current state of affairs is slim. Precedents date back to the Revolutionary War, through the War of 1812, the Mexican-American War, of course, and the Spanish-American War. Involvement by Hispanic *norteamericanos* in inter-American relations virtually disappeared after the turn of the century. Subsequent incidents of U.S.–Latino involvement was quite indirect. Pro and con sentiment was evident in Spanish-language newspapers at the time of the Mexican Revolution—many were founded by political exiles of Mexico. Diplomatic or administrative participation, particularly by Mexican Americans, was not evident until the Kennedy years when the Kennedy-influenced Peace Corps placed many Chicanos in foreign posts worldwide.

One of the early stories of an Hispanic presence in foreign affairs involved Victoria Davis de Sanchez, probably the highest-ranking woman and Hispana in the then International Cooperation Administration (ICA), predecessor of the Agency for International Development (AID). Mrs. Davis de Sanchez, whose family originally had settled in Santa Fe, New Mexico, has to be credited with inspiring her son, Leveo Sanchez, now head of the Hemisphere National Bank in Washington, D.C., to enter the international field. In 1965, mother and son were featured in AID's newsletter as an unique duo—both boasting highest ranking in their respective areas, she as a program director in Nicaragua and he as youngest staff person in the ICA director's office. Of course, both were the only Latinos in those divisions.

According to Leveo Sanchez, who served as a deputy regional director in the Peace Corps, the Peace Corps drew upon the talents and skills of numerous Hispanic persons. He knew of eight technicians in Peru and seventeen in Bolivia alone. A large portion of the contingent was recruited from New Mexico. In a 1963–64 survey of Peace Corps personnel, California held the largest number; New Mexico, the second largest, accounted for primarily because of the large number of Hispanic recruits from the state. Mrs. Davis de Sanchez attributes this phenomenon to their better preparation and their maintenance of Spanish and English, which enabled them to obtain Latin American assignments.

Levo Sanchez, following graduation from George Washington University in Washington, D.C., with a Masters in Foreign Affairs, worked three years for the Organization of American States as an economic researcher (his B.A. from New Mexico Highlands University was in economics), before joining the Foreign Service Reserve in 1959. He served as an assistant program officer in Peru for three years with the title of Acting Program Officer at the time he returned in 1962 to the position of evaluator for all of Latin America in the Peace Corps, followed by assignments as chief for Central America and the Caribbean and for West Coast Central America programs, and finally as Deputy Director for Latin America. He took the post as director of the Alliance for Progress' Office of Institutional Development in State-AID (during the period of five years both State and AID experimented with merger), but left foreign service in January 1967 for a position with the Office of Economic Opportunity.

Sanchez perceived little if any increase in Latino participation in international assignments since the heyday of the Peace Corps' early years, or even before during the Institute for Interamerican Affairs (IIA), founded by Nelson Rockefeller, who stimulated the hiring of Latinos to serve in Latin America. Sanchez believes that two figures, Rockefeller and John F. Kennedy, have been the major sources of Hispanic involvement in Latin America. However, little continuity has been built into these programs, particularly the Peace Corps.

Realistically, he observes, Hispanic participation and influence in international policy may not actually evolve until Latinos undergo the cycle of survival through group awareness, preparation in the pertinent fields (and schools), coupled with economic advancement of this generation of parents, which might lead to our children seeking access to world activities. "After all, the State Department is exclusive even toward Anglos. You have to come from the right schools and have good grades."[3] He recalls taking the Foreign Service exam in 1958 and failing it by two points. A year later, he took the examination for a position with the ICA's management overseas intern program and passed—the only nonwhite of 16 persons admitted.

According to Sanchez, whose bank boasts half of its deposits from Latin America, economic power may be the ultimate answer. Through financial development within the Hispanic community, the cycle of survival can be broken so that Latinos can in fact look beyond the U.S. borders to their historical roots.

Speaking of a unique problem among Mexican-Americans, Sanchez cautioned:

> Mejicanos in the U.S. think only of Mexico when we refer to U.S. policy toward Latin America. There is a barrier of culture and language that exists among Mexican-Americans toward involvement with other Latinos. We view ourselves as belonging neither to Mexico nor to the U.S., and because of a lack of ability to speak Spanish and often English, we shy away from situations where we have to mix with other Latinos.

Dr. Hector García, founder of the American G.I. Forum, now one of the largest Hispanic organizations in the United States, was the first Hispanic person to be named as a delegate, an alternate specifically, to the U.S. delegation to the United Nations in 1968. Subsequently, under Nixon and Ford, Hispanic involvement in foreign matters centered primarily on ambassadorial appointments.

A characteristic of these appointments, a trait later to change radically, was the fact that few of the persons involved were out of the Foreign Service corps or even had an international politics background. In other words, candidates were selected predominantly on the basis of political connections. What did begin to occur in the later 1960s and early 1970s was the development of a small but growing number of individuals with deep Hispanic roots who began to form that vital element, a base for a future cadre of well-trained but sensitive Latino scholars, political scientists, lawyers, and economists. A case in point is that of the present chief of protocol to the president, which holds the rank of ambassador, Abelardo Valdez. Sworn in as assistant administrator of the Latin American Bureau of AID in May 1977, Valdez represented at the time the highest-placed Latino in the State Department.

Commenting on his new-found status, as a focus for Hispanic activism in inter-American affairs, Valdez said at the time of his appointment, "Up to now, for the Hispanic community to think about Latin American issues has been a luxury. We have been concerned, and rightly so, with survival; social and economic survival has been at stake."[4] As the son of immigrant farm worker parents from Floresville, Texas, Valdez spent his first thirteen years in the farmworker circuit, through Oklahoma, Kansas, the Dakotas, and Montana.

When his father, who came from Torreon, Mexico, in 1928 as a legal immigrant, took up truck farming, "Lalo" Valdez left farmwork. In 1960 he graduated with honors from Floresville High School, earned a B.S. degree in civil engineering from Texas A&M in 1965, and, commissioned as an army lieutenant, was assigned to Fort Belvoir, Virginia, just across the Potomac River from the White House, where he now serves as Chief of Protocol.

En route to Fort Belvoir, he fell into conversation with a man who turned out to be a friend of then President Lyndon Johnson. This led to his being recommended in November 1965 to the White House staff as a military aide-de-camp. As such, he attended the Conference of the American Presidents at Punta del Este in April 1967. As he puts it, "That started everything. I didn't see any engineers advising the president and it appeared his advisors were all lawyers or economists — I figured I'd better get myself a law degree."

True to his word, Valdez acquired the Juris Doctor in 1970 from Baylor Law School. During his second year of studies he participated in an advanced course in international studies at the Academy of International Law, The Hague. A scholarship for advanced work in international law helped him obtain the LLM at Harvard Law School in 1974. Before stepping into the AID position, he had served as general counsel to the Inter-American Foundation and as an attorney to the Overseas Private Investment Corporation.

Valdez indicated that as of May 1977, 0.8 percent of the AID and 0.7 percent overall of the State Department personnel were of Hispanic origin. In order to increase the Hispanic presence on State Department rosters, he stressed that Latino organizations and individuals must organize around international issues, as has occurred on domestic problems in order to raise the Hispanic public's consciousness toward playing a more substantive role in world affairs.

The past ten years among Latinos has been characterized by feeling our way through differences and similarities, a searching for mutual goals and aspirations as a starting point for joint efforts. The Unidos Conference in October 1971, held in Washington, D.C., was the first major attempt at dealing with broad common issues and with felt differences.[5] The results were nearly catastrophic: Chicanos, Puerto Ricans, Cubans, and a few Latino Americans all under one roof; but much was gained from the standpoint of cultural interchange. For the first time, Chicanos learned about the severity of conflict over the issue of Puerto Rico's status and of the massive impact of anti-Castro feelings on the Cuban sociopolitical thought. Puerto Ricans and Cubans let flare some of the pent-up resentment toward each other and yet also discovered the tremendous deprivation Chicanos had suffered as victims of oppressive U.S. institutions—the police, political machines, agribusiness, school systems—that had denied them their language and heritage. Altogether, they discovered how much Latinos had in common.

Unidos represented a first step toward consolidation of the Hispanic peoples in the United States and essentially set the stage for our turning attention as a natural sequence toward affairs of fellow peoples of Hispanic origin. Important subsequent steps of national scale have followed; there have been numerous efforts bringing together Hispanic peoples of all origins to deliberate over common concerns and goals. The National Hispanic Leadership Conference in Dallas, July 1978, the grape boycott, and a national communications buildup are a few examples.

At least since the Viva Kennedy committees of 1960, Hispanic political alliances have largely maintained a symbiosis with Democratic administrations. Traditionally of Democratic persuasion, Latinos, especially Chicanos, have tended to improve their standing under each successive Democratic president since Kennedy. However, even under Richard Nixon and Gerald Ford, Latinos continued to augment their presence in Executive Office and Cabinet department positions. Under the Carter Administration, Latinos had reached a peak of nearly 200 appointments by the November 1980 elections, the highest number of presidential appointees of Hispanic heritage persons in history.

The current level of Hispanic influence on U.S. foreign policy is directly linked to the increased political clout of Latinos in the Carter administration. In fact, few other events demonstrate the importance of the ethnic vote to foreign policy as does the case of Hispanic outrage when, during the transition phase between the Ford and Carter administrations, Latinos began to clamor for a variety of high-level appointments, among them key Foreign Service spots.

Latinos had cause and evidence to complain. A survey of minority hiring and affirmative action opportunities was published by the Task Force on Equal Employment Opportunity, a panel set up by former Secretary of State Cyrus R. Vance; Valdez represented AID on the panel.

The study, entitled "Executive Leadership and Equal Opportunity in AID," was made public on September 15, 1977, by the then AID administrator, John J. Gilligan, former governor of Michigan. Findings in the report indicated widespread patterns of discrimination throughout the Foreign Service establishment. In general, neither blacks, Asians, Native Americans, nor Latinos fared well anywhere in AID, with minority groups bearing the brunt of unequal treatment in hiring, promotions, job assignments, and training opportunities. In fact, 85.1 percent of all supervisory positions were staffed by nonminority males. The report labeled this statistic "a quota by informal preference which given the law is subject to challenge."[6]

In short, as far as AID is concerned, there are Latinos on the staff, and they are far from holding policy-making decisions. No similar study exists of the State Department staff, but generally State can be considered relatively on a par with AID in its provision of opportunity for Latinos. With a history no different from State, AID reflects the standard approach to hiring and promoting:

> Supervisors recruiting new employees for direct-hire positions are often unaware, or choose to ignore, formal procedures. Informal and often misleading practices tend to pre-selection, totally obstructing the conduct of merit procedures. For example, where 90 percent of supervisory staff are non-minorities, and almost all unfamiliar with minority talent sources, the natural inclination is to informally recruit only non-minorities for direct-hire positions.[7]

In other words, AID has functioned through an "old buddy" system, with supervisors recruiting by word of mouth from their own talent banks and hiring on a preselective basis persons who may have met basic requirements but had not been subjected to a formal and rigorous screening and interviewing procedure. The end result historically has been the foundation of an institution governed predominantly by white, Anglo-Saxon males with strongly similar personal profiles — "the old school tie" syndrome.

THE TODMAN AFFAIR

Rather portentously, the Hispanic communities' first break with President Carter arose over inter-American affairs even before the president had learned where the Rose Garden was located at the White House. This political confrontation had its roots in the transition period from the Ford-Nixon administration.

Latino leaders had begun to pressure the White House for top-level positions including Cabinet-level appointments immediately after the November 1976 elections. President-elect Carter issued a telegram to all Cabinet designates on January 8, 1977, asking them to review at this time your lists of prospective appointees to policy-level decisions in your department, and to renew efforts to recruit and place Hispanics who want to serve in this Administration. I want you to draw upon the talent and resources of Hispanic citizens to extend their opportunity and involvement in this Administration.[8]

Despite Carter's urging, appointments continued to be made with little attention to Hispanic hopefuls; no Cabinet-level and only a few sub-Cabinet positions at the assistant secretary level emerged. Hispanic factions split on the candidates; infighting over the choicest plums resulted in lost opportunities for all.

Of great significance in the aftermath of the failure of the Carter transition team to fulfill Carter's promises to Latinos has been the heightened attention by U.S. Latinos to Latin America. Everything came to a head when Terence Todman, ambassador to Costa Rica, a black career officer who had spent about two years in Latin America, was nominated as assistant secretary on inter-American affairs in the State Department. Several Latino groups and foreign affairs groups had proposed Esteban Torres, an official of the United Auto Workers International Department, to the office.

Manny Fierro, director of the National Congress of Hispanic American Citizens (El Congreso), labeled the appointment "a kick in the teeth" for Latino aspirations, not only for that one office but for the whole prospect of finally achieving some solid advances at the upper levels of the new administration.

In a press conference, Larry Birns, director of the Council on Hispanic Affairs, disclosed that he had learned of a strong anti-Hispanic bias against Torres among transition teamsters and State Department insiders, because he was a Mexican-American.

According to Fierro, the selection of a black was specifically intended to stave off any Chicano or Latino counterattack. This divide and rule strategy, used effectively by the white establishment for generations, worked again.

Nevertheless, Latino activists became incensed by what was perceived as a bold rejection of a better candidate because he was a Chicano. Out of the experience of the catastrophic transition period came some sharply defined questions:

How do Latinos build linkages with Latin America that will raise the consciousness of the Spanish-speaking communities throughout the Western Hemisphere?

Where are the true pressure points that will lead to success in the future?

How can Latinos build solid support for their goals, in Latin America or otherwise when it appears that votes are of little consequence when it comes to appointments? (Chicano votes went 85 percent for Carter in Texas; Puerto Rican areas in New York went as high as 95 percent. Carter won narrowly in both states. The only high-level appointee was from northern California, an area Carter lost in 1976.)

The Todman experience should have convinced Latinos that even ethnicity backed up by votes is not enough. Success will come only by way of strategy and action directed at convincing, removing, or sidestepping those who feel essentially no debt to the Hispanic population nor responsibility for its status.

In a related event, Manny Fierro, speaking as president of El Congreso, and as a trustee of the Council on Hemisphere Affairs, addressed the Senate Foreign Relations Committee on the occasion of Cyrus Vance's confirmation hearings. Aside from his vigorous opposition to Todman's nomination, while supporting Esteban Torres, he expressed some revealing insights into the trend of Hispanic participation in international interests:

> we are vitally interested in every aspect of our U.S.–Latin American policy. . . . our people in the past have been delinquent in establishing a proper sense of identification with our brothers and sisters to the South of us. We were too preoccupied with our own domestic sense of survival to realize as Black-Americans, Irish-Americans, Italian-Americans, Jewish-Americans, and Greek-Americans—among many other ethnic groups—have realized that an *identity with one's ancestral roots augments one's self esteem and collective power rather than diminishes it. We have suffered from this oversight and we also admit that Latin America has as well. We intend to rectify this.* (Emphasis added.)

Citing U.S. interventions in Guatemala, Brazil, the Dominican Republic, and Chile, Fierro added:

> As these acts were taking place behind a veil of secrecy and deception, our Hispanic community, like the rest of the nation, was barely aware of what was happening. We didn't permit a sense of natural kinship to develop, or respect the processes of history which linked our fate with those of our kinsmen. Regrettably, our conduct deceived people into thinking that we were ashamed to be of Latin American descent.[9]

Fierro asserted that the days of a general Hispanic ignorance or disinterest toward Latin American affairs had passed. His words echoed mine in *Chicano Manifesto,* written seven years earlier:

Chicanos should have something particularly insightful to say about U.S. policy because we are as much victims of the U.S. attitude as *la raza* in South America. We are treated as foreigners; Spanish is taught as a foreign language although it predates English in the Americas. Revolutionary forces in South American countries consider the United States—this includes the Chicano people—the worst enemy of their people.

Do people of Latin America realize that a distinct Chicano community exists in the United States? Have Chicanos done anything to make our Latin American brothers aware of our existence? Chicanos can fulfill in part the desire for freedom of *la raza* all over the Americas by making ourselves more aware of their history and struggle, of which we are so much a part.[10]

What is apparent from these two commentaries, seven years apart, is the movement from philosophical insight to political confrontation at the highest levels of government. Although Latinos lost this early round with the Carter administration, their diligence was later rewarded with Torres being named Special Assistant on Hispanic Affairs in the president's inner circle of advisors after Torres had spent two years as U.S. Ambassador to UNESCO in France.[11]

NATIONALIST CONCERNS AMONG LATINOS

While Latinos in general appear more thoughtful and determined in achieving the important goals of exerting greater influence at least in inter-American affairs, certain historical factors continue to distract and divide interests among the largest nationality groups: Mexican-Americans, Puerto Ricans, and Cubans.

For Cubans, the possible reestablishment of U.S. relations with Cuba is the source of virulent debate within the community, a verbal infighting that has often erupted into death-dealing violence involving Cubans and non-Cubans as its victims.

The Cuban presence has been forced upon the United States. Prior to the takeover of Cuba by Fidel Castro in 1959, the Cuban population was hardly significant in the United States. As a result of the exile immigration and more than two decades of births, Cubans virtually control Miami and other communities in Florida and, nationally, wield a political and economic influence disproportionate to their numbers. The U.S. policy toward the island remains a jarring point of contention, but more and more, many Cubans (with resignation by some older exiles and as a matter of fact by those raised in the United States) are concentrating on domestic interests, establishing viable alternatives as Americans to the unsettled nature of Cubanos interminably fighting for vindication against a regime they thoroughly revile.

In a very real sense, then, the major "foreign" concern among Cuban Americans is their homeland, their relatives and friends there, its future, and their desire to return. It is perhaps too much of a simplification to suggest that this is the overriding factor in Cuban attitudes toward international affairs, but it certainly colors all questions of U.S. involvement in Latin America. Cuban Americans, in short, are opposed to renewal of ties with Cuba. Nevertheless, diplomatic "interests sections" were established in September 1977, with a liaison group set up within the Swiss Embassy in Havana representing the United States, and a similar contingent representing Cuba in the Czech Embassy in Washington. The United States also has granted visas to selected Cuban citizens to visit the United States, lifted the ban on U.S. travel to Cuba, and further modified, but not lifted, the U.S. trade embargo. As far as Cuban Americans are concerned, such steps toward "normalization" of U.S.–Cuban relations will only tend to "help perpetuate Communism and thus keep the people of Cuba even longer under the terrible plague."[12]

Perhaps the most complex internal issue of an international dimension is the situation of Puerto Rico as an island home for 3 million persons and motherland for perhaps as many *puertorriqueños* on the mainland. Natives of the island furiously contend among themselves as to what ultimate form of government is most practical or most desired for Puerto Rico: continued commonwealth status, statehood, or independence. Political party affiliations are intensely maintained and appear inextricably complicated to the observer. A Chicano probing islander sentiments senses that if Puerto Ricans could have their way, independence would be their heartfelt choice. *El Grito de Lares* still seems to resound as a rallying cry, recalling the island's brief moment in 1868 when the Republic of Puerto Rico was declared only to become shortly afterward an "aborted revolution."[13] Yet, elections featuring *independentista* referendum or candidates result only in strong showings for both statehood and commonwealth advocates.

A unique amalgam of international-domestic issues, Puerto Rico continues to baffle presidents and would-be candidates as they stumble over the complexity of the three factions. Latinos in general tend to remain neutral toward the island's status, preferring that Puerto Ricans of the island be permitted to decide their own fate, but not all are sure that the island's people are enjoying sufficient freedom from mainland influence to enable them to choose freely.

Furthermore, marked differences of perception exist between island-born and mainland Puerto Ricans, although disparities have become less distinct in recent years. Capabilities in language, education, and political awareness have tended to be more pronounced among island *puertorriqueños,* many of those coming to the mainland having graduated from the island's university system with professional training and bilingual speaking skills. Island-born *puertorriqueños* boast a broader sense of world affairs since they have had to deal within the context of an ambience that is looked upon as a U.S. territory and yet falling within the sphere of Latin American interests.

Chicanos have a unique combination of factors to face that distinguishes them not only from other Hispanic groups but also from other international concerns of Cubans and Puerto Ricans. The motherland specifically is not off the mainland—it is adjacent to the United States and, as some Mexican-Americans perceive it, a part of the United States by virtue of conquest. Mexican-Americans became such as of February 2, 1848, with the signing of the Treaty of Guadalupe-Hidalgo, which brought the U.S. war against Mexico to an inglorious end. As with every other treaty the United States entered into with native peoples in North America, that treaty was breached almost before the wax seals cooled. Guarantees of land, culture, and language rights were violated from the start; Mejicanos living on their side of the new border became Americans by default—they refused to leave their homesteads and automatically became U.S. citizens at the end of the year following the signing of the treaty.

Only recently have U.S. Mejicanos become aware of the treaty's existence—litigation and violent confrontations have occurred such as the courthouse raid and takeover by Reies Lopez Tijerina in Tierra Amarilla, New Mexico, in June 1967. In a sense, Chicanos derive their existence from an international treaty yet have never been enabled to benefit from that status either through governmental recognition of their rights or through litigation initiated by Mexican-American organizations. For example, there is some question as to whether the treaty was ever properly constituted as a legal binding document.

This historical setting serves as a backdrop for what is now the largest Hispanic nationality group in the United States (at least 7.3 million, according to official figures based on the 1970 census).[14] Perhaps the most confusing characteristic to the observer is the complexity of titles for persons of Mexican origin: Mexican-American, Mejicano, Chicano, Latin American, Raza, Hispano, and others less complimentary. Represented among these labels is an ethnicity run rampant; multiple terms to designate the same people yet with each reflecting a variance in cultural, political, and historical background and group perception. These variations among people of Mexican heritage can be the cause of friction within the overall population although goals, and needs, are generally similar.

Despite these ethnic nuances, Chicanos (my personal preference) do rally together on certain substantive issues: the predominance of U.S.– Mexican relations as a critical factor in the influence value of Chicanos in the future; the inherent fellowship felt toward the plight of undocumented Latinos; the overall effects of discrimination in jobs, schools, health care, social services, training, and politics, which ultimately touch all Hispanic peoples, documented and undocumented, in some way.

The impact of Mexican oil on U.S. attitudes and attention to Mexico's economic and geopolitical circumstances is only now beginning to become apparent. The U.S. government has long been aware of the benign approach we as a nation have taken toward Mexico, along with the other Latin American countries. As long as Mexico was dependent on U.S. imports and the necessity to export its manpower, a cheap labor force that has long depressed wages and undercut the union movement along *la frontera*, the United States was content to ignore the long-festering inequities that its foreign policy has imposed on Mexico and other Third World nations. But this is no longer the case.

An almost direct result of this new perspective in U.S.–Mexican relations was the nomination of Julian Nava, a distinguished California educator and former member of the Los Angeles City Board of Education, as U.S. ambassador to Mexico. Nava was confirmed in March 1980, the first person of Mexican origin to fill the position, thereby fulfilling a long-sought objective to Chicanos specifically but of Hispanic activists in general. The Mexican ambassadorship had been a contention with the Carter administration since it began. In early 1977, when the former ambassador, Patrick Lucey of Wisconsin, was named, the story Latinos got as an explanation was that Mexico itself did not wish to have an Hispanic-origin person in the position—not enough clout and experience, and so on. It seemed Mexicans preferred a non-Spanish-speaking Anglo with party connections.

However, as Eduardo Peña, head of an international law firm in Washington, D.C., and one of the most consistent activists on inter-American affairs, writes:

> State Department officials have long maintained that Mexico would not accept a Mexican-American as Ambassador. In fact, they once went so far as to leak word that Mexico's President, Jose Lopez Portillo, had rebuffed such a suggestion. President Lopez Portillo denied the allegation to me personally. He told me that he would welcome a U.S. Ambassador of Mexican background. . . .
>
> Just as Americans of ethnic European origin have been tapped as ambassadors to the capitals of Europe, Hispanics are belatedly being recognized for the part their special talents and ties can play in presenting our nation's policies abroad.[15]

A factor accelerating the Carter nomination of Nava, of course, has been the usual election-year ploy of appointing representatives from special interest groups in order to affect voting preferences. Whether or not Nava's appointment has the impact hoped for by the Carter administration, its long-term value is in bringing Hispanic concerns to a higher level of attention. Mexico symbolizes a major breakthrough for Chicanos; other ambassadorial posts are important, but for Chicanos, Mexico is the big one. Within the historic perspective of 132 years since Guadalupe-Hidalgo, the Mexico appointment is like a vindication. It has taken a mixture of factors to achieve this recognition: Mexican oil, election-year politics, growing Chicano activism, and general Latino assertiveness are all facets of an ethnic community's overall coming of age on the world front.

On the other side of the Nava appointment, interest in Chicano affairs should increase among the Mexican press and other observers of the U.S. scene. Because of the importance of this type of attention, interaction, and increased understanding between Mexicans and Mexican-Americans bodes well for the advancement of transborder relations between these peoples of common heritage. The ingrained knowledge of how America ticks should be a valuable asset for Chicanos working with Mexican economic and political interests; Mexicans should be able to collaborate with Chicanos in advancing Mexican interests through their intimate knowledge of Mexico's ethos.

The fourth segment of Hispanicity in the United States is composed of immigrants from every Spanish-speaking country in the world. Cities such as Washington, D.C., with its embassies, and San Francisco, with its cosmopolitan attractiveness, boast significant populations from Latin America. The U.S. Capital represents a microcosm of Hispanidad because it houses an embassy for every nation in the Western Hemisphere and Spain. A Cuban contingent was long established before Castro. The non-diplomatic immigrants, particularly in Washington, D.C., tend to maintain strong emotional and cultural ties to the homeland. Often, Latinos (the term is used with greater accuracy in Washington) in the Capital are political refugees who continue to campaign against injustice and deprivation in their home countries. Salvadorans, Chileans, Nicaraguans, Paraguayans, and others enlist the aid of the larger Hispanic and general communities, stage media events, and lobby national and local politicians. In 1978 Washington was the site of the assassination of Orlando Letelier, political exile and an outspoken critic of Chile. When the Somoza regime fell, the person appointed interim chargé d'affaires had been active in several Latino causes as well as continually prodding Latinos to support the struggle to oust Somoza.

Latinos, in the specific sense of Latin American immigrants, then, provide additional complexity to any effort to understand Hispanic involvement and interest in international affairs from the ethnic perspective. Strategies and activities are as sophisticated and outspoken as those of Chicanos who marked for recognition by the Carter administration in 1978, *puertorriqueños* who demonstrated for the island's independence in 1976, and Cuban-Americans who flooded the White House with calls in April 1980 to demand that the United States take in thousands of Cubanos marooned in the Peruvian Embassy in Havana.

None of the issues is easily solvable; each adds to the complexity not only of dealing with the issue itself, but also of forging a common policy or even viewpoint among the varied Hispanic peoples in the United States.

Chicanos, *puertorriqueños,* Cubanos, and Latinos, then, have distinct points of reference to concerns of hemispheric if not global dimensions. The inborn cultural and historic ties of their ethnicity naturally cause Latinos to look beyond the U.S. mainland or across fictional borders – not merely as foreign affairs specialists, but as *hermanos,* brothers under the skin, linked professionally and emotionally with the futures of our hemispheric neighbors. As a group, in turn, Latinos have begun to act jointly in achieving a greater influence in foreign policy.

In the spring of 1980, the State Department convened an advisory committee of Hispanic leaders and experts to provide insight and recommendations to Secretary Vance on broad foreign policy matters. Previously, the State Department had assembled ad hoc groups, either providing them with orientation on certain issues, for example, during the drive for congressional approval of the Panama Canal Treaties, or asking advice as in the case of Rosalynn Carter's trip to seven Latin American countries in May 1978. The appointment of Esteban Torres, a Chicano, as ambassador to UNESCO and later as Carter's Special Assistant for Hispanic Affairs; the presence of Oscar García-Rivera, a *puertorriqueño* with an eye to foreign affairs slots in the presidential appointments branch; and Valdez's proximity to Carter as Chief of Protocol all suggest a strong and solid combination of internationally astute presidential advisors who can, over time, have a marked effect on foreign affairs appointments and policy.

On the community level, ten members of the National Forum of Hispanic Organizations, an umbrella group of more than seventy national Latino non-profit agencies, formed on February 18, 1980, the U.S. Hispanic-Mexican Commission to institute social, cultural, and educational activities between the Hispanics in the United States and the Mexican government. Comprising the group are: American G.I. Forum, ASPIRA, IMAGE, League of United Latin American Citizens, Mexican-American Legal Defense and Educational Fund, Mexican-American Women's National Association, National Association of Farmworker Organizations, National

Council of La Raza, National Forum of Hispanic Organizations, and Project Ser.

The Commission resulted from a meeting, September 27, 1979, between various representatives of the National Forum and President Jose Lopez Portillo of Mexico in New York City. The joint venture represents the first inter-American effort for mutual advancement between a Hispanic-controlled group and a nation of Latin America.

FUTURE TRENDS

Bogged down by issues of life and death until now, the Hispanic American has paid little heed to international affairs, let alone inter-American concerns. That myopia of ours is being corrected. As an ethnic political force, we can no longer allow one administration after the other to downplay the importance of nations in Latin America or view them as a monolith.

In fact, future foreign and domestic policy toward Latinos on either side of the U.S. border is intimately linked, as are the fortunes of Hispanic peoples throughout the hemisphere. Whatever U.S. Latinos can accomplish in raising the consciousness of American society about our needs, our views, our aspirations, and our common stake in the future will have an impact on the progress of Latin America's peoples. The reverse is also true for Hispanic *norteamericanos.*

What Latinos must bear in mind is that with demographic trends as they are, the U.S. Latino population is expected to be the largest minority ethnic group in the United States by the end of the century. The population of Latin America will exceed that of the United States by the year 2000. A reassessment, a balancing of values and strengths, must be undertaken by the United States toward Latin America, either through cooperative deliberations or under the pressures of inter-American crises.

Latinos can carry out a decisive role in the evolution of policy, issue identification, and goal setting if, as a group of diverse peoples, they assert humane values and amass the necessary political clout toward resolution of their common problems. What do Latinos have to say about Soviet intervention in the Americas, Mexican oil, illegal immigration, and the prevalence of military governments? Can we help attain a political symbiosis with Latin America to displace the lingering imperialist "big stick" policy perception of Latin Americans toward the U.S.?

The current administration and those that are to come must be informed as to how U.S. policy toward Latin America affects all Latinos, U.S. Latinos included. Foreign policy toward the other Americas affects

Chicanos, Puerto Ricans, Cubans, and all the other nationalities of Hispanic origin.

The United States, it must be understood by our policy makers, is not a one-dimensional society, however hard its schools and governments have sought to make it such through discriminatory practices. The Latino presence, an ever-growing element, makes the United States the fourth largest Spanish-speaking country in the world. Chicanos alone comprise a larger single population than several countries in Central and South America.

Perhaps the Hispanic American is too little understood by the United States at large to be taken into account. Latinos internally, of course, are hard pressed to establish one single self-identifying label all can accept. Nevertheless, Latinos are simply not going to melt down or fade away. Their presence will become increasingly felt and appreciated by the nation at large.

Finally, if there is a single abiding goal of U.S. Latinos actively engaged in the field of international affairs, it is to remake the Americas by reshaping the United States from within and ultimately to have an impact on the world. As an ethnic group, Latinos believe they have many positive contributions to bestow upon the hemisphere — in this, they would wholeheartedly reaffirm the long-term purpose that the more activist Latinos have determined for their cause.

The record of Hispanic interest and involvement in the foreign policy field is momentarily thin in terms of individual accomplishments and substantive research and writing. Clearly, though, the trends indicate that there will be much more to record and analyze as Hispanic Americans acquire the academic and experiential background to become technocrats in the international field and as Latinos can begin to afford to pay greater attention to how U.S. foreign policy affects them. We are no longer isolated from our fellow Hispanic peoples. We know that foreign and domestic policy are related. And, as an ethnic group, we are on the verge of putting together immense political clout in all spheres of interest.

NOTES

1. See Magnus Mörner, *Race Mixture in the History of Latin America* (Boston: Little, Brown, 1967), especially pp. 139–150, for a discussion of the racial history of Latinos; also Armando B. Rendón, *Chicano Manifesto* (New York: Macmillan, 1971), especially chap. 4: "Genesis, According to Chicano," pp. 58–62, for a Chicano perspective on the racial background affecting current Hispanic thought.

2. For a Chicano view of this history, see Ernesto Galarza, *Merchants of Labor* (McNally & Loftin, 1964); also, Cary McWilliams, *North from Mexico* (New York: Greenwood Press, 1968).

3. Leveo Sanchez.

4. Abelardo Valdez.

5. The author was a member of the multinational steering committee that planned and conducted the conference, held October 19–20, 1971.

6. "Executive Leadership and Equal Opportunity in AID," Equal Employment Opportunity Task Force (Washington, D.C.: AID, September 17, 1973), p. II 6.

7. Ibid. p. II 2.

8. Mailgram to members of the Cabinet designate, President Jimmy Carter, Americus, Georgia, January 8, 1977.

9. Statement by Manuel D. Fierro, Senate Foreign Relations Committee (Washington, D.C., January 11, 1977).

10. Rendón, op. cit., p. 300.

11. Overall, Hispanic successes in placing Latinos in significant international positions have been limited: ambassadorships are held by Raul Castro, Argentina; Mari-Luci Jaramillo, Honduras; and Diego C. Ascencio, Colombia. The latter was among several diplomats taken hostage on February 27, 1980, in the Dominican Republic embassy in Bogota. Along with Valdez as chief of protocol, other Foreign Service-related positions were held by Tomas Rivera, member of the board of Foreign Scholarships; Alberto Ibarguen, members of the board, Inter-American Foundation; Frank V. Ortiz, representative to Antigua, Dominica, St. Christopher-Nevis-Anguilla; Frank H. Perez, representative to U.S. delegation to SALT; Vilma Martinez and Maurice Ferre, Mayor of Miami, members, President's Advisory Board on Ambassadorial Appointments; and Cruz Reynoso, member, Select Commission on Immigration and Refugee Policy.

12. Question posed to Cyrus R. Vance, question and answer session, New Orleans Hilton, January 12, 1978.

13. Manual Maldonado-Denis, *Puerto Rico: A Socio-Historic Interpretation* (New York: Vintage Books, 1972), p. 43.

14. Puerto Ricans are at 1.7 million and Cubans at 0.8 million; Central, South American, and other Hispanic-origin peoples account for 2.4 million, for a total of 12.1 million. U.S. Bureau of the Census, *Current Population Reports,* March 1979 Series P-20, No. 347, issued October 1979.

15. Eduardo Peña, "Our Man in Mexico City," *Hispanic Link* (Washington, D.C., April 7, 1980).

PART V

Feedback:
Outcomes and Reactions

THE POLITICAL SYSTEM OF THE United States is an ever changing dynamic set of interrelationships. It is impossible to present on the printed page the manifold relationships and vitality of the millions of actors and activities which are involved in the constant operations of our political system. We have examined how one significant portion of the United States population, Americans of Latino/Hispanic ancestry, have been relating to and operating within the American political system. Unfortunately, the mode of presentation may imply that this relationship is a static one, one that occurs in discrete stages, when in fact this is not the case.

To take just one small example, every time a political decision is made, that is, when Latino wants and needs are converted into public policies, this immediately has effects throughout the entire political system. Inevitably, the new policy affects the total environment in which Latino politics occur. There are a multitude of reactions to a new policy. A policy may be implemented to a greater or lesser extent or completely ignored. Its implementation has significant ramifications for the rest of the system as well as for Latino politics specifically. As the system accommodates to a new policy, an *outcome* begins to take shape. Latinos may either benefit or lose from the new policy. This not only affects the way Latinos then think about government, but as they and others react, it also shapes their new inputs into the system. The outcomes of governmental decisions not only affect new inputs into the system, but they also have direct effects on the decision makers themselves. Although it is difficult to comprehend precisely, one can imagine how the thousands of decisions that are being made each day across the United States by all branches of government at national, state, and local levels produce varying outcomes which give the political environment new shapes and which in turn cause reactions that influence the political activities of all those who participate in politics, including Latinos.

461

Latinos' politics up to the "Decade of the Hispanics" certainly have produced many major and visible outcomes, and these in turn affected and are affecting the politics of Latinos in the 1980s. Where did Latinos find themselves in the initial years of the decade of the Hispanics? Latinos certainly had gained many more resources than were possessed before the "movement" period of the 1960s and early 1970s. Their economic status was somewhat improved as was their educational level. Latinos gained expertise and experience in areas of leadership and organization. A relatively few of them gained influential, if not powerful, positions in some of our major institutions. And these accomplishments made Latinos a little more optimistic about their future. Yet, much of the national and world environment changed to the disadvantage of Latinos.

There can be little doubt that the political activities of the Latino "movement" did produce some beneficial outcomes for Latinos. Any perusal of the indicators of social, political, and economic well-being would show a significant improvement for Latinos over the past two decades. These gains, however, have been far from revolutionary. They have not altered substantially the basic distribution of power between Latinos and core cultural society. There have been few, if any, major institutional reforms aimed at eliminating the institutional racism still prevalent in American society. Nor, for that matter, have all, or even most, of the needs and demands of the Latino people been met in the 1960s, 1970s, and 1980s. In fact, the improvements have been piecemeal and relatively minor. It may be that the advances have been just substantial enough to preempt further demands and deplete much of the energy from the movement. Nevertheless, Latino politics has produced some gainful outcomes, and in all fairness they should be recognized.

Almost all the leading socioeconomic indicators in the United States have shown some improvement for Latinos vis-à-vis national averages over the past quarter century. For example, by 1985 the average level of educational attainment for Latinos had increased from less than ten years in 1965 to 11.5 years. The overall national average was 12.7 years completed. In 1960, 34 percent of Mexican-American males had completed high school compared with 69 percent of the males in the majority population; by 1970, 55 percent of Chicano males and 83 percent of core culture males had graduated; by 1976, these figures stood at 64 percent and 84 percent, respectively. In 1982, among Hispanics 25 years old and over, 46 percent had completed high school compared to 72 percent of non-Hispanics. Moreover, 8 percent of Latinos had completed four or more years of college compared to 18 percent of non-Hispanics. Reviews of curricular materials in the schools will show that materials relevant to Latino culture are now included in at least some of our classrooms. There is an increased number of Latino faculty members in our educational institutions, and there are even a few Latinos in educational administrative positions. Chicano and Latino studies programs still exist in many of the nation's colleges and universities. It is certainly evident then that there has been both a qualitative and quantitative improvement in the educational status of Latinos during the past two decades. However, it must also be noted that the educational gap between Hispanics and Anglos is far from being closed.

Latinos also made definite gains during the past twenty-five years in the all-important area of economic status. There is some evidence, albeit indirect, that Latino job holders have increased their very slow movement into higher prestige and income occupations, including white collar, managerial, and professional positions. Nevertheless, in the mid-1980s, the overwhelming majority of Latinos were still in less desirable, lower-paying positions. For examples, in 1978, 57 percent of Hispanic men were in the blue collar work force compared to 45 percent of the total male working population. From 1964 to 1979, there was only an 0.08 percent increase in the number of Chicanos in the professions, up to 8 percent, compared to 17 percent for non-Hispanics. The proportion of Hispanic men employed in white-collar occupations in 1982 was 26 percent compared to 46 percent for non-Hispanic men. In contrast, among "operators, fabricators, and laborers," 31.6 percent of Latino males were in this category compared to 20.5 percent of male workers in the total population.

This depressed labor position was reflected in income statistics. The median income of Latino families in the 1960s was only about 60 percent of the median family income of all Americans. By the late 1970s, that percentage had climbed to almost 70 percent where it seemed to level off. In 1984 the median income of Hispanic families was only slightly over 70 percent of that of all families— $18,883 for Latinos and $26,951 for non-Latinos. In 1959 median per capita income for Latinos was just 50 percent of the majority median per capita income. By 1969 the proportion rose to 51 percent, but in 1980 the figure fell to 49 percent. Twenty-eight percent of Mexican-Americans were in the poverty category in 1969 compared to 13 percent of majority Americans. By 1974 these figures were down to 24 percent and 9 percent respectively, but in 1985 poverty rates were back up to 25 percent for Hispanics, 14 percent for all Americans, and 11 percent for Anglos. Throughout the past two decades, unemployment among Latinos also remained higher than that for Anglo Americans. The unemployment rate for Hispanics in 1985, for example, was 11.3 percent compared to 7.4 percent for the total non-Latino work force. Therefore, there was some statistical improvement, but again expectations of equity fell short of realization.

In addition to positive outcomes in educational and economic areas, however incomplete, Latinos also made some more substantial political gains. More Latinos were elected to positions in state and local government in the 1970s and early 1980s than had been elected in the previous one hundred years. State legislatures evidenced an increasing Latino representation. For example, of the only thirty-eight Latinos elected to the California State Legislature between 1860 and 1979 (out of more than 4,000 persons who were members of the legislature during that century), seven were serving in 1984. In Texas, Latino representation improved from six legislators in 1962 to twenty-five in 1984. In Arizona, Latino representation in the legislature went from three to eleven between 1962 and 1984. The number of Latinos in the Colorado legislature increased from zero to eight in the period 1962 to 1978 and then to six in 1984. The proportion of Latinos in the New Mexico legislature remained relatively unchanged in the same period, although the total number of Latino legislators increased from twenty-three in 1962 to thirty-two in 1984. Overall, while Latino representation in the southwestern state legislatures remained small and fairly constant from 1932 to 1962, it more than doubled between 1962 and 1978, from a total of thirty-two legislators in the five southwestern states to a total of eighty legislators in 1978 and eighty-one in 1984. Although there were definite gains for Latinos in these years, it should be noted that in all the states of the Southwest the proportion of Latino lawmakers in the state legislatures remains far below the proportion of Latinos in the total population of each state.

Political gains for Latinos at other levels of government were also much in evidence in the last twenty-five years. In the first half of the 1970s, two of the five southwestern governorships were held by Latinos, as Raul Castro served as governor of Arizona at the same time that Jerry Apodaca was the governor of New Mexico. In 1984 there was one Latino governor and four other Latino elected state governmental executives, all in New Mexico. Major gains were also made at the local level. Significant here were the early gains made in rural counties and small rural towns such as Crystal City, Texas, and Parlier, California, where Latinos were able to gain majority representation on the city councils. Of course, these communities did have overwhelmingly Latino populations. Some gains also have been made in the larger cities of the United States with Latinos gaining a seat or two on city councils in El Paso, San Antonio, Houston, Denver, and other cities and winning the mayorships in Denver (Pena) and San Antonio (Sisneros). Still in these larger metropolitan areas, Latinos remain badly underrepresented.

Overall, from 1973 to 1984, there was an average gain of 118 percent in the number of Hispanic elected officeholders in the states of Arizona, California, Florida, New Mexico, New York, and Texas, from 1,280 to

2,793. Most of these were at the local level—municipalities, counties, and school boards. Particularly in the late 1970s and early 1980s, this increase had been abetted by litigation which produced single-member, districted elective constituencies from previous at-large, multimember districts. Groups such as MALDEF and SVREP were in the forefront of these challenges through the courts. Fairer reapportionments following the 1980 census had also promoted Latino electoral success.

Because Latinos are perceived as becoming an increasingly important political factor in the United States, an increasing number of Latinos also have been appointed to office at the national, state, and local levels. Presidential appointments to relatively high positions in the federal bureaucracy increased dramatically during the Nixon, Ford, Carter, and Reagan administrations. Many of these appointments were mainly symbolic, since the positions in question either were in special Latino or minority-oriented agencies or they offered the appointee little or no significant influence in policy formulation. But at minimum the appointments do provide some additional opportunities for Latinos to have an impact on major institutions. Also, such appointments are useful in that the appointees serve as public role models to which other Latinos, especially the young, can relate.

One can see that the outcome of Latino politics up to the 1980s reflects some noteworthy gains. However, much remains to be done, and one related question in how Latinos should best employ their relatively limited political resources to have maximum impacts on the political system. In his article, Santillan postulates the styles and strategies which he feels have been most effective in various settings in the Midwest and suggests that these may serve as valuable lessons for other regions and for national politics as a whole. In the rural areas, the political leadership by women and the unified politics of "collective preservation" have been employed effectively. In the large urban settings, organizational bases are very important, and unions seem to offer significant opportunities in those areas as do effective interactions with both the Democratic and Republican parties. Additionally, alliances need to be sought with other ethnic minorities. In the middle-sized cities, the situation seems likely to evoke the best of the previous two strategies, which incorporates the effective involvement of Latinas, successful coalitions with organizations, such as both the Democratic and Republican parties, and increasingly effective attempts to form coalitions among the various Latino nationality groups. Lessons learned in the Midwest, its being in several ways a microcosm of the national Latino political setting, may be particularly valuable and insightful.

In our last selection, Jennings makes some observations about Puerto Rican politics and policies in the United States that apply more generally to Latino politics and even to the politics of other ethnic groups. A contrast is drawn between traditional ethnic politics of the recent and distant past and future progressive politics. While traditional ethnic politics have, in one form or another, simply sought to become a part of the current political and economic structures in the United States, the new progressive politics calls for the *empowerment* of Puerto Ricans and Latinos in general, so that both the public and private sectors' structural arrangements can be altered to empower virtually all of the people. Empowerment of the previously powerless will replace access and patronage politics that basically have benefited the middle-class Latinos. In order to attain this empowerment, a multitude of varying political strategies must be employed, including electoral participation. However, this electoral participation will be used not as a short-term means in itself but as an intermediate strategy that also will lead to further structural and policy victories, that is, to more favorable policy outcomes.

26. Styles and Strategies

Richard Santillan

THE CURRENT STATE OF Mexican-American politics in the Midwest can best be described as a unique collage comprising three distinct political styles and strategies. The calculated decision to adopt all three approaches in the Midwest appears at first glance to be both adversely competitive and reflecting a lack of regional cooperation among Latinos. A closer examination, however, reveals that this political mixture actually demonstrates the versatile ability of the Mexican-American leadership to systematically adapt itself to particular types of social environments.

Midwest Mexican-American communities fall into three basic categories: rural, urban, and rural-urban. The selection of one of three political strategy variations seems to be largely contingent on both the historical and the economic conditions within each of these three general environments.

The following three Midwest models, notwithstanding their inherent weaknesses, provide a regional mosaic of valuable lessons, suggesting methodical ways for increasing the political voice of Latino communities nationwide.

RURAL MODEL: COLLECTIVE PRESERVATION

There are presently several rural communities scattered throughout the Midwest in which Mexican-Americans are escalating their political participation. The majority of these small towns are located within the western portion of the Midwest (Kansas, Iowa, Missouri, Nebraska, and Oklahoma), and are represented by such communities as Scottsbluff, Nebraska; Muscatine, Iowa; Hutchinson, Kansas; Albert Lea, Minnesota; Lansing, Michigan; and South Bend, Indiana. The first wave of Mexican immigrants arrived in many of these states during the latter part of the nineteenth century, primarily as railroad workers.[1] After the completion of the railroad systems, the majority of these Mexican-American railroad workers eventually found employment with the large steel companies near the Great Lakes region. The post–Mexican revolution period witnessed further penetration of Mexican immigrants into these rural communities. The arrival of these new political refugees during the 1920s coincided with the recruitment of Mexican-Americans from South Texas as workers in the expanding agricultural industry.[2] These two groups continue to serve as the backbone of the agricultural labor force in the Midwest today.

The harmful effects of both mechanization and the farm crisis, however, have swiftly forced the majority of these migrant workers to seek permanent year-round employment and residency in nonagricultural jobs in the Midwest. The farm crisis alone has resulted in the loss of 350,000 farmworker jobs between 1979–1985.[3] This economic and social resettlement has significantly inflated the Mexican-American population in several Midwest farming communities during the past two decades.

The rapid cultural transformation of many of these rural communities has served to heighten the political distrust between Anglo and Mexican-American leadership, largely due to deep-seated prejudice and nationalistic pride on both sides.[4] These cultural misunderstandings, along with refined forms of social discrimination, have resulted in the geographical quarantine, cutting off many Mexican-American communities from the political mainstream of these towns.

This social demarcation has produced two unique traits among Mexican-Americans in these Grain Belt states. The first characteristic is that the sense of "community" is a very tangible experience, and not one merely reduced to an abstract notion. The residents of these Mexican-American neighborhoods are politically linked by strong family friendship ties.[5]

Second, the Mexican culture and Spanish language remain the dominant lifestyle in these communities, and it appears that the Catholic church plays an influential role in preserving many of these indigenous traditions.

These two social traits largely determine both the character and the tactics of Mexican-American political behavior in these rural communities. Mexican-American candidates, for example, nearly always seek elected office by strongly articulating Mexican-American grievances and issues. The nationalistic tone of these campaigns, however, generally results in heartbreaking defeats because of the expected political backlash of Anglo voters. This political situation poses an electoral dilemma for many Mexican-American candidates, because any attempt to forge political alliances with certain Anglo leaders is likely to be negatively interpreted as catering to Anglo concerns at the expense of the Mexican-American community.

Moreover, both the working-class nature and the migratory history of these Mexican-American communities unfairly place them at a political and economic disadvantage against the well-financed local power elites, i.e., lack of campaign funds, discriminatory at-large district election systems, unequal press coverage, political alienation, and the talents of only a handful of college-educated Mexican-American professionals.[6]

The Mexican-American community also suffers from the lack of natural political allies generally found in larger urban Midwest cities. The Democratic Party and labor unions, for example, are nearly voiceless in many of these heavily Republican right-to-work states. In addition, the Catholic Church tends to shy away from social activism and prefers to concentrate its community efforts primarily on cultural and social events. Last, other sizeable minority groups, including Puerto Ricans and blacks, are virtually nonexistent in many of these rural areas. There are small pockets of Native Americans; they are, however, sadly devoid of the political resources to help even themselves, let alone assist the political aims of Mexican-Americans.

The Mexican-American community, nevertheless, is slowly making political headway in these small cities, despite these social roadblocks. A major contributing factor for this gradual progress is the inventive utilization of nontraditional strategies generally overlooked by the Latino leadership in larger Midwest communities. First and foremost is the impressive leadership role currently being demonstrated by Mexican-American women. A possible explanation for this particular situation is that many of these women came from migrant experiences where traditional gender roles were often blurred by the social equality of labor between women and men.[7] Furthermore, these women had strong female role models to emulate during their childhood. This social background has taught both rural Mexican-American men and women that political survival, like economic survival, is deeply rooted in collective cooperation and respect for each other's participation.

The participation of women in leadership roles also appears to have the instinctual support of many Mexican-American men, primarily because they see themselves as the prime beneficiaries of such a political arrangement. The Mexican-American male leadership fully realizes, for example, that its political self-interests, including appointments, are intertwined with the voting and leadership power of Mexican-American women simply because men alone are numerically insignificant in this rural context in achieving political power. Moreover, the kinship nature of these small Mexican-American communities realistically forecloses the capability of any group to exclude a vocal constituency patiently determined to take its rightful place in local political affairs.

Furthermore, and most importantly, both Mexican-American men and women share the communal awareness that gender segmentation would seriously jeopardize conjointly their ability to achieve a better life for their children. This down-to-earth realism regarding the social welfare of their children and other pressing issues transcends the traditional habit of arbitrarily dispensing community influence according to gender.[8]

Finally, the Mexican-American leadership in these agricultural towns also realizes that it cannot politically afford to be fragmented on the basis of partisan, organizational, and class conflicts given the blight of its limited number of community activists. This demographic fact of life has produced the politics of collective preservation, which almost always places the social well-being of the entire community above the self-centered interests of any particular organization or individual. The ultimate outcome of this unorthodox policy of political compromise has been the ability of rural Mexican-Americans to create the public image of speaking with a common voice, although the image makers are simultaneously disagreeing among themselves behind closed doors in their respective communities. This shrewd defense mechanism, which multiplies the actual power of Mexican-Americans, is notably responsible for the few political gains achieved by Mexican-Americans in these predominantly Anglo communities.[9]

For the moment, there exists one major downside to small-town Mexican-American politics. This can be characterized as the "insiders-outsiders" syndrome. The vast majority of Midwest-born Mexican-American leaders have expressed a subtle suspicion of the influx of newly arriving Mexican-Americans from the Southwest, especially white-collar professionals. This regional mistrust is understandable given the deeply embedded local perception that these "intruders" often flout their social, cultural, political, and linguistic abilities over those of the native population.

In addition, many of these transient middle-class Mexican-Americans have often disassociated themselves from community issues as a result of the fact that they reside outside the Mexican-American section of town. This class behavior is often perceived as clannish, which further antagonizes the local Mexican-American leadership. However, there are many incoming Mexican-Americans who have communicated a sincere willingness to participate in community activities, only to be made to feel unwelcome because of the stereotype which unfairly portrays almost all non-natives as politically aloof and culturally arrogant. This parochial tug-of-war denies the Mexican-American community the precious resources and talents cooperatively needed for amplifying its political voice inside these rural towns.

URBAN MODEL: COALITION OR EXCLUSION?

These Mexican-American communities border the Great Lakes and are represented by such cities as Milwaukee, Wisconsin; Chicago, Illinois; East Chicago and Gary, Indiana; Detroit, Michigan; and Lorain and Cleveland, Ohio.[10] Mexicans have been arriving into these urban centers since the early 1900s seeking work in the steel, auto, railroad, textile, and mining industries.

Currently, these Mexican-American communities are steadily making their political influence felt in local elected and appointed positions and are presently aiming their electoral sights higher toward state and congressional seats. The bulk of elected and appointed Mexican-American officials in the Midwest is from this eastern portion.[11] The urban Mexican-American leadership has clearly profited from the following historical factors, which are generally absent in the political experience of rural Mexican-Americans.

To begin with, the Mexican-American urban community can trace its organizational roots back nearly seventy-five years, as compared with the recent settlement of immigrants in rural towns. This longevity has enabled the Mexican-American urban leadership to draw upon both the firm foundation and the rich resources of numerous social and civic organizations.

Second, the Mexican-American urban leadership has benefited from closely observing and gaining political acumen from many politically successful ethnic groups, including the Italians, the Irish, the Jews, and the Polish. Moreover, Black Civil Rights, along with the election of black mayors to the cities of Chicago, Detroit, and Gary, has provided the Mexican-American leadership with additional strategic options for achieving political influence.

Third, Mexican-Americans are gradually penetrating the union hierarchy as a strategy for increasing their political clout.[12] Historically, the union movement has resisted minority participation and often ignored the social and economic needs of its minority rank and file members.

This minority exclusion by labor unions was largely based on racial discrimination, job competition, and the historical fact that some Mexican workers were unknowingly recruited as strikebreakers. Currently, these past union practices and backward attitudes are gradually changing due to the establishment of aggressive minority caucuses within the labor movement.

These unions possess several valuable resources which are presently being redirected in a manner designed to supplement the political aims of the Mexican-American leadership. This union support system includes funds for voter registration programs, leadership training, financial assistance for campaigns, newsletters for disseminating information, the selection of delegates for local, state, and national conventions, and accessibility to elected officials.[13] Many Midwest Mexican-American elected officials and community leaders received the political baptism through the union ranks and, more importantly, are utilizing these union skills and resources in promoting electoral participation among Mexican-Americans.

Fourth, some Mexican-American communities have improved their political fortunes by forging temporary alliances with the Puerto Rican community. These Latino coalitions appear to take place in cities where Mexican-Americans and Puerto Ricans are residentially integrated, i.e., Milwaukee, East Chicago, and Lorain.[14] This social intermixture seems to significantly reduce the problems of political competition, social distrust, and cultural misunderstanding between these two Spanish-speaking groups, and therefore enhances the opportunities for political cooperation. The opposite condition is also valid—as the geographical distance widens between Mexican-Americans and Puerto Ricans, so does the possibility for joint political activities.

Last, the Midwest Democratic Party, unlike its weaker counterpart in rural Mexican-American communities, is currently undertaking certain responsive measures as a means of incorporating within the party structure a number of urban Mexican-American interests.[15] These new reforms include the establishment of Hispanic caucuses, platform issues, committee appointments, support for voter registration, and delegates to local, state, and national conventions. These recent changes by the Democrats, however, appear mainly to be short-sighted alterations designed merely for taking immediate advantage of the growing importance of the Mexican-American vote for both the 1988 and 1990 Midwest elections.

The efforts of the Republican Party to recruit among professional and middle-class Mexican-Americans in the Sunbelt states are well publicized, but it is almost politically invisible within these Midwest Mexican-American communities. This lack of serious outreach in the urban Midwest by the GOP is strongly influenced by three overriding factors: first, the vast majority of Midwest Mexican-Americans are blue-collar workers, who remain a loyal bloc vote to both the Democratic Party and their unions; second, the Reagan Administration is largely blamed for the severe economic crisis in both the urban and rural Midwest, which has negatively affected nearly every Mexican-American and Puerto Rican household; and third, upward political mobility is extremely limited for Latinos who join the Republican ranks in these tough Democratic strongholds.[16]

The preceding social and political benefits are mainly responsible for helping increase the electoral advancement of urban Mexican-Americans in the Midwest. There are, however, both social liabilities and self-imposed shortcomings which partly neutralize the political effectiveness derived from these urban advantages.

The Mexican-American metropolitan populations are, for example, both widely dispersed and geographically fragmented within these huge cities, which greatly reduces the sense of a community of common interests — a striking deficiency of the social fellowship generally indigenous to rural Mexican-Americans. These scattered Mexican-American urban neighborhoods were chronologically established according to both the industry and the decade when Mexican-Americans arrived into these industrial areas seeking employment.[17] This historical pattern of uneven settlement has also divided Mexican-American residents with respect to their social degree of cultural and linguistic assimilation.

The condition of cultural and social diversity among these splintered Mexican-American communities has spawned a number of local power brokers who seem to be more interested in protecting their own particular "turf" than promoting the general welfare of the entire community. This decentralization of power has promoted the politics of self-indulgence, which reduces the ability of the Mexican-American leadership to maximize their collective resources and talents for achieving long-lasting reforms rather than the short-lived cosmetic changes offered by the Democratic Party.

The Puerto Rican community, for example, has achieved more elected and appointed positions than the much older and larger Mexican-American communities in some of these cities. One possible explanation for this difference appears to be the ability of the Puerto Rican leadership to submerge their social distinctions at times for the betterment of the overall Puerto Rican community.

Furthermore, Mexican-American and Puerto Rican women are almost voiceless in the urban decision-making process, largely because of the economic history of these industrial centers. These urban cities have been and continue to be viewed as rugged "beer and shot" towns, where backbreaking jobs are considered for men only.[18] More importantly, the adequate wages earned by men as a result of exhausting work and plenty of overtime afforded Mexican-American and Puerto Rican male workers the economic independence to be the sole providers for their large families.

Women's roles in these urban cities, unlike those of Mexican-American and Puerto Rican migrant women, were considered secondary and without monetary value, and consisted of domestically supporting the labor force, reproducing laborers, as well as some employment in both pink-collar occupations and light factory work, with the notable exception of World War II, when many Latinas worked in the war industry.[19]

This social inequality of labor based on both gender and wages has naturally spilled over into the urban political arena where Latino men are self-appointed as community leaders while women are relegated to the level of campaign supporters. As a result of this political discouragement, many Mexican-American and Puerto Rican women are redirecting their resources and energies into the fields of education, social services, law, and the private sector. The near total absence of Latinas in community politics seems almost to guarantee the delay of any substantial social progress in these urban communities for the present.

Also, the Mexican-American leadership is uncertain regarding its appropriate political relationship with the larger black community. This long standing policy of indecision has denied the Mexican-American community the unique opportunity to join political forces with black voters, who are currently making significant electoral strides, with examples being the mayorships of Chicago, Detroit, and Gary.[20] The failure to establish strong black-brown coalitions in the urban Midwest lies squarely with racial prejudice on both sides and group rivalry for limited social resources. Moreover, Mexican-American leaders have voiced strong complaints that most black elected and appointed officials have often ignored the community concerns and issues of Mexican-Americans in favor of promoting their own political agendas.

There are, however, some Mexican-American and black leaders who are presently discussing the political ground rules for establishing possible alliances in upcoming elections, especially in the city of Chicago.[21] These positive steps, nevertheless, are largely overshadowed by the overall political mistrust in the Midwest between these two minority constituencies. This ongoing contest between urban blacks and Mexican-Americans considerably impedes their collaborative capability for broadening their political horizons.

In addition, the urban Catholic Church does not seem to be active in the political affairs of the Latino community. This lack of social support can be traced back to the racial antagonism between Europeans and Mexican Catholics during the labor movement and competition for skilled and unskilled jobs. Naturally, many of the European Catholic priests took the side of the European Catholics, which alienated many Mexican Catholics from the Catholic Church and into the ranks of other Midwest religions.[22]

Finally, the urban Mexican-American and Puerto Rican communities suffer from a continuous "brain drain," mainly because the vast majority of their college graduates are leaving for more lucrative opportunities outside the Midwest.[23] This depletion of much-needed human resources has dramatically slowed the political and economic progress of Latinos in the Midwest. Ironically, many Latin-American professionals, including Cuban-Americans from Florida, are immigrating into the Midwest for work in the fields of medicine, law, education, business, and the media—valuable resources desperately needed by the Mexican-American and Puerto Rican communities. These Latin American professionals, with a few noticeable exceptions, do not socially identify themselves as a linguistic and ethnic "minority," and consequently, they make little effort to join Mexican-American and Puerto Rican civil rights and community-based organizations.[24] Furthermore, many of these Latin and Cuban-American newcomers seem to be politically conservative, and this difference also places them in ideological conflict with the more liberal Mexican-American and Puerto Rican leadership over social and foreign policy issues and militant strategies. The Mexican-American leadership is also partly at fault for this harmful situation as its community organizations and cultural activities primarily focus on Mexican culture and issues, which usually alienates the broader Latin American community.

There is one more side to this Mexican-American brain drain: Mexican-American professionals who choose to remain in the Midwest are moving out to the surrounding predominantly Anglo suburbs. The majority of these Mexican-Americans, however, continue to remain active in the political affairs of the Mexican-American community, largely because of strong family ties and social commitment.

RURAL-URBAN MODEL: ECLECTIC

These middle-sized cities are a rich mixture of both the rural and urban Mexican-American experiences, and are represented by such municipalities as St. Paul, Minnesota; Kansas City, Kansas; Des Moines and Council Bluffs, Iowa; Grand Rapids, Michigan; Omaha and North Platte, Nebraska; Waukesha and Racine, Wisconsin; Toledo, Ohio; Kansas City, Missouri; and Fort Wayne, Indiana.[25]

Mexicans originally arrived in these towns during the 1920s for work in light and heavy industries, including textiles, meatpacking, electronics, tanneries, railroads, and mining.[26] The initial Mexican population has substantially increased due to the resettlement of thousands of migrant workers since the 1960s. Moreover, the past decade has seen large numbers of Cuban and Latin American professionals moving into these cities for employment, especially in the business sector.

These Mexican-American communities, as a result of this rural-urban-

Latin fusion, are gradually inheriting the combined strengths of both of the models discussed earlier, with the political benefits clearly overshadowing the organizational shortcomings.[27] Equally important to these political advantages is the demographic fact that these Mexican-American communities are neither large enough to pose a direct threat to the Anglo leadership nor small enough to be ignored during local elections—a very healthy political posture for the Mexican-American leadership.[28]

These special Mexican-American communities are the closest examples to a classical casebook study for maximizing organizational resources and human talents in order to achieve a louder political voice for the Latino community. Some of the following strategies of these medium cities appear to be applicable elsewhere in the Midwest and U.S. for escalating Latino political influence, across varying social and economic environments.

First, Mexican-American women play a vital leadership role and serve as positive role models for the entire community. Second, there is a sincere willingness between Mexican-American Democrats and Republicans to set aside partisan typecasting in order to work together on common issues. Third, the "insiders-outsiders" syndrome does not seem to be a major hindrance to the normal growth and development in these communities. Fourth, there has been a genuine attempt by some of the Mexican-American leadership to broaden its political base by reaching out to the Puerto Rican, Cuban-American, and Latin American communities. Fifth, many Mexican-American college graduates and professionals are choosing to remain and invest their human and financial resources, largely because of the expanding economic opportunities in nonfarming and high-tech occupations. Finally, there is the tactical effort by the Mexican-American leadership to socially cooperate with the Anglo leadership, including membership interaction in civic and business associations. The weak spots are surprisingly minimal and include the lack of cooperation between the Latino and black leadership, and the failure to take full advantage of the church and union resources.

CONCLUSION

Mexican-Americans in both the Southwest and Midwest paradoxically are historical partners and contemporary strangers. Both groups have been common victims of social and economic discrimination and currently share several problems, including unemployment, high drop-out rates, voting rights abuses, police and immigration harassment, and lack of adequate housing and health care. Nonetheless, Mexican-Americans of both regions are almost completely unacquainted with each other's rich history and present problems.

Mexican-American political trends in the Southwest, especially in Texas, have largely molded the political character of the Midwest between the 1920s and 1970s, i.e., mutual aid associations, G.I. Forum, LULAC, and La Raza Unida Party. The decade of the 1980s, however, is witnessing a gradual reversal of this long standing one-way political influence, whereas Midwest Latino political ideology and behavior now appear to be providing some tangible organizational guidance for Latinos on both coasts.

The major reason for this political turnabout is that the Midwest is the geographical crossroads where Mexican-Americans, Puerto Ricans, and Cuban-Americans are socially interblending, with the result being the emergence of several ingenious political strategies. The political value of this Latino cultural merger is becoming increasingly apparent for Latinos elsewhere because Midwest Latino political success may provide a "sneak preview" for other Latinos as their demographic diversity begins to slowly mirror that of the Midwest.

All in all, the political destiny of all Latinos is inherently linked, regardless of geographic region, and this common bond only serves to underscore the present need for a national political agenda as Latinos enter soon into the twenty-first century.

NOTES

1. Interview with Esther Valladorid Wolf, September 3, 1986, Kansas City, Kansas. Also see Elvira Valenzuela Crocker, "Small Town Hispanic America," *Vista,* July 1986.

2. Interview with Alfredo and Linda Lares, July 2, 1986, Albert Lea, Minnesota.

3. Keith Schneider, "Upheaval in U.S. Food Industry Forces A Hard Look at its Future," *The New York Times,* October 9, 1986; and Harvey M. Choldin and Grafton D. Trout, *Mexican-Americans in Transition Migration and Employment in Michigan Cities, Part I: Introduction and Summary* (Michigan State University, East Lansing, March 1971).

4. Interview with Joe Romero, June 11, 1986, Scottsbluff, Nebraska.

5. Ibid.

6. Interview with Miguel Teran, June 18, 1986, Des Moines, Iowa. Also, Albert Sanchez, *The Effect of "Reformed" Government Structures on Minority Political Recruitment and Policy Outputs: The Case of Scottsbluff, Nebraska,* (Honors Thesis: University of Nebraska–Lincoln, 1984); and N. Steven King, *Hispanic Voter Registration Project—City of Scottsbluff,* Mexican-American Commission, 1983.

7. Interviews with Olga Villa Parra, August 10, 1986, South Bend, Indiana, and Irma Guerra, July 11, 1986, Milwaukee, Wisconsin. Both women are former migrant workers.

8. Interview with Raul Cardova, Jr., July 2, 1986, Albert Lea, Minnesota.

9. Interview with Juan Andrade, October 11, 1986, Chicago, Illinois.

10. Ibid. Also, Frank Jacinto, *The Mexican Community in Lorain, Ohio* (unpublished paper), June 1981; Louise Año Nuevo de Kerr, "Chicano Settlements in Chicago: A Brief History," *Journal of Ethnic Studies* (1982); and Julian Samora and Richard A. Lamanna, *Mexican-Americans in a Midwest Metropolis: A Study of East Chicago* (University of California, Los Angeles, 1967).

11. Ibid.

12. Interviews with Oscar Sanchez, August 5, 1986, East Chicago, Indiana, and Eva Zavala, June 25, 1986, East Moline, Illinois.

13. Interview with John "Buck" Serrano, June 23, 1986, Davenport, Iowa.

14. Interviews with Dagoberto Ibarra, July 11, 1986, Waukesha, Wisconsin; Ricardo Diaz, July 10, 1986, Milwaukee, Wisconsin; and Peter Martinez, October 10, 1986, Chicago, Illinois.

15. Interviews with Jose Estrada, September 6, 1985, Detroit, Michigan; Albert Quintela, August 23, 1985, St. Paul, Minnesota; Al Sanchez, August 25, 1985, Chicago, Illinois; and Raynae Lagunas, August 19, 1985, Des Moines, Iowa.

16. Interview with Ness Flores, July 10, 1986, Waukesha, Wisconsin.

17. Interview with John Attinasi, October 10, 1986, Chicago, Illinois.

18. Interviews with Carol Padilla, July 20, 1986, Highland, Indiana; Jesse Villalpando, July 21, 1986, Griffith, Indiana; and John "Buck" Serrano, June 23, 1986, Davenport, Iowa.

19. Interviews with Luis and Martha Gonzales, October 11, 1986, Chicago, Illinois, and Carmen Fernandez, August 7, 1986, East Chicago, Indiana.

20. Interview with Enrique Rodriguez, September 5, 1985, Detroit, Michigan. Mr. Rodriguez is an assistant to Mayor Coleman Young.

21. Interviews with Edwin Claudio, October 9, 1986, Chicago, Illinois, and Ray Romero, October 11, 1986, Chicago, Illinois. Also see *Al Filo/At the Cutting Edge: The Empowerment of Chicago's Latino Electorate*, Latino Institute, Chicago, Illinois, September 1986.

22. Interview with Oscar Cervera, August 21, 1986, Milwaukee, Wisconsin.

23. Interviews with Ricardo Parra, August 12, 1986, South Bend, Indiana, and Nancy Barcelo, June 26, 1986, Iowa City, Iowa.

24. Interview with Walter Salva, August 18, 1986, Waukesha, Wisconsin.

25. Interviews with JoAnn Cardenas Enos, August 22, 1985, St. Paul, Minnesota; Paula Campos Cortez, August 21, 1985, Des Moines, Iowa; Eloise Gomez, August 24, 1985, Madison, Wisconsin; Lupe Gonzales, August 16, 1985, Kansas City, Kansas; Miguel Carranza, August 17, 1985, Lincoln, Nebraska; Fred J. Sanchez, August 14, 1985, Kansas City, Missouri; Steven Corona, August 14, 1986, Fort Wayne, Indiana; Becky Ramirez, August 18, 1986, Waukesha, Wisconsin; Arturo Martinez, August 20, 1986, Racine, Wisconsin, and Helen Julie Rodriguez, Hutchinson, Kansas, August 15, 1985.

26. Nina L. Nixon, *The Mexican-American Settlement Of Omaha,* Omaha City Planning Department, August, 1979; and *Latin-Americans in Kansas City, Missouri,* Council of Churches of Metropolitan Kansas City, March 1965.

27. Interviews with Richard J. Hernandez and Jose Cuevas, August 18, 1986, Waukesha, Wisconsin.

28. Interview with Juan Andrade, August 11, 1986, Chicago, Illinois.

27. Future Directions for Puerto Rican Politics in the U.S. and Puerto Rico

James Jennings

MANY PEOPLE OF COLOR AND poor people in our society are facing worsening economic and social living conditions. Certain groups are also perceived as culturally and intellectually inferior by the media, scholarly community, and government officials. At the same time that socioeconomic conditions are worsening for Puerto Ricans, for example, sectors of the intelligentsia in this country are attacking what they perceive to be Puerto Rican culture or group attitudes. Raising the possibility that Puerto Ricans are culturally inferior serves to justify decisions by those responsible for public policy resulting in adverse impact on the well-being of the Puerto Rican community.

America is in a stage of racial and social relations in which Puerto Ricans find themselves increasingly powerless to change or even arrest worsening living conditions. The suggestion that Puerto Ricans should respond with strategies based on changing the hierarchy of power and the distribution of wealth in order to arrest the deterioration of living conditions has not been cited extensively; in fact this notion is challenged or even ridiculed by various academic and political thinkers. Some researchers and governmental leaders will claim, instead, that the reasons Puerto Ricans suffer from adverse social conditions has more to do with the level of education, inability to speak English, or as stated earlier, simply having inappropriate attitudes for the realization of mobility in America.

For the most part, Puerto Rican intellectuals have argued that this kind of analysis is basically erroneous. Sociologist Jose Hernandez has suggested instead that

> the major question is how greater power can be obtained. . . . [A] most convincing argument for empowerment is that we now have the solution at hand. After so many years of research, thinking and prac-

> tical efforts, we know what we want. . . . our experience generally shows that the 'how' reduces to political power.[1]

Many Puerto Rican leaders have proposed that it is lack of power or lack of control over institutions influencing life in Puerto Rican communities, rather than attitudes or level of English proficiency that explains negative living conditions. This viewpoint is seldom reflected by the media or in academic sectors.

Debates regarding the causes of social and economic conditions of poor people and people of color is cast by the media and scholarly community almost exclusively within what could be referred to as the "standard" liberal-conservative public policy framework. Even when so-called "radicals" join these debates, a "Puerto Rican" perspective of the problems facing Puerto Ricans is not proposed. What follows is an attempt to develop a political framework by which strategies of empowerment can be proposed as responses to the living conditions of Puerto Ricans.

This proposed conceptualization is appropriate for analyzing the current status and future directions of Puerto Rican politics in this country. It is also useful and relevant to the perennial questions regarding the status of Puerto Rico and the political relationship between the Puerto Rican community in the U.S. and Puerto Rico. Several questions raised by leaders and activists in Puerto Rican communities can be approached within the framework:

- The advantages of electoral vs. non-electoral political participation for Puerto Ricans
- The relevance of analysis of Puerto Rican politics based on racial/ethnic vs. class concepts and approaches
- The lack or low level of political participation on the part of Puerto Ricans
- The differential rate of socio-economic progress for Puerto Ricans, Mexican-Americans, and Cubans
- The relationship between Puerto Rican politics in the continental U.S. and Puerto Rico
- The possibilities, or lack thereof, of coalitions with other groups, especially with blacks

There are many other political questions and issues which could be approached under an analysis of power in American society. But before explaining this further a brief overview of current public policy frameworks is appropriate.

There are currently three well-known conceptual public policy frameworks which can be summarized in political terms for the purpose of this essay. Although two of these approaches have been the basis of public policy impacting on Puerto Ricans, they all are inadequate in various ways for understanding the political or social experiences of Puerto Ricans, or for proposing future directions for Puerto Rican politics in the United States. These three frameworks or conceptualizations can be summarized as the "conservative," "liberal," and "radical" schools. This taxonomy may be but a more current terminology for the prominent debate among political scientists in the 1950s and 1960s regarding the concepts of "pluralism" and "elitism."

The terms "liberal" or "conservative" suggest related ideas of what is known as the pluralist school reflected in the writings of Robert Dahl, David Truman, Nelson Polsby, Ray Wolfinger, and others; the "radical" orientation to public policy has some antecedents in the works of C. Wright Mills and E. E. Schattschneider.[2] In discussing public policy today these three terms can be utilized to refer to various packages of ideas; each term reflects a general orientation regarding the relationship between the socioeconomic needs of citizen groups, politics, and the metropolitan economy. There is, of course, much overlap in these political summaries.

Generally speaking, proponents of these three approaches have not developed a comprehensive and interrelated set of information and ideas which would allow us to understand adequately the political experiences of Puerto Ricans in the United States. The liberal, conservative, and radical frameworks suffer from common weaknesses. These weaknesses include historical inaccuracies regarding the experiences of Puerto Ricans in the United States, cultural bias, and, most importantly, an underestimating of the organization of power as critical in understanding socioeconomic characteristics of Puerto Rican life. It may be helpful to describe and discuss these frameworks by selecting various theoretical issues facing Puerto Rican leaders and activists and examining how such issues are approached by proponents of liberal, conservative, and radical orientations.

Issues such as the advantages of electoral vs. non-electoral political participation and the levels of voter registration and turnout among Puerto Ricans are important concerns. In many cities Puerto Ricans tend to be characterized by low registration and turnout rates. According to the Hispanic Policy Development Project most Latino officials feel that the reason for this is the general belief among Latinos that voting does not significantly impact on the general quality of urban life. In a survey of 448 elected and appointed Hispanic officials a few years ago 73 percent of the respondents supported this claim. This survey found that "the chief obstacle Hispanic officials say they face is the need to convince their people that political participation can make a difference. . . . The single greatest cause of low voting participation rates is a widespread feeling that votes simply won't make a difference."[3] The feeling of estrangement among Puerto Ricans poses problems for those reflecting the liberal orientation who argue that the right to vote is fundamental to American society. The right to vote is indeed fundamental to American democracy; but among Puerto Ricans there seems to be a major sentiment that voting is not functional in meeting basic social and economic needs. Some liberal theorists would argue, however, that Puerto Ricans should seek to become conscientious voters and participants in the electoral processes available to them—not merely out of civic responsibility, but because there is indeed a linkage between political participation and policy outcome. That is, the more Puerto Ricans vote, the more beneficial governmental and public policy outcomes can be expected. Puerto Ricans, as an identifiable group in American society, are yet to be convinced of this claim.

Those espousing a conservative orientation toward public policy posit that once the right to vote is guaranteed, it is up to the individual to vote or not to vote. If Puerto Ricans choose not to vote, then it is completely their choice and should not be lamented—and government should certainly not intercede merely because a group is not voting at expected levels given certain social and economic conditions. Others reflecting the conservative orientation might even propose that the reason Puerto Ricans do not vote as extensively as others may be due to a relative degree of satisfaction with governmental services and urban life conditions. Furthermore, the social and economic problems faced by Puerto Ricans may not be susceptible to political responses or social tinkering. It is claimed, for example, that Puerto Ricans may have cultural attributes that are responsible for unemployment, high levels of crime, and general social dislocation, and until these cultural attitudes change even a relative high level electoral participation may not be effective in improving life conditions for this group. This view has been expressed by both conservative and liberal thinkers.

The "radicals" generally take the position that attitudes of the minority group are not critical; political participation in the electoral arena supports the social and economic status-quo, and therefore higher levels of electoral activism may not be functional in responding to the needs of an impoverished group like Puerto Ricans. This is because effective responses to an impoverished group is contradictory with maintaining or even reforming the social and economic status quo. Thus, traditional electoral activism has made it possible for Puerto Ricans to participate to some degree in managing the American political system without necessarily receiving significant benefits for this participation. The capturing of electoral or appointive positions at the local and state levels by Puerto Ricans may be viewed simply as a process for managing political and economic tensions between groups enjoying dominant status and those characterized by sub-dominant social and economic status. This process allows Puerto Ricans to make demands through electoral mobilization without realizing the resources necessary to improve significantly their life conditions. And it is possible to obtain certain kinds of benefits as a result of electoral mobilization. But these benefits are either responsive to the interests of elites in an impoverished community, or are distributed in such a way as to keep masses of people politically neutralized. In other words, even when benefits are made available to masses rather than elites, city political machines — or the federal government—will distribute resources in ways which encourage "political recipiency" rather than "political clientelism."[4] The benefits possible from electoral mobilization should not be deemphasized or ignored, but electoral mobilization has yet to illustrate its value in changing or even arresting deteriorating social conditions such as unemployment, poverty, ill health, or inadequate housing in Puerto Rican communities.

Some on the American left have argued this very proposition, which has led to the suggestion that electoral mobilization as a mass strategy is ineffective. Electoral activism on the part of Puerto Ricans or blacks has been perceived by sectors in the American left with suspicion, and sometimes arrogance. Radical proponents have not been involved extensively with organizations seeking to register more Puerto Ricans as voters or to increase levels of participation in traditional electoral activities.

Each of these general approaches reflects several valid ideas about American politics and social relations. Policies and practices that eliminate formal and informal barriers to greater levels of political participation should be pursued, even if the direct socioeconomic benefit resulting from this activity is not apparent. Struggles organized in response to a "politics of rights" or "access" issues, such as easier and more open voter registration procedures, "fair" district boundaries which are not gerrymandered, and bilingual services to assist non-English speaking groups in voter registration procedures are very important.[5] But the claim that voting will not make a substantial difference in the everyday lives of poor people has validity to a certain degree. To be sure, even 90 percent Puerto Rican voter registration and turn-out rates, by itself, may not necessarily have significant impact on crime, high school drop-out rates, unemployment, or the dearth of decent and affordable housing. If a 90 percent voter registration and turnout among Puerto Ricans does not arrest worsening living conditions, then should not community and organizational resources by expended in ways other than attempting to rectify voter registration rates currently in the range of 20 to 30 percent? As some would propose, community resources available for electoral mobilization should be directed at the organization of protest activities.

In studying this question many researchers have utilized an approach which incorrectly poses "electoral activism" as contradictory with "protest." The question then becomes which is more timely, or effective, or longer lasting: electoral mobilization or protest? A number of important studies on black politics are marred by a gross insistence on focusing on struggles between the "protest" leaders and the "electoral" leaders. This dichotomy is erroneous for the black community today, as well as for the Puerto Rican community.

The major weakness of the three conceptualizations cited earlier is that neither the liberal, conservative, or radical frameworks consider community-based "power" as critical in analysis of the social status of Puerto Ricans. The key question is not electoral vs. non-electoral mobilization, or even what particular level of political participation is appropriate or adequate for the Puerto Rican community—the important question is what strategies and what kinds of social situations will allow for a change in society's hierarchy of power, that is, a qualitative change in the social relations between powerful groups and relatively powerless groups. What are the political activities, in other words, which can lead to change in hierarchical relations between dominant and sub-dominant groups in American society? Both liberal and conservative thinkers virtually ignore this question. While not denying the importance of this question theoretically, the radicals can never seem to accept that certain kinds of electoral strategies and tactics may allow Puerto Ricans—as "Puerto Ricans" rather than "workers"—to challenge the hierarchical arrangements of power in American society.

Should Puerto Rican politics be approached within racial/ethnic or class-based analysis? The answer has many implications for those seeking to organize Puerto Ricans and resolving the human service crisis facing this community. But the question is simplistic and inappropriate. We can most certainly utilize both approaches to analyze socio-economic conditions of Puerto Ricans. Liberal strategies tend to posit that Puerto Rican experiences are basically a racial/ethnic phenomenon; Puerto Ricans are but one of many ethnic groups which must pass through certain stages of social and economic development in order to realize assimilation into mainstream America. For the most part the radical school has rejected this and instead argued that Puerto Ricans are but a sector among the poor and workers and that Puerto Ricans therefore should be organized not as Puerto Ricans necessarily, but rather as workers. Conservative thinkers such as Edward Banfield have also utilized "class" analysis to explain the "lower class" experiences of Puerto Ricans.[6] But the conservative school does not define "class" as does the American left. "Class" to conservatives is not determined by a group's relationships to "means of production," but rather as a conglomeration of social attitudes.

Conservatives feel that government tinkering with public policy will not necessarily improve life conditions for Puerto Ricans and, in fact, would worsen such conditions. Depressed life conditions reflect Puerto Rican group attitudes towards authority, education, and work. These attitudes are imbedded in a group's history and psyche and may not be susceptible to change or improvement, except perhaps for a few individuals. Liberal thinkers have also proposed that Puerto Rican life experiences reflect negative group attitudes, but they would argue that social engineering can perhaps bring these attitudes closer to those of middle-class whites. Thus, liberals may also propose that the problems of depressed life conditions are consequence of the group attitudes of Puerto Ricans.

An extreme position of some in the American left is the argument that Puerto Ricans should minimize their ethnicity or nationalist-oriented tactics, such as the development of Puerto Rican-led and Puerto Rican-controlled political organizations. Puerto Ricans, they argue, should not seek to organize themselves along racial/ethnic (i.e., "nationalist") lines, or seek public policy that responds to this experience rather than to class interests. They point out that ethnicity is a tool under capitalism that keeps the working class divided. What is not pointed out, however, is that the white working class has also utilized "ethnicity" and race to maintain social and economic hierarchy among the American working class.

There are problems with all three approaches regarding the experiences and politics of Puerto Ricans. None of the three schools offers strategies or tactics by which Puerto Ricans can challenge the hierarchies of power in their own communities. Furthermore, all of these approaches are culturally biased. The radicals ask Puerto Ricans to forget their culture and history; the liberals seem to treat Puerto Ricans as poor, misguided children; and the conservatives seem to suggest that Puerto Ricans are a socially disorganized group with attitudes and cultural orientation not appropriate for modern American society.

These schools have not offered programs that allow Puerto Ricans to challenge effectively their social position in American society. As a matter of fact, proponents of all three schools have histories of being opposed to changing power relationships between Puerto Ricans and powerful white groups in the American city. Perhaps a good example of this is the Community Control Movement in New York City during the late 1960s and early 1970s. Some radicals in the white community simply could not support what they considered to be the nationalist orientation of Puerto Rican parents in Community School District #1 in the Lower East Side. Many liberals quickly abandoned the concept of community control when they discovered that Puerto Ricans were utilizing this concept to challenge the hierarchy of political power in New York City. And conservatives seem to have been affronted by the idea that Puerto Ricans would seek to control their own communities on their own terms.

The Puerto Rican community can no longer afford to get stuck in political or public policy debates that are confined by the conceptual boundaries of these three schools of thought. Puerto Rican activists must now attempt a conceptualization of political and social experiences that allows a vision and strategy of Puerto Rican empowerment in America. Only through "empowerment" can the Puerto Rican community begin to resolve depressing living conditions that are continually worsening. But empowerment can only take place through effective challenges to current arrangements and organization of power.

A conceptualization of political activities that is built on "power analysis" and is culturally relevant for Puerto Ricans can be developed utilizing theory and empirical data. Unfortunately this is beyond the scope of this brief essay. But aside from theoretical and empirical factors there are several demographic and social developments that will make it increasingly difficult for traditional public policy approaches to be effective in improving the quality of life for Puerto Ricans in the U.S. These same developments are also providing a foundation for critiques of the standard liberal or conservative public policy approaches to problems like unemployment, crime, and poverty.

Various demographic patterns emerging in some places are encouraging activists to mold political strategies which move the Puerto Rican community from the pursuit of "access" to positions challenging hierarchies of social and economic power in the American city. One factor is the number of Puerto Ricans in certain major American cities. Between 1980 and 1985 the total population of the U.S. grew by 3 percent, but the number of Puerto Ricans grew by 28 percent. In cities like Philadelphia, New York, Chicago, Hartford, Baltimore, Boston, and other big cities, Puerto Ricans are increasing in number and beginning to reflect significant size within the total population. But related to increasing numbers are two other demographic factors. It is important to note that the growth in the Puerto Rican population is taking place in locations critical to the future economic viability of this society and of major strategic value to the U.S. economy, that is, big cities in the Northeast. Furthermore, cities like New York, Chicago, and Philadelphia will continue to have significant impact on national politics.

The migratory movement of Puerto Ricans between the U.S. and Puerto Rico also has major implications for the kind of politics which will characterize this community. Between the end of World War II and the current period over 25 percent of the total population in Puerto Rico has migrated, primarily for economic improvement. But the search for economic improvement has also motivated many to return to Puerto Rico. Thus, rather than the experience of immigrants who increasingly were torn away from their homeland, the Puerto Rican experience reflects converse development—Puerto Ricans in both locales are being drawn closer together. Conceivably, one result of this could be greater availability of resources utilized for political action by Puerto Ricans in the U.S. But another result can also be a renewed sense of the international context of Puerto Rico's status and its relationship with Puerto Ricans in the U.S. It is possible that Puerto Ricans focusing on domestic issues will at some point integrate these issues with the status of Puerto Rico and other international issues. This would represent a change from the current practice of Puerto Ricans involved with politics in American cities taking somewhat of a "hands off" approach to the question of Puerto Rico's status.[7] The numbers, the locale of these numbers, and the youthfulness of these numbers cannot be ignored as significant political developments in assessing the future directions of Puerto Rican politics.

There are social conditions challenging Puerto Rican political leaders to move toward new strategies for changing status-quo power relationships between Puerto Ricans and mainstream American society. The first is a situation of worsening life conditions for the overwhelming majority of Puerto Ricans. In 1976 the U.S. Commission on Civil Rights reported that

> mainland Puerto Ricans generally continue to be mired in the poverty facing first generations of all immigrant or migrant groups. Expectations were that succeeding generations of mainland Puerto Ricans would have achieved upward mobility. One generation later, the essential fact of poverty remains little changed. Indeed, the economic situation of the mainland Puerto Ricans has worsened over the last decade.[8]

Louis Nunez, President of the National Puerto Rican Coalition and the Staff Director of the Civil Rights Commission's 1976 report, reported ten years after its release that

> the situation for mainland Puerto Ricans has not improved notably in the 80's—we are still disproportionately represented amongst the poor and that new class "the underclass." At the same time the island community has also been mired in stagnation with little or no growth.[9]

In the areas of employment, poverty, education, and health, we find that social and economic indices reflect deteriorating living conditions for the majority of Puerto Ricans whether living in the U.S. or Puerto Rico.

Certain political conditions also require a response from Puerto Rican leaders today. One such condition is indeed the general failure of electoral activism to resolve the human service crisis in Puerto Rican communities.

Electoral activism cannot solve, *ipso facto,* systemic failures and problems like crime and unemployment. This does not mean that electoral politics is unimportant or insignificant as some on the left have suggested. On the other hand, electoral mobilization should not be approached "noncritically." In a recent and most important essay "Is Anything Enough?" the authors state that electoral mobilization coupled with coalitions may lead to political incorporation. Rufus P. Browning and Dale Rogers Marshall argue further that

> political incorporation in cities is not everything, and sometimes it is very little—but it is not nothing. The agenda of possibilities is still being created. Improvements in the economic position of minorities resulting from political incorporation may be slow and small, but they may gradually cumulate as accommodations are made by both the political and economic sectors.[10]

The authors suggest, in effect, that electoral mobilization should be pursued by minorities because it may, at some point, result in policy responsiveness on the part of government. This liberal conceptualization of electoral politics is becoming increasingly useless in mobilizing masses of Puerto Ricans or other minorities.

Electoral politics, however, are fundamental to any strategy of empowerment. It must be first acknowledged, however, that merely electing individuals who are "socially descriptive" with Puerto Ricans may have but little impact on the quality of life in Puerto Rican communities. Electoral activism can be organized in such ways as to provide the Puerto Rican community opportunities to challenge policy making and implementation in both government and the private sector. Electoral mobilization can be directed at allowing progressive activists to control the land and political economy of Puerto Rican communities.

Electoral positions that allow relatively powerless groups to challenge public decisionmakers are important because they raise the level of public debate and informational consciousness. Electoral positions also allow relatively powerless groups to challenge private sector decisions that impact directly on urban life conditions. Government not only regulates the private sector but also determines the legal and political context in which the private sector operates. This was suggested by Charles Lindblom in his classic study, *Politics and Markets,* in which he argued that the control of government ultimately implies control over property and wealth.[11] Governments authorize the arrangements which make property or wealth fundamental to the development of power in modern society. It follows, then, that electoral activism can indeed be significant in the development of group power, insofar as that activity allows people to control their gov-

ernment and their communities. The difference between the call for electoral mobilization by some civic leaders, and a growing number of grassroots activists, is that the approaches of the former serve to maintain the
power status quo, while the latter challenge it.

Today the electoral arena is fundamental in advancing the interests
of Puerto Ricans in cities—this does not mean that it is the *only* means,
but certainly one of several necessary tools for strategies of empowerment.
Electoral activism will not necessarily improve socioeconomic conditions
among Puerto Ricans. Electoral activism is simply a political tool that Puerto
Ricans must utilize to make other things happen. It is a tool that could
bring Puerto Ricans closer to those interests, public and private, that have
a direct impact on Puerto Rican life conditions. But traditional politics
as we understand and have practiced it is not sufficient to maximize the
"empowering" potential of electoral positions. To simply register voters,
and then ask them to turn out and vote for individuals seeking access and
influence is an ineffective way to resolve the human service crisis in Puerto
Rican communities, and it does not begin to effectively empower the Puerto
Rican community.

Demographic and economic changes and conditions provide a foundation for the emergence of two types of "politics"; one has been referred
to as the "traditional" face of urban politics, the other, the "progressive"
face of politics.[12] These two urban political orientations involve different
styles, values, and public policy strategies. One "face" of local politics is
quite traditional. It basically seeks to maintain the arrangement of power
which has characterized major American cities since World War II. Initially, the important actors in American local politics were private interest
groups, the federal government, and mayors and their machines. In the
late 1950s the public service unions were added to this urban "executive
coalition," to use Robert Salisbury's term.[13] During the 1960s the black
thrust for political participation culminated in the community control movement and the call for "Black Power" in major American cities. Although
the post–World War II urban "executive coalition" acceded some political
concessions to blacks, Puerto Ricans, and other citizen groups, in fact, an
institutionalization of membership into the ruling partnership was never
offered. Local government leaders did not invite blacks, Puerto Ricans, or
the poor to join the partnerships of the powerful; instead, temporary political arrangements and reforms were offered to quell the anger of racial
and ethnic minorities.

Many of these reforms have not resulted in qualitative change of the
urban executive coalition or in life conditions for Puerto Ricans. The urban executive coalition, which still manages American cities, can be referred to as reflective of the "old" face of local politics. Within this context

the problems of the city are approached in ways which do not threaten or interrupt the arrangements, distribution, or flow of power, money, status, or privilege. It is the "traditional" face of urban politics that may no longer be useful in responding to either the socioeconomic or political needs of Puerto Ricans. Clarence Stone, in *Economic Growth and Neighborhood Discontent* has shown convincingly how a minority group—in this case blacks in Atlanta—can capture political positions and acquire limited economic benefits for middle-class elements even within a context which does not challenge prevailing social and economic arrangements.[14] But even in Atlanta the problems of crime, high unemployment, malnutrition, illiteracy, and poverty are found at high levels among the majority of blacks.

Under the traditional face of politics, electoral challengers to incumbents usually present themselves as "better" managers or technicians; under this face of local politics, seekers of electoral office do not offer themselves as leaders of the citizenry against private interests, but as effective brokers. The basic problem faced by these managers is how to accommodate the social and economic problems facing blacks, Puerto Ricans, the poor, and the working class within the present hierarchy of power and wealth.

Traditional politics develops strategies in the pursuit of "access" to public decision makers in ways that do not challenge the rules of the game or the hierarchical position of the major players. When Puerto Ricans seek public office, but do not seek also to challenge the legal and political context in which the private sector operates, it implies the acceptance of a "junior partner" status. This is the major role reserved for minorities in urban America's political arena. Puerto Ricans then become merely another ethnic group trying to climb up a given socioeconomic ladder. The problem with this is that the ethnic analogy model is not relevant or useful for Puerto Ricans. The history and culture of Puerto Ricans simply do not fit into this kind of theoretical explanation.

The "progressive" face of politics seeks not mere access, but "empowerment." Under the progressive face of local politics, activists attempt to show the fiscal links between the militarization of American society and the quality of life in the city. Nuclear proliferation, business investments in South Africa, and military adventurism in Central America are local issues for progressive activists seeking to utilize the electoral arena for change. Though access to public and private decision makers is important and should be continually sought, access by itself does not change the qualitative or social relationship between the Puerto Rican community and those sectors or interest groups—public and private—considered "powerful." Empowerment suggests that Puerto Ricans and their leaders can utilize government to change the legal and political context in which the private sector conducts its business. This is what will change the social position of Puerto Ricans vis-à-vis other groups. Empowerment, in other words, includes those activities and goals that will change the social and economic relations between the Puerto Ricans as a community and the white power structures which manage the American city. And for this to happen empowerment strategies must also focus on activities that challenge the accumulation, ownership, management, and distribution of wealth in the metropolitan locale.

The questions that are placed before a city's public agenda within the rules of traditional local politics are well known and repetitive throughout urban America: "How can we attract big business for 'downtown' economic development?" "How can we build more office space and high rise luxury hotels?" "How can we make life easier for those who don't live in the city, but control the city?" "Which human and social services can be reduced in order to relieve the partners of the executive coalition of fiscal pressures?" "How can the public schools become more responsive to the needs of the business community?" These are the important questions under a local politics that seeks to maintain arrangements of wealth and power. Many Puerto Rican leaders continue to pursue influence within traditional electoral activism; they will continue to ask, for example, "How can we get a piece of the pie?" "How can we maintain our junior partner status in the urban executive coalition?" "How can we be given access to the powerful?" "How can we assist in reforming white power structures managing American cities?" The implications of these kinds of questions are very different than questions directed at changing the distribution of wealth and, therefore, power, in America.

Political participation may be either directed at structural change in the distribution of wealth and power, or at the maintenance of the status quo. The latter may be characterized by limited flexibility (liberalism), or resistance (conservatism), but it is the maintenance of social continuity and political stability that is emphasized in both cases. The politics characterizing increasing numbers of grassroots activists focuses instead on the well-being and empowerment of people regardless of effects on the executive coalition's political stability.

This emerging conceptualization of Puerto Rican politics in urban America allows us to approach effectively and systematically related political questions. For example, we know that there is major concern by activists regarding the political relationship between blacks and Puerto Ricans. Will ensuing political and social relationships reflect cooperation or conflict? A progressive conceptualization suggests strategies for those involved with mobilizing efforts in both communities. According to the progressive framework, the dichotomy is not between blacks and Puerto Ricans, but rather between activists oriented toward the "traditional" face of politics, and those oriented toward the "progressive" face of urban politics in both communities.

Traditional politics demands that blacks look out for blacks, and Puerto Ricans look out for Puerto Ricans. In many social and economic situations this immediately creates conflict. If political careers can be built in both communities upon sniping at the other powerless group, then so be it — this is what traditional politics is all about in the American city. By merely pursuing access and patronage, rather than empowerment, politicians in both communities adopt positions and pursue public policies which ultimately will be ethnically divisive. Progressive activists, however, seek policies that change qualitatively the subdominant status of racial and ethnic minorities; the public policies which are pursued tend to enjoin the interests of Puerto Ricans, with blacks and other powerless groups. The agenda, although ethnically organized, is not essentially an "ethnic" agenda, but a "power" agenda.

We can use this conceptualization of politics to look at several questions posed at the beginning of this essay. If increasing numbers of Puerto Rican grassroots activists continue to experiment with electoral mobilization, then we will see a resurgence of interest on the particular status of Puerto Rico. This is because American foreign policy becomes an important and relevant issue for progressive activists involved in electoral politics at the local level. There has been an artificial separation, even a mythology, regarding foreign policy and local politics. Many citizens approach local issues as totally separate from world political and economic developments. This is erroneous; and the more this country becomes militarized, the harder it will be for this mythology to be maintained. Progressive activists already have been successful in raising international issues in various local electoral campaigns. Political developments in Central America will lead to greater attention on the part of Puerto Rican activists in this country regarding the status of Puerto Rico and its relationship to the U.S. Under traditional politics locally based electoral activists basically adopt a "no comment" approach regarding the status of Puerto Rico. This will become increasingly difficult — not only because of greater attention on the part of activists to the international arena, but also because younger Puerto Ricans, representing, in part, alienated sectors, will also be entering the electoral arena to express themselves in increasing numbers as issues of power, rather than mere access, are presented to them.

Electoral politics based on changing the social position of the Puerto Rican community rather than seeking a mere "piece of the pie" will attract younger and poorer Puerto Ricans. Electoral politics organized around giving Puerto Ricans control over institutions that have major impact in molding the quality of life at the local level eventually will attract the other

50, 60, and in some cases 70 percent of the voting age population, which have not registered or turned out in local elections. If this possibility materializes, then it will have an impact on politics in Puerto Rico. It is conceivable that as Puerto Ricans develop an electoral politics that challenges the distribution of wealth and the hierarchies of power in the U.S., that similar questions—with renewed vigor—will be raised about Puerto Rico.

CONCLUSION

In arguing that a new orientation to political power is emerging in Puerto Rican communities one might ask if this is also the case with other Latino groups such as Cubans, Dominicans, and Mexican-Americans. Despite the commonality of language background it cannot be overlooked that these groups have (1) different types of migration patterns into the U.S., (2) do not share uniform socioeconomic characteristics, and (3) do not share uniformly common social and cultural backgrounds. These particular groups have also exhibited diverse political attitudes and behavior. In some areas of public policy, these groups hold positions which are competitive with each other.

Spanish-speaking groups arrived in this country under varying social and historical circumstances. Part of Mexico, like Puerto Rico, was colonized by the United States. While Puerto Ricans were granted citizenship a few years after the annexation of their country, however, the border between the U.S. and Mexico was closed to free movement after the annexation of Texas and New Mexico. Mexican-Americans are legally separate from Mexico—this is not the case with Puerto Ricans and Puerto Rico. Cubans have a unique migration history among Latinos. Although not granted blanket citizenship, they were virtually invited into the country after Fidel Castro's rise to power in Cuba. There are significant differences in patterns of migration. In many cases Mexican immigrants have had to sneak into the country; Puerto Ricans were forced to accept American citizenship in order to perform low wage and menial labor, and Cubans fleeing Castro in the 1960s were treated, relatively speaking, as political heroes.

Another major factor to consider are the socioeconomic characteristics of various Latino groups. Significant economic differences among Latinos led to a recent report sponsored by the National Puerto Rican Forum, Inc., which sought "to clearly differentiate between the Puerto Rican and other ethnic groups that comprise the 'Hispanic' community, for purposes of establishing the fact that the Puerto Rican community is the most disadvantaged of all groups, inside or outside the Hispanic community."[15] The report criticized officials who "have broadly used the term 'Hispanic' to describe all Spanish-speaking ethnic groups in the mainland United States, and based their conclusions upon the median incomes, ages, family size, labor force participation, or employment rates of the entire Spanish-speaking community as a whole." Based on census data and various kinds of reports and surveys this is a valid argument in the areas of income, poverty, education, and employment.

Comparison of political and social attitudes of different Latino groups seems to suggest major differences between Cubans, Dominicans, and Puerto Ricans. One study found that in New York City, for example,

> Puerto Ricans generally exhibit higher levels of political conscious-
> ness than either Cubans or Dominicans. Puerto Ricans are most likely
> to express strong support for ethnic political action, to believe that
> governmental officials would give preferential treatment to members
> of their own ethnic group, and to believe that local government dis-
> criminates against their ethnic group in treatment and jobs.[16]

Due to the differences between these three Latino groups the study concluded that

> the term "Hispanic" political attitudes was of little conceptual help
> in describing the attitudes analyzed, at least in reference to Puerto
> Ricans, Cubans and Dominicans in New York City.[17]

But differences in political attitudes and behavior are also suggested at the national level when the presidential preferences of Cubans, Puerto Ricans, and Mexican-Americans are compared.[18]

Despite these kinds of significant differences there are also substantial similarities. One can argue that future directions of Puerto Rican politics will be paralleled in other Latino communities. The Puerto Rican community may be more "advanced" in moving from a politics of access to "empowerment" due to several reasons. One is that it is the most impoverished of the Latino groups in America, and therefore those public policies that are responsive to mass needs rather than beneficial merely to elites will enjoy a greater degree of acceptance and legitimacy. Another reason is that Puerto Ricans are not as large a group as Mexican-Americans, and Puerto Ricans are geographically concentrated to a greater extent. These demographic conditions may encourage Puerto Rican communities to be more receptive to alternative views of politics. If Puerto Ricans were as large a group as Mexican-Americans in the Southwest, or Cubans in Miami, for example, their level of political efficacy in traditional electoral politics might discourage politics focusing on challenging the distribution of wealth, rather than merely electing representatives into public office. Finally, there is a degree of economic success in both the Cuban and

Mexican-American communities which has not characterized Puerto Ricans. This group has not been as effectively economically "mainstreamed" as the two other groups; thus the "American Dream" is not as realistic for Puerto Ricans as it might be for Cubans and Mexican-Americans. This may encourage community activists to utilize electoral politics to challenge the "rules of the game." But as Puerto Ricans move toward a new conceptualization of politics they could have the effect of encouraging the more impoverished sectors of other Latino communities to also examine electoral activism within the kind of progressive framework outlined in this essay. The dynamics of social movement are quite contagious. If the electoral arena becomes a stage for the unfolding of a social movement in Puerto Rican (and black) communities, then other Latino groups will follow. As has already been suggested, what will create parallel movements for progressive electoral activism in these other communities will not be the commonality of language or culture; instead, it will reflect responses to the arrangements of power and wealth in American society that are contributing to worsening living conditions for minorities.

NOTES

This article is based on a presentation made at a National Symposium held at Temple University and sponsored by the Institute for Puerto Rican Policy in the fall of 1986.

1. "Puerto Rican Youth Empowerment" in *Puerto Ricans in the Mid '80's: An American Challenge* (Alexandria, Va.: National Puerto Rican Coalition, 1985), p. 50.

2. See C. Wright Mills, *The Power Elite* (New York: Oxford University Press, 1956), and E. E. Schattschneider, *The Semi Sovereign People* (Hinsdale, Illinois: Dryden Press, 1960).

3. "Moving Into the Political Mainstream," Hispanic Policy Development Project (New York: February 1984), p. 12.

4. These terms are described in Charles V. Hamilton, "The Patron-Recipient Relationship and Minority Politics In New York City," *Political Science Quarterly* (Summer 1979).

5. Charles V. Hamilton has proposed that minority politics has, or is moving, from a "politics of rights," to a "politics of resources." See his article "New Elites and Pluralism" in Richard M. Pious (ed.), *The Power To Govern: Assessing Reform in the U.S.* (New York: The Academy of Political Science, 1981). I have argued that minority activists are beginning to emphasize "power" issues, over "access" issues. See "Black Politics in America: From Access to Power" in James Jennings and Mel King, *From Access to Power: Black Politics In Boston* (Cambridge, Mass.: Schenkman Books, 1986).

6. See Edward C. Banfield, *The Unheavenly City* (Boston: Little, Brown and Co., 1970).

7. Generally speaking, Puerto Rican politicians have shied away from issues such as the status of Puerto Rico, as they become more integrated with U.S. local politics. See "The Emergence of Puerto Rican Electoral Activism in Urban America" in James Jennings and Monte Rivera, *Puerto Rican Politics in Urban America* (Westport, Conn.: Greenwood Press, 1981).

8. Quoted by Louis Nunez in *Puerto Ricans in the Mid 80's: An American Challenge* (Alexandria, Va.: National Puerto Rican Coalition, 1985), p. vii.

9. *Puerto Ricans in the Mid '80's: An American Challenge* (Alexandria, Va.: National Puerto Rican Coalition, Inc., 1985), p. vii.

10. This and related ideas are presented more fully in Rufus P. Browning, Dale Rogers Marshall, and David H. Tabb, *Protest Is Not Enough: The Struggle of Blacks and Hispanics for Equality in Urban Politics* (Berkeley, Calif.: University of California Press, 1984).

11. Charles E. Lindblom, *Politics and Markets* (New York: Basic Books, Inc., 1977), chapter two, "Authority and State."

12. For a discussion of the two types of urban politics today, see James Jennings, "Black Power and Electoral Activism" in Rod Bush, ed., *The New Black Vote* (San Francisco: Synthesis Publications, 1984) and "The Struggle for Equality: From Access To Power," *Suffolk Law Review* (Winter 1984).

13. Robert Salisbury, "The New Convergence of Power In Urban Politics," *Journal of Politics* (November 1964).

14. Clarence Stone, *Economic Growth and Neighborhood Discontent* (Chapel Hill, N.C.: University of North Carolina Press, 1976).

15. Mae T. Lee, "The First Step Toward Equality" (New York: National Puerto Rican Forum, 1979).

16. Dale Nelson, "Hispanic Political Behavior: A Comparison of Cubans, Dominicans, and Puerto Ricans." Paper presented at the Annual Meeting of the American Political Science Association (Washington, D.C.: 1979), p. 21.

17. Ibid., p. 37.

18. See James Jennings, "Black and Hispanic Voters: Competition or Cooperation?" unpublished manuscript (1983).

Conclusion

WHAT IS THE STATUS OF Latinos in the United States political system in the decade of the 1980s? What are likely to be the parameters of Latino politics in the remaining two decades of the twentieth century? Some possibilities are less ambiguous than others. First, Latinos do have many more resources than ever before. Latinos' economic status has been improved; significant educational and social gains have been attained. There is a cadre of Latinos with good educations, training in community and large-scale organizations, and leadership experience in a variety of settings. Yet, progress the past few years has been less than optimal, as the environment in the United States has changed to make it more difficult for Latinos to make additional gains easily. Although the 1980s decade seems to be a period of retrenchment in America, that does not mean that Latinos will allow these ten years to be a period of regression. Latinos who are concerned with their situation have renewed their efforts and worked as hard as in the past, but their tactics are taking more conventional or traditional forms. Tactics that were used successfully in the late 1960s and early 1970s probably would bring forth negative reactions from the majority culture in the 1980s rather than produce sympathetic understanding and support. The economic situation has become a tight one with little or no slack to afford majority culture people the luxury of supporting causes which do not serve their own immediate interests. Competition not cooperation, egocentrism rather than social concern, ethnocentrism rather than toleration of diversity seem to be descriptive of the 1980s. In light of this situation, it seems incumbent for Latinos to use more accommodative and conventional tactics in pursuing their political, social, and economic goals. That is not to say that the goals will be pursued with any less vigor or tenacity. Attempts to increase Latino influence in electoral politics will be continued and fortified. Voter registration and get-out-the-vote drives will continue to be important and necessary, if not sufficient, for the attainment of at least one base of political power. However, the limitations as well as the benefits of accommodation politics must be realized, and either a new style of elec-

9445

toral politics such as that which leads to empowerment of the Latino communities must be employed or else other political strategies must be used. Also, efforts should be continued to recruit candidates for public office who are at one and the same time genuinely concerned with the needs of the Latino people and who still are at least minimally acceptable to the core culture.

Increased efforts will be made to influence the electoral process through the judicious use of political parties. More pressure might be exerted on the Democratic Party to be responsive to a group most of which has long been its staunch supporter. As for the Republican Party, although it has made some pronouncements about increased Latino affiliation based on a shared conservative ideology, it has not seemed able to shed its conservative, elitist, and ethnocentric values which preclude the party's acceptance of Latinos (with the exception of Cubans) or Latinos' needs in any significant numbers. However, it is interesting that there is some evidence that at least among younger Latinos an increased identification with the GOP is evident. Meanwhile, the hope for a successful "third" party or for an imminent major realignment of the current parties has become increasingly slim. Conceivably, a minor party could recruit Latinos to its cause as a way of exerting pressure on both major parties and on other established institutions. Such a party would probably meet its greatest success in its role as a kind of electorally oriented pressure group. Marxist-oriented minor parties could continue to remind the dominant institutions in America about the hardships Latinos have undergone in this capitalist system. All of these minor parties could contribute innovative alternatives to the consensus-constrained, majority-oriented approaches of the major parties.

Coalition politics must be one of the major strategies of a relatively powerless minority group. Latinos will continue to explore alliances with other reform-minded groups. Other colored ethnic groups, such as Native Americans and blacks, remain potential allies, since many of the problems of the Latinos are shared by these other excluded groups. Labor unions and religious organizations also could be natural organizational allies for challenging the historical exclusivity of major American institutions.

With regard to alliances, it is not entirely clear that the various nationality groups within the Latino rubric actually constitute a cohesive "community." Certainly, Mexican-Americans, Cuban-Americans, Puerto Ricans and other Spanish ancestry groups have a great deal in common, including language and other cultural manifestations, as well as similar treatment by the majority culture in most cases. Yet, it is also evident that there are significant differences between each of the groups' historical, demographic, and socioeconomic circumstances. Indeed, although we have done so, one cannot speak with complete confidence about a unified Latino political community. Much research is needed to clarify the precise parameters of political and cultural identifications within and among Latino groups, how these groups feel about themselves and other Latino groups, as well as their identifications with the United States political community. Similarities and differences in their attitudes toward various governments, and their other political values and opinions on issues must be delineated. Basic investigations into fundamental cultural and political orientations are needed before the term "Latino" or "Hispanic" is completely meaningful. At this point it seems likely that there are bases for cohesion and cooperation which at least allow one to speak generally of Latino politics.

Latinos can continue to support traditional Hispanic "interest group" organizations that have become increasingly concerned with political, economic, and educational advancement. Increased levels of education and income should allow more support through donations and memberships for these longstanding associations such as LULAC and the GI Forum. Newer associations, such as NALEO, the National Council of La Raza, and the Congressional Hispanic Caucus are also increasingly in the forefront of representing the views of Latinos to national leaders in Washington. This kind of interest group activity is important, since it remains essential that the media, national political authorities, and federal bureaucracies continue to be reminded of the presence and plight of the nation's second largest ethnic minority.

It will be at the local community level where most of Latino involvement in interest group politics will take place. Those issues which are at the top of many Latino community agencies—jobs, housing, health, law enforcement, municipal services, and education—are conducive to the activation of issue-oriented community interest groups. Those political resources gained over the past two decades, such as education, leadership training, organizing skills, and material resources, can be employed effectively to exert pressure on community politicians and other decision makers.

Successful political outcomes still will be difficult to achieve. The time and effort required will be substantial, and the opposition still will be widespread and powerful. For example, public support for such programs as affirmative action and bilingual education is not what it was in the 1960s and 1970s. One dramatic, if shortsighted, manifestation of this is the "English only" movement that has proposed an amendment to the U.S. Constitution which would make this nation officially monolingual. In fact, in 1986 through a statewide referendum, California made English the only legal language in that state.

Some potential bright spots do exist. One is the new recognition of the importance of Latin America, including Mexico, in United States policy considerations and the consequent possible roles that Latinos can play in the relationships between Latin America and the United States. Another is the demographic reports which, although varying in details, agree that Latinos are the fastest growing minority group in the United States. Sheer numbers can be an extremely valuable political resource. One traditional way that population resources can be used to affect politics is through elections where numbers are of utmost importance. Latinos historically have registered and voted in much lower numbers than non-Hispanics, with the exception of Cubans and Mexican-Americans in a few areas of the Southwest. In the 1980s, major efforts are being made to register Latinos by organizations such as the Southwest and Midwest Voter Registration Education Projects, and notable increases have been the result. For example, in California Hispanic registration has increased from 715,600 in 1976 to 988,130 in 1980 and 1,136,497 in 1984. In Texas the increase was from 488,200 in 1976 to 798,563 in 1980, to 1,034,922 in 1984. In Texas the Hispanic registration rate climbed from 32 percent in 1976 to 51 percent in 1984. Across the nation from 1972 to 1984, Latino registration increased by 27 percent compared to a 24 percent increase in black and a 9 percent increase in white voters. The Latino population is much younger than the national average and thus an increase in Latino registration and participation in the future is more likely on that basis alone. In sum, Latinos are not only the fastest growing minority in population but also in voter registration.

Victories continue to be won in court decisions which have struck down multimember, at-large electoral districts. Redistricting continues to allow Latinos to have more and more responsive representation at all levels of government.

There is no doubt that the United States is undergoing a Latinization the cumulative effects of which will be major if subtle. In a society in which distinctive minorities may well become the majority over the next century, Latinos likely will constitute the largest proportion of those.

Over the past several years, it has become most apparent that Latinos are a large and significant group in the American political system and that they have the potential for substantial political and economic power. The leaders of our society and much of the attentive public are being made to realize the significance of this situation. As throughout their history, Latinos will persist in their efforts to better their lives and to create in the United States a social and political environment conducive to the realization of these goals. Latinos' efforts toward achieving equality will continue and inexorably will lead to that achievement. The path may be long and uneven, but the belief of the vast majority of Americans in the basic concepts of liberty, justice, equality, and prosperity, in addition to Latinos' historical determination and perseverance, inevitably will result in a society in which equality and justice are much closer to being realities for all U.S. citizens, including Latinos.